THE ROUTLEDGE HANDBOOK OF ENERGY SECURITY

This Handbook examines the subject of energy security: its definition, dimensions, ways to measure and index it, and the complicating factors that are often overlooked.

The volume identifies varying definitions and dimensions of energy security, including those that prioritize security of supply and affordability alongside those that emphasize availability, energy efficiency, trade, environmental quality, and social and political stewardship. It also explores the various metrics that can be used to give energy security more coherence, and also to enable it to be quantified, including recent attempts to measure energy security progress at the national level, with a special emphasis placed on countries within the Organisation for Economic Co-operation and Development (OECD), countries within Asia, and industrialized countries worldwide.

This Handbook:

- Broadens existing discussions of energy security that center on access to fuels, including "oil security" and "coal security;"
- Focuses not only on the supply side of energy but also the demand side, taking a hard look at energy services and politics along with technologies and infrastructure;
- Investigates energy security issues such as energy poverty, equity and access, and sustainable development;
- Analyzes ways to index and measure energy security progress at the national and international level.

This book will be of much interest to students of energy security, energy policy, economics, environmental studies, and IR/Security Studies in general.

Benjamin K. Sovacool is an Assistant Professor at the Lee Kuan Yew School of Public Policy at the National University of Singapore. He is also a Research Fellow in the Energy Governance Program at the Centre on Asia and Globalization. He is author or editor of four books on energy issues.

THE ROUTLEDGE HANDBOOK OF ENERGY SECURITY

Edited by Benjamin K. Sovacool

Routledge
Taylor & Francis Group

LONDON AND NEW YORK

First published 2011
by Routledge
2 Park Square, Milton Park, Abingdon, Oxon, OX14 4RN

Simultaneously published in the USA and Canada
by Routledge
711 Third Avenue, New York, NY 10017

Routledge is an imprint of the Taylor & Francis Group, an informa business

© 2011 Benjamin K. Sovacool
for selection and editorial matter, individual contributors; their contributions

Typeset in Bembo by
Integra Software Services Pvt. Ltd, Pondicherry, India
Printed and bound in Great Britain by
CPI Antony Rowe, Chippenham, Wiltshire

British Library Cataloguing in Publication Data
A catalogue record for this book is available from the British Library

Library of Congress Cataloging-in-Publication Data
The Routledge handbook of energy security / edited by
Benjamin K. Sovacool.
p. cm.
Includes indexes.
1. Energy development. 2. Energy consumption. 3. Energy policy.
4. Energy industries. 5. Supply and demand. I. Sovacool, Benjamin K.
HD9502.A2R68 2010
333.79--dc22
2010026134

ISBN13: 978-0-415-59117-1 (hbk)
ISBN13: 978-0-203-83460-2 (ebk)

CONTENTS

ILLUSTRATIONS

Figures

Tables

CONTRIBUTORS

Anthony D'Agostino is a Research Associate at the Centre on Asia and Globalisation, Lee Kuan Yew School of Public Policy, National University of Singapore. His current research focuses on energy security developments in Southeast Asia and the intersection of energy and development needs in the Asia-Pacific region. He has held positions with the United Nations Environment Program, the World Resources Institute's Greenhouse Gas Protocol, and the Institute of Water Policy. He has worked in India, Australia, New Zealand, and the U.S. with rural development and sustainable agriculture organizations.

Marilyn A. Brown is an endowed Professor of Energy Policy in the School of Public Policy at the Georgia Institute of Technology, and a Visiting Distinguished Scientist at the Oak Ridge National Laboratory. She has led several energy technology and policy scenario studies, testified before both houses of the U.S. Congress, and penned more than 200 publications relating to energy policy, sustainable development, and climate change. She was designated a co-recipient of the Nobel Peace Prize for her work on the Intergovernmental Panel on Climate Change in 2007. She is the co-editor with Benjamin K. Sovacool of *Energy and American Society: Thirteen Myths* (2007) and is the lead author of *Climate Change and Global Energy Security: Technology and Policy Options* (forthcoming 2011).

Aleh Cherp is Professor, Academic Secretary, and Research Director at Central European University, Budapest, Hungary. He is also the Coordinating Lead Author (Energy Security) of the Global Energy Assessment. In addition to energy security, he is interested in environmental sustainability of transition societies, sustainable development strategies and environmental assessment in Central Asia and Central and Eastern Europe. He has undertaken professional work for groups as diverse as the European Environment Agency and World Bank to the United Nations Development Program and Organization for Security and Cooperation in Europe. He also serves or has served on the editorial boards of *Impact Assessment and Project Appraisal*, the *Environmental Impact Assessment Review* and the *Environmental Management and Engineering Journal*.

Bert J. M. de Vries is a Professor at the Department of Science, Technology, and Society at Utrecht University and Professor of Global Change and Energy at the Copernicus Institute for Sustainable Development and Innovation. Since 1990 he has also been a senior scientist at the Netherlands Environmental Assessment Agency. He is the co-founder of the Institute for Energy and Environment at the University of Groningen. His publications include *Perspectives on Global Futures* (1997) and (with Johan Goudsbloem) *Mappae Mundi: Humans and Their Habitats in a Socio-Ecological Perspective. Myths, Maps, and Models* (2002), as well as a lead author for the Intergovernmental Panel on Climate Change's Third Assessment.

Michael Dworkin is Director and Founder of the Institute for Energy and the Environment and Professor of Law at the Vermont Law School. He is also Director of the American Council for an Energy Efficient Economy and Director of the Electric Power Research Institute. He spent five years in the U.S. EPA's Office of General Counsel, where he focused on the development and appellate defense of standards that reduced air and water pollution, including appellate defense of the rules that removed most toxic metals from U.S. waste streams. He has also served as general counsel and chair of the Vermont Public Service Board.

Dwi Ari Fauzi is a researcher at the Indonesian Institute for Energy Economics, Jakarta. His research focuses on energy policy, renewable energy, sustainability, and climate change. He also manages and edits the *Indonesian Energy Economics Review*.

Alfa Firdaus is a researcher at the Indonesian Institute for Energy Economics and a lecturer at Mercu Buana University, Jakarta. His research interests include renewable energy, energy policy and sustainability. He is the co-author of the *Indonesia Biofuels Program Evaluation and Future Challenges*.

Edgard Gnansounou is head of the Bioenergy and Energy Planning Research Group at the Ecole Polytechnique Féderale de Lausanne in Switzerland. He is also an Associate Professor at the Shandong Electric Power Research Institute in China. His research relates to the planning of energy systems, particularly modeling uncertainty, imprecision and stakeholders' behavior in the process of matching energy supply to demand. He is a member of several professional associations: International Hydropower Association. International Association for Energy Economics, and the Swiss Committee of the World Energy Council.

Andreas Goldthau is an Associate Professor with the Department of Public Policy at Central European University, Hungary. He is also a Fellow with the Global Public Policy Institute (Berlin and Geneva), co-heading the institute's Global Energy Governance program. His academic interests focus on energy security and on global governance issues related to oil and gas. He is the author of *OPEC and Power: How the Prize Eludes the Cartel* (2011), *Imported Oil and National Security* (2009) and *OPEC. Macht und Ohnmacht des Oelkartells* (2009), and the co-editor of *Global Energy Governance: The New Rules of the Game* (2010).

Heleen Groenenberg is a Senior Researcher at the Energy research Center of the Netherlands (ECN). Her activities currently involve the development of guidelines for monitoring and verifying carbon dioxide storage, the assessment of costs, and public perspectives on carbon capture and storage. She earned her graduate degree in Soil, Water and Atmosphere at Wageningen University, and finished her dissertation on post-Kyoto commitments for the industrialized and developing world at Utrecht University in 2002. She joined ECN after working as a post-doc Global Change and Energy at the European Commission's Joint Research Center in Seville.

Eshita Gupta is currently finishing her Ph.D. in economics from the Indian Statistical Institute in New Delhi. She has also served as a Research Fellow at the Centre for Development Economics and a Research Associate at the Energy and Resources Institute (TERI) in New Delhi. Her research interests include development economics, environmental economics, industrial organization, and energy economics.

Peter Hayes is Executive Director of the Nautilus Institute for Security and Sustainable Development, a non-governmental policy-oriented research and advocacy group. Professionally active as an environment and energy consultant in developing countries (working for United Nations Environment Program, Asian Development Bank, World Bank, Canadian International Development Research Council, U.S. Agency for International Development, United Nations Development Program), he also writes widely about security affairs in the Asian-Pacific region. He was first executive director of the Environment Liaison Centre in Nairobi, Kenya in 1974–76. He was Deputy Director of the Commission for the Future (Australian Government) from 1989 to 1991. He is co-author of *American Lake: Nuclear Peril in the Pacific* (1987) and *The Global Greenhouse Regime* (1993).

Larry Hughes is a Professor in the Department of Electrical and Computer Engineering at Dalhousie University in Halifax, Nova Scotia, Canada, where he leads the department's Energy and Environment Research Group and is a Fellow of Dalhousie's College of Sustainability. He has applied systems analysis techniques to researching energy security and environmental problems over the past 20 years. He has advised government officials in both Canada and Sweden on energy security, while also conducting research on wind and biomass for various levels of government in Canada. His publications cover many different energy issues, including approaches to dealing with heating emergencies in Canada, ways of improving energy security, the use of wind for space and water heating, and a classification scheme for net metering.

Asclepias R. S. Indriyanto has been the Executive Director of the Indonesian Institute for Energy Economics since 2003. Her research interests include energy economics, energy security, sustainable development, climate change and renewable energy development. She has advised government officials and a state-owned electricity company in Indonesia, as well as several multilateral organizations.

Jaap C. Jansen is a Senior Research Fellow at the Energy research Centre of the Netherlands (ECN). His research interests include energy-related environmental markets (renewable energy certificates, guarantees of origin, emission allowances) and regulatory frameworks for market stimulation and network integration of renewable energy as well as security of supply. Mr. Jansen has worked in some 30 countries as an adviser and consultant for government authorities, multilateral organizations including the World Bank, European Union, UNIDO and Asian Development Bank. He is (co-)author of many scientific publications, including peer-reviewed articles and book chapters.

Jessica Jewell is a Ph.D. student at Central European University where her research focuses on understanding energy security under energy transitions and as a driver for policy change. In conjunction with her research, she is a Lead Author of the Global Energy Assessment Energy Security knowledge module and a contributing author to the Global Energy Assessment Scenarios module. She also has been a visiting researcher at the International Institute for Applied Systems Analysis, where she worked on designing a method to characterize energy security risks of future energy systems.

John Kessels is a senior analyst at the International Energy Agency Clean Coal Centre based in London. His research interests include carbon abatement and management issues pertaining to emissions trading, international agreements and frameworks that could accelerate the use of clean coal technologies. He has also been an advisor to the Intergovernmental Panel on Climate Change (IPCC)'s Working Group III. Some of the reports he has written for the IEA Clean Coal Centre include "Clean Coal Technologies for a Carbon-constrained World: The Role of Power Sector Clean Coal Technologies in Climate Policy" and "Energy Security and the Role of Coal".

Anne Korin is co-director of the Institute for the Analysis of Global Security (IAGS). She is also chair of the Set America Free Coalition, an alliance of national security, environmental, labor and religious groups promoting ways to reduce America's dependence on oil. She focuses on energy supply vulnerabilities, energy security, and technological innovation. She appears in the media frequently and has written articles for *Foreign Affairs*, the *American Interest*, the *National Review, Commentary Magazine*, and the *Journal of International Security Affairs*. She also appears often on Capitol Hill and her advice is sought by members of Congress. She is co-author of *Energy Security Challenges for the 21st Century* (2009) and *Turning Oil into Salt: Energy Independence Through Fuel Choice* (2009).

Bert Kruyt is an energy consultant for BECO, a consultancy specializing in sustainable development. At Utrecht University, he has worked on topics in the field of energy technology, policy, modeling and economics as well as the physics and mitigation of climate change. For his Master's thesis on indicators for energy security he worked at the department Policy Studies from the Energy Research Centre of the Netherlands (ECN), as well as the Climate & Global Sustainability team of the Netherlands Environmental Assessment Agency (MNP). There he researches indicators for energy security and the modeling of future energy security in the TIMER energy model.

Tai Wei Lim is an Assistant Professor at the Chinese University of Hong Kong. He is the associate editor for book reviews at *Asian Politics and Policy*, and Academic Member of the India China Economic and Cultural Council, Chief Editor of the *Cambodia Journal of International Affairs* and a reviewer for Inderscience's *International Journal of Global Energy Issues*.

Carolin Liss is a Research Fellow at the Griffith Asia Institute and the Centre for Governance and Public Policy, Griffith University. She is the author of articles on maritime piracy and the privatization of maritime security in Asia and Africa and terrorism in Southeast Asia. Her Ph.D. thesis will be published as *Oceans of Crime. Maritime Piracy and Transnational Security in Southeast Asia and Bangladesh* by ISEAS/IIAS in late 2010.

Gal Luft is executive director of the Institute for the Analysis of Global Security, a Washington DC-based think-tank focused on energy security and co-founder of the Set America Free Coalition, an alliance of national security, environmental, labor and religious groups promoting ways to reduce America's dependence on oil. He is co-editor of *Energy Security Challenges for the 21st Century* (2009), co-author of *Turning Oil into Salt: Energy Independence Through Fuel Choice* (2009) and author of *Beer, Bacon and Bullets: Culture in Coalition Warfare from Gallipoli to Iraq* (2010.) He also publishes the *Journal of Energy Security*.

Shonali Pachauri is an energy and environmental economist working at the International Institute for Applied Systems Analysis in Austria. She also serves on the Executive Committee of the Global Energy Assessment. Her work includes the analysis of the socio-economics of energy access, use and choice; resource use and access in relationship to lifestyles, poverty and development; energy demand and fuel choice modeling; and the analysis of embodied energy of household consumption in developing countries. She is author of *An Energy Analysis of Household Consumption: Changing Patterns of Direct and Indirect Use in India* (2007) and is also author or co-author of several scientific journal articles.

Geoffrey Pakiam is a Research Associate at the Energy Studies Institute at the National University of Singapore. His current interests include the political economy of energy systems, state-society relations and the politics of development, with particular emphases on Southeast Asian polities and their interactions with the international system. His other publications include "The Power System Problématique in Southeast Asia," in H. Peimani (ed.), *Energy Infrastructure Security in Asia* (forthcoming).

Martin J. Pasqualetti is Professor in the School of Geographical Sciences and Urban Planning at Arizona State University. He has advised several government agencies and serves on the editorial boards of five journals. His most recent research includes work in Mexico, Scotland, Canada, and the U.S. on the water/energy nexus, social barriers to renewable energy, energy landscapes of the southwestern U.S., and the environmental impacts of energy mega-projects such as the Albert oil sands. At Arizona State University, he regularly teaches courses on energy and other natural resources.

Timothy Savage is Deputy Director of the Seoul branch of the Nautilus Institute for Security & Sustainable Development. From 1997-2002, he worked as Senior Program Officer for Northeast Asia at Institute's headquarters in Berkeley, California, where he coordinated cooperative engagement programs with North Korea. He also works as Associate Editor at OhmyNews International, an Internet-based newspaper. From 2004 to 2005, he was Senior Analyst at the Northeast Asia Office of the International Crisis Group.

Darren Shupe is a recent graduate of the Master of Planning program at Dalhousie University in Halifax, Nova Scotia, Canada. His interests in energy security were influenced initially by James Howard Kunstler, Thomas Homer Dixon, and Robert Hirsch. Searching for a local researcher in this field led him to Larry Hughes, with whom he has further explored energy analysis, specifically energy security indices. He hopes to carry forward to his career in planning, the urgency of the imagined energy future, to develop strategies to help mitigate the most harmful effects to our communities of fossil fuel depletion.

Benjamin K. Sovacool is an Assistant Professor at the Lee Kuan Yew School of Public Policy at the National University of Singapore. He is also a Research Fellow in the Energy Governance Program at the Centre on Asia and Globalization. He has worked as a researcher, professor, and consultant on issues pertaining to energy policy and security, climate change, the environment, sustainability, and science and technology policy. He is the co-editor of *Energy and American Society* (2007) and the editor, author, or co-author of *The Dirty Energy Dilemma* (2008), *Powering the Green Economy* (2009), *Contesting the Future of Nuclear Power* (2010), and *Climate Change and Global Energy Security* (forthcoming 2011).

Andy Stirling is Director of Research for Science and Technology Policy Research (SPRU) at the University of Sussex. He also co-directs the Sussex-based ESRC Centre on Social, Technological and Environmental Pathways to Sustainability (STEPS) and is a member of the Sussex Energy Group. He is an interdisciplinary researcher, publishing on a range of issues in science, technology and energy policy. He has served on a number of governmental advisory bodies including the EU Energy Policy Consultative Committee, Science in Society Committee and Expert Group on Science and Governance. In the U.K., he has served on the Advisory Committee on Toxic Substances, GM Science Review Panel, DEFRA Science Advisory Council and the Advisory Board of the BIS Sciencewise Programme.

Tatsujiro Suzuki is a Vice Chairman of Japan Atomic Energy Commission of the Japanese government since January 2010. Until then, he was an Associate Vice President of the Central Research Institute of Electric Power Industry in Japan as well as a Senior Research Fellow at the Institute of Energy Economics of Japan and Visiting Professor at the Graduate School of Public Policy, University of Tokyo. He was Associate Director of MIT's International Program on Enhanced Nuclear Power Safety from 1988 to 1993 and a Research Associate at MIT's Center for International Studies (1993–95) where he co-authored a report on Japan's plutonium program. He was a member of International Panel on Fissile Materials (IPFM) and co-authored reports including "Fast Breeder Reactor Programs: History and Status" (2009) and "Japan's Spent Fuel and Plutonium Management Challenges" (2006). He was a member of the Ministry of Economy, Trade and Industry's Advisory Committee on Energy (Nuclear Policy Subcommittee) until December 2009.

Peter G. Taylor is Head of the Energy Technology Policy Division at the International Energy Agency in Paris, France. He is responsible for leading work to analyze and promote the role of energy technologies in achieving the three goals of the IEA: energy security, economic development, and environmental protection. This includes major activities on energy efficiency indicators and technology roadmaps, as well as the Energy Technology Perspectives project, which develops scenarios and strategies for dramatically reducing global greenhouse gas emissions. Prior to working at the IEA, he was the Technical Director of Future Energy Solutions, a leading UK energy and environmental consultancy. He has also spent 15 years working in research and consultancy on a range of national and international policy issues related to energy and climate change.

Nathalie Trudeau joined the Energy Technology Policy Division of the International Energy Agency in January 2008 as energy analyst. She is responsible for the development and analysis of energy and energy efficiency indicators, including development of methodologies, analysis of current and past energy and efficiency trends and potential savings assessment. She also lead the work on the development of the industrial technology model used for the IEA *Energy Technology Perspective* project. Prior to joining the IEA, she worked for over ten years on numerous energy-related files such as development of detailed energy end-use databases and modeling frameworks, energy efficiency indicators development and analysis, and modeling and analysis of climate change policies.

Scott Victor Valentine is currently an Assistant Professor and Assistant Director of the International Master of Public Policy program at the Graduate School of Public Policy, University of Tokyo. He has over 20 years of diverse international business experience specializing in business development and organizational development. His research focus is broadly in the areas of sustainable development policy, environmental policy and public management. In the field of energy policy research he has published a number of papers in journals such as *Energy Policy*, *Energy*, and *Energy for Sustainable Development*. He is also a contributing author of *Critical Issues in Climate Change and the Kyoto Protocol*.

Adriaan J. van der Welle works as a scientific researcher at the Energy research Centre of the Netherlands (ECN). His research interests include the integration of intermittent renewable generation in electricity markets and grids, network regulation, energy markets design and security of supply. He has contributed to many European research projects about the market and network integration of distributed generation. He is (co-)author of papers and book chapters about distributed generation (INTECH) and security of supply (FEEM).

Detlef van Vuuren is a Senior Researcher at the Netherlands Environmental Assessment Agency. His work concentrates on global environmental change scenarios, in particular the possible pathways for the world energy system in relation to climate change. He is the author of the *Global Environment Outlook* of the United Nations Environment Program and Coordinating Lead Author of the *Millennium Ecosystem Assessment*. He is now involved as Lead Author in the *Fourth Assessment Report* of the Intergovernmental Panel on Climate Change and Coordinating Lead Author of the *Agriculture Assessment* for the World Bank. He has also played a coordinating role in the development of new scenarios for climate research and participates regularly in studies of the Stanford University-based Energy Modeling Forum. In total, Detlef van Vuuren has published more than 75 articles in peer-reviewed scientific journals.

David F. von Hippel is a Senior Associate with the Nautilus Institute and independent consultant working in Eugene, Oregon. His work with Nautilus has centered on energy and environmental issues in Asia, and particularly in Northeast Asia, including in the multi-nation Asia Energy Security Project, centered around national and regional energy paths analysis, and the related East Asia Science and Security project, which focuses on potential nuclear materials issues in the region. He is a co-editor of the forthcoming *Asian Energy Security Special Issue* of the journal *Energy Policy*, the lead author of the forthcoming (2010) Nautilus report, *Future Regional Nuclear Fuel Cycle Cooperation in East Asia: Energy Security Costs and Benefits*, and the lead author of the 2007 Nautilus report, *Fueling DPRK Energy Futures and Energy Security: 2005 Energy Balance, Engagement Options, and Future Paths*, as well as numerous articles, presentations, book chapters, and reports on energy security and related topics.

James H. Williams is an Associate Professor at the Monterey Institute of International Studies. Dr. Williams has worked in the energy and climate change field for more than 20 years as an academic researcher, teacher, consultant, and practitioner. Before joining the faculty, he worked at Energy and Environmental Economics where he was lead analyst on the implementation of California's Global Warming Solutions Act for California state agencies. He is a specialist in regulatory policy and clean energy technologies for electric power systems, with experience in carbon market design, renewable generation and transmission, energy efficiency and demand response, plug-in hybrid electric vehicles, energy storage, and distribution automation.

INTRODUCTION

Defining, measuring, and exploring energy security

Benjamin K. Sovacool

Introduction to the book

As I write this introduction in the summer of 2010, in the past week 104,500 barrels of crude oil spilled from the Trans-Alaska Pipeline System after a battery failed to properly recharge an electronic valve. A few days earlier, the Malaysian oil tanker MT *Bunga Kelana 3* collided with the Grenadine cargo ship MV *Waily* in the Singapore Strait, spewing 2,500 tons of crude oil that created a four square kilometer slick that traversed into coral reefs, fisheries, parks, and beaches around Singapore and Malaysia. In the Gulf of Mexico, British Petroleum engineers were trying to stop the *Deepwater Horizon* spill from leaking 5,000 barrels of oil per day, oil that is already washing ashore and damaging wetlands and fisheries in Alabama, Louisiana, and Florida. The international community was still considering sanctions against North Korea and Iran for their nuclear energy programs, shortages of coal in China remain a pressing concern, and the US Congress had more than ten energy and climate-related bills that they will soon debate.

Indeed, the perceived global energy security challenges have become so severe that some experts have called for military action. Writing from Hungary, one government official proposed militarizing energy security as part of the North Atlantic Treaty Organization (NATO), desiring to assign NATO with the task of formally ensuring a secure supply of energy fuels, surveying maritime transportation corridors, securing pipelines, and interdicting energy terrorists.[1] One officer from the US military even went so far as to claim that "responsible access to energy could be the single largest US strategic security issue short of full-scale nuclear war."[2] Others have argued that new institutions, such as a global Energy Stability Board, are required to coordinate energy investments and minimize energy security risks.[3]

What is behind the resurgence of concern over energy security, and what are the most prominent energy security challenges around the world? How does energy security differ from other closely related concepts such as sustainability or national security? How can it be measured and tracked? How do energy security concerns differ by countries and according to technologies? How can best practices at improving energy security be identified? How can countries improve their energy security relative to others?

This book tackles these questions directly. It explores the dimensions to energy security, attempts at measuring it on a national and international scale, and particular case studies and complications related to energy security in practice. The book begins by identifying varying definitions and dimensions of energy security, including those that prioritize security of supply and affordability alongside those that emphasize availability, energy efficiency, trade, environmental quality, and social and political stewardship. The final part of the book explores the various metrics that can be used to give energy security more coherence, including recent attempts to measure energy security progress at the national level, with a special emphasis placed on countries within the Organization of Economic Cooperation and Development (OECD), countries within Asia, and industrialized countries worldwide.

The main themes and objectives of the book are to:

- broaden beyond existing discussions of energy security that center exclusively on access to fuels, or things like "oil security" or "coal security." These fall under "security of supply" and are important, but ignore other dimensions related to the environment, efficiency, trade, innovation, climate change, and affordability;
- focus not only on the supply side of energy but also the demand side, taking a hard look at energy services and politics along with technologies and infrastructure;
- investigate oft-ignored issues such as energy poverty, equity and access, and development alongside the more common elements of energy consumption, industrialization, and interruptions in energy supply;
- analyze ways to index and measure energy security progress at the national and international level.

The book is therefore unique in at least five senses. First, it looks not only at differing dimensions and national challenges to energy security but also at systematic ways to measure it and evaluate performance. Second is scale or the unit of analysis. Chapters focus not only on the traditional energy security culprits of nations and energy infrastructure, but also households, communities, and global linkages of energy systems and technologies. Third, as well as being academics and scholars, contributors are also practitioners and analysts working at places such as the International Energy Agency, making the book truly interdisciplinary. Fourth, the book focuses on energy security issues for Western and industrialized countries alongside numerous perspectives from the developing world, with case studies investigating Indonesia, India, Southeast Asia, and other emerging economies. Fifth, whereas many works treat energy security from purely a technological perspective or a geopolitical perspective, this book combines social, political, economic, and technical factors to look at how technologies, policies, and values interact in a mutually constitutive role with energy security concerns.

To get started, this introductory chapter defines energy security, exploring its meaning in contemporary policy and scholarly literature, along with some of its dimensions. It describes a few competing frameworks or paradigms driving different meanings of energy security. The chapter then illustrates a series of energy security challenges at three different scales. It explores one set of threats at the *macro* level of the international global system. These threats include things like geopolitical struggles over resources, transboundary environmental pollution, and climate change. It then iterates another set of threats at the *micro* scale of households, exploring the nexus between energy poverty, pollution, equity, and access to energy services. A final set of challenges exist at the *meso* scale between the level of households and the global energy system, where specific energy technologies and fuel chains present unique risks, from those connected to nuclear energy and fossil fuels to hydroelectric power and small-scale renewable energy. The final section of the chapter previews the contents of the book.

Navigating the contested terrain of energy security

Aristotle is reputed once to have said that "he who controls the definition, controls the debate." Oddly, however, some politicians refuse to define energy security at all. Although the Food and

Energy Security Act of 2007 in the United States was 1,362 pages long and the Energy Independence and Security Act of 2007 218 pages long, neither offered any definitions of the term "energy security."[4] Yet in the policy and scholarly literature, there seems to be no shortage of definitions. My own cursory review, along with a few research interviews with energy experts, has so far found 45 different definitions, presented below in Table I.1 (to be fair, though, many of these definitions are very close to each other). Whether it's the five 'S's, the four 'A's, or the four 'R's of energy security, this multitude of definitions serves some strategic value; it enables people to advance very different notions of energy security so that they can then justify actions and policies on energy security grounds. But one implication is that the concept has become diffuse and often incoherent. Some authors, including myself, have not even defined it consistently in their own work. Or, as Professor David Victor at Stanford University told the author, "Energy security is like a Rorschach inkblot test—you can see whatever you want to see in it."[5]

Table I.1 Forty-five definitions of energy security

Source	Definition
Asia Pacific Energy Research Centre[6]	Ability of an economy to guarantee the ability of energy resource supply in a sustainable and timely manner with the energy price being at a level that will not adversely affect the economic performance of the economy, spread across the four As of availability, accessibility, acceptability, and affordability
Barton *et al.*[7]	A condition in which a nation and all, or most, of its citizens and businesses have access to sufficient energy resources at reasonable prices for the foreseeable future free from serious risk of major disruption of service
Bazilian *et al.*[8]	Energy fuels and services at reasonable and stable prices, in sufficient quantity, free from imports and indigenously provided, attuned to increases in future demand, delivered at the right time
Bielecki[9]	Reliable and adequate supply of energy at reasonable prices
Bohi and Toman[10]	Loss of welfare that may occur as a result of a change in price or availability of energy
Brown and Sovacool[11]	Adequate energy supply and affordable prices as well as social and cultural sustainability and environmental preservation
CNA[12]	Diversity, or a mix of fuel sources; stability, or stable sources of reserves and technology; intelligence, or the use of energy efficiency and smart meters; reliability, or having strong distribution networks; electrification of ground transport through plug-in hybrids; and bio-based mobility liquid fuels for military applications and aviation
Deutch[13]	Connection between the economic activity that occurs in both domestic and international energy markets and the foreign policy response of nations
Drezel[14]	The five Ss: *supply*, having resources, such as fossil fuels, alternative energy, and renewable energy; *sufficiency*, adequate quantity of fuel and services from these sources; *surety*, having access to them; *survivability*, resilient and durable sources of energy in the face of disruption or damage; and *sustainability*, reducing waste and limiting damage to the environment

Table I.1 (continued)

Source	Definition
European Commission[15]	Uninterrupted physical availability of energy products on the market at an affordable price for all consumers
Florini[16]	Reliable and affordable access to energy supplies
Hughes[17]	The four Rs: review (understanding the problem), reduce (using less energy), replace (shifting to secure sources), and restrict (limiting new demand to secure sources)
International Atomic Energy Agency[18]	Secure supply of energy fuels as well as imports, technologies that promote self-sufficiency as well as protection against disruptions, including those that hedge against price volatility, encourage diversity of technologies and sources, reduce threats to and/ or from neighboring states, enable well-functioning markets, and improve environmental sustainability
International Energy Agency[19]	Adequate, affordable, and reliable access to energy fuels and services, it includes *availability* of resources, decreasing *dependence* on imports, decreasing pressures on the *environment*, *competition* and market efficiency, reliance on indigenous resources that are *environmentally clean*, and energy services that are affordable and equitably shared
International Institute of Applied Systems Analysis[20]	The term may be defined in terms of access to secure, stable, and reliable supplies of efficient and modern energy supplies and appliances at prices that are affordable and in amounts adequate to meet demands for basic energy services in full to ensure human health and well-being and without detriment to the environment
Jacobson[21]	Managing global warming, air pollution mortality, security of supply, water availability, land use, disruption of wildlife, resource availability, thermal pollution, water chemical pollution, nuclear proliferation, and malnutrition
Jansen[22]	The extent to which the population in a defined area can have access to affordably and competitively priced, environmentally acceptable energy services of adequate quality
Jegen[23]	A term that involves three aspects: interconnectedness and promoting market liberalization, regulating climate change, and improving external governance. It entails four aspects: (1) sufficiency of supply, connected to diversification; (2) affordable prices, reasonable for most people; (3) public utility, so that most citizens and users have access to energy services, and (4) time, a distinction between short-term and long-term energy security needs
Kalicki and Goldwyn[24]	Access to stable and affordable supplies of fuel for transportation and electrification
Kalicki and Goldwyn[25]	Assurance of the ability to access the energy resources required for the continued development of national power ... it is the provision of affordable, reliable, diverse, and ample supplies of oil and gas and their future equivalents and adequate infrastructure to deliver these supplies to market
Kemmler and Spreng[26]	Promoting energy efficiency and reducing energy intensity, protecting the natural environment, reducing pollution, and distributing energy to all who need it so that standards of living can be improved

Table I.1 (continued)

Source	Definition
Kessels et al.[27]	Diversification of supply sources, robust security margins (including spare capacity, emergency stocks, redundancy of infrastructure), flexible and competitive energy markets, mutual interdependence among companies and governments, mutual interdependence between suppliers and consumers, physical security for consumers and producers, quality of information to the public, investments in new technologies, lowered energy imports
Konoplyanik[28]	Stable, cheap, and environmentally friendly energy cycle including primary suppliers, transportation, refining, transformation, and final consumption
Lovins[29]	A term that rests on three pillars: making domestic energy infrastructure resilient, improving reliability by phasing out vulnerable facilities and fuel sources, and eliminating reliance on oil from any source
Medlock[30]	Maintaining a stable supply of energy at a reasonable price to avoid the macroeconomic costs associated with interruption of energy supply or increases in energy price
Muller-Kraenner[31]	Provision of reasonably priced, reliable, and environmentally friendly energy
Nuclear Energy Agency [32]	Minimizing vulnerability to unique and unforeseeable events threatening the physical integrity of energy flows or leading to discontinuous energy price rises, independent of economic fundamentals
Omorogbe[33]	Provision of adequate, affordable, efficient, and reliable energy services with minimal adverse impacts on the environment
Orr[34]	Seriously pushing energy efficiency, energy systems that rely on renewable and non-depletable fuels, decentralization and small-scale supply, and financing the ability to shift away from fossil fuels and conventional energy systems
Scheepers et al.[35]	Diversification of energy sources, diversification of imports, long-term political stability of importing regions, and the resource base in those regions
Shrestha and Kumar[36]	Ensuring the availability of energy resources that are diverse, in sustainable quantities, at affordable prices, that support economic growth, assist in poverty alleviation, and do not harm the environment
Sovacool[37]	Technical feasibility, affordability, environmental protection, reliability, and security of supply
Tonn et al.[38]	The elimination of imports and diversity of domestic energy sources
US Agency for International Development[39]	Availability of usable energy supplies, at the point of final consumption, in sufficient quantity and timeliness so that, given due regard for encouraging energy efficiency, the economic and social development of the country is not materially constrained
US Congress[40]	A future where abundant, reliable, and affordable energy is produced with little impact on the environment and no dependence on the goodwill of hostile nations
US Department of Defense[41]	Capacity to avoid adverse impact of energy disruptions caused either by natural, accidental, or intentional events affecting energy and utility supply and distribution systems

Table I.1 (continued)

Source	Definition
US Department of Energy[42]	Promoting America's energy security through reliable, clean, and affordable energy
United Kingdom Department of Trade and Industry[43]	Environmental sustainability, or carbon dioxide emissions; reliability, or having the "right" infrastructure, regulatory system, and liberalized market; competitiveness and productivity, or energy costs that do not discourage investment and growth; social equity, or minimal fuel poverty
United Nations[44]	Protection against shortages of affordable fuel and energy resources
White[45]	A term that encompasses the various aspects of electricity reliability and transmission, energy storage, renewable energy and domestic supply, the penetration of non-carbon-based fuels, political consistency, adequate research budgets for energy, protection of intellectual property rights for energy technologies, development and economic growth, and equity and access
World Bank[46]	Access to secure supplies of fuel, a competitive market that distributes those fuels, stability of resource flows and transit points, and efficiency of end use
World Economic Forum[47]	*Autonomy*, energy supply that is within the control of a country and free from disruption by external agents; *reliability*, or distribution that is safe and meets demand without interruption; *affordability*, or prices commensurable with the buying power of consumers; and *sustainability*, or sufficient supply of energy to support a high quality of life without damaging the environment
World Energy Assessment[48]	Availability of energy at all times in various forms, in sufficient quantities, at affordable prices
World Resources Institute[49]	Sufficiency of supply as well as reliability, affordability, environmental sustainability, geopolitical stability, and social acceptability
Yergin[50]	Reliable and affordable access to energy supplies, diversification, integration into energy markets, and the provision of information

What accounts for such a broad range of definitions, with some arguing energy security is as narrow as meaning secure supplies of fuel and others positing that it involves environmental and social quality or competitive markets, to still others purporting that it necessitates research in new technologies? Part of the difficulty seems to be that energy itself is a politicized and multifaceted concept. In their work after the energy crises of the 1970s, for example, two psychologists identified a *scientific* view of physicists and engineers who see energy as a property of heat, motion, and electrical potential, measurable in joules and British Thermal Units (BTUs).[51] According to this view, energy can be neither produced nor consumed, quantity is always conserved, quality is always declining, and energy security is a matter of understanding thermodynamics and physics.

But they also identified an *economic* view which sees energy as a commodity, or a collection of commodities such as electricity, coal, oil, and natural gas, traded on the market. This view emphasizes the value of choice for consumers and producers and assumes the marketplace allocates choices efficiently. According to this view, when prices rise, fuel substitutes will be found. Energy security is a matter of analyzing transactions between buyers and sellers and minimizing the external costs of these transactions.

Stern and Aronson further identified an *ecological* view which rejects framing energy as scientific or economic, and instead classifies energy resources as renewable or non-renewable, clean or polluting, and inexhaustible or depletable. This view prioritizes the values of sustainability, frugality, and future choice. Energy security is a matter of recognizing that energy resources are finite and interdependent and that present use endangers the planet and future generations.

As if three views were not enough, two additional ones were categorized. The *social welfare* view sees energy services as a social necessity. This view suggests that people have a fundamental right to energy for home heating, cooling, lighting, cooking, transportation, and essential purposes. The central value here is one of equity, and energy security becomes a matter of distributing energy services to all social classes. The hard *political* view focuses on the geographical location of energy resources, the stability of producing and consuming countries, and availability of fuel substitutes. Energy security is seen as a key component of national security, and correct policy becomes a matter of maintaining economic vitality and military strength.

These varying views are not confined to the 1970s and 1980s, and were confirmed in a recent survey of attitudes towards energy.[52] This study, much like the work before it, identified at least seven different perspectives in the United States. "America-firsters" made energy decisions primarily directed at making the country more energy independent; "bottom liners" supported the portfolio of technologies with the lowest cost; "entrepreneurs" supported creativity and research in solving problems through innovation and advancements in technology; "environ-mentalists" sought to minimize pollution and made decisions based on mitigating or adapting to climate change; "individualists" desired a high quality of life and consumption; "politicians" supported energy systems that accommodated as many interests as possible; and "technophiles" sought big engineering approaches to energy problems.

Herein lays the rub: many of these views are incommensurable with each other. Those who believe in economic growth and increased energy use, for instance, see an expanding economy underpinning constant improvements in average living standards, upward social and economic mobility, and a general aura of progress. Those who advocate energy efficiency and conservation see restricted capacity of the environment to absorb pollution from energy processes, adverse effects on human health and safety, and a growing risk of full-fledged catastrophe in a complex, centralized, and independent world.[53] A similar tension exists between treating energy as a commodity and regarding it as a public service. If a commodity, it would make sense for energy companies to choose their customers carefully and focus only on distributing energy services where they can maximize profits, even if it means the exclusion of poor and rural areas. If a public service, then energy companies should have an obligation to supply everyone regardless of cost.[54]

One study looked intently at the "debate" over energy in the world's largest consumer, the United States, and identified three very different views (see Table I.2).[55] Proponents of a "supply" perspective desired to produce more energy to avoid a repeat of the crises, saw resources as inexhaustible and believed that technology was improving in its ability to discover and harvest them, and envisioned government intervention as harmful and disruptive to the free market. The principal actors for the supply perspective are energy companies and corporations, the end goal is to achieve abundant supplies of cheap energy, and the most serious risk is interruption to that supply. Proponents of a "conservation" perspective sought a technical fix to energy problems and high-lighted the need to use energy more judiciously, seeking to break the historic tie between energy consumption and economic growth. The principal actors for the conservation perspective are government agencies in charge of research, and their role is to drive basic science and innovation that will lead to a more energy-efficient society, the most serious risk being waste and inefficiency. Proponents of the "energetics" perspective were more critical and viewed the energy problem not as resource driven or technological problem, but as a social problem of an energy system incompatible

Table I.2 Three different perspectives on energy in the United States

Perspective	Principal Actors	Goal	Most Serious Perceived Problem
Supply	Corporations	Achieve an inexhaustible supply of cheap energy	Interruption to energy supply
Conservation	Government	Create a more energy-efficient society through technical breakthroughs and a decoupling of economic growth from energy consumption	Inefficient energy use
Energetics	Energy Users and Individuals	Promote a more egalitarian, decentralized, democratic, and participatory society that qualitatively matches energy needs with end uses	Resource exhaustion, pollution, and social and community destruction

with democratic values and the physical laws of science. The important actors here are energy users and individuals, the goal is to create a more egalitarian, decentralized, participatory society, and the most serious risk is resource exhaustion and social and community destruction.

Consider public reaction to the energy crisis of 1973. The American public tended to see the oil crisis primarily as a maneuver of oil companies to reap the benefits of higher prices. Anti-environmentalists saw it as a blessing of their war against environmental organizations (such as the Sierra Club) and their allies. Environmentalists saw high prices as a boon for discouraging oil consumption. Independent oil companies saw it as a way to attack the "major" oil companies such as Exxon and Shell. Tax reformers saw it as a chance to end certain provisions that benefited the major oil companies abroad. In essence, there was something in the energy crisis for everyone, but none of "it" was consistent. [56]

It gets worse. A similar survey of 130 "energy advocates" found that many had diametrically opposed views.[57] When asked about the perceived causes of the nation's energy problem, some strongly believed that we waste too much energy while others firmly argued that the restrictions in production were to blame. When asked what technologies the United States should focus on developing, some said exclusively conservation and solar power while others said exclusively fossil fuels and nuclear power. Asked if economic growth required increased energy consumption, 90 percent of "solar" activists said economic growth was possible with reduced consumption, but 80 percent of "conventional" activists felt that economic growth demanded increased consumption. All "advocates" had exceptionally high levels of education, had similar incomes, and represented a broad spectrum of interests, implying that their views could not be explained by education, class, or political affiliation. The researchers concluded that two virtually dichotomous networks of energy researchers were emerging, separated by deep epistemic gulfs.

Another study also found that "education" did little to ameliorate differences between advocates of conventional and alternative energy technologies. Researchers discovered that the two groups that had the most in common, petrochemical industry executives and conservationists, were on both extremes of the energy policy gamut. Both groups were constituted with educated, fairly affluent, strongly committed individuals who believed the nation was confronting a serious and lasting crisis; they just concluded the opposite about what should be done about it.[58]

So given the contested and politicized notion of energy itself, how does one therefore navigate this rich but treacherous terrain of defining or conceptualizing energy security? One novel way is to match differing energy security dimensions with threats. Jonathan Elkind, principal deputy assistant secretary for policy and international energy at the US Department of Energy, has done this nicely in recent research on energy security conducted for the Brookings Institution.[59] He has argued that energy security is composed of four elements: availability, reliability, affordability, and sustainability. Availability refers to the ability for consumers and users to secure the energy that they need. It requires an extensive commercial market, buyers and sellers trading goods, parties that agree on terms, as well as sufficient physical resources, investments, technology, and legal and regulatory frameworks to back them up. Reliability refers to the extent that energy services are protected from disruption, predicated on a number of interrelated criteria including:

- diversification of sources of supply (various fuels and technologies);
- diversification of supply chains;
- resilience or the ability to handle shocks and recover from failures;
- reducing energy demand to ease the burden on infrastructure;
- redundancy in case failures occur;
- distributing timely information to markets.

Affordability involves not only low or equitable prices relative to income but also stable prices that are non-volatile. Sustainability refers to minimizing the social, environmental, and economic damage that can result from long-lived energy infrastructure. Table I.3 shows that each of these four elements can be correlated with different components and threats.

Like Elkind, I propose that energy security should include the interconnected dimensions of availability, affordability, efficiency, and stewardship.[61] This allows the concept to cut across the various dimensions of energy production and use discussed above, but still retains coherence. It is no longer appropriate to envision and practice energy security as merely direct national control over energy supply, and instead necessitates carefully cultivating respect for human rights and the preservation of natural ecosystems along with keeping prices low and fuel supplies abundant, issues that extend beyond individual states. Table I.4 summarizes these criteria.

For me, *availability* relates to the relative independence and diversification of energy fuels and services. Part of ensuring availability entails procuring "sufficient and uninterrupted supply" and minimizing reliance on imported fuels.[62] A related aspect of availability is diversification, or preventing the sabotage and attack of critical infrastructure, such as power plants, pipelines, dams, and transmission and distribution networks so that the services they provide are available. Diversification encompasses at least three dimensions. Source diversification requires utilizing a mix of different energy sources, fuels, types, and fuel cycles (i.e., relying not just on nuclear power or natural gas but also coal, oil, wind, biomass, geothermal, etc.). Supplier diversification refers to developing multiple points of energy production so that no single company or provider has control over the market (i.e., purchasing natural gas from not just one or two companies but a diversified mix of dozens of energy firms). Spatial diversification means spreading out the locations of individual facilities so that they are not disrupted by single attack, event, malfunction, or failure (i.e., spreading refineries across the country instead of placing all of them along the same coast). Typically, an "optimized" level of diversification is achieved when all three dimensions are promoted at once, or certain portfolios of energy systems are arranged to explicitly minimize risk across the entire sector at the lowest cost.

A second component of energy security extends beyond availability to include the basic *affordability* of energy services, a term that means not just lower prices so that people can afford energy services but also stable prices and equitable access to energy services. When fuel prices swing wildly, suppliers find it difficult to plan prudent investments. The enormous price spikes for natural gas, coal, and oil seen over the past few years have made many power plants uneconomic to operate, and have resulted in significant increases in electricity prices in several areas. High levels of access to electricity and energy services also correlates with higher levels of energy consumption and lower rates of energy poverty, while lower levels of access and minimal choice correlate with low levels of use, reliance on biomass, and lack of efficient equipment.

Table I.3 Elements, components, and threats to energy security[60]

Elements	Components	Threats
Availability	Physical endowment of producers	Exhaustion of reserves that can be extracted cost-effectively
	Ability of producers, transit countries, and consumers to agree on terms of trade	Limits on development opportunities such as resource-nationalist policies and state-to-state contracts
	Technological solutions for production, transportation, conversion, storage, and distribution	Problems in siting infrastructure including NIMBY syndrome
	Capital investment	Financial, legal, regulatory, or policy environments that inhibit investment
	Viable legal and regulatory structures	
	Compliance with environmental and other regulatory requirements	
Reliability	Robust, diversified energy value chain	Failure of energy systems due to severe weather and natural disasters
	Adequate reserve capacity	Failure due to poor maintenance or underinvestment
	Protection from terrorist attacks and political disruptions	Attack or threat of attack by military forces and terrorist organizations
	Adequate information about global energy markets	Political interventions such as embargoes and sanctions
Affordability	Minimal price volatility	Exhaustion of reserves that can be extracted cost-effectively
	Equitable prices	Energy prices that require lower income households to expend large shares of their income
	Transparent pricing	Excessive subsidies that distort prices
	Realistic expectations about future prices	Failure to institute sound pricing policies
	Prices that reflect full costs	Failure to incorporate environmental and social costs to energy production and use
Sustainability	Low emissions of greenhouse gases	Adoption and promotion of carbon-intensive energy infrastructure
	Minimal contribution to local, regional, and global forms of environmental pollution	Impacts of indoor and outdoor air pollution associated with energy use
	Protection of energy systems from climate change	Impacts of a changing climate such as rises in sea level, storm surges, and severe weather events

A third component relates to *efficiency*, or the improved performance and increased deployment of more efficient energy equipment and changes in behavior. Energy efficiency enables the most economically efficient use of energy to perform a certain task (such as light, torque, or heat) by minimizing unit of resources per unit of output. Energy efficiency can include substituting resource inputs or fuels, changing habits and preferences, or altering the mix of goods and services to demand less energy.

A fourth component encompasses *stewardship*, and it emphasizes the importance of sustainability. Stewardship means ensuring that energy systems are socially acceptable; that harvest rates

Table I.4 The four criteria of energy security

Criteria	Underlying Values	Explanation
Availability	Independence and diversification	Diversifying the fuels used to provide energy services as well as the location of facilities using those fuels, promoting energy systems that can recover quickly from attack or disruption, and minimizing dependence on foreign suppliers
Affordability	Equity	Providing energy services that are affordable for consumers and minimizing price volatility
Energy efficiency	Innovation and education	Improving the performance of energy equipment and altering consumer attitudes
Stewardship	Social and environmental sustainability	Protecting the natural environment, communities, and future generations

of renewable resources do not exceed regeneration rates; making sure that pollution and environmental degradation do not exceed relevant assimilative capacities of ecosystems; and guaranteeing that non-renewable resources are only depleted at a rate equal to the creation of renewable ones. It also prioritizes energy systems that operate with minimal damage to the natural environment.

Contemporary energy security challenges

When energy security is viewed this way—as involving availability, affordability, efficiency and technology, and environmental and social stewardship—a number of stark energy security challenges become apparent. These occur primarily at three scales: the macro (meant to encompass global, transnational, and supranational threats), the micro (encompassing local threats at the household level), and the meso (encompassing mid-level threats to energy systems and specific technologies).

Global energy security threats

Global energy security threats can be roughly divided into three areas:[63] geopolitics and war, global investment barriers, and transboundary externalities (environmental and social damages that extend across countries, such as climate change).

Geopolitics and war

Modern economies rely heavily on oil, natural gas, coal, and uranium, which are often imported. The resulting pattern of extensive international trade in energy sources—particularly oil—engenders major security concerns whenever supplies are concentrated or production capacities constrained. The world's known oil reserves are concentrated in a handful of largely volatile countries—notably the Middle East, Russia, Nigeria, and Venezuela—whose governments have been known to yield to the temptation to use their control of this vital resource for political ends.

Consider the situation with oil and gas pipelines. Russia, for example, restricted natural gas transmission to Turkmenistan in 1997 to coerce higher prices after a dispute over contracts. Russia, again, used control of their natural gas pipelines in 2005 to manipulate the market to their advantage and gain concessions on gas prices from Ukraine, even at the risk of blackouts and international outrage.[64] Russia has since used the same tactic at least five times in natural gas disputes with Belarus, Georgia, Moldova, and Ukraine in 2007 and in an oil pricing dispute with Germany in 2008.[65] The lesson is simple: suppliers and transporters frequently manipulate dependency to their advantage. One study on the behavior of energy transit pipeline countries found that if countries are taking oil and gas directly from the pipeline, they are continually tempted to always try to take more. Countries transiting oil and gas that have no stake in using it at all, conversely, eventually "play games" and try to squeeze the suppliers for more rent.[66] Worryingly, the study noted that international law and contracts do not mitigate these risks since the rewards often outweigh the costs, especially when the damage inflicted by punitive sanctions is less than what the countries would gain by renegotiating prices.

Similarly, after assessing the performance pipelines in Europe, Asia, South America, the Caribbean, and the Middle East, researchers at Stanford University concluded that in *every* case they looked at, natural gas pipelines were prone to frequent contract interruptions due to price increases and gluts in the market.[67] They also found that such a "gas weapon" was available equally to suppliers, transit countries, or importers, with each attempting to use interruptions to renegotiate contracts to lower or raise prices.

Another review of the financial performance of natural gas companies operating gas pipelines and liquefied natural gas (LNG) terminals in Algeria, Afghanistan, Argentina, Belarus, Bolivia, Indonesia, Iran, Italy, Qatar, Russia, Tobago, Trinidad, and Turkmenistan found that long-term contracts and other mechanisms needed to ensure stable supply could not provide security for investors and governments.[68] In other words, in each of these countries legal and economic protections did not offset the inherent political risks with natural gas infrastructure.

Finally, an assessment of transit pipeline performance in Iraq, Jordan, Lebanon, Saudi Arabia, Syria, Tunisia, and Turkey found much the same situation from 1970 to 2000.[69] During this period, the study noted that when oil and gas prices were high, producers and transit countries tended to want to increase volumes to earn greater returns, placing greater stress on renegotiating contracts to take advantage of high prices and inducing more spills and accidents. When prices were low, in contrast, the study noted that operators tended to cut back on maintenance expenses, causing corrosion and damage so that they could use the degraded pipeline infrastructure to create negotiating leverage for higher transit prices. The study concluded that "the operating experience of such pipelines had been abysmal in terms of interruptions to flow."[70]

The tenuousness of pipelines, and the ability of those who control reserves to manipulate their price, creates strong incentives for countries to claim as many energy resources as they can. Asian countries, for instance, are already embroiled in intensive interstate rivalries over oil among themselves and with regional superpowers such as China.[71] Picking just a few of the most prominent examples, in 1992 China formally stated its right to the "use of force" to protect its claims to oil and gas resources in the South China Sea. In 1995, China seized a chunk of Philippine land and attacked a few fishing vessels to procure offshore oil and gas reserves. In the "Kikeh oil dispute," competing efforts between Brunei and Malaysia to sign contracts with oil companies deteriorated into a tense naval standoff in April and May 2003. In 2007 demonstrations in Vietnam over China's attempts to claim the Spratly Islands in the South China Sea convinced their national oil and gas companies to withdraw from the region.

These recent anecdotes ignore the far more serious historical examples where energy resources have provoked and/or escalated major international conflicts, including both of the world wars. In

World War I, Entente and Central powers both believed control of coal, oil, and gas resources was key to victory. Before World War II, Japan, suffering from a dearth of available raw materials, invaded Manchuria in 1931 to acquire their coal reserves. In response to Japan's later invasion of China in 1937 and to show support for the United Kingdom, in January 1940 the Roosevelt Administration abrogated the 1911 Treaty of Commerce and Navigation with Japan. This meant licenses for the export of gasoline and aviation fuel as well as machine tools to Japan were suspended. Without domestic resources, Japan invaded the oil-rich Indonesian islands, and the resulting tensions were a contributory factor in the Japanese decision to attack Pearl Harbor. That same year, Adolf Hitler declared war on the Soviet Union in part to secure oil for his war machine, and he launched *Operation Blau* to protect German oilfields in Romania while securing new ones in the Central Caucasus. The Soviet Union attempted to invade northern Iran in 1945 and 1946 to acquire control of their oil resources precisely to reduce their own dependence.

Historian Vaclav Smil has traced the role of energy and war, and documented numerous examples where energy reserves prompted or exacerbated international conflict.[72] Apart from identifying the interconnections between energy reserves and the world wars, Smil argues that energy and energy resources were factors in the Korean War (North Korea is the coal-rich part of the peninsula), the Vietnam War (waged by France until 1954, the US after 1964; at stake were Vietnamese oil and gas reserves), the Soviet occupation of Afghanistan (which had significant energy and mineral resources), and the first Gulf War (explicitly about oil, with the Iraqi occupation of Kuwait). Smil also suggests that almost "all" recent cross-border wars of the twentieth century were energy-related, including the conflict between India and Pakistan, Eritrea and Ethiopia, China and India, and also civil wars such as those in Sri Lanka, Uganda, Angola, and Colombia.

Finally, energy is implicated in military action and international conflict in three other ways: wars represent the most concentrated and devastating releases of energy, military operations need mobilization of energy for resources, and a common consequence of war is disruption of energy services.[73] First, energy is embodied in weapons and projectiles, which release all of it at once to inflict damage. As Table I.5 shows, the evolution of weaponry, in a way, is also an evolution of the ability of weapons to release destructive energy. Concomitant with the destructive power unleashed in war is an increase in battlefield deaths, which grew from less than 200 per 1,000 soldiers of armed forces fielded at the beginning of conflict during the Crimean War of 1853–1856 and the Franco-Prussian War of 1870–1871 to more than 1,500 during World War I and 2,000 for World War II (and for some particular campaigns, like the German invasion of Russia, surpassed 4,000 deaths).[74] These latter numbers reveal the bloody nature of these conflicts, with deaths surpassing the number of soldiers fielded.

Second, modern wars rely on weapons whose construction requires energy and energy-intensive materials. Once built, such technologies need flows of liquid fuels and electricity to function. As a "conservative estimate," Smil calculates that about 5 percent of all US and Soviet commercial energy consumed between 1950 and 1990 went to developing and amassing weapons and their delivery mechanisms.[76] The American military now risks most of its casualties in combat from convoys and their guards, primarily distributing inefficiently used fuel,[77] and by one estimate 50 percent of the energy used by the US Air Force is spent hauling energy fuels.[78]

Third, and finally, wars damage energy infrastructure. In the current American military campaigns in Afghanistan and Iraq, determined insurgents have learned to destroy critical energy infrastructure faster than American contractors can rebuild it. John Robb, a former "black ops" agent and expert in counterterrorism, warns that a terrorist–criminal symbiosis is developing whereby terrorists have learned to fight nation states strategically without weapons of mass

Table I.5 Kinetic energy released by weapons and explosives[75]

Weapon	Projectile/Explosive	Kinetic Energy (J)
Bow and arrow	Arrow	20
Heavy crossbow	Arrow	100
Civil war musket	Bullet	1×10^3
M16 assault rifle	Bullet	2×10^3
Medieval cannon	Stone ball	50×10^3
Eighteenth century cannon	Iron ball	300×10^3
World War I artillery gun	Shrapnel shell	1×10^6
Hand grenade	TNT	2×10^6
World War II heavy AA gun	High-explosive shell	6×10^6
M1A1 Abrams Tank	Depleted uranium shell	6×10^6
Unguided World War II rocket	Missile with payload	18×10^6
Suicide bomber	TDX	100×10^6
500 kg truck bomb	ANFO	2×10^9
Boeing 767 (September 11, 2001)	Hijacked plane	4×10^9
Hiroshima atomic bomb (1945)	Fission	52×10^{12}
US nuclear intercontinental ballistic missile	Fusion	1×10^{15}
Novaya Zemlya bomb (1961)	Fusion	240×10^{15}

destruction, using a new method of "systems disruption," a simple way of attacking critical services (electricity, gas, water, communications, etc.) that require centralized coordination of complex networks.[79]

Military planners also often strategically select energy infrastructures as priority targets during attacks and invasions. A post-war study of the 1991 air campaign during the Gulf War revealed that the American strategy went beyond bombing armed forces and military targets and concluded that (a) some targets were attacked to destroy or damage facilities that would require foreign assistance to repair; (b) many targets were selected to amplify economic and psychological impact; (c) targets were selected to do great harm to Iraq's ability to support itself.[80] More than 20 power plants and 3 nuclear plants were attacked in the initial wave of air strikes in 1991, releasing large quantities of radiation, fuel, and debris into the local population.[81] Subsequent World Health Organization investigations estimated that 31 percent of animal resources were directly exposed to hazardous radiation and that 42 percent of arable soil was contaminated, and a United Nations commission visiting Iraq after the Gulf War admitted, "Iraq has, for some time to come, been relegated to a pre-industrial age, but with all the disabilities of post-industrial dependency on intensive use of energy and technology."[82]

Trade and investment barriers

Meeting the growing global demand for energy will require massive investments of trillions of dollars, with significant challenges relating to anachronistic regulations, trade constraints, and intellectual property rights. Moreover, national subsidies currently encourage the channeling of energy investments heavily in the direction of fossil fuels and nuclear energy. Decisions about cross-border energy investment are influenced by multiple sets of actors, both private and public. Investments in cross-border energy infrastructure (and indeed many other forms of infrastructure) are regulated primarily by a large, interlocking web of bilateral investment treaties, whose terms can actively discourage governments from making the regulatory changes needed to encourage the development of cleaner and less polluting systems. The treaties aim to protect the foreign investor from any financial loss arising as a result of state action. Those state actions include not only direct expropriation, but also the enactment of new laws or regulatory policies that force the investor to make changes that result in a loss. Thus, regulatory changes aimed at encouraging the development of "clean" energy could lead to expensive expropriation claims. Under most bilateral investment treaties, such claims are settled by international arbitration panels that have generally favored investor interests.

In addition, the current global structure of intellectual property rights creates impediments to the diffusion of new energy technologies across countries. A debate has been raging in many industries over the role of intellectual property in innovation, with some arguing that strong intellectual property protections spur innovation, while others posit that strong patents deter innovation and raise prices. In the case of energy technologies, intellectual property rights have been used to block entry into the wind turbine, solar panel, and hybrid electric vehicle markets in Japan and the United States, and prevent the acquisition of clean coal technology by Chinese firms.[83] Many countries in the developing world, moreover, do not own the intellectual property rights for the newest or most efficient energy systems, meaning that they have to license Western technology to avoid reliance on fossil fuels, particularly in markets such as China and India. One assessment of the barriers facing greenhouse gas-reducing energy systems (such as clean coal and carbon capture and sequestration, nuclear power, energy efficiency, and renewable power plants) found that many firms were reluctant to distribute new energy technologies to developing markets for fear that their intellectual property rights would not be respected and enforced by the World Trade Organization and other relevant authorities.[84]

Yet at the same time, perverse but long-established subsidies—which benefit fossil fuel and nuclear energy sources at the expense of emerging alternatives—abound. Indeed, among the most pernicious entrenched factors militating against a rapid transformation to a secure and sustainable global energy future is the widespread use of energy subsidies supporting exactly the opposite. The global energy industry receives at least $328 billion in subsidies per year. These subsidies distort the price signals that consumers receive for energy fuels and services, and artificially create demand for both energy and its associated infrastructure. Moreover, existing energy subsidies have heavily favored those technologies that are the least efficient (from a thermodynamic standpoint) and most destructive to the environment, with the bulk of research subsidies going towards nuclear and fossil fuel systems.

In many industrialized countries, especially the United States, coal producers still receive a percentage depletion allowance for mining operations, deductions for mining exploration and development costs, special capital gains treatment for coal and iron ore, a special deduction for mine reclamation and closing, research subsidies, and black-lung benefits paid for by national governments. Oil and gas producers still receive a similar depletion allowance, bonuses for enhanced oil recovery, tax reductions for drilling and development costs, fuel production credits, and research subsidies. Nuclear energy operators and manufacturers benefit from massive loan guarantees, research funds, public insurance and compensation against construction delays, tax breaks for decommissioning, tax credits for operation, and government-funded off-site security and nuclear waste storage. From 1974 to 2002, nuclear power received almost 50 percent of *all* government subsidies related to energy, and fossil fuels received about 15 percent; cleaner sources of energy such as wind farms received about 1 percent.[85] And such distortions are not limited to rich countries. The world's poorer countries (non-OECD members) subsidize oil exploration and production at more than $90 billion a year.

Transboundary externalities

The environmental externalities imposed by current energy systems are beginning to rival security issues in importance on the global agenda. This is due largely to the powerful and increasingly alarming evidence on the scale and pace of climate change, which threatens the entire planet with altered temperatures and weather patterns, rises in sea level, the loss of species, and the destruction of habitats. But energy systems are also at the heart of numerous other common problems: catastrophic risks such as nuclear meltdowns, oil spills, coal mine collapses, natural gas wellhead explosions, and dam breaches that cross national borders; the movement of toxic pollutants such as mercury and acid rain, which do not respect national borders and cause chronic disease, morbidity, and mortality among humans, destroy crops, and damage ecosystems; and continual maintenance of caches of spent nuclear fuel, a common heritage issue because of the long-lived radioactive nature of high-level nuclear waste, to name just some.

Yet climate change is arguably the most challenging collective action problem ever to hit the international stage. The institutional development and political will needed to bring about a global climate agreement, and, crucially, address the temptation to free ride, is still lacking. Moreover, *agreement* on a post-Kyoto Protocol pact to mitigate climate change is, relatively speaking, the easy part. *Implementation* of an accord that is sufficiently ambitious to address the problem may be much harder. Experiments with novel transborder governance approaches such as cap and trade systems and the Kyoto Protocol's Clean Development Mechanism have shown limited efficacy to date, as has the Kyoto Protocol itself.[86] Industrialized countries that signed up to the Kyoto Protocol agreed to collectively reduce greenhouse gas emissions by 5.2 percent below 1990 levels by 2008 to 2012, but to date their collective emissions have increased 8.4 percent over 1990 levels.[87] Given that Kyoto imposed only minor reductions on the handful of countries most able and willing to afford such reductions, this track record does not bode well for the implementation of more ambitious agreements.

Even if climate change were not an issue, current fossil fuel dependence would still impose very costly environmental externalities that often cross borders. One meta-study of the peer-reviewed literature found that negative externalities from just the electricity sector in the United States amounted to $420 billion in damages in 2006, some $143 billion more than that sector's entire revenue for the year.[88] For some fuels such as coal or oil, the negative externalities associated with their use are even greater than the existing market price for the electricity that they produce.

A final compelling transboundary externality is the issue of water. Although energy and water are addressed by almost entirely separate communities of scholars and policymakers, in fact the two are deeply intertwined. Energy fuels and production cannot be managed without attention to water, with every single energy source (including energy efficiency practices and renewable resources) using at least some water, and many components of the water sector (conveyance, treatment, purification, desalination, pumping, distribution) reliant on electricity and energy. Fifty-plus countries rely primarily on hydroelectric dams to generate power and their electricity sectors depend on predictable water supplies. Beyond this, ambitious expansion of conventional power plants and transportation fuels would require vast amounts of water. Thermoelectric power plants running on coal, natural gas, oil, and uranium are water-cooled, withdrawing trillions of gallons of water from rivers and streams, consuming billions of gallons of water from local aquifers and lakes, and contaminating water supplies at various parts of their fuel cycle. Oil and gas production facilities, refineries, ethanol distilleries, and manufacturing firms also rely on prodigious amounts of water to transform raw commodities into usable energy fuels, services, and technologies.

But the water these energy facilities need may not be available. Nearly a billion people already lack adequate access to water, a figure that may rise to more than 3 billion by 2015. Water tables for major grain producing areas in northern China are dropping at a rate of 5 feet per year, and per capita water availability in India is expected to drop 50 to 75 percent over the next decade.[89] About two-thirds of groundwater withdrawals in India, responsible for one-quarter of the country's harvest, are rapidly depleting aquifers and could soon run out. Groundwater consumption in Yemen exceeds the natural recharge rate by more than 70 percent, and other "crisis" levels could soon exist in urban areas across Asia, parts of Mexico, the Oglalla aquifer in the Midwestern United States, and Saudi Arabia.[90] Some of the driest and poorest countries completely reliant on water for agriculture also lack water supply. Ninety percent of water use in Egypt, Libya, and the Sudan supports irrigation and agricultural systems, meaning droughts and shortages can cause widespread shortages of food.[91] By 2025, demographers, geologists, and water managers anticipate that more than 60 percent of the global population will live in countries with significant imbalances between water supply and demand.[92]

Local energy security threats

At the scale of individuals and households, energy security threats take a markedly different form. These types of threats center on lack of equitable access to energy services, energy poverty, and pollution, and are especially prominent in the developing world.

Improved access to energy services is arguably the key defining characteristic of economic development. As Fatih Birol, the Chief Economist for the International Energy Agency, put it:

> Up to now, the energy-economics community has devoted considerable time and effort to analyzing the challenges of energy security and environmental sustainability [for the industrialized world] … Unfortunately, the energy-economics community has given far less attention to the challenge of energy poverty among the world's poorest people.[93]

Worldwide, Table I.6 depicts that nearly 2.4 billion people use traditional biomass fuels for cooking and heating, and 1.6 billion people do not have access to electricity. Even accounting for significant increases in development assistance and rural electrification programs in emerging economies, by 2030 about 1.4 billion people will still be at risk of having to live without modern energy services.[94] When correlated with the amount of energy consumed per capita, Figure I.1 shows that a person living in North America consumes almost 20 times the amount a person does in India. And as Figure I.2 highlights, more than half the population in developing countries such

Table I.6 Number of people relying on traditional biomass in developing countries[95]

	Million	*% Total Population*
China	706	56
Indonesia	155	74
Rest of East Asia	137	37
India	585	58
Rest of South Asia	128	41
Latin America	96	23
North Africa/Middle East	8	0.05
Sub-Saharan Africa	575	89
Total	2,390	52

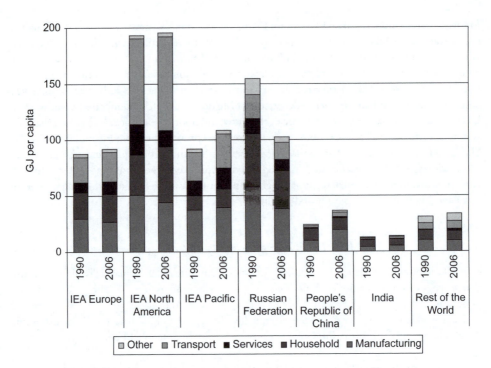

Figure I.1 Energy consumption per capita for selected countries, 1990 and 2006.[96]

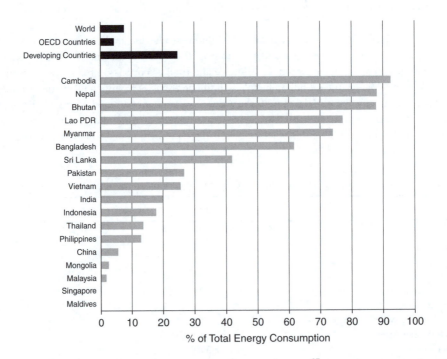

Figure I.2 Proportion of primary energy supplied by traditional biomass.[97]

as Cambodia, Nepal, Bhutan, Laos, Myanmar, and Bangladesh relies on traditional fuels for their primary energy supply.

Energy poverty intersects with other pressing problems including gender equity, social justice, and environmental degradation. Without modern energy carriers, women and children, typically, are forced to spend significant amounts of time searching for firewood, and then burning wood and charcoal indoors to heat their homes or prepare meals. Tragically, this presents many occupational hazards. Ten thousand fuel-wood carriers in Addis Ababa supply one-third of the wood consumed by the city and suffer frequent falls, bone fractures, eye problems, headaches, anemia, internal body disorders, and miscarriages from carrying loads often equal to their body weights. Fuel collection also places women in areas of physical or psychological violence. Hundreds of Somali women have reportedly been raped while collecting fuel, and women in Sarajevo faced sniper fire to collect wood for cooking.[98]

From a health perspective, since such fuels are typically combusted indoors in simple household cooking stoves, without flues or hoods, and burn fuel inefficiently, they concentrate pollution within homes. Such stoves are used for several hours each day at times when people are present indoors, resulting in serious public heath, environmental, and economic repercussions. The availability of cooking fuels is also linked to hunger, as the poorest families must devote a higher share of their income to purchasing fuel, leaving less money for actual food, and making them vulnerable to sudden changes in fuel prices. One study looking at the effects of increases in the price of fuels in four developing Asian economies from 2002 to 2005 found that poorer households paid 171 percent more of their income for cooking fuels and 120 percent more for transportation, 67 percent more for electricity and 33 percent more for fertilizers when compared with the expenditures on energy from middle- and upper-class households.[99] Reliance on traditional fuels and indoor combustion is monumental and the health consequences are dire: indoor air pollution kills more than 2 million people every year, almost equal to the number dying annually from HIV/AIDS.[100] Table I.7 presents these deaths broken down by region and for 18 Asian countries. Put into a daily context, about 4,000 unnecessary deaths, mostly women and children, occur every day from dependence on fuel-wood, charcoal, agricultural waste, and animal dung for energy, and in some countries more than 90 percent of households rely exclusively on these types of health-impairing fuels.[101]

Indeed, even within highly industrialized countries access to energy services is unequal. The poor must expend a larger proportion of their income on energy services even though they generally use less energy than the rich. Using a metric known as a Gini coefficient or Lorenz curve, which looks at the degree of income concentration related to energy (varying between 0 for perfect equality and 1 for maximum inequality), one study looked at the equity of energy use in El Salvador, Kenya, Norway, Thailand, and the United States.[103] The study found that *no* country was equitable in its energy use. The best country was Norway (where half of residential electricity was used by the top 38 percent of household customers), followed by the United States (half of its electricity consumed by 25 percent of customers), El Salvador (15 percent), Thailand (13 percent), and Kenya (6 percent).

The lack of access to modern energy services can worsen poverty, and research has shown that the relationship between energy and poverty is mutually constitutive. That is, high levels of poverty are associated with patterns of energy consumption in households: low levels of use, lack of access to cleaner fuels, lack of efficient equipment, and reliance on biomass occur primarily in lower income homes.[104] Conversely, the provision of clean and reliable energy is a key aspect of poverty alleviation and development.

Many, if not most, developing countries lack the capacity and technology to shift to more sustainable and affordable supplies of energy without external assistance. One survey of the 24 least developed countries in the world found that 22 of them had less than 1 percent of their region's total

Table I.7 Health impacts of energy-related indoor and outdoor air pollutants[102]

Country	Population using solid fuel (%)	Deaths per year	Annual concentrations of PM 10 (ug/m³)	Deaths per year	Total
Bangladesh	89	46,000	157	8,200	54,446
Cambodia	95	1,600	51	200	1,946
China	80	380,700	80	275,600	656,460
Democratic People's Republic of Korea	–	–	88	4,900	4,988
India	82	407,100	84	120,600	527,866
Indonesia	72	15,300	114	28,800	44,286
Japan	5	–	33	23,800	23,838
Laos	95	2,400	25	100	2,620
Malaysia	5	100	28	500	633
Myanmar	95	14,700	75	3,900	18,770
Nepal	81	7,500	161	700	8,442
Pakistan	81	70,700	165	28,700	99,646
Philippines	45	6,900	34	3,900	10,879
Republic of Korea	5	–	43	6,800	6,848
Singapore	5	–	48	1,000	1,053
Sri Lanka	67	3,100	93	1,000	4,260
Thailand	72	4,600	77	2,800	7,549
Vietnam	70	10,600	66	6,300	17,036
Asia	77	972,200	–	517,700	1,489,977
World	52	1,497,000	61	865,000	2,362,113

energy resources.[105] The good news, though, is that low-cost interventions can greatly enhance access and minimize energy poverty. As just one example, liquefied petroleum gas is much better (from a health standpoint) than fuel-wood or kerosene. Providing LPG cylinders and stoves to all the people who currently rely on biomass for cooking by 2030 would cost $18 billion per year but save 1.3 million lives.[106]

Technology-based energy security threats

A final category of threats cuts across global and local scales, and relates to vertically and horizontally integrated energy systems. Many of these threats, such as those facing fossil fuels, nuclear power, hydroelectric dams, and small-scale renewable energy technologies, are unique to each energy system.

The complicated aspect of these threats is that they are generally influenced by multiple scales, or events occurring at the local, community, state, national, regional, and global levels. Energy market instabilities, for example, can be caused by unforeseen changes in geopolitical factors or concentration of fossil fuels at the global level, but also occur due to political unrest, conflict, trade embargoes, and successful negotiation for unilateral deals at the national or sub-national level.[107] Technical system failures can include power outages caused by grid malfunction (local), faults in supply systems (local), accidents or human error (local), or shortages of fuel and disruptions in transit (global). Physical security threats such as terrorism and extreme weather events, sabotage, theft, piracy, earthquakes, hurricanes, volcanoes, and climate change can affect any part of the supply chain, including power stations, transmission lines, refineries, oil and gas wells, rail or road networks, terminals and ports, and shipping tankers. Such threats become even more pronounced when pipelines, cables, and offshore installations traverse multiple countries and straddle national and international boundaries.[108]

Fossil fuels

Global trade in oil, gas, coal, and uranium amounted to $900 billion in 2006, including almost two-thirds of the oil produced in the world.[109] As a result, few countries in the world are truly energy independent, and reserves of fossil fuels are heavily concentrated. The world's known 1.2 trillion barrels of oil reserves are concentrated in volatile regions, as are the world's largest petroleum companies. The three largest of these—Saudi Arabian Oil Company, National Iranian Oil Company, and Qatar Petroleum—own more crude oil than the next 40 largest oil companies. The 12 largest oil companies control roughly 80 percent of petroleum reserves and are all state owned. Oil and gas, although internationally traded in what superficially resembles a free market, therefore do not operate as such, given that most supplies are controlled by a handful of government-dominated firms. The distribution of other conventional energy resources, such as coal, natural gas, and uranium, is equally concentrated. When looked at by country, Figure I.3 vividly shows that 80 percent of the world's oil can be found in 9 countries with only 5 percent of the world population; 80 percent of the world's natural gas in 13 countries; and 85.1 percent of the world's coal can be found in the United States, Russia, China, India, Australia, and South Africa.[110] Six countries control more than 80 percent of global uranium resources.[111] Figure I.4 exhibits the geographic distribution of fossil fuels on the world map.

While these reserves may appear plentiful, in truth they will run out soon. Looking at current reserve to production ratios for proven fossil fuel reserves and identified uranium resources, with a zero increase in production the world has 137 years of coal left, 60 years of natural gas, 43 years of petroleum, and 85 years

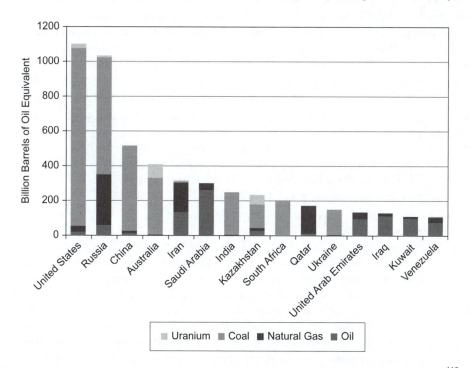

Figure I.3   Proven energy reserves for the largest 15 countries, 2008 (billion barrels of oil equivalent).[112]

	Oil	Natural Gas	Coal	Uranium	Total
United States	21	37	1018	23	1099
Russia	60	294	668	13	1035
China	16	14	487	4	521
Australia	2	5	326	77	410
Iran	136	171	6	1	314
Saudi Arabia	262	42	0	0	304
India	0	7	240	5	252
Kazakhstan	30	18	133	55	236
South Africa	0	0	204	0	204
Qatar	15	159	0	0	174
Ukraine	0	7	144	0	151
United Arab Emirates	98	38	0	0	136
Iraq	115	20	0	0	135
Kuwait	102	10	0	0	112
Venezuela	80	27	2	0	109
Total	937	849	3228	178	5192

Figure I.3   (continued)

of uranium. As Table I.8 shows, however, such numbers become much smaller with only a 5 percent growth in production, dropping to 42 years for coal, 28 for natural gas, and 23 for petroleum. For this reason, Tim Jackson has referred to fossil fuel reserves as "thermodynamic time-bombs."[114]

The impact of the concentration of energy fuels, as well as their rates of depletion, is twofold. First, it makes certain energy systems vulnerable to disruptions in supply. To cite a few prominent examples, oil transit supplies were disrupted in Latvia in 1998, natural gas pipelines shut off between Russia and Ukraine in 2005 and 2006, shortages of coal occurred in China in 2007, lack of rain and snow caused hydropower shortfalls in California, Brazil, and Fiji, blackouts hit North America in 2003 and Europe in 2005, and Hurricane Katrina caused a substantial number of refinery shutdowns.[116] A multitude of serious oil supply shocks averaging eight months in duration and affecting almost 4 percent of global supply have occurred from 1950 to 2003.[117] One study identified five major disruptions in the global oil market in the two decades *after* the famed oil shocks of the 1970s:

- the Gulf War of 1990 and 1991, which removed 4.3 million barrels per day (mbd) of oil production from the market;
- suspension of Iraqi oil exports in 2001, which removed 2.1 mbd;
- a Venezuelan strike in 2003 and 2004, which removed 2.6 mbd;
- the Gulf War of 2003, which removed 2.3 mbd;
- Hurricane Katrina in 2005, which removed 1.5 mbd.[118]

In the electricity sector, another study identified 17 major disruptions in supply in North America alone from 1965 to 2003, or an average number of 700,000 customers per year that suffered disruptions in service.[119]

Second, resource concentration makes the prices of fossil fuels volatile. While it is unclear how long the world can produce enough oil (and even coal, natural gas, and uranium) to meet growing global demand, it is clear that a growing percentage of global oil demand will be met using resources from the Middle East since almost half (45 percent) of the world's proven reserves of conventional oil are located in Saudi Arabia, Iraq, and Iran. If transportation remains oil-dependent and if surplus oil production in the world is limited to one or two million barrels per day,[120] oil-importing nations across the world will continue to be vulnerable to oil price shocks

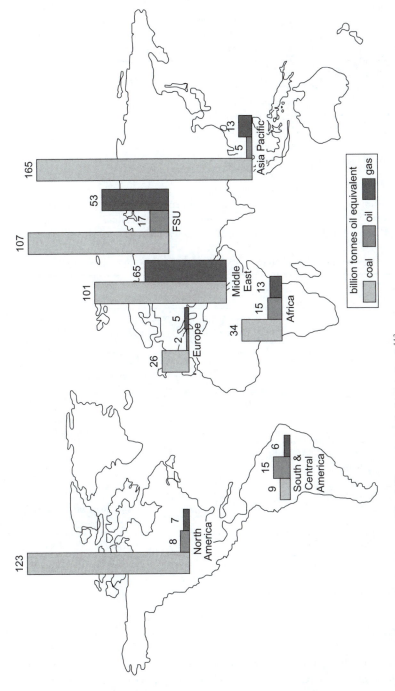

Figure I.4 Worldwide coal, oil, and gas reserves (billion tonnes of oil equivalent).[113]

Table I.8 Life expectancy of proved fossil fuel and identified uranium reserves[115]

	Proved Reserves (2005)	Current Production (2006)	Life Expectancy		
			0% Annual Rate of Growth of Production	2.5% Rate of Growth of Production	5% Rate of Growth of Production
Coal	930,400 million short tons	6,807 million short tons	137	60	42
Natural Gas	6,189 trillion cubic feet	104.0 trillion cubic feet	60	37	28
Petroleum	1317 billion barrels	30.560 billion barrels	43	29	23
	Identified Resources at <USD 130/kgU (2005)	Current Production (2005)	With identified uranium resources (2004)	With total conventional resources (2004)	With total conventional resources and phosphates (2004)
Uranium	4,743,000 tons	40,260 tons	85	270	675

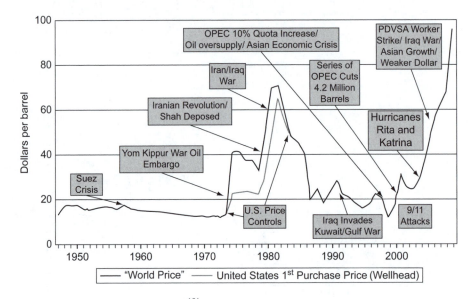

Figure I.5 Crude oil prices 1945 to 2008.[121]

and volatility, as has been the case since the Yom Kippur War and oil embargo of 1973, as seen in Figure I.5.

Natural gas prices have also been extremely volatile, especially given the speculation about the quality and location of gas reserves. Figure I.6 shows that the price of natural gas at the Henry Hub in New York, one of its trading points, jumped from $6.20 per million BTUs (MMBtu) in 1998 to $14.50 per MMBtu in 2001, then dropped precipitously for almost a year only to rebound yet

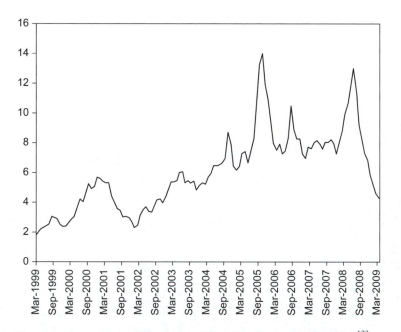

Figure I.6   Natural gas futures prices 1999 to March 2009 (US dollars per million BTU).[123]

again.[122] Hurricane Katrina caused similar price spikes when it disrupted natural gas refining and reprocessing infrastructure in the southeastern part of the United States.

Figure I.7 shows that coal prices have also been volatile, jumping from $50 per short ton in Central Appalachia in November 2007 to $140 per short ton in August 2008, almost tripling in nine months.[124] Transportation bottlenecks and demand surges in developing countries such as India and China were partly to blame. From 2001 to 2006, coal use around the world grew by 30 percent, and 88 percent of this increase came from Asia (with 72 percent of the increase from China alone).[125] In 2004 China shifted from a net exporter to an importer of coal, creating a severe shortage of oceanworthy bulk carriers and causing the global price of coal (as well as other commodities such as iron, ore, and steel) to jump drastically as freight prices soared.[126] Other contributing factors included (a) dwindling reserves of coal in some parts of the United States and Europe, (b) constricted rail service, (c) flooding and hurricanes hitting barge routes, (d) bankruptcies and resulting consolidation and restructuring within the industry, (e) permitting, bonding, and insurance issues, (f) mine closures, (g) more stringent environmental regulations concerning mine planning and the posting of reclamation bonds, and (h) restrictions on mountain top removal.[127] A comprehensive International Energy Agency (IEA) study revealed that more than half of coal-powered plants reported significant price fluctuations in coal, varying by almost a factor of 20.[128]

Nuclear power

Nuclear energy is proving popular as a response both to soaring energy demand and to the need to develop less carbon-intensive energy sources. In 2008, more than 440 nuclear power plants operated in 31 countries and supplied about 15 percent of the world's electricity. Additionally, 60-plus countries, including Egypt, Indonesia, and Turkey, have formally expressed interest in

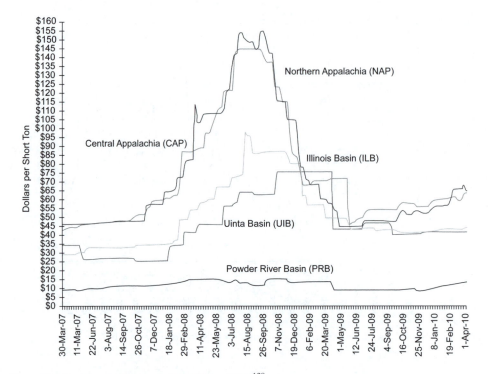

Figure I.7   Coal commodity spot prices, 2007 to 2010.[129]

Notes:
Key to Coal Commodities by Region

Central Appalachia:	Big Sandy/Kanawha	Powder River Basin:	8,800 Btu, 0.8 lb SO2/mmBtu
Northern Appalachia:	12,500 Btu, 1.2 lb SO2/mmBtu	Uinta Basin in Colo:	11,700 Btu, 0.8 lb SO2/mmBtu
Illinois Basin:	Pittsburgh Seam 13,000 Btu, <3.0 lb SO2/mmBtu 11,800 Btu, 5.0 lb SO2/mmBtu		

introducing nuclear power to their energy systems. Countries such as France and the United States are actively marketing their nuclear power technology. If one takes all government proclamations at face value, 319 new nuclear power plants have been planned and proposed totaling 325,488 MW of capacity that would need more than 64,000 additional tons of uranium each year to operate, with the fastest growth rates expected to occur in China, India, Japan, and South Korea.[130]

Yet nuclear power facilities face their own set of risks.[131] One unique to nuclear power is the connection between reactors and weapons of mass destruction. The twin pillars of the nuclear non-proliferation regime—the Nonproliferation Treaty (NPT) and the formation of the International Atomic Energy Agency (IAEA)—are nowhere near sufficiently robust to stand up to such a vast increase in reliance on nuclear energy. A recent high-level commission found that the IAEA is already badly overstretched and needs to be strengthened considerably to address the need for monitoring and safeguarding what is likely to be an explosion in the number and size of nuclear energy programs, particularly in Asia.[132] The agency's 2,000 or so full-time staff have been struggling under a zero-growth budget and spread thin across very different mandates. The IAEA, for example, must not only devise technical safeguards relating to nuclear power plant safety and perfect tools for assessing the economics and planning for new nuclear reactors, but also oversee the use of nuclear isotopes for medical diagnostics and treatment, manage research programs on new waste management systems, and undertake basic science in experimental nuclear physics. Yet at a time when the IAEA urgently needs additional resources to carry out its mandates, consensus on the basic bargain that underlies the non-proliferation regime and legitimizes the IAEA—that nuclear-weapon states will pursue disarmament and help other states with peaceful nuclear technology on a non-discriminatory basis and with defense against threats of nuclear attack—is breaking down.[133]

A second major energy security challenge is cost. While historic costs of producing nuclear energy are relatively low—due in large part to generous subsidies and almost five decades of commercial operating experience—the expense of building new nuclear plants is immense. Although the industry reports construction costs of about $2,000 per installed kilowatt (kW), independent assessments suggest about $5,500 to $8,100 per installed kilowatt—translating into a whopping $6 to $9 billion for each 1,100 MW plant. Unlike other energy sources, capacity costs are rising across time. The Keystone Center, an independent think tank, estimated in 2007 that operating costs for these plants would be 30¢ kilowatt-hour (kWh) for the first 13 years, followed by 18¢/kWh after the plants have been paid off.[134] This makes nuclear more expensive than natural gas, coal, and even wind, biomass, geothermal, landfill capture, and new hydroelectric power plants.

The assessments above still exclude things like decommissioning, unexpected delays, cost overruns, insurance, interest on loans, early retirements, and building transmission and distribution networks to nuclear facilities. The average construction time for all 376 nuclear power plants built from 1976 to 2007 was greater than seven years and some have dragged on for more than 20 years.[135] Over the same period of time, 5 gas-fired combined cycle plants or 18 wind farms of comparable size could have been completed. Because of this incredible time frame, nuclear plants are exceptionally prone to cost overruns. The independent Congressional Budget Office in the United States has estimated that actual construction costs for American reactors are *twice* as much as expected and that the risk of default on loan guarantees exceeds 50 percent.[136]

The proverbial elephant in the room when it comes to the challenges facing nuclear energy is waste. No one has yet worked out a satisfactory solution to the nuclear waste problem. The world's nuclear fleet creates about 10,000 metric tons of high-level spent nuclear fuel each year. Eighty-five percent of this waste is *not* reprocessed and most is stored on-site in special facilities at nuclear power plants.[137]

As for climate change, nuclear energy is not climate-neutral. Yes, its life-cycle carbon footprint is considerably better than equivalently sized coal, natural gas, and oil-fired facilities. But this point obscures two very disturbing facts. For one, the nuclear life cycle consists of many activities that emit substantial amounts of greenhouse gas into our atmosphere, such as uranium mining and milling and spent fuel conditioning. When these are calculated along with the emissions associated with plant construction, operation, and decommissioning, the typical reactor emits about 66 grams of carbon dioxide equivalent for every kW of electricity it produces.[138] That may not sound like much, but it demonstrates that nuclear energy is worse from a climate perspective than every single source of renewable electricity, as well as small-scale distributed generators that rely on fossil fuels. For two, the carbon footprint of nuclear power is expected to rise significantly as high-quality uranium ores are exhausted and uranium enrichment becomes more energy-intensive. If the Oxford Research Group is to be believed, by 2050 the total life-cycle carbon footprint for a kWh of nuclear electricity will be the *same* for a kWh from natural gas, hardly a smart choice for a carbon-constrained world, given the only direction for nuclear life-cycle emissions is upwards.[139]

Renewable energy

Even small-scale and hydroelectric forms of renewable energy present distinct energy security challenges. Perhaps the most vociferous environmental concern associated with wind energy relates to the death of birds resulting from collisions with wind turbine blades, an issue termed "avian mortality." Onshore and offshore wind turbines present direct and indirect hazards to birds and other avian species. Birds can directly fly into a turbine blade when they are fixated on perching or hunting and pass through its rotor plane; they can strike its support structure; they can hit part of its tower; or they can collide with its associated transmission lines. These risks are exacerbated when turbines are placed on ridges and upwind slopes, close to migration routes, and when there are periods of poor visibility such as fog, rain, and at night. Indirectly, wind farms can physically alter natural habitats, the quantity and quality of prey, and the availability of nesting sites.[140]

Others find wind turbines visually unattractive, especially in significant tourist or recreational destinations where the human-built turbines impose obtrusively on the natural environment. The regions in the United States with the most offshore wind potential include areas along the eastern seaboard, coastlines highly valued for their fisheries, esthetics, and recreational activities. One recent study noted that for many people, "fears of three hundred foot spinning turbines and blinking navigational lights blanketing the horizon have caused an uproar that threatens to drown out wind power's loudest advocates." [141]

For hydroelectric dams, the most extensively debated and complex problems relate to habitat and ecosystem destruction, emissions from reservoirs, water quality, and sedimentation.[142] All these concerns arise because of a dam's role as a physical barrier interrupting water flows for lakes, rivers, and streams. Consequently, dams can drastically disrupt the movement of species and change upstream and downstream habitats. Such barriers also result in modified habitats with environments more conducive to invasive plant, fish, snail, insect, and animal species, all of which may overwhelm local ecosystems. To maintain an adequate supply of energy resources in reserve, most dams impound water in extensive reservoirs. However, these reservoirs can also emit greenhouse gases from rotting vegetation.[143]

While biomass combustion has the advantage of not releasing any net CO_2 into the atmosphere (and thus contributes little to the global inventory of greenhouse gases), it releases measurable levels of a wide variety of pollutants to air, land, and water.[144] These air pollution issues parallel esthetic concerns about land use, smell, and traffic congestion. The combustion of biomass has been noted to release foul odors near some plants, and they can contribute to traffic congestion when large amounts of fuel must be delivered by trucks.[145] The use of agricultural wastes, forest residues, and energy crops such as sugar, legumes, and vineyard grain to generate electricity, when harvested improperly, can strip local ecosystems of needed nutrients and minerals. Widespread use of these crops can also contribute to habitat destruction and deforestation.[146]

For geothermal energy, plants can emit small amounts of hydrogen sulfide and CO_2 along with toxic sludge containing sulfur, silica compounds, arsenic, and mercury (depending on the type of plant).[147] Geothermal systems require water during drilling and fracturing processes, and are ill-suited for desert areas or regions with low levels of water.[148] Extra land may also be required for the disposal of waste salts from geothermal brines, and contamination of groundwater and freshwater can occur if plants are poorly designed.[149]

For solar power, the life cycle for solar photovoltaic systems requires the use of hazardous materials which must be mined from the earth and can contaminate areas of land when such systems break down or are destroyed, such as during hurricanes and tornados.[150] Chemical pollution has also been noted to occur during the manufacturing phase of solar cells and modules.[151]

Lastly, for liquid biofuels, concerns center on land use and food security. The use of corn, rice, and sugarcane as feedstocks for biofuel production has been blamed, at least partly, for rising global food prices.[152] Others have argued that biofuel production in places like Brazil directly contributes to illegal logging and the destruction of the Amazonian and Atlantic rainforests.[153]

Systemic vulnerability

Of course, energy production and use occurs at the nexus of all three of these scales: the macro, micro, and meso, or at the global, local, and technological levels. A constitutive or interstitial systemic vulnerability therefore occurs when all three types of threats and challenges interact with each other. Put another way, the threats are compounded when different energy sources are put into a portfolio. The resulting global energy system thus remains vulnerable to many different types of systemic threats.[154]

Indeed, most existing energy infrastructure is inherently vulnerable to deliberate and accidental disruptions. Systems operators, planners, and energy firms still adhere to a "classic" mentality of building tightly coupled, centralized, capital-intensive forms of energy supply that can easily be disrupted by changing weather, small animals, balloons, rocks, and bullets. Electricity suppliers, for example, have clustered generating units geographically near oil fields, coal mines, sources of water, demand centers, and each other, interconnecting them sparsely and thereby making them heavily dependent on a few critical nodes and links. Operators have provided little storage to buffer successive stages of energy conversion and distribution, meaning that failures tend to be abrupt and unexpected rather than gradual and predictable. Companies and firms have also located generators remotely from users, so that supply-chain links have to be long and the overall system lacks the qualities of user controllability, comprehensibility, and interdependence.[155] Systems are centralized, meaning that power plants and refineries are often far from users, which necessitates longer transmission and distribution distances. The average power plant, for example, delivers its electricity a distance of 220 miles.[156] Centralized supply for electricity therefore cannot discriminate well between end-users. Electricity for a water heater is unaffected by a few hours of interruption, but must bear the high cost of extreme reliability needed for subways and hospitals. Other energy systems are not well adapted to changes in throughput. Natural gas is a good example—if pressure falls below a certain level, a pipeline no longer works, and many forms of transport (pipelines, tankers) are built to move only one type of fuel. Moreover, systems often involve highly hazardous and combustible fuels that corrode and explode or contaminate (indeed, many have been designed to be combustible). Facilities can be opposed by communities that do not want them permitted or built near their homes and neighborhoods. Minnesota farmers in the 1970s, for example, dismantled high voltage power lines once a night that had been built across their land as a sign of political protest.[157]

This complexity and interdependence can be a curse as much as a blessing, for systems can interact in unforeseen and unplanned ways. Some technologies, dependent on multiple fuels at once, can fail due to lack of any one of them, such as a furnace that burns oil or natural gas but needs electricity to ignite and pump the fuel, or gasoline pumps that rely on electricity. Others are physically dependent, meaning the lack of one affects the other, for example municipal water treatment systems need lots of electricity, but thermoelectric power plants need water. When built too closely together, failures in one system can cascade to the other. Broken water mains, for instance, can short out circuits or electric cables, fires and explosions can ignite entire pipeline networks, earthquakes cause gas mains to rupture and explode destroying facilities that survived the initial shock. In the United Kingdom, when Britain converted to natural gas from the North Sea, some public telephone booths actually started exploding. Higher gas pressure was too much for old joints, causing gas to leak into adjacent telephone cable conduits, seep into booths, and become set ablaze by phone users smoking cigarettes.[158]

Our energy systems are also capital-intensive. This makes it difficult to improve energy security, as designers are less able to afford much redundancy. Capital intensity creates a strong temptation to keep facilities running to pay off debt, and avoid routine maintenance that disrupts operation. This is often practiced at nuclear reactors and refineries, where addressing minor leaks is not deemed important. It also creates a push to run facilities at maximum capacity, operating them closer to their technical limits. And the long lead times for such infrastructure require foreknowledge of demand, technological, and political conditions, and also shortens learning since there will be longer periods between cycles of development.[159]

What results is an energy system that is inherently vulnerable to multiple types of disruption. Nuclear reactors and facilities have been attacked or bombed in Argentina, France, Italy, Spain, and the United States. Fourteen transmission towers in rural Oregon were bombed and toppled in 1974 by two extortionists threatening to black out Portland if they were not paid $1 million.[160] Transmission lines were cut in Ireland during a jailbreak orchestrated by the Irish Republican Army, and transmission towers have been bombed and attacked in Alabama, California, Louisiana, New Jersey, Ohio, Washington, and Wisconsin. The bombing of a single substation enabled a military coup in Chile. In an ironic reversal, an attempted military coup in El Salvador failed because the principals blew up all the main substations, and could no longer use telephones or broadcasting to communicate with each other. Indeed, attacks on critical energy infrastructure have occurred in Afghanistan, Angola, Argentina, Bolivia, Brazil, Chile, Cyprus, Egypt, El Salvador, Germany, Guatemala, France, India, Iran, Ireland, Iraq, Israel, Italy, Japan, Korea, Kuwait, Lebanon, Libya, Mozambique, Netherlands, Nicaragua, Nigeria, Portugal, Puerto Rico, Qatar, Saudi Arabia, Singapore, Spain, Sweden, Syria, Taiwan, Turkey, Uganda, United Kingdom, United States, Vietnam, and Zimbabwe.[161]

A few more examples are telling. The US Federal Bureau of Investigation reports that about 15,000 actual or attempted bombings occur in the United States each year, with about 2 percent directed at electric utilities. These bombings peaked in 1978, ostensibly over frustration at higher energy prices, with an American utility being bombed every 12 days over the course of the year.[162] In 1975 the New World Liberation Front bombed pipelines of the Pacific Gas and Electric Company in California more than ten times, and members of the Ku Klux Klan and San Joaquin Militia have been convicted of attempting to attack natural gas infrastructure throughout Mexico and the United States.[163] In 1997 in Texas, police prevented the bombing of natural gas storage tanks at a processing plant by Ku Klux Klan members seeking to create a diversion for a robbery.[164] In 1999 Vancouver police arrested a man for planning to blow up the trans-Alaskan pipeline for personal profit in oil futures.[165] In 2001, an attack on the trans-Alaskan pipeline with a high-powered rifle forced a two-day shutdown and caused extensive economic and environmental damage—all apparently part of a hunting trip gone awry.[166]

Beyond North America, in the 1970s during the Russian invasion of Afghanistan, the mujahidin conducted so many attacks on Soviet oil and gas pipelines that the Russians lost more than 500 tons of petroleum every day. A few decades later in the midst of the Russian–Chechen conflict, both sides exploited pipelines as a way to intensify their military campaign, with the Chechens tapping the Baku-Grozny-Novorossiysk pipeline hundreds of times to draw away oil to hidden refineries where it could be processed into cheap gasoline and then sold in Grozny to purchase weapons.[167] The government of Saudi Arabia, which manages more than 11,000 miles of gas and oil pipelines, has repelled at least 30 attempts in the past four years to destroy or damage their pipelines by "insurgents".[168] Next door, in Iraq, more than 150 attacks on the country's 4,000-mile pipeline system occurred over the course of 12 months.[169] Suicide bombers have attacked natural gas infrastructure in Nigeria, Sri Lanka, and Yemen,[170] and in Pakistan gunmen have frequently stormed Pakistan Petroleum Limited natural gas facilities, fired rockets at pipelines, and kidnapped employees of the Water and Power Development Authority.[171] In Colombia, in South America, the 480-mile Cano Limon-Covenas pipeline has had so many holes blown in it that the locals jokingly refer to it as "the flute."[172] In the Sudan,

Arakis Energy Corporation and Greater Nile Petroleum Company have to repel daily attacks on their oil and gas pipelines.[173] Also, London Police foiled a plot by the Irish Republican Army in 1996 to bomb gas pipelines and other utilities across the city with 36 explosive devices.[174] A strike at Petróleos de Venezuela during the winter of 2002–2003 brought to a halt the country's entire oil sector and temporarily reduced global oil supplies by 3 percent.[175]

Attacks do not have to be "physical." As energy companies and electricity operators have come to rely more on Supervisory Control and Data Acquisition (SCADA) systems with computers, telemetry, radio, and dedicated telephone lines to monitor system elements and transmit information, they become more vulnerable to cyber terrorism. For example, Robert F. Dacey, Director of Information Security Issues at the US General Accounting Office (GAO), recently noted that:

> For several years, security risks have been reported in [SCADA] control systems, upon which many of the nation's critical infrastructures rely to monitor and control sensitive processes and physical functions. In addition to general cyber threats, which have been steadily increasing, several factors have contributed to the escalation of risks specific to control systems, including the (1) adoption of standardized technologies with known vulnerabilities, (2) connectivity of control systems to other networks, (3) constraints on the use of existing security technologies and practices, (4) insecure remote connections, and (5) widespread availability of technical information about control systems.[176]

The report goes on to identify several serious flaws with SCADA technologies employed by electric utilities and other institutions, including (a) unexplained system downtime and loss of operations, (b) deletion of key data from the system, and (c) use of SCADA servers to attack other systems within corporate networks.

The National Transportation Safety Board (NTSB) confirmed this finding when they examined the role of SCADA systems in 13 hazardous liquid pipeline accidents between 1992 and 2004. The NTSB found that in ten of these accidents—that is, more than 75 percent—some aspect of the SCADA system actually "contributed to the severity of the accident," most frequently due to human error in evaluating SCADA information.[177]

It should come as no surprise, therefore, that there have been multiple (and somewhat famous) incidents of SCADA systems being hacked, infiltrated, manipulated, or destroyed:

- computers and manuals seized in al-Qaeda training camps had numerous SCADA manuals and information related to dams and other critical infrastructure;
- the Davis–Besse nuclear power plant in Ohio was offline for five hours due to a virus affecting its SCADA system in January 2003;
- hackers broke in to SCADA systems of the world's largest natural gas pipeline network operated by Gazprom in Russia.[178]

Idaho National Laboratory and the New York State Office of Cyber Security have both warned that the problems with SCADA could be severely underestimated, given the secrecy of how the systems operate. Vulnerabilities with SCADA systems are seldom disclosed, and incidents affecting such systems are rarely reported. One security expert stated that "massive security shortcomings in critical systems are more the norm than the exception."[179]

Preview of chapters

So how ought policymakers to address these various energy security vulnerabilities? Which dimensions of energy security are truly the most important? How can energy security be measured, and which countries are doing the best at improving it? With these questions and issues in mind, the following 20 chapters of the book are divided into three primary sections. The first section presents chapters that define and conceptualize energy security. The second section investigates the various dimensions of energy security. The third section surveys existing metrics and indices in place for measuring energy security performance.

Part 1: *definitions and concepts*

In Chapter 1, "Energy security and climate change—a tenuous link," Gal Luft, Ann Korin, and Eshita Gupta argue that while energy security and reducing greenhouse gas emissions have synergies, tradeoffs between them also occur. The first part of the chapter defines energy security, stating that while consumers, producers, and transit states might have a different outlook on energy security, they all conform to a definition that emphasizes availability and affordability of fossil fuels, which are currently the primary sources of energy used throughout the world. The second section argues that climate change should not be factored into the energy security debate.

In Chapter 2, "The fuzzy nature of energy security," Scott Victor Valentine argues that energy security is far too ideologically nuanced to permit agreement. Rather, the best that energy security analysts can hope for is to produce transparent assessments that clearly define what type of "energy security" is being evaluated, specify the temporal scale that is incorporated into the analysis, and explicate any critical ideological assumptions that influenced the analysis. Unless such ideological disclosure takes place, the clouds of bias surrounding national energy assessments cast a gray hue on an exercise that should be intended to enlighten.

In Chapter 3, "Evaluating the energy security impacts of energy policies," David F. von Hippel and colleagues contend that security has become less useful to policy formation due to increasingly global, diverse energy markets combined with emerging, energy-related transnational problems. Moreover, a policy-oriented rationale for "energy security" must also encompass global issues such as climate change and many other economic, technological, and international security considerations—a conceptual task that is tackled in their chapter. The chapter proceeds to present a more comprehensive operating definition of "energy security," along with a workable frame-work for analyzing future energy paths and scenarios. The chapter also describes a set of methodological tools for evaluating the relative energy security costs and benefits of different energy policies.

Part 2: *dimensions of energy security*

In Chapter 4, "The sustainable development dimension of energy security," Asclepias R. S. Indriyanto, Dwi Ari Fauzi, and Alfa Firdaus suggest that the energy security paradigm now relates very closely with the sustainable development paradigm. Combining the availability, accessibility, affordability, and acceptability elements in the energy security view with the social, economic, and environmental dimensions of the sustainable development perspective allows energy security concerns to be interlinked with wider and longer-term considerations. The chapter then uses Indonesia as a case study to show how both perspectives can be incorporated together.

In Chapter 5, "The maritime dimension of energy security," Caroline Liss traces the linkages between the safety of shipping and sea lines of communication and energy security. The chapter primarily explores two key maritime-based energy security threats: piracy and terrorism. It begins by providing an overview of the role of shipping in transporting energy fuels around the world. It then discusses key security challenges to the safe transit of merchant vessels carrying energy resources, with particular attention to the threat posed by pirates and terrorists in the Malacca Strait and Gulf of Aden area. The chapter concludes by evaluating the threat to energy security posed by these non-state actors.

In Chapter 6, "The public policy dimension of energy security," Andreas Goldthau comments that energy security by definition has strong public policy characteristics. These may occur due to imperfect competition; negative externalities; lack of information; or the presence of public goods. Cases in point are the existence of market-distorting cartels; a lack of data on the global oil market; economic costs related to price shocks; the security of global transport routes; or the maintenance of crucial reserve capacity. In many of these cases, classical free-rider problems arise and "energy security" risks are underprovided by the market altogether. His chapter then draws conclusions on implications for global public policy.

In Chapter 7, "The diversification dimension of energy security," Andy Stirling offers a systematic, comprehensive, and transparent framework through which to address diversity in energy security analysis. Energy diversity is well recognized in many different disciplines—and has been for many decades in the field of energy security—and deliberate diversification has presented a means to hedge against even the most intractable forms of uncertainty, ambiguity, and ignorance. The chapter explores the implications of diversification for attempts to derive a systematic understanding of energy diversity, of a kind that could be employed in the quest for portfolios of indicators as a means to help strengthen energy governance.

In Chapter 8, "The environmental dimension of energy security," Marilyn A. Brown and Michael Dworkin posit that environmental sustainability is an energy security issue. The world's conventional energy supply is limited, and the waste and damage from energy production and use are beginning to exceed the assimilative capacity of the Earth and its atmosphere. The chapter suggests a range of metrics to help governments, investors, and policymakers manage these risks. In particular, the chapter examines three environmental "threat multipliers": climate change, air pollution, and water issues. These security threats can trigger different types of impacts, ranging from large-scale migration of climate refugees to instabilities caused by shrinking supplies of safe drinking water, food, and breathable indoor air. The chapter argues that through energy efficiency and renewable energy measures, countries can mitigate the energy security risks caused by environmental damage.

In Chapter 9, "The energy poverty dimension of energy security," Shonali Pachauri contends that the energy insecurity of the poor remains a neglected issue. Her chapter discusses energy security from the perspective of households and analyzes its access and poverty dimensions. Empirical examples and analysis from India are presented to illustrate many of the issues and indicators involved with energy poverty. The chapter discusses the implications of a continued dependence on traditional fuels for the well-being of households and the multiple benefits that can accrue from access to modern energy.

In Chapter 10, "The social development dimension of energy security," Anthony D'Agostino notes that public policy intervention to improve affordability via energy subsidies is commonly justified on social grounds, but in isolation obscures the broader range of social impacts felt by affected populations. Concurrently, impacts like forced displacement, public health threats, and pollution-related damages stemming from energy systems have largely been ignored by energy security discussions. Using a case study format with examples from Southeast Asia, his chapter argues that the social development dimension of energy security is more all-encompassing than acknowledged; affordability is not the exclusive social spillover of energy systems. Policymakers should therefore factor in the broad range of potential and realized social development impacts to improve energy and human security.

In Chapter 11, "The energy efficiency dimension of energy security," Nathalie Trudeau and Peter G. Taylor suggest that improving energy efficiency is often the most economic, proven, and readily available means of achieving the goal of energy security. They argue that establishing and maintaining sound policy requires the availability of good quality, timely, comparable, and detailed data that go well beyond those currently included in the statistics of energy balances, and must reflect the distinct characteristics of economic activity and resources available in each country. The chapter summarizes research conducted at the International Energy Agency for the past decade on developing in-depth indicators for energy efficiency and energy reduction potential.

In Chapter 12, "The energy services dimension of energy security," Jaap C. Jansen and Adriaan J. Van der Welle note that official energy projections sketch a picture of relentless growing energy demand in their baseline scenarios. Yet several analysts predict serious supply bottlenecks, what-ever the future world energy mix might be. This warrants a paradigm shift in the approach of the "energy security" issue towards a more integrated demand-side and supply-side one, making the heart of the matter energy services security rather than energy security. The chapter argues that such a shift must involve influencing consumer choices towards spending disposable income on less fuel (resource)-intensive consumption packages; substitution into less fuel(resource)-intensive ways to meet given needs for energy services; and improving security of supply of energy resources.

In Chapter 13, "The industrial dimension of energy security," Geoffrey K. Pakiam analyzes the interplay between national energy security concerns and industrial policies for energy technolo-gies. Energy technologies are being continuously incubated, developed, and produced for deployment. Many of these processes are influenced by industrial policies. National energy security concerns may influence the industrial development of energy technologies and vice versa. Based on a case study of the USA's wind energy sector between 1977 and 2010, his chapter outlines a number of complications and ambiguities in the relationship. He argues that industrial policies motivated by energy security concerns have made important contributions to the devel-opment of clean energy technologies, but great care must be taken to ensure that appropriate policies are chosen for tasks with multiple goals.

In Chapter 14, "The competing dimensions of energy security," Martin J. Pasqualetti notes that energy security influences everything from military deployments to offshore oil drilling, from coal burning and carbon dioxide emissions to alternative energy, from political unrest to high-seas piracy, from dung-gathering to uranium mining. His chapter investigates the definition of energy security, methods of indexing and measurement, time, environmental quality, geographic varia-bility, socio-economic variability, and topics deserving further discussion. The chapter concludes that the achievement of sustainability, economic prosperity, and world order is impossible without energy security. Whether in Asia, Africa, Europe, North or South America, we all need energy security. It is at the core of our individual and collective survival.

Part 3: energy security metrics and indexing

In Chapter 15, "Indicators for energy security," Bert Kruyt and colleagues comment that while the concept of energy security is widely used, there is no consensus on its precise interpretation. Their chapter provides an overview of available indicators for long-term security of supply. It distinguishes four dimensions of energy security that relate to the availability, accessibility, affordability, and acceptability of energy respectively, and classify indicators for energy security according to this taxonomy. There is no single ideal indicator, as the notion of energy security is highly context-dependent. Incorporating these indicators in model-based scenario analysis shows accelerated depletion of currently known fossil resources due to increasing global demand. Coupled with increasing spatial discrepancy between consumption and production, international trade in energy carriers is projected to increase by nearly 150 percent in 2050 as compared with 2008. Oil production is projected to become increasingly concentrated in a few countries up to 2030, after which production from other regions may diversify.

In Chapter 16, "Measuring security of energy supply with two diversity indexes," John Kessels notes that climate change and energy supply security policy are currently not integrated in most countries, despite possible synergies. The Energy Security and Climate Policy Evaluation (ESCAPE) approach suggests that linking climate change policy with security of energy supply could improve at both national and international levels. The ESCAPE approach also explores the interaction between policies of energy security and climate change, and the options of inclusion of energy security issues into national and international post-2012 climate negotiations. His chapter discusses the importance of energy security using two measurement tools, the Shannon diversity index and the Supply/Demand Index.

In Chapter 17, "Measuring energy security: From universal indicators to contextualized frameworks," Aleh Cherp and Jessica Jewell describe the assumptions concerning energy systems and their possible futures, as well as choices about priorities and assumptions that are made in measuring energy security. This chapter is illustrated with references to some of the most common energy security discourses and their related indicators. The limitations of de-contextualized indicators of energy security are also discussed. The second part of the chapter proposes an energy security assessment framework where the global knowledge about energy security is contextualized with respect to national energy systems. The chapter is situated within the preliminary findings of the worldwide energy security assessment carried out by the International Institute for Applied Systems Analysis.

In Chapter 18, "Applying the four 'A's of energy security as criteria in an energy security ranking method," Larry Hughes and Darren Shupe describe how APERC's (Asia-Pacific Energy Research Center) four 'A's originally developed as security indicators for fossil fuels and nuclear power can be broadened to act as criteria, each with its own quantitative metric and weight, for a novel, general-purpose energy security analysis method. The chapter shows how applying a range of weights to the criteria allows for a better understanding of the sensitivity of a jurisdiction's energy sources to changes in any of the criteria. The method is applied to the energy sources used in Canada's four Atlantic Provinces.

In Chapter 19, "Measuring energy security performance in the OECD," Marilyn A. Brown and I investigate how well industrialized nations are doing in terms of their energy security. We propose the creation of an Energy Security Index to inform policymakers, investors, and analysts about the status of energy conditions. Using the United States and 21 other member countries of the Organisation for Economic Co-operation and Development (OECD) as an example, and looking at energy security from 1970 to 2007, our index shows that only four countries—Belgium, Denmark, Japan, and the United Kingdom—have made progress on multiple dimensions of the energy security problem. The remaining 18 have either made no improvement or are less secure. The chapter then analyzes the relative performance of four countries: Denmark (the top performer), Japan (which performed well), the United States (which performed poorly), and Spain (the worst performer). The chapter concludes by offering implications for policy.

In Chapter 20, "Measuring energy security vulnerability," Edgard Gnansounou suggests that the emergence of new large consumer countries on energy markets and the perspective of oil and gas depletion at the end of the current century raise concerns about fair distribution of resources. Measures are needed, mainly in industrialized countries, to develop alternative and sustainable energy sources, enable technology transfer towards emerging and developing countries, and avoid the struggle for energy procurement. In his chapter an aggregate index of energy demand / supply weaknesses is defined as a proxy of energy vulnerability. The proposed index is based on five indicators: energy intensity, oil and gas import dependency, CO_2 content of primary energy supply, electricity supply weaknesses, and non-diversity in transport fuels. The application of the index for selected industrialized countries is discussed as well as the sensitivity to various factors.

Finally, the Conclusion, written by Tai Wei Lim and myself, distills five points of contention and three points of convergence found within the book. Points of contention include what energy security is and ought to be, energy fuels and technologies of preference, the role of technology, the role of government, and how an optimal level of energy security ought to be accomplished. Points of convergence include an admission by almost all authors that energy security is a multidimensional concept encompassing multiple scales and time frames, that energy security concerns and policies are heterogeneous and that existing approaches and indicators for energy security suffer from limitations.

Notes

1 Nagy, Karoly. 2009. "The Additional Benefits of Setting Up an Energy Security Centre," *Energy* 34: 1715–1720.
2 Triola, Larry C. 2008. "Energy and National Security: An Exploration of Threats, Solutions, and Alternative Futures," *IEEE Energy 2030* (November 17–18): 13–35.
3 Victor, David G. and Linda Yueh. 2010. "The New Energy Order," *Foreign Affairs* 89(1) (January/ February): 61–74.
4 Ciuta, Felix. 2009. "From Oil Wars to Total Security: Energy in Three Logics of Security," *Paper Presented at the 2009 International Studies Association Convention in New York, February 16.*
5 Interview with author, Stanford University, Palo Alto, California, March 6, 2009.
6 Asia Pacific Energy Research Centre. 2007. *A Quest for Energy Security in the 21st Century: Resources and Constraints* (Tokyo: APERC).
7 Barton, Barry, Catherine Redgwell, Anita Ronne, and Donald N. Zillman. 2004. "Introduction." In Barton, Barry, Catherine Redgwell, Anita Ronne, and Donald N. Zillman (eds.) *Energy Security: Managing Risk in a Dynamic Legal and Regulatory Environment* (Oxford: Oxford University Press), p. 5.
8 Bazilian, Morgan, Fergal O'Leary, Brian O'Gallachoir, and Martin Howley. 2006. *Security of Supply Metrics* (Dublin: Sustainable Energy Ireland, January).
9 Bielecki, J. 2002. "Energy Security: Is the Wolf at the Door?" *Quarterly Review of Economics and Finance* 42: 235–250.
10 Bohi, D. R. and M. A. Toman. 1996. *The Economics of Energy Supply Security* (Norwell: Kluwer).
11 Brown, Marilyn A. and Benjamin K. Sovacool. 2007. "Developing an 'Energy Sustainability Index' to Evaluate Energy Policy," *Interdisciplinary Science Reviews* 32 (4 (December)): 335–349.
12 CNA. 2009. *Powering America's Defense: Energy and the Risks to National Security* (Alexandria, Maryland: CNA Corporation).
13 Deutch, John. 2007. "Priority Energy Security Issues." In John Deutch, Anne Lauvergeon, and Widhyawan Prawiraatmadja (eds), *Energy Security and Climate Change* (Washington, DC: Trilateral Commission), p. 1.
14 Kleber, Drezel. 2009. "The U.S. Department of Defense: Valuing Energy Security," *Journal of Energy Security* (June): 12–22.
15 Quoted in Olz, Samantha, Ralph Sims, and Nicolai Kirchner. 2007. *Contributions of Renewables to Energy Security: International Energy Agency Information Paper* (Paris: OECD, April), p. 13.
16 Florini, Ann. 2010. "Global Governance and Energy." In Carlos Pascual and Jonathan Elkind (eds), *Energy Security: Economics, Politics, Strategies, and Implications* (Washington, DC: Brookings Institution), p. 151.
17 Hughes, Larry. 2009. "The Four R's of Energy Security," *Energy Policy* 37(6) (June): 2459–2461.
18 Rogner, Hans-Holger, Lucille M. Langlois, Alan McDonald, Daniel Weisser, and Mark Howells. 2006. *The Costs of Energy Supply Security* (Vienna: International Atomic Energy Agency, December 27).

19 Based on Olz *et al.*, *Contributions of Renewables to Energy Security*; International Energy Agency. 2006. *Energy Technology Perspectives: Scenarios and Strategies to 2050* (Paris: OECD); as well as personal interview with author, International Energy Agency, Paris, France, April 28, 2009.

20 Personal interview with author, International Institute for Applied Systems Analysis, Vienna, Austria, May 5, 2009.

21 Jacobson, Mark Z. 2009. "Review of Solutions to Global Warming, Air Pollution, and Energy Security," *Energy & Environmental Science* 2: 148–173.

22 Jansen, J. C. 2009. *Energy Services Security Concepts and Metrics* (Vienna: International Atomic Energy Agency Project on Selecting and Defining Integrated Indicators for Nuclear Energy, October, ECN-E-09-080), p. 7.

23 Jegen, Maya. 2009. "Framing Energy Security: The Case of the European Union." *Paper Presented at the 2009 International Studies Association Convention in New York, February 16.*

24 Kalicki, J. H. and D. L. Goldwyn. 2005. "Energy, Security, and Foreign Policy." In J. H. Kalicki and D. L. Goldwyn (eds) *Energy Security – Toward a New Foreign Policy Strategy* (Baltimore: Johns Hopkins Press), p. 561.

25 Kalicki and Goldwyn. "Energy, Security, and Foreign Policy," p. 9.

26 Kemmler, Andreas and Daniel Spreng. 2007. "Energy Indicators for Tracking Sustainability in Developing Countries," *Energy Policy* 35: 2466–2480.

27 Kessels, John, Stefan Bakker, and Bas Wetzelaer. 2008. *Energy Security and the Role of Coal* (London: IEA Clean Coal Centre CCC/131).

28 Konoplyanik, Andrei. 2004. "Energy Security and the Development of International Energy Markets." In Barton, Barry, Catherine Redgwell, Anita Ronne, and Donald N. Zillman (Eds.) *Energy Security: Managing Risk in a Dynamic Legal and Regulatory Environment* (Oxford: Oxford University Press), p. 64.

29 Lovins, Amory. 2006. "How Innovative Technologies, Business Strategies, and Policies can Dramatically Enhance Energy Security and Prosperity," *Invited Testimony to the U.S. Senate Committee on Energy and Natural Resources*, March 7.

30 Medlock, Kenneth B. 2004. "Economics of Energy Demand." In Cutler Cleveland (ed.), *Encyclopedia of Energy* (New York: Elsevier), vol. 2, p. 65.

31 Muller-Kraenner, Sascha. 2007. *Energy Security: Re-Measuring the World* (London: Earthscan), p. xi.

32 Keppler, Jan Horst. 2007. *Energy Supply Security and Nuclear Energy: Concepts, Indicators, Policies* (Paris: Nuclear Energy Agency, October), p. 3.

33 Omorogbe, Yinka. 2004. "Regional and National Frameworks for Energy Security in Africa." In Barton, Barry, Catherine Redgwell, Anita Ronne, and Donald N. Zillman (Eds.) *Energy Security: Managing Risk in a Dynamic Legal and Regulatory Environment* (Oxford: Oxford University Press), p. 124.

34 David Orr, interview with author, Oberlin College, Oberlin, Ohio, March 10, 2009.

35 Scheepers, Martin, Ad Seebregts, Jacques de Jong, and Hans Maters. 2006. *EU Standards for Energy Security of Supply* (Netherlands: ECN).

36 Shrestha, Ram M. and S. Kumar. 2008. "Energy Security for Developing Countries," *Presentation to the GNESD Expert Meeting and Assembly, December 9, Poznan, Poland.*

37 Sovacool, Benjamin K. 2007. "Coal and Nuclear Technologies: Creating a False Dichotomy for American Energy Policy," *Policy Sciences* 40 (2) (June): 101–122.

38 Tonn, Bruce, K. C. Healy, Amy Gibson, Ashutosh Ashish, Preston Cody, Drew Beres, Sam Lulla, Jim Mazur, and A. J. Ritter. 2009. "Power from Perspective: Potential Future United States Energy Portfolios," *Energy Policy* 37: 1432–1443.

39 U.S. Agency for International Development. 2008. *Energy Security Quarterly: USAID South Asia Regional Initiative for Energy* (Washington, DC: USAID, January), p. 2.

40 Kessels, John, Stefan Bakker and Bas Wetzelaer. 2008. *Energy Security and the Role of Coal* (London: IEA Clean Coal Centre CCC/131), p. 7.

41 Kleber, Drezel. 2009. "The U.S. Department of Defense: Valuing Energy Security," *Journal of Energy Security* (June): 12–22.

42 U.S. Department of Energy. 2010. "About the Department of Energy." March. Available at http://www.energy.gov/about/index.htm (accessed May 4, 2010).

43 United Kingdom Department of Trade and Industry. 2006. *UK Energy Sector Indicators 2006* (London: DTI).

44 United Nations Economic and Social Commission for Asia and the Pacific [UNESCAP]. 2008. *Energy Security and Sustainable Development in Asia and the Pacific* (Geneva: UNESCAP, April, ST/ESCAP/2494).

45 Joseph White, interview with author, Case Western Reserve University, Cleveland, Ohio, March 9, 2009.

46 Personal interview with author, World Bank Group, Washington, DC, November 5, 2009.

47 World Economic Forum. 2009. *Global Risks 2009: A Global Risk Network Report* (Davos: World Economic Forum, January).

48 World Energy Assessment. 2000. *Energy and the Challenge of Sustainability* (New York: United Nations Development Program).

49 Logan, Jeffrey and John Venezia. 2007. "Weighing U.S. Energy Options: The WRI Bubble Chart," *WRI Policy Note on Energy Security and Climate Change* (Washington, DC: World Resources Institute, July).

50 Yergin, Daniel. 2006. "Ensuring Energy Security," *Foreign Affairs* 85 (2) (March/April): 69–82.

51 Stern, Paul C. and Elliot Aronson. 1984. *Energy Use: The Human Dimension* (New York: Freeman & Company).

52 Tonn, Bruce, K. C. Healy, Amy Gibson, Ashutosh Ashish, Preston Cody, Drew Beres, Sam Lulla, Jim Mazur, and A. J. Ritter. 2009. "Power from Perspective: Potential Future United States Energy Portfolios," *Energy Policy* 37: 1432–1443.

53 Schurr, Sam H., Joel Darmstadter, Harry Perry, William Ramsay, and Milton Russell. 1979. *Energy in America's Future: The Choices Before Us* (Baltimore, MD: Johns Hopkins University Press); Bultena, Gordon. 1976. *Public Response to the Energy Crisis: A Study of Citizens' Attitudes and Adaptive Behaviors* (Ames, IA: Iowa State University, July).

54 Patterson, Walt. 1999. *Can Public Service Survive the Market? Issues for Liberalized Electricity* (London: Chatham House Briefing Paper).

55 Orr, David W. 1979. "U.S. Energy Policy and the Political Economy of Participation," *Journal of Politics* 41: 1027–1056.

56 See Smith, William D. 1973. "Shortage amid Plenty," *Proceedings of the Academy of Political Science* 31 (2) (December): 41–50; Temkin, Benny. 1983. "State, Ecology and Independence: Policy Responses to the Energy Crisis in the U.S.," *British Journal of Political Science* 13(4) (October): 441–462; Kash, Don E. and Robert W. Rycroft. 1984. *U.S. Energy Policy: Crisis and Complacency* (New York: University of Oklahoma Press).

57 Dunlap, Riley E. and Marvin E. Olsen. 1984. "Hard-Path Versus Soft-Path Advocates: A Study of Energy Activists," *Policy Studies Journal* 13(2): 413–428.

58 Gottlieb, David and Marc Matre. 1976. *Sociological Dimensions of the Energy Crisis: A Follow-Up Study* (Houston, TX: University of Houston, The Energy Institute, April 30).

59 Elkind, Jonathan. 2010. "Energy Security: Call for a Broader Agenda." In Carlos Pascual and Jonathan Elkind (eds), *Energy Security: Economics, Politics, Strategies, and Implications* (Washington, DC: Brookings Institution Press), pp. 119–148.

60 Source: Slightly modified from Elkind, "Energy Security: Call for a Broader Agenda," p. 122.

61 This approach is presented in Sovacool, Benjamin K. 2009. "Reassessing Energy Security and the Trans-ASEAN Natural Gas Pipeline Network in Southeast Asia," *Pacific Affairs* 82(3) (Fall): 467–486.

62 Klare, Michael T. 2007. "The Futile Pursuit of Energy Security by Military Force," *Brown Journal of World Affairs* 13 (2) (Spring/Summer): 139.

63 Parts of this section are based on Florini, Ann E. and Benjamin K. Sovacool. In press. "Bridging the Gaps in Global Energy Governance." *Global Governance* 17(1) (Winter).

64 Pamir, Necdet. 2006. *Energy (In)Security and the Most Recent Lesson: The Russia-Ukraine Gas Crisis* (Ankara: Center for Eurasian Strategic Studies), pp. 6–7; Gelb, Bernard A. 2007. "Russian Natural Gas: Regional Dependence," *CRS Report for Congress* (Washington, DC: January 5, Congressional Research Service Report Number RS22562).

65 "Lukoil Stops German Delivery," *Financial Times*, February 20, 2008, p. 5.

66 Omonbude, Ekpen J. 2007. "The Transit Oil and Gas Pipeline and the Role of Bargaining: A Non-Technical Discussion," *Energy Policy* 35: 6188–6194.

67 Hayes, Mark H. and David G. Victor. 2006. "Politics, Markets, and the Shift to Gas: Insights from the Seven Historical Case Studies," *Natural Gas and Geopolitics: From 1970 to 2040* (Cambridge: Cambridge University Press), pp. 319–353.

68 Barnes, Joe, Mark H. Hayes, Amy M. Jaffe, and David G. Victor. 2006. "Introduction to the Study." In Barnes, Joe, Mark H. Hayes, Amy M. Jaffe, and David G. Victor (eds.) *Natural Gas and Geopolitics: From 1970 to 2040* (Cambridge: Cambridge University Press), pp. 3–24.

69 Stevens, Paul. 2000. "Pipelines or Pipedreams? Lessons from the History of Arab Transit Pipelines," *Middle East Journal* 54(2): 224–241.

70 Stevens, Paul. 2000. "Pipelines or Pipedreams? Lessons from the History of Arab Transit Pipelines," *Middle East Journal* 54(2): 224–241.

71 Sovacool 2009. "Reassessing Energy Security."

72 Smil, Vaclav. 2004. "War and Energy." In Cutler Cleveland (ed.), *Encyclopedia of Energy* (New York: Elsevier), vol. 2, pp. 363–371.

73 Smil, "War and Energy."

74 Smil, "War and Energy," p. 369.

75 Source: Smil, "War and Energy," pp. 364–367.

76 Smil, "War and Energy," pp. 364–367.

77 Lovins, Amory. 2009. Preface to the Chinese Edition of *Winning the Oil Endgame*, (Snowmass, CO: Rocky Mountain Institute, February 29).

78 Interview with Michal Quah, Energy Studies Institute, Singapore, June 14, 2009.

79 Robb, John. 2006. "Security: Power to the People," *Fast Company Magazine* 103 (March): 120.

80 Sovacool, BK and S Halfon. 2007. "Reconstructing Iraq: Merging Discourses of Security and Development," *Review of International Studies* 33(2) (April), pp. 223–243.

81 Ibid.

82 Ibid.

83 Sovacool, Benjamin K. 2008. "Placing a Glove on the Invisible Hand: How Intellectual Property Rights May Impede Innovation in Energy Research and Development (R&D)," *Albany Law Journal of Science & Technology* 18(2) (Fall): 381–440.

84 Brown, Marilyn A., Jess Chandler, Melissa V. Lapsa, and Benjamin K. Sovacool. November 2007. *Carbon Lock-In: Barriers to the Deployment of Climate Change Mitigation Technologies*. (Oak Ridge, TN: Oak Ridge National Laboratory, ORNL/TM-2007/124).

85 International Energy Agency. 2008. *World Energy Outlook 2008* (Paris: OECD/IEA).

86 Wara, Michael. 2007. "Is the Global Carbon Market Working?" *Nature* 445 (February 8): 595–596; Wara, Michael W. and David G. Victor. 2008. "A Realistic Policy on International Carbon Offsets," *Stanford University Program on Energy and Sustainable Development Working Paper #74*, April.

87 Hepburn, Cameron. 2007. "Carbon Trading: A Review of the Kyoto Mechanisms," *Annual Review of Environment and Resources* 32: 375–393; Huq, Saleemul and Mozaharul Alam. 2008. *Climate Change Adaptation in Post-2012 Architecture*. London: Progressive Governance.

88 Sovacool, Benjamin K. 2008. "Renewable Energy: Economically Sound, Politically Difficult," *Electricity Journal* 21(5) (June), pp. 18–29.

89 Pope, Carl. 2005. "The State of Nature: Our Roof is Caving In," *Foreign Policy* July/August: 67.

90 Boberg, Jill. 2005. *Liquid Assets: How Demographic Changes and Water Management Policies Affect Freshwater Resources* (Santa Monica, CA: RAND Corporation), p. 20.

91 Gleick, Peter H. 2003. "Water Use," *Annual Review of Environment and Resources* 28: 275–314.

92 Feeley, Thomas J. *et al.* 2008. "Water: A Critical Resource in the Thermoelectric Power Industry," *Energy* 33: 1–11, p. 1.

93 Birol, Fatih 2007. "Energy Economics: A Place for Energy Poverty on the Agenda?" *The Energy Journal* 28(3) pp. 1–6.

94 Vijay Modi, Susan McDade, Dominique Lallement, Jamal Saghir.. 2005. *Energy Services for the Millennium Development Goals*. Washington and New York: The International Bank for Reconstruction and Development/The World Bank and the United Nations Development Programme.

95 Source: Modi *et al.*, *Energy Services*, p. 13.

96 Source: Trudeau, Nathalie. 2009. "Measuring National Energy Efficiency and Energy Reduction Potentials," Presentation to the International Workshop on Energy Security Concepts and Indicators for Asia, Lee Kuan Yew School of Public Policy, National University of Singapore November 14–16, 2009.

97 Source: UNESCAP, *Energy Security and Sustainable Development*, p. 17.

98 United Nations Development Programme. 1997. "Energy and Major Global Issues," Energy After Rio: Prospects and Challenges (Geneva: United Nations), pp. 87–115.

99 UNESCAP, *Energy Security and Sustainable Development*.

100 Holdren, John P. and Kirk R. Smith. 2000. "Energy, the Environment, and Health." In Tord Kjellstrom, David Streets, and Xiadong Wang (eds), *World Energy Assessment: Energy and the Challenge of Sustainability*. (New York: United Nations Development Programme), pp. 61–110.

101 Malyshev, Teresa. 2009. *Looking Ahead: Energy, Climate, and Pro-Poor Responses* (Bellagio: Rockefeller Foundation).

102 Source: Zhang, Zhong Xiang. 2008. "Asian Energy and Environmental Policy: Promoting Growth While Preserving the Environment," *Energy Policy* 36: 3905–3924.

103 Jacobson, Arne, Anita Milman, and Daniel M. Kammen. 2005. "Letting the (Energy) Gini Out of the Bottle: Lorenz Curves of Cumulative Electricity Consumption and Gini Coefficients as Metrics of Energy Distribution and Equity," *Energy Policy* 33(14): 1825–1832.

104 Pachauri, S., A Mueller, A. Kemmler, and D. Spreng. 2004. "On Measuring Energy Poverty in Indian Households," *World Development* 32(12): 2083–2104.

105 United Nations Economic and Social Commission for Asia and the Pacific (UNESCAP). 2008. *Energy Security and Sustainable Development in Asia and the Pacific* (Geneva: UNESCAP, ST/ESCAP/ 2494, April), p. 185.

106 Birol, "Energy Economics".

107 Olz, Samantha, Ralph Sims, and Nicolai Kirchner. 2007. *Contributions of Renewables to Energy Security: International Energy Agency Information Paper* (Paris: OECD, April).

108 Redgwell, Catherine. 2004. "International Energy Security." In Barton, Barry, Catherine Redgwell, Anita Ronne, and Donald N. Zillman (Eds.) *Energy Security: Managing Risk in a Dynamic Legal and Regulatory Environment* (Oxford: Oxford University Press), pp. 17–46.

109 Verrastro, Frank and Sarah Ladislaw. 2007. "Providing Energy Security in an Interdependent World," *The Washington Quarterly* 30(4): 95–104.

110 Kessels, John, Stefan Bakker, and Bas Wetzelaer. 2008. *Energy Security and the Role of Coal* (London: IEA Clean Coal Centre CCC/131), p. 31.

111 Energy Information Administration (EIA), "Short-Term Energy Outlook, September 2006." Available at http://www.eia.doe.gov/pub/forecasting/steo/oldsteos/sep06.pdf (accessed March 3, 2010).

112 Brown, Marilyn A. and BK Sovacool. 2011. *Climate Change and Global Energy Security: Technology and Policy Options* (Cambridge, MA: MIT Press).

113 Source: Kessels, *et al.*, *Energy Security and the Role of Coal*.

114 Jackson, Tim. 1991."Renewable Energy: Great Hope or False Promise?" *Energy Policy* (January/ February): 7.

115 Source: Energy Information Administration. 2006. *International Energy Annual 2006* (Washington, DC: U.S. Department of Energy). Uranium taken from International Atomic Energy Agency, *Uranium 2005 – Resources, Production, and Demand* (Vienna: International Atomic Energy Agency)); Echávarri, Luis and Yuri Sokolov. 2006. *Uranium Resources: Plenty to Sustain Growth of Nuclear Power* (Vienna: Nuclear Energy Agency and IAEA), p. 13.

116 Rogner, Hans-Holger, Lucille M. Langlois, Alan McDonald, Daniel Weisser, and Mark Howells. 2006. *The Costs of Energy Supply Security* (Vienna: International Atomic Energy Agency, December 27).

117 Leiby, P. N., D. W. Jones, T. R. Curlee, and R. Lee. 1997. *Oil Imports: An Assessment of Benefits and Costs* (Oak Ridge: Oak Ridge National Laboratory ORNL-6851); Jones, D. W., P. N. Leiby, and I. K. Paik. 2004. "Oil Price Shocks and the Macroeconomy: What Has Been Learned Since 1996?" *The Energy Journal* 25(2): 1–32.

118 Loschel, Andreas, Ulf Moslener, and Dirk Rubbelke. 2010. "Indicators of Energy Security in Industrialized Countries," *Energy Policy* 38: 1665–1671.

119 Amin, Massoud. 2003. "North America's Electricity Infrastructure." *IEEE Security and Privacy* (September/October): 19–25.

120 Energy Information Administration, "Short-Term Energy Outlook, September 2006." Available at http://www.eia.doe.gov/pub/forecasting/steo/oldsteos/sep06.pdf (accessed March 3, 2010).

121 Source: Brown and Sovacool *Climate Change and Global Energy Security*.

122 U.S. Energy Information Administration. 2006. *Annual Energy Outlook 2006* (Washington, DC: U.S. Department of Energy).

123 Source: Sovacool, Benjamin K. 2009. "Reassessing Energy Security and the Trans-ASEAN Natural Gas Pipeline Network in Southeast Asia," *Pacific Affairs* 82(3) (Fall), pp. 467–486.

124 CNA, *Powering America's Defense*.

125 Worldwide Fund for Nature. 2007. *Coming Clean: The Truth and Future of Coal in the Asia Pacific* (Washington, DC: WWF).

126 Ryan, M.,2005. "Volatile Coal Prices Reflect Supply, Demand Uncertainties," *Platt's Insights Magazine* (March 30,). pp. 10–11.

127 Ryan, "Volatile Coal Prices."

128 International Energy Agency. 2003. "Investment in the Coal Industry," *Background Paper on the Meeting with the IEA Governing Board* (November).

129 Source: U.S. Energy Information Administration. 2010. *Coal News and Markets*, (Washington, DC: U.S. Department of Energy, April).

130 Sovacool, Benjamin K. and Christopher Cooper. 2008. "Nuclear Nonsense: Why Nuclear Power is No Answer to Climate Change and the World's Post-Kyoto Energy Challenges," *William & Mary Environmental Law & Policy Review* 33(1) (Fall): 1–119.

131 Parts of this section are based on Sovacool, Benjamin K. and Anthony D'Agostino. 2010. "Nuclear Renaissance: a Flawed Proposition," *Chemical Engineering Progress* 106(7) (July), pp. 29–35.

132 International Atomic Energy Agency (IAEA). 2008. *Reinforcing the Global Nuclear Order for Peace and Prosperity: The Role of the IAEA to 2020 and Beyond* (Vienna: IAEA).

133 Perkovich, George. 2006. "The End of the Nonproliferation Regime?" *Current History* 105 (694) (November): 355–362.

134 Russell, P. R. 2008. "Prices Are Rising: Nuclear Cost Estimates Under Pressure," *EnergyBiz Insider*, May–June: 22.

135 Ramana, M. V. 2009. "Nuclear Power: Economic, Safety, Health, and Environmental Issues of Near-Term Technologies," *Annual Review of Environment and Resources* 34: 127–152.

136 U.S. Congressional Budget Office (CBO). 2008. *Nuclear Power's Role in Generating Electricity* (Washington, DC: CBO, May).

137 Sovacool and Cooper, "Nuclear Nonsense."

138 Sovacool, B. K. 2008. "Valuing the Greenhouse Gas Emissions from Nuclear Power: A Critical Survey," *Energy Policy* 36 (8) (August): 2940–2953.

139 Barnaby, F. and J. Kemp. 2007. *Secure Energy? Civil Nuclear Power, Security, and Global Warming* (Oxford: Oxford Research Group, March).

140 Sovacool, B. K. 2009. "Contextualizing Avian Mortality: A Preliminary Appraisal of Bird and Bat Fatalities from Wind, Fossil-Fuel, and Nuclear Electricity," *Energy Policy* 37: 2241–2248.

141 Kaplan, C. S. 2004. "Coastal Wind Energy Generation: Conflict and Capacity," *Boston College Environmental Affairs Law Review* 31: 134–212.

142 World Commission on Dams. 2000. *Dams and Development: A New Framework for Decision-making* (London: Earthscan).

143 Gagnon, L. and J. F. van de Vate. 1997. "Greenhouse Gas Emissions from Hydropower: The State of Research in 1996," *Energy Policy* 25: 7–13.

144 Pimentel, D., G. Rodrigues, T. Wane, R. Abrams, K. Goldberg, H. Staecker, E. Ma, L. Brueckner, L.Trovato, C. Chow, U. Govindarajulu, and S. Boerke. 1994. "Renewable Energy: Economic and Environmental Issues," *BioScience* 44: 42–48.

145 Karmis, M. et. al. 2005. *A Study of Increased Use of Renewable Energy Resources in Virginia* (Blacksburg, VA: Virginia Center for Coal and Energy Research).

146 Mahapatra, A. K. and C. P. Mitchell. 1999. "Biofuel Consumption, Deforestation, and Farm Level Tree Growing in Rural India," *Biomass Bioengineering*. 17: 291–303.

147 Berinstein, P. 2001. *Alternative Energy: Facts, Statistics, and Issues* (New York: Oryx Press).

148 Green, B. D. and R. G. Nix. 2006. *Geothermal – The Energy Under Our Feet* (Golden, CO: National Renewable Energy Laboratory).

149 Duffield, W. A. and J. H. Sass. 2003. *Geothermal Energy: Clean Power from the Earth's Heat* (Washington, DC: U.S. Geological Survey).

150 See Fthenakis, V. M. and E. Alsema. 2006. "Photovoltaics Energy Payback Times, Greenhouse Gas Emissions, and External Costs," *Progress in Photovoltaics Research Applications* 14: 275–280; Fthenakis, V. M. and H. C. Kim. 2007. "Greenhouse-Gas Emissions from Solar Electric – and Nuclear Power: A Life-Cycle Study," *Energy Policy* 35: 2549–2557; Fthenakis, V. M., H. C. Kim and M. Alsema. 2008. "Emissions from Photovoltaic Life Cycles," *Environmental Science & Technology*. 42: 2168–2174.

151 Fthenakis, V. M. 2001. "Multilayer Protection Analysis for Photovoltaic Manufacturing Facilities," *Process Safety Progress*. 20: 87–94.

152 See Naylor, Rosamond L., Adam J. Liska, Marshall B. Burke, Walter P. Falcon, Joanne C. Gaskell, Scott D. Rozelle, and Kenneth G. Cassman. 2007. "The Ripple Effect: Biofuels, Food Security, and the Environment," *Environment* 49(9): 30–43; Runge, Ford and Benjamin Senauer. 2007. "How Biofuels Could Starve the Poor," *Foreign Affairs* 86(3) (May/June): 41–54.

153 McGowan, Chris. 2007. "Biofuel could Eat Brazil's Savannas and Deforest the Amazon," *The Huffington Post*, September 14.

154 These threats are identified elegantly in Amory B. Lovins and L. Hunter Lovins. 1982. *Brittle Power: Energy Strategy for National Security* (Andover, MA: Brick House Publishing Company).

155 Sovacool, Benjamin K. 2008a. *The Dirty Energy Dilemma: What's Blocking Clean Power in the United States* (Westport, CT: Praeger).

156 Sovacool, *Dirty Energy Dilemma*, p. 35.

157 Lovins and Lovins, *Brittle Power*.

158 Lovins and Lovins, *Brittle Power*, p. 43.

159 Lovins and Lovins, *Brittle Power*.

160 Lovins and Lovins, *Brittle Power*, p. 128.

161 Lovins and Lovins, *Brittle Power*.

162 Lovins and Lovins, *Brittle Power*, p. 131.

163 Farrell, Alexander, Hisham Zerriffi, and Hadi Dowlatabadi. 2004. "Energy Infrastructure and Security," *Annual Review of Environment and Resources* 29: 421–422.

164 Parfomak, Paul W. 2004. "Pipeline Security: An Overview of Federal Activities and Current Policy Issues," *CRS Report for Congress* (Washington, DC: RL31990, February 5), pp. 1–6. [Author query: please provide publisher.]

165 Parfomak, "Pipeline Security."

166 Parfomak, "Pipeline Security."

167 Grau, Lester W. 2001. "Hydrocarbons and a New Strategic Region: The Caspian Sea and Central Asia," *Military Review* (May–June). pp. 17–26.

168 U.S. Energy Information Administration. 2007. *Country Analysis Brief: Saudi Arabia* (Washington, DC: U.S. Department of Energy, February).

169 Luft, Gal and Anne Korin. 2004. "Terrorism Goes to Sea." *Foreign Affairs* (November/December), pp. 71–82 "Terrorism"; Parfomak, "Pipeline Security."

170 Luft and Korin "Terrorism."

171 Luft, Gal. 2005."Iran-Pakistan-India Pipeline: The Baloch Wildcard," *Institute for the Analysis of Global Security Policy Brief* (Washington, DC: IAGS, January 12).

172 Luft and Korin, "Terrorism," p. 65.

173 Amnesty International. 2000. "Sudan: The Human Price of Oil." (May 3). Available at: http://web.amnesty.org/library/Index/engAFR540042000?OpenDocument&of=COUNTRIES%5CSUDAN (accessed May 2, 2010).

174 Parfomak, "Pipeline Security."

175 U.S. Government Accountability Office. 2006b. "*Energy Security. Issues Related to Potential Reductions in Venezuelan Oil Production.*" Report to the Chairman (Washington DC: Committee on Foreign Relations, U.S. Senate), 12.

176 Office of the Manager of the National Communications System. 2004. *National Communications System Bulletin 04–1: Supervisory Control and Data Acquisition Systems* (Washington, DC: U.S. National Communications System, October).

177 National Transportation Safety Board. 2005. *Supervisory Control and Data Acquisition (SCADA) in Liquid Pipelines* (Washington, DC: NTSP Safety Study, NTSP/SS-05/02, November 29).

178 Internet Security Systems. 2006. *SCADA Security and Terrorism: We're Not Crying Wolf.* Available at http://www.blackhat.com/presentations/bh-federal-06/BH-Fed-06-Maynor-Graham-up.pdf. [Accessed August 28, 2010].

179 Lemos, Robert. 2006. "SCADA System Makers Pushed Toward Security," *Security Focus News*, July 26.

1

ENERGY SECURITY AND CLIMATE CHANGE

A tenuous link

Gal Luft, Anne Korin, and Eshita Gupta

Rising concern by many around the world about global warming has brought with it attempts to broaden the definition of energy security and use security/energy security arguments as yet another tool to advance economic policies aimed at curbing greenhouse gas emissions. The terms climate change and security/energy security are being increasingly tied together and discussed in similar contexts, creating the impression that there is a direct and inextricable link between the two. Furthermore, this alleged linkage suggests that climate policy and energy security share a common solution: moving to a low carbon economy. This linkage has become an article of faith among government officials, pundits, and academics creating fertile ground for a new school of thought within the energy security community, one which promotes a broader definition of energy security. Those who view climate change as a global security threat of equal urgency to the current energy security challenge demand that the potential national security consequences of climate change be fully integrated into national security and energy security strategies, and that energy security solutions should only be applied if they also address climate change concerns.

As we will argue in this chapter, the link between climate security and energy security is more tenuous than one may think. Energy security and greenhouse gas reduction have many complementarities, but there are also many trade-offs between them, and contrary to popular belief, it is not self-evident that climate change will necessarily lead to energy insecurity, or vice versa. It is also incorrect to contend that we may be able to achieve both reduction in greenhouse gas emissions and improvement in energy security with one strike. In fact, too much emphasis on one could compromise the other.

The first section of this chapter attempts to encompass what energy security is, making the case that while consumers, producers, and transit states might have a different outlook on energy security, they all conform to the purist definition of energy security, the one that emphasizes availability and affordability of fossil fuels, which are currently the primary sources of energy used throughout the world. The second section is about what energy security is not. We argue that factoring climate change into the energy security debate is based on flawed logic, selective information, and weak conjunctions. We will show that those who try to make the linkage between energy security and climate change deliberately highlight the potential negative impact of climate change on energy security while failing to account for the potential positive impact. They also ignore the negative impact climate policy might have on energy security in some parts of the world. Worst of all, they repeatedly and manipulatively masquerade climate change solutions as energy security ones.

The purist approach to energy security

After decades in which researchers and politicians have limited the concept of energy security to consuming countries, it is broadly accepted today that energy security is a primary concern to every country regardless of whether it is a producer, consumer, or transit state. It is also commonly accepted that there is no uniform definition of energy security as this concept means different things to different nations based on their state of development, geographical location, their natural endowments, political system, and international relations.[1] While energy importers want security of supply and low prices, energy exporters seek security of demand—the assurance that their production will be purchased at what it considers to be a fair price over the long term—so that national budgets can anticipate a steady and predictable revenue flow. It is also worth remembering that many of the energy exporting nations also face domestic supply problems of their own driven by economic expansion, high population growth, and extremely large subsidies of electricity and transportation fuel prices. Hence, a country's definition of energy security has much to do with its own particular energy situation and how it views its vulnerability to energy supply disruptions.

In this, it is important to realize that there are two primary energy usage sectors which pose two different types of energy security challenges. The first sector is electricity. Throughout the world today electricity is generated from coal (43 percent), natural gas (20 percent), renewables like hydroelectric, biomass, solar, wind, and geothermal power (19 percent), and nuclear power (13 percent). Contrary to popular belief, in most countries electricity is essentially no longer produced from oil. Only 5 percent of world electricity is generated from petroleum.[2] This diversity of sources does not exist in the second major sector of energy use—transportation. Transportation energy makes the world go around. It fuels the flow of individuals goods and services on board cars, trucks, ships, airplanes, and many trains. Here oil is king, accounting for over 95 percent of the energy used. In fact, the vast majority of the cars sold around the world today cannot even run on something other than petroleum fuel, be it in the form of gasoline or diesel.

The distinction between electricity and transportation energy shapes countries' perception of energy security. Some countries like Russia and Saudi Arabia are almost fully self-sufficient with respect to energy, relying on their vast domestic resources of oil and natural gas and, in the case of Russia, coal, for both their power and transportation sectors. Others, like the US and France—the former thanks to its massive coal reserves and the latter due to an expanded nuclear power industry—are almost self-sufficient when it comes to their electricity supply but are heavily dependent on foreign oil imports to fuel their transportation sector. And then there are the most vulnerable countries, which are dependent on imports both of electricity sources like coal and natural gas as well as oil for their transportation needs. In the worst position are those members of the last group that are not only completely dependent on foreign energy but whose energy supply lines are facing constant threat of cut-off.

What shapes countries' perceptions of energy security is how they view their vulnerabilities. Europeans and Americans are similarly dependent on imported oil, but Europeans' thinking on energy security is mainly influenced by their dependence on Russian natural gas. Americans are almost self sufficient when it comes to their electricity generation but their way of life depends on private automobiles and cheap fuel. Therefore while Europeans think about gas, Americans are primarily concerned about gasoline.

Despite the variations in countries' perceptions of energy security, most governments, when pressed to point out what energy security means to them, tend to view the concept as a "reliable and adequate supply of energy at reasonable prices" or as Barry Barton *et al.* defined energy security: "a condition in which a nation and all, or most, of its citizens and businesses have access to sufficient energy resources at reasonable prices for the foreseeable future free from serious risk of major disruption of service."[3] The term "sufficient energy resources" is clear. But what are "reasonable prices"? What seems to be reasonable to producers may be unreasonable to consumers. What may be reasonable to the rich may be unreasonable to the poor.

This brings us to the often neglected link between poverty and energy security. While large numbers of people in both developed and developing countries today enjoy modern forms of energy, there are still about 2.5 billion people who continue to rely heavily on traditional cooking fuels such as dung and wood, and about 1.6 billion people who have no access to electricity. Most of these people reside in remote rural areas, have low incomes, and are largely dependent on agriculture for their livelihoods. India, home to more than a quarter of the world's poor, alone accounts for approximately 50 percent of people with high dependence on traditional cooking fuels and 31 percent of those without access to electricity. Enabling the poor to escape the "energy poverty trap" is a primary objective of energy policy decisions in these countries.[4] While in relatively more developed parts of the world energy security is more about reliability of energy supply, for the poor, energy security means ensuring affordable primary energy access to meet basic consumption and production needs like clean drinking water, cooking, lighting, irrigation, and public transportation.

In sum, where countries stand on energy security depends on where they sit. Perceptions of energy security include considerations varying from availability of supply of energy at an afford-able price to improving access of the poor to modern energy resources, to activities that allow countries to produce and use energy at reasonable cost—diversification of energy sources, reducing risk of energy supply disruption by reducing dependence on imported energy supplies, maintaining the physical security of energy sea lanes and pipelines, keeping spare capacity and emergency stocks, enhancing efficiency, and conservation measures. With such a spectrum of issues to consider, burdening discussion with an additional layer of constraints such as climate would only cause sluggishness, if not total paralysis, in energy security decision-making.

The climate-inclusive approach to energy security

The "holistic" approach to energy security is based on the following narrative: humanity's growing use of energy generated from fossil fuels causes global warming. This rise in global temperatures causes an array of erratic weather conditions like rise in sea level, droughts, floods, and violent storms that, in turn, breed security problems from migration to border disputes to ethnic violence and wars. According to one report, "climate change is a threat multiplier [which] has the potential to cause multiple chronic, destabilizing conditions to occur globally."[5] According to this view, climate change should therefore be recognized as an international security problem. To highlight the causality between global warming and security, climate advocates have recruited military brass and senior defense officials. This helped generate momentum to include discussion of national security threats posed by climate change in many nations' military and national security assessments. In the US, the Congress ordered the National Intelligence Council, which produces government-wide intelligence analyses, to include in its 2008 report the first assessment of the national security implications of climate change.[6] Intelligence agencies were tasked with preparing a series of reports on the issue. The Pentagon was instructed by Congress to include a climate section in the Quadrennial Defense Review, and the State Department addressed the issue in its Quadrennial Diplomacy and Development Review. This politically ordered embrace of climate change by the defense and diplomatic communities has, in turn, given fodder and cover to lawmakers working to make the national security argument for approving climate change legislation.

The holistic narrative goes further to suggest that climate change is not only a threat to global security but also a threat multiplier in terms of energy security. The rationale: "Mass migration of refugees seeking asylum from ecological disasters could destabilize regions of the world, threatening energy as well as national security."[7] Similar arguments are applied to other environmental phenomena like air pollution, water pollution, land pollution, forestry, and diversity loss. Therefore, according to this argument, climate change solutions should become part and parcel of any reasonable national and international energy security strategy.

Holes in holisticism

The notion that climate change is a driver behind some global security problems is valid and can be easily supported. Indeed, any change in climatic conditions would have some impact on some humans in some parts of the planet. But from here to assume that climate change has an overarching negative impact on energy security requires a leap of logic that must be carefully scrutinized. If a certain variable impacts *security* this does not necessarily mean that it also impacts *energy security*. Take religion for example. Since the dawn of history religion has been a driver of conflicts and ethnic strife around the world. Indeed, religion impacts global security. But does that make religion a threat to energy security? If one judges this based on the purist definition of energy security, religion can only be relevant to the energy security debate if it affects energy supply or a nation's ability to access energy. If religious strife occurring in an energy-producing region actually caused supply disruption, or if one can prove that an attack against an energy facility was religiously motivated, then religion would indeed have a first-order impact on energy security. If, however, religion only happened to contribute to a challenging security environment, causing problems like forced migration, and as a result some of the migrants suffered from lack of access to energy, then that would be a second-order effect.

Hence, assessing the influence of climate change (or religion for that matter) on energy security should be done through one prism: does climate affect the supply, demand, affordability, or reliability of energy supply? If so, is the effect one of first or second order?

For example, if global warming thaws the permafrost in northern Russia, causing damage to oil and gas pipelines and other energy infrastructure, this is a first-order effect. So also is the case if global warming dries rivers that communities rely upon for hydroelectric power. In both cases it is demonstrable that environmental changes adversely impact energy supply. But if a global warming-induced drought forced people to migrate, infringing on other people's territory, and resulting in a tribal war, that would not be considered as a first-order effect on energy security, even if, among the other hardships suffered by those people (disease, starvation, etc.), there was also shortage of energy.

The danger of including second-order effects of climate change (or any other driver for that matter) in energy security analysis is that such methodology opens the floodgate to multiple second-order effects caused by each and every transnational phenomenon from illegal immigration to organized crime. Such a broad canvas would add hundreds of new variables to the energy security analysis, complicating international dialogue on energy security and making policies designed to enhance energy security much more difficult to agree upon and implement. Say that a suggested path of a pipeline project that would greatly contribute to energy security of country X happens to run through a forest area and thousands of trees soaking up carbon dioxide would have to be cut down in order to complete its construction, hence contributing to global greenhouse gas emissions. Under the climate-inclusive approach to energy security (which generally assumes that climate change hinders energy security) the energy security value of the pipeline project would, by definition, be diminished. Including climate change considerations would therefore serve to cloud rather than illuminate the trade-offs inherent in building the pipeline. By redefining the term energy security, reducing the perceived energy security value of such a pipeline, the terminology would serve as an Orwellian obstacle to a decision to build the pipeline for its energy security benefits despite its environmental impact.

Failure to account for positives

Supporters of the climate–inclusive approach to energy security operate under the assumption that climate change impedes energy security. Based on this assumption, policies that combat climate change would surely bolster energy security. But how certain are we that the warming of the planet threatens global energy security? Could it be the exact opposite? Unfortunately, thus far research on the topic has presented only a partial picture, omitting the positive impact climate change has on energy security. This tendency to count the "losers" and leave out the "winners" is symptomatic of the highly subjective debate on climate change. Changes in global temperature certainly have impacts on energy production and use, and therefore in some cases an impact, first or later order, on energy security. But in order to assess the net impact of climate change on energy security it is imperative that we weigh the negatives against the positives.

A few examples of how climate change would benefit energy security are as follows:

1. Average warming can be expected to increase energy requirements for cooling, but at the same time it can also be expected to reduce energy requirements for heating. People living in cold areas such as northern Europe, North America, and Russia would benefit from the milder winter conditions caused by global warming. In the US, heating and cooling represent roughly one third of the average household electricity consumption.[8] A number of studies that examined the impact of rising temperatures on the consumption of energy in residential heating in the US revealed decreases of 2.8 percent to 14 percent for every 1 °C increase in temperature.[9] Of course, these numbers are subject to regional variations. A 2005 study, for example, projected a 7 percent to 33 percent decline in space heating in the 2020s in Massachusetts, which has a long heating season. In areas where winter temperatures are more moderate, smaller declines are expected. Either way, when it comes to heating, warmer temperatures would reduce the demand for fossil energy which, in turn, could lead to lower energy prices—a clear benefit to energy security.
2. Melting of the glaciers in the Arctic and particularly in Alaska creates new trade routes for energy. As ice sheets disappear, the Bering Strait emerges as a potential oceanic highway between the western and eastern hemispheres. The gain for global energy security could be profound. Sea routes across northern Russia could soon become practical alternatives to shipping oil and gas freight from the Pacific Rim to Europe, cutting the distance of marine routes and circumventing critical and increasingly congested and threatened chokepoints like the Suez Canal, the Bosporus, and the Strait of Malacca.
3. Defrosting of areas like the Arctic Ocean as well as Siberia and Greenland will open new areas for exploration of oil, gas, and minerals, both onshore and offshore. According to the US Geological Survey the area north of the Arctic Circle alone is home to about 30 percent of the world's undiscovered gas and 13 percent of the world's undiscovered oil. Most of these reserves can be tapped in depths of less than 500 meters of water.[10] This considerable amount of hydrocarbons, which would no doubt greatly contribute to energy security, would never be commercially viable if not for global warming.
4. Increased concentration of carbon dioxide in the atmosphere, combined with longer growing seasons and fewer frosts, would increase the amount of biomass material available for electricity generation and for alternative fuel production, hence alleviating the demand

for fossil fuels in the power sector and for crude oil in the transportation sector. This is good news for the energy security of many poor oil-importing countries in Africa, Latin America, and South Asia. With their strong agricultural base, such countries will be able to grow their fuel instead of importing it.

5. In some parts of the world, such as California, global warming-induced offshore current changes are likely to intensify summer winds and thus increase wind energy potential.[11]

Obviously all those benefits and others would be checked against the all-familiar negatives, of which there are many. But to date, no such analysis has been conducted.

Let's get back to the pipeline example at the end of the previous section. Suppose that it was discovered that the net impact of climate change on energy security was positive. If this were the case, should the chopping down of trees, subsequent greenhouse gas release, and postulated resulting climate impact be counted as an energy security enhancer for the pipeline? Should it raise its perceived energy security value? Or should the potential positive and negative impacts of climate change on energy supply cancel each other out? Who decides? Existing studies do not even agree on whether there would be a net increase or decrease in energy consumption with a changed climate because a variety of methodologies have been used. Furthermore, many of the effects of climate change on energy security are not well understood and will not be fully understood for many years to come. Until such balanced analysis is conducted, using a widely accepted methodology, it would be unscientific to conclude categorically that climate change is to the detriment of energy security.

Impact of climate change policies: failure to account for negatives

As climate advocates trumpet the benefits for both global security and energy security of their favored policies they conveniently ignore those cases where such policies undermine security. A variety of policies and technologies to address climate change are being floated by governments throughout the world. Some, like cap-and-trade or carbon tax, are aimed at artificially raising the cost of using fossil fuels in the hope of creating a competitive advantage for low-carbon energy sources and promoting energy efficiency. Other policies aim to encourage the use of renewable energy through direct subsidies, loan guarantees, and various tax incentives, making it more affordable and competitive with fossil fuels. All of these interventions in the economy are

Table 1.1 The balance sheet of climate and energy security

Negative impact of warming	Positive impact of warming
Flooding and storms will damage critical energy infrastructure. Defrosting of permafrost causes damage to oil and gas pipelines.	Defrosting of areas like the Arctic Ocean as well as Siberia and Greenland will open new areas for exploration of oil, gas, and minerals.
Warming increases energy requirements for cooling.	Warming reduces energy requirements for heating.
Warming dries rivers that communities rely upon for hydroelectric power and cooling of nuclear reactors.	Melting of glaciers creates new trade routes for energy.
In some parts of the world, warming decreases the amount of biomass material available for electricity generation and for alternative fuel production.	In other parts of the world, warming increases the amount of biomass material available for electricity generation and for alternative fuel production.

promoted on the grounds that the externalities of climate change should be better reflected in the cost of fossil fuel energy. Many of the above policies do just that. When fossil fuels artificially become more expensive and renewable energy artificially becomes cheaper, market forces are likely to shift in the latter's direction. In some cases this will no doubt offer tangible security as well as energy security benefits. Take oil for example. There is no doubt that the world's dependence on a small group of non-democratic oil exporting countries, operating in unison as part of a cartel, is a threat to global security. As Arab oil-exporting countries demonstrated in 1973, under certain conditions oil can become a weapon. Provided that cars are fuel flexible—able to run on alternative fuels in addition to gasoline—and provided that alternative fuel producers enjoy, at a minimum, free access to the market and are able to use existing refueling infrastructure, alternative fuels could compete at the pump with petroleum and hence break its virtual monopoly over transportation fuels. This means that environmental policies that open the market to alternative fuels offer direct national security benefits. There are other similar examples. Yet, there are also cases in which environmental policy generates the opposite outcome. To extend the example just discussed, environmental policies that thwart the production of high-carbon non-petroleum fuels, like coal-to-liquids, would, by reducing the ability of consuming countries to open their markets to competitors to conventional petroleum-based fuels, have a detrimental impact on national security.

Some examples of how climate policy could undermine human security are as follows:

1. *Nuclear power:* Shifting away from greenhouse gas-emitting fossil fuels puts nuclear power at the center stage as the only near zero emission source of base-load electricity. There is talk of a "nuclear renaissance" should the world move to a low-carbon economy. But a possible wider use of nuclear energy for power generation might raise new concerns about pro-liferation, in the context of a non-proliferation regime that is already under pressure. In no other place does such development pose more security challenges than in the Middle East. There, major oil- and gas-producing countries like Iran, Kuwait, and Saudi Arabia are developing nuclear power for "peaceful purposes," in what they describe as an attempt to reduce their fossil fuel consumption. Other than the traditional risks of nuclear proliferation, including the danger of nuclear materials reaching the hands of terrorists, the shift to nuclear power allows those countries to develop the scientific and industrial base that can be used for development of nuclear weapons. Further, by shifting to nuclear electricity such countries hope to divert more of their oil and gas for export purposes, which in turn would increase their geopolitical power.

2. *India's shift to natural gas:* Heavily dependent on coal for 53 percent of its installed power generation capacity, India is the world's fourth largest carbon dioxide emitter. Facing international pressure to reduce its emissions as well as domestic pressure to expand access to electricity to its poor, India is considering switching coal with cleaner burning natural gas. In doing so it runs the risk of becoming increasingly dependent on Iran as the nearest and largest source of natural gas. In March 2010, after nearly 15 years of negotiations, Iran and Pakistan signed a deal to connect their economies via a 1,300-mile natural gas pipeline. The so called Peace Pipeline will initially transfer 30 million cubic meters of gas per day to Pakistan, but will eventually increase the transfer to 60 million cubic meters per day, generating a hefty income for Tehran. Both Iran and Pakistan hope to extend the pipeline into India. This would give Iran a foothold in the Asian gas market and ensure that millions of energy-impoverished Indians are beholden to Iran's gas. For Iran, such Indian depen-dency would be a major geopolitical gain. Hence, India's shift from coal to Iranian natural gas may slow down the melting of the ice caps, but from a global security perspective it

would be a major setback, especially at a time when the international community struggles to weaken Iran economically.

3. *Carbon sequestration*: The goal of this lavishly funded approach is to inject carbon dioxide collected in power stations into deep underground rock formations and storage sites with the hope that it will stay there forever. The concept is essentially to treat carbon dioxide as a hazardous waste and bury it underground or underwater. But carbon dioxide is a leaky gas that tends to migrate to the surface. Sequestration proponents promise that leakage would be minimal, but such promises are no more reassuring than those coming from mobile phone companies telling us that there is no long-term link between cell phone use and brain cancer. Even an MIT report on the future of coal, which overall was bullish about the prospect of sequestration, admitted that it is not yet possible to provide quantitative estimates of the possibility of leakage from storage sites and that high carbon dioxide concentrations could cause adverse health, safety, and environmental consequences.[12] A leakage of as little as 2 percent per year means that within 50 years most of the stored carbon dioxide will be back in the atmosphere, making sequestration an expensive feel-good solution but one that will have minimal impact on long-term dialing back of carbon dioxide emissions. With more significant leakage, sequestration can be outright dangerous. If an underground carbon dioxide bubble slips to the surface as a result of a weak earthquake the outcome could be devastating. In 1986 a gigantic natural carbon dioxide bubble that emerged from Lake Nyos in Cameroon caused the death of 1,700 people and 3,500 livestock. One can only imagine what the impact might be of such a release in a seismically sensitive place like California.

The examples above demonstrate that the climate–security picture is more nuanced than many believe. Climate change policy cuts both ways. Policies to address climate change—especially a global embrace of nuclear power—could be as much a threat multiplier as climate change itself. The same is true for the climate–energy security nexus.

A few examples of how climate policy could undermine energy security follow:

1. *Increasing energy poverty*: Climate rhetoric aside, as long as coal is the cheapest form of base-load electricity, policies that raise its costs will in fact deny millions of poor people basic electricity and fuel security, hence undermining their energy security and condemning them to perpetual poverty. We illustrate this with two examples. First, consider a farmer who wants to purchase a pump for irrigating his fields. He can buy an electric pump or a diesel pump. But what are the most important factors guiding his choice? Is it affordability (fuel cost) or availability of the fuel in his village or reliability of fuel supply or greenhouse gas emissions associated with burning these fuels? For sure his choice will not be determined by the related greenhouse gas emissions. Despite being a more expensive fuel (as compared with electricity which is highly subsidized in India), diesel (which is supposed to be associated with a higher degree of greenhouse gas emissions as compared with electricity) is used in many northeastern Indian states where the supply of electricity is highly unreliable. In such a situation a carbon tax on diesel pumps without improvement in electricity supply will further escalate energy expenditures of the poor and reduce their energy affordability. Second, one observes that many rural households, including rural rich, use modern fuels along with traditional fuels for cooking and lighting. At the household level, multiple fuel usage can provide energy security. Whole dependence on commercially traded fuels makes rural households extremely vulnerable to changeable prices and frequently unreliable service. Although inefficient burning of biomass is extremely bad for the user's health and may be responsible for the frequent appearance in winters of dense brown clouds over South

Asia, any climate policy or energy policy that reduces availability of biomass for household use without providing affordable alternatives is likely to undermine the security of the poor.

2. *Making coal-to-liquids and unconventional oil prohibitive*: Today, coal-rich countries like China and the US eager to cut petroleum dependence are increasingly interested in coal-to-liquids technology, which is profitable as long as crude oil remains above $70 a barrel. But, coal-derived fuel produces twice as much carbon dioxide as petroleum-based fuel, and proposed climate policy would make coal-to-liquid technologies far less economic. Coal is not the only source of energy that improves energy security while increasing carbon dioxide emissions. Canadian tar-sands and oil shale have tremendous potential for expanded liquid fuel supply, but the environmental impact of extracting them far exceeds that of conventional oil. Carbon mitigation policies could deny global energy markets billions of barrels of new oil.

3. *Germany's out-of-balance energy policy*: Germany's energy policy offers a good example of how carbon-mitigating strategies could increase energy security vulnerabilities. Climate prioritization is gradually driving the country away from coal, while traditional anti-nuclear sentiment has brought the practical demise of the country's nuclear industry. German Chancellor Angela Merkel announced an ambitious policy strategy to curb greenhouse gas emissions by up to 40 percent by 2020, promoting aggressive policies to meet this goal. As Frank Umbach has pointed out, "Germany's energy policies have concurrently been idealistic, ambitious, provincial and overly optimistic."[13] Germany, while a true leader in renewable energy deployment, is utterly dependent on Russian natural gas supply and its energy security is now at the mercy of Russian leaders who have repeatedly demonstrated their willingness to use energy as a tool of coercion and intimidation. As a result of this dependence, Germany's policies have become much more timid when it comes to issues that would upset the Russians, such as NATO enlargement and Russia's invasion of Georgia.

4. *Shifting from base-load to intermittent power*: Renewable energy is viewed by many as both an energy security and climate change panacea. But while its benefits to greenhouse gas reduction are undisputed, when it comes to energy security it is not always a net winner. A US government report concluded that "because renewable energy depends directly on ambient natural resources such as hydrological resources, wind patterns and intensity, and solar radiation, it is likely to be more sensitive to climate variability than fossil or nuclear energy systems that rely on geological stores."[14] Beyond that, wind and solar power, the two most popular forms of expanded renewable energy capacity, are intermittent sources of power. The wind does not blow 24 hours a day and the sun does not shine at night. While in theory this intermittency could be managed and mitigated, under current political, technological, and regulatory conditions, in the absence of adequate electric storage capacity or backup power generators, wind and solar, with the exception of solar thermal plants, are unable to provide base-load electricity and are prone to supply interruptions. Therefore, they cannot always be counted upon as energy security enhancers.

Table 1.2 The unintended security consequences of climate policy

---

Increasing coal prices could deny poor communities in the developing world access to cheap base-load electricity.

Shifting from base-load to intermittent sources of power like solar and wind can cause reliability problems.

Shift to low-carbon nuclear power increases the risk of nuclear proliferation.

Climate policy makes coal-to-liquids and unconventional oil like shale and tar sands prohibitive.

The shift from coal to natural gas can create dependency on unreliable natural gas exporters like Russia and Iran, increasing these countries' geopolitical power.

Why does all this matter?

At this point some readers might ask why we insist on such a guarded perimeter for energy security. What is the downside of a broader definition of energy security which can bring into the fold environmental activists and other constituencies that could potentially help build at least some subset of the case for energy security?

If there is an inconvenient truth relating to our energy system it is that we may not be able to address both climate change and energy security in one strike, and too much emphasis on one could worsen the other. This is not to say that there are no policies and technologies that could successfully address both. Efficiency, conservation, and clean technology are generally beneficial to both emissions reduction energy security. So are technologies to recycle carbon dioxide into usable liquid fuels like methanol and to feed it to algae to make biodiesel. But if one is to look at the big picture, such agreeable-to-all-sides remedies in and of themselves cannot solve problems of this magnitude. Unfortunately, none of the breakthrough technologies can be brought to commercialization without substantial investment in R&D. Yet, the current level of energy R&D is too little to spur a technological revolution.[15]

One reason for this is that climate has characteristics pertinent to public goods, and therefore any effective approach to greenhouse gas emission reduction requires concerted efforts at an international level. Action would require global recognition that greenhouse gas emissions are externalities due to human activities (such as burning of fossil fuels required for growth) and a political willingness across at least major energy consuming countries to embody this externality by taxation. It is total stocks of greenhouse gases that matter, not their place of origin. On the other hand, energy security exhibits attributes close to a private good, and is largely addressed at the national level. When it comes to economic development and security, global concerns and interests generally come second to national interests. Poor regions such as Africa (that contribute least to greenhouse gas emissions) are most vulnerable to climate change.[16] At the same time, their marginal benefit from energy consumption growth and energy access (resulting in higher growth) dominates those obtained from addressing climate change concerns. Any attempt to impose climate policy would thwart the use of fossil fuels and is likely to give rise to inequities in energy and to jeopardize economic growth in many developing nations. As was demonstrated in the December 2009 failed climate summit in Copenhagen, this gap between the developed and developing world is the main stumbling block on the road to a global

Table 1.3 Top ten carbon dioxide emitters 2006

Ranking	Country	Total emissions in million metric tons of CO_2	Per capita emissions (tons/capita)
1	China	6017.69	4.58
2	United States	5902.75	19.78
3	Russia	1704.36	12.00
4	India	1293.17	1.16
5	Japan	1246.76	9.78
6	Germany	857.60	10.40
7	Canada	614.33	18.81
8	United Kingdom	585.71	9.66
9	South Korea	514.53	10.53
10	Iran	471.48	7.25

Source: Union of Concerned Scientists.

binding agreement on climate policy. This means that any attempt to internationalize energy security policy by adding to it climate constraints would make energy security solutions more difficult to accomplish.

There is also a challenge in the allocation of resources. In normal times, security and the environment tend to compete for resources and public support and the challenge policymakers face is to find an optimal balance between the two. As geopolitical and economic concerns loom larger, environmental concerns are pushed to the back burner in favor of more immediate needs like employment, shelter, and security. The current economic recession which started in 2008 brought a noticeable decline in the public's concern about climate change and in its willingness to support climate policies.[17] This forces climate activists to invest a great deal of money in trying to portray climate mitigation policies as ways to strengthen national security, economic security ("green jobs" is today's buzzword), and energy security. The tactics vary from recruitment of retired generals and admirals with no particular training or expertise in energy policy as public spokespeople for the cause of climate legislation, to TV ads juxtaposing national security with clean energy. One TV ad run in the US by an organization called VoteVet.org begins with a military vehicle exploding on a road in Iraq. A decorated Iraq War veteran explains that the armor-penetrating explosive device which nearly took his life and earned him a Purple Heart was made in "oil rich Iran." Images of Iran's notorious president Mahmoud Ahmadinejad are shown on the screen to drive home the oil-security nexus. "Every time oil goes up $1, Iran gets $1.5 billion to use against us. The connection between oil and our enemy couldn't be clearer," the veteran says. At this point images of wind turbines and solar panels appear on the screen and he continues: "We need to break this connection by breaking our addiction and we can by passing a clean energy climate plan." The message in such advertisements is: support for climate legislation will deliver energy security and spare us the need to fight for oil in the Middle East. The fact that only 2 percent of US electricity is generated from oil and therefore solutions like solar and wind power will not do anything to address oil dependence is conveniently hidden in this willful manipulation of the public. Yet, this attempt to masquerade climate change solutions as cures to America's national security challenges is not an isolated case but part of an ongoing cynical and intellectually dishonest effort by the environmental movement.

Unfortunately these tactics have been quite successful. Knowing that climate change polls far lower than national security, many politicians in the US promoting climate legislation are using the national security rationale to bolster their case. In June 2009, the U.S House of Representatives approved the American Clean Energy and Security Act of 2009, a bill that would establish a cap-and-trade plan for greenhouse gases to address climate change. The US Environmental Protection Agency which analyzed the bill found that it did not reduce petroleum prices and usage in any perceptible way.[18] Yet, the bill was sold to the American public, both in name as well as in spirit, as energy security legislation. In March 2010, a few weeks after VoteVets.org ran its ads and while the bill was being deliberated in the US Senate, a poll of Iraq and Afghanistan veterans found that 79 percent believe that ending US dependence on foreign oil is important to national security. An almost similar percentage of those polled believed that passing the cap-and-trade bill would help eliminate America's vulnerability. In other words, most Americans were misled into believing that the problem they care about—oil dependence/ national security—could be solved through climate policy which demonstrably has no impact whatsoever on energy security.

Energy security and climate change are only two challenges in the menu of issues that dominate our policy discourse. Injecting large doses of climate change into every dish on that menu would inevitably cause indigestion, at least to some around the table. Important as climate change may be, it should not be confused with other, no less pressing, concerns, particularly not with energy security. This is particularly necessary since climate change has thus far proven to be a variable of relatively minor impact on energy security. A close look at the major energy challenges the world has faced in the past 100 years—the US oil embargo on Japan prior to World War II, the 1973 Arab Oil Embargo, the Iran–Iraq War, the Iraqi invasion of Kuwait and the subsequent Gulf War, Russia's gas cutoff to Ukraine, insurgencies in Iraq and Nigeria, strikes in Venezuela—reveals that none of those threats was related to climate change. Looking into the crystal ball one can already identify many of the threats to energy security that loom on the horizon—nuclear war in the Middle East, Sunni–Shi'ite violence in the Persian Gulf, successful terror attacks against oil installations in Saudi Arabia, major disruption in energy shipping, collapse of Nigeria, energy embargos, to name a few. Here, too, none of these is related to climate change. This is not to say that energy security is immune from the wrath of Mother Nature. It isn't, and as climate shows a greater impact on energy availability and pricing, so it would merit a reassessment of its role in energy security analysis. But until that happens, a more factual and dispassionate discourse, one which enables a better understanding of the trade-offs associated with linking climate and energy security policy, is needed. In order to accomplish coherent discussion that could result in tangible and effective energy security policies, we should recognize that progress in addressing large-caliber problems can only be achieved not just when those problems are narrowly delineated but also when their solutions are widely accepted.

Notes

1 Luft, Gal and Anne Korin (eds). 2009. *Energy Security Challenges for the 21st Century: A Reference Handbook* (Santa Barbara, CA: Praeger), pp. 5–7.

2 U.S. Department of Energy. 2009. *International Energy Outlook 2009*, Energy Information Administration Report #:DOE/EIA-0484(2009). Available at: http://www.eia.doe.gov/oiaf/ieo/electricity.html (accessed August 28, 2010).

3 Barton, Barry, Catherine Redgwell, Anita Ronne, and Donald N. Zillman 2004. *Energy Security: Managing Risk in a Dynamic Legal and Regulatory Environment*, (New York: Oxford University Press), p. 5.

4 Gupta, Eshita and Anant Sudarshan. 2009. "Energy and Poverty in India." In Ligia Noronha and Anant Sudarshan (eds), *India's Energy Security* (New York: Routledge), pp. 29–48.

5 CNA Corporation Center for Naval Analysis (CNA), "National Security and the Threat of Climate Change." Available at: http://securityandclimate.cna.org (accessed August 28, 2010). See also Jeffrey Mazo. 2010. *Climate Conflict: How Global Warming Threatens Security and What to Do About It*, Adelphi Paper 409 (London: International Institute for Strategic Studies).

6 Broder, John. 2009. "Climate Change Seen as Threat to US Security," *New York Times*, August 8.

7 Brown, Marilyn. 2009. "The Environmental Dimension of Energy Security." White paper presented before an International Workshop on Energy Security Concepts and Indicators for Asia, Center on Asia and Globalization, Lee Kuan Yew School of Public Policy, National University of Singapore, November 15.

8 U.S. Department of Energy. Energy Information Administration, *U.S. Household Electricity Report, 2005*. Available at: http://www.eia.doe.gov/emeu/reps/enduse/er01_us_figs.html (accessed August 28, 2010).

9 *Effects of Climate Change on Energy Production and Use in the United States*, Synthesis and Assessment Product 4.5, Report by the U.S. Climate Change Science Program and the Subcommittee on Global Change Research. Available at: http://www.climatescience.gov/Library/sap/sap4-5/final-report/sap4-5-final-all.pdf, p. 13, October 2007 (accessed August 28, 2010).

10 U.S. Geological Survey (USGS) Release. 2008. "90 Billion Barrels of Oil and 1,670 Trillion Cubic Feet of Natural Gas Assessed in the Arctic," July 23. Available at: http://www.usgs.gov/newsroom/article_pf.asp?ID=1980 (accessed August 28, 2010).

11 Edwards, Allen G. 1991. *Global Warming from an Energy Perspective, Global Climate Change and California* (Berkeley: University of California Press), chapter 8.

12 Massachusetts Institue of Technology (MIT) Report, *The Future of Coal*. Available at: http://web.mit.edu/coal/, March 2007 (accessed August 28, 2010).

13 Umbach, Frank. 2008. "Germany's Energy Insecurity," *Journal of Energy Security*, October.

14 U.S. Climate Change Science Program *Effects of Climate Change*.

15 Barrett, Scott. 2009. "The Coming Global Climate-Technology Revolution," *Journal of Economic Perspectives* 23(2): 69.

16 Mendelsohn, Robert, Ariel Dinar, and Larry Williams. 2006. "The Distributional Impact of Climate Change on Rich and Poor Countries," *Environment and Development Economics*, April: 159.

17 Pew Research Center for the Public and the Press. 2009. Public Opinion Poll: "Fewer Americans See Solid Evidence of Global Warming," October. Available at: http://people-press.org/report/556/global-warming (accessed August 28, 2010).

18 *EPA Analysis of the American Clean Energy and Security Act of 2009 H.R. 2454 in the 111th Congress,* June 23, 2009, p. 60. Available at: http://www.epa.gov/climatechange/economics/pdfs/HR2454_Analysis_Appendix.pdf (accessed August 28, 2010).

2

THE FUZZY NATURE OF ENERGY SECURITY

Scott Victor Valentine

Introduction

In Plato's *Republic*, a conversation takes place between Socrates and Plato's brother, Glaucon, wherein Socrates asks Glaucon to imagine a scenario in which a group of men have been imprisoned in a cave and rendered immobile since birth.[1] Hands and legs are bound and their heads are immobilized by devices that fix their respective gazes on a stone wall in front of them.[2]

Behind the prisoners in Socrates' scenario is a blazing fire. Between this fire and the backs of the prisoners, individuals silently pass carrying objects on their heads. Socrates, while putting down his figurative water bong, rhetorically asks if it would not be unreasonable for these prisoners (who have known no other reality) to perceive the shadows cast on the wall within their respective frames of sight to be real things rather than mere reflections of reality.

Plato's Allegory of the Cave presents a delightfully obscure metaphor for describing the manner in which past experiences, levels of education, social contacts, and a host of other influential forces alter individual perception. The allegory also serves as a cautionary tale for those of us who are tasked with the challenge of somehow evaluating energy security in order to somehow "speak truth to power"[3] and help decision-makers to develop *rationalizable* national energy strategies. Lynne Chester summarizes the quandary facing energy security analysts: "an examination of explicit and inferred definitions finds that the concept of *energy security* is inherently slippery because it is polysemic in nature, capable of holding multiple dimensions and taking on different specificities depending on the country (or continent), time frame or energy source to which it is applied."[4]

In short, those in the energy security analysis field who are searching for one comprehensive methodology for analyzing a given nation's energy security will find themselves spending many a long night sobbing ruefully into their pillows. There will be no definitive methodology for assessing national energy security because "energy security" is a malleable concept that has even led some to question the usefulness and meaningfulness of the term.[5] How one assesses energy security depends explicitly on choices made regarding *inter alia*: (1) the scope of the term "energy security", (2) the temporal scale that is adopted for assessing national energy security, and (3) critical assumptions underpinning the assessment. As Ciuta points out, "energy security clearly means many different things to different authors and actors, and even at times to the same author or actor."[6]

Some analysts have attempted to address the fuzzy nature of energy security by creating aggregate indices that conflate a number of different energy security criteria. Unfortunately, approaching energy security analysis through the application of multiple indicators does not lead to the "broader understanding" that some colleagues purport;[7] rather, adding more indicators to an energy security assessment simply serves to enhance intellectual discord by introducing contentious debate over the weighting of multiple indicators and inveigling academic tantrums over criteria that was unfairly omitted or thoughtlessly added to the assessment. Comprehensive indices or methodologies for measuring energy security merely represent more complex mobilization of ideological bias. A good illustration is demonstrated by considering Jansen and colleagues'[8] well-argued and detailed reformulation of the Shannon Index. The researchers created an index consisting of four broad criteria: diversification of energy sources in energy supply, diversification of imports with respect to imported energy sources, long-term political stability in import regions, and the resource base in regions of origin. Although the index itself was well defined, clearly justified, and useful for some analytical purposes, the end result is an energy security assessment tool that is heavily predisposed toward the importance of political stability.[9] In fact, all of the recently advanced aggregate indices—for example, the IEA Energy Security Index, Scheepers and colleagues' Supply-Demand (SD) Index,[10] Bollen's MERGE model,[11] Gupta's Oil Vulnerability Index[12] – suffer from the same unavoidable quality of mobilizing ideological bias through the choice of criteria to include in the index and the weightings given to each variable. This is not in any way intended to be critical of the above-mentioned indices. Despite the inherent truth in Ralph Waldo Emerson's observation that "the only sin that we never forgive in each other is a difference in opinion,"[13] those of us in the social sciences should actively seek to nurture interactions with those who hold different ideological biases. However, in public presentation of our theses, we should also be prepared to make our biases known to our audience.

This chapter pursues two objectives. First, the passages that follow will seek to clarify how different choices made in the process of (1) defining energy security, (2) establishing temporal scale, and (3) establishing criteria for assessing energy security can significantly influence energy security analysis. Second, it is hoped that the expatiations presented in this chapter embolden energy analysts to explore the environs of the ontological caves in which they reside intellectually and encourage them to both reflect upon and communicate their ideological leanings through sufficient transparency in any energy security analysis that they undertake. In doing so, "new levels of understanding will enrich the policy debate to deal with obstacles impacting on the constantly evolving nature of energy security."[14] Success in achieving these two objectives will be measured by any future invitations that I receive to meetings of "the Association of Ideologically Introspective Energy Security Analysts," preferably held in serene retreats intended to pay suitable tribute to Bacchus.

Due to the obdurate nature of word limits, it is a certainty that informed readers will experience a degree of dissonance over the apparent omission of a critical assumption or two (or ten) which would alter the nature of energy security assessment. I make no apologies for such omissions, not because of underdeveloped skills of self-reflection but because the ontological perspectives introduced in this chapter are not intended to represent an exhaustive list of elements that shape the nature of energy security assessment. The illustrations introduced in this chapter are introduced as evidence to belabor the point that the creation of national energy security assessments is an inherently political, subjective, biased, and coercive undertaking that simultaneously exhibits the capacity to *speak truth to power* (encourage optimized national energy strategies based on transparent but ideologically bound criteria) and *speak the truths of those in power* (justify biased national energy strategies through manipulation of assessment criteria).

The failure of creators of national energy security assessments to transparently disclose the critical assumptions that have been made in developing such assessments is an act that warrants an intellectual wrap across the wrists with a wooden ruler. In a world where well-funded special interest groups routinely scour media sources in search of "unbiased" support for the ideologies that they espouse and where media sources increasingly appear amenable to publishing academic detritus, the responsibility for ensuring that national security assessments clearly communicate ideological and perceptual biases increasingly becomes an exercise in self-policing. My appeal to energy security analysts here is straightforward: take the time to create one paragraph (or two) that explicates the ontological influences and assumptions underlying one's work.

So, with this appeal firmly ensconced, let us take a moment to examine the term "energy security" and some of the conceptual rascals that tend to complicate what would otherwise be a simple mathematical exercise of setting evaluative metrics, collecting quantitative data on the metrics, and then conflating the metrics.

Defining the scope of "energy security"

Some intrepid academics have proffered conceptual frameworks intended to clarify perspectives on "energy security." Recent contributions include Ciuta's three logics of energy security (a logic of war, a logic of subsistence, and a "total" security logic)[15] and Kruyt's and colleagues' four dimensions of energy security (availability, accessibility, affordability, acceptability).[16] However, these and others fall short when it comes to comprehensiveness. William Blake once noted that "if the doors of perception were cleansed, everything would appear to man as it is, infinite."[17] If the doors of perception were cleansed in regard to assessing energy security, one would find a boundless array of perspectives on what constitutes energy security (Figure 2.1). This section hopes to introduce the reader to a sampling of these perspectives.

International energy security or national energy security?

Perhaps the first fundamental choice that needs to be made when undertaking energy security analysis is whether the assessment should emphasize global energy security or national energy security. On the one hand, from a global perspective, the progressive drawdown of fossil fuel reserves driven by a seemingly insatiable demand for energy and its trappings implies that there is a looming crisis ahead in the transportation and electricity generation sectors and solving this

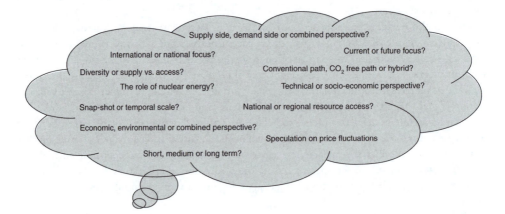

Figure 2.1 A sampling of critical choices when defining "energy security".

crisis will require wide-scale reconfiguration of energy generation technologies.[18,19] In short, global reliance on fossil fuels for primary energy generation places *all* nations in extremely insecure circumstances.[20] On the other hand, from a national perspective, some nations are far less insecure than other nations in regard to the sustainability of their respective energy portfolios. For example, Japan has virtually no domestic petroleum resources,[21] while Canada boasts an abundance of untapped oil potential in its Albertan tar sands and enjoys the increasingly rare attribute of being a net exporter of crude oil.[22] Clearly, as global demand for petroleum begins to outpace the expansion of supply capabilities, the cost of petroleum will rise. We have already felt the first tremors of this demand-led economic earthquake in petroleum markets in recent years.[23] Under a business as usual scenario, price inflation in petroleum will not be met with the same level of economic anxiety in petroleum-rich Canada as it will in petroleum-indigent Japan.

Differing international energy security perspectives

Deciding to nest an evaluation of energy security within a global perspective represents only the first of a host of ideologically infused decision points. From this first conceptual fork in the road, more ideological choices need to be made in regard to what exactly constitutes international energy security. As this section will demonstrate, assessing energy security from an international perspective represents an analytical path that is laden with divergent conceptual tributaries, all of which are capable of producing useful and actionable insight. Such analysis is far more complex than critics contend when accusing international energy security analysts of being "an entire foreign-policy cottage industry that obsesses about the need for nations and their diplomats to worry about and attempt to manage petroleum markets."[24] International energy security assessment is an important aspect of energy security analysis but it is far from an invariable undertaking.

Consider the following five possible assessment approaches stemming from different interpretations of the term "international energy security." First, it could be defined as an analysis of the aggregate capacity to fulfill energy demand through *existing sources* of supply.[25] Under this conceptualization of "international energy security," the assessment process would include evaluation of the nexus between aggregate conventional fuel supply and demand trends, either in the present time or projected some time into the future.[26] Such an analysis would also likely include an evaluation of the capacity of the international energy community to protect global energy resources from terrorist threat and respond to unexpected supply disruptions.[27] Although critics may argue that analysis of the aggregate global capacity to maintain sufficient supply of conventional fuel sources does nothing to shed light on disparities with national access, an analysis of this type sheds valuable light on supply chain risk that is likely of high interest to decision-makers in any current energy regime. In short, an analysis of this type has its use, albeit limited.

A second approach to conceptualizing international energy security is to assess certainty of access on a nation-by-nation basis[28] in order to shed light on disparities of access and supply chain risk that exist within the global energy supply chain. Popular metrics that appear in such assessments include *inter alia* resource availability analysis, fuel diversity indices, and measures of import dependence.[29] This second approach would also likely incorporate both an evaluation of the strength of the underlying trading relationships between the host nation and nations from which energy resources are imported[30] and an evaluation of political stability in nations from which energy is imported.[31] As with the first approach, critics could condemn such an assessment as failing to consider non-conventional energy options. However, for nations that are plotting investment strategies that entail the construction of infrastructure for supporting conventional energy services, an analysis of this type would be of high value. Once again, as limited as this approach may be in the eyes of some critics, it does have an audience to serve.

A third approach aimed at overcoming the strategic planning weakness of an energy security analysis that focuses only on conventional fuels is to evaluate the capacity of individual nations to satisfy national energy requirements through access to energy resources of any type. Frequently, scenario analysis is employed for such analysis in order to examine the options that a nation has to its avail[32,33] and speculate on how this will influence global energy markets. Such an analysis can be useful for helping decision-makers understand how decisions made in other nations will impact domestic strategic energy options. Therefore, this approach has a place in energy security analysis even if interpreting international energy security as a function of supply accessibility of any type ignores the question of economic optimality.

A fourth approach to international energy security analysis could address this economic over-sight by reinterpreting international energy security as a challenge of balancing the attributes of availability, accessibility, and affordability,[34] either from an aggregate perspective or from a nationally aggregated perspective. Many traditional energy security analysts would agree that these three attributes represent crucial goals of international energy security analysis.[35,36] Indeed, these criteria essentially form the foundation of the International Energy Agency's (IEA) Energy Security assessment methodology. However, to prioritize such elements appropriately tends to result in a clash of intellectual horns involving competing ideological perspectives. This does not render such assessments ineffective but it does make them susceptible to ideological bias and commercially driven distortion. Transparent disclosure of critical assumptions is the way to prevent such useful tools from being misapplied.

Finally, there is a strong argument to be made in favor of an international security perspective that views long-term global reliance on fossil fuels as untenable in the face of the threats posed by global warming.[37,38] Accordingly, a fifth approach to international energy security might be founded on a premise that a balance must be sought between availability, accessibility, and affordability within constraints posed by our global ecosystem.[39]

The truth is that scenarios of how to approach international energy security could be constructed *ad nauseam*, with each scenario characterized as serving select decision-making purposes. Furthermore, each conceptualization of "international energy security" requires some contentious choices to be made in terms of which variables should be included in the analysis and how multiple variables should be weighted.

The long and the short of this discussion is that any international energy security assessment springs from a specific, ideology-infused definition of what international energy security actually entails. The act of creating such a definition sires perceptual discord that is not vastly dissimilar from attempting to resolve disagreement over which rock group is the greatest rock group of all time. Unfortunately, as the next section will demonstrate, shifting the scope of energy security analysis from an international scale to a national scale does little to infuse a degree of harmony to such perceptual discord.

Differing national energy security perspectives

National energy security analyses typically range from technical to socio-economic assessments. Technical analyses focus on evaluating the efficiency, effectiveness, and inherent risks associated with energy networks.[40] Evaluative criteria would include assessment of network resiliency, diversity of energy technologies, diversity of energy supply, surplus capacity within a given energy system, and technical capacity to respond to unexpected demand fluctuations.[41,42] Although, technological perspectives are not the focus of this chapter, it suffices to point out that the term "national energy security" means something entirely different to the average electrical engineer than it does to the average energy policy expert. Going back to our analogy of identifying the greatest rock group of all time, this ontological difference is the equivalent of one person responding with "The Beatles" and another responding with "the cluster at Stonehenge."

From a socio-economic perspective (which constitutes the focus of this chapter), interpretation of what constitutes "national energy security" also represents a multifaceted foray into theoretical rationality and the structure of cognition.[43]

Undoubtedly, the dominant perspective of national energy security over the past few decades has been rooted in economic rationality, with sustainable risk-free access to the cheapest forms of energy representing the holy grail of national energy security.[44] Even national energy security assessments designed to feed into assessments of national defense capabilities depend ineluctably on attaining sustainable risk-free access to the cheapest forms of energy.[45,46] Under this traditional perspective, nations that boast an abundance of domestic energy resources of any type can be considered to possess a high degree of national energy security.[47] Obviously the shortcoming of such a high-level perspective of national energy security is that it fails to distinguish between sustainable and unsustainable energy resource governance practice. For example, both Australia and Canada currently enjoy the potential to satisfy domestic electricity demand through domestic energy resources. However, Australia's self-sufficiency in electricity generation is achieved through the continued depletion of finite coal reserves,[48] while Canada's self-sufficiency in electricity generation is achieved largely through sustainable exploitation of hydropower capacity.[49] One does not need to have an advanced degree in cleverness from Oxford University to understand which of these two nations has a higher capacity to enjoy longer-term national security in the electricity generation sector.

So already we see a fracturing of perspectives involving the term "national energy security," with traditionalists arguing that economic optimization in the short run represents a state of high security and critics countering that the sustainability of resource use over a longer term needs to be factored into such an analysis.[50,51]

While it might be intuitively appealing to side with the "sustainable use" camp, there is a valid argument that can be made to justify short-term economic maximization. Minimizing costs in the short term provides a nation with the financial leverage necessary to facilitate technological transitions to alternative energy sources in the future. Moreover, speculating on the prospects of domestically available energy resources to support the future needs of a nation also requires speculative analysis of energy system technological development. For example, technological advances in nuclear fusion could theoretically render an analysis of a nation's capacity to support long-term reliance on current energy generation technologies moot. In short, the technological wild card could turn long-term sustainability analysis into a scenario analysis exercise that is about as objective as a Jackson Pollock painting.

A further perspective on national energy security stems from the belief that global response to the threat of climate change needs to be factored into any medium- to long-term assessment of national energy security for at least three economic reasons that even traditional analysts who are committed to supporting the prevailing economic rational perspective are obliged to consider.[52] First, global climate change negotiations could, in one fell swoop, alter energy market dynamics. Widespread commitments to capping CO_2 emissions could (and likely will) catalyze a resurgence in nuclear power and may alter the economics of this energy source.[53] Similarly, the World Wind Energy Association contends that costs of wind power are expected to fall below costs of all fossil fuel resources if externalities associated with fossil fuel combustion are adequately internalized.[54] Second, altering fossil fuel energy technologies to mitigate CO_2 emissions (i.e. carbon capture and sequestration) either through national or sub-national mandates will undermine the economic attractiveness of fossil fuel energy systems.[55] Third, as new technologies emerge and new alliances develop around alternative energy sources, even nations committed to conventional sources will be forced to diversify technologies in order to mitigate the risk of being left behind technologically.

A fourth perspective of national energy security stems from the premise that the manner in which a nation's energy strategy influences social capital should be considered because the evolution of social capital in a given nation has ramifications both for the economic development and the socio-political stability of a nation.[56] By logical extension then, anything that significantly influences a nation's social capital will also significantly influence a nation's national security, which, in turn, will influence national energy security.

Energy has three characteristics that can influence the evolution of social capital in a given nation. First, energy is an essential service. As such, access to affordable supplies of energy plays a vital role in supporting human activity; and therefore it is an indicator of the well-being of a given society.[57] This attribute of energy is the basis upon which The Energy Research Institute's (TERI) Lighting a Billion Lives campaign is built. The campaign contends that providing solar lanterns to impoverished communities can rapidly improve both productivity and education levels in impoverished communities.[58]

Second, the energy service sector is a key employer in many nations. A *very* conservative estimate put forth in a study commissioned by Greenpeace estimated that in 2010 there were approximately 9.1 million jobs related to the provision of electricity alone, which is broken down into coal (4.65 million), gas (1.95 million), renewables (1.8 million), and nuclear, oil and diesel (0.61 million).[59]

Third, there are numerous adverse environmental externalities associated with the energy supply chain and, in extreme cases, these externalities can have a significant impact on social welfare. For example, in China, air pollution is so severe that it is now the leading cause of death in the country.[60] Worldwide, 16 of the 20 cities with the worst air pollution are found in China.[61] Thus, China's energy strategy exacerbates social and health costs.

Given the link between energy and the development of social capital in a given nation, an argument can be made for assessment of a nation's energy strategy in the context of evaluating the extent to which the strategy either bolsters or degrades national social capital. Enhanced social capital implies improved economic development prospects and higher levels of political stability. Progress in these two areas, in turn, implies a higher level of national energy security because healthier economies permit the level of investment necessary to optimize energy networks, and politically stable economies reduce the risk of disruption—be it through dysfunctional planning or civic protest—to energy networks.

Whether one agrees with this ideological perspective is beside the point. An analysis that includes an assessment of the impact that a nation's energy strategy has on social capital development has valid uses. For example, the Danish government, in defending its support for wide-scale transition to renewable energy (wind power in particular), would likely find it useful to include social capital enhancement data to defend this strategy on the basis of job creation, support for the technological evolution of the Danish workforce, reduced health costs associated with fuel stock combustion, and improved self-sufficiency in electricity generation.[62,63]

Another ideological perspective on what should or should not be included into national energy security assessments argues for the importance of including evaluation of climate change impacts. Arguments for this can be quite convincing. For example, one could argue that the economic, physical, and social welfare of citizens around the world will be predominantly adversely affected as the effects of climate change become more pronounced. In nations that are particularly hard hit by the adverse impacts of global warming, social protest may have real and unexpected consequences for parties in power. For example, it is not inconceivable that civic unrest could destabilize a country such as Bangladesh if rising sea levels begin to displace hordes of already poverty-stricken citizens.

For any given nation, how international relations evolve in reaction to climate change mitigation and abatement policies may wind up having more severe national security consequences than the estimated physical impacts attributed to climate change might have. As nations begin to experience the adverse economic impacts associated with global warming, one can anticipate a degree of international antagonism toward nations that are slow to adopt responsible CO_2 emission abatement policies.[64] Furthermore, as nations jostle to improve national energy security, intergovernmental relationships will change. On the one hand, some trading relationships—such as that which exists between Canada and the United States—will likely strengthen.[65] On the other hand, other existing alliances will weaken. Conceivably, many European nations that have close ties with Russia, such as the Ukraine, may begin to seek new strategic relationships in order to insulate themselves from an overreliance on energy flows from a nation that has a history of using such dependence for political gain.[66] Meanwhile, new collaborative relationships will also emerge. Take China as an example. It is actively courting partners that have the ability to help supply China's accelerating demand for energy, and its proactive engagement with rogue nations such as Sudan is viewed as a potentially destabilizing influence on global politics.[67]

All of these examples reflect foreseeable possibilities based on existing trends that can be objectively confirmed. However, it is reasonable to expect that a host of other unexpected alliances, collaborations, and conflicts will form as competition for dwindling supplies of fossil fuel resources heats up.[68] In such a world, energy security and national security cannot be cleanly separated.[69] Given this contextual background, it should be apparent that there is an argument to be made in support of including climate change impact assessment in long-term national energy security assessments.

It is useful in concluding this section to remind the reader that the conjectures put forward in this section regarding what may or may not be included appropriately in a national energy security assessment are not intended to lend support to any given perspective. Rather, the intent of this discussion is (1) to highlight how the simple act of defining "energy security" is not so simple after all, and (2) to demonstrate how the definition of "energy security" has widespread implications with regard to how an energy security assessment ought to be undertaken and the purposes that such an assessment effectively serves. If the act of defining energy security has such catalytic strength, it is only logical that any energy security assessment should begin with the author's definition of "energy security." Without explicating interpretation of this term, readers are placed in the unenviable position of trying to understand the scope and boundaries of a nation's energy security assessment. Stated in simpler terms, it is impossible to evaluate suitably the contention that The Beatles are the greatest rock group of all time without explaining the basis upon which "greatest" has been assessed.

The temporal nature of national energy security assessment

It should be clear from the discussion to this point that there is a temporal dimension to energy security analysis which poses severe conceptualization challenges.[70,71] Simply put, a secure energy portfolio today will likely differ from a secure energy portfolio ten years from now. And a secure energy portfolio ten years from now will undoubtedly differ from a secure energy portfolio 50 years from now.

Woody Allen once quipped, that time is nature's way of keeping everything from happening at once. This is certainly an appropriate sentiment when it comes to evaluating energy security. If an energy security analyst were to take a "quantitative snapshot" of today's global energy picture and use the data from this snapshot to guide development of a set of metrics for evaluating national energy security, risk-free access to adequate supplies of fossil fuels or uranium would likely play a central role in determining the extent of energy security in any given nation.

However, if one were to assess energy security over a 30-year time span, speculation regarding the extent to which fossil fuel prices will escalate would likely be required to evaluate energy security with the same energy mix. From this medium-term perspective, nations that boast an abundance of hydropower might be assessed as enjoying a greater degree of energy security than nations that boast an abundance of coal, simply because the risk of price escalation with coal-fired energy is much higher than with hydropower. Similarly, if one were to take an even longer-term perspective of energy security, an analyst might be tempted to speculate on the impact that global warming will have on a given nation's energy security.

So if one is tasked with the job of assessing energy security for a given nation, which time frame should one use? Or should analysts simply reject analyses employing a single temporal perspective and instead incorporate multiple temporal dimensions into each study?[72] Blissfully, this chapter does not aim to resolve these difficult questions. However, it does seek to mercilessly pound home the point that there are many viable perspectives regarding which temporal scale to employ in energy security analysis that are fully justifiable based on the purpose for which the analysis is being undertaken.

The directional bias of critical assumptions

An assessment of energy security of any type requires some path-wobbling assumptions to be made regarding future events. Even energy security assessments that are based on business as usual scenarios embrace a critical assumption that circumstances will not change.

Much to the consternation of analysts who conduct such assessments, the trouble with assessing future developments is that—and here comes the key insight—the future has not happened yet. In the time that passes between now and any given future development, a horde of bawdy, unanticipated influences tend to disrupt our expectations. Therefore, successfully predicting future trends requires considerably more work than simply putting a ruler down next to a graph of historical trends and drawing a pencil line into the future. Success depends on the ability of analysts to predict how thousands if not millions of catalytic variables influence the evolution of complex adaptive systems. Of course, the difficulty in compiling and processing so much data renders the vast majority of energy analysts as prognostically effective as dart-throwing monkeys who are standing in front of scenario projections. Fortunately, energy security analysts have a leg up on dart-throwing monkeys when competing for credibility, human analysts can at least explicate the methodology behind their assessments, whereas monkeys cannot.

This section will demonstrate through some select examples how assumptions made in regard to a nation's capacity for change, technological developments, environmental trends, energy market trends, aggregate economic trends, and global political developments can all *significantly* (again in the Janusian sense) influence the conclusions of an energy security assessment (see Figure 2.2).

Once again the reader is reminded that this is not meant to be an exhaustive list of assumptions that influence energy security analysis; rather, it provides the reader with a sense of how extensive an impact these assumptions can have on energy security analysis. Making the nature of such assumptions clear at least gives the reader a general idea of the direction in which analytical darts are being thrown.

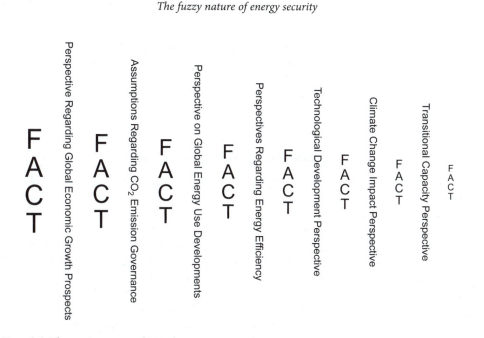

Figure 2.2 The erosive nature of critical assumptions on factual reporting.

Technological development perspective

Although most social scientists aspire to be detached observers of the human condition, the truth is that social scientists are not immune from bias and personal mindsets.[73] When it comes to questioning the extent to which technological developments may obviate current trends of resource depletion or environmental degradation, the spectacles worn by some social scientists will simply be rosier than those worn by others. The reason that this is applicable to a discussion on energy security assessment is because due to the fluid nature of energy security, critical assumptions need to be made regarding the scale and scope of technological development in order to speculate on future energy security crisis points.

A concrete example demonstrates how assumptions related to technological development can alter energy security assessments. As we all know by now, like a little boy who has awoken hours before the rest of the household and now sits in front of a Christmas tree adorned with a sea of unopened presents, Canada is currently perched on top of a vast reservoir of petroleum resources in the form of tar sands.[74] Given the current cost of extracting oil from Canada's tar sands, recent Canadian government initiatives to support accelerated development of the tar sands can be seen as either enhancing or undermining national energy security depending on one's technological development perspective. Technological optimists could argue that technological developments within the next two decades could reduce the cost of processing oil from tar sands to a level that would place Canada in an enviable position of having backyard access to massive reserves of cheap energy. Conversely, technological skeptics could argue that research and development funding spent on tar sand development will not produce such a desirable outcome. These skeptics could argue that not only has technology, to date, failed to render exploitation of the tar sands commercially viable, the economic evolution of renewable technologies such as wind power and third-generation biofuels will render the prospect of economically competitive extraction of tar sands to be sillier than a Marx Brothers' film.[75]

The insight to be drawn from the example of Canada's tar sands should be apparent, but just in case it isn't, I will make it so: explicating assumptions regarding the anticipated path of energy technology development should be included in any energy security assessment because such assumptions impact the manner in which current energy strategies contribute to, or detract from, future energy security.

Transitional capacity perspective

Perhaps of all the nations in the world, over the next few decades, China stands to have the greatest impact on energy security analysis.[76] Not only does Chinese demand for energy possess the potential to significantly influence global energy prices, but also choices made in China in regard to energy mix can have significant consequences for the global environment.[77] The challenge of predicting developments in China's energy market is complicated by both a general lack of understanding amongst Western energy security analysts regarding the drivers behind China's national energy strategy and the historical unpredictability associated with Chinese energy development strategy. Twenty years ago, who would have predicted that installed wind power capacity in China would rank second only to the US in the world by 2009? Government pro-wind policy over the past four years in China has resulted in aggregate installed capacity doubling each year.[78]

Different interpretations of the scale and scope of energy technology transition in China can lead to significantly disparate evaluations. For example, on the one hand, one energy security analyst could view current developmental trends in China's energy market and conclude that the pace at which China is transitioning to less carbon-intensive energy systems (1) is insufficient given the need to expediently reduce atmospheric CO_2 concentration levels, (2) will undoubtedly place upward pressure on global energy prices, and (3) will exacerbate dwindling supplies of conventional energy resources, thereby giving rise to political tension over competition for access to energy resources.[79] On the other hand, another energy security analyst could conclude that (1) the economic might that is currently being amassed in China will provide Chinese leadership with the financial resources necessary to support a larger-scale transition in the future, and (2) public backlash over environmental problems associated with fossil fuel combustion and the impressive development of wind power in the Chinese government to date speaks to the likelihood of such a transition taking place.[80] The data used to arrive at these disparate assessments could theoretically be the same, with the disparity stemming from differences in transitional capacity perspective. The first analyst assumes that energy technology in China will evolve in a more or less linear manner based on aggregate energy consumption data; the second analyst interprets the exponential growth of wind power capacity as support evidence to infer a rapid transition away from fossil fuel technologies. "Two energy security wunderkinder: one reveres coal, the other reveres wind."

Climate change impact perspective

Mark Twain once noted, "There is something fascinating about science. One gets such wholesale returns of conjecture out of such a trifling investment of fact."[81] Regrettably, this observation largely reflects the state of affairs in terms of predicting the changes that will occur to our planet as global warming intensifies. Of perhaps greatest consternation is the observation that, as climate change knowledge improves, past conjectures regarding adverse ecological repercussions are proven to be understated:

Oops, we forgot to factor in the impact of methane escaping from our warming oceans. Well that might add a few degrees to global warming over the next few decades … Oh, by the way, it looks like there is a possibility that the oceanic thermohaline circulation in the Atlantic may actually be altered to the point where the entire climate of Western Europe is changed … Hey, the Northwest Passage is free of ice, gosh we didn't expect that to happen so early!

The point is that we are dealing with a phenomenon that is not well understood and, unfortunately for energy security analysts (and energy consumers!), fossil fuel energy combustion is the primary culprit behind humanity's role in global warming.[82] Due to this ineluctable relationship, strategies to respond to global warming will undoubtedly result in dynamic changes to national energy mixes and these changes could significantly influence energy security from both national and international perspectives.

How energy security analysts interpret the impact that global warming will have on the evolution of global energy markets can significantly influence the manner in which any given nation's energy strategy is evaluated. For example, if an analyst believes that a high degree of resilience still exists in regard to atmospheric and terrestrial capacity to assimilate greenhouse gas emissions, the analyst may be tempted to downplay the influence that global warming developments will have on energy portfolios around the world. However, if an analyst accepts IPCC (Intergovernmental Panel on Climate Change) estimates of ecological and economic damage caused by climate change,[83] any nation that is not enacting a strategic transition away from carbon-intensive energy technologies should be evaluated as placing itself in a disadvantageous position in the future, should an international pact emerge which forces countries to abandon fossil fuel energy technologies.

Obviously, economic problems caused by global warming will also have national security and energy security repercussions that differ by nation. For example, India is expected to be severely impacted by higher levels of global warming due to concerns over flooding of population centers such as Mumbai (Bombay), Chennai, and Kolkata (Calcutta).[84] Not only would the large-scale displacement of citizens have adverse social and economic repercussions for the nation, both international and civic pressures would likely come to bear on India's leadership to play a more active role in facilitating a transition away from fossil fuel energy technologies. A nation that has already embarked on the road to energy technology transition (such as India exhibits in wind power, nuclear power, and biomass research) stands to be less exposed to political and security risks compared with a nation that is still digging vast quantities of coal out of the ground and holding mass meetings to chant "drill baby drill."

Any elements that influence the energy security of a nation should be included in a national energy security assessment, whether these elements are capable of being fully managed by a nation or not. When it comes to the role that global warming might play in energy security analysis, analysts should clearly communicate the assumptions they are making regarding anticipated impact. It should be left to the reader of the analysis to decide whether the assumptions are valid or not.

Perspective on global energy use developments

A nation's energy security is undermined if the nation's main sources of energy are being depleted on a global scale or are in such high demand that the comparative cost of generating energy from these main sources is expected to change. Understandably, then, the manner in which energy security analysts interpret energy market trends can significantly alter comparative assessments of national energy security.

Estimations regarding existing reserves of fossil fuels and uranium, along with projections made regarding global demand for these resources over the next few decades, will influence the assessed potential for conventional fuel sources to continue to play a dominant role in global energy supply. For example, if an energy security analyst were to estimate that a global shift to natural gas would catalyze a tripling of demand for this dwindling resource over the next two decades, energy security in a country such as Singapore, which is largely dependent on natural gas for electricity generation,[85] would have to be assessed as being in a state of decline. However, if the energy security analyst were to assume that, over the same period, a global shift to nuclear power will eclipse a shift to natural gas, then the global supply of natural gas in the future would not be subject to the same intense demand pressures. Under such a scenario, energy security in Singapore would be considered to be more stable than in the previous scenario.

In a similar vein, assumptions made concerning the evolution of international alliances in regard to energy supply and demand can have significant consequences for national energy security assessment.[86] For example, assessing national energy security in nations such as China and Japan depends significantly on critical assumptions made regarding the development of supply alliances between these countries and conventional fuel supplier nations such as Russia and Kazakhstan. In this respect, projections that assume deeper alliances between China and these supplier nations would also have to devalue national energy security in Japan, and vice versa.[87]

Perspective regarding global economic growth prospects

Although a few nations (notably Japan) have managed to achieve a degree of decoupling between economic growth and energy utilization,[88] most nations exhibit a high correlation between these two variables.[89] Accordingly, assumptions made regarding global economic growth rates significantly influence assumptions made regarding rates of energy resource depletion and energy price trends. Therefore, global economic growth prospects have an influential role in national energy security assessment.

It is perhaps of interest to note, given the context of this section, that the nexus between global economic growth projections, conventional fuel prices, and energy mix transition represents perhaps the one area where assumptions are transparently recognized in global energy assessments. Annual global energy assessments from the International Energy Agency,[90] US Energy Information Administration,[91] and BP all detail the assumptions made in regard to economic growth in the prefaces, footnotes, or appendices to their global energy assessments. It begs the question, why aren't other critical assumptions treated with the same due diligence?

Perspectives regarding energy efficiency

Many energy experts view energy efficiency improvements as a pseudo form of energy reserve.[92] After all, a technology that reduces energy utilization and saves 10 billion barrels of oil per year can indeed be considered to be the equivalent of stumbling across a massive oilfield. Logically, then, if statistics on domestic energy reserves are essential for evaluating the national energy security of a given nation, the potential for that nation to foster enhanced levels of energy efficiency should also be included in national energy security assessment.[93]

The trouble with evaluating a nation's potential to foster enhanced levels of energy efficiency is that some critical assumptions need to be made regarding how to estimate "potential." An analyst can employ a benchmarking approach and use the most efficient nation's accomplishments to date (i.e. Japan) in order to estimate potential. However, such an approach ignores disparities in social structure (i.e. Japan is a densely populated nation that can exploit concentrated population clusters to enhance energy efficiency), climatic conditions (i.e. anyone who has lived in Singapore understands the indispensable nature of those energy-sucking air conditioners), geographic characteristics (i.e. visiting a neighbor in Tokyo can be done by popping one's head out of a window while visiting a neighbor in Manitoba; Canada may require a car with a full fuel tank), and political structure (i.e. Japanese industrial policy has been guided by the same government party for 53 of the past 55 years), to name but a few influences.

Benchmarking with the most efficient nations also ignores the capacity for improvement in these efficient nations. Energy efficiency in Japan, for example, improved by approximately 30 percent over the past 30 years and the government is aiming to further enhance energy efficiency by 30 percent by 2030.[94] In short, energy efficiency is a fluid measure and somehow methodologies have to be created to estimate the progress that will actually be made in a given country within the time frame covered by any energy security assessment. Unfortunately, methodologies for predicting events in the social sciences require the application of critical assumptions which are subject *inter alia* to ideological bias, human error, and predictive inaccuracy.[95] Nevertheless, regardless of the accuracy of the assumptions that have gone into predictions of national energy efficiency, explicating the nature of these assumptions gives the reader the chance to evaluate the credibility of the assessment. This is certainly a better standard of research to aspire to than simply leaving the assumptions unaddressed, which appears to be the modus operandi for most current energy security assessments.

Assumptions regarding CO_2 emission governance

The extent to which costs associated with CO_2 emissions are internalized by national energy regimes has enormous potential repercussions for energy security for at least two notable reasons. First, assumptions made regarding the extent to which conventional energy costs will increase due to carbon price internalization affecting the comparative economic well-being of any nation committed to such initiatives. In particular, CO_2 emission regulation can influence the comparative industrial competitiveness of a nation if other nations adopt less economically abrasive governance policies. Clearly, changes in a nation's comparative industrial cost structure of this sort represent a threat to national energy security because economic deterioration implies a reduced capacity to optimize energy systems and respond effectively to unforeseen developments in the energy market.

Second, assumptions made regarding CO_2 emission regulatory policies also influence global economic modeling of conventional fuel demand. A scenario wherein high taxes are applied globally to fossil fuel combustion implies that demand for fossil fuel energy will decrease, while demand for alternative fuel sources will increase. This has national energy security implications for all nations.

Conclusion

In Plato's Allegory of the Cave, Socrates introduces one further scenario to Glaucon for consideration. Socrates asks Glaucon to consider what would happen if one of the prisoners was forcefully dragged out of the cave into the light of day. Rhetorically, Socrates muses that it may be reasonable to assume that the prisoner would first be distressed and angered by the environmental changes enforced upon him. Yet, over time, the prisoner would acclimatize to the environment and begin to understand how narrow his initial perception of reality truly was.

This chapter has really been about the need (and indeed the responsibility) to drag the assumptions upon which energy security analysis is conducted out from the ontological caves inhabited by energy security analysts and into the light of day. As was pointed out in Plato's Allegory of the Cave, the admonition presented in this chapter is certain to cause a degree of distress and denial from some security analysts. However, the fact remains that most energy security assessments fail to meet acceptable standards of academic rigor because the studies fail to acknowledge critical assumptions that skew or bias the findings.

However, if those security analysts offended by this criticism took a moment to consider the implications associated with heightened due diligence in disclosing critical assumptions influencing energy security assessments, they may come to realize that practicing heightened due diligence would actually make them better analysts. The process of explicating critical assumptions undoubtedly improves the quality of the assessment because it forces analysts to formally dissect the logic upon which their analyses are based. So in addition to the benefit of alerting users of the analysis to the possibility that other interpretations may exist, heightened transparency actually provides real benefits to the security analysts themselves.

In considering what may become of the hapless victim of enlightenment in Plato's allegory, Socrates concludes with the following:

> Wouldn't he remember his first home, what passed for wisdom there, and his fellow prisoners, and consider himself happy and them pitiable? And wouldn't he disdain whatever honors, praises, and prizes were awarded there to the ones who guessed best which shadows followed which? Moreover, were he to return there, wouldn't he be rather bad at their game, no longer being accustomed to the darkness? Wouldn't it be said of him that he went up and came back with his eyes corrupted, and that it's not even worth trying to go up?[96]

One can only hope that in the social science of energy security analysis, at least a few analysts will be willing to break free from the intellectual fetters that bind analysts to the practice of presenting their assessments as if they reflect absolute objectivity. After all, why spend all of one's time in a cave when there is so much more of the world to experience and understand? Why sip from a tea cup when one can drink from the river?

Notes

1 Plato. 2007. *The Republic*, translated by Desmond Lee (New York: Penguin Books).
2 It is of passing interest that in an age where many of us spend our days with eyes transfixed to a computer, that this scenario has actually become far less surreal than when I first read Plato's *Republic*, 30 years ago.
3 Wildavsky, A. 1987. *Speaking Truth to Power: The Art and Craft of Policy Analysis* (New York: Transaction Publishers USA).
4 Chester, L. 2010. "Conceptualising Energy Security and Making Explicit its Polysemic Nature," *Energy Policy* 38(2): 887.
5 Ciuta, F. 2010. "Conceptual Notes on Energy Security: Total or Banal Security?" *Security Dialogue* 41(2): 123–144.
6 Ciuta, "Conceptual Notes on Energy Security", pp. 127.
7 Kruyt B., van Vuuren D. P., de Vries H. J. M., and Groenenberg H. 2009. "Indicators for Energy Security," *Energy Policy* 37(6): 2166–2181.
8 Jansen J. C., and Seebregts A. J. 2010. "Long-Term Energy Services Security: What is it and How Can it be Measured and Valued?" *Energy Policy* 38(4): 1654–1664.
9 Kruyt *et al.*, "Indicators for Energy Security," pp. 2166–2181.
10 Scheepers, M., Seebregts, A., deJong, J., and Maters, H. 1974. *EU Standards for Energy Security of Supply – Updates on the Crisis Capability Index and the Supply / Demand Index Quantification for EU*

(The Hague, the Netherlands: Energy Research Centre of the Netherlands (ERC), Report no. ECN-E-07-004-27).

11 Bollen, J. 1974. *Energy Security, Air Pollution, and Climate Change: An Integrated Cost-benefit Approach* (Bilthoven, the Netherlands: Milieu-en Natuurplanbureau (MNP)).

12 Gupta, E. 2008. "Oil Vulnerability Index of Oil-Importing Countries," *Energy Policy* 36(3): 1195–1211.

13 Emerson, Ralph Waldo. 2004. *The Ralph Waldo Emerson Reader* (New York: Freeman Press), p. ix.

14 Chester, "Conceptualising Energy Security," p. 887.

15 Ciuta, F. 2010. "Conceptual Notes on Energy Security: Total or Banal Security?" *Security Dialogue* 41(2): 123–144.

16 Kruyt *et al.*, "Indicators for Energy Security," pp. 2166–2181.

17 Blake, William. 1984. *The Philosophy and Poetry of William Blake* (New York: Penguin).

18 Roberts, P. 2004. *The End of Oil* (Boston, MA: Houghton Mifflin Company).

19 Sovacool, B. K. 2008. *The Dirty Energy Dilemma: What's Blocking Clean Power in the United States* (Santa Barbara, CA: Praeger Publishers).

20 Campbell, K. M. and J. Price. 2008. "The Global Politics of Energy: An Aspen Strategy Group Workshop." In K. M. Campbell and J. Price (eds.), *The Global Politics of Energy* (Aspen, CO: The Aspen Institute), pp. 11–23.

21 Valentine, S. V. [2010]. "Japanese Wind Energy Development Policy: Grand Plan or Group Think?" *Energy Policy* (in press).

22 Hughes, L. 2010. "Eastern Canadian Crude Oil Supply and its Implications for Regional Energy Security," *Energy Policy* 38(6): 2692–2699.

23 Deffeyes, K. S. 2005. *Beyond Oil: The View from Hubbert's Peak* (New York: Hill and Wang).

24 van Doren, P. 2006. "Book Reveiw of Jan H. Kalicki and David L. Goldwyn (eds.), *Energy & Security: Toward a New Foreign Policy Strategy*," *The Energy Journal* 27(2): 187.

25 Nuttall, W. J. and D. L. Manz. 2008. *A New Energy Security Paradigm for the Twenty-First Century* (Cambridge: Judge Business School, University of Cambridge), pp. 1–13.

26 Jansen and Seebregts, "Long-Term Energy Services Security," pp. 1654–1664.

27 Yergin, D. 2005. "Energy Security and Markets." In J. Kalicki and D. Goldwyn (eds.), *Energy and Security: Toward a New Foreign Policy Strategy* (Washington, DC: Woodrow Wilson Center Press).

28 Chester, "Conceptualising Energy Security," pp. 887–895.

29 Kruyt *et al.*, "Indicators for Energy Security," pp. 2166–2181.

30 Yergin, D. 2006. "Ensuring Energy Security," *Foreign Affairs* 85: 69–82.

31 Kruyt *et al.*, "Indicators for Energy Security," pp. 2166–2181.

32 Resch, G., A. Held, T. Faber, C. Panzer, F. Toro, and R. Haas. 2008. "Potentials and Prospects for Renewable Energies at the Global Scale," *Energy Policy* 36(11): 4048–4056.

33 Tonn, B., K. C. Healy, A. Gibson, A. Ashish, P. Cody, D. Beres, *et al.* 2009. "Power from Perspective: Potential Future United States Energy Portfolios," *Energy Policy* 37(4): 1432–1443.

34 Kruyt *et al.*, "Indicators for Energy Security," pp. 2166–2181.

35 Campbell, K. M. and J. Price J. (eds.). 2008. *The Global Politics of Energy* (Aspen, CO: The Aspen Institute).

36 Yergin, D. 2006. "Ensuring Energy Security," *Foreign Affairs* 85: 69–82.

37 Resch *et al.*, "Potentials and Prospects," pp. 4048–4056.

38 Stern, N. 2007. "The Global Climate Change Imperative," *Business Week*, April 16: 90.

39 Kruyt *et al.*, "Indicators for Energy Security," pp. 2166–2181.

40 Brennan, T. J. 1974. *Discussion Paper: Electricity Markets and Energy Security: Friends or Foes?* (Washington: Resources for the Future, Report no. RFFDP07).

41 Boyle, G., B. Everett, and J. Ramage (eds.). 2004. *Energy Systems and Sustainability: Power for a Sustainable Future* (Oxford: Oxford University Press).

42 Ackerman, T. 2005. *Wind Power in Power Systems* (Chichester: John Wiley and Sons).

43 Mele, A. R. and P. Rawling (eds.). 2004. *The Oxford Handbook of Rationality* (New York: Oxford University Press).

44 Yergin, D. 1993. *The Prize: The Epic Quest for Oil, Money & Power* (New York: The Free Press).

45 Bielecki, J. 2002. "Energy Security: Is the Wolf at the Door?" *The Quarterly Review of Economics and Finance* 42(2): 235–250.

46 Ciuta, "Conceptual Notes on Energy Security," pp. 123–144.

47 Yergin, "Ensuring Energy Security," pp. 69–82.

48 Valentine, S. V. 2010."Braking Wind in Australia: A Critical Evaluation of the National Renewable Energy Target," *Energy Policy* 38(7): 3668–3675.

49 Valentine, S. V. 2010. "Canada's Constitutional Separation of (Wind) Power," *Energy Policy* 38(4): 1918–1930.

50 Li, Z. 2010. "Quantitative Analysis of Sustainable Energy Strategies in China," *Energy Policy* 38(5): 2149–2160.

51 Jansen and Seebregts, "Long-Term Energy Services Security," pp. 1654–1664.

52 Shrestha, R. M. and S. Pradhan. 2010. "Co-benefits of CO_2 Emission Reduction in a Developing Country," *Energy Policy* 38(5): 2586–2597.

53 See the World Nuclear Association website for updates on the growth of nuclear power. Available at: http://www.world-nuclear.org

54 World Wind Energy Association (WWEA). 2009. *World Wind Energy Report 2008* (Bonn: WWEA).

55 Capoor, K. and P. Ambrosi. 2009. *State and Trends of the Carbon Market 2008* (Washington, DC: World Bank).

56 Fukuyama, F. 1999. "Social Capital and Civil Society," *Proceedings of the IMF Conference on Second Generation Reforms* (Washington: International Monetary Fund (IMF)).

57 Oh, T. H., S. Y. Pang, and S. C. Chua. 2010. "Energy Policy and Alternative Energy in Malaysia: Issues and Challenges for Sustainable Growth," *Renewable and Sustainable Energy Reviews* 14(4): 1241–1252.

58 For more on this refer to the Lighting a Billion Lives website at: http://labl.teriin.org/

59 Rutovitz, J. and A. Atherton. 2009. *Energy Sector Jobs to 2030: A Global Analysis* (Sydney: Institute for Sustainable Futures).

60 Fairley, P. 2007. "China's Coal Future," *Technology Review*, e-publication ahead of print, July 28.

61 Bader, J. A. 2008. "Rising China and Rising Oil Demand: Real and Imagined Problems for the International System." In K. M. Campbell and J. Price (eds.), *The Global Politics of Energy* (Aspen, CO: The Aspen Institute), pp. 97–111.

62 Dismukes, John P., Lawrence K. Miller, Andrew Solocha, Sandeep Jagani, and John A. Bers. 2007. "Wind Energy Electrical Power Generation: Industrial Life Cycle of a Radical Innovation." Paper presented at the PICMET 2007 Proceedings, Portland, Oregon, August 5–9.

63 Lipp, J. 2007. "Lessons for Effective Renewable Electricity Policy from Denmark, Germany and United Kingdom," *Energy Policy* 35(11): 5481–5495.

64 Nuttall, W. J. and D. L. Manz. 2008. *A New Energy Security Paradigm for the Twenty-First Century* (Cambridge: Judge Business School, University of Cambridge), pp. 1–13.

65 Farrell, D. and I. Bozon. 2008. "Demand-Side Economics: The Case for a New US Energy Policy Direction." In K. M. Campbell and J. Price (eds.), *The Global Politics of Energy* (The Aspen Institute), pp. 45–61.

66 Stent, A. 2008. "An Energy Superpower? Russia and Europe." In K. M. Campbell and J. Price (eds.), *The Global Politics of Energy* (The Aspen Institute), pp. 77–95.

67 Bader, "Rising China and Rising Oil Demand," pp. 97–111.

68 Campbell and Price, *The Global Politics of Energy.*

69 Vivoda, V. 2009. "Diversification of Oil Import Sources and Energy Security: A Key Strategy or an Elusive Objective?" *Energy Policy* 37(11): 4615–4623.

70 Bielecki, "Energy Security: Is the Wolf at the Door?" pp. 235–250.

71 Chester, "Conceptualising Energy Security," pp. 887–895.

72 Brennan, T. J. 1974. *Discussion Paper: Electricity Markets and Energy Security: Friends or Foes?* (Washington, DC: Resources for the Future, Report no. RFFDP07).

73 Oakley, A. 1999. "Paradigm Wars: Some Thoughts on a Personal and Public Trajectory," *International Journal of Social Research Methodology* 2(3): 247–254.

74 Hughes, L. 2010. "Eastern Canadian Crude Oil Supply and its Implications for Regional Energy Security," *Energy Policy* 38(6): 2692–2699.

75 Morthorst, P.-E. and S. Awerbuch. 2009. *The Economics of Wind Energy* (European Wind Energy Association, Belgium); Valentine, "Canada's Constitutional Separation of (Wind) Power," pp. 1918–1930.

76 Bader, "Rising China and Rising Oil Demand," pp. 97–111.

77 Li, "Quantitative Analysis," pp. 2149–2160.

78 World Wind Energy Association (WWEA). 2010. *World Wind Energy Report 2009* (WWEA, Germany).

79 Fairley, "China's Coal Future"; Bader, "Rising China and Rising Oil Demand," pp. 97–111.
80 Fairley, "China's Coal Future."; National Renewable Energy Laboratory (NREL). 2004. *Renewable Energy Policy in China: Overview* (US Department of Energy (NREL); Yang, J. 2006. "China Speeds Up Renewable Energy Development." Available at: http://www.worldwatch.org/node/4691 (accessed January 2, 2009).
81 Clemens, Samuel. 1954. *The Work of Mark Twain* (Chicago: Freeman Publishers), p. 4.
82 Boyle, G. 2004. *Renewable Energy: A Power for a Sustainable Future*, 2nd edn. (Oxford: Oxford University Press).
83 Intergovernmental Panel on Climate Change (IPCC). 2008. *Climate Change 2007: Synthesis Report.* (Geneva: IPCC).
84 See the India Water Portal for more on this story: http://www.indiawaterportal.org/node/6478 (accessed August 28, 2010).
85 Singapore Ministry of Environment and Water Resources. 2006. *Singapore's National Climate Change Strategy: Consultation Paper* (Government of Singapore).
86 Yergin, "Ensuring Energy Security," pp. 69–82.
87 Calder, K. E. 2006. "China and Japan's Simmering Rivalry," *Foreign Affairs* 85: 129–139.
88 International Energy Agency (IEA). 2004. *Energy Efficiency Updates* (Paris: IEA).
89 Shrestha, R. M. and Pradhan, S. 2010. "Co-benefits of CO2 Emission Reduction in a Developing Country," *Energy Policy* 38(5): 2586–2597.
90 For example see: IEA. 2008. *World Energy Outlook 2007*. Available at: http://www.iea.org/Textbase/nppdf/free/2007/WEO_2007.pdf (Accessed March 17, 2009).
91 For example see: Energy Information Administration (EIA). 2009. *International Energy Outlook 2008* (Washington, DC: US Department of Energy).
92 Boyle, G., B. Everett, and J. Ramage (eds.). 2004. *Energy Systems and Sustainability: Power for a Sustainable Future* (Oxford: Oxford University Press).
93 Yergin, "Ensuring Energy Security," pp. 69–82.
94 International Energy Agency (IEA). 2009. *Global Renewable Energy: Policies and Measures.* (Paris: IEA).
95 Oakley, A. 1999. "Paradigm Wars: Some Thoughts on a Personal and Public Trajectory," *International Journal of Social Research Methodology* 2(3): 247–254; Blaikie, N. 2000. Designing Social Research (Cambridge: Polity Press).
96 Plato. 1941. *The Republic*, ed. B. Jowett (New York: The Modern Library), p. 516. Quotation available at: http://en.wikipedia.org/wiki/Allegory_of_the_Cave (accessed May 1, 2010.)

3

EVALUATING THE ENERGY SECURITY IMPACTS OF ENERGY POLICIES

David F. von Hippel, Tatsujiro Suzuki, James H. Williams,
Timothy Savage, and Peter Hayes

Introduction

For policymakers, the term "energy security" refers mostly to assured access to oil, coal, and gas. This conventional energy security concept, however, has become less useful to policy formation due to increasingly global, diverse energy markets combined with emerging, energy-related transnational problems (such as acid rain). Moreover, a policy-oriented rationale for "energy security" must also encompass global issues such as climate change and many other economic, technological, and international security considerations. As a consequence, a more comprehensive operating definition of "energy security" is needed, along with a workable framework for analysis of which future energy paths or scenarios are likely to yield greater energy security in a broader, more comprehensive sense.[1]

Defining energy security

Many of the existing definitions of energy security begin, and usually end, with a focus on maintaining energy supplies—and particularly supplies of oil.[2] This supply-based focus has as its cornerstones reducing vulnerability to foreign threats or pressure, preventing a supply crisis (including either or both of restrictions in physical supply or an abrupt and significant increase in energy prices) from occurring, and minimizing the economic and military impact of a supply crisis once it has occurred. Current national and international energy policies, however, have been facing many new challenges, and as such need to have their effectiveness judged by additional criteria. This broader array of criteria needs to be considered as a key component of new energy security concepts.

Why has oil been the primary focus of energy security policy? There are good reasons behind this particular focus. First, oil is still the dominant fuel (~35 percent) in global primary energy supply (as of 2008[3]). Second, the Middle East, where the largest oil reserves exist, is still one of the most unstable areas in the world. Third, and related to the second reason, oil supply and prices are often influenced by political decisions of oil suppliers and buyers. Fourth, world economic conditions, as aptly demonstrated in the last several years, are still vulnerable to oil price volatility, since there are certain key sectors that are heavily dependent on oil (such as transportation,

74

petrochemicals, agriculture, and others), with limited short-term alternatives for substitution. Fifth, the key words here are "volatility" and "instability." Although globalization has improved the transparency of the oil market, oil prices remain to some extent at the mercy of speculators, as well as being affected by fluctuations in currency values, subject to manipulation by oil suppliers and, of course, sensitive to the forces of market supply and demand (for a discussion of the impact of speculation on the oil market, see Harris[4]). This has been dramatically shown recently, with oil prices roughly doubling between mid-2007 and mid-2008, followed by a 75 percent decline in price by early 2009, followed by a return to Fall 2007 price levels by early 2010.[5]

Few works have made a serious attempt to clarify the concept of energy security. One attempt at a clear definition of energy security was that by the Working Group on Asian Energy and Security at the Massachusetts Institute of Technology's (MIT) Center for International Studies. The MIT Working Group defined three distinct goals of energy security:[6]

1. reducing vulnerability to foreign threats or pressure;
2. preventing a supply crisis from occurring; and
3. minimizing the economic and military impact of a supply crisis once it has occurred.

These goals implicitly assume that an "oil supply crisis" is the central focus of energy security policy. In essence, the central tenets of conventional energy security policy are: (1) reduction of threats to oil supply, and (2) operating in a mode of crisis management. These tenets constitute a shared view among key energy policymakers in both the East and the West.

Differences in energy security policies

If the above characterization of conventional energy security thinking is shared by the major energy consuming/importing countries, does this mean that there are no critical differences in energy security policy among them? No. Although many countries share the above broad characteristics, it is also true that there are significant differences. What are the differences and why do they exist? One important factor is, of course, natural and geopolitical conditions. One country might have abundant natural resources and another might not. Some consumer countries are located close to energy-producing countries, while some are distant and thus need transportation of fuel over long distances. Those conditional differences can lead to basic differences in energy security perceptions.

In sum, there are three major attributes that define the differences in energy security thinking between countries: (1) the degree to which a country is energy resource-rich or energy resource-poor, (2) the degree to which market forces are allowed to operate as compared with the use of government intervention to set prices, and (3) the degree to which long-term versus short-term planning is employed.[7] Despite these differences in thinking, however, energy policies in both resource-poor countries and resource-rich countries are arguably converging, as both types of countries recognize the need to face a new paradigm in energy policy.

Emerging paradigm: toward comprehensive energy security

National energy policies in the new century are facing challenges on multiple fronts. The substance of these challenges needs to be incorporated into a new concept of energy security. It is important to note here that energy security policies in various countries are now showing trends of "convergence" rather than "divergence," despite the basic differences in concepts of energy security as discussed above. This convergence does not eliminate regional and national differences, of course, but it is an encouraging sign with regard to minimizing the potential conflict that may come from differences in energy security concepts, as reflected in the different energy security policies that countries adopt.

The following is a quick review of the major challenges that will help to bring about a new energy security concept.

Environment

Perhaps the most serious challenge to traditional (supply-security-oriented) energy policy thinking is the need to protect the environment. If environmental problems are to be solved, energy policies will have to be reformulated. International environmental problems present the greatest impetus for change. Two international environmental problems inherently linked with energy consumption, in particular fossil fuel consumption, are acid rain and global climate change.[8] Transboundary air pollution (acid rain) has been an international issue in Europe and North America, is a developing issue in East Asia, and even has trans-Pacific elements.[9]

Global climate change poses an even broader and more complex challenge to energy policy than transboundary air pollution. Although there are relatively straightforward (though often not cheap) technical solutions—including flue gas desulfurization devices—to reduce the emissions of acid rain precursors, greenhouse gas emissions cannot so easily be abated by "end-of-pipe" methods. A comprehensive approach toward greenhouse gas emissions is necessary. The climate change issue also brings in a much longer time perspective than business and governments are used to dealing with. Other environmental issues, such as radioactive waste management, also require long-term perspectives. In sum, environmental issues must be incorporated into the energy security concept.[10]

Technology

Risks associated with development and deployment of advanced technologies challenge current energy policy thinking. Conventional thinking understates such risks and tends to see them as short term, not long term. Risks include nuclear accidents such as those at Three Mile Island in the United States (1979) and Chernobyl in the former Soviet Union (1986), natural disasters with impacts on energy infrastructure (such as Hurricane Katrina's impacts on oil and gas production in the Gulf of Mexico, and the impact of the July 2007 earthquake near Niigata, Japan on the seven-unit Kashiwazaki-Kariwa nuclear plant), and the failure of R&D efforts (such as the synthetic fuel, fast breeder reactor, and solar thermal programs in the US during the 1970s and 1980s) to perform as expected. Technological risks can be transnational; the accident at Chernobyl is a good example of an incident with decidedly cross-boundary implications. Also, markets for advanced technologies are becoming global and, as a result, technological risks can be exported. Nuclear technology, for example, is being exported to a number of developing countries, most notably China and India, but also potentially including Vietnam, Indonesia, Thailand, Pakistan, and Malaysia,[11] as well as Middle Eastern nations including the United Arab Emirates.[12] As the world moves rapidly toward a "technology intensive" energy society, a new energy security concept must address the various domestic and international risks associated with advanced technologies.

Demand-side management

Another challenge to energy policy thinking is the need to address energy demand itself. Conventional energy policy seeks to assure supply while assuming that demand is a given. This notion has been changing since the mid-1980s, when the concept of demand-side management

(DSM) was first incorporated into energy planning. Now, management of energy demand is almost on an equal footing with management of supply—new technologies such as distributed generation and "smart grids," in fact, blur the distinction between demand and supply—and is recognized as a key tool in the achievement of climate change mitigation and other environmental goals. DSM does not, however, eliminate uncertainties that are inherent in energy policy planning. Unexpected demand surges and drops occur depending on, for instance, changes in weather patterns and economic conditions.

There are risks associated with energy demand just as with supply. Conventional energy policy thinking has tended to underestimate demand-side risks. Risks stem from, for example, demand surges (periods of peak demand in response to extreme conditions). These are a serious concern for utility management, but managing peak demand is not easy, particularly given uncertainties in consumer behavior. Long recessions are another major concern for energy industry managers, since recession means large supply capacity surpluses. Uncertainty (risk) in the demand-side of the total energy picture is therefore a key component of a new concept of energy security.

Social–cultural factors

"Not in my backyard" (NIMBY) and environmental justice concerns are becoming global phenomena, making it increasingly difficult, time-consuming, and costly to site "nuisance facilities" such as large power plants, waste treatment and disposal facilities, oil refineries, or liquefied natural gas terminals (for example). Although people may recognize the need for such facilities, many communities prefer not to have the actual plants in their neighborhood. Opposition to plant siting has elevated the importance of local politics in energy policy planning. Who has the right to decide where to locate such facilities? Who has the right to refuse? Can any rational policymaking process satisfy all stakeholders? These questions pose not only a challenge to energy security policy, but also to democratic institutions themselves. NIMBY epitomizes the "social and cultural" risks that need to be recognized in policymaking agendas. Various social–cultural factors present a challenge to current energy policy thinking.

There are "enviro-economic" concerns as well. It is often the case that the party who bears the risk should get economic compensation. But how much compensation is reasonable, and who should be qualified to receive such compensation? These issues are often difficult to decide.

Public confidence is also a social factor influencing energy policy; once lost, it is hard to recover. "Public confidence" should be distinguished from "public acceptance," which is commonly used in traditional energy policy thinking. Promoting public acceptance is often the object of public relations campaigns. Promoting public confidence involves more than public relations. Examples of efforts to increase public confidence in energy decisions include, for example, efforts by the US Department of Energy (DOE) to increase information disclosure, as well as the effort by the Japanese government to make the nuclear policymaking process more transparent (for instance, by holding roundtable discussions). Accounting for social–cultural factors and increasing public confidence in energy choices are therefore central components of a new concept of energy security.

International relations—military

New dimensions in international relations and new military risks are challenging traditional energy policymaking. The end of the Cold War has brought in its wake a new level of uncertainty in international politics. Although the risk of a world war has been drastically reduced, the threat of regional clashes has increased, as demonstrated by ongoing conflicts in the Middle East, the Balkans, and the former Soviet states of the Caucasus, to name just a few. The international politics of plutonium fuel-cycle development, with its associated risks of nuclear terrorism and proliferation, remains an area where energy security and military security issues meet. The brave new world of post-Cold War international relations must be accounted for in a new concept of energy security.

Comprehensive concept of energy security

The above five key components—environment, technology, demand-side management, social and cultural factors, and post-Cold War international relations—are central additions to the traditional supply-side point of view in a new comprehensive energy security concept.

A nation state is energy secure to the degree that fuel and energy services are available to ensure: (a) survival of the nation, (b) protection of national welfare, and (c) minimization of risks associated with supply and use of fuel and energy services. The six dimensions of energy security include energy supply, economic, technological, environmental, social and cultural, and military/security dimensions. Energy policies must address the domestic and international (regional and global) implications of each of these dimensions.

What distinguishes this energy security definition is its emphasis on the imperative to consider extra-territorial implications of the provision of energy and energy services, while recognizing the complexity of implementing national energy security policies and measuring national energy security. The definition is also designed to include emerging concepts of environmental security, which include the effects of the state of the environment on human security and military security, and the effects of security institutions on the environment and on prospects for international environmental cooperation.[13]

Sustainability and sustainable development

As environmental and other considerations, apart from energy supply, play increasing roles in the development of energy policies in both industrialized and developing nations, the concepts of sustainability and sustainable development are becoming intimately entwined with the goals of energy policy. An understanding of what these concepts mean, and what they may mean for energy security, is therefore helpful.

Sustainability

A strict definition of sustainability is as follows:[14] "A sustainable process or condition is one that can be maintained indefinitely without progressive diminution of valued qualities inside or outside the system in which the process operates or the condition prevails." Further, from a biophysical perspective, sustainability means "maintaining or improving the life support systems of earth." Due to recent "intense and pervasive" human activity, "biophysical sustainability must, therefore, mean the sustainability of the biosphere minus humanity. Humanity's role has to be considered separately as economic or social sustainability. Likewise, sustainable development should mean both sustainability of the biophysical medium or environment and sustainability of human development, with the latter sustaining the former."

Sustainable development

As defined in the report of the 1987 World Commission on Environment and Development, sustainable development is "development that meets the needs of the present without compromising the ability of future generations to meet their own needs."[15] Other recent definitions of this concept have spanned the range from "corporate sustainability," meaning "responsible environmental and labor management practices" in business, to a definition of sustainable development that includes "a vast, diverse set of goals, such as poverty elimination and fair and transparent governance."[16]

Like ensuring energy security, pursuing sustainable development includes addressing numerous, often conflicting issues, including[17] human poverty, impoverishment of the environment, the possibility of wars on all different spatial scales, oppression of human rights, and wastage of human potential. The forces driving these issues—which are also forces affecting energy security—include excessive population growth, poor distribution of consumption and investment, misuse of technology, corruption and mismanagement, and lack of knowledge/power on the part of victims.

Though sustainable development, arguably, will never have a single, clear definition, as "sustainability" depends on what is being sustained and "development" depends on the desired outcomes, it is clear that achieving sustainable development, like enhancing energy security, depends on addressing a variety of economic, social, and environmental goals—and these goals are often in conflict.

There are sustainable development/energy security challenges related to actually accomplishing the goals of sustainable development policies. For example, Smil[18] underlines some of the formidable challenges involved in replacing fossil fuels with renewable fuels to move toward sustainable development, including the scale of the shift in fuel use required, the relative energy and power densities of fossil versus renewable fuels and power systems, the intermittency of many renewable fuels, and the geographical distribution of renewable resources relative to where fossil fuels are currently used. These challenges may ultimately mean that a truly sustainable economy must actually produce less in the way of goods and services than our global economy does today, rather than using alternative resources to sustain or expand the existing level of output.

The International Atomic Energy Agency (IAEA), in cooperation with other agencies, has assembled a list of indicators for sustainable energy development.[19] The IAEA list starts with a consideration of the economic, environmental, social, and institutional dimensions of sustainable development, and develops 30 different indicators, most with several subcomponents. Many of these indicators touch upon the issues and perspectives noted above, and many are reflected in the discussion of methods and parameters for evaluating energy security that are presented in the next section of this chapter.

No matter how it is defined and measured, sustainable development will require increasing understanding of the interlinked nature of environmental, social, and economic problems—as addressing single problems without consideration of linkages to other problems may be risky. Sustainable development—and addressing energy security—will also require increasing transparency in planning and decision-making of all types, particularly for large projects, and building human capacity (and societal support for such education) to ensure that the capabilities exist in all "stakeholder" groups (those affected by decisions) in order to address multifaceted problems and participate in planning processes.

Evaluating and measuring energy security

Given the multiple dimensions of energy security identified above, and the linkages/overlaps between energy security dimensions and the dimensions of sustainability and sustainable development, a framework for evaluating and measuring—or at least comparing—the relative attributes of different approaches to energy sector development is needed. Such a framework should be designed to help to identify the relative costs and benefits of different "energy futures" – essentially, future scenarios driven by suites of energy (and other social) policies. Below we identify some of the policy issues associated with the dimensions of energy policy presented earlier, and present a framework for evaluating energy security, as broadly defined.

An energy policy conceptual framework

A listing of each dimension of energy security—broadly defined as above—is provided in Table 3.1, which also offers a sampling of the policy issues with which each dimension of energy security is associated. The two right-hand columns of Table 3.1 provide examples, many drawn from the energy security approaches described above, that might be used to address the types of "routine" and "radical" risk and uncertainty that are faced in the planning, construction, and operation of energy systems. It should be noted that while Table 3.1 provides what is intended to be a broad, but by no means complete, list of policy issues, even the categories shown are often not necessarily independent. Certain energy technologies will be affected by climate change (hydroelectric power and inland nuclear power plants, for example, may be affected by changes in water availability), and there are many other examples of interdependence that need to be carefully thought through in a full consideration of the energy security impacts of candidate energy policies.

Testing the energy security impacts of different energy scenarios

Given the broad definition of energy security provided above, how should a framework for evaluation of energy security impacts of different policy approaches be organized? Some of the challenges in setting up such a framework include deciding on manageable but useful level of detail, incorporation of uncertainty, risk considerations, comparison of tangible and intangible costs/benefits, comparing impacts across different spatial levels and timescales, and balancing analytical comprehensiveness and transparency. To meet these challenges, a framework was devised based on a variety of tools, including the elaboration and evaluation of alternative energy/environmental "paths" or "scenarios" for a nation and/or region (for example, with the LEAP[20] software tool used in the Asian Energy Security project), diversity indices, and multiple-attribute (tradeoff) analyses, as described below. Central to the application of the framework is its application to search for "robust" solutions—a set of policies that meet multiple energy security and other objectives at the same time.

The framework for the analysis of energy security (broadly defined) includes the following steps:

1. Define objective and subjective measures of energy (and environmental) security to be evaluated. Within the overall categories presented in Table 3.1, these measures could vary significantly between different analyses.
2. Collect data, and develop candidate energy paths/scenarios that yield roughly consistent energy services, but use assumptions different enough to illuminate the policy approaches being explored.
3. Test the relative performance of paths/scenarios for each energy security measure included in the analysis.
4. Incorporate elements of risk.
5. Compare path and scenario results.
6. Eliminate paths that lead to clearly suboptimal or unacceptable results, and iterate the analysis as necessary to reach clear conclusions.

Table 3.1 Energy security conceptual framework

Dimension/Criterion of Risk and Uncertainty Associated with Energy Security	Energy Security Policy Issues	Energy Security Strategies/Measures	
		Reduction and Management of Routine Risk	Identification and Management of Radical Uncertainty
1. Energy Supply	• Domestic/imported • Absolute scarcity • Technology/fuel intensive? • Incremental, market-friendly, fast, cheap, sustainable?	• Substitute technology for energy • Efficiency first	• Technological breakthroughs • Exploration and new reserves
2. Economic	• Cost-benefit analysis • Risk-benefit analysis • Social opportunity cost of supply disruption • Local manufacturing of equipment • Labor • Financing aspects • No regrets	• Compare costs/benefits of insurance strategies to reduce loss-of-supply disruption • Investment to create supplier–consumer inter-dependence • Insurance by fuel (U, oil, gas, coal) stockpiling, global (IEA) or regional quotas (energy charters)	• Export energy-intensive industries • Focus on information-intensive industries • Export energy or energy technology

(Continued on next page)

Table 3.1 (continued)

Dimension/Criterion of Risk and Uncertainty Associated with Energy Security	Energy Security Policy Issues	Energy Security Strategies/Measures	
		Reduction and Management of Routine Risk	Identification and Management of Radical Uncertainty
3. Technological	• R&D failure • Technological monoculture vs. diversification • New materials dependency in technological substitution strategies • Catastrophic failure • Adoption/diffusion or commercialization failure	• Invest in renewables • Mixed oxide fuels recycling • Plutonium /fast breeder reactors • Uranium from seawater • Spent fuel management issues	• Ultimate nuclear waste storage
4. Environmental	• Local externalities • Regional externalities, both atmospheric and maritime • Global externalities • Precautionary principle	• Risk-benefit analysis and local pollution control • Treaties • Mitigation • Technology transfer	• Thresholds and radical shifts of state such as sea level rise and polar ice melt rate

(Continued on next page)

Table 3.1 (continued)

Dimension/Criterion of Risk and Uncertainty Associated with Energy Security	Energy Security Policy Issues	Energy Security Strategies/Measures	
		Reduction and Management of Routine Risk	Identification and Management of Radical Uncertainty

5. Social–Cultural	• Consensus/conflict in domestic or foreign policymaking coalitions
	• Institutional capacities
	• Siting and downwind distributional impacts
	• Populist revulsion or rejection of technocratic strategies
	  ○ Perceptions and historical lessons
		• Transparency
		• Participation
		• Accountability
		• Side payments and compensation
		• Education
		  ○ Training	

6. Military–Security	• International management of plutonium • Proliferation potential • Sea lanes and energy shipping • Geopolitics of oil/gas supplies	• Non-Proliferation Treaty regime • Terrorism and energy facilities • Status • Security alliances • Naval power projection • Transparency and confidence building • Terrorism	• Disposition and disposal of excess nuclear warhead fissile materials • Military options for resolving energy-related conflicts, securing infrastructure

Some of the possible dimensions of energy security, and potential measures and attributes of those dimensions, are summarized in Table 3.2. The table also includes, in its right-hand column, a listing of possible "interpretations"—that is, a listing of what direction in a given measure would typically indicate greater energy security. It should be noted that many of these dimensions and measures can and do interact—and a solution to one problem may exacerbate another. Formal or informal application of analytical methods such as "systems thinking" can be used

Table 3.2 Dimensions and measures/attributes of energy security

Dimension of Energy Security	Measures/Attributes	Interpretation
Energy Supply	Total primary energy	Higher = indicator of other impacts
	Fraction of primary energy as imports	Lower = preferred
	Diversification index (by fuel type, primary energy)	Lower index value (indicating greater diversity)
	Diversification index (by supplier, key fuel types)	Lower index value preferred (see above)
	Stocks as a fraction of imports (key fuels)	Higher = greater resilience to supply interruption
Economic	Total energy system internal costs	Lower = preferred
	Total fuel costs	Lower = preferred
	Import fuel costs	Lower = preferred
	Economic impact of fuel price increase (as fraction of GNP)	Lower = preferred
Technological	Diversification indices for key industries (such as power generation) by technology type	Lower = preferred
	Diversity of R&D spending	Qualitative–Higher preferred
	Reliance on proven technologies	Qualitative–Higher preferred
	Technological adaptability	Qualitative–Higher preferred
Environmental	GHG emissions (tonnes CO_2, CH_4)	Lower = preferred
	Acid gas emissions (tonnes SOx, NOx)	Lower = preferred
	Local air pollutants (tonnes particulates, hydrocarbons, others)	Lower = preferred
	Other air and water pollutants (including marine oil pollution)	Lower = preferred
	Solid wastes (tonnes bottom ash, fly ash, scrubber sludge)	Lower = preferred (or at worst neutral, with safe re-use)
	Nuclear waste (tonnes or Curies, by type)	Lower = preferred, but qualitative component for waste isolation scheme
	Ecosystem and aesthetic impacts	Largely Qualitative–Lower preferred
	Exposure to environmental risk	Qualitative–Lower preferred
Social and Cultural	Exposure to risk of social or cultural conflict over energy systems	Qualitative–Lower preferred
Military/Security	Exposure to military/security risks	Qualitative–Lower preferred
	Relative level of spending on energy-related security arrangements	Lower = preferred

to assist in carrying out steps 4 and 5, above. These methods allow the interaction of the different elements of complex processes, and the way that those elements affect and feed back on each other, to be seen more clearly than if a pair of systems interactions are viewed independently.[21]

There is often a temptation, in step 5, to attempt to put the attributes of energy security into a common metric, for example an index of relative energy security calculated through a ranking and weighting system. We would recommend avoiding this temptation, as such systems almost invariably involve procedures that amplify small differences between paths/scenarios, play down large differences, and give an illusion of objectivity to weighting choices that are by their nature quite subjective. Instead, as described below, we recommend laying out the energy security attributes of each path/scenario side by side, which allows reviewers, stakeholders, and decision-makers to see the differences and similarities between different energy futures for themselves, and to apply their own perspectives and knowledge, in consultation with each other, to determine what is most important in making energy policy choices. Also not explicitly included in steps 5 or 6 are mathematical tools for optimizing energy security results over a set of paths or scenarios. Optimization can be attractive, as it appears to identify one "best" path for moving forward. Optimization models can in some cases offer useful insights, provided that the underlying assumptions and algorithms in the analysis are well understood by the users of the results. Optimization, however, like weighting and ranking, involves subjective choices made to appear objective, especially when applied across a range of different energy security attributes, and as such should be employed only with caution and with a thorough understanding of its limitations in a given application.

Development of paths/scenarios to test and evaluate future energy security impacts

An energy path or scenario describes the evolution—or potential evolution—of a country's energy sector assuming that a specific set of energy policies are (or are not) put in place. The level of detail with which an energy path/scenario is described will be a function of the degree of realism required to make the path analysis plausible to an audience of policymakers, as well as the analytical resources (person-time) and data available to do the analysis. "Bottom-up" quantitative descriptions of energy paths offer the possibility to specify fuels and technologies used, as well as energy system costs and key environmental emissions, in some detail, but can require a considerable amount of work. Simpler econometric models (or models that combine econometric and end-use elements) can also be used, providing that model outputs can include measures of energy security like those presented above. A major criterion to keep in mind, when developing energy paths/scenarios, is that the paths chosen should be both reasonably plausible, yet different enough from each other to yield, when their attributes are compared, significant insight into the ramifications of the energy policy choices that the paths describe.

Some of the data requirements in defining an energy path/scenario can include:

- data on *current demand for and supply of fuels*, by sector, in the area (state, country, or region, for example) under study;
- existing *projections and scenarios* for the evolution of the *energy system* (over the next 15 to 30 years, for example) in the area;
- costs, applicability, availability, inputs, and efficiencies of the *technologies*, energy-efficiency measures, and fuels to be used in scenarios;
- information on *environmental impacts* expected (or derivation of impact estimates) from discrete levels of pollutant emissions (local, regional, and global);

- estimates of the *environmental costs of major accidents*, such as nuclear reactor meltdowns or major oil tanker accidents;
- existing methods for *ascribing costs to environmental impacts*;
- existing estimates of *climate change impacts* and their ramifications;
- existing scenarios and analysis of the likely *security impacts of proliferation* of nuclear power in the region;
- costs of *security arrangements*, including military hardware, armed forces readiness.

Of course, not all of the above information may be applicable to (or available for) a particular energy security analysis. Once the energy paths are specified, the next step is to evaluate the objective and subjective measures listed in Table 3.2 (or a similar set as defined by the researcher), or as large a subset of those measures as is practicable and desirable. In many cases, the use of economic models (or adaptation of existing results of such models) or other computational tools will be in order to perform measures evaluations.

Energy policy goals and problems to address in preparation of energy paths/scenarios

A key goal of energy policy is to improve energy security—whether broadly or narrowly defined—and thus to reduce existing (or looming) "energy insecurity." Development (and modeling) of energy policies that accomplish this goal, at the global, national, or sub-national scales, begins with a review of the problems to be addressed, the attributes and inertias in the current energy system, and the likely determinants of the energy future that policies will hope to address. For example, problems to be addressed range from global climate change to local/regional/global air pollution, land and water resource stresses, war and other conflicts, nuclear weapons proliferation, and stresses on national and international financial systems, along with a daunting host of other issues. Inertias that must be reflected in energy paths include consideration of population growth, existing stocks of energy-using equipment and energy supply infrastructure, current patterns of energy consumption, and other existing trends among a host of factors contributing to the "momentum" of future energy supply and demand. Determinants of future energy use include those that are more predictable (but still, often, potentially addressed by policies), such as changes in demographics, changes in the need for energy goods and services, and changes in the intensity with which energy is used to produce goods and services. Less predictable determinants are those influences on energy supply and demand that are hard to predict with any degree of confidence at present, or that come as complete surprises, such as changes in resource scarcity, dramatic evidence of climate change (and/or abrupt changes in responses to climate change), conflict flare-ups in key energy supplier nations, acts of terrorism against energy systems, and major technological breakthroughs. These considerations shape future paths/scenarios for analysis.[22]

Tools and methods

As noted above, Nautilus Institute's ongoing Asian Energy Security and East Asia Science and Security projects continue to use the LEAP energy/environment planning software system as an organizing/calculation tool for the elaboration of future energy paths ("scenarios" in LEAP) and for the evaluation of some (but by no means all) of the energy security attributes of different paths. The energy security analysis approach above, however, can accommodate a range of tools or approaches for developing and evaluating energy paths, from simple spreadsheet tools to more complex models. Whatever tool is used, the key is to develop energy paths so as to provide comprehensive accounting of how energy is consumed, converted, and produced in a given region or economy under a range of alternative assumptions with regard to population, economic development, technology, fuel prices, costs of energy-consuming and energy conversion equipment, and other factors. Energy paths/scenarios should be self-consistent storylines of how an energy system might evolve over time in a particular socio-economic setting and under a particular set of policy conditions. Paths/scenarios can be built and then compared, using the energy security analysis framework above, to assess parameters such as energy requirements, social costs and benefits, and environmental impacts.

Application of paths outputs for energy security analysis

The outputs of energy paths analysis prepared using LEAP and/or other tools can be used directly for some of the measures of energy security described above. Typically, results from two or more different energy paths within a country or region are compared to indicate which path is preferable with regard to different direct measures of energy security, such as cost, physical energy output, fuels imports and exports, or environmental emissions. Depending on the energy security measure, a combination of direct use of model outputs, "off-line" quantitative analysis based on model output and other parameters, and the use of qualitative techniques based on the consideration of energy paths, together provide a powerful suite of tools for the evaluation of the impacts of different policies on energy security.

Other tools and methods for energy security analysis

One set of analyses critical to the comprehensive evaluation of energy security, but not directly performed by LEAP or similar tools, is the evaluation of the energy security impacts of risk for different energy paths. The incorporation of the elements of risk in energy security analysis can involve more qualitative but systematic **consideration of different potential futures** to "arrive at policy decisions that remain valid under a large set of plausible scenarios"; **sensitivity analysis** —where variations in one or more plans (or paths) are studied when key uncertain parameters are varied; **probabilistic analysis**—in which "probabilities are assigned to different values of uncertain variables, and outcomes are obtained through probabilistic simulations"; "**stochastic optimization**"—in which a probability distribution for each uncertain variable is assigned during an optimization exercise, **incorporating uncertainty** in the discount rate used in an economic analysis; and **search for a robust solution**—which Hossein Razavi describes as using "the technique of trade-off analysis to eliminate uncertainties that do not matter and to concentrate on the ranges of uncertainty which are most relevant to corresponding objective attributes."[23]

Although any or all of these six techniques could be applied within the energy security analysis framework that we suggest, probably the most broadly applicable and transparent of the techniques above are scenario analysis, sensitivity analysis, and "search for a robust solution". In the PARES analysis of the energy security implications of two different medium-term energy paths for Japan for example, a combination of paths analyses and sensitivity analyses was used to test the response of the different energy paths to extreme changes in key variables.

Diversification indices

In a paper prepared for the PARES project, Thomas Neff borrows from the economics and financial analysis communities and other disciplines to create a set of tools, based on diversity indices,[24] that can help to provide a metric for the energy security implications of different energy supply strategies.

Neff starts with a simple diversification index, the Herfindahl index, written in mathematical terms as:

$$H = \sum_i x_i^2$$

where x_i is the fraction of total supply from source "i." This index can measure the diversity of, for example, the types of fuels used in an economy (where x_i would then be the fraction of primary energy or final demand by fuel type). Alternatively, within a single type of fuel (such as oil), the index can be applied to the pattern of imports of a particular country by supplier nation. The index has a maximum value of 1 (when there is only one supplier or fuel type), and goes down with increasing diversity of number of suppliers or fuel types, so that a lower value of the index indicates more diverse, and (perhaps) more robust, supply conditions.

Consideration of risk in specific fuel import patterns can be worked into the above index, Neff argues, through consideration of the variance in the behavior of each supplier, and by application of correlation coefficients that describe how variance in the behavior of pairs of suppliers (for example, oil exporters Saudi Arabia and Indonesia) are or might be related. The correlation might be positive, for countries that tend to raise and lower their exports together, or negative, as when supplier "A" would tend to increase production to compensate for decreased production by supplier "B."

Neff also addresses the topic of market, or systematic risk, that is, the risk associated with the whole market—be it a market for stocks, oil, or uranium—changing at once. Applying parameters that describe the degree to which individual suppliers are likely to change their output when the market as a whole shifts (the contribution of the variance of an individual supplier to overall market variance), allows the calculation of the variance of a given energy supply pattern. Hence, calculation of "portfolio variance," for example, provides a measure of the relative risk inherent in any given fuel supplier pattern versus any other.

Multiple-attribute analysis and matrices

Deciding upon a single set of energy policies (or a few top options) from a wide range of choices is a complex process, necessarily with both qualitative and quantitative aspects, and should be approached systematically if the result of the choice is to be credible. There are many different methods, with many gradations, for deciding which set of policies or which energy path is the most desirable. These range from simply listing each attribute of each policy set or path in a large matrix (for example, on a chalkboard in a conference room) and methodically eliminating candidate paths (noting why each is eliminated), to more quantitative approaches involving "multiple-attribute analysis."

In one type of application of multiple-attribute analysis, each criterion (attribute) used to evaluate energy policies or paths is assigned a numerical value. For objective criteria, the values of the attributes are used directly (present value costs are an example), while subjective criteria can be assigned a value based (for example) on a scale of 1 to 10. Once each attribute has a value, a weight is assigned to each attribute. These weights should reflect a consensus as to which attributes are the most important in planning. Multiplying the values of the attribute by the weights assigned, then summing over the attributes, yields "scores" for each individual policy set or path that can be compared. Although this process may seem like an attractive way to organize and make more objective a complicated decision/evaluation process, great care must be taken to apply the analysis so that (1) all subjective decisions—for example, the decisions that go into defining the system of weights used—are carefully and fully documented, and (2) the system used avoids magnifying small differences (or minimizing large differences) between policy or path alternatives.

Whatever tool or technique is used to decide between policy sets or paths, it is ultimately the policymakers and their constituencies who will decide which policies are to be implemented, or which energy path is worth pursuing. As a consequence, one of the most important rules of the application of multiple-attribute analysis to an evaluation of policies is to present the analytical process in an open, clear, and complete manner, so that others who wish to review the decisions and assumptions made along the way can do so.

The most straightforward approach to comparing paths is to simply line up the attributes values for each path side by side, and review the differences between paths, focusing on differences that are truly significant. For example, if the difference in net present value (NPV) cost of plan "A" is one billion dollars greater than that of plan "B," it may seem, at first glance, like a lot of money, but the difference must be examined relative to the overall cost of the energy system, or to the cost of the economy as a whole. To an energy system that has, say, one trillion (10^{12}) dollars in capital, operating and maintenance, and fuel costs over 20 years, a difference between plans of one billion (10^9) dollars is not only trivial, it is dwarfed by the uncertainties in even the most certain elements of the analysis. The key, then, is to search for differences between the attributes of the plans—taking care to include both qualitative and quantitative attributes—that are truly meaningful.

One straightforward way to visualize the similarities and differences between paths, both quantitative and qualitative, is the use of a comparison matrix (or a set of matrices). These tables show, for example, the different attributes and measures of each path (cost, environmental emissions, military security, and others) as rows, while the results for each scenario/path form a column in the table. Table 3.3 shows an example of a comparison of two energy paths for Japan (done for the

Table 3.3 Energy security comparison for Japan: BAU versus alternative path

Dimension of Energy Security	Attributes	BAU Path Result	Alternative Path Result
Energy Supply	Total primary energy	2010: 26.2 EJ; 2020: 28.7 EJ	2010: 22.0 EJ; 2020: 28.7 PJ
	Fraction primary energy as imports	2020: 96% of fuel use	2020: 85% of fuel use
	Diversification index (by fuel type, primary energy)	2010: 0.254 2020: 0.240	2010: 0.262; 2020: 0.230, 0.213 and 0.175 (separate accounting for pipeline gas, energy efficiency)
	Diversification index (by supplier, key fuel types)		Not quantified, but probably lower
	Stocks as a fraction of imports (key fuels)	Oil: 150 days' stocks in 1995 lasts for 110 days in 2020	Oil: 150 days' stocks in 1995 lasts for 187 days in 2020
Economic	Total energy system internal costs		27 trillion Yen (net present value) *less* than BAU path over 1990 to 2020
	Total fuel costs		32 trillion Yen (net present value) *less* than BAU path over 1990 to 2020
	Import fuel costs		About the same as total fuel costs
	Economic impact of fuel price increase (as fraction of GNP)	In 2015, energy resource costs about 1% of GDP *more* than in alternative path	Impact of 2010 oil price rise to 4,725 Yen per bbl about 27 trillion Yen NPV *less* than BAU path, 1990 to 2020.

Table 3.3 (continued)

Dimension of Energy Security	Attributes	BAU Path Result	Alternative Path Result
Technological	Diversification indices for key industries by technology type	For electricity generation: 2010: 0.166 2020: 0.138	For electricity generation: 2010: 0.153 2020: 0.105
	Diversity of R&D spending		Probably higher
	Reliance on proven technologies	Higher	
	Technological adaptability		Probably higher
Environmental	GHG emissions	In 2020: 1,600 Mte CO_2, 300 kte CH_4, 120 kte N_2O	In 2020: 1,000 Mte CO_2, 310 kte CH_4, 82 kte N_2O
	Acid gas emissions	In 2020: 2.0 Mte SO_x, 5.2 Mte NO_x	In 2020: 1.1 Mte SO_x, 3.2 Mte NO_x
	Local air pollutants	In 2020: 3.8 Mte CO, 1.1 Mte hydrocarbons, 0.94 Mte particulates	In 2020: 2.8 Mte CO, 0.55 Mte hydrocarbons, 0.54 Mte particulates
	Other air and water pollutants (including marine oil pollution)		Somewhat lower to substantially lower, depending on pollutant and pollutant source
	Solid wastes (tonnes bottom ash, fly ash, scrubber sludge)		Likely somewhat lower (depends on fuel sulfur, ash contents, degree of scrubbing)
	Nuclear waste (tonnes or curies, by type)		Somewhat (~5–10 percent over 1990 to 2020) lower; on-site spent fuel isolation means less waste transport
	Ecosystem and esthetic impacts	More large-infrastructure-related impacts	More indigenous energy-related esthetic impacts; less ecosystem impacts due to pollutants
	Exposure to environmental risk		Lower
Social and Cultural	Exposure to risk of social or cultural conflict over energy systems		Likely lower overall, but may require more social and cultural adjustment
Military/ Security	Exposure to Military/ Security risks		Likely somewhat lower
	Relative level of spending on energy-related security arrangements		Likely somewhat lower

Notes:
One exajoule, or EJ, is equal to one billion gigajoules, or 10^{18} joules.
mte = million tons equivalent. Kte = thousand tons equivalent.

PARES project in the late 1990s) laid out in a "matrix" format. The "BAU" path roughly echoed Japanese government plans at the time, while the "Alternative" path featured an emphasis on aggressive application of energy efficiency and renewable energy in end-use demand and electricity (and heat) supply.[25] The matrix format allows, in theory, the comparison of a large number of different attributes for a large number of different paths, but in practice the more that the number of attributes can be reduced to the most significant few, and the more that the number of paths can be reduced to those that show clear differences relative to each other, the more easily comprehended and useful the comparison matrix will be. The matrix format is also compatible with the use of other tools and methods for evaluating aspects of energy security, including, but by no means limited to, the sampling of tools and methods presented above.

The side-by-side comparison of candidate paths/scenarios should, if the original set of paths considered was sufficiently broad, allow the elimination of paths that are clearly worse, in several (or key) attribute dimensions, than other candidates. The process of elimination of paths should, however, be approached in a systematic, transparent, and well-documented way.

Qualitative analysis

One advantage of the "matrix" method of paths comparison shown above is that it allows input on both quantitative and qualitative attributes and measures of energy security. In some cases, comparing attributes quantitatively across paths is theoretically possible (for example, employment impacts or spending on security arrangements), but not feasible from a practical perspective, at least for the study at hand. In other cases (exposure to social and cultural risk, for example), quantitative measures may simply not exist. In these types of cases, the only option for measuring the relative attributes of different paths may be qualitative analysis. There is no one correct way to accomplish a qualitative analysis, but such an analysis should attempt to address the issue from different points of view (for example, cultural impacts on different segments of society), should clearly define operating assumptions, and should clearly show a thinking-through of the relationship between cause (differences between energy paths) and effect (differences in attribute outcome). Qualitative analysis is by definition subjective, but is a necessary part of the overall analysis of different energy paths, which otherwise runs the risk of confusing the attributes that are *countable* with the issues that *count*.

Methods yet to be developed

The consideration of different energy paths and their outcomes is an inexact science, as noted above, with both objective and subjective components. Possible areas of research into methods of evaluating energy paths results include:

- developing better ways to summarize and visualize multiple energy security dimensions and attributes, including tabular, statistical, and graphical methods;
- developing statistical data on correlations between fuel exporter behavior for supply diversification analyses (for example, on correlations between the pricing and supply behavior of different groups of oil exporters);
- improving the analysis of economic interactions (for example, the impacts of using different energy sources—renewable fuels versus fossil fuels as a case in point—on employment and on other sectors of the economy) within candidate energy paths;
- identifying more effective ways of evaluating energy security impacts of risks of different types;

- exploring analytical methods for evaluating military security impacts and costs, including case studies of past energy choices with military security linkages;
- exploring the analytical use of the types of "scenario-building" processes to help to evaluate the differences between energy paths.

Conclusion

Energy security, if defined more comprehensively, has many overlaps with the concept of sustainability. As a consequence, many policies that seek to enhance future energy security, be it at the global, regional, national, or sub-national levels, also have the effect of enhancing (or moving toward) sustainability. In order to determine—to the extent possible with any forward-looking activity—whether future national, regional, and global energy policies will lead to improved energy security and sustainability, a systematic approach to evaluating the performance of different energy paths/scenarios with regard to the many dimensions of comprehensive energy security is needed. The analytical tools and methods described above (and summarized in Table 3.4), applied to evaluate and take into account both quantitative and qualitative factors

Table 3.4 Tools and methodologies for energy security analysis

Tool or Method	Description	Advantages	Disadvantages
Optimization Modeling	Mathematical modeling to determine the optimal solution (for example, by minimizing costs or pollutant emissions) from among a range of options that meet certain criteria (for example, for the development of electricity generation capacity)	Provides a single, "optimal" result that is easy to understand	Result depends very strongly on inputs and modeling parameters, which are often not easy for the users of the results to review
Energy Paths Analysis	Allows comparison of selected results related to energy security across different "paths" for the evolution of an energy system that (ideally) provides the same energy services to society	Flexible enough to allow a range of different policy options to be modeled, and to incorporate non-quantitive considerations in the design of "paths"	Requires care in design of paths so as to yield a result that is relevant to energy security policy, and is at an appropriate level of detail
Diversification Indicies	Mathematical formulae that allow the degree of diversification in a system— for example diversification among energy sources, or suppliers of imported energy – to be expressed as an index value	Relatively easy to use to compare the evolution of diversification over time in key parameters across energy paths driven by alternative policies	Provides only part of the energy security picture. Also must be applied with care, as some types of diversification – for example among suppliers feeding gas into the same pipeline—may yield similar results, but provide less real energy security than others

Table 3.4 (continued)

Tool or Method	Description	Advantages	Disadvantages
Multiple-Attribute Analysis with Factor Ranking and/or Weighting	Applies ranking and/or weighting procedures to potentially diverse attributes of a system to provide a set of overall numerical scores for use in ranking energy policy plans/paths/scenarios	Provides a single comprehensive metric that is easy to use in presenting options to policymakers or stakeholders	Rankings can unreasonably exaggerate small differences between choices, and/or downplay large difference; also can mask what are inherently subjective choices (weightings) as objective
"Matrix" Approach to Paths Comparison	Compare the results of energy paths that yield (roughly) the same benefits in a table that displays results for each path considered across a broad and representative range of energy security attributes	Allows the review of both quantitative and qualitative measures in the same table, without (or with limited) hidden judgments as to the importance of specific attributes	Depends on the user of the results to judge which attributes in the comparison are most important, and on the analyst to evaluate a representative set of attributes

and measures in multiple-attribute, side-by-side analyses of different candidate energy paths, provide at least the beginnings of such an approach. Together with other tools, this approach can be used to help to guide energy policy by placing the different dimensions of energy decisions before policymakers in a clear and transparent fashion.

Notes

1 This chapter draws from previous work done as part of the Nautilus Institute's "Pacific Asia Regional Energy Security" project, including a summary of the PARES energy security analysis approach published earlier, and developed in related articles, as well as articles scheduled for publication in an upcoming Asian Energy Security Special Issue of the journal *Energy Policy*. See, for example, von Hippel, D. F. 2004. "Energy Security Analysis: A New Framework," *reCOMMEND* 1(2) (December): 4–6; Hayes, P. and D. von Hippel. 2006. "Energy Security in Northeast Asia," *Global Asia* 1(1): 91–105; von Hippel, D. F., T. Suzuki, J. H. Williams, T. Savage, and P. Hayes. Forthcoming. "Energy Security and Sustainability in Northeast Asia," Asian Energy Security Special Issue of *Energy Policy*; and von Hippel, D. F., T. Savage, and P. Hayes. Forthcoming. "Introduction to the Asian Energy Security Project: Project Organization and Methodologies," Asian Energy Security Special Issue of *Energy Policy*.

2 See, for example, Clawson, P. 1997. "Energy Security in a Time of Plenty", *National Defense University Institute for National Strategic Studies Strategic Forum*, Number 130, November. Available at: https://digitalndulibrary.ndu.edu/cdm4/document.php?CISOROOT=/ndupress&CISOPTR=10329&REC= 9 (accessed August 28, 2010).

3 British Petroleum Co. 2009. *BP Statistical Review of World Energy*, June. Downloaded as Excel workbook "statistical_review_of_world_energy_full_report_2009.xls" from: http://www.bp.com/multipleimagesection.do?categoryId=9023755&contentId=7044552. (Accessed August 28, 2010).

4 See Harris, J. 2008. *Written Testimony of Jeffrey Harris, Chief Economist, Before the Committee on Energy and Natural Resources United States Senate*, April 3. Available at: http://www.cftc.gov/stellent/groups/public/@newsroom/documents/speechandtestimony/opaharris040308.pdf. (accessed August 28, 2010).

5 For example, Reuters. 2008. "FOREX–Dollar Falls as Oil Prices Rise on Iran News," July 9. Available at: http://www.reuters.com/article/usDollarRpt/idUSN0943813620080709; Reuters. 2008. "Oil Hits Record above $147," July 11. Available at: http://www.reuters.com/article/topNews/idUST14048520080711; United States Department of Energy, Energy Information Administration (USDOE EIA). 2010. "NYMEX Light Sweet Crude Oil Futures Prices." Available at: http://www.eia.doe.gov/emeu/international/crude2.html (accessed March 31, 2010).

6 Samuels, R. 1997. "Securing Asian Energy Investments," *The MIT Japan Program Science, Technology and Management Report* 4(2) (September/October).

7 For a more comprehensive discussion of these attributes, see von Hippel, D. F., T. Suzuki, J. H. Williams, T. Savage, and P. Hayes. Forthcoming. "Energy Security and Sustainability in Northeast Asia," Asian Energy Security Special Issue of *Energy Policy*, currently available at: http://dx.doi.org/10.1016/j.enpol.2009.07 (accessed August 28, 2010).

8 Asuka, J. 1997. *A Brief Memo on Environmental Security Regimes in the Asian Region*; and Yamaji, K. 1997. *Long-Term Techno-Management for Mitigating Global Warming*, both prepared as background to the PARES project, Nautilus Institute, December.

9 Wilkening, K. E., L., A. Barrie, and M. Engle. 2000. "Trans-Pacific Air Pollution," *Science* 290 (5489) (October 6): 65–67.

10 Khatib, H. 2000. "Energy Security." In J. Goldemberg, J. Holdren, and K. Smith l. (eds.), *World Energy Assessment* (New York: UNDP/CSD/WEC, United Nations Development Programme), chapter 4. Available at: http://stone.undp.org/undpweb/seed/wea/pdfs/chapter4.pdf (accessed August 28, 2010).

11 International Atomic Energy Agency (IAEA). 2007. "Asia Leads Way in Nuclear Power Development: Japan, South Korea, China and India Driving Present Global Nuclear Power Expansion." Staff report, October 30. Available at: http://www.iaea.org/NewsCenter/News/2007/asialeads.html (accessed August 28, 2010).

12 World Nuclear Association. 2010. "Nuclear Power in the United Arab Emirates." February. Available at: http://www.world-nuclear.org/info/UAE_nuclear_power_inf123.html (accessed August 28, 2010).

13 Matthew, R. 1995. "Environmental Security: Demystifying the Concept, Clarifying the Stakes." In *Environmental Change and Security Project Report* (Washington, DC: Woodrow Wilson Center for International Scholars), pp. 14–23.

14 Holdren, J. P., G. Daily, and P. E. Ehrlich. 1995. *The Meaning of Sustainability: Biogeophysical Aspects*, ed. Mohan Munasinghe and Walter Shearer (Washington, DC: distributed for the United Nations University by the World Bank). Available at: http://www.ufrgs.br/iph/Holdren_Daily_Ehrlich_The_meaning_of_sustainability_biogeophysical_aspects.pdf (accessed August 28, 2010).

15 Brundtland GH. 1987. *Our Common Future: World Commission on Environment and Development*. Oxford, UK: Oxford Univ. Press, p. 3.

16 Marshall, J. D. and M. W. Toffel. 2005. "Framing the Elusive Concept of Sustainability: A Sustainability Hierarchy," *Environmental Science and Technology* 39(3): 673–682.

17 Holdren *et al.*, *The Meaning of Sustainability*.

18 Smil, V. 2006. "21st Century Energy: Some Sobering Thoughts," *OECD Observer* No. 258/259, December. Available at: http://www.oecdobserver.org/news/fullstory.php/aid/2083/21st_century_energy:_Some_sobering_thoughts.html (accessed August 28, 2010).

19 As described in, for example, International Atomic Energy Agency (IAEA). 2005. *Energy Indicators for Sustainable Development: Guidelines and Methodologies*, prepared in collaboration with the United Nations Department of Economic and Social Affairs, the International Energy Agency, Eurostat, and the European Environment Agency, report number STI/PUB/1222, April. Available at: http://www-pub.iaea.org/MTCD/publications/PDF/Pub1222_web.pdf; Vera, I, and L. Langlois. 2007. "Energy Indicators for Sustainable Development," *Energy* 32(6) (June): 875–882; and Vera, I. A., L. M. Langlois, H. H. Rogner, A. I. Jalal, and F. L. Toth. 2005. "Indicators for Sustainable Energy Development: An Initiative by the International Atomic Energy Agency," *Natural Resources Forum* 29: 274–283. Available at: http://www.iaea.or.at/OurWork/ST/NE/Pess/assets/NRF_indicators_art05.pdf (acessed August 28, 2010).

20 LEAP is the Long-range Energy Alternatives Planning software system, developed and distributed by the Stockholm Environment Institute in the United States (see http://www.energycommunity.org/) (accessed August 28, 2010).

21 See, for example, Aronson, D. 1998. "Overview of Systems Thinking." Available at: http://www.thinking.net/Systems_Thinking/OverviewSTarticle.pdf (accessed August 28, 2010).

22 See von Hippel *et al.*, "Energy Security and Sustainability in Northeast Asia," for a more detailed discussion of these considerations.

23 Razavi, H. 1997. *Economic, Security and Environmental Aspects of Energy Supply: A Conceptual Framework for Strategic Analysis of Fossil Fuels.* Commissioned by the Pacific Asia Regional Energy Security (PARES) Project, December. Available at: http://www.nautilus.org/archives/papers/energy/RazaviPARES.pdf.

24 Neff, T. L. 1997. *Improving Energy Security in Pacific Asia: Diversification and Risk Reduction for Fossil and Nuclear Fuels.* Commissioned by the Pacific Asia Regional Energy Security (PARES) Project, December. Available at: http://www.nautilus.org/archives/papers/energy/NeffPARES.pdf (accessed August 28, 2010).

25 For readers interested in more detailed descriptions of updated versions of these paths for Japan, see Nakata, M., J. Oda, C. Heaps, and D. von Hippel. 2003. *Carbon Dioxide Emissions Reduction Potential in Japan's Power Sector—Estimating Carbon Emissions Avoided by a Fuel-Switch Scenario*, prepared for Worldwidefund for Nature (WWF)—Japan, October. Available at: www.energycommunity.org/documents/PowerSwitchJapan.pdf; Takase, K. and T. Suzuki. Forthcoming. "The Japanese Energy Sector: Current Situation, and Future Paths," Asian Energy Security Special Issue of *Energy Policy*. Available at: http://dx.doi.org/10.1016/j.enpol.2010.01.036 (accessed August 28, 2010).

4

THE SUSTAINABLE DEVELOPMENT DIMENSION OF ENERGY SECURITY

Asclepias R. S. Indriyanto, Dwi Ari Fauzi, and Alfa Firdaus

Introduction

The world's historic reliance on oil has influenced many aspects of human life, from political platforms and economic policies to business practices and the daily energy decisions of individuals. The world is now facing manifold energy-related challenges from many directions and in various forms, as our fondness for oil and other fossil fuels has been identified as a significant contributor to global warming. This chapter highlights three wide-ranging principles, namely energy security, sustainable development, and governance, that can help us see through the complexities of the energy challenges we are facing.

As many other chapters in this book reveal, perspectives on energy security evolve through time. Energy security concerns were initially centered on the availability of energy, and the center of attention was on the primary energy supply side, especially crude oil. However, in recent years it has been widely recognized that energy availability can be affected by various factors in each segment of the energy industry, as well as in interactions among those segments. Major concerns remain in relation to the sufficiency of supply and the quality of energy services. However, prices and various economic arrangements are also important since they dictate the quantity and quality of energy provision, as well as the pattern of energy consumption. Further, activities in all segments of the energy sector impact society, ecology, and the environment in general, which in turn directly or indirectly affect the supply and demand of energy and therefore energy security as well. The new paradigm of energy security pays attention to the whole chain of the energy industry, since any mishap caused by or affecting any of the elements may disrupt energy security at various magnitudes in the short as well as long term.

At this point in understanding the conditions that encompass energy security, it becomes clear that there are some essential linkages between energy security and the principles of sustainable development. Balancing economic, social, and environmental objectives is crucial to maintaining sustainable development, and similar concerns also apply to retaining energy security. However, the two paradigms may have a slightly different emphasis attributed to the origin of those concepts. Energy security may put more weight on the short- and medium-term issues, while sustainable development addresses long-term concerns. Recognizing the similarities, as well as the differences, between the two would enhance our tools for a better understanding about the complex energy challenges facing us.

Energy for sustainable development

This chapter adopts the energy security and sustainable development (ESSD) framework, which is a synthesis of the four As approach (availability, accessibility, affordability, and acceptability) to energy security[1] and the sustainable development dimensions (social, economics, and environment).[2] The energy security view represented by the four As tends to focus on physical terms and has more short-term objectives, although some longer-term elements are included. In contrast, the sustainable development dimension is much longer term than the energy security point of view, since it also considers inter-temporal and inter-generational allocation of available resources, and addresses much wider issues of development. This analytical framework has represented the three layers of energy securities identified by the Asia Pacific Energy Research Centre (APERC), which are: (a) physical availability, (b) economics of energy security, and (c) environmental sustainability.

In assessing ESSD indicators for Indonesia, some technical indicators can be measured quantitatively using accessible statistical data. However, some other indicators are evaluated qualitatively since there is currently no suitable formula or data available. These qualitative measures may be developed into more quantitative measures, but further elaboration of the methodology and sets of publicly available data is required. This framework allows evaluation of the cross-links between energy security principles and the sustainable development dimension to be explored, both in terms of the specific time frame and for other periods of observation. Table 4.1 presents a summary of this framework.

Energy security and sustainable development analysis

This section explores the ESSD condition in Indonesia based on the indicators and other related information gathered by IIEE under the framework explained in the previous section.[3] Each of the four 'A's is discussed in a pair with either social, economic, or environmental dimensions. Each pair is represented by one or more issues, while each issue is evaluated through one or more indicators.

Table 4.1 Energy security and sustainable development framework

	Social	Economy	Environment
Availability	Implication of diversification and physical supply disruption on social life	• Diversification • Dependency • Physical Supply Disruption • Energy Use Pattern	Implication of diversification and energy use pattern on environment
Accessibility	Household access	Infrastructure & Transportation	Influence of environmental factors and natural disaster in accessibility of energy
Affordability	Share of household on energy	Energy Price	Implication of energy use pattern on environment
Acceptability	Quantity and quality of energy	Role of Energy to Economics	• Fossil dependency • Global warming adaptation & mitigation
Governance	• Institutional arrangement	• Decision-making process	• Substantive Issues

Source: Indriyanto, Ascelpias R.S., Bobby A.T. Wattimena, H. Batih, and I. Sari Triandi. 2007. "Rising Demand, Uncertain Supply, and Price Management." In Subroto (ed.), *Contesting Energy Security* (Jakarta: Indonesian Institute for Energy Economics), pp. 17–34.

Evaluation of the Indonesian circumstance in every issue will be presented in tables by arrows implying its influence towards ESSD. A downward arrow indicates a tendency to deteriorate ESSD, a flat arrow suggests neutral impact, and an upward arrow indicates a favorable situation that would support ESSD. Some of these arrows are linked to a quantitative assessment approach, while others are supported by qualitative data and information.

Availability

The focus of availability concern is the presence of energy commodity and services presented to consumers. Two main issues are of particular interest, namely diversification and supply disruption. Diversification would allow for more flexibility since it refers to either multiple types of energy, various sources of supply, or different modes of transport; hence it substantiates availability. However, supply disruption directly denies availability. Table 4.2 summarizes the influence of each availability issue and the respective indicators towards ESSD, while the subsections below explain how the direction of the arrows is assigned.

Table 4.2 The social, economic, and environmental dimension of availability

Dimension	Issue	Indicators	Influence on ESSD
Social	Diversification	• Social impact of diversification program	
	Supply Disruption	• Share of subsidized fuel	↓
		Social unrest	↓
Economic	Diversification	Diversification of Primary Energy Demand (DoPED)★	↑
		Diversification of Power Generation (DoPG)★	↓
	Dependency	Net Oil Import Dependency (NOID)★	↓
		Middle East Oil Import Dependency (MEOID)★	↑↑
	Supply Disruption	System average interruption duration index (SAIDI) and system average interruption frequency index (SAIFI)	↑
		Kerosene shortage	↓
		Electricity crisis	↓
		Coal supply	↓
		Gas supply	↓
	Energy Use Pattern	Oil & Gas Reserve to Production Ratio (R/P)★	→
		Coal Reserve to Production Ratio (R/P)★	↓
		Productivity of Final Energy Consumption:	
		• Intensity per GDP★	↓
		• Intensity per Capita★	↓
		• Elasticity of Final Energy★	↓
Environment	Diversification	Non-Carbon-Based Fuel Portfolio	↑
	Supply Disruption	Fuel substitution (gas to fuel, kerosene to biomass)	↓

Source: Indriyanto *et al.* "Rising Demand, Uncertain Supply."
Note:
Indicators with asterisks are based on historical figures, others are derived from recent reports and news media.

Availability–social

This pair portrays the link of energy availability and social life. The selected two indicators for the energy diversification issue are social impacts of energy diversification programs and share of subsidized fuels in total energy consumption. The indicator for social impacts of supply disruption is frequency or severity of social unrest.

In social impacts of energy diversification, the assessment is linked to the introduction of an energy diversification program, especially in the household sector. Increasing demand for and price of oil directly affects the size of subsidy requirement and presents a major burden to the state budget. To manage this pressure, the government adjusted fuel prices in 2005; and in the following years the parliament agreed to limit the supply of subsidized fuels.

Energy diversification programs have been launched to accompany these policies, hence the main context is to quickly reduce the subsidy burden. Kerosene price adjustment in 2005 was accompanied by a program to promote coal briquettes. Starting in 2006 the kerosene supply cap is operating in tandem with the program of providing LPG in 3kg containers and the respective stove to households in several areas. The coal briquette promotion was short-lived, causing small domestic industries to incur financial losses . Both the briquette promotion and the program to switch to LPG do not match the widespread impacts of price adjustment and supply limitation in terms of magnitude, time, and spread of locations.

This condition created long queues to buy kerosene in several areas of Indonesia, public rallies to express dissatisfaction with the unavailability of kerosene, loss of jobs and income, and forced consumption reduction mostly affecting low income households and small businesses. Further, the media reported evidence linking the shortage to the higher cost of meeting basic needs, an indication of increased cases of malnutrition, and some incidences of mental breakdown.

The other indicator related to social impacts of the diversification program is the share of subsidized fuels in relation to the total final energy consumption. Figure 4.1 shows that the share of kerosene in household energy consumption during 1995–2008 decreased, but it still represented a major portion. This shows the magnitude of the social implications of the above-mentioned energy diversification programs. Severe social impacts are also a consequence of the fact that alternative forms of energy were not available to the majority of these consumers at the time the

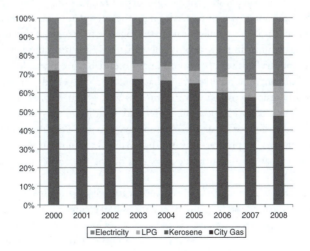

Figure 4.1 Share of subsidized kerosene and electricity in household sector.
Source: Handbook of Energy Economics Statistics 2006.

changes took place. In the mean time, technical difficulties and consumer behavior reportedly have reduced the implementation effectiveness of the effort to shift to LPG in areas affected by this program.

This particular energy diversification program resulted in unfavorable social impact. Security of energy supply was compromised, with widespread difficulties affecting vulnerable groups. Hence, these programs and the way they were implemented have had a negative influence on ESSD.

Energy supply disruption also appeared outside the energy diversification context. Various energy supply disruptions have affected every province in Indonesia. The severity of this situation can be measured, for example, by the frequency and magnitude of social unrest. Frequent electricity blackouts in West Kalimantan outraged PLN's customers and triggered their attempt to occupy its regional office building. Prolonged electricity disruption in some regions, for example North Sumatra, has forced some customers to take legal action against their electricity provider. The energy fuel price adjustment induced adulteration, such as mixing diesel oil with kerosene and hoarding, which lead to widespread unavailability of kerosene and encouraged public protest. This evidence shows the negative social impacts of energy supply disruption, which undermine ESSD.

Availability–economy

This pair reflects the implication of energy availability to the economy. Diversification is measured by the indicators of Diversification of Primary Energy Demand (DoPED) and Diversification of Power Generation (DoPG), which adopt the Shannon index formula that applies the higher number for the more diversified condition.

The DoPED index measures the dependency of a country on specific primary energy resources. From the energy security perspective, the more variety of primary energy in the supply mix will increase the flexibility and availability of a country to meet its energy needs. Figure 4.2 shows that the DoPED index for Indonesia tended to improve from 1995 to 2005, since the declining share of oil was replaced primarily by coal and later by geothermal energy. The dominance of oil had been reduced during the period.

However, some remarks should be made with regard to availability indicators. First, such indicators measure the diversification of energy-mix without taking into account whether they are depleted or renewable energy resources. Although the energy-mix has improved in Indonesia, the role of fossil fuel energy is still significant since the increase in coal share replaces the decrease in oil share. Second, availability indicators only show the existing utilization of energy resources in isolation of the country's other energy resource potentials. For example, as a tropical country, Indonesia has abundant potential sun rays that could be converted into electricity generation. Similarly, a country residing on the volcanic rim has large geothermal energy potential. Although a good DoPED index means a good energy security condition, these two limitations imply that this measurement applies for a partial or temporary security condition and therefore it is not sufficient for benchmarking progress towards sustainable development. Aside from the limitations, this indicator shows that the Indonesian energy mix during the period 1995–2006 gives a positive influence on ESSD.

In contrast to DoPED which measures diversification by the energy-mix at a macro level, the DoPG measures diversification by primary energy uses in electricity generation, which is at sector level. Energy-mix in power generation is affected by technology selection, load pattern and load factor of the system, and resource availability. The DoPG index for Indonesia declined during 1995–2005 due to an increase in oil fuel uses. The increase in oil consumption in power generation, especially by PLN, relates to the decreasing supply of gas to the existing gas-based

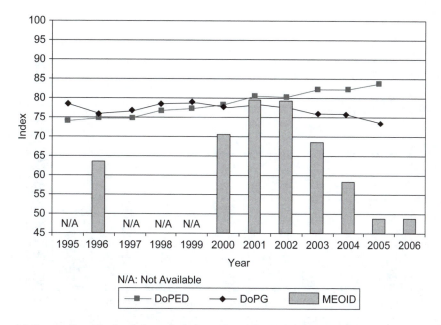

Figure 4.2 Energy diversification indexes for Indonesia.
Source: Handbook of Energy Economics Statistics 2006, PLN Statistics, PERTAMINA, IIEE Study.

power plants. Further, the installed capacity in geothermal plants has only been 800 MW, while the rest of the generating capacity, including the new additions in recent years, depends on fossil fuels. The declining DoPG index indicates that from a diversification point of view, the electricity sector contributed a negative influence to ESSD.

Another measure on the linkage of energy availability and the economy is import dependency, such as the Net Oil Import Dependency (NOID) and Middle East Oil Import Dependency (MEOID). The NOID index for Indonesia is relatively stable when only crude oil import is taken into account, as it has remained at around 30 percent of total crude consumption during the past decade, reflecting no increase in refinery capacity in Indonesia. However, if imported fuel products are included in the figure, then as Indonesia becomes a net oil-importing country the NOID index will deteriorate. A higher NOID index also indicates insecurity in the highly volatile international oil market. Based on these considerations, Indonesia's NOID measure has had a negative impact on ESSD as a whole.

The MEOID index measures dependency on supply source of oil import, in this case from the Middle East. Indonesia has diversified its source of crude import. Middle Eastern countries supplied 63 percent of Indonesia's imported crude in 1996; this increased to 80 percent in 2001 and 2002, and then declined to 48 percent in 2006. The current crude import suppliers for Indonesia include countries in the Asia and Australia regions. The trend during 2002–2006 provides a positive contribution towards ESSD.

The physical energy unavailability can also be seen from the indicators of the System Average Interruption Duration Index (SAIDI), System Average Interruption Frequency Index (SAIFI), kerosene shortage, electricity supply crises, coal supply disruption, and lack of gas supply in various instances. SAIDI and SAIFI for the overall electricity system in Indonesia tended to decrease during 2001–2004 (see Figure 4.3), which means an improvement in reliability of electricity services and therefore they provide positive influences on ESSD. However, limited expansion in

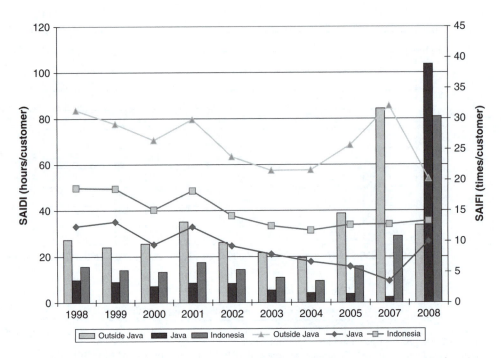

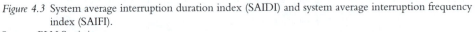

Figure 4.3 System average interruption duration index (SAIDI) and system average interruption frequency index (SAIFI).
Source: PLN Statistics.

generating and transmission/distribution capacity after 2004 has caused both indexes to deteriorate, which is likely to continue if capacity expansion cannot catch up with the growth in demand for electricity. Electricity services deteriorated significantly during 2006–07 on the islands outside Java, and during 2008–09 in Java itself. There are also some disparities between Java and non-Java regions, whereby both SAIDI and SAIFI in Java are lower due to the fact that the electricity infrastructure is more developed in Java. These SAIDI and SAIFI conditions provide a negative contribution to ESSD.

The occurrences of kerosene shortage in some regions of Indonesia led to various adverse effects for the economy. The direct impact for consumers includes the higher cost of meeting domestic needs. Kerosene price disparity has led subsidized household consumers to face a scarcity of supply, since some non-subsidized industrial users managed to divert the distribution for their own purposes. This condition also created the economic incentive to smuggle the subsidized goods onto the international market. The overall impact of the kerosene shortage to ESSD is negative.

The economic impact of energy availability can also be measured through energy use patterns, such as by the reserve to production ratio (R/P) and the productivity of final energy consumption. The R/P ratios for oil and natural gas in Indonesia during the period 1995–2005 were relatively constant due to decreasing production and a lack of new reserves (see Figure 4.4). Using the coal production figure for 2004 and the estimated reserve capacity, coal can support economic development for more than 100 years.[4] However, an increase in domestic consumption and the attractiveness of the export market have boosted the production rate from 135 million tons in 2004 to 215 million tons in 2007. If the increase in production is not followed by expansion in coal reserves, then the coal production life will decrease significantly. From the perspective of energy security, a low R/P ratio for oil and gas and an attractive export market for coal could create energy insecurity.

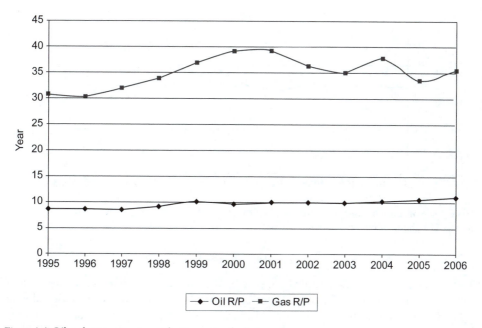

Figure 4.4 Oil and gas reserve to production ratios for Indonesia.
Source: BP Statistics Review of World Energy 2007.

Energy intensity in Indonesia generally increased during 1995–2005. Before the economic crisis in 1998, the energy intensity was relatively lower than it was after the crisis. During the recovery periods, the energy intensity increased significantly as the GDP growth was relatively low, but the energy consumption growth remained strong. However, the energy intensity growth rates slowed down during 2000–2003, which was linked to a periodical energy price consumption elasticity of 1.49, which means the energy consumption growth rate exceeded GDP growth. In the current National Energy Policy, the Indonesian government plans for a gradual improvement in efficiency and productivity such that energy elasticity will become less than 1 by 2025. The upward trend of the final energy consumption intensity gives a negative influence on ESSD.

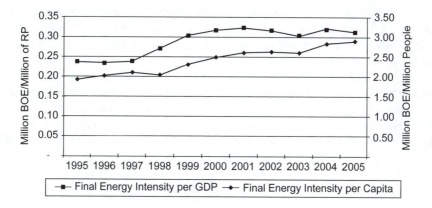

Figure 4.5 Energy intensity per GDP and energy intensity per capita (BOE = billion barrels of oil equivalent).
Source: Handbook of Energy Economics Statistics 2006.

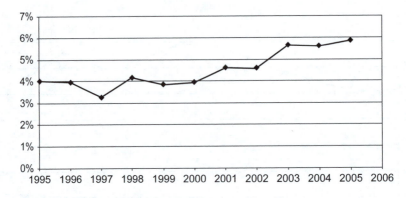

Figure 4.6 Non-carbon-based fuel portfolio (NCFP).
Source: Handbook of Energy Economics Statistics 2006.

Availability–environment

This pair links energy selection with the respective environmental implication, considering the local and global impacts of energy utilization. Non-Carbon-Based Fuel Portfolio (NCFP) is selected as the indicator to measure the share of non-fossil fuel primary energy use, taking into account only modern energy (excluding biomass). Lack of access and supply disruption can cause energy unavailability, which may cause fuel substitution to the less environmentally friendly choices. The unavailability of gas supply for several gas power plants leads to increased use of oil fuels in electricity generation. Degradation of many catchment areas throughout Indonesia has increased the sedimentation rate of some dams and the deterioration of hydropower performance, forcing more utilization of coal and diesel for power generation. Figure 4.6 shows a relatively constant NCFP at 4 percent during 1995–1996, reaching the lowest level at approximately 3.5 percent in 1997 due to a significant decrease in hydropower operation during that dry year. During 1998–2005 the NCFP tended to improve continuously following additions in geothermal power plants. Referring to this condition, progress in the NCFP indicator for Indonesia during the early 2000s has a positive influence on ESSD.

Accessibility

Accessibility is important towards aiming for energy security and sustainable development, since access to energy makes energy utilization possible. Without access, the presence of energy resources per se does not imply any benefits in meeting human needs. Energy infrastructure and transport mode pose a significant role in this respect. This section will explore the social, economic, and environmental dimensions of accessibility. Accessibility in the perspective of social dimension highlights the provision of energy access to households, reflecting the ability of the population to use energy and take advantage of its service. The economic dimension of accessibility focuses on infrastructure and transportation mode for moving energy to end-users. Environment dimension reviews the disturbance of access that may be triggered either by man-made actions or natural disasters or their combination. Table 4.3 summarizes the influence of each issue and the indicators of accessibility on ESSD.

Accessibility–social

The link of energy accessibility to social implication can be expected from the multiplier effects that energy would bring to a household, a community, and eventually the whole population. In

Table 4.3 The social, economic, and environmental dimensions of accessibility

Dimension	Issue	Indicators	Influence on ESSD
Social	Household Access	Electrification ratio to population growth	→
Economic	Infrastructure & Transportation	Bottleneck at infrastructure	→
		Transportation mode dependency	→
Environmental	Infrastructure & Transportation	Impact of natural and man-made actions	→

Source: Indriyanto, Ascelpias R.S., Bobby A.T. Wattimena, H. Batih, and I. Sari Triandi. 2007. "Rising Demand, Uncertain Supply, and Price Management." In Subroto (ed.), *Contesting Energy Security* (Jakarta: Indonesian Institute for Energy Economics), pp. 17–34.

this study the focus for this link is on electricity access, which is commonly measured by the electrification ratio. In 2005, the electrification ratio in Indonesia was around 54 percent, comprising a ratio of 58 percent in Java and an average of 48 percent for the other islands. This means nearly half of the population was without electricity access.

In the past decade the electrification ratio in Indonesia has increased by close to twice as much as the GDP growth. During 1995–1998 (before the economic crisis), the relative amount of electrification ratio growth to population growth was 3.51; but this index decreased significantly to only 0.55 during 1999–2005 (after the economic crisis). The latter implies that although electricity access expanded, the speed of expansion did not match the population growth during this period. These statistics indicate a declining performance of electricity access expansion during the early 2000s, and therefore a negative contribution towards achieving ESSD.

Accessibility–economy

The correlation between accessibility and economy can be viewed from the coverage and quality of the infrastructure and mode of transport. The existence of a bottleneck in the infrastructure can obstruct the energy supply from the production regions to the demand regions and end-users. For example, coal consumption in Indonesia increased almost sixfold from nearly 9 million tons in 1995 to around 52 million tons in 2007. Coal production has increased more than fivefold, from 41 million tons in 1995 to 215 million tons in 2007, when nearly two-thirds was designated for export.

However, the main mode of transport from the production region in South Sumatra has been the railroad, which has had the same capacity for many years, and in South Kalimantan public roads. Escalation of traffic frequency has put an increasing burden on these infrastructures, leading to deterioration in rail and road services that affects the whole of the economic activities in the region. The dependency on a single mode of transport is not limited to coal supply; distribution of oil fuel in Java, for example, depends heavily on the railway and road networks. In other regions, fuel distribution is even more difficult as it is dependent on sea conditions, water level in the rivers, and air transport which can carry limited supplies. All the above indicate limited infrastructure coverage and quality of transport for the supply of energy to end-users, which undermines the reliability of the energy supply and consequently inhibits economic activities. This means a negative contribution to ESSD.

Accessibility–environment

Man-made actions and natural disasters can also affect energy infrastructures. The linkage between accessibility and the environment is in general neutral, as it may result in both positive and negative implications. A positive implication of the expansion of energy access is through benefits to people as the end-users of energy services. A negative implication may arise from imprudent development planning and implementation processes.

The mud flooding still ongoing (as of August 2010) from the gas field owned by Lapindo Brantas, Inc. in Sidoardjo is an extreme case. Without entering into the dispute concerning its root cause, the facts show that the mud flood has damaged various infrastructures in the surrounding area. The explosion at Indonesia's state-owned energy company Pertamina's gas pipeline there disrupted the operation of several industries in East Java and some power plants owned by PLN that supply electricity to the Java–Bali grid system.

In contrast, efforts to expand energy access may also affect the surrounding environment. The media reported various incidents of public protests related to the erection of transmission and distribution power lines over their lands, with concerns ranging from the legal aspects on land ownership and the health implications of electrical and magnetic influence, to the expectation of economic benefits.

More specific criteria need to be developed for assessing the overall linkage of accessibility and the environment with regard to achieving ESSD, and for evaluating the Indonesian situation in that respect. For the time being, the contribution is considered neutral.

Affordability

Energy security addresses affordability as one of the four main concerns due to the fact that it determines the final condition of being able to consume energy. Affordability applies to both energy producers as well as consumers. Without affordability, energy availability and accessibility will only result in selected or limited service provision. Since every human being needs energy to live, non-affordability is a contra factor for energy security and sustainable development. Table 4.4 summarizes the assessment on energy affordability.

Affordability–social

From the consumer's point of view, the purchasing ability for obtaining energy services can be assessed through the share of energy consumption spending in the total expenditure for each income category. Lower income households, relatively, spent a higher proportion of their income on energy-related goods than other income groups.

Table 4.4 The social, economic, and environmental dimension of affordability

Dimension	Issue	Indicators	Influence on ESSD
Social	Energy Price	Share of energy consumption for income groups	↓
Economic	Energy Price	Electricity price (cost vs. revenue)	↓
		Oil fuel price	↓
		Coal price (domestic vs. export)	↓
		Gas price: industry vs. PLN	↓
		Energy subsidy in the state budget	↑
Environmental	Energy Price	Choices of energy utilization and pattern	→

Source: Indriyanto, Ascelpias R.S., Bobby A.T. Wattimena, H. Batih, and I. Sari Triandi. 2007. "Rising Demand, Uncertain Supply, and Price Management." In Subroto (ed.), *Contesting Energy Security* (Jakarta: Indonesian Institute for Energy Economics), pp. 17–34.

This shows that an increase in price will impact heavily on low-income households, or, in the other words, it will increase energy insecurity for this group. A drastic price adjustment in October 2005 that increased fuel prices by an average of 120 percent is expected to have wide social implications. Government efforts to lessen this impact were through the direct distribution of cash. Nevertheless, this short-term remedy may not address the magnitude of inflation and scarcity of supply of kerosene that followed. Moreover, direct distribution of cash will not be able to absorb the continuous increase in the international oil price.

A recent program to promote Jatropha for biofuel production was designed to alleviate poverty. However, this program faced major challenges including a lack of coordination, insufficient information dissemination, and no firm financial support. This drawback has not resulted in any improvement in economic conditions for farmers. In addition, all the findings from the various research projects carried out in the global context, especially the US and EU, identify biofuels development as one of the causes of food scarcity. It is related to food price which increased drastically and to the competition over supplies between food and biofuels feedstock.

It is a challenge for Indonesia that must considered with care, since developing and developed countries have quite different circumstances with regard to developing biofuels. Indonesia's biofuels development program was intended to reduce poverty and unemployment, and support sustainable economic growth through biofuel provision in a sufficient quantity and quality, at a rational price, and in an efficient, reliable, harmless, and environmentally friendly manner, thus reducing domestic consumption of oil fuels.

Based on the above considerations, the affordability and social dimension of the existing policy and programs in Indonesia have not been able to support ESSD.

Affordability–economy

The linkage of affordability to the economy can be represented by examining the position of the energy producer and the government budget allocation. Indonesia adopts a uniform tariff policy in the electricity sector, which results in similar charges throughout the archipelago regardless of the wide range of costs associated with providing electricity in different areas. This condition provides no incentive to service the remote and smaller areas of the country, leading to a low electrification ratio. Similarly, the government also determines the range of acceptable prices for liquid fuels, while distributing liquid fuels from the refinery to consumers in distant locations requires time, effort, and various modes of transport. The gap between the cost of supply and the end-user charges paid by the consumer should be covered by energy subsidy.

Over the years the energy subsidy policy has survived, but recently it has become more and more difficult to sustain. As energy consumption is continually increasing and limitations in energy production continue, the budget allocation for energy subsidy is ballooning, as shown in Figure 4.7. This is a tough call during the surge in the international oil price and at a time when the country is becoming a net oil importer. As a response from the government, Presidential Decree no. 5 of 2006 on National Energy Policy and its Blueprint of National Energy Management 2005–2025 sets out the energy policy objectives as follows: to reduce significantly the use of oil to below 20 percent; to reduce energy elasticity to below 1; to improve energy infrastructure; and to increase the use of coal, natural gas, and renewables.

From the point ov view of the producer, PLN is in a difficult position when electricity prices cannot be increased and subsidy payment is being squeezed, while consumers are getting increasingly impatient over the long waiting lists to get connected and suboptimum service reliability. Similarly, a reduced energy subsidy implies a lower profit for Pertamina, but it has to continue its service to both the lucrative market as well as the hard-to-reach consumers.

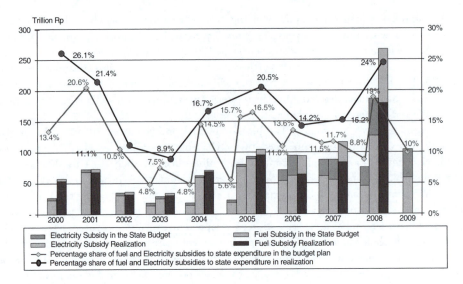

Figure 4.7 Fuel subsidies in the state budget.
Source: Various documents issued by the Ministry of Finance and the Ministry of Energy and Mineral Resources.
Notes:
1) Realization in 2008 is estimation based on Financial Notes and the draft of state budget 2009.
2) Electricity and fuel subsidies 2009 is based on state budget 2009 set by GOI.

Affordability–environment

Choices of energy utilization and pattern will have implications on the environment. The above discussion on the link of economy with affordability indicates that all parties are under budget pressure, and cheap options are most likely to be attractive as a short-term remedy for this burden. Coal is now considered as the most viable option to support Indonesian economic development, replacing the role of oil in the past. Coal share in the total energy mix has risen from 3.99 percent in 1995 to 14.15 percent in 2005.

Nevertheless, there are several caveats to this energy selection. First, competition with strong demands in the international market is likely to challenge the supply security and increase the price in the domestic market. Second, similar to oil, coal is also a form of non-renewable energy. Increasing the rate of production as has happened in the past several years will directly shorten the lifetime of coal production. Third, the global concern on climate change may induce compliance for adopting clean technology that will imply a higher cost than initially estimated for the various coal projects in the country. These factors may undermine the affordability consideration that was taken as the base to promote coal in the first place.

Significant changes in world geopolitics and energy constellation may result in a different set of global constraints and opportunities. The decision to focus mainly on coal has various potential drawbacks as mentioned above. For this reason, the electricity from the geothermal plant in the second phase of power plant development acceleration program will displace the dependency on electricity produced by an equivalent coal-fired thermal plant. Considering these aspects, the decision to rely on coal poses a significant risk to ESSD and it will be displaced by geothermal energy to be rolled out soon.

Table 4.5 The social, economic, and environmental dimensions of acceptability

Dimension	Issue	Indicators	Influence on ESSD
Social	Energy subsidy	Effective allocation	↓
Economic	Energy subsidy	Energy subsidy in the state budget	↓
Environmental	GHG emission	GHG emission from power generation	↑
		GHG from energy uses	↑
	Efforts to reduce global warming	Demand-side management programs (17–22, compact fluorescent lightbulb promotion, etc)	↑
Governance	Legal framework	Institutional arrangement	↑
		Decision-making process	→
		Substantive issues	→

Source: Indriyanto, Ascelpias R.S., Bobby A.T. Wattimena, H. Batih, and I. Sari Triandi. 2007. "Rising Demand, Uncertain Supply, and Price Management." In Subroto (ed.), *Contesting Energy Security* (Jakarta: Indonesian Institute for Energy Economics), pp. 17–34.

Acceptability

Acceptability is important in the efforts towards achieving energy security and sustainable development since it refers to the support needed to enable a certain decision to survive over time. In this study, the focus for acceptability assessment is on energy subsidy. Slightly different from the affordability assessment discussed above, acceptability with regard to the government policy to subsidize energy prices relates to fairness, improved welfare of the general public, and protection of the planet to allow for healthy and wealthy future generations.

Acceptability–social and economic

While it is justifiable to protect access to energy for the vulnerable groups, the existing energy subsidy mechanism is non-proportional since it also subsidizes the higher income groups and the latter enjoy even more benefit from the subsidy than the other groups since their lifestyle means that they consume more energy. Some of the government efforts to improve the allocation of energy subsidy were implemented through the substitution program of coal briquettes for kerosene and later on LPG in 3kg tanks.

The previous subsections on availability highlight several adverse social impacts of these programs during their initial implementation period, despite the deployment of significant resources to accompany these programs. These programs are not merely about changing technology or commodity distribution; rather they involve an important aspect of changing perceptions and cultural shifts. Apprehensiveness in using new equipment is normal in the early stages in this kind of transition, and will naturally subside when more successful shifts in the surrounding neighborhood can be looked upon as good and safe examples. For this reason, information dissemination and technical assistance should become major parts of the approach, directed towards both consumers and local suppliers of appliances and other technical components.

Reducing kerosene supply drastically prior to sufficient adaptation on both the consumer and the local supplier sides was an unwise decision. When there is no energy alternative available for the low income group, this pressure is no less than torture for them since their basic needs are more difficult to obtain and more costly. This is in contrast to the initial objective which was to improve the subsidy benefit for the needy. Based on this consideration, the existing effort to improve subsidy allocation effectiveness does not support ESSD.

Acceptability–environment

The environmental concerns about utilizing energy resources, relate to the greenhouse gas (GHG) emission from burning coal, oil fuels, and natural gas in particular as they create global and local atmospheric abnormalities. The implications of the existing energy choices affect the environment negatively, and acceptability would mean the ability to manage and control these adverse impacts. CO_2 emissions from power plants in 2000 reached almost 60 million tons and this number increased, along with an increase in energy consumption, to reach 92.88 million tons by 2007 (see Figure 4.8). Energy consumption in the transportation sector has also produced CO_2 emissions at about 54.4 million tons in 2000, increasing to 67.7 million tons of CO_2 in 2005.

As increasing CO_2 will aggravate GHG emission and impact on global warming, the increasing demand of energy, including electricity, can be a serious problem. The Indonesian government has made some efforts to reduce the impact of global warming. For example, an energy efficiency and demand-side management program has been conducted by PT. PLN (Persero). While PLN has no specific policy, it does have efficiency improvement programs, including replacing older less-efficient plants, retrofitting more modern control systems, and component upgrades on both thermal and hydroelectric power plants.

Public campaigns to reduce electricity consumption during the daily peak load period of 17:00 to22:00 hours have proven to be effective following the implementation of advertising and other formsof public outreach programs. In 2005 Indonesia developed a policy of energy efficiency in government buildings. Another measure has involved switching appliances, for example switching from incandescent lamps to compact fluorescent lamps (CFLs) in households, which was reported to haveresulted in an increase in CFL imports from 9.9 million units in 2001 to more than 64 million units in 2005.

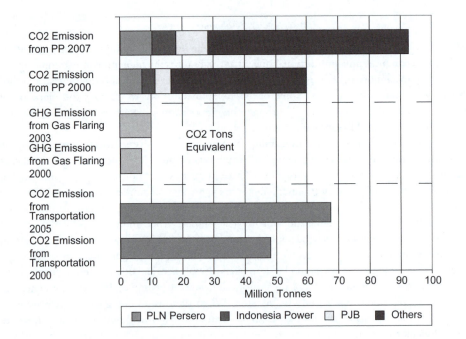

Figure 4.8 CO_2 emissions in Indonesia.
Source: Indriyanto *et al.* "Rising Demand, Uncertain Supply."

The establishment of the National Council for Climate Change in 2008 was an important step with regard to the climate change issue. Another major landmark was a remark by President Susilo Bambang Yudhoyono at the G-20 summit in Pittsburg in September 2009, stating that Indonesia pledged a 26 percent voluntary emission reduction by 2020 to be funded by its state budget and a higher target of 41 percent with financial support from other countries. The Second National Communication (SNC) document launched in November 2009 contains a breakdown by sectors and other explanations about these targets. The Ministry of Finance Green Paper was also issued in November 2009, which put forward economic and fiscal policy strategies for climate change mitigation in Indonesia. Later that year, the Climate Change Sectoral Road Map was published by The National Planning Agency (Bappenas).

These documents are key references depicting Indonesian government policy on climate change. It is interesting to note that these documents select only mitigation in the energy sector while stating the importance of understanding the interaction of climate change policies with development objectives. If development objectives refer to merely GDP growth, this statement may not be contradictory. But various government documents mention that Indonesia's development objectives include other crucial matters such as eradication of poverty. In the energy context, this means everybody has the right to access energy as stipulated in article 19 of Law 30/ 2007 on energy. Focusing only on mitigation in the energy sector will not serve this objective.

The decision to set very few priorities in such high-level national policies is dangerously misleading the development path of this country. It denies the fact that Indonesia has specific challenges as a developing country, being an archipelago with thousands of small islands, scattered populations, and many inhabitants who do not have access to modern energy. The current policy approach therefore limits the possibilities to synergize energy programs in the context of climate change with the wider national development context.

Many energy policies and actions are as relevant for adaptation consideration as they are for mitigation. In an archipelago country like Indonesia, potential disruption of energy supply due to extreme weather affecting the rivers, shorelines, and oceans is an important and strategic matter. Utilization of indigenous energy sources, on both a small and large scale, is particularly important to shorten the chain of energy distribution. Hence energy diversification, the Self-Sufficient Energy Village, and various actions to enable renewable energy development and decentralized energy supply sources are as important as CO_2 emission reduction where national development is concerned. Synergizing this issue with climate change policy actions will enhance public benefit and therefore increase grass-roots support for government policy actions overall.

Governance

The incorporation of the energy security concepts and sustainable development dimensions implicitly calls for the application of principles of good governance. There are many elements of good governance, but in this study we focus on the institutional arrangement, decision-making process, and substantive issues. Recent government efforts to separate the role and functions of the regulator from those of the executives and the state-owned companies are a positive improvement from the institutional arrangement point of view.

However, inconsistencies, overlapping jurisdiction, and unclear arrangements for institutional roles and responsibility appear in many areas as consequences of the existing segregated or sector-based legal framework. Key to the success of policies is having clarity around objectives and lines of responsibility, and strong institutions (government and regulators). Coordination among policy-makers is also seen as essential. Indonesia has clear targets on innovation to develop key technologies, with anticipated strong and active private sector participation. The enactment of Law No. 30/2007 on energy is expected to integrate the energy management in Indonesia, both at macro and micro levels.

Based on an assessment of governance implementation in the electricity sector,[5] the decision-making process is now more open to public participation, although access is still limited to selected groups or individuals. Political interest and ad hoc decisions are easily influencing the public decision-making process, for example the National Development Program in 2000 stated that the energy subsidy program would be concluded in 2004 but it was abandoned in 2003 due to the approaching election in 2004. There is a lack of monitoring and evaluation processes during the decision-making process, and there is no clear mechanism on how the decision-makers should accommodate public input and reflect this in any proposed policies or regulations. On the substantive issues, the Indonesian energy sector is currently still facing uncertainty on where the reform will be and how regulation should be synchronized, both within the energy sector and across other sectors. These uncertainties must be resolved soon to enable a revival of investment in the energy sector that has been stagnant for the last ten years.

Concluding remarks

The above exercise is an initial attempt to portray the various elements that collectively form a benchmark towards energy security (ES) and sustainable development (SD). This approach is expected to allow for development of linkages between the short-term and longer-term considerations in energy policy and implementation decisions. As this is an initial step, more work is required to test this approach and make use of it in a more practical way.

Some of the indicators can be measured quantitatively by a specific formula, but most require a combination of some quantitative work and qualitative assessments. Based on this preliminary exercise, many indicators have a downward arrow sign implying that they are unsupportive towards ESSD. This may be due to the selection of the focus of assessment, or the way we see the issue fitting into the ESSD framework. Nevertheless, these indicators can also be used to identify which areas need improvements.

Many of the existing government programs may be improved by more comprehensive planning and preparation, adjusting to a more reasonable time frame and achievement target, and involving wider pubic participation to support the program implementation. Strategic coordination is crucial in order to minimize waste of resources. A regular monitoring and evaluation process should not be taken lightly, as it would provide useful feedbacks over time.

From a wider perspective, the authors and IIEE believe that the ESSD objectives would be best approached by triggering regional (sub-national) economic activities through indigenous energy resource development, considering the archipelagic nature of the country. Focusing economic development too heavily on Java will not support ESSD since it will soon be limited by its carrying capacity, while transporting energy from other islands to meet the enormous needs of Java's population would be cost-ineffective and limit the nation's growth.

Notes

1 Asia Pacific Energy Research Centre (APERC). 2007. *A Quest for Energy Security in the 21st Century* (Tokyo: APERC, Institute of Energy Economics).

2 International Atomic Energy Agency (IAEA). 2005. *Energy Security Indicators and Sustainable Development: Guidelines and Methodologies* (Vienna: IAEA).

3 Indriyanto, Ascelpias R.S., Bobby A.T. Wattimena, H. Batih, and I. Sari Triandi. 2007. "Rising Demand, Uncertain Supply, and Price Management." In Subroto (ed.), *Contesting Energy Security* (Jakarta: Indonesian Institute for Energy Economics), pp. 17–34.

4 Legowo, Evita. 2007. "Coal Use in Indonesia." In *Annual Meeting on National Energy Management*. (Jakarta, National Energy Management Institute, December).

5 The World Resources Institute. 2005. *Electricity Governance Initiatives: Case of Indonesia* (Jakarta: The World Resource Institute).

5

THE MARITIME DIMENSION OF ENERGY SECURITY

Carolin Liss

In 2004, a Chinese newspaper declared that "It is no exaggeration to say that whoever controls the Strait of Malacca will also have a stranglehold on the energy route of China."[1] This quote illustrates that the transport of energy resources is of crucial importance to China and that there is an acute awareness of the dependence on, and vulnerability of, essential goods such as oil and gas transported by ships through waters like the Malacca Strait.

Like China, many countries around the world today rely on (imported) oil, gas, and other energy resources transported by sea. This makes the safety of shipping and sea lines of communication (SLOC) crucially important, linking maritime security closely to energy security. This chapter examines that link, focusing on the safety of transporting energy resources by merchant vessels.[2] While there are numerous threats to shipping, this chapter is particularly concerned with two of the new and now widely discussed threats: modern piracy and maritime terrorism. It examines whether the activities of pirates and terrorists can disrupt maritime transport to such a degree that transporting energy resources is jeopardized and energy security is adversely affected. The chapter first provides a brief overview of the role of shipping in transporting resources such as oil and gas across the globe. It then discusses key security challenges to the safe transit of merchant vessels carrying energy resources, with particular attention to the threat posed by pirates and terrorists in the Malacca Strait and Gulf of Aden area. Finally, the chapter offers an evaluation of the threat to energy security posed by these non-state actors.

The importance of maritime transport

As Stopford points out, "[s]eaborne trade is, in a sense, at the apex of world economic activity."[3] In fact, more than 90 percent of world trade is transported by ships, with around 50,000 merchant vessels plying the world's oceans. Among them are bulk carriers transporting raw materials such as coal, and tankers carrying goods that include chemicals, oil, and gas. The volume of trade by sea has increased significantly over the past few decades, due to the industrialization of countries around the world and the expansion of the capitalist world system, which has brought with it the liberalization of trade and an ever increasing demand for consumer goods.[4] Shipping has remained the cornerstone of international trade because transport by sea is comparatively reliable, fast, and cheap—enabling goods to be transported speedily from one end of the world to the other without significantly increasing the price for the consumer. Technological advances

113

and changes such as the introduction of containers, the construction of safer and larger vessels, as well as high-speed cargo handling systems have been largely responsible for ensuring that shipping remains, in many instances, significantly cheaper than transporting goods over land.[5] As Stopford observes, "it is often cheaper for industries to import raw materials by sea from suppliers thousands of miles away than by land from suppliers only a few hundred miles away."[6]

Accelerating industrialization and economic development in countries around the world has led over the years to increasing demand for energy and the resources needed to satisfy that demand.[7] To satisfy their energy hunger, many countries rely on imported oil, gas, and other energy resources,[8] with these commodities today forming a substantial part of seaborne trade. "Energy trades," encompassing trade in goods such as oil products, crude oil, liquefied gas, and thermal coal used for generating electricity, account for 45 percent of maritime trade.[9] While the volume of these imported and exported commodities varies between countries, the fact that 45 percent of all seaborne commerce is in energy trades indicates the vast quantity of such goods traded internationally and, by association, the importance of these commodities for both the world economy and individual states. The safety of maritime trade is consequently of concern to governments around the world, particularly those that rely heavily on imported energy resources, such as the United States, China, and Japan.[10] In fact, the safety of shipping and SLOCs is becoming more and more important, with increasing attention being paid to an expanding range of maritime security threats that can adversely affect the safety of maritime trade and consequently the energy supply and energy security of countries around the world.

Threats and dangers to international shipping

Seafaring and shipping have always been associated with adventure and hazard. Indeed, any voyage of a ship anywhere in the world has its dangers. Rough seas and weather continuously threaten the safety of shipping in oceans and waterways around the globe. Other risks, mainly those associated with navigation, are also a concern. The grounding on April 3, 2010 of the Chinese coal carrier *Shen Neng 1* on Australia's Great Barrier Reef is but one example.[11] Congestion in some sea lanes and waterways also makes collision of merchant vessels still a real danger.

However, improvements in ship design and construction, as well as technological advances such as modern navigation equipment, have vastly improved the safety of shipping. Regulation of maritime traffic, including the introduction of traffic separation schemes in congested waterways, also contributes significantly to safe conduct of the large number of vessels plying the world's oceans and waterways today.[12] This is why, even though issues such as the construction of vessels and navigation remain important, the focus in securing international maritime trade has arguably shifted in recent years to increasingly include threats from beyond the realm of shipbuilding and regulation of maritime traffic. Among those "external" threats, two are of particular importance at present, namely maritime piracy and terrorism.

Piracy

Defining piracy is essential, but difficult. "Piracy" remains a highly contested term, with no standardized definition agreed upon by institutions, academics, and governments around the world. One of the most controversial issues concerning a uniform definition of piracy is still whether the motive behind a pirate attack should be a defining factor. Equally contested is whether only attacks committed on the high seas should be considered piracy or whether attacks on vessels in territorial waters, within Exclusive Economic Zones (EEZs), and in ports, also qualify as piracy.

Nevertheless, two definitions of piracy can be considered the most prominent and commonly used at present. The first is the legal definition of piracy implemented in both the 1958 Geneva Convention on the Law of the Sea and the 1982 UN Convention on the Law of the Sea (UNCLOS).[13] Article 101 of UNCLOS defines piracy as:

Piracy consists of any of the following acts:

(a) any illegal acts of violence or detention, or any act of depredation, committed for private ends by the crew or the passengers of a private ship or a private aircraft, and directed:

    (i) on the high seas, against another ship or aircraft, or against persons or property on board such ship or aircraft;

    (ii) against a ship, aircraft, persons or property in a place outside the jurisdiction of any State;

(b) any act of voluntary participation in the operation of a ship or of an aircraft with knowledge of facts making it a pirate ship or aircraft;

(c) any act of inciting or of intentionally facilitating an act described in subparagraph (a) or (b).[14]

Many observers see the UNCLOS definition as problematic and impractical as it only includes attacks on the high seas "outside the jurisdiction of any State." Yet the majority of contemporary reported pirate attacks on vessels are conducted in territorial waters, EEZs, or ports, and are therefore clearly within the jurisdiction of coastal states.

The second commonly used definition of piracy is the more inclusive version of the Piracy Reporting Centre (PRC) of the International Maritime Bureau (IMB). The rising number of pirate attacks in Asia in the 1980s prompted the establishment of the IMB's Regional Piracy Reporting Centre in Kuala Lumpur in October 1992. The Centre initially provided services only for the East Asian Region, including Northeast and Southeast Asia. However, in 1998 the name of the agency was changed to PRC and the Centre began to collect reports on piracy and armed robbery at sea from all around the world. Today the PRC also issues warnings to seafarers, liaises with law enforcement authorities, issues consolidated reports to interested bodies, and regularly publishes reports on piracy and armed robbery at sea.[15] In these reports, the IMB relies on its own definition of piracy, and includes in its analysis any "act of boarding any vessel with the intent to commit theft or any other crime and with the intent or capability to use force in the furtherance of that act."[16] The IMB's reports therefore include information on attempted attacks, attacks on vessels at anchorage or at berth, simple hit-and-run robberies in territorial waters, as well as hijackings of vessels, and, controversially, certain acts of maritime terrorism. The IMB's definition of piracy will be adopted here with the proviso that those acts have to be committed for private— as opposed to political—ends.

The IMB's definition of piracy and its data are controversial, not only because they include terrorist attacks. Some observers have, for example, pointed to the serious problem of under-reporting of attacks, suggesting that the actual number of pirate attacks worldwide may be substantially higher than presented in the IMB's reports. Regional Manager of the PRC, Noel Choong, claims that more than 50 percent of all pirate attacks remain unreported.[17] Some shipowners are reluctant to report attacks as they fear an investigation will delay their vessels' operation, resulting in additional costs. Many also do not want to be branded as unreliable carriers of freight or they fear rising insurance costs. Governments and law enforcement agencies in the

Table 5.1 Attacks and attempted attacks worldwide, the Asian region, and African region, 1995–2006

	'97	'98	'99	'00	'01	'02	'03	'04	'05	'06	'07	'08	'09
Actual and attempted* attacks worldwide	247	202	300	469	335	370	445	329	276	239	263	293	406
Actual attacks worldwide	205	166	242	318	238	286	332	237	205	176	187	200	202
Actual and attempted attacks Asian Region*	117	105	191	314	190	197	246	188	143	134	93	77	85
Actual attacks Asian Region	94	78	152	208	138	155	177	136	112	100	75	68	70
Actual and attempted attacks African Region**	37	38	49	67	85	73	93	72	79	61	120	189	264
Actual attacks African Region	28	34	36	40	59	51	66	50	47	41	77	108	86

Source: International Chamber of Commerce, *Piracy and Armed Robbery against Ships. Annual Reports 1995–2009.*
Notes:
* The Asian Region here includes: Indonesia, Malaysia, Malacca Strait, Myanmar, Philippines, Singapore Straits, Thailand, South China Sea, China, Cambodia, HLH Area, Bangladesh, and Vietnam.
** Includes: Algeria, Angola, Benin, Cameroon, Congo, Dem. Republic Congo, Egypt, Eritrea, Equatorial Guinea, Gabon, Ghana, Guinea, Guinea Bissau, Gulf of Aden, Ivory Coast, Kenya, Liberia, Madagascar, Mauritania, Morocco, Mozambique, Nigeria, Red Sea, Senegal, Sierra Leone, Somalia, South Africa, Tanzania, Togo, and Zaire.

region are also often reluctant to disclose the number of attacks in their respective countries to preserve their reputations as safe places for trade and passage.[18]Acknowledging these limits on data collection, the IMB arguably offers the most comprehensive database on contemporary piracy.

According to the IMB, the number of actual and attempted pirate attacks reported between 1992 and 2009 ranges from 90 in 1994 to 469 in 2000 (Table 5.1). Piracy is concentrated in specific geographic areas, with most attacks reported in developing countries in Asia and Africa. IMB statistics show that until recently, Asia—including Southeast Asia, the South China Seas, and China—has been the most "pirate-infested" region in the world, with piracy hot spots in this area shifting over time. The waters between the Malacca and Singapore Straits have been identified as the world's most pirate-prone seas between 1990 and 1992, but after the initiation of coordinated anti-piracy patrols in this area, the focus of piracy shifted to the South China Sea, where a high proportion of reported attacks took place between 1993 and 1995. Particularly affected were the territorial waters of Hong Kong and Macau and the so-called HLH "terror triangle," encompassing the waters between Hong Kong, Luzon in the Philippines, and the Chinese island of Hainan.[19] After Chinese authorities tightened control in their waters, pirate attacks in Chinese waters ceased by the mid-1990s. Since the mid-1990s, as Suharto's New Order regime unravelled, Indonesian ports and territorial waters have been identified as the world's most pirate-infested seas.[20] In 2004, for instance, Indonesia accounted for 93 out of 325 attacks recorded worldwide.[21] Outside Indonesia, Bangladesh's waters were the site of a spate of attacks in the early twenty-first century, while high numbers of attacks in the busy Malacca and Singapore Straits rekindled earlier concerns (Table 5.2).

Since 2007, pirate attacks in Asia have been overshadowed by large numbers of serious incidents off the coast of Africa (Table 5.1). Pirate attacks in this region occurred throughout the 1990s and into the twenty-first century, but with the exception of Nigeria where significant numbers of pirate attacks occurred throughout these years,[22] generally only very small numbers of

Table 5.2 Attacks and attempted attacks: Gulf of Aden area and Malacca Strait

	'97	'98	'99	'00	'01	'02	'03	'04	'05	'06	'07	'08	'09
Gulf of Aden and Red Sea (actual and attempted)	0	0	0	13	11	11	18	8	10	10	13	92	111
Gulf of Aden and Red Sea (actual)	0	0	0	0	1	1	3	2	0	1	1	34	20
Somalia (actual and attempted)	4	9*	11*	9*	8*	6*	3*	2*	35	10	31	19	80
Somalia (actual)	2	6*	5*	2*	3*	4	3*	1*	16	5	11	10	27
Malacca Strait (actual and attempted attacks)		1	2	75	17	16	28	37	12	11	7	2	2
Malacca Strait (actual attacks)		1		37	8	13	9	17	7	6	3		2

Source: International Chamber of Commerce, *Piracy and Armed Robbery against Ships. Annual Reports 1995–2009.*
Note:
★ Somalia/Djibouti

attacks were reported from African countries. This changed in 2007, when the number of serious attacks reported from the waters off Somalia, including the Gulf of Aden and the Red Sea, began to surge (Table 5.2).[23]

Terrorism

The second kind of non-state actors who pose a threat to shipping are terrorists. As in defining piracy, defining terrorism is difficult. Part of the problem, as Walter Laqueur points out, is that terrorism is not an ideology but an insurrectional strategy, which can be used by people of very different political convictions.[24] Moreover, the meaning and use of the word terrorism have been changed from the time of the French Revolution, when the term was first brought into common political usage, to accommodate the ideological vernacular and discourse of subsequent eras.[25] The search for a satisfactory definition is further complicated by the fact that many so-called terrorists do not consider themselves to be terrorists, but rather prefer other terms such as freedom fighters or militants.[26] Acknowledging these semantic, albeit political–cultural, difficulties, Hoffman suggests that:

> We may ... attempt to define terrorism as the deliberate creation and exploitation of fear through violence or the threat of violence in the pursuit of political change. All terrorist acts involve violence or the threat of violence. Terrorism is specifically designed to have far-reaching psychological effects beyond the immediate victim(s) or object of the terrorist attack. It is meant to instil fear within, and thereby intimidate, a wider "target audience" that might include a rival ethnic or religious group, an entire country, a national government or political party, or public opinion in general.[27]

The motives of terrorists therefore distinguish these actors from ordinary criminals, including pirates, who are mainly interested in personal financial gain.[28] However, the boundaries between politically motivated and criminally motivated acts and groups can be blurred, as exemplified by the increasing criminalization of terrorist movements.

Terrorist organizations have conducted a range of maritime attacks in different parts of the world. For example, the Philippines-based group Abu Sayyaf was responsible for the bombing off Corregidor Island in February 2004 of the *SuperFerry 14*, in which more than 100 people lost their lives.[29] Passenger vessels such as ferries, and even more so cruise ships, are believed to be particularly likely terrorist targets because they carry a large number of often middle-class Western passengers.[30] The threat to, or killing of, these passengers would certainly create a media spectacle, focusing worldwide attention on the terrorist act and the group responsible. Merchant vessels with their skeleton crews are in this respect less likely targets. Yet ocean vessels transporting energy supplies—oil tankers and LNG carriers in particular—present different opportunities to create fear and terror. These vessels are also believed to be high-profile targets since they can be, it is feared, turned into floating bombs and exploded in ports. However, such a scenario is not easy to achieve, particularly with LNG carriers which are particularly difficult to set on fire.[31]

According to the RAND Terrorism Database, only 2 percent of terrorist attacks have targeted maritime installations or vessels in the past 30 years.[32] The low percentage of maritime attacks is accounted for by the fact that overall, maritime attacks are more difficult to conduct, as the "recondite nature of the sea compared to the familiarity of land, ... complicates terrorist operations."[33] Maritime targets are also often out of sight of witnesses, spectators, and media representatives and are consequently less appealing to terrorists seeking media spectacle and international attention.[34]

Piracy and terrorism: the threat to shipping

With only around 2 percent of terrorist attacks carried out in the maritime sphere, the question arises as to whether terrorism today is a serious threat to international shipping. Indeed, RAND's Database of Worldwide Terrorism Incidents lists "only" 26 attacks on maritime targets between 1990 and 2007.[35] A closer look at the threat posed by pirates leads to similar questions. While significantly more pirate attacks than maritime terrorist incidents are reported, closer examination of the IMB data reveals that many attacks included in the statistics are only "attempted" attacks. Furthermore, most of the actual incidents recorded in these data are simple hit-and-run robberies conducted either at sea or in harbors, and in which nothing but a length of rope or a can of paint is stolen. The pirates responsible for such attacks are mostly opportunistic thieves or fishermen trying to top-up their income in times of need. The incidents included in the IMB statistics and the low number of maritime terrorist attacks also appear insignificant when compared with the large number of vessels and seafarers involved in the global shipping industry, particularly if fishing vessels and other small craft are included in the calculation. Yet despite these considerations, piracy and maritime terrorism are taken seriously and are regarded as threats to international shipping, mainly because of two interconnected factors.

First, particularly in terms of terrorism, the threat is taken seriously because of the scale and nature of transnational terrorist attacks in recent years, which have increased the feeling of insecurity among people in targeted countries and places believed to be potential targets. These developments have also led to the identification of "high profile" or "likely" terrorist targets on the basis of what is perceived to be their strategic, cultural, or economic importance. Such likely targets include some in the maritime sphere, mainly because of the economic significance of seaborne trade and major ports. Organizations such as al-Qaeda have therefore accomplished one of their goals by spreading fear through perceived vulnerability, even in places that have not been targeted and where the risk of an attack is comparatively low, such as in the maritime sphere. The most "successful" terrorist act in this regard was the September 11 attack in the US. Examining the perceived threat of terrorism since September 11, 2001, Jackson concludes that: "In a world of multiple threats, many of which pose a far greater risk to individual safety, the fact that terrorism is widely seen as posing the greatest and most immediate threat is due to the deliberate construction of a discourse of danger."[36] It can be argued that fear of a major maritime terrorist attack is, at least in part, a direct result of this discourse.

Piracy, too, has drawn attention in this context, with a number of observers conflating piracy and terrorism, arguing that a high number of pirate attacks in a certain area translates directly into heightened risk of a maritime terrorist attack.[37] Despite the absence of factual evidence, such observers claim that, for example, pirates and terrorists could cooperate with each other. The level of likely collusion is contested. Moderate observers have argued that terrorists can learn from pirates by observing their activities and copying their practices.[38] Others have suggested that pirates may work directly for (or with) terrorists, helping terrorists in actual attacks on merchant vessels and/or in navigating hijacked ships.[39] More tendentious illustrations of such an event envision "pirates" hijacking a tanker which is then turned into a floating bomb and exploded in a United States port.[40] It has also been argued that "pirates could sell assets such as maritime and littoral knowledge, stolen vessels (such as tugs) and stolen documentation to conventional terrorists, who could then leverage these assets into a large-scale terrorist attack on a port."[41]

Second, piracy and maritime terrorism are mostly a concern in specific waters, including those identified as high-profile terrorist targets such as major US ports,[42] and so-called piracy hot spots such as the waters of Indonesia where a large number of pirate attacks occur. However, achieving a complete shutdown of a port is extremely difficult for terrorists, and major ports in developed countries are reasonably well protected.[43] Also, in countries where high numbers of pirate attacks are recorded, ships may be able to avoid high-risk waters if the potential attacks are serious enough to justify this move. Concerns about attacks at sea therefore center, arguably, on maritime chokepoints such as strategic waterways/straits, particularly those in politically volatile regions. It is more difficult for ships to avoid such chokepoints since alternative routes substantially prolong a ship's journey. Furthermore, unlike major ports in economically developed countries where security is comparatively tight, waterways in politically volatile areas, while also of strategic importance, are generally less well protected. Pirates and terrorists, who have their bases in such areas, greatly benefit from such an environment. For instance, it is easier for pirates or terrorists to obtain weapons to conduct their operations in areas of civil conflict or war where weapons are widely available.

Ships are particularly vulnerable when passing through such chokepoints/straits because they have to slow down to traverse these areas and travel fairly close to the coast. Here ships are easier targets for pirates or terrorists to approach and board. There is also no shortage of targets as chokepoints are often rather congested. Also, the consequences of attacks in such vulnerable areas can potentially be more severe than those of attacks in other waters, and in a worst case scenario can result in the temporary closure of a strait or chokepoint. Although very difficult for them technically, terrorists may plan to sink vessels in such strategic areas to prevent merchant ships from passing through.[44] Pirate attacks, even though not motivated by the intent to block a passage, could possibly lead to a maritime accident with similar outcomes. For countries relying on energy resources shipped through such vulnerable areas, blockage caused by pirates or terrorists can have significant consequences, including delays in the delivery of energy resources.

Two maritime chokepoints are currently the focus of concern about pirate/terrorist activities: the Malacca Strait and the Gulf of Aden area.

The Malacca Strait and the Gulf of Aden

The Malacca Strait and the Gulf of Aden are strategically important waterways and play a significant role in international trade. Both have been considered piracy hot spots in recent years and because of their global importance as transit routes, these waterways have also been identified as high risk areas for a maritime terrorist attack.

The Malacca Strait

The Malacca Strait, which connects the Indian Ocean with the South China Sea, is one of the busiest waterways in the world. More than 60,000 merchant vessels transit the strait each year. Tankers carrying oil from the Middle East to countries such as China and Japan, which rely heavily on imported oil, are just some of the vessels passing through the waterway each day.[45] In fact, about 90 percent of Japan's crude oil imports and up to 80 percent of China's oil imports travel this route.[46] Singapore harbor and other ports in Asia, such as Hong Kong, Shanghai, and Shenzen, rank among those with the highest container turnover rate and total cargo volume in the world.[47] Vessels bound for these ports, or for other major East and Southeast Asian harbors, pass through the Malacca Strait. The area also has oil, gas, and mineral resources, with both onshore and offshore energy installations in operation. Companies extracting oil, gas, or other natural resources therefore depend on offshore platforms or terminals along the coast from which the extracted goods are shipped around the world.

Security is a concern in the Malacca Strait because criminal gangs as well as politically motivated groups, such as the terrorist group Jemaah Islamiyah (JI) and (at least until recently) the guerrilla group Free Aceh Movement (Gerakan Aceh Merdeka or GAM), are active in the vicinity of the waterway. Marginalization of parts of the population and persistent poverty in a number of places along the strait, such as the Riau Archipelago, Indonesia, are conducive to radical politically motivated groups and criminal activities. Such criminal activities include pirate attacks conducted by both opportunistic sea robbers and organized pirate gangs that hijack vessels or kidnap crew. As discussed previously, piracy was a concern in the Malacca Strait in the early 1990s and again in the early twentieth century. According to IMB data, the number of reported pirate attacks in the Malacca Strait jumped from 2 in 1999 to 75 in 2000. In the following six years, the numbers remained worrisome: with 17 incidents reported in 2001, 16 in 2002, 28 in 2003, 37 in 2004, 12 in 2005, and 11 in 2006. In the three years following, the numbers sank below ten attacks a year (Table 5.2).

The attacks in the Malacca Strait are a major concern because some of them have been serious, including the kidnapping of crew for ransom.[48] Although the vast majority of pirate attacks in the Malacca Strait have been simple "hit-and-run" robberies, some were conducted by organized pirate gangs—or syndicates—that attack predominantly medium-sized vessels including cargo ships, bulk carriers, and tankers. In these cases, a vessel and its crew are held hostage for a limited time, or the entire vessel is hijacked by pirates and is then turned into a "phantom ship." The attack on the Japanese-owned tanker *Global Mars* is one such serious incident. On February 23, 2000, the *Global Mars* was attacked in the Malacca Strait by a gang of 20 pirates who overpowered the 18-man crew and took control of the vessel. The pirates repainted the tanker, renamed it *Bulawan*, and replaced its Panamanian flag with the colours of Honduras. After completing the change of identity, the pirates sailed the *Bulawan* to an unidentified port where the cargo was sold. After 13 days in captivity, the crew were moved to a smaller fishing boat, set adrift, and ultimately rescued off the coast of Phuket. The *Bulawan* was eventually found in Chinese waters and the local authorities, acting on information from the IMB, seized the ship and arrested the "crew" onboard on May 30.[49]

Politically motivated groups, too, are active near the Malacca Strait. The GAM, which signed a peace agreement with the Indonesian authorities in 2005 after almost three decades of struggle for independence of the Aceh region from Indonesia, has been blamed for a number of attacks on fishing boats and merchant vessels in the strait. These include an attack with an explicitly political agenda—the assault in June 2002 on a supply vessel chartered by oil company ExxonMobil, whose activities in Aceh GAM are regarded as very problematic.[50] However, the vast majority of attacks allegedly involving the GAM appear to have economic rather than political motivations. Examples include the attacks on the Malaysian MT *Penrider* in August 2003 and the Indonesian MT *Tri Samudra* in March 2005. In both cases, hostages were taken, a ransom was demanded, and the kidnapped crew were released unharmed after the ransom was paid.[51] Allegations that the kidnappers were GAM members have been voiced by the shipowner of the *Tri Samudra* and the sailors taken hostage from the *Penrider*, who described their captors as uniformed men who spoke Acehnese. Some of the captives were reportedly taken to a GAM camp in the jungle of Aceh.[52] Yet whether the GAM was really responsible for these attacks remains contested, with alternative explanations blaming actors such as rogue GAM fighters or members of the Indonesian military intentionally posing as GAM members to tarnish the group's reputation. Overall these and similar attacks allegedly conducted by the GAM can probably be described better as "piracy" rather than terrorism as the motive was financial gain. It is believed that the purpose of such attacks by politically motivated groups is to gain funds to finance their operations or simply to provide an income for group members. Clearly, the boundaries between a pirate attack and a politically motivated act are blurred in these cases, since the money from such attacks may have been used to finance the GAM's politically motivated struggle. Nevertheless, the pirate attacks allegedly conducted by GAM demonstrate the difference between attacks conducted for financial gain and terrorist acts. The difference in motivation between terrorists and pirates (including members of politically motivated movements taking action to acquire funds) is reflected in the perpetrators' modus operandi. Unlike terrorists who seek media spectacle and self-projection, those responsible for pirate attacks shun public attention and do not exploit the kidnapping of crews to voice their grievances or political demands.

Apart from the GAM, no other politically motivated group has yet been involved in—or accused of—attacks on shipping in the Malacca Strait. However, groups such as JI and al-Qaeda are believed to be interested in targeting ships in the strait. Indeed, only a few months after the September 11, 2001 attacks, Singaporean intelligence discovered al-Qaeda plans for a series of attacks, including on a US warship visiting Singapore.[53] The most recent Malacca Strait terror alert was issued in early 2010, warning of attacks on oil tankers in the waterway. While no details were made public, JI is widely suspected to be the group planning such attacks.[54]

The Gulf of Aden

The Gulf of Aden is also of vital strategic importance, with more than 20,000 vessels passing through every year while travelling between Europe and the Middle East, Asia, and Australia, carrying, among other goods, oil from the Middle East.[55] The security concerns about the safety of ships passing the Horn of Africa stem largely from the political instability of Somalia. The country has often been described as a failed state, and has been without effective government since 1991. Since the end of the Cold War when the country's central government collapsed, Somalia has been ruled by a succession of varying coalitions of politicians and local warlords. With weapons widely available, armed conflict and violence have been a constant component of "politics" in Somalia. Famine and other natural and man-made disasters have been a further long-term burden for the country's population. Hundreds of thousands of Somali people have lost their lives and an estimated 2.5 million urgently need assistance.[56] Given the political instability, to the limited extent that authorities in Somalia exist and function, they are unable to provide security for shipping in the nation's waters, particularly because there are more pressing issues to address.

The waters off the coast of Somalia have also not remained trouble free. Indeed, the world's most blatant pirate attacks currently take place in the Gulf of Aden area, encompassing the Gulf of Aden, the Red Sea, and Somali waters. In the two years of 2008 and 2009, more than

300 ships were attacked in this dangerous area (see Table 5.2). These attacks included more than 85 hijackings of merchant and fishing vessels, with the pirates receiving millions of US dollars in ransom money for kidnapped crew and hijacked ships. Pirates in the area hold several ships at a time, while negotiating ransoms with shipowners. The negotiation processes can take months, while crews are held hostage. Among the vessels attacked are the Ukrainian freighter *La Faina*, hijacked on September 25, 2008 while carrying 33 combat tanks and other weaponry, and the supertanker *Sirius Star*, hijacked less than two months later. The *Sirius Star*, a new ship worth approximately US$150 million, was at the time the largest vessel ever taken by pirates and was carrying a cargo of crude oil valued at US$100 million. While the *Sirius Star* was released in January 2009 after a ransom payment of reportedly US$3 million, the hijacking of the supertanker clearly demonstrated the capacity of Somali pirates to attack ships of any size.[57]

The pirates responsible for these attacks are mostly Somali fishermen and other local residents. They are well equipped with firearms and have used mother ships to conduct attacks too far from the coast for speedboats to reach. The use of mother ships has become increasingly important as pirates attack ships further and further out at sea. Many attacks no longer take place in the Gulf of Aden; instead the targets are ships travelling to and from the chokepoint. There is little indication that piracy in these waters will cease because the attacks are extremely lucrative and therefore "successful" for the pirates. It is believed that pirates now use their newfound wealth to buy additional boats and weapons for future attacks, as well as personal goods. With few exceptions, the pirate attacks have not resulted in deaths or major physical injuries of crew members. The perpetrators have so far treated their hostages comparatively well and have released the hostages once ransoms are paid. Nonetheless, the pirates have made serious threats to ensure that the ransom is paid. Among the most serious is the recent threat to blow up the hijacked Korean-owned supertanker *Samho Dream*. The 320,000 tonne tanker was on its way from Iraq to the United States, carrying a cargo of oil valued at US$170 million, when it was hijacked on April 4, 2010. The perpetrators have demanded US$20 million in exchange for the tanker and the 24 crew members onboard.[58]

Despite the serious nature of these threats, the pirates' objective remains the collection of ransom money and no political demands have been voiced by pirates. Some speculation has linked pirates with politically motivated groups but this remains unsubstantiated. Like the Malacca Strait, the Gulf of Aden is a strategic maritime chokepoint and may therefore be regarded as a potential target for terrorist groups that are active in the vicinity, including al-Qaeda.[59] Certainly, fear of maritime terrorist attacks in this area intensified after two such attacks in Yemen just inside the new century. First was the bombing of the guided-missile destroyer USS *Cole* in October 2000 by al-Qaeda. Second was the attack on the French tanker *Limburg* in 2002, for which both Al-Qaeda and the Aden Abyan Islamic Army (AAIA) have been blamed.[60]

Impact on energy security—a conclusion

Terrorism and piracy are clearly concerns in the Gulf of Aden area and the Malacca Strait, and should be taken seriously. However, it can be argued that in the Malacca Strait, the current level of attacks does not pose a significant threat to energy security. The number of pirate attacks is small when compared with the large number of vessels passing through this area. For example, in 2004 when 37 attempted and actual attacks were reported in the Malacca Strait, the risk of a vessel being targeted in this waterway was less than 0.06 percent.[61] Furthermore, most pirate attacks are minor hit-and-run affairs that can be traumatic for seafarers onboard, but do not seriously affect maritime transport of energy resources. Major attacks, such as the attack on the tanker *Global Mars*, are clearly more dangerous. Such

Table 5.3 Maritime terrorism

Potential Maritime Terrorist Targets	Examples
Passenger vessels (ferries, cruise ships)	Unknown: August 28, 2005, Philippines. Thirty people were injured when a bomb exploded on a passenger ferry in Lamitan, Basilan.
Merchant vessels (container ships, tankers, etc.)	Al-Fatah: December 25, 1993, Israel. An Israeli vessel was bombed while in the port of Eilat.
Ports	Harkat ul-Mujahidin: May 25, 2004, Pakistan. Two people were killed and two injured when a bomb exploded in the port of Karachi.
Offshore oil/gas platforms and supply vessels	NA
Maritime workers/personnel	Al-Qaeda: September 7, 2008, Algeria. At least 30 Coast Guard troops were killed in an explosion.

Source: RAND, "RAND Database of Worldwide Terrorism Incidents." Available at: http://smapp.rand.org/rwtid (accessed April 18, 2010).

attacks, however, only occur occasionally in the Malacca Strait and while the loss of a tanker is a concern, it will not disrupt maritime trade or energy supply.

However, in regard to major attacks such as hijackings and temporary seizures of ships, another factor may be more significant in relation to energy security. In these attacks the pirates overpower the crew and take control of the vessel or simply leave it at sea with no one in control. Unmanned floating ships can easily produce accidents, including collisions with other vessels or major oil spills that can adversely affect shipping in the strait temporarily. Terrorist attacks could have a similar effect, though as yet no politically motivated group has been involved in a serious attack in the Malacca Strait. Also, blocking the strait by sinking vessels is a difficult task, and even though "almost half of the world's fleet would have to travel further" if the Malacca Strait was closed,[62] bypassing the waterway requires only an extra two to five days of steaming.[63] Such a delay could cause short-term problems in those economies relying on just-in-time delivery of energy resources and it would increase freight costs, but, as Chalk writes, a "long-term or widespread disruption to the global economy is unlikely."[64]

Today the level of threat to shipping is considerably higher in the Gulf of Aden area than in the Malacca Strait. While terrorists planning to target vessels in the Gulf area would face problems similar to those facing terrorists in the Malacca Strait, the level and seriousness of pirate attacks in the Gulf area at present are unprecedented. Never before have modern pirates been able to hijack such a large number of vessels, including supertankers. The incidents cause concern for the safety of shipping, of the crews on board vessels, and of the environment, and have consequently increased insurance costs for ships passing through the Gulf area. Furthermore, unlike in the Malacca Strait, the risk of being targeted in these waters is now perceived to be so high that some major shipping companies have considered or even decided to reroute their vessels around the Cape of Good Hope, adding an additional 12 to 20 days to the journey. Rerouting vessels also increases transport costs, with one shipping company estimating that using the longer route may increase these costs by up to 40 percent.[65] Attacks in the Gulf of Aden area therefore affect energy security more severely than attacks in the Malacca Strait, causing additional costs, longer transport time and, in cases where tankers or other ships carrying energy resources are hijacked, a delay in delivery or a possible loss of the cargo. Generally, the additional time at sea is a serious problem only for the delivery of some perishable goods, such as LNG. As Forbes writes:

The LNG trade depends on rapid transport to the shore infrastructure before the gas degrades. Any delays to scheduled delivery would have a two-fold impact. First, reducing the quality of the gas delivered (which might affect the energy infrastructure and/or future export contracts); and second, where an economy is geared to just-in-time deliveries for energy products, delays could severely impact the general economy.[66]

However, piracy has so far not prevented ships from passing through the Gulf of Aden area. This situation gives shipping companies time to consider their options, taking into account longer routes and delivery times. Although the comparatively low cost of maritime transport ensures that longer voyages are still financially tenable, longer travelling times may mean that shipping companies require more ships and have to draw on the surplus of ships available. This may raise concern when the world economy is booming, but finding surplus vessels is not likely to be a major challenge in times like the present (early 2010) when the adverse effects of financial crisis have reduced the volume of maritime trade.[67]

The attacks in the Gulf of Aden area are also a reminder why it is important to ensure that piracy does not escalate, and while maritime terrorist attacks are rare, they are possible in all waters around the world. Securing SLOCs, and particularly maritime chokepoints, is therefore extremely important. While shipping companies carry some responsibility to ensure the safety of their vessels, states and law enforcement agencies are, overall, the primary providers of security for ships in ports and waters under their jurisdiction. Unfortunately, the weaknesses of states where attacks take place make it difficult for them to address the problem. In fact, while the scale of pirate attacks differs between the Gulf of Aden area and the Malacca Strait, in both locations pirates are predominantly operating from one country, that is, the weakest of the littoral states. In the Malacca Strait, the majority of pirates are based in Indonesia, while sea robbers from Somalia are mainly responsible for attacks in the Gulf of Aden.

Nevertheless there are also major differences between the two waterways and their respective littoral states, which shape the character of pirate attacks. Southeast Asian countries, including those bordering the Malacca Strait, have comparatively stable governments and have in recent decades experienced rapid economic development. Economic success has enabled Southeast Asian countries to strengthen and modernize their defence forces, including their navies.[68] Over the past years the Malacca Strait's littoral states have implemented a number of anti-piracy and anti-terrorism measures, including coordinated air and sea patrols. Authorities in Somalia, on the contrary, were not able to combat piracy or terrorism at sea and the international community has taken steps to address these problems. Multilateral anti-terrorism operations, such as those conducted by the Combined Task Force 150, have been in place for years, many being part of the so-called "War on Terrorism."[69] The frequent and serious attacks on vessels off the coast of Somalia over the past two years have also led nations around the world to send warships to combat piracy in the area. These nations include the US, Canada, Britain, Germany, France, Russia, Malaysia, China, and India. Many of their patrol vessels are part of missions sanctioned or organized by multilateral organizations, including NATO and the EU.[70]

Yet, the continuation of serious pirate attacks in the Gulf of Aden area suggests that current efforts to combat piracy in the region—even including involvement of naval forces from countries around the world—are not sufficient to prevent major attacks. Likewise in the Malacca Strait, despite the efforts of the littoral states, piracy has not been eradicated and maritime terrorism remains a concern. In the Malacca Strait and Gulf of Aden area (as well as all other waters) careful consideration therefore needs to be given to new measures to combat piracy and terrorism that will also address the root causes of these threats to ensure the safety of all shipping, including vessels carrying energy resources.

Notes

1 Quoted in Storey, Ian. 2006. "China's 'Malacca Dilemma'," *China Brief* VI (8) (11 April). Available at: http://www.jamestown.org/programs/chinabrief/single/?tx_ttnews[tt_news]=31575&tx_ttnews [backPid]=196&no_cache=1 (accessed April 16, 2010).

2 While the focus of this discussion is the safety of transporting energy resources by merchant vessels, it is important to note here other significant related issues such as the safety of offshore oil platforms and links between energy security, maritime security, and environmental security. These remain beyond the ambit of this chapter given its specific focus.

3 Stopford, Martin. 2004. *Maritime Economics*, 2nd edn. (London: Routledge), p. 2.

4 Maritime International Secretariat Services Limited (Marisec),"Shipping and World Trade. Value of Volume of World Trade by Sea." 2010, Available at: http://www.marisec.org/shippingfacts/world-trade/volume-world-trade-sea.php?SID=a6012e9a0145fe8c15d3e9d4f5ba181a (accessed April 16, 2010); Maritime International Secretariat Services Limited (Marisec), "Key Facts. Overview of the International Shipping Industry." Available at: http://www.marisec.org/shippingfacts/keyfacts/ (accessed April 16, 2010).

5 Stopford, *Maritime Economics*, pp. 2–6.

6 Stopford, *Maritime Economics*, p. 4.

7 For statistics on increasing energy consumption see: US Energy Information Administration (EIA). 2009. "International Energy Outlook 2009," Report #:DOE/EIA-0484(2009), May 27. Available at: http://www.eia.doe.gov/oiaf/ieo/world.html (accessed April 16, 2010). However, EIA data can be controversial, see: Aleklett, Kjell, Mikael Höök, Kristofer Jakobsson, Michael Lardelli, Simon Snowden, and Bengt Söderbergh. 2010. "The Peak of the Oil Age—Analyzing the World Oil Production Reference Scenario in World Energy Outlook 2008," *Energy Policy* 38(3) (March): 1398–1414.

8 For statistics/graphs showing the amount of oil imported by countries, see: Central Intelligence Agency (US), "The World Fact Book." 2009, Available at: https://www.cia.gov/library/publications/the-world-factbook/rankorder/2175rank.html?countryName=United%20States&countryCode=us& regionCode=na&rank=1#us (accessed April 16, 2010); NationMaster, "Energy Statistics 'Oil' Imports (Most Recent) by Country." 2010, Available at: http://www.nationmaster.com/red/graph/ene_oil_ imp-energy-oil-imports&b_printable=1 (accessed April 16, 2010).

9 Stopford, *Maritime Economics*, p.11.

10 Central Intelligence Agency (US), "The World Fact Book."

11 Fraser, Andrew. 2010. "Shen Neng 1's Masters Charged Over Reef," *The Australian*, April 15. Available at: http://www.theaustralian.com.au/news/nation/shen-neng-1s-masters-charged-over-reef/story-e6frg6nf-1225853839670 (accessed April 16, 2010).

12 International Maritime Organisation, "Ships' Routeing." Available at: http://www.imo.org/safety/ mainframe.asp?topic_id=770 (accessed April 27, 2010).

13 This definition is derived from a long history of anti-piracy laws of European countries and the United States. Young, Adam J. 2005. "Roots of Contemporary Maritime Piracy in Southeast Asia." In Derek Johnson and Mark Valencia (eds.), *Piracy in Southeast Asia. Status, Issues, and Responses* (Singapore: ISEAS Publications), pp. 3–8.

14 United Nations. 1982. "United Nations Convention on the Law of the Sea." Available at: http://www.un.org/Depts/los/convention_agreements/texts/unclos/closindx.htm (accessed July 4, 2005).

15 Keyuan, Zou. 1998. "Enforcing the Law of Piracy in the South China Sea," EAI Background Brief no. 19 (Singapore: East Asian Institute, National University of Singapore, August 24), p. 13.

16 International Chamber of Commerce (ICC). 1998. "Piracy and Armed Robbery against Ships: A Special Report," rev. edn (Geneva: International Chamber of Commerce, International Maritime Bureau, March), p. 2.

17 Author's interview with Noel Choong, Regional Manager, International Maritime Bureau, Piracy Reporting Centre, October 23, 2002, Kuala Lumpur, Malaysia.

18 Centre for Strategic Studies. 2000. *Piracy in Southeast Asia*, CSS Strategic Briefing Papers (Wellington: University of Wellington, June), pp.1–2.

19 Chalk, Peter. 2000. *Non-military Security and Global Order: The Impact of Extremism, Violence and Chaos on National and International Security* (New York: St. Martin's Press, LLC), pp. 68–71.

20 Chalk, *Non-military Security and Global Order*, pp. 68–71.

21 ICC.2005. "Piracy and Armed Robbery against Ships. Annual Report 1 January–31 December 2004" (Barking, Essex: International Chamber of Commerce, International Maritime Bureau), p. 16.

22 The number of actual and attempted attacks reported in Nigeria are as follows: 1997: 9, 1998: 1, 1999: 11, 2000: 9, 2001: 19, 2002: 14, 2003: 39, 2004: 16, 2005: 16, 2006: 12, 2007: 42, 2008: 40, and 2009: 28. See International Maritime Boad Annual Piracy Statistics 1997–2010 (Geneva: IMB).

23 Ibid.

24 Laqueur, Walter. 1977. *Terrorism* (London: Weidenfeld & Nicolson), pp. 4, 79.

25 Juergensmeyer, Mark. 2000. *Terror in the Mind of God: The Global Rise of Religious Violence* (Berkeley: University of California Press), p. 5.

26 Hoffman, Bruce. 1998. *Inside Terrorism* (London: Victor Gollancz), pp. 29–30; Juergensmeyer, *Terror in the Mind of God*, pp. 9, 188–190.

27 Hoffman, *Inside Terrorism*, pp. 43–44.

28 Hoffman, *Inside Terrorism*, pp. 41–43.

29 Labog-Javellana, Juliet and Philip Tubeza. 2004. "SuperFerry 14 Bombing Solved, Says Arroyo," *Philippine Daily Inquirer*, October 12, p. A1.

30 Chalk, Peter. 2008. "The Maritime Dimension of International Security" (RAND Corporation). Available at: http://www.rand.org/pubs/monographs/2008/RAND_MG697.pdf (accessed April 17, 2010), pp. 25–26.

31 Forbes, Andrew. 2008. "The Economic Impact of Disruptions to Seaborne Energy Flows." In Andrew Forbes (ed.), *Asian Energy Security: Regional Cooperation in the Malacca Strait*, Papers in Australian Maritime Affairs No. 23 (Sea Power Centre, Australia), pp. 62–63, 66–67.

32 Chalk, "The Maritime Dimension of International Security," p.19; Chalk, Peter. 2006. "Maritime Terrorism in the Contemporary Era: Threat and Potential Future Contingencies." In National Memorial Institute for the Prevention of Terrorism (ed.), *The MIPT Terrorism Annual 2006* (Oklahoma City: National Memorial Institute for the Prevention of Terrorism), pp. 19–42 (p. 21).

33 Pelkofski, James. 2005. "Before the Storm: Al Qaeda's Coming Maritime Campaign," *Proceedings*, December, n. p.

34 Pelkofski, "Before the Storm"; Blanche, Ed. 2002. "Terror Attacks Threaten Gulf's Oil Routes," *Jane's Intelligence Review* 14(12): 8.

35 RAND, "RAND Database of Worldwide Terrorism Incidents." Available at: http://smapp.rand.org/rwtid (accessed April 18, 2010). The database is currently being updated.

36 Jackson, Richard. 2005. "Security, Democracy, and the Rhetoric of Counter Terrorism," *Democracy and Security* 1: 157. This does not imply that the threat should not be taken seriously, or that maritime terrorist attacks cannot occur, rather that it should be placed into proper historical and contextual perspective.

37 See: Young, Adam J. and Mark J. Valencia. 2003. "Conflation of Piracy and Terrorism in Southeast Asia," *Contemporary Southeast Asia* 25(2): 269–283; Ong, Graham Gerard. 2005. "Ships Can Be Dangerous, Too: Coupling Piracy and Terrorism in Southeast Asia's Maritime Security Framework." In Derek Johnson and Mark J. Valencia (eds), *Piracy in Southeast Asia: Status, Issues, and Responses* (Singapore: Institute of Southeast Asian Studies), pp. 63–67.

38 Goodenough, Patrick. 2005. "Maritime Terror Concerns Prompt New Initiatives in SE Asia," *CNSNews.com*, 2 March. Available at: http://www.cnsnews.com/ViewForeignBureaus.asp?Page= %5CForeignBureaus%5Carchive%5C200503%5CFOR20050302a.html (accessed March 3, 2005).

39 Furthermore, some observers believe that, given the violence and type of attacks they conduct, pirates should more accurately be labeled terrorists. Herbert-Burns, Rupert and Lauren Zucker. 2004. "Malevolent Tide: Fusion and Overlaps in Piracy and Maritime Terrorism" (Washington, DC: Marine Intelligence Group, July 30), pp. 1–2.

40 The example is taken from an article written by Rupert Herbert-Burns and Lauren Zucker in 2004. The authors describe the attack, set to occur on November 25, 2007, in great detail. Herbert-Burns and Zucker, "Malevolent Tide." See also Halloran, Richard. 2003. "Threat of Terrorism Adds to Piracy Fears," *Baltimore Sun*, May 18. Available at: http://www.sunspot.net/news/opinion/oped/bal-pe.piracy18may18,0,7746135.story?coll=bal%2Doped%2Dheadlines (accessed May 19, 2003).

41 Herbert-Burns and Zucker, "Malevolent Tide," p. 10.

42 The World Economic Forum, for example, states that an attack on a major port may force it to close down for several weeks and have "severe economic consequences on world trade because it would inflict major disruptions in complex just-in-time supply chains that comprise the global economy": World Economic Forum.2010. "Global Risks 2010: A Global Risk Network Report" (Geneva,

January), p. 23. Available at: http://www.weforum.org/pdf/globalrisk/globalrisks2010.pdf (accessed April 25, 2010).

43   Chalk, "The Maritime Dimension of International Security," p. 23. An attack on a port from land may in some respects be a greater threat.

44   See: Chalk, "The Maritime Dimension of International Security," pp. 22–23.

45   On its website, the Malaysian Marine Department publishes the numbers of vessels that transited the Malacca Strait from 1999 to 2004. In this period, the number increased from 43,964 in 1999 to 63,636 in 2004. See: Marine Department Malaysia, "Mandatory Ship Reporting System in the Straits of Malacca and Singapore." Available at: http://www.marine.gov.my/service/index.html (accessed June 22, 2007).

46   "Maritime Terrorism Could Have Global Economic Impact" (sidebar), *Straits Times*, March 4, 2010. Available at: http://www.straitstimes.com/BreakingNews/SEAsia/Story/STIStory_497928.html (accessed April 16, 2010).

47   American Association of Port Authorities, "World Port Ranking—2008." Available at: http://aapa. files.cms-plus.com/Statistics/WORLD_PORT_RANKINGS_20081.pdf (accessed March 30, 2010).

48   Stehr, Michael. 2004. *Piraterie und Terror auf See. Nicht-Staatliche Gewalt auf den Weltmeeren 1990 bis 2004* (Berlin: Verlag Dr. Koester), pp. 58–59. In 2005, the attacks were deemed to be so serious that the Joint War Committee (JWC) – a body constituted of members of the Lloyds Market Association and the International Underwriting Association—included the Malacca Straits in its Hull War, Strikes, Terrorism and Related Perils Listed Areas. Following international protest, the strait was removed from the list the following year. Burton, John. 2006. "Lloyd's Drops War Rating on Malacca Strait," August 9. Available at: http://bpms.kempen.gov.my/index.php?option=com_content&task= view&id=7070&Itemid=0 (accessed August 13, 2006).

49   International Chamber of Commerce (ICC). 2001. *Piracy and Armed Robbery against Ships. Annual Report 1 January–31 December 2000* (Barking, Essex: ICC, International Maritime Bureau), p. 15.

50   International Chamber of Commerce (ICC). 2003. *Piracy and Armed Robbery against Ships. Annual Report 1 January–31 December 2002* (Barking, Essex: ICC, International Maritime Bureau), p. 34; Raymond, Catherine Zara. 2005. *Piracy in Southeast Asia. New Trends, Issues, and Responses*, Working Paper no. 89 (Singapore: Institute of Defence and Strategic Studies, October), p. 9. Available at: http://www.ntu.edu.sg/idss/publications/WorkingPapers/WP89.pdf (accessed December 28, 2005).

51   US$100,000 was demanded for the release of the crew kidnapped from the *Penrider*. ICC, "Piracy and Armed Robbery against Ships. Annual Report 1 January–31 December 2003", Barking, Essex: International Chamber of Commerce, International Maritime Bureau, 2004, p. 20. ICC, "Piracy and Armed Robbery against Ships. Annual Report 1 January–31 December 2005," Barking, Essex: International Chamber of Commerce, International Maritime Bureau, 2006, p. 17.

52   Vijay Sakhuja, "The Sea Muggers Are Back in Malacca Strait", Paper no. 1300, South Asia Analysis Group, 23 March 2005, http://www.saag.org/papers13/paper1300.html (accessed 24 August 2006). Leslie Lau, "Aceh Rebels Behind Spate of Pirate Attacks", *Straits Times*, 14 August 2003, n. p. Kate McGeown, "Aceh Rebels Blamed for Piracy", BBC News Online, 8 September 2003, http://news. bbc.co.uk/1/hi/world/asia-pacific/3090136.stm (accessed 14 August 2006).

53   Bradford, John F. 2005. "The Growing Prospects for Maritime Security Cooperation in Southeast Asia," *Naval War College Review* 2005 (6) (Summer): 67.

54   See: "Straits Terror Attack Alert," *Straits Times*, March 4, 2010. Available at: http://www.straitstimes. com/BreakingNews/SEAsia/Story/STIStory_497928.html (accessed March 25, 2010); "On High Alert for Possible JI Attacks on Oil Tankers," *New Straits Times*, March 6, 2010. Available at: http:// news.asiaone.com/print/News/AsiaOne%2BNews/Malaysia/Story/A1Story20100306-202882.html (accessed April 22, 2010).

55   Smiles, Sarah. 2009. "Navy Plans Pirate Fight," *Age*, January 9. Available at: http://www.theage.com. au/national/navy-plans-pirate-fight-20090108-7cw7.html (accessed January 13, 2009).

56   International Crisis Group, "Conflict History: Somalia," updated September 2008. Available at: http://www.crisisgroup.org/home/index.cfm?action=conflict_search&l=1&t=1&c_country=98 (accessed November 20, 2008); Kroslak, Daniela and Andrew Stroehlein, "Oh my Gosh, Pirates!" 2008. *International Herald Tribune*, April 28. Available at: http://www.iht.com/bin/printfriendly. php?id=12399900 (accessed April 30, 2008). Perry, Alex. 2008. "The Suffering of Somalia," *Time Online*, November 13. Available at: http://www.time.com/printout/0,8816,1858874,00.html (accessed November 20, 2008).

57 "Pirate Boat Destroyed after New Raid," *Australian*, November 20, 2008; Panti, Llanesca T. 2009. "Somali Pirates Release Philippine Ship and Crew," *Manila Times*, January 14. Available at: http://www.manilatimes.net/national/2009/jan/14/yehey/metro/20090114met1.html (accessed January 15, 2009); Office of Naval Intelligence. 2009. *Worldwide Threat to Shipping Mariner Warning Information* (United States: Civil Maritime Analysis Department, January 8).

58 "Piraten drohen mit Sprengung von Supertanker," *Spiegel Online*, April 22, 2010. Available at: http://www.spiegel.de/panorama/justiz/0,1518,druck-690477,00.html (accessed April 22, 2010).

59 For one of the latest terror warnings see: "US Warns Gulf of Aden Shipping at Risk of Al Qaeda Bombing," World Cargo Insurance, March 22, 2010. Available at: http://worldcargoinsurance.com/wordpress/us-warns-gulf-of-aden-shipping-at-risk-of-al-qaeda-bombing/ (accessed April 27, 2010).

60 Bradford, "The Growing Prospects for Maritime Security Cooperation in Southeast Asia," pp. 67, 71; RAND, "RAND Database of Worldwide Terrorism Incidents."

61 Data used for this calculation was taken from the Malaysian Marine Department website, which only includes vessels weighing 300 gt and above, or being 50 meters in length or above. Marine Department Malaysia, "Mandatory Ship Reporting System in the Straits of Malacca and Singapore." Available at: http://www.marine.gov.my/service/index.html (accessed June 22, 2007).

62 Forbes, "The Economic Impact of Disruptions to Seaborne Energy Flows," p. 63.

63 Forbes, "The Economic Impact of Disruptions to Seaborne Energy Flows," p. 72. Chalk, "The Maritime Dimension of International Security," p. 23.

64 Chalk, "The Maritime Dimension of International Security," p. 23.

65 "Piraten haben schon 150 Millionen Dollar erpresst," *Spiegel Online*, November 21, 2008. Available at: http://www.spiegel.de/panorama/justiz/0,1518,druck-591992,00.html (accessed November 22, 2008); Philp, Catherine. 2008. "Somali Pirates Seize Saudi Oil Supertanker," *Australian*, November 18. Available at: http://www.theaustralian.news.com.au/story/0,25197,24668477-2703,00.html (accessed November 18, 2008).

66 Forbes, "The Economic Impact of Disruptions to Seaborne Energy Flows," p. 64.

67 Forbes, "The Economic Impact of Disruptions to Seaborne Energy Flows," p. 63; United Nations. 2008. "New UN Report on Maritime Transport Reveals Effects of Financial Crisis" (UN News Centre, November 4). Available at: http://www.un.org/apps/news/story.asp?NewsID=28817&Cr=unctad&Cr1 (accessed April 28, 2010); "Shipping Industry Drowning in Financial Woes," originally published in *Spiegel*, August 14, 2009. Available at: http://www.presseurop.eu/en/content/article/76921-shipping-industry-drowning-financial-woes (accessed April 28, 2010).

68 Simon, Sheldon W. 2001. "Asian Armed Forces: Internal and External Tasks and Capabilities." In Sheldon W. Simon (ed.), *The Many Faces of Security* (Lanham, MD: Rowman & Littlefield), p. 51; Carolin Liss, Carolin. 2007. "Southeast Asia's Maritime Security Dilemma: State or Market?" *Japan Focus*, June 8. Available at: http://japanfocus.org/products/details/2444.

69 See: Commander, Combined Maritime Forces Public Affairs, "Pakistan Assumes Command of Combined Task Force 150," April 15, 2010. Available at:http://www.cusnc.navy.mil/articles/2010/CMF029.html (accessed April 25, 2010).

70 Sorge, Petra. 2008. "Alliierte gehen ohne Deutschland auf Piratenjagd," *Spiegel Online*, October 27. Available at: http://www.spiegel.de/politik/ausland/0,1518,druck-584554,00.html (accessed October 28, 2008); North Atlantic Treaty Organization. 2008. "Somalia: Successful Completion of NATO Mission Operation Allied Provider," December 12. Available at:http://www.reliefweb.int/rw/rwb.nsf/db900SID/JBRN-7M9K2N?OpenDocument (accessed January 17, 2009).

6

THE PUBLIC POLICY DIMENSION OF ENERGY SECURITY[1]

Andreas Goldthau

A public policy perspective on global energy security

Energy security has made it atop of national policy agendas. It is particularly the rise of new and spectacularly hungry energy consumers such as China and India, along with dwindling low cost fossil reserves, that dominates current debates on energy security. As a consequence, the latter tend to be characterized by two defining elements: they put special emphasis on the demand side, implicitly defining energy security as "security of supply"; and they regard energy as a "hard security" issue, and subject to geopolitical scheming. Ever since Great Britain led the way in opening the Middle East for oil production in the early twentieth century, energy security has been assessed mainly on a national level, focusing on policy imperatives for governments whose perceived job it has been to improve the energy security situation of their respective countries. Yet, the world has changed since then. Energy markets, and particularly oil, have globalized. Energy production, processing, transmission, and marketing have become highly complex and nowadays are truly transnational processes. As a consequence, energy security has become more than a national affair. In fact, it would be outright dangerous for policy prescriptions to narrow energy matters down to national security concerns. Most of the risks modern economies face by far exceed both the regulatory and interventionist capacity of individual national governments. Risks stemming from oil price volatility, a lack in transport infrastructure, or insufficient upstream investments certainly are of truly transnational or global scope. These risks can best be conceptionalized as classical market failure. In that, they require and justify public intervention. Energy security therefore, first and foremost, has strong public policy characteristics, whether from the perspective of a consuming nation aiming at securing its supply of vital energy input; or from the perspective of a producing nation, aiming at securing demand for its energy exports and products. Compared with the pre-globalization era, these public policies—and this certainly is the challenge both in scholarly as well as in policy terms—now require a truly transnational or even global answer.

The scholarly literature does not take much note of that. As mentioned, global energy challenges tend to enter debates mostly in geopolitical and hard-nosed security terms, not in global public policy ones.[2] By contrast, available studies on global public goods and global public policy by and large fail to apply available concepts to the case of energy at all.[3] Whatever the reason, with oil markets being of a global nature, gas markets of at least a regional nature, and hence supply-side, demand-side or price-related fluctuations of transnational scope, there is an urgent need to explore energy security from a global public policy angle.

The aim of this chapter is twofold. First, it conceptualizes global energy security in classic public policy terms, that is, it assesses possible incidents of global market failure.[4] Rather than informing the theoretical debate on public policy, this conceptual discussion primarily aims at exploring energy security from a public policy lens. It draws from textbook concepts on normative causes of public policy and on economic justifications for public action based on incidents of imperfect competition, the existence of externalities or information asymmetry, and of public goods characteristics.

Second, acknowledging the fact that by definition market failure tends to result in under-provision of the good in question, this chapter will elaborate on the imperatives for (global) public action. The focus of discussion will be on sketching what policies may be suitable and required to address key problems inherent in, for instance, the provision of public goods, such as free riding.

Before starting the discussion, a few disclaimers may be in order. First, discussions in this chapter deliberately focus on oil and gas. This focus mirrors the fact that both fuels make up for 60 percent of global primary energy demand;[5] that they are politicized like no other fuel; and that there exists cross-border trade of global scale and volume, which suggests that the effective provision of supply (or demand) also is a transnational or global policy issue. Further, while acknowledging that climate change is part of the global energy equation, this fact is accounted for only to the extent it affects energy security proper. In other words, the detrimental environmental effects of burning fossil fuels as such are not subject of this chapter's deliberations; by contrast, the question as to whether carbon markets and climate change-induced legislation (or the lack thereof) affect investment in fossil fuels and renewables, certainly is. Finally, while acknowledging that there are numerous forms of government failure in energy, including regulatory failure,[6] subsidy policies,[7] or rent seeking, this contribution does not explicitly account for these aspects. Rather, its key concern is to assess various forms and formats of global market failure and to draw conclusions on the form and scope of call for public policy of a global scale. In a nutshell: rather than asking "who governs" global energy,[8] the starting point of this chapter is to assess what actually is "to be governed," and to draw conclusions on policies.

The next section assesses incidents of market failure in global energy.

Market failure in global energy

While obvious, it is an often forgotten fact that energy resources such as oil and gas are commodities. As such they are primarily private goods, and subject to (private) market interaction, whether on a local, national, regional, or global level.[9] Yet, as any other market, energy markets may fail in providing for a good at the price or quantity demanded. While the role of government in modern economies remains contested and controversial, market failure is widely regarded as a justification for state action. In fact, in standard public policy literature, market failure is a key incident for states or state agencies to intervene in a particular market in order to ensure the delivery of a good, welfare, or security of citizens.[10] Classic public policy models center on four key causes of market failure: imperfect competition, the existence of externalities, incomplete information, and public goods characteristics. The following section briefly discusses these four incidents of market failure and applies them to the case of global energy. The aim is certainly not to comprehensively treat the issue from a theoretical perspective, for which textbooks may be the more appropriate place; rather, the goal is to illustrate what market failure means for global energy security and what lessons are to be drawn from this for public action.

Imperfect competition

Markets can fail due to imperfect competition, arising from a concentration of market power. The latter usually appears in the form of monopolies or producer cartels on the supply side, and monopsonies or consumer cartels on the demand side. As a consequence, the market price is either pushed above or below competitive levels, that is, either producers are able to extract additional rents, or consumers may be able to dictate the terms of market exchange to their suppliers.

In the global oil market, two classic examples of imperfect competition come to mind: the Organization of Oil Exporting Countries (OPEC), a supplier cartel, and the buyers' cartel of the Seven Sisters. OPEC, though not a perfect cartel, has arguably been able to put a premium on each barrel of consumed oil.[11] To the same extent, members of the Seven Sisters for a long time managed to maintain an internal transfer pricing scheme, which secured enormous rents for participating oil companies.[12] In both cases, market failure of a global scope occurred—in the case of OPEC to the detriment of consumers, who had to bear a higher than optimal price; in the case of the Seven Sisters to the detriment of producers who did not earn an optimal income from their resource exports.

In contrast to the global and liquid oil market, natural gas markets have by and large remained regional in nature. This is mainly due to the fact that natural gas is a less fungible commodity than oil and critically relies on one single form of transport infrastructure: pipelines.[13] With the notable exception of the North American gas market, long-term contracts, based on take-off agreements, dominate the scene. They usually also peg the price of natural gas to the price of a substitute, mostly oil. On the Eurasian gas market, the supply side tends to be concentrated among few suppliers, with the most dominant one being Russia's state-owned Gazprom; the (net) demand side is, by contrast, characterized rather by actor fragmentation. Interestingly, and with the notable exception of some Former Soviet Union (FSU) countries, this apparent imbalance in market power does not translate primarily into price distortions. Rather, it creates a veritable supply risk. Since the base price for gas is not formed on the basis of a Eurasian supply and demand balance, any tinkering on the supply side simply does not translate into price hikes. As we shall see when discussing the case of the European gas conflicts, instead it limits available volumes.

Addressing global market failures related to imperfect competition obviously faces clear limits in terms of public policy and state intervention. Supply-side problems caused by a producer cartel may simply not be subject to public policy actions of consumer nations; likewise, buyer cartels can usually not be broken up by producers. As a second best option, scholars have, however, made the case for the establishment and use of a countervailing monopsony if a cartel or monopoly exploits its market power, and vice versa.[14] As for oil, the creation of OPEC in 1960 was a direct response to the oil market dominance of the Seven Sisters. In turn, the establishment of the International Energy Agency (IEA) in 1974, following the first oil shock, may be an example of an attempt to pool demand-sided market power.[15] Likewise, a recent proposal launched by the European Commission to set up a "Caspian Development Corporation" (CDC) as a "block purchasing mechanism for Caspian gas"[16] can certainly be interpreted as a European attempt to establish a buyer's cartel in gas in order to re-shift the power balance on the Eurasian gas market.[17]

Externalities

Externalities generally refer to spillover costs or benefits of an actor's (economic) activity on some other actor's welfare. Put differently: a problem caused by one person may negatively affect a second, uninvolved person; or a second person may profit from the action of a first one. Examples in the literature would, for instance, refer to pollution in the first case; and to education in the second.[18] Externalities related to oil would materialize primarily as a movement in the price. In that, they impact on the fiscal situation or the economic activity of a nation—in a positive or negative way.[19] Since oil is a fungible commodity and traded on an integrated global market, a disruption of supplies anywhere in the world translates into higher prices for *all* consumers— whether citizens of an importing nation or of a self-sufficient one. In other words, while profiting from additional revenue during a price hike, oil exporting nations also face a higher domestic price for oil—unless they possibly decide to leverage the latter through subsidies. Events triggering sudden price increases include domestic turmoil (e.g. Nigeria's ongoing domestic conflict), political quarrels (e.g. Venezuela's oil workers' strike of December 2002–February 2003), or regime change (e.g. the Iranian Islamic Revolution of 1979), all of which—despite being limited to a single nation—affected oil prices on a global scale. As a corollary, a sudden drop in demand in some parts of the world certainly has a revenue impact on all producer nations, not only on the ones supplying the economically depressed region. The 1998 price slope in oil, for instance, was partly triggered by a regional economic depression in Asia, but eventually translated into globally depressed crude prices. A change in global prices can even occur if actual supply is not altered at all. Sheer perceptions and the fact that market participants factor future uncertainties into the price formation may well translate locally restricted events into veritable externalities for third parties.

Externalities of such kind are inherently direct in nature. Yet, they can also be more indirect. In that case, price externalities materialize differently for producers/ exporters and consumers/ importers. An oil-importing nation, affected by a price hike, would probably experience an economic slump due to sharply rising costs of a key economic input factor; it would suffer from rising inflation, or experience an increase in unemployment. In fact, as Brown pointedly notes, 10 out of 11 post-World War II recessions in the US followed sharp oil price increases.[20] Producer nations, in turn, being affected by the same price hike, and while profiting from additional revenue, may experience an appreciation of their currency, due to additional income in foreign money. As a corollary, they may see deteriorating terms of trade of domestic industry. The much discussed "Dutch disease," describing a situation in which a dominant extracting industry depresses economic activity in a country's other sectors, is an infamous case in point of such a negative price externality for oil-exporting nations.[21] Several studies have estimated various types of cost impacts of oil price increases, and have modeled the "energy security gain" of reduced crude imports for major consumer nations. While it is beyond the scope of this chapter to discuss these studies' findings in detail, it is worth noting that the bulk of price-related externalities occur as macroeconomic adjustment costs.[22] What follows from this is that the more frequently an economy needs to adjust, up or down, the more often these costs occur. Hence, it is a high volatility of oil prices in particular that creates externality costs. In other words, it is not necessarily the oil price level as such that matters in the long run (as an economy can, over time, adjust to a new input factor price), but the extent to which and how frequently the oil price deviates from the standard. Price volatility has, however, yet another effect that qualifies as (negative) externality, this time on energy security proper: it disincentivizes investment into costly upstream projects. During periods of high volatility, the oil price tells little about future price levels.[23] As a consequence of this uncertainty about future revenues, and given the fact that upstream projects are very costly and have lead times of several years, companies may simply abstain from investing in new projects.

As studies have proven, oil prices have indeed become more volatile since the mid-1990s, and particularly since mid-2008. Since then, the world has witnessed a roller coaster from an all-time high of almost $150 per barrel in July 2008, to around $30 by the end of the same year, and up again to some $80 by the end of 2009. This is in fact bad news for energy security, as an estimated $26 trillion—roughly equivalent to twice the entire annual US GDP—will need to be spent until 2030 to meet projected global energy demand, with an additional $10.5 trillion if climate goals are to be met.[24] Yet, since late 2008, capital spending on energy projects has been massively cut. Over 20 large-scale upstream oil and gas projects have been put on hold or cancelled. Investment in renewables fell even over-proportionately.[25] True, it is certainly not only volatility that has caused this development, and the ongoing financial and economic crisis can partly be blamed for this slope in investment. Yet, faltering energy investment now will have serious effects on energy security ten years down the line. And it will defer the necessary shift towards a low-carbon future. For policies aimed at addressing externalities stemming from oil price changes it is therefore of crucial importance not only to address the extent to which the oil price changes in absolute terms, but also the frequency it does so.

Turning to natural gas, externalities look still somewhat different. They tend to arise particularly from the prevalent characteristics of market arrangements in Eurasia and Asia and the pipeline-bound nature of these markets. First, externalities may occur due to the fact that the bulk of gas volumes is not directly traded between two contractual partners (i.e. the producer and the consumer), but transited through third countries. As a consequence and neatly demonstrated by the recent frictions observed on the Eurasian gas market, disputes involving a transit nation easily translate into negative externalities for the two main contractual partners. As some 80 percent of Russian gas exports transit through the Ukraine, and the remaining 20 percent through Belarus, conflicts between Russian monopolist Gazprom, Kyiv, and Minsk severely affect third parties in Eastern, Central and Western Europe further down the line.[26] Given the prevalent oil price peg, such externalities have no implications in terms of changing gas prices but they do in terms of physical supply.[27] In this way, externalities in gas differ considerably from those in oil. In January 2009, following a dispute over price schemes and payments between Russia and the Ukraine, natural gas supplies to consumers in Moldova, Bulgaria, Romania, Serbia, and Bosnia-Herzegovina were cut off for two weeks. This led to the shutdown of these countries' industries, the closure of schools and other public institutions, and deeply affected public life. In addition to lost revenues amounting to some $1.5bn for Gazprom, the economic costs of the gas cut-off, particularly for southeastern Europe, were considered to be substantial.[28]

Second, externalities may be caused by the above-mentioned price peg that characterizes most take-off agreements in natural gas. As discussed, the base gas price does not reflect a supply and demand balance in the Eurasian gas market. By contrast, it basically reflects movements in the oil market, usually lagged by some six months. A straightforward spillover effect following from this is price fluctuations that are caused by totally unrelated market fundamentals. In other words, gas price hikes of up to $380 per thousand cubic meters (tcm), as observed in 2008, reflected nothing else than a tight oil market and its futures being in constant contango.

Public goods

Technically, "pure" public goods are defined as goods that are non-rival and non-excludable in consumption. Put differently, a public good can be consumed without reducing the amount available for others; and it cannot be withheld from anyone who does not pay for it.[29] Classic examples of public goods are lighthouses—once they are there, all ships profit from their presence, regardless of whether the respective shipowners have paid for the provision of the lighthouse or not. What follows from this, and this is the tricky issue characterizing public goods, is that their provision creates a free-rider problem. As a consequence, they are barely produced by the market, or not at the quantities or the price that consumers are willing to pay. For sure, oil as such is not a public good, nor is gas. Both are private in nature, as their use by one consumer affects the amount available to others, and as it is certainly feasible to exclude consumers from benefiting from them. Yet, in both the oil and the gas market, a number of examples can be found where market failure occurs due to the public goods' character of issues related to oil and gas.

A classic example in this regard is petroleum stocks. These stocks are created and maintained by consumer nations to buffer sudden supply shortages and resulting price shocks. In that, they are a mechanism to fix a market failure stemming from externalities of a kind discussed earlier.[30] Yet, ironically, these mechanisms themselves can fall prey to market failure. As Leiby *et al.* note, oil price stabilization is nothing else than a public good that benefits all oil-using economies.[31] And so is strategic stock-piling, as its costs are concentrated, while its benefits are dispersed. In other words, for the same reasons that negative price externalities are of global scope, measures taken to buffer sudden supply shocks are non-rival and non-excludable in consumption. Apparently, such free-riding is a particular problem with regard to small economies, as they benefit over-proportionally from stocks held and released by larger consumer nations.[32] Yet, against the backdrop of rising consumers such as India and China, the problem gains additional traction. Following the 1973–1974 oil price shocks, major energy-consuming nations established the International Energy Agency (IEA) which introduced distinct rules to provide a framework for two specific mechanisms of short-term supply (risk) management: the International Energy Program (IEP, founded in 1974) and the Coordinated Response Mechanism (CRP, set up in 1979). The linchpin of the system is national emergency oil stocks among members (Strategic Petroleum Reserves, SPR) equivalent to at least 90 days of oil imports. This strict system responded to the problem of free-riding discussed earlier and ensured that all participating members contribute their individual share. As participation in the IEA is linked to OECD membership, emerging consumers such as India and China are currently excluded from this system for formal reasons. Yet, even more importantly, both countries should have little incentive to build up their own stocks and align them with the IEA system. In fact, they can easily free-ride on stocks held and paid for by OECD countries. True, both China and India have recently begun building up strategic reserves for petroleum. China completed a first phase in 2008, whereas India is still in the process of developing stocks. Yet, in total, Chinese crude reserves account for only some 30 days of current net imports, whereas India's stock is equal to approximately three weeks of its current net oil imports.[33] Therefore China and India not only fall far short of the IEA's 90-day requirement, they also constitute an increasingly pressing problem to the security of all global oil consumers, as both countries represent the fastest growing consumer heavyweights in the market.[34]

A related problem occurs with regard to supply-side mechanisms to calm down the oil market: spare capacity. Spare capacity is an essential element of oil market psychology, as it determines how "safe" market participants are against a price shock stemming from severe supply-side problems. Some observers have even called spare capacity "the most important single asset for the world's supply security."[35] Most of the world's spare capacity is currently held by Saudi Arabia. How crucial Saudi Arabia's spare capacity is for world markets became evident particularly in the first Gulf War, during which Riyadh considerably ramped up production to buffer the supply losses from Iraq and Kuwait. As a consequence, price impacts have remained rather modest. Yet, reserve capacity, as strategic stocks, has a public goods character. While a certain country needs to develop the capacity and pay for it, no market participant can be excluded from the benefits of this additional, supply-side buffer. In addition, for the producer country holding reserve capacity, this additional capacity costs money but does not create any return for investment.

As such, reserve capacity should simply not exist, as no country or industry has an incentive to build it up in the first place, or hold its unused capacity. The primary reason why Saudi Arabia is apparently still willing to bear related costs but socialize the benefits is that reserve capacity is a welcome tool to enforce discipline within OPEC. The sheer fact that Saudi Arabia can threaten its fellow producers to create an oil glut, similar to the one in 1986, gives this country an unmatched power status within the cartel. A second reason may lie in the fact that Saudi Arabia, the world's largest reserve holder, has an interest in keeping consumers "hooked" on oil for decades to come. Hence, holding reserve capacity is an investment it makes in future demand security, enabling Riyadh to calm down markets and stabilize prices at an affordable level for consumers.[36] In other words, holding reserve capacity is still a highly rational move for the Saudis, but the underlying rationale is of a different nature than the one primarily discussed here.

A third global good by and large of public nature is secure sea lanes. Key to the smooth functioning of the global oil market, secure transport routes are hardly provided for by the collective of global producers and consumers. By contrast, the same collective action problem occurs as in the provision of strategic stocks or reserve capacity. Securing critical sea lanes is costly, as it requires a sizeable naval fleet that is able credibly to enforce free transit. Once one actor has taken on the task of investing in secure maritime transport routes, all other actors profit. Interestingly, the task of securing the Straits of Malacca and of Hormuz, the world's most famous chokepoints and crucial maritime transit routes for some 33 mbd out of 43 mbd of the globe's crude shipped daily by tankers is taken on by one single market participant: the US.[37] In other words, world consumers and producers pass on the costs of energy security in transportation to the American tax payer. While estimates on the related costs vary widely and range from $13 billion to $143 billion per year, it can certainly be said that this translates into an additional cost chunk for the American budget.[38] In the case of the Persian Gulf, the costs associated with maintaining the presence of the 5th Fleet may serve as a direct proxy to a price tag for securing sea lanes in this region. The reason why the US takes on these costs is, again, twofold. First, securing maritime routes may serve other purposes than supply security. In fact, many of the military forces included in planning for Gulf-based missions are included in plans for defending US interests in other world regions as well.[39] In that, as a by-product, they provide for the public good of energy security in maritime transportation. Second, the US regards secure oil supplies as part of its interest and mission, and therefore includes global oil transit in its force planning. As a positive externality of this, the world is provided with a global public good.

Turning to the Eurasian gas market again, one main public goods–related problem arises in infrastructure investment. An individual consumer in, say, Bulgaria, aiming at enhancing his energy security in gas supplies, would need to invest in diversifying sources: in infrastructure that would bring these alternative supplies to Bulgaria; in interconnectors that would link the Bulgarian grid to the neighboring pipeline systems; and in storage capacities that would hedge the country against short-term supply risks. Obviously, the benefits of these investments are by definition non-excludable and non-rival in consumption. In that, there is an inherent collective action problem related to the public goods character of the infrastructure investment needed to improve energy security in supply.

Regarding storage infrastructure, another collective action problem among European consumer countries arises. Storage of gas is more expensive than of oil. Hence, setting up storage facilities requires clear prioritization of public policies (read: investments), in which storage may sometimes fall prey to zero sum games in state budgets. In view of this, certain—particularly smaller and less wealthy—European countries have a clear incentive to "outsource" the costs of gas storage to other, wealthier, fellow Europeans. In fact, as the last gas crises have demonstrated, some European gas consumers simply disguise their refusal to pay for expensive storage capacities with calls for "solidarity" once they are faced with a supply shortage. In all, setting up individual storage capacity in Europe may easily end up being bound with a public goods character.

Lack of information

Finally, market failure in global energy can arise due to imperfect information. Information is key for market actors to find the right price for a product, to estimate risks effectively, or to judge whether to make an investment or not. A number of reasons can lead to a low level of information for energy market participants. Centrally, these include insufficient data on supply and demand fundamentals characterizing the market, regulatory uncertainty in key producer and/or consumer markets, or arrangements that render price signals ineffective.

The oil market, while having become the world's most integrated, highly fungible, and globalized energy market, has at the same time remained notoriously non-transparent. Key producer countries such as Saudi Arabia abstain from officially reporting output levels, while data from key consumer nations such as China tend to lack accuracy.[40] In addition, state companies have come to control the bulk of global oil and gas reserves.[41] National oil companies (NOCs) tend not to have the same reporting requirements as their stock market listed international private competitors, which adds to the non-transparency problem. In addition, "energy diplomacy" has experienced a vivid renaissance during the last decade. In particular, new consumers tend to resort to bilateral deals and diplomacy when it comes to securing supply, with China's "going out" efforts being a case in point. To be sure, energy diplomacy is not a problem with regard to globally available supply. Crude brought onstream by, say, Chinese NOCs either ends up on the global market, thus strengthening the supply side, or it is shipped back to the Chinese home market, thus taking pressure off global demand. In other words, it does not matter who gets the crude out of the ground but rather how much oil becomes part of the global balance. Yet, bilateral deals that Chinese NOCs strike in Africa, Central Asia, and elsewhere severely limit data availability, as this crude is no longer made "visible." In that, energy diplomacy adds to the already existing transparency problems in the oil market. As a consequence, market participants are left with somewhat educated guesses on key fundamentals on the supply and demand side. Yet, as upstream investments in oil have long lead times and are highly capital-intensive, insufficient data, a lack of accurate projections on supply and demand, and a general lack of transparency decrease the planning security of investors and companies. As a result, necessary investment, even if profitable, may not take place, leading to market failure on the supply side.

Energy diplomacy may also entail an additional problem: it sidelines prices as key drivers of investment. In fact, investment decisions based on political calculations ignore some of the underlying business fundamentals of upstream projects. Chinese upstream investments in Africa tend to be informed by political opportunity influencing both investment location and volume. Projects identified on political rather than economic grounds are often characterized by a lower return on investment compared with exploration and production projects driven by hard business fundamentals. As a result, and as elaborated in more detail elsewhere, energy diplomacy may negatively impact on effective allocation of investment since money risks flowing into the "wrong" projects.[42] For an individual consumer country such as China, this may simply add an additional price chunk on the barrel, a bearable burden from a political point of view, which is driven by the goal to secure supply and not to optimize costs. Yet if this strategy is pursued by a large number of market participants, including producers, the overall effect can be highly detrimental. Allocation of capital becomes suboptimal, which, in turn, implies a suboptimal development of available offer, eventually even translating into a supply gap. As a corollary, politically motivated and driven exploration and production projects may crowd out private sector investments, adding to the overall negative supply effect. In particular, financial state backing may be detrimental as capital markets may abstain from financing large-scale projects, which further decreases transparency regarding not only volume of investment but also business fundamentals.[43]

Further, and though this chapter does not explicitly account for government-induced policy failure, it is important to note that regulatory uncertainty may negatively affect available information on markets, too. Cases in point are policies related to carbon emissions. Attempts to establish cap-and-trade (C&T) systems remain in their infancy and regionally fragmented. The EU's Emission's Trading System (ETS), while widely regarded as a role model and frontrunner in C&T, is restricted to 27 countries (with the 3 non-EU countries of Norway, Iceland, and Liechtenstein joining in 2007) and covers not even half the EU's CO_2 emissions.[44] In the US, by contrast, the establishment of a similar system became stuck in political quarrels in the Senate. Even if the latter did get off the ground, however, the chances of linking both regional markets to emerging ones in Australia and elsewhere are generally low, given their politico-economic incompatibility.[45] Finally, recent attempts in Copenhagen to come to grips with a global C&T system have ended in no more than a vague and non-binding political statement, falling way short of establishing a global level playing field on carbon pricing. This, as a consequence, leads to uncertainty among businesses on how future carbon policies will affect their costs, which—if standard economic theory holds true—will negatively impact investment decisions.[46] Uncertainty will likely stem from fuel price risk, will lower incentives for low-carbon technologies, and put in question the competitiveness of both carbon- and non-carbon-based products. In that, it will impact businesses in both fossil fuel exporting and importing nations alike.

Turning to natural gas, a different kind of regulatory uncertainty exists on the Eurasian gas market, arising from the European Commission's efforts to liberalize gas markets within EU jurisdiction. Initiated to create a level playing field and to foster the establishment of a liquid and competitive European gas market, the Commission's liberalization efforts have got stuck in a hybrid of deregulation and protectionism. While Brussels' explicit goal was to unbundle gas sales from infrastructure—and though EU member countries tend to regularly pay lip service to this goal—nation states have shielded their national gas markets against "foreign" competition, and have managed to retain oligopolistic structures on these markets. Yet, while European governments tend to justify their protectionist stance on the grounds of enhancing national energy security in gas, this current deadlock in liberalization efforts may in fact have long-term effects on available supply. Crucially, it remains unclear whether the market structure based on long-term take-off contracts will prevail or not. Gas-to-gas competition in a liberalized and liquid European gas market will centrally require cracking up these take-off arrangements, and particularly their entailed destination clauses. In the case of a crack-up of take-off arrangements, there no longer exists certainty on long-term contracted volumes. Key producer companies such as Gazprom may therefore be less incentivized to spend billions of dollars on expensive and technically demanding upstream projects in the Yamal peninsula or elsewhere. Even if long-term contracts remain untouched, however, producers are left with the current regulatory hybrid and a Commission's looming liberalization agenda. Hence, in both cases planning security among producers may suffer. In sum, regulatory uncertainty on the demand side may lead to market failure in the sense that gas supplies are not brought onstream in the volumes needed.

Finally, prevalent Eurasian gas market arrangements and particularly its price peg come with an additional, information-related risk for market failure: the price ceases to function as a market signal. To be sure, take-off agreements and the entailed price peg have their own rights. Given lead times of no less than a decade in many major upstream projects, these arrangements allow splitting the risks related to uncertainties about the market environment ten years down the line. Yet, while strengthening planning security on produced and contracted volumes, this risk-hedging arrangement obviously comes with a price: it levers out the price mechanism. This has an important consequence as the price mechanism plays no role in valuing "energy security." In theory, some consumers may value supply security highly and be willing to spend money now,

Table 6.1 Summary of public policy issues related to energy security

	Market imbalance	Externalities	Public goods	Lack of information
Principal problem	Monopolies, monopsonies, cartels push price above or below competitive level	(Negative) spillover effects on third parties	Free-riding, underprovision	Insufficient data on market fundamentals; regulatory uncertainty; blurred price signals
Incident	OPEC, Seven Sisters, IEA, CDG	Direct and indirect price and supply externalities on oil market and Eurasian gas market	Petroleum stocks; spare capacity; security of sea lanes; transnational infrastructure; European gas storage	Non-transparent oil market; NOCs; "energy diplomacy"; uncertainty on carbon price; EU's flawed gas market liberalization; gas price peg

thus improving their future security situation. Others may put more value on present consumption and regard potential future supply disruptions as a risk they are willing to accept and for whose mitigation they are not willing to pay. Yet, to the extent the individual "valuation" of energy security is concerned, the price peg in prevalent gas market arrangements renders price signals meaningless. In fact, it prevents differing preferences from being catered for. No European consumer can effectively account for his individual degree of risk aversion and pay less or more for energy security in gas supplies. In addition, and as discussed above, if one consumer decided to invest in more individual energy security, any other consumer would be able to profit—stressing once again the public goods character of energy security in gas. In turn, suppliers such as Russia's Gazprom face the opposite problem: it does not receive any price signals on which it could base investment decisions. In other words, the prevalent market arrangements in natural gas limit available information on consumer preferences, and thus may lead to market failure.

Table 6.1 summarizes the main points of this section.

Implications for public policy in global energy security

As our discussion has revealed, market failure on a global or regional scale can occur due to the reasons of imperfect competition, externalities, lack of information, and public goods characteristics. And it can do so along the entire "energy value chain," and among all components of the global energy system, including finance, production, transmission, and consumption. As illustrating examples have shown, not all incidents of market failure need to be addressed or require action. Some of them may simply consist in tradeoffs between competing goals, with the discussed Eurasian gas market arrangements being a case in point. Others, such as the security of sea lanes, are "taken care of" by actors whose decision to provide for the public good in question is based on a different rationale.

Nevertheless, incidents of market failure, by definition, make the case for public policy and public action. In light of this, a number of principal conclusions can be drawn from the above discussion for public policy in global energy security. First, four key areas should ideally be addressed and "governed" by global public policy as global fossil fuel energy markets may fall short therein: market transparency and planning security; negative spill-over effects of a global scale; free-rider problems; and the existence of global market imbalances caused by cartels. Second, and this is where "reality" kicks in, out of these four areas only three may at best be policy-relevant. As scholars like Bohi *et al.* clearly stress, incidents of policy-relevant market failure refer to situations that can actually be dealt with, compared with ones in which no cost-effective option is available at the very moment in time the market failure occurs.[47] The existence of OPEC, for instance, would clearly qualify for the latter category. Third, while separated in theoretical debates, different incidents of market failure may be strongly interlinked and hence be addressed by similar policies.

Turning to global public policy, what are the implications of these findings, and what are the possible instruments for dealing with the obvious challenges?

Market transparency and planning security

As regards information and planning security, the call on (global) public policy is clear and straightforward: as discussed, investment challenges are tremendous—both to satisfy projected future primary energy demand and to meet climate targets of curbing global warming at 2 degrees Celsius. A lack of information and market transparency inevitably translates into lower inclination among risk-averse market participants to invest. Three issues are key in this context: transparency in the oil market, transparency on carbon pricing, and transparency on energy choices. Since the oil market is the globe's key energy market, its price signals are a key determinant for any other competing fossil or non-fossil fuel. A lack of available data on oil market fundamentals therefore simply translates into flawed price signals, for upstream investments in both fossil fuels and in non-fossil ones. Flawed or incomplete information also translates into price volatility as traders tend to work under incomplete information and adjust their positions in a constant search process for "true" data and market equilibria. Further, as carbon pricing mechanisms play a crucial role in determining the competitiveness of carbon and non-carbon fuels, reducing regulatory uncertainty on emerging carbon markets is key to investments in fossil fuels and renewables. Finally, necessary investments, both in fossil fuels and renewables, crucially require full information on future energy paths consuming nations will be taking. From a global public policy perspective it is therefore essential to provide for planning security for producers, investors, and consumers alike, to provide for effective pricing signals and to channel sufficient investment into energy supplies and services.

Policy instruments and mechanisms providing for a greater degree of information do already exist, notably the IEA's energy data-generating efforts, OPEC's oil market statistics, or BP's world energy yearbook. In addition, new instruments, notably the Joint Oil Data Initiative (JODI), can emerge to reduce information asymmetries in the oil market. Yet, challenges remain. Methodologies need to be brought in line, and countries currently not reporting need to be brought into the system. Further, to effectively price in CO_2-related externalities and put a global price tag on carbon, the flawed Consultation of Parties (COP) process needs to give way to a more effective mechanism. A way to deal with this is recent suggestions to simply gather the globe's top polluters—the industrialized economies and emerging economies accounting for, say, some two-thirds of global emissions—and to have them agree on a binding reduction target.[48]

Negative spillover effects of a global scale

Next, and with regard to negative spillover effects, a key externality identified relates to oil price volatility. As discussed, volatility may be detrimental to energy investments. Producer countries, often relying almost exclusively on resource revenues, will only invest billions of dollars into finding new resources if they can expect a stable and sufficient return on their investment. Shifting towards low carbon, in turn, also requires a reliable price environment. To facilitate a transition towards low carbon, not only clear price signals are needed, but also a stable and reliable price floor for fossil fuels. Moreover, volatility-induced adjustment costs tend to be the higher the more reliant an economy is on oil inputs, that is, the higher its oil intensity. In that, it is certainly not

Western car drivers at the pump that suffer the most from repeated price hikes, but rather developing countries, which need comparatively more oil to produce their GDP. Here, the call on global public policy lies in calming down volatility and to provide for a stable price environment in oil. Finally, however, global public policies addressing externalities also need to account for different and in fact diametric risk patterns among producers and consumers. While for consumers cost risks related to overinvestment are generally relatively small, considerable risks lie in underinvestment as it is susceptible of causing price hikes. For producers, in turn, costs related to underinvestment tend to be the smaller problem, whereas overinvestment and potential resulting price slumps may put their economies in danger.[49]

Global public policies addressing this problem may be found along similar lines to the ones discussed above related to information and planning security; they may also be related to public goods aspects discussed further below. As for spillover effects in natural gas, challenges rather seem to stem from a veritable supply risk. In that case, the call on global public policy would rather consist in providing for a mechanism that enables market participants to settle disputes in a smooth and cooperative manner. In particular with regard to previous Eurasian gas crises, in which various involved parties tended to resort to Rambo strategies, mechanisms allowing for win-win situations rather than zero-sum ones seem to be urgently required. By the very virtue of natural gas markets, this is a rather regionally defined task; yet, if working effectively, a regional dispute settlement mechanism can still provide for a role model on a global level, aiming at facilitating win-win situations. An institution does indeed exist that would be well suited to enhance the time horizons of, and the trust among, market participants: the Energy Charter Treaty (ECT). It is a prime example of a rule-setting institution that explicitly addresses the energy sector, most importantly natural gas, petroleum, and petroleum products. It basically links free market policies with an open access investment regime and a transit regime. Yet, and as Victor pointedly notes, the Treaty violates the "first rule of effective institution building": it alienates the key player.[50] Yet, the ECT in fact has great potential: it establishes a clearly defined set of rules for investment, transit, and trade in the energy sector, which is complemented by a dispute settlement mechanism. More recently, Russian president Medvedev has openly contemplated a new Eurasian energy regime—which may, though not openly stated, lead out of the deadlock and to an ECT II. In addition, and discussed further below, externalities stemming from short-term supply risks may be buffered by building up gas storage.

Public goods and free-rider problems

Interestingly, public goods, are not necessarily underprovided, with global spare capacity in oil or secure oil transport routes being cases in point. Yet, as the underlying rationale of their provision is linked to different motives (e.g. Saudi Arabia holding reserve capacity to dominate OPEC; the US securing sea lanes to serve its national security interests), these motives can change. In other words, a change in preferences (e.g. due to regime change in Riyadh) or cost structures (e.g. due to financial distress in the US budget) will inevitably lead to a harmful collective action problem in the provision of the global public good in question. Hence, the call on global public policy will be to find mechanisms of burden sharing. This will include making consumer nations co-finance maintenance of unused spare capacity, the cost of which at present lies entirely with the producers; it will include finding collective mandates to secure crucial transport routes and hence a smooth functioning of the oil market; and it will include accommodating new consumer heavyweights such as China and India in collective mechanisms to buffer sudden supply shocks in the oil market, and align them with the IEA's emergency response mechanisms. As argued by Harks, the International Energy Forum (IEF) in Riyadh may be a promising place to facilitate mutual exchange between producers and consumers on these matters, particularly spare capacity issues and ways to accommodate the newcomers in the system.[51]

Such buffers will need to be provided for gas, too—on a regional level. As for the entailed free-rider problem, there is apparently no need for a global institutional answer. Up to now, only a few European countries have started to establish such stocks. This collective action problem may eventually be solved by a top-down approach, that is, a European directive. Eurasian energy security in gas, however, does not necessarily require infrastructure, that is, public goods-related policies per se. Rather, it is planning security that will be key in order to limit (public) investments in storage to the volumes needed to adjust for minor, "normal" market changes caused by, say, a frosty winter, not for permanent or fundamental ones such as the January 2009 gas crisis. In that case, part of the answer to public goods problems related to the Eurasian gas market simply lies in providing for mutual planning security and in building up trust, not in infrastructure investments as such. As regards the latter, things are indeed also highly contextual. From a theoretical perspective, it is hard to make a general case for public action for infrastructure investments, even for transnational ones. The planned Nabucco project is a case in point here. Proponents of the pipeline tend to argue implicitly on the basis of its alleged public goods character.[52] There is certainly some truth to this argument, particularly with regard to the fact that—given the high upfront costs and entailed political risks—individual companies may not have enough incentive to build the interconnector that would foster gas-to-gas competition, to build markets, and to improve the energy security situation of European consumers. However, there is also the danger of private companies socializing the costs and privatizing the benefits of that project—literally free-riding on the market failure argument. In other words, complex transnational infrastructure projects require tailored and regional public policy answers, not necessarily global ones. Yet, when it comes to identifying a policy framework that would facilitate a smooth implementation of such multibillion-dollar infrastructure projects and its effective running across national and supranational jurisdictions, an institutional arrangement providing for an effective dispute settlement mechanism seems to be in order. This, again, seems particularly crucial with regard to previous Eurasian gas crises, in which transit countries used a geographical monopoly to foster their own interests vis-à-vis producer and consumer countries. In this case, and as discussed earlier, the public good produced by such an institutional framework would no longer be infrastructure as such; rather, it would consist in planning security for involved actors and lie in overcoming collective action problems related to transnational infrastructure projects.

Conclusion

This contribution has attempted to conceptualize energy security in classic public policy terms, that is, by assessing possible incidents of global market failure. To this end, it has drawn from textbook concepts on imperfect competition, the existence of externalities or information asymmetry, and of public goods characteristics. Discussions have focused on fossil fuels, that is, oil and gas, reflecting the dominant role these energy resources play in primary energy demand. Based on this, the chapter has identified four key areas that ideally should be addressed by global public policy: market transparency and planning security, negative spillover effects of a global scale, free-rider problems, and the existence of global market imbalances caused by cartels. Acknowledging the fact that global, and for that matter also collective global public action, may not be able effectively to address the existence of cartels, the latter have been excluded from further discussions. Finally, and though the primary concern of this chapter was a conceptual one, some implications of the "call" on global public policy have been discussed.

In conclusion it can be stated that energy security can successfully be assessed from a public policy lens. It is a potent framework that leads to results and allows the generating of clear-cut policy recommendations. The latter also differ substantially from the ones stemming from predominantly geopolitical approaches in energy policy debates. These tend to center on "security of supply," suggesting that nations are locked into a competition over access to energy resources, key to economic prosperity and, maybe even more importantly, state power. A public policy framework, by contrast, not only treats energy security more holistically in the sense that it comprises supply as well as demand-side aspects. It also points to the crucial importance of both markets *and* states in ensuring the delivery of energy security—for producers and consumers alike. Following that, it points to units and levels of analysis that matter, that is, state as well as non-state actors; to the rationales that make them tick; to the possible unintended global side effects of state and non-state action; and to the issues of real concern in energy, that is, planning security, investment levels, detrimental price volatility or collective actions problems. True, this framework is more complex than models that tend to think of states as black boxes, of energy as a means of power, and of the world as an arena of zero-sum games. Yet, in turn, it also allows developing more sophisticated policy instruments in providing energy security than the overall reductive and hard security-related toolbox suggested by geopolitical scholars.

Addressing and eventually correcting energy market failures on a global scale by definition also is a global exercise—and one that requires both a strong commitment and major efforts among producing and consuming states. It is a thoroughly political exercise and will require major efforts by all involved players. Will these materialize? In fact, and going back to a key concern addressed in this chapter, incentives for collective action do clearly exist: it is not only Western or Chinese imports that are at stake in the event of a major upward oil price shock. It is also state coffers in producer countries such as Saudi Arabia or Kuwait, depending up to 100 percent on oil revenues, that suffer to the same extent in the case of a counter-shock—not to mention the detrimental effects such an event would have on consumers' efforts to go low carbon and make renewable fuels competitive.[53] In other words, highly volatile oil prices entail considerable dangers for both producer and consumer states alike. Providing for a reliable price environment involves establishing mechanisms along many of the fronts discussed, from strengthening information to accounting for diametric risk patterns.

Yet, it is important to stress that there are also limits to a public policy approach to global energy security. First, it is of course subject to further discussion as to what extent the concept of (global) market failure can and should inform public policymaking.[54] Second, some incidents of market failure may simply fall prey to a global collective action problem which it is hard to overcome by institutional arrangements. Third, and finally, perceptions matter, as do paradigms. Depending on which of the latter policymakers subscribe to, policy prescriptions differ. A public policy approach, focusing on making markets work, on producing public goods, and on preventing public bads may be analytically compelling and may also provide for powerful policy advice. Yet, at the very end it is up to policymakers to make the choice—in favor of a paradigm focusing on markets or the more simplistic but equally intuitive zero-sum rationales informed by hard security approaches.

Notes

1 The author would like to thank Marc Thurber for his valuable comments to an earlier version of this chapter. Special thanks also go to the participants of the Global Energy Governance panel at the Annual Convention of the International Studies Association in New Orleans, February 18, 2010, and to the participants of the CEU Energy Policy Research Group workshop in March 2010. This chapter draws to a large extent on an article entitled "Market failure in energy: a global public policy perspective on energy security," to be published in 2011, as well as on previous works.
2 Among others: Bahgat, Gawdat. 2003. "Pipeline Diplomacy: The Geopolitics of the Caspian Sea Region," *International Studies Perspectives* 3(3): 310–327; Barnes, Jo, and Amy Myers Jaffe. 2006. "The Persian Gulf and the Geopolitics of Oil," *Survival* 48(1): 143–162; Smith, Keith. 2006. "Defuse Russia's Energy Weapon," *International Herald Tribune*, January 16; Deutch, John M., James

R. Schlesinger, and David G. Victor. 2006. *National Security Consequences of U.S. Oil Dependency: Report of an Independent Task Force* (New York: Council on Foreign Relations).

3 For an almost classical piece on global public goods and policymaking see Kaul, Inge, Isabelle Grunberg, and Marc A. Stern. 1999. *Global Public Goods: International Cooperation in the 21st Century* (Oxford: Oxford University Press), and its more recent sequel Kaul, Inge, Pedro Conceição, Katell Le Goulven, and Ronald U. Mendoza. 2003. *Providing Global Public Goods: Managing Globalization* (New York: Oxford University Press); see also Barrett, Scott. 2007. *For Why Cooperate? The Incentive to Supply Global Public Goods* (Oxford: Oxford University Press); for a conceptual overview see Stone, Diane L. 2008. "Global Public Policy, Transnational Policy Communities and their Networks," *Policy Studies Journal* 36 (10): 19–38. Available empirical studies tend to center on aid, development, global health or global financial stability; energy, however, is not subject to analysis. Bohi, Douglas R., Michael A. Toman, and Margaret A. Walls. 1995. *The Economics of Energy Security* (New York: Springer) is, to my best knowledge, the only attempt to conceptualize energy security in terms of market failure – even if not consistently from a global perspective. Please note that the climate nexus has been the subject of in-depth research from a global public goods angle. Climate policy is, however, not the primary subject of this chapter.

4 Reflecting the fact that energy security comprises both producer and consumer nations, this contribution defines energy security as "reliable access to energy supplies and services at affordable prices for consuming nations and as reliable demand of energy products and services at sustainable prices for exporting ones."

5 BP. 2009. *Statistical Review of World Energy* (London: British Petroleum), p. 41.

6 A clear case of a "government failure" on a global level would be the fact that there is a lack of a clear classification for biofuels within the World Trade Organization's (WTO) multilateral trading system, which restricts the emergence of a fungible and veritably global market for biofuels. See Zarrilli, Simonetta. 2010. "The Emerging Biofuels Market and its Development Implications." In A. Goldthau and J. M. Witte (eds.), *Global Energy Governance: The New Rules of the Game* (Washington, DC: Brookings Press), pp. 73–98.

7 Subsidies tend to distort price incentives and to encourage the over-usage of finite resources; a case in point is the subsidy policy in the Gulf States. See Mitchell, John V, and Paul Stevens. 2008. *Ending Dependence: Hard Choices for Oil-Exporting States* (London: Chatham House).

8 Florini, Ann, and Benjamin K. Sovacool. 2009. "Who Governs Energy? The Challenges Facing Global Energy Governance," *Energy Policy* 37(12): 5239–5248.

9 Private goods are characterized as rivalrous and excludable in consumption.

10 For a classic piece see Bator, Francis M. 1985. "The Anatomy of Market Failure," *The Quarterly Journal of Economics* 72(3): 351–379.

11 Since the early 1970s, oil prices have remained far above marginal production costs, which would be a direct indicator for the existence of such a premium.

12 The Seven Sisters consisted of Standard Oil of New Jersey (later Exxon), Royal Dutch Shell, the Anglo-Persian Oil Company (APOC, later BP), Standard Oil of New York (Socony, later Mobil), Standard Oil of California (Socal, later Chevron), Gulf Oil, and Texaco. For a history of the oil market see Yergin, Daniel. 1991. *The Prize: The Epic Quest for Oil, Money, and Power* (New York: Simon & Schuster); Maugeri, Leonardo. 2006. *Age of Oil: The Mythology History and Future of the World's Most Controversial Resource* (Westport, CT: Praeger); and Parra, Francisco. 2004. *Oil Politics: A Modern History of Petroleum* (London: I. B. Tauris).

13 For a discussion of the evolving Liquefied Natural Gas (LNG) market: Jong, Dick de, Coby van der Linde, and Tom Smeenk. 2010. "The Evolving Role of LNG in the Gas Market: The EU Gas Market as a Case Study." In A. Goldthau and J. M. Witte (eds), *Global Energy Governance: The New Rules of the Game* (Washington, DC: Brookings Press), pp. 221–246.

14 Bohi *et al.*, *The Economics of Energy Security*, p. 15.

15 For a classic piece on the IEA see Keohane, Robert. 1984. "The Consumers' Oil Regime, 1974–81." In his *After Hegemony: Cooperation and Discord in the World Political Economy* (Princeton, NJ: Princeton University Press); for a discussion on current challenges facing the IEA see Kohl, Wilfrid. 2010. "The International Energy Agency and the Global Energy Order." In A. Goldthau and J. M. Witte (eds.), *Global Energy Governance: The New Rules of the Game* (Washington, DC: Brookings Institution Press); and Colgan, Jeff. 2009. *The International Energy Agency: Challenges for the 21st Century*, GPPi Energy Policy Paper 6.

16 Barroso, José Manuel Durão. 2008. "Opening Remarks of President Barroso on the 2nd Strategic Energy Review." Paper read at press conference on the Strategic Energy Review Package, November 13, at Brussels.

17 EU Commission. 2008. *EU Energy Security and Solidarity Action Plan: 2nd Strategic Energy Review* (Brussels: Commission of the European Communities).

18 For a classic piece see Buchanan, James, and William C. Stubblebine. 1969. "Externality," *Economica* 29: 371–384.

19 See Bohi *et al.*, *The Economics of Energy Security* for an in-depth discussion of externalities in energy security. In addition, oil consumption as such creates other externalities, notably detrimental greenhouse gas emissions. As these types of externalities do not, however, directly affect energy security and are prominently discussed elsewhere, they are not of primary concern to this chapter. For an overview of externalities, particularly regarding the environmental dimension of energy policy, see Pearce, David. 2001. "Energy Policy and Externalities: An Overview." Paper read at OECD Nuclear Energy Agency Workshop on Energy Policy and Externalities: "the Life Cycle Analysis Approach," November 15–16, at Paris.

20 Brown, Stephen P. A. 2009. "Reassessing Oil Security," *Resources for the Future Weekly Commentary* (October 5), available at http://206.205.47.99/Publications/WPC/Pages/Reassessing-Oil-Security-Stephen-P.A.-Brown.aspx (accessed August 28, 2010).

21 Corden, W. Max, and J. Peter Neary. 1982. "Booming Sector and De-industrialisation in a Small Open Economy," *The Economic Journal* 92 (December): 825–848.

22 For recent papers on the EU see Arnold, Steve, and Alistair Hunt. 2009. *National and EU-Level Estimates of Energy Supply Externalities*, CEPS Policy Brief 186; or Hedenus, Fredrik, Christian Azar, and Daniel J.A. Johansson. 2010. "Energy Security Policies in EU-25: The Expected Cost of Oil Supply Disruptions," *Energy Policy* 38: 1241–1250; for the US see Leiby, Paul N. 2007. *Estimating the Energy Security Benefits of Reduced U.S. Oil Imports* (Oak Ridge: Oak Ridge National Laboratory); Beccue, Phillip and Hillard G. Huntington. 2005. "Oil Disruption Risk Assessment." In *Energy Modeling Forum Special Report* (Stanford, CA: Stanford University), available at http://emf.stanford.edu/publications/emf_sr_8_an_assessment_of_oil_market_disruption_risks/ (accessed August 28, 2010); or Brown, Stephen P. A. and Hillard G. Huntington. 2009. *Estimating U.S. Oil Security Premiums* (Stanford, CA: Stanford University, Energy Modeling Forum). For a literature survey see Sauter, Raphael and Shimon Awerbuch. 2002. *Oil Price Volatility and Economic Activity: A Survey and Literature Review*, IEA Working Paper (Paris: IEA). As for natural gas, and for reasons discussed below, it is very hard to quantify the externality costs associated with supply insecurities.

23 Hunt, Alistair and Anil Markandya. 2004. *Final Report on Work Package 3: The Externalities of Energy Insecurity*, European Commission, p. 10.

24 International Energy Agency (IEA). 2009. *World Energy Outlook 2009* (Paris: International Energy Agency).

25 International Energy Agency, *World Energy Outlook 2009*.

26 Among others: Stern, Jonathan, Simon Pirani, and Katja Yafimava. 2009. *The Russo-Ukrainian Gas Dispute of January 2009: A Comprehensive Assessment* (Oxford: Oxford Institute for Energy Studies); Yafimava, Katja and Jonathan Stern. 2007. "The 2007 Russia-Belarus Gas Agreement," *Oxford Energy Comment* (January); Stern, Jonathan. 2007. "Gas-OPEC: A Distraction from Important Issues of Russian Gas Supply to Europe," *Oxford Energy Comment* 2; and Goldthau, Andreas. 2008. "Resurgent Russia? Rethinking Energy Inc. Five myths about the 'energy superpower'," *Policy Review* 147 (February/ March): 53–63.

27 This is not an externality in strictly economic terms. Yet, as it distorts the effective allocation of resources on a market, it still qualifies as an externality.

28 Stern *et al.*, *The Russo-Ukrainian Gas Dispute of January 2009*, p. 61; Kovacevic, Aleksandar. 2009. *The Impact of the Russia–Ukraine Gas Crisis in South Eastern Europe* (Oxford: Oxford Institute for Energy Studies), p. 19.

29 For a classical read on public goods see Paul Samuelson. "The Pure Theory of Public Expenditure," *Review of Economics and Statistics* 36(4) (1954), pp. 387–389; Samuelson, Paul and Mancur Olson. *The Logic of Collective Action: Public Goods and the Theory of Groups* (Cambridge, MA: Harvard University Press, 1965). It is, however, important to note that, due to the fact that very few public goods are "pure," impure public goods such as club goods are also subject to this discussion.

30 See also Jaffe, Amy Myers, and Ronald Soligo. 2002. "The Role of Inventories in Oil Market Stability," *The Quarterly Review of Economics and Finance* 42(2): 401–415.

31 Leiby, Paul N., David Bowman, and Donald W. Jones. 2002. "Improving Energy Security Through an International Cooperative Approach to Emergency Oil Stockpiling." Paper read at 25th Annual IAEE International Conference, June 26–29, at Aberdeen, Scotland.

32 In fact, as Leiby *et al.* note, only some few countries such as the US are big enough for the benefits of holding stocks to exceed related costs: "Improving Energy Security," p. 9.

33 Colgan, *The International Energy Agency: Challenges for the 21st Century*.

34 The entire projected increment in global oil demand until 2030 will stem from non-OECD countries, notably Asia. By that time, China's oil consumption alone will about double. IEA, *World Energy Outlook 2009*, p. 73.

35 Harks, Enno. 2010. "The International Energy Forum and the mitigation of oil market risks." In A. Goldthau and J. M. Witte (eds.), *Global Energy Governance: The new Rules of the Game* (Washington DC: Brookings Press), p. 253.

36 A painful lesson from the first and second oil shocks in the 1970s for the producers was that consumers started to invest in energy efficiency, demand-reducing technology, and in alternative supplies.

37 U.S. Energy Information Administration, *World Oil Transit Chokepoints* (Washington, DC: U.S. Department of Energy), January, 2008. Available at: http://www.eia.doe.gov/cabs/World_Oil_Transit_Chokepoints/Background.html (accessed August 28, 2010).

38 See Crane, Keith, Andreas Goldthau, and Michael Toman, 2009. *Imported Oil and National Security* (Washington DC: RAND Corporation), p. 63f.

39 Crane et al., *Imported Oil and National Security*, p. 74.

40 International Energy Agency (IEA). 2009. *Oil Market Report* (Paris: IEA), p. 17; Holscher, Jens, Ray Bachan, and Andrew Stimpson. 2008. "Oil Demand in China: An Econometric Approach," *International Journal of Emerging Markets* 31(1): 54–70.

41 Energy Intelligence. 2009. *Energy Intelligence Top 100: Ranking The World's Oil Companies* (New York: Energy Intelligence).

42 Goldthau, Andreas. 2010. "Energy Diplomacy in Trade and Investment of Oil and Gas. In A. Goldthau and J. M. Witte (eds.), *Global Energy Governance: The New Rules of the Game* (Washington DC: Brookings Press), pp 25–48.

43 Evans, Peter C., and Erica S. Downs. 2006. Untangling China's quest for oil through state-backed financial deals. *Brookings Policy Brief* 154.

44 As Albert Bressand notes pointedly, Europe makes up for some 13 percent of global carbon emissions only and is just too clean already to make a difference. Bresssand, Albert. 2010. "European Integration and the Development of a European External Energy Policy in Eurasia," *GPPi Policy Paper* 7: 31.

45 Witte, Jan Martin, Timo Behr, Wade Hoxtell, and Jamie Manzer. 2009. "Towards a Global Carbon Market? The Potential and Limits of Carbon Market Integration," *GPPi Policy Paper* 7.

46 "CO2 Pact Leaves Businesses Feeling Up in the Air," *Wall Street Journal*, December 21, 2009; Blyth, William. 2010. "How do Carbon Markets Influence Energy Sector Investments." In A. Goldthau and J. M. Witte (eds), *Global Energy Governance: The New Rules of the Game* (Washington DC: Brookings Press); International Energy Agency. 2007. *Climate Policy Uncertainty and Investment Risk* (Paris: IEA). For a theoretical approach see also Dixit, Avinsash K., and Robert S. Pindyck. 1994. *Investment under Uncertainty* (Princeton, NJ: Princeton University Press).

47 Bohi *et al.*, *The Economics of Energy Security*, p. 10.

48 Antypas, Alexios. 2010. The Copenhagen Accord: "Inclusive, Meaningful and an Important Step Forward," *Environmental Law and Management* (21): 295–301.

49 In natural gas, take-off agreements make sure that the contracted and produced volumes are indeed absorbed by the consumer, whether needed or not. However, the price risks still exist, though only indirectly, through the price-peg mechanism.

50 Victor, David, and Linda Yueh. 2010. "The New Energy Order: Managing Insecurities in the Twenty-First Century," *Foreign Affairs*, January/February.

51 Harks, "The International Energy Forum and the Mitigation of Oil Market Risks."

52 Among others: Socor, Vladimir. 2009. "Chancellor Merkel Says Nein to Nabucco," *Eurasia Daily Monitor* 6 (45); Mirow, Thomas. 2009. "Bringing the Pipeline into the Pipeline – Conditions for an EBRD Participation in the Nabucco Project." Speech at Nabucco Summit of Heads of State and Government, January 26–27, Budapest.

53 See the EIA's Country Analysis Briefs on Saudi Arabia and Kuwait, available at http://www.eia.doe.gov/emeu/cabs/ (accessed January 31, 2010).

54 For a critical perspective on market failures see Cowen, Tyler. 1988. *The Theory of Market Failure: A Critical Examination* (Washington, DC: George Mason University Press).

7

THE DIVERSIFICATION DIMENSION OF ENERGY SECURITY

Andy Stirling

Diversity and ignorance

Energy diversity is not an end in itself, but offers different means to a variety of ends. Although energy security is often treated as if it were the exclusive rationale for deliberate diversification (Spicer, 1987; Parkinson, 1989; PIU, 2001; DTI, 2006), it is actually only one reason for policy interest in diversity (IEA, 1985; CEC, 1990, 2007; Stirling, 1994; Verrastro and Ladislaw, 2007; Bazilian and Roques, 2008). Yet even with respect to the particular domain of energy security, different notions of energy diversity are invoked in contrasting policy contexts. Surprisingly often, energy diversity remains entirely undefined—both in high-level policymaking and associated analysis. Being curiously underscrutinized in this way, diversity is particularly vulnerable to special pleading in highly politicized energy security debates. Drawing closely on earlier work (Stirling, 2010), the aim of this chapter is to explore the challenges of diversity in their wider policy context and identify a systematic, comprehensive, and transparent framework through which to address them in a practical way.

The chapter will begin by examining the variety of contexts and approaches for the analysis of energy diversity. It will start by considering in the present section the often-neglected dimensions and implications of incomplete knowledge (concerning energy security as well as other strategic issues). Attention will then turn to some wider strategic and policy considerations bearing on diversification in energy infrastructures. This will then form a basis for indentifying some underlying common elements of diversity—applicable with respect to any policy domain. Criteria will be developed for the rigorous aggregation, accommodation, and articulation of these multiple dimensions of energy diversity. These will then present a formal framework under which will be derived a novel quantitative diversity heuristic, which can be applied to the task of exploring contrasting energy portfolios using a method called multicriteria diversity analysis (Stirling, 2010). This approach will be illustrated using a schematic empirical example of direct relevance to current practical policymaking on energy security.

As a starting point, we should begin by clarifying the general concept of energy diversity itself. Despite the complexities, ambiguities, and expediencies, international policy discussions of energy diversity are all in various ways about pursuit of "an evenly balanced reliance on a variety of mutually disparate options" (Stirling, 2010). In principle, such "options" may be recognized equally in the form of technologies or policies, sources or fuels, suppliers or infrastructures, or on the supply or demand side. It follows from this that there lies a crucial difference between diversity and other key themes in energy policy. Unlike many other aspects of performance under energy security criteria—as well as financial, economic, environmental, or wider strategic issues—diversity is an inherent and irreducible feature of an energy system taken as a whole (Stirling, 1994). For reasons that will be discussed later, evenness of "balance," the scale of mutual "disparities," and even the partitioning of "variety" are all holistic system-level properties. These may each be understood in different ways. But, irrespective of context or perspective, diversity cannot legitimately be reduced to simple aggregates of the attributes of individual technological, resource, or institutional "options" within a given energy system.

To elaborate this more specifically in the context of energy security, diversity is seen in this area as a means simultaneously to help *prevent* disruptions to energy supply and to *mitigate* their effects should they occur (IEA, 1985). Attention tends to focus on what are held to be relatively well-known sources of disruption, like fuel price fluctuations, constraints on the availability of specific primary resources, or a restricted number of clearly identified threats (Lucas *et al.*, 1995). However, to focus exclusively on these relatively readily characterized parameters in some ways circum-scribes the real value of diversification (Stirling, 1995). As distinct from a range of more specific and targeted preventive and mitigative strategies, diversity remains effective (at least in part) *even if the sources or modalities of the prospective disruptions are effectively unknown*. By maintaining an evenly balanced reliance across a variety of mutually disparate options, we may hope to resist impacts on any subset of these, *even if we do not know in advance exactly what impacts we are seeking to hedge* (Stirling, 1996). It is in these ways that energy diversity is best addressed as an irreducible system-level quality (however construed), rather than as an aggregate property of individual energy options.

The essential quality of diversity thus lies simply in "putting eggs in different baskets." Although the value of this strategy rests on spreading dependencies across a variety of different "baskets," it applies irrespective of the particularities of any individual basket. This has profound implications for analytical methodology. There exists a host of specific, structured, targeted techniques for addressing well-determined energy security threats—and corresponding attributes of individual options. These include sophisticated quantitative tools, offering powerful responses under conditions where the relevant parameters may confidently be *reduced* to single metrics and definitively *aggregated* across different dimensions (Stirling, 2003). Yet, for this same fundamental reason, such "reductive aggregative" techniques offer a poor general basis for thinking about energy diversity. This is because the particular value of diversification lies in addressing conditions under which precisely these kinds of required data inputs or calculative procedure may not be possible with any confidence. In order to appreciate this point, it is necessary to consider in a little more detail the contrasting ways in which knowledge may be incomplete—as much in relation to energy security as in other areas.

As already mentioned, the principal stated reasons for policy interest in energy diversity have traditionally lain in the hedging of uncertainties concerning the security of energy supplies (eg: CEC, 1990, 2007; IEA, 2007; NERA, 2002; PMSU, 2002; DTI, 2003a). Here, the conventional way to represent incomplete knowledge is through a particular suite of reductive aggregative "probabilistic risk assessment" techniques (CEC, 2007; NERA, 2002). With parti-cular respect to analysis of diversity, this includes various forms of Monte Carlo analysis and portfolio theory (Ulph, 1988, 1989; NERA, 1995; ERM, 1995; Awerbuch and Berger, 2003; Awerbuch and Yang, 2007). Yet, the representation of all forms of incomplete knowledge as if they were the very specific and circumscribed condition of risk raises several serious issues that are too rarely discussed—or even acknowledged—in discussions of policy analysis for energy security.

knowledge about outcomes

unproblematic   problematic

unproblematic	**RISK**	**AMBIGUITY**
	variability under giving conditions	**contested assumptions**
	BERR: "primarily about measuring risk"	*disaggregated indicators*
	market signals/responses	*appraisal bias*
	'spark-spread' indicators	*institutional interests*
	probabilistic event trees	*contending disciplines*
	'expected energy unserved' calculus	*divergent values*
	'mean-variance portfolio theory'	*mulitiple perspectives*
	benefit-cost analysis	
	'optimal security' models	

knowledge about likelihoods

specified new possibilities
safety intervals/multipliers
capacity/demand margins
vulnerability assessment   **surprises and unknowns**
fixed forms of flexibility/adaptation   *open reversibility/adaptiveness*
single indicator scenarios   *redundancy, agility, suppleness*
deterministic sensitivity envelopes   *diversity, resilience, robustness*

problematic   **UNCERTAINTY**   **IGNORANCE**

Figure 7.1 Contrasting aspects of incomplete knowledge (and associated responses in energy security analysis).

Figure 7.1 presents one heuristic way to think about this challenge (Stirling, 1999c). In order to highlight how the issues that arise are intrinsic to any probabilistic approach, the picture is framed according to the two fundamental defining parameters for the condition of "risk": probabilities and outcomes. In short (and whether acknowledged or not), these highlight two distinct ways in which knowledge about energy security threats may be incomplete: concerning the accurate derivation of probabilities, or the meaningful or complete definition of the possible outcomes themselves. Contemplating conditions under which knowledge may variously be conceived as "problematic" or "unproblematic" under each of these twin parameters thus yields four ideal-typical aspects of a wider challenge of "incertitude," extending well beyond the confines of conventional notions of "risk"—or even the strict definition of "uncertainty" (Stirling, 2003). Under conditions where we can be confident in our knowledges concerning both probability and outcomes (in the top left quadrant), then, conventional probabilistic techniques can offer powerful tools for policy analysis. These include risk assessment itself (von Winterfeldt and Edwards, 1986), more elaborate Bayesian procedures (Jaynes, 1986), cost-benefit analysis (Hanley and Spash, 1993), life cycle assessment (van den Berg *et al.*, 1995), multi-attribute evaluation (Dodgson *et al.*, 2001), and decision-tree methods (Clemen, 1996). All of these "reductive aggregative" techniques are routinely used effectively to treat all incertitude as if it were "risk" (Stirling, 2007b). Figure 7.1 provides some indicative illustrations of typical energy security interventions (mentioned in recent UK energy security policy documentation, e.g.: JESS, 2004; Wicks, 2006) that represent this kind of "reductive aggregative" treatment of "risk".

Moving to the lower left of Figure 7.1, we find the strictly defined condition of uncertainty. Here, we are confident in our knowledges of the range of possibilities. But the available empirical information or analytical models are recognized not to present definitive grounds for assigning probabilities (Knight, 1921; Keynes, 1921; Rowe, 1994). Examples may be found precisely in the complex, dynamic, open, indeterminate systems that typically characterize energy security problems. It is under these conditions—according to the celebrated probability theorist de Finetti (1974)—that "probability does not exist." Of course, we can still exercise subjective judgments and treat these as a basis for systematic analysis (Luce and Raiffa, 1957; Morgan, *et al.*, 1990). However, the challenge of this strict state of uncertainty is that such judgments may take different equally plausible forms (Wynne, 1992; Stirling and Mayer, 2001). Use of conventional risk-based approaches to reduce and aggregate this subjective diversity may give the appearance of objectivity, but can raise serious questions over both rigour and reliability (Stirling, 2008a; 2008b).

Insistence on treating uncertainty in analysis as if it were risk is curious, since there exists under these conditions, a wide range of more appropriate methods. These include sensitivity (Saltelli, 2004), scenario (Werner, 2004), and interval analysis (Jaulin *et al.*, 2001), all of which can serve to "open up" the limits to probabilistic reduction and aggregation. Various "decision heuristics" provide frameworks for thinking about the normative implications of comparing different likelihoods, including "maximax" (Pearce and Nash, 1981) and "minimum regret" (Forster, 1999) or "maximin" (Rawls, 1997) criteria. Taken together, these methods help respond practically to challenges of irreducible uncertainty that otherwise remain entirely unaddressed in conventional risk assessment. Also drawing on recent high-profile UK government documentation on energy security policy, Figure 7.1 lists in the uncertainty quadrant, some well-known measures that offer to avoid treating uncertainty as if it were risk (JESS, 2004; BERR, 2006; Wicks, 2006).

Under conditions of ambiguity (top right quadrant in Figure 7.1), it is not knowledges of likelihoods, but of the possible energy security threats themselves, that are problematic. Ambiguities may be found, for instance, where outcomes are thought to be certain—or have even occurred already. The question in the latter case is not "what might happen?" but "exactly what did happen?" For instance, a violent war may be agreed to have occurred, but (even when seen only under perspectives extant in the perpetrating country) was this more about "liberating foreign populations," "defending domestic security," "dominating strategic regions," or "controlling key energy resources"? Although often invisible in analysis, such questions arise ubiquitously in characterizing different dimensions of energy security and interpreting their normative meanings: for instance in selecting, partitioning, prioritizing, or measuring different rationales for and implications of energy security and their respective possible consequences (Wynne, 2002; Stirling, 2003). They are independent of any consideration of relative likelihood, and thus about ambiguity rather than uncertainty.

Put simply, ambiguity raises the thorny problem of "apples and oranges." How should we prioritize security as compared with economic or environmental issues? How might we best define and articulate different forms of, needs for, or perspectives on, "energy security" (like those associated with households, livelihoods, business, regions, governments, social groups, political constituencies)? Such dilemmas are routine in energy security debates, where radically divergent pictures are yielded under contrasting viewpoints. These may each also vary, when seen through the lenses of different disciplines (such as policy analysis, international studies, social science and various branches of economics, decision theory, and operations research)—each itself often represented by contending individual experts. Interestingly, it is a prominent but neglected feature of rational choice theory (on which probabilistic risk-based techniques are founded), that there can in principle exist no definitive analytical means to guarantee the validity of any particular aggregation of these kinds of "incommensurable" issues (Arrow, 1963; Kelly, 1978; Mackay, 1980; Collingridge, 1982; Bonner, 1986). In this light, it is an intriguing—but equally neglected—feature of diversity that it offers a means to help accommodate otherwise irreconcilable values and interests. There are few areas of policymaking where this is more salient than in the field of energy security.

Alongside diversification, however, there exist a wide range of alternatives to "risk-based" techniques for addressing challenges of ambiguity. These include both qualitative elicitation in (expert or lay) focus groups (Grove-White *et al.*, 2000), dissensus panels (Canary, *et al.*, 1987; Meyers, 1997), Delphi procedures (Renn *et al.*, 1995), open space methods (Owen, 1997), and do-it-yourself juries (Wakeford, 2002, as well as various forms of interactive modeling (de Marchi *et al.*, 1998) and hybrid techniques like Q-method (McKeown and Thomas, 1988), repertory grid (Fransella *et al.*, 2004), multicriteria mapping (Stirling and Mayer, 2001), and deliberative mapping (Burgess *et al.*, 2007). In different ways, these help enable more broad-based "reflective" attention and more recursively self-aware "reflexive" deliberation over the different dimensions of energy security (Stirling, 2006a). It is therefore doubly curious that policy analysis for energy security issues should tend to favor reductive aggregative risk-based techniques, which are as formally inapplicable under ambiguity as they are under uncertainty. Some measures alluded to obliquely and intermittently in the UK government energy security literature are also mentioned under "ambiguity" in Figure 7.1.

Finally, in the bottom right corner of Figure 7.1, there is the condition of ignorance. Here there lie some of the most profound challenges in energy security policy: where neither probabilities nor possibilities can be definitively characterized (Keynes, 1921; Loasby, 1976; Collingridge, 1980). This acknowledges the prospect of developments that are not merely uncertain or ambiguous, but utterly unexpected (Rosenberg, 1996). It is a condition where "we don't know what we don't know" (Wynne, 1992, 2002)—invoking the ever-present (but otherwise excluded) possibility of surprise (Brooks, 1986). This differs from uncertainty, which focuses on agreed known parameters like resource availability or fuel price variability (Funtowicz and Ravetz, 1990). It differs from ambiguity in that salient parameters are acknowledged not just to be contestable, undercharacterized, or incommensurable in their relative importance, but unbounded, indeterminate, unknown, or unknowable (Faber and Proops, 1994). It is under conditions of ignorance that the routine risk-based tools used in energy security analysis are least applicable of all (Stirling, 1999c). To paraphrase a notorious recent remark in a field not unrelated to energy policy (Rumsfeld, 2002), there emerges here the strongest rationale for diversification. When we don't know what we don't know, we shouldn't put all our eggs in one basket! Figure 7.1 indicates in this last quadrant alongside diversity, some wider strategic responses to ignorance, of a kind that also challenge reliance on risk-based analysis, but which each remain similarly neglected (JESS, 2004; BERR, 2006; Wicks, 2006). Indeed, taken as a whole, Figure 7.1 illustrates a more general phenomenon under which institutional pressures act to lead incumbents preferentially to represent open, indeterminate forms of incertitude as if they were more tractable than they really are (Stirling, 2009a). Without appreciating these multiple aspects of incertitude and their intractability to conventional risk-based analysis, it is difficult fully to appreciate the multivalent benefits of energy diversity as a robust general strategy for energy security.

Broader contexts for security and diversity

All this said, it is important to acknowledge that—despite the importance of diversity to debates over energy security—there exist many other dimensions of energy security that extend beyond the issue of diversity alone. Internationally ubiquitous aims around achieving "availability of energy at all times in various forms in sufficient quantities and at affordable prices" (Umbach, 2004) can be pursued by many different strategies. A number of these are entirely distinct from— and sometimes even in tension with—diversification. For instance, reliance on indigenous resources has been advocated as an energy security strategy, even if this reduces diversity (IEA, 1980). By contrast, efficient functioning of energy markets is often highlighted as a means to achieve "optimal" levels of energy security, without the need for extraneous policy interventions to foster diversity (Helm, 2002, 2007). Despite this, it is well established that (even under agendas of liberalization) states do continue to seek to structure more "secure" energy markets—for instance through promotion of economic interdependence on the part of supplier interests (European Energy Charter, 2004) or more effective international planning of responses to disruption (Adelman, 1995). In this way, strategic stockpiles are often crucial (Greene *et al.*, 1998), as are efforts to exercise greater control over energy supply chains (Lawson, 1992). Irrespective of their diversity, a security premium is often paid for more flexible supply options (Costello, 2004): redundant infrastructures (Farrell *et al.*, 2004) or demand-side efficiency programs (Lovins and Lovins, 1982). Finally, although less openly acknowledged, there is the potential for violent action—both as resisted in "resilient" domestic energy infrastructures (JESS, 2004) and as perpetrated in offensive military interventions against perceived energy security threats (Plummer, 1983).

Diversity is thus only one—albeit prominent—factor among a wide range of different dimensions of energy security. However, it is important to note that references to diversity also feature prominently in a number of parallel policy debates (Stirling, 1998). Some of these are highly relevant to the energy sector, and should therefore also be set alongside historic preoccupations with energy security as reasons for interest in energy diversity. As shown in Figure 7.2, the relationship between energy diversity and security is therefore somewhat more complex than often assumed.

In considering claims over the multiple benefits of diversity, it must be remembered that—in any single context—diversity rarely offers a "free lunch" (Weitzman, 1992). Those options that are marginal in any given energy system are often in this position for reasons of poor performance. Contingent differences in resource endowments or institutional environments thus condition

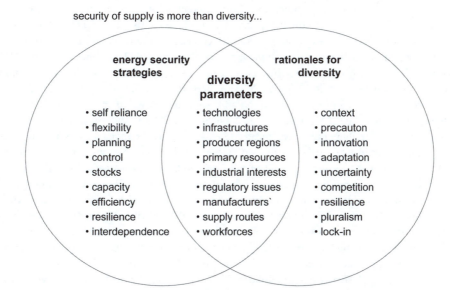

Figure 7.2 Schematic summary of relationships between energy diversity and security.

different patterns of emergent diversity in different geographical, socio-economic, or cultural contexts. To enlarge the contributions of marginal options in any given context will thus—under any given perspective—often incur some performance penalty (David and Rothwell, 1996). In addition, there are typically further tradeoffs between diversity and transaction costs (Williamson, 1993) and with foregone benefits like coherence (Cohendet, *et al.*, 1992), accountability (Grabher and Stark, 1997), standardization (Cowan, 1991), and economies of scale (Matthews and McGowan, 1990). Diversification may retard enhanced learning about incumbent technologies in favor of learning about more marginal options (Jacobsson and Johnson, 2000). The crucial challenge thus lies in striking a balance between the benefits of diversity and these countervailing aspects of portfolio performance (Geroski, 1989). The value of the "diversity premium" (Ulph, 1988, 1989) that is warranted in any particular energy mix may be appraised under a variety of strategic criteria—including financial, economic, environmental, health, or broader social impacts (COLA, 1994). Indeed, the situation may even arise where tradeoffs are made between the general security benefits of enhanced energy diversity and more particular security penalties associated with specific options through which diversification is achieved (IEA, 1980). In the end, all such issues are judgmental, offering ample scope for legitimate disagreement. A crucial challenge for policy analysis of energy diversity is therefore to examine these multidimensional interactions and tradeoffs.

Thus qualified, it remains to substantiate the potential benefits of energy diversity identified in Figure 7.2, beyond the traditional preoccupations with preventing or mitigating service disruptions. The first kinds of benefit arise quite naturally from the rationale conventionally discussed with respect to supply security. Putting "eggs in different baskets" hedges against "surprises" (Brooks, 1986)—including operational, environmental, economic, or wider strategic uncertainties that are not directly relevant to supply security (Rosenberg, 1996). This underscores increasing associations between diversity, sustainability, and precaution in energy strategies (Stirling, 1999c, 2008b; Bird, 2007; Helm, 2002, 2007; IEA, 2007). Second, it is true in the energy sector as elsewhere, that reducing concentration in technology, service or commodity markets is an important means to promote competition. Indeed, competitive diversity in energy markets is often presented as significant to the competitiveness of the wider economy (DTI, 2003a, 2006). Third, a growing literature shows how general technical, institutional, and functional heterogeneity can help foster more effective innovation (Rosenberg, 1982; Grabher and Stark, 1997; Kauffman, 1995). This is of crucial interest equally where policy attention focuses on moves towards "the knowledge society" (CEC, 2005) or in driving specific radical transformations like those involved in environmental innovation and transitions to sustainable energy (Bird, 2007; Patterson, 1999; Mitchell, 2007; Grubb *et al.*, 2006; Stirling, 2008b). Indeed, with moves towards sustainability intrinsically requiring enhanced context-sensitivity (Brundtland, 1987), there arises a further, fourth, distinct rationale for diversity in better tailoring energy systems to diverse local cultural, ecological, and geopolitical and geophysical conditions (Landau *et al.*, 1996).

This leads to a fifth and final important role for energy diversity. By sustaining a plurality of disparate techno-institutional strategies, we may better accommodate otherwise irreconcilable socio-economic interests—not just on energy security itself (as discussed in the last section), but in relation to other important political domains (Stirling, 1997). Energy policy has long served as a site for deeply entrenched and protracted general cultural, institutional, and political conflicts around technology choice (MacKerron and Scrase, 2009). Issues around nuclear power provide an iconic, but not exclusive, example (Elliott, 2007). Far from being attenuated by growing consensus over the general imperatives for transitions to "sustainable energy," the role of the energy sector as an arena for public contention may actually be amplified by the many questions that follow from this (Smith *et al.*, 2005). What really counts as "sustainable"? Which strategies are most viable? Far from diminishing the resulting dilemmas of social choice, the scale and urgency of the proposed transformations and associated public policy interventions actually compounds and renders more acute the essential political challenges. What roles are to be played, for instance, by: alternative fluid fuels; carbon capture and storage; "new generation" nuclear power; centralized renewable energy; distributed intelligent networks; or novel "energy service" institutions? Even within the disparate category of "renewable energy" there lies a host of strategic choices. All the above options are variously seen as feasible or desirable routes to "sustainable energy" under at least some influential perspective. Yet we cannot equally pursue all to their full potential (Stirling, 2009b).

This crucial role for deliberate social choice is seriously downplayed by current official and incumbent discourses in energy policy. Senior figures routinely understate the scope for agency, for instance promoting nuclear strategies for the paradoxically contradictory reasons that there is "no alternative" (King, 2006) or that policymaking should "do everything" (King, 2007). In fact, not only is contemporary energy policy dominated by dilemmas of choice, but the stakes are rendered even higher and more urgent by the fact that each possible sustainable energy pathway displays dynamics of "increasing returns" (Arthur, 1989, 1994). Early patterns in economic investment (Cowan, 1991), learning by doing (Jacobsson and Johnson, 2000), institutional momentum (Hughes, 1983), political commitment (Walker, 2000), or cultural expectations (Brown and Michael, 2003) may strongly condition the prospects of success in any one of a number of equally viable paths. With the implications of contending values and interests thus accentuated, it becomes more imperative to make these social choices in a deliberate and accountable fashion—without detracting from the efficacy of moves towards sustainability. The way to achieve this is to pursue a judicious diversity of pathways. These will prioritize only some of the array of possible trajectories (Stirling, 2009b). Just as no single option is unique in offering diversity, so none is individually imperative. Diverse strategies towards sustainability do not therefore mean "doing everything" in a blanket fashion, but involve pursuit of a "requisite variety" (Ashby, 1956) among possible pathways. Arguments that any single option is rendered inevitable by the general desirability of diversity are thus just as spuriously expedient as the claim that there is "no alternative."

Given this remarkable conjunction of reasons for interest, it should be no surprise that the concept of diversity is as prominent as it is in energy policy. There clearly exists a challenging imperative to understand the various synergies, complexities, constraints, and tradeoffs. Yet—despite notable exceptions (DTI, 1995; Jansen *et al.*, 2004; IEA, 2007)—it is curious that systematic appraisal of diversity occupies only a relatively minor niche in official energy policy analysis. When compared, for instance, with entire sub-disciplines and literatures formed around analysis of energy-specific financial evaluation, external costs assessment, risk analysis, and environmental appraisal, rigorous attention to diversity itself remains relatively neglected. This may be understood, perhaps, partly as a reflection of political pressures for expedient exploitation of the "apple pie" connotations of diversity (Matthews and McGowan, 1990). For instance, past high-profile UK government diversity rhetorics have later been acknowledged by the Ministers involved, to have been "code" for the less widely supported aims of promoting nuclear power and neutralizing organized labor (Lawson, 1992). Under this kind of political dynamic, systematic policy analysis is actually inconvenient to potential sponsors. Despite the many substantive reasons for interest in diversity, then, such overbearing instrumentalism may serve to discourage serious academic attention.

None of these political factors diminish the pressing underlying need for more comprehensive, rigorous, and transparent policy analysis of energy diversity. Consequently, despite any inhibitions, many important and honorable such initiatives do, of course, exist (Ulph, 1988, 1989; Stirling, 1994, 1996; COLA, 1994; NERA, 1995; ERM, 1995; Awerbuch and Berger, 2003; Jansen *et al.*,

2004; Scheepers *et al.*, 2007; Markandya *et al.*, 2005; Awerbuch and Yang, 2007; Grubb *et al.*, 2006; Hubberke, 2007; IEA, 2007; Bazilian and Roques, 2008; Yoshizawa *et al.*, 2008). These will be discussed in the next section. As with any analysis in such a complex, dynamic, uncertain, and contested field, however, different studies typically yield highly variable outcomes, under entirely reasonable divergences in input assumptions. This is often downplayed as a pathology, with individual studies and approaches remaining relatively silent on the possible sources of volatility. Yet when seen from the general view of policy appraisal, such plurality can in some ways actually be a positive general quality. Collectively, the concurrence of diverse analytical frameworks provides a useful means both to enrich and qualify what might otherwise tend to be myopic, blinkered or manipulative institutional, political or economic interests.

Approached in a mature, transparent, and plural fashion, then, openness in policymaking to a multiplicity of valid appraisals of energy diversity can help calibrate apparent risks, identify boundary conditions, reveal sensitivities to particular assumptions, values or prejudices, and so triangulate prescriptive conclusions (Stirling, 2008a). Handled in the right way, this kind of more pluralistic policy discourse can enhance the robustness and accountability of high-level decision-making over contending possible energy strategies. What is needed is a framework under which the contending approaches may be articulated, such as more transparently to reveal their specific idiosyncrasies, conditionalities, and possible sources of bias. This will be the topic of the following sections (based on Stirling, 2008b).

General properties of energy diversity: variety, balance, and disparity

Energy diversity was defined at the outset of this chapter as an evenly balanced reliance on a variety of mutually disparate options. As such, diversity is a property of any system whose elements may be apportioned into categories. Energy systems are simply one example of this. Disciplines like ecology, economics, taxonomy, paleontology, complexity, and information theory have all developed sophisticated frameworks for analyzing various aspects in contrasting contexts (Stirling, 1998). The analysis of energy diversity may therefore gain much through building on the approaches developed in other fields. This is all the more the case, because the parameters of interest are—as we have seen—so wide-ranging within energy policy itself. This breadth in the policy salience of energy diversity presents an inherent advantage for the most generally applicable frameworks.

To take the electricity sector as an example, discussions of diversity span an array of disparate supply- and demand-side technologies and primary resources. The scope of diversity analysis is, as we have seen, further extended by a variety of other relevant factors, including: the regional sourcing of fuel and associated supply routes; concentration among trading, supplier or service companies; reliance on generic equipment or component vendors; dependencies on monopoly utilities, shareowners, or labour unions; and the configurations and spatial distribution of infra-structures (PIU, 2001; Farrell *et al.*, 2004; Verrastro and Ladislaw, 2007; Helm, 2007; CEC, 2007). Each of these parameters is potentially relevant to diversity as a means to hedge ignorance, foster innovation, mitigate lock-in, or accommodate plural values and interests, in the broader senses also discussed earlier. It is therefore desirable that any framework for the analysis of energy diversity be equally applicable in principle across all these aspects.

Fortunately, it is precisely when approached in this most general fashion (as a fundamental property of any system apportioned among elements), that experience in other disciplines holds the clearest lessons for analyzing energy diversity. In short, diversity concepts employed across the full range of sciences mentioned above, display some combination of the three basic properties included in our present definition: "variety," "balance," and "disparity" (Stirling, 1994; Grubb *et al.*, 2006). Each is a necessary but individually insufficient property of diversity (Stirling, 1998). Though addressed in different vocabularies, each is applicable across a range of contexts. Each is aggregated in various permutations and degrees in quantitative indices (Hill, 1978). Despite the multiple disciplines and divergent empirical details, there seems no other obvious candidate for a fourth important general property of diversity beyond these three (Stirling, 1998: 47). They are summarized schematically in Figure 7.3.

In terms of electricity supply portfolios, variety is the number of diverse categories of "option" into which an energy system may be apportioned. It is the answer to the question: "how many options do we have?" This aspect of diversity is highlighted (for instance) in conventional approaches based on the simple counting of named categories like "coal," "gas," "nuclear," and "renewable energy." All else being equal, the greater the variety of distinct types of energy option, the greater the system diversity. For instance, in 1990, standard OECD statistics partitioned national member state electricity supply systems among six options—"coal," "oil," "gas," "nuclear," "hydro/geothermal," and "other" (IEA, 1991). For more specific purposes in 2001, the resolution of reporting increased to 11 options—"coal," "oil," "gas," "nuclear," "hydro," "geothermal," "solar," "tide/wave/ocean," "wind," "combustion renewables and waste," and "other (e.g. fuel cells)" (IEA, 2002). Each scheme provides a different basis for counting variety.

Balance is a function of the apportionment of the energy system across the identified options. It is the answer to the question: "how much do we rely on each option?" The denominator here may (depending on the context) be expressed as energy inputs or outputs, power capacity, economic value, or services delivered. Either way, balance (like statistical variance—Pielou, 1977), is simply represented by a set of positive fractions, which sum to one (Laxton, 1978). This dimension appears most frequently in energy debates, in discussions around a possible role for designating the contributions of different supply options (Helm, 2007). It is captured in more detail in a variety of "concentration" or "entropy" measures that are nowadays quite widely applied in energy policy, like the Shannon-Wiener (Stirling, 1994; COLA, 1994; NERA, 1995; DTI, 1995, 2003b; Markandya *et al.*, 2005; Scheepers *et al.*, 2007) and/or (Grubb *et al.*, 2006) Herfindahl–Hirschman (IEA, 2007; Hubberke, 2007) indices. All else being equal, the more even is the balance across energy options, the greater the system diversity. An example of the importance of considering balance, lies in the contrasting stories of Japanese and French electricity supply systems following the 1973 "oil shock." Over the 27-year period up to 2000, both Japan and France moved away from oil-dominated systems with nuclear at the margin (2 percent of

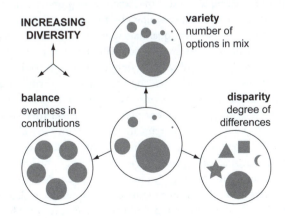

Figure 7.3 A schematic picture of three co-constituting properties of energy diversity.

delivered electricity in Japan, 8 percent in France). In the Japanese case, the diversification strategy led to a roughly even balance across nuclear, coal, and gas as modal options (Suzuki, 2001). In France, however, the "diversification" strategy simply substituted an initial 40 percent dependence on oil for an even greater 77 percent dependence on nuclear at the end, involving an eventual decrease in diversity over this period (Stirling, 1994).

Disparity refers to the manner and degree in which energy options may be distinguished (Runnegar, 1987). It is the answer to the question: "how different are our options from each other?" This is the most fundamental—and yet most frequently neglected—aspect of energy diversity. After all, it is judgments over disparity that necessarily govern the resolving of the categories of energy option, which underlie characterizations of variety and balance. It is this aspect of diversity that is addressed by applications of portfolio theory, which (deliberately or inadvertently) take fossil fuel price covariance as a stochastic proxy for wider disparities, such as those mentioned above (Ulph, 1988, 1989; NERA, 1995; ERM, 1995; Awerbuch and Berger, 2003; Awerbuch *et al.*, 2006; Awerbuch and Yang, 2007). This method will be returned to below. Alternative approaches to this property in other disciplines are usually based on some more general form of scalar distance measure. Either way, all else being equal, the more disparate are the energy options, the greater the system diversity. In other words, an electricity supply system divided equally among gas, nuclear, wind, and biomass power is more disparate than one divided equally among coal, oil, and Norwegian and Russian gas.

The consequence of this threefold understanding of diversity is recognition that—though disparity is fundamental—each property helps constitute the other two (Stirling, 1998). This in turn highlights difficulties with diversity concepts and associated indices that focus exclusively on subsets of these properties (Eldredge, 1992), an illustrative selection of which are displayed in Table 7.1. The resulting ambiguities or hidden assumptions can exacerbate the tendency already noted for insufficiently rigorous treatments of diversity to serve as a vehicle for special pleading.

Variety and balance, for instance, cannot be characterized without first partitioning the system on the basis of disparity (May, 1990). An electricity system may be assigned a nominal variety of four, if it is divided into categories labeled "coal," "gas," "nuclear," and "renewable energy" (Stirling, 1994). Yet "renewables" might readily be further divided into numerous other nested categories (like "hydro," "wind," "biomass," and "tide"). The mutual disparities between many of these ostensibly subordinate taxa might reasonably be thought greater than those between large centralized thermal nuclear and fossil fuel plant.

For similar reasons, considerations of disparity also hold crucial importance for the resolving of balance. These hinge on the simple fact that the structures of proportional contributions are—like counting the categories themselves—determined by the ways and degrees in which options are divided up. Though the more complex quantitative form may confer an apparent authority, an index of balance (like Shannon or Simpson/Herfindahl–Hirschman) is no less arbitrary than the simple counting of variety. It will yield radically different results depending on the partitioning of options. The implications may be addressed by systematic sensitivity analysis and by adopting explicitly conservative assumptions on disparity with respect to the argument propounded or the hypothesis under test (Stirling, 1994). However, the fact remains that taking measures of variety and/or balance as proxies for diversity thus remains highly sensitive to tacitly subjective taxonomies and arbitrary linguistic conventions concerning the implicit bounding of categories.

Conversely, the importance of disparity to energy diversity is itself typically qualified by the pattern of apportionment across options. For instance, an electricity supply portfolio comprising a 95 percent contribution from one of four highly disparate resources (like Russian gas with the residual 5 percent made up of nuclear, wind, and hydro) might reasonably, under some perspectives, be judged less diverse than a portfolio comprising even contributions from four much less

Table 7.1 Selected indices of contrasting subordinate properties of diversity

Property	Name and/or Reference	Form
Variety	Category Count (MacArthur, 1965)	N
Balance	Shannon Evenness (Pielou, 1969)	$\dfrac{-\Sigma_i\ p_i\ \ln p_i}{\ln N}$
variety/balance	Shannon-Wiener (Shannon & Weaver, 1962)	$-\Sigma_i\ p_i\ \ln p_i$
	Simpson/Herfindahl-Hirschman (Simpson, 1949; Herfindahl, 1959; Hirschman, 1964)	$\Sigma_i\ p_i^2$
	Gini diversity index (1912)	$1 - \Sigma_i\ p_i^2$
	Hill (1973)	$\Sigma_I(p_i^a)^{1/(1-a)}$
disparity	Weitzman (1992)	$\max\ i\epsilon S\{\mathbf{D}_w(S\backslash i) + \mathbf{d}_w(i, S\backslash i)\}$
	Solow & Polasky (1994)	$f(\mathbf{d}_{ij})$
variety/balance/ disparity	Junge (1994)	$\left(\dfrac{\sigma}{\mu.\sqrt{n-1}}\right)\cdot\left(\dfrac{1}{\sqrt{N}}\right)\cdot$ $\left(\sqrt{N-1} - \sqrt{N\Sigma_i p_i^2 - 1}\right)$
	Stirling (2007a)	$\Sigma_{Ij}\ \mathbf{d}_{ij}{}^{\alpha}.(p_i.\ p_j)^{\beta}$

Key to Table 7.1

Notation	Interpretation in terms of energy portfolios
N	number of categories of energy options
$\ln$	logarithm (usually natural)
p_I	proportion of energy system comprised of option category i
a	a parameter governing relative weighting on variety and balance
n	number of attributes displayed by options
σ	standard deviation of attributes within option categories
μ	mean of attributes within option categories
$f(\mathbf{d}_{ij})$	function of disparity distance between option categories i and j ($\mathbf{d}_{ij}$)
$\mathbf{D}_W(S)$	aggregate disparity of energy system S
$\mathbf{d}_W(i,\ S/i)$	disparity distance between option i and nearest option in S if i is excluded
α, β	parameters governing relative weightings on variety, balance and disparity

disparate options (like piped Russian, Norwegian, and UK gas with internationally traded and transported LNG) (PIU, 2001). Likewise, the balance of a portfolio is neglected where attention is restricted to variety alone—as is the case in much of the literature. At what scale of contribution is an option considered to add to system diversity? Does the installation of the first household rooftop photovoltaic panel increase the diversity of a national energy portfolio by the same degree as the construction of the first 1.5 GWe new nuclear power station? If not, at what scale of contribution does any given option begin to be counted? How do we avoid perverse threshold effects? Different indices of balance treat this crucial threshold issue in quite radically different ways (Skea, 2007). Taking disparity (or variety) as proxies for diversity ignores the balance with which a system is apportioned. It therefore seems that the only robust approach to thinking about energy diversity is to think about variety, balance, and disparity together.

Aggregating, accommodating, and articulating different aspects of energy diversity

Thus far, we have established a definition of energy diversity in terms of three necessary but individually insufficient properties of disparity, variety, and balance. A series of methodological questions follow from this. How can these quite distinct aspects of diversity be aggregated into a single coherent framework? How might such an analytical framework be applied such as to accommodate the range of relevant perspectives typically engaged in real debates over energy strategy? And how can the results of any diversity analysis on these lines be articulated with wider policy considerations—such as the performance of individual generating options under criteria of economic efficiency, environmental quality, social impact, and security of supply raised earlier in relation to broad sustainability goals? The present section will consider these challenges of aggregation, accommodation, and articulation.

With regard to aggregation, most contemporary approaches to analyzing energy diversity focus on variety and/or balance alone (e.g. Stirling, 1994, 1996; COLA, 1994; DTI, 2003b; Markandya, 2007; Grubb *et al.*, 2006; Scheepers *et al.*, 2007; Hubberke, 2007; IEA, 2007). Even where disparity is thus neglected, however, it is far from straightforward what relative emphasis to place on variety as compared with balance. How much weight should be assigned to small contributions from additional options, compared with enhanced balance among dominant options? It is a little-recognized property of widely used sum-of-the-squares concentration indices (like Simpson, 1949), the Herfindahl-Hirschman index ('HHI'—Herfindahl, 1959; Hirschman, 1964), and the Gini diversity index (Gini, 1912; Sen, 2005: this chapter, Table 7.1), that different exponent powers yield divergent rank orderings for portfolios displaying different patterns of composition across marginal and dominant options (Stirling, 1998: 56). That such divergent rankings may not arise in practice for certain particular portfolios (Grubb *et al.*, 2006) does not resolve this concern. Yet there exists no firmly grounded theoretical or empirical reason for taking the commonly used exponent value of two rather than, say, three, four, or so on.

Logarithmic entropy functions (like Shannon-Wiener) avoid similar ranking sensitivities across different logarithm bases (Stirling, 1998: 56). But there still arises the question as to why the particular implicit weighting embodied in such indices should necessarily reflect the appropriate weighting for real energy systems or stakeholder perspectives. Theoretical work in mathematical ecology derives generalizations of these kinds of index, in which this crucial issue is dealt with by explicit weighting parameters (e.g. Hill, 1978 in Table 7.1) Just because such parameters are not recognized in the conventional indices used in the energy sector does not remove this problem. To ignore this, risks straying into mathematical mysticism, where contingently privileged algorithms are ascribed transcendent authority concerning appropriate interests and priorities in the real world.

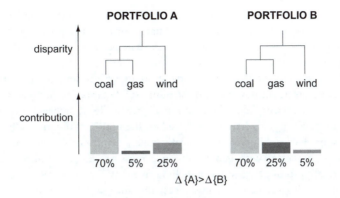

Figure 7.4 A case where varying diversity is not discriminated by conventional indices.

Beyond this, however, the most serious difficulty with conventional variety-balance indices concerns the neglect of the crucial property of disparity. Where attention is restricted to the enumeration or concentration of options, the assumption is effectively made that all options are equally disparate. This can yield manifestly perverse results, such as that represented in Figure 7.4. Here, any index restricted to variety and/or balance alone will entirely fail to address the fact that the enhanced representation of the more disparate option makes Portfolio A more diverse than Portfolio B. This point is returned to in comparing Figures 7.6 and 7.7 below.

Of course, the salience of the example illustrated in Figure 7.4 rests on the understanding (illustrated with the stylized dendrograms) that wind is more disparate from coal and gas than either of these fossil fuels is from the other. This may seem reasonable at an immediate intuitive level. But how can we be sure? And any practically useful diversity analysis must also be clear about the degree to which this is the case. In other words, in contemplating an increase in diversity in moving from Portfolio B to Portfolio A where gas is rated as the best-performing option, exactly what value of performance on the part of gas might be sacrificed as a premium for the additional diversity conferred by wind? This raises the second challenge identified above—that of accommodating the divergent perspectives on disparity (as well as performance) that typically characterize even the most specialist discussions of energy strategy.

This is essentially the problem that many seek to address through the exploratory application of probabilistic risk modeling techniques (NERA, 2002)—and especially portfolio theory—to the analysis of contending possible electricity supply mixes (Ulph, 1988, 1989; NERA, 1995; ERM, 1995; Awerbuch and Berger, 2003; Awerbuch and Yang, 2007). In brief, what this does is take the single parameter of covariance in fuel price risk as a stochastic proxy for a range of multidimensional economic, physical, environmental, technical, institutional, and geographical disparities between electricity options (Awerbuch *et al.*, 2006). Such elegant shorthand may suffice for short-term decisions by private firms, dominated simply by financial risks due to fuel price shocks (Awerbuch, 2000b). It has the benefit, at least in principle, of requiring only relatively objectively attested data (Lucas *et al.*, 1995; Brower, 1995). However, as strategic interests grow wider and time frames longer, serious questions arise over the sufficiency (and even validity) of this approach. To what extent can the historic behavior of fuel prices be taken as a reliable guide even to the future trajectories of this one parameter, let alone the host of other factors invoked by wider sustainability agendas (Brower, 1995)? How do we address options whose attributes are simply not reflected in fossil fuel markets (Stirling, 1996)? Where diversity is undertaken as a response to strict uncertainty and ignorance, the use of probabilistic concepts like covariance coefficients is by definition invalid (Stirling, 2003). Despite its applicability where attention is confined to near-term fluctuations in fuel prices, portfolio theory is a highly circumscribed basis for addressing the full strategic scope of energy diversity (Awerbuch *et al.*, 2006).

Though rarely integrated with consideration of variety and balance, the challenge of accommodating divergent possible understandings of disparity is quite well addressed in other disciplines. Approaches in fields like taxonomy, paleontology, archaeology, and conservation biology all routinely adopt a framework based on the notion of distance. Often, there exists in such fields some well-established or even objectively determinable criterion of disparity. This is the case, for instance, with genetic distance measures in evolutionary ecology, assumed (often incorrectly) to display a strict branching form (Weitzmann, 1992; Solow and Polasky, 1994). Under such expedient circumstances, the analysis of diversity can be quite strictly codified in terms of "disparity distances" between elements and relatively unambiguous answers derived.

Elsewhere, however, the picture is much more similar to that in the energy field, where options are not differentiated by strictly branching genetic processes and where typically there exist a variety of different views over the relevant aspects of disparity and their respective degrees of importance (Stirling, 1998). Even here, however, it is possible to use the simple concept of distance. Options are characterized in terms of whatever are held to be the salient attributes of difference, such that each can be represented as a coordinate in a multidimensional "disparity space" (Stirling, 2007a). With the different disparity attributes weighted to reflect their relative importance, the simple Euclidean distances separating options in this space can be taken as a reflection of their mutual disparity. By appropriate normalization and weighting procedures, a "disparity space" of this kind can be constructed so as accurately to reflect any conceivable perspective on the distinguishing features of different energy options (Kruskal, 1964). Indeed, fuel price covariance might be seen just as one such possible dimension of disparity.

As a starting point for implementing this broader disparity-distance approach in the analysis of energy diversity, it is useful to consider the nature of existing datasets concerning the economic and/or wider sustainability performance of different energy options (e.g. Externe, 2004). Encompassing different aspects of financial, operational, environmental, health, and broader social impacts, many such datasets have been generated over past years by a range of different disciplines – including cost-benefit, environmental impact and technology assessment, and comparative risk, life cycle and multi-criteria analysis. To the extent that the performance of each energy option is structured differently under the various performance criteria, each of these datasets contains potentially useful information over their disparities. If the different criteria are normalized such that all options are reassigned nominally equal performance, then the distances in the resulting multidimensional space will provide a robust indication of broader disparities according to the perspective in question on salient strategic attributes. Figure 7.5 provides a schematic illustration of this approach. Of course, none of this precludes use of non-normalized performance data as a basis for determining tradeoffs between performance and diversity (Stirling, 2007a).

The kind of disparity structures that pilot work indicates may be yielded by such performance data are illustrated in Figure 7.6. Distances between successively more remote pairs of options in disparity space can be represented using standard cluster analysis techniques and represented as a dendrogram (with disparity distance indicated on the horizontal axis labeled "d"). The actual underlying distances used in diversity analysis will not be affected by the sometimes slightly contrasting representations yielded by different clustering metrics, algorithms, and procedures (Sneath and Sokal, 1973).

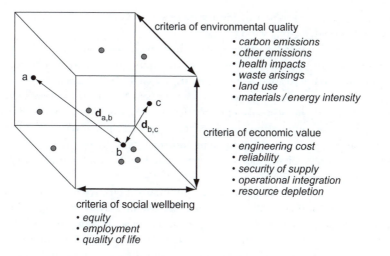

Figure 7.5 A disparity space generated by normalized sustainability performance data.

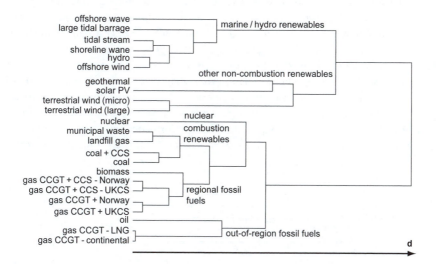

Figure 7.6 Indicative disparities in multi–criteria performance of electricity options.
Notes:
CCGT=combined cycle gas turbine; CCS=carbon capture and storage; UKCS=UK Continental Shelf;
LNG=liquefied natural gas

More importantly, however, different performance datasets can be expected to generate different disparity structures. Similarly, given the broad strategic scope required in considering diversity, it may also be expected that the different dimensions of such analysis will be weighted differently under different perspectives. This is a matter for empirical investigation, of a kind recently piloted by the author in collaboration with colleagues Go Yoshizawa and Tatsujiro Suzuki (Yoshizawa *et al.*, 2008). For the moment, early indications are that direct elicitation from interviewees, by reference to typical detailed sustainability performance datasets, consistently yields intuitively meaningful structures, such as those indicated in Figure 7.6. Existing performance datasets provide a useful starting point to the construction of meaningful patterns of disparity, which may readily be followed up by direct elicitation of further more specific disparity attributes in an intensive interview or deliberative group setting.

In considering the many possible queries that might be raised over detailed disparity structures such as that illustrated in Figure 7.6, two things must be remembered. The first is that the point here is not to assert that there exists any single well-defined "objective" disparity structure that applies irrespective of context or perspective across real-world energy options. Instead, the value of this general approach lies in the possibility of more systematic and transparent ways of accommodating inevitably divergent viewpoints on disparity. It is interesting and potentially significant that existing performance datasets—backed up by direct elicitation and deliberation involving specialists—may quite readily yield intuitively robust disparity structures.

For those to whom this seems like an uncomfortably subjective or open-ended approach, the second point is that these challenges are unavoidably intrinsic to the complexities of energy disparity itself. Simply to ignore this challenge—for instance through the conventional restriction of attention to variety and balance alone or a single circumscribed parameter like fuel price covariance—does not avoid assumptions over option disparity. It simply conceals them. If indices like Shannon or Simpson/Herfindahl–Hirschman are used to analyze diversity among a set of electricity supply options like that resolved in Figure 7.6, for instance, this simply amounts to treating all identified options as equally disparate—as represented in Figure 7.7. The choice is therefore not whether to respond to the challenge of accommodating divergent perspectives on disparity but how—and with what degree of rigour and openness. The resulting questions concern not the absolute precision of any given directly elicited disparity structure, but its relative plausibility in relation to a default picture like that in Figure 7.7.

The third and final challenge raised at the beginning of this section, concerns the articulation of diversity with other properties of strategic interest in the appraisal of energy portfolios. As already noted, the key dimensions of portfolio performance will often be quite distinct from diversity—concerning criteria such as operational efficacy, financial performance,

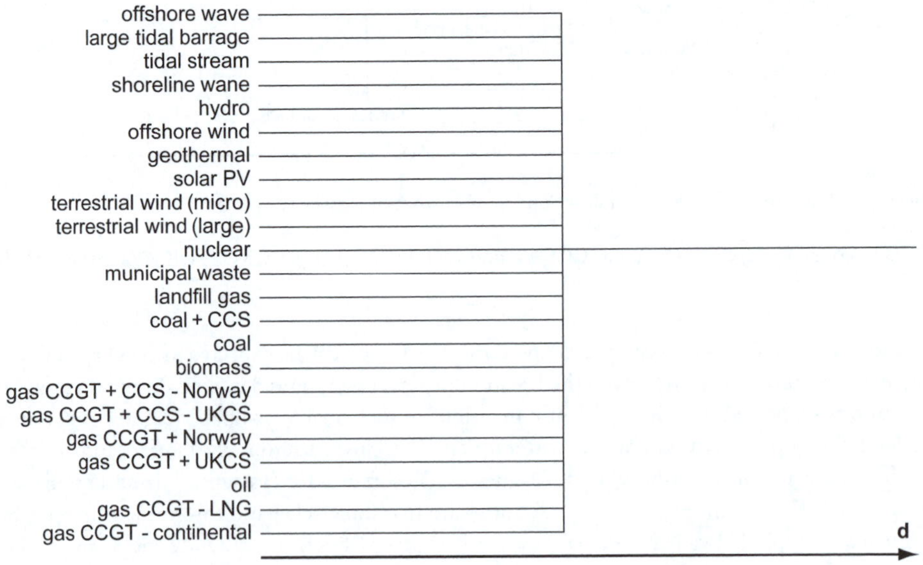

Figure 7.7 Indicative disparities implicit in the use of Shannon or Herfindahl indices.

environmental impacts, and other aspects of supply security. The challenge is particularly acute as attention extends to the full range of pressing issues invoked by sustainability agendas. Aggregate option performance under such criteria (under any perspective) will typically be a function of the performance of the individual options. This will therefore be subject to important tradeoffs as deliberate diversification draws larger contributions from what appear under the perspective in question to be lower-performing options. In order to be useful, therefore, any practical framework for the analysis of energy diversity should not be applied in isolation, but should articulate directly with these broader appraisal criteria, such as to allow systematic exploration of relevant tradeoffs, interactions, and operational effects. It is to one possible framework for addressing these challenges of aggregation, accommodation, and articulation that attention will now turn.

A novel diversity heuristic for strategic appraisal of energy portfolios

To take seriously these problems of aggregation, accommodation, and articulation does not necessarily lead to a counsel of despair over the potential for systematic general characterizations – or even quantifications—of energy diversity. A more positive starting point is the observation that the futility of deriving a single definitive diversity *index*, need not preclude the possibility of a flexible general *heuristic*. Like an index, a heuristic may be quantitative. But rather than aiming to measure diversity in some unconditional objective fashion, it offers an explicit, systematic basis for exploring sensitivities to the assumptions conditioning aggregation, accommodation, and articulation (Stirling, 2007a).

For any particular perspective on the appropriate weightings for variety and balance and the salient dimensions of disparity, such a heuristic would behave as an index. It would accommodate different views on the relevant attributes of disparity, aggregate these with consideration of variety and balance, and allow systematic articulation with important system-level properties other than diversity (like portfolio interactions). For applications involving a range of perspectives, this heuristic would allow clear comparisons to be made between the implications of contending judgments. In other words, a heuristic characterization of energy diversity aims to combine the rigour, transparency, and specificity of quantification with the scope, applicability, flexibility, and symmetry of qualitative approaches. The real challenge lies in achieving this, whilst minimizing the introduction of further complexity and contingency.

No existing diversity index addresses all three properties of variety, balance, and disparity in an unproblematic way. However, based on well-established criteria applied to the treatment of these individual diversity properties by researchers such as Hill (1978), Laxton (1978), Pielou (1977), Weitzman (1992), and Solow and Polasky (1994), a series of non-trivial requirements are quite readily developed. For instance, some significant desirable features of a general diversity heuristic Δ that help explicitly to address challenges of aggregation, accommodation, and articulation as defined here, are outlined in Table 7.2.

No established diversity index satisfies all the criteria summarized in Table 7.2. Yet there is one relatively straightforward quantitative heuristic, independently derived in different disciplines (Rao, 1982; Stirling, 1998), which does offer a starting point. This is the sum of pairwise option disparities, weighted in proportion to option contributions (D):

$$D = \sum_{ij\,(i \neq j)} d_{ij} \cdot p_i \cdot p_j \qquad (1)$$

Table 7.2 Formal conditions for a robust general heuristic of energy diversity, Δ

Condition	Description (see references in Stirling, 2007a)
1: Scaling of variety	Where option variety is equal to one, Δ takes a value of zero.
2: Monotonicity of variety	Where energy options are evenly balanced and equally disparate, Δ increases monotonically with variety.
3: Monotonicity of balance	For given option variety and disparity, Δ increases monotonically with balance (ie: Δ is maximal for equal reliance on all options).
4: Monotonicity of disparity	For given variety and balance, Δ increases monotonically with the aggregate disparity between energy options.
5: Scaling of disparity	Where aggregate disparity is zero (ie: where all energy options are effectively identical), Δ takes a value of zero.
6: Open accommodation	Δ accommodates any perspective on salient dimensions of disparity under which energy options can be differentiated.
7: Insensitivity to partitioning	For any given perspective on taxonomy, Δ is insensitive to alternative partitionings of options into categories.
8: Parsimony of form	Δ is as uncomplicated in structure and parsimonious in form as necessary to fulfil the above conditions.
9: Explicit aggregation	Δ permits explicit aggregation of variety, balance and disparity, by reflecting divergent contexts or perspectives using weightings.
10: Ready articulation	Δ allows unconstrained articulations of diversity with other salient properties of individual options or the energy system as a whole.

where p_i and p_j are proportional representations of options i and j in the energy system (balance), and d_{ij} is the distance separating options i and j in a particular disparity space (Figure 7.5). The summation is across the half-matrix of $((n-1)^2/2)$ non-identical pairs of n options (i≠j). In the special case where all d_{ij} are equal (scalable to unity), D reduces to half Gini (Table 7.1).

It is readily demonstrated that this heuristic, D, complies with criteria (1) to (7). Compliance with criterion (8) remains a matter of judgment, but it is difficult to imagine a solution to these criteria that is simpler or more parsimonious. As to criterion (9), this raises a final notable feature of D that can be illustrated by introducing just two further terms (Stirling, 2007a):

$$\Delta = \sum_{ij\,(i \neq j)} (d_{ij})^{\alpha} \cdot (p_i \cdot p_j)^{\beta} \tag{2}$$

If exponents α and β are allowed to take all possible permutations of the values 0 and 1, this yields four variants of the heuristic Δ. Each of these usefully captures one of the four properties of interest: variety, balance, disparity, and diversity (Table 7.3).

Shifting values of exponents α and β between 0 and 1 yields further variants of Δ, collectively addressing all possible relative weightings on variety, balance, and disparity. Of these, the reference case, D ($\alpha = \beta = 1$), does the same job as other widely used non-parametric measures like Gini, Shannon, and Simpson, but with the major additional feature that it also captures disparity. Unlike the disparity measures proposed by Weitzman or Solow and Polasky (Table 7.1), Δ also addresses variety and balance. Unlike the "triple concept" proposed by Junge (1994; see this chapter, Table 7.1), Δ accommodates radically divergent perspectives on disparity itself, yet is relatively parsimonious in form. An entirely novel feature of Δ is that it systematically addresses alternative possible aggregations of these subordinate properties, according to perspective and context.

Table 7.3 Four variants of Δ and their relationships with diversity properties

Property	α	β	$\Delta =$	Equivalents [cf: Table 1]	Interpretation
variety	0	0	$\Sigma_{ij}\, d_{ij}^{\,0}$	([category count]-1)^2/2	scaled variety
balance	0	1	$\Sigma_{ij}\, p_i \cdot p_j$	[Gini] / 2	variety-weighted balance
disparity	1	0	$\Sigma_{ij}\, d_{ij}$	[Solow & Polasky]	variety-weighted disparity
diversity	1	1	$\Sigma_{ij}\, d_{ij} \cdot p_i \cdot p_j$	D	balance-weighted disparity

Articulating energy diversity with other aspects of strategic performance

Of the formal criteria identified for a general heuristic of energy diversity in Table 7.2, the discussion in the last section leaves only criterion (10) unaddressed—concerning the articulation of diversity with other relevant system-level properties. As already mentioned, energy diversity is rarely a free lunch. The overall strategic performance of a portfolio as a whole will be a function not only of diversity but of other system properties and the performance of individual options. For instance, there will typically be portfolio effects resulting from interactions between subsets of options—such as potentially negative feedbacks between high penetrations from intermittent renewables and the inflexibility of large, predominantly base-load plant like nuclear power (Gross *et al.*, 2006); and competition between contending technology strategies or more specific institutional and industrial tensions through which, for instance, nuclear power can "crowd out" large-scale commitments to renewable energy (Mitchell and Woodman, 2006). Of course, there can also be positive synergies between disparate energy options, such as those often argued to benefit joint pursuit of distributed generation and demand-side energy efficiency measures.(Prindle *et al.*, 2007) Diversity itself may provide a strategic response to supply security challenges, as well as hedging more general sources of ignorance, fostering innovation, mitigating lock-in, and accommodating pluralism. But it will typically require some compromise on other aspects of performance, like financial costs, operational efficacy, environmental impacts, or wider economic factors.

In addition, many energy options will be constrained in their possible contributions. A number of renewable energy sources, for instance, are in this position. Rather than being static in nature, such constraints will take the form of a dynamic resource curve, under which successive increments are available at varying levels of performance. The shape of this curve will reflect the performance attributed to successive incremental "tranches" for these options. This will be a function of two contending factors. On the one hand, there are the combined negative effects of using successively less favorable sites (OXERA, 2004; DTI, 2005). On the other hand, there are learning effects and other increasing returns processes, which will yield countervailing positive improvements as experience accumulates with increasing use (Jacobsson and Johnson, 2000).

To take account of these factors, then, the value assigned under any given perspective to any particular energy system under specific conditions ($V\{S\}$) can be expressed as the sum of the value due to the aggregate performance of individual options ($V\{E\}$) and an incremental value attached to irreducible portfolio-level properties including diversity ($V\{P\}$). If the net implications of diversity are adverse, then $V\{P\}$ can be negative.

$$V\{S\}=V\{E\}+V\{P\} \tag{3}$$

It has already been mentioned in discussing disparity distances, that there exist numerous well-tried methods—and extensive bodies of data—addressing the multi-criteria performance of energy options. Long experience in the field of decision analysis (Vincke et al, 1992) shows that—just as divergent notions of difference can be represented as co-ordinates in an *n*-dimensional Euclidean disparity space (Figure 4)—so can divergent valuations of individual system elements be represented as co-ordinates in an *m*-dimensional Euclidean performance space (Stirling, 2006a). The dimensions of this space represent any set of *m* relevant performance criteria, each weighted to reflect their respective importance (Stirling, 1998:81). As with disparity, the selection, characterisation and scaling of these criteria will vary across context and perspective (Stirling, 1997). Although it is difficult to justify any single approach to aggregating *across* perspectives, decision analysis has shown that any single perspective can be uniquely captured by means of the following expression for the overall value attached to the performance of individual system elements $V\{E\}$:

$$\mathbf{V}\{E\} = \text{\r{a}}_i\text{\r{a}}_c(w_c \cdot s_{ic}) \cdot p_i \tag{4}$$

where s_{ic} is the value attached to the performance of option i under criterion c; w_c is a scalar weighting reflecting the effective relative importance of criterion c (under the perspective and context in question) and p_i is (as in equations (1) and (2)), the proportional representation of option i in the energy system in question. It follows from equation (2) that the corresponding value attached to irreducible portfolio-level properties including diversity ($V\{P\}$), can then be expressed follows:

$$\mathbf{V}\{P\} = \mathbf{d} \cdot \mathbf{D}¢$$

$$= \mathbf{d} \cdot \text{\r{a}}_{ij(i^1j)}\left(d_{ij}\right)^a \cdot \left(p_i \cdot p_j\right)^b \cdot i_{ij} \tag{5}$$

where $\mathbf{D}¢$ represents an augmented form of the diversity heuristic $\mathbf{D}$ given in equation (2), which includes an additional term to reflect portfolio interactions (i_{ij}). i_{ij} is an array of scalar multipliers exploiting the pairwise structure of $\mathbf{D}¢$ to express the effect on system value of synergies or tensions between options i and j, respectively, as marginal positive or negative departures from a default of unity ($i_{ij} = 1 \pm \P_i$: for most systems $\P_i \ll 1$). This serves as a means to capture a variety of system-level properties that—like diversity—are irreducible to individual options. The coefficient $\mathbf{d}$ scales expressions of portfolio value to render them commensurable with aggregate values of individual options in equation (4). For positive assessments of portfolio value, $0 < \mathbf{d} < ¥$. From equations (3), (4) and (5), we therefore obtain the following heuristic system-level articulation ($V\{S\}$) of the value attached to diversity together with that assigned to other portfolio properties ($V\{P\}$) and the value attached to the performance of individual energy options ($V\{E\}$).

$$\mathbf{V}\{S\} = \text{\r{a}}_i\text{\r{a}}_c(w_c \cdot s_{ic}) \cdot p_i + \mathbf{d} \cdot \text{\r{a}}_{ij(i^1j)}\left(d_{ij}\right)^a \cdot \left(p_i \cdot p_j\right)^b \cdot i_{ij} \tag{6}$$

It is in $V\{S\}$ that we have a means to address the final criterion (10) developed above for a heuristic of energy diversity, in that it should allow systematic unconstrained articulation of system diversity with alternative characterisations of other salient properties of the energy system as a whole (interactions) or its component options (individual performance). Under such an approach, the 'systems' and 'options' in question may equally be defined to address contexts like primary energy mixes, electricity supply portfolios, energy service provision and transport systems modalities. The approach can as readily focus on specific economic performance or broader criteria of energy sustainability.

The interest of the heuristic $V\{S\}$, lies not in any attempt to derive some unconditional 'optimal' balance between the performance of individual options, system interactions and portfolio diversity. Instead, $V\{S\}$ can be used systematically to explore different possible perspectives and assumptions concerning the contributions of these components to the overall value of an energy system. For each perspective on the available options, their individual performance, dynamic resource curves, joint interactions, mutual disparities, aggregations of diversity properties and the performance-diversity trade-off, there will exists a particular apportionment of options that yields some maximum overall value. By varying **d** between zero and infinity, $V\{S\}$ yields a set of all possible conditionally optimal energy systems ranging (respectively) from those that maximise value due to aggregate performance of individual.

Reflecting work currently in progress (Yoshizawa *et al.*, 2008), Figure 7.8 provides a schematic illustration of the kind of picture that arises from this analysis. For purposes of exposition, it focuses on the mix of generating technologies at the level of the UK electricity supply system taken as a whole. It is constructed on the basis of economic and resource data developed for the UK government's recent Energy Reviews (PIU, 2001; DTI, 2005). Broader sustainability criteria are also included under one particular perspective on the weighting of different aspects of performance (Stirling, 2007a). Such an approach might as easily be addressed with respect to regional or international systems, to primary energy mixes in a broad sense, or to include information on demand-side options for the provision of energy services. Either way, disparities will be conceived in a fashion similar to that represented in Figure 7.4: concerning a wide range of attributes of the resources and technologies involved, together with their geographical, commercial, institutional, and socio-political contexts (Stirling, 1996). Positive and negative economic, organizational, and operational synergies between different technologies inform the modeling of interactions (using term i_{ij} in equations 5 and 6). Certain options are tightly constrained in terms of the available resource, or display reductions (from learning or scale) or increases (from depletion) in costs or impacts as the contributions rise. For now, the point is not to assert the empirical particularities, but simply to illustrate the method. Figure 7.8 shows—for a particular hypothetical perspective—how the resulting conditionally optimal electricity portfolios vary as greater or lesser priority is placed on diversity.

Low values of δ in Figure 7.8 may express high confidence in performance appraisals of individual technologies, with little concern over deep uncertainties and ignorance, to which diversity is a reasonable response (Awerbuch *et al.*, 2006). Likewise, low values of δ may imply that priority is attached to maximizing this performance, rather than the other benefits of diversity (in fostering innovation, mitigating lock-in, or accommodating pluralism). High values of δ, on the other hand, reflect a dominant interest in these benefits of diversity, with little concern over the resulting compromises on performance. Again, the value of this kind of heuristic framework is as a means, more explicitly and systematically, to inform analysis under individual perspectives, and to provide a basis for more effective and transparent deliberation between contending positions.

Summary and conclusions

This chapter began by noting some of the principal challenges in seeking to address intractable uncertainties concerning different forms and sources of energy security. In particular, it discussed the dangers of overemphasis on reductive aggregative "risk-based" measures that imply complete

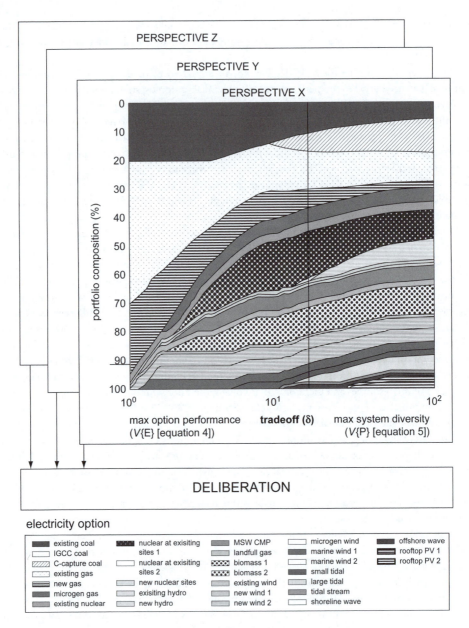

Figure 7.8 Illustrative performance-diversity tradeoffs
Source: Yoshizawa *et al.* (2008).

knowledge with respect both to possibilities and their respective probabilities. There emerges from this analysis a particular value in deliberate diversification that remains robust, even where possibilities and likelihoods remain unknown. Also noted were a number of other reasons for interest in energy diversity, extending beyond security considerations alone. These include well-established benefits such as: hedging ignorance, promoting competition, accommodating plural interests, fostering innovation, nurturing context-sensitivity, and mitigating lock-in. In order to address this diversity of reasons for an interest in energy diversity—and rigorously explore the associated tensions and tradeoffs—the chapter outlined a novel general framework for analysis of energy diversity. The resulting method may be especially useful in helping to inform integrated policy interventions seeking to address a variety of different challenges, such as to achieve large-scale transitions to sustainable energy infrastructures.

Based on the recognition of three necessary but individually insufficient properties of diversity (variety, balance, and disparity), the analytical framework proposed here is applicable in a wide range of different energy policy contexts. It can be focused equally at the level of primary energy mixes, electricity supply portfolios, or energy service delivery. Unlike other approaches, it is not constrained to address only certain specific performance criteria (like the fuel prices highlighted in portfolio theory). Whilst it may be applied in purely economic terms if this is thought appropriate, the method can also be readily extended to encompass any range of issues addressed in well-established multi-criteria appraisal techniques. Nor is this approach dependent on assumptions that past experience necessarily provides a reliable guide to future performance. The pictures of disparity that underlie this analysis can be informed by extensive bodies of existing multivariate performance data, building only on the general underlying structures in this performance, rather than the specific values. Finally, it can be seen that the framework allows attention to be given to more detailed properties such as dynamic resource curves and system-level interactions between options.

Perhaps most importantly, the present framework for multi-criteria diversity analysis can be applied flexibly to an unconstrained array of different specialist, institutional, or stakeholder perspectives. This amenability to more open and plural processes of engagement is also central to agendas around democratization and sustainability. As a framework for quantification, the approach is compliant with a series of rigorous formal quality criteria (Table 7.2). However, as a heuristic approach, it does not purport to derive a single definitively objective indicator of energy diversity, irrespective of context or perspective. Indeed, in a complex, uncertain dynamic and contested arena like energy security policy, any such aims (and claims) might be regarded as misleading and spurious. Instead, the present framework might be taken as a basis for deriving conditional indicators, by reference to particular datasets concerning whatever appear to preset salient dimensions of disparity under any given context and perspective. In particular, it offers a way rigorously, symmetrically, and transparently to articulate a variety of disparate perspectives on diversity. It is in these ways that this diversity analysis approach may offer a concrete basis for further research.

In the end, however, the present methodology is not so much an alternative to other approaches to the appraisal of energy diversity, as it is a complement—and potential integrative framework. It was reported at the beginning of this chapter, that—even within particular approaches—the profusion of different methods and framings for assessment of diversity and option performance often yield radically different policy implications. Where policymaking is based (either contingently or strategically) on a circumscribed subset of such technical perspectives, then it risks delivering results that are at best lacking in robustness. At worst, they present a vulnerability to manipulation by special interests of the kind (as we have seen) that is not unknown in the analysis of diversity. Here, as in other areas of policy appraisal, we need to move away from simplistic and hubristic prescriptive methods, which neglect uncertainties and presume consensus around a particular asserted set of priorities and value judgments. Instead, the present general heuristic framework provides a means to articulate an unlimited variety of different approaches to the assessment of performance and appraisal of disparity. By revealing the legitimate scope for disagreement and identifying areas of common ground, multi-criteria diversity analysis may help build a framework for more robust and accountable policymaking on energy diversity.

Acknowledgements

With thanks to the editors and publishers at Elsevier, part of this chapter is reproduced with permission from an earlier article published by the author: A. Stirling. 2010. "Multicriteria Diversity Analysis: A Novel Heuristic Framework for Appraising Energy Portfolios," *Energy Policy* 38: 1622–1634, available at: doi:10.1016/j.enpol.2009.02.023. The author would also like to thank the present editor, Benjamin Sovacool, for his patience and support and the UK ESRC, who funded the research published here.

References

Adelman, M. 1995. *The Genie Out of the Bottle: World Oil Since 1970* (Cambridge, MA: MIT Press).

Arrow, K. 1963. *Social Choice and Individual Values* (New Haven, CT: Yale University Press).

Arthur, W. 1989. "Competing Technologies, Increasing Returns, and Lock-in by Historical Events," *Economic Journal* 99: 116–131.

Arthur, W. 1994. *Increasing Returns and Path Dependence in the Economy* (Ann Arbor: University of Michigan Press).

Ashby, W. 1956. *An Introduction to Cybernetics* (London: Chapman and Hall).

Awerbuch, S. 2000a. "Investing in Photovoltaics: Risk, Accounting and the Value of New Technology," *Energy Policy* 28: 1023–1035.

Awerbuch, S. 2000b. "Investing in Distributed Generation." In E. Bietry, J. Donaldson, J. Gururaja, J. Hurt, and V. Mubayi (eds.), *Decentralized Energy Alternatives: Proceedings of the Decentralized Energy Alternative Symposium* (New York: Columbia School of Business Sustainable Development Initiative), pp. 34–47.

Awerbuch, S. and M. Berger. 2003. *Applying Portfolio Theory to EU Electricity Planning and Policy Making*, Report No. EET/2003/03 (Paris: International Energy Agency).

Awerbuch, S. and S. Yang. 2007. "Efficient Electricity Generating Portfolios for Europe: Maximising Energy Security and Climate Change Mitigation," *EIB Papers* 12(2): 8–37.

Awerbuch, S., A. Stirling, J. Jansen, and L. Beurskens. 2006. "Portfolio and Diversity Analysis of Energy Technologies Using Full-Spectrum Uncertainty Measures." In D. Bodde and K. Leggio (eds.), *Understanding and Managing Business Risk in the Electric Sector* (Amsterdam: Elsevier), pp. 202–222.

Bazilian, M. and F. Roques (eds.). 2008. *Analytical Methods for Energy Diversity and Security* (Oxford: Elsevier).

Bird, J. 2007. *Energy Security in the UK* (London: Institute for Public Policy Research).

Bonner, J. 1986. *Politics, Economics and Welfare: An Elementary Introduction to Social Choice* (Brighton: Harvester Press).

Brooks, H. 1986. "The Typology of Surprises in Technology, Institutions and Development." In W. Clark and R. Munn (eds.), *Sustainable Development of the Biosphere* (Cambridge: Cambridge University Press), pp. 325–350.

Brower, M. 1995. "Comments on Stirling's 'Diversity and Ignorance in Electricity Supply Investment'," *Energy Policy* 23(2): 115–116.

Brown, N. and M. Michael. 2003. "A Sociology of Expectations: Retrospecting Prospects and Prospecting Retrospects," *Technology Analysis and Strategic Management* 15(1): 3–18.

Brundtland, G. (ed.). 1987. *Our Common Future: Report of the United Nations Commission on Environment and Development* (Oxford: Oxford University Press).

Burgess, J., A. Stirling, J. Clark, D. Davies, M. Eames, K. Staley, and S. Williamson. 2007. "Deliberative Mapping: Developing an Analytic-Deliberative Methodology to Support Contested Science-Policy Decisions," *Public Understanding of Science* 16(3): 299–322.

California Energy Commission (CEC). 1998. *Final Report: Diversity and Risk Analysis in a Restructured California Electricity Market*, Contract #500-96-019 (San Francisco: Resource Decisions, October).

Canary, D., B. Brossmann, and D. Seibold. 1987. "Argument Structures in Decision-making Groups," *Southern Speech Communication Journal* 53: 18–37.

Clemen, R. 1996. *Making Hard Decisions*, 2nd edn (Belmont: Duxbury).

Cohendet, P., P. Llerena, and A. Sorge. 1992. "Technological Diversity and Coherence in Europe: An Analytical Overview," *Revue d Economie Industrielle* 59: 9–26.

Collingridge, D. 1980. *The Social Control of Technology* (Milton Keynes: Open University Press).

Collingridge, D. 1982. *Critical Decision Making: A New Theory of Social Choice* (London: Pinter).

Commission of the European Communities (CEC). 1990. *Security of Supply*, SEC(90)548 (Brussels: European Commission).

Commission of the European Communities (CEC). 2005. *Working Together for Growth and Jobs: A New Start for the Lisbon Strategy: Communication from the President*, (2005) (Brussels: European Comission).

Commission of the European Communities (CEC). 2007. *An Energy Policy for Europe*, Communication from the Commission to the European Council and the European Parliament, SEC(2007)12 (Brussels: European Commission).

Consortium of Local Authorities (COLA), 1994. *New Nuclear Investment and Electricity Portfolio Diversity*, submission to the UK Government Review of Nuclear Power Policy by Consortium of Local Authorities, Gwent, September.

Costello, K. (2004). *Increased Dependence on Natural Gas for Electric Generation: Meeting the Challenge* (Columbia, OH: National Regulatory Research Institute, Ohio State University).

Cowan, R. 1991. "Tortoises and Hares: Choice Among Technologies of Unknown Merit," *Economic Journal* 101: 801–814.

David, P. and G. Rothwell. 1996. "Standardisation, Diversity and Learning: Strategies for the Co-evolution of Technology and Industrial Capacity," *International Journal of Industrial Organization* 14: 181–201.

De Finetti, N. 1974. *Theory of Probability* (New York: Wiley).

De Marchi, B., S. Funtowicz, C. Gough, A. Guimaraes Pereira, and E. Rota. 1998. *The Ulysses Voyage*, ULYSSES at JRC EUR 17760EN, Ispra, Joint Research Centre.

Department of Business, Enterprise and Regulatory Reform (BERR). 2006. *The Energy Challenge: Report of the UK Government Energy Review* (London: BERR).

Department of Trade and Industry (DTI). 1995. *The Prospects for Nuclear Power in the UK: Conclusions of the Government's Nuclear Review*, Cmnd 2860 (London: HMSO).

Department of Trade and Industry (DTI). 2003a. *Energy White Paper: Our Energy Future: Creating a Low Carbon Economy* (London, HMSO, March).

Department of Trade and Industry (DTI). 2003b. *Digest of UK Energy Statistics* (London: HMSO).

Department of Trade and Industry (DTI). 2005. *The Role of Fossil Fuel Carbon Abatement Technologies (CATs) in a Low Carbon Energy System: A Report on the Analysis Undertaken to Advise the DTI's CAT Strategy* (London: DTI, December).

Department of Trade and Industry (DTI). 2006. *Our Energy Future: Creating a Low Carbon Economy*, Energy White Paper (London: HMSO). Available at: http://www.dti.gov.uk/files/file10719.pdf (accessed August 28, 2010).

Dodgson, J., M. Spackman, A. Pearman, and L. Phillips. 2001. *Multi-Criteria Analysis: A Manual* (London: Department for Transport, Local Government and the Regions and HMSO).

Eldredge, N. 1992. *Systematics, Ecology and the Biodiversity Crisis* (New York: Columbia University Press).

Elliott, D. (ed.). 2007. *Nuclear or Not? Does Nuclear Power Have a Place in a Sustainable Energy Future?* (London: Palgrave).

Environmental Resources Management (ERM). 1995. *Diversity in UK Electricity Generation: A Portfolio Analysis*, report commissioned by Scottish Nuclear Ltd, Environmental Resources Management, December.

European Energy Charter Secretariat. 2004. *The European Energy Charter Treaty and Related Documents: A Legal Framework for International Co-operation* (Brussels: European Commission). Available at: <http://www.encharter.org/fileadmin/user_upload/document/EN.pdf#page=211> (accessed July 12, 2009).

Externe Project. 2004. *New Elements for the Assessment of External Costs from Energy Technologies*, report to EC DG Research, Technological Development and Demonstration (RTD), Brussels. Available at: <http://www.ier.uni-stuttgart.de/forschung/projektwebsites/newext/> (accessed July 2008).

Faber, M. and J. Proops. 1994. *Evolution, Time, Production and the Environment* (Berlin: Springer).

Farrell, A., H. Zerriffi, and H. Dowlatabadi. 2004. "Energy Infrastructure and Security," *Annual Review of Environment and Resources* 29: 421–469.

Forster, M. 1999. "How do Simple Rules 'Fit to Reality' in a Complex World?" *Minds and Machines* 9: 543–556.

Fransella, F., R. Bell, and D. Bannister. 2004. *A Manual for Repertory Grid Technique*, 2nd edn. (Chichester: John Wiley).

Funtowicz, S. and J. Ravetz. 1990. *Uncertainty and Quality in Science for Policy* (Amsterdam: Kluwer).

Geroski P. 1989. "The Choice between Diversity and Scale." In E. Davis (ed.), *1992: Myths and Realities* (London: Centre for Business Strategy, London Business School), pp. 29–45.

Gini, C. 1913. "Variabilita e Mutabilita", *Journal of the Royal Statistical Society* 76(3) (February): 326–327.

Grabher, G. and D. Stark. 1997. "Organizing Diversity: Evolutionary Theory, Network Analysis and Postsocialism," *Regional Studies* 31(5): 533–544.

Green, D. and P. Leiby. 2007. "Measuring Energy Security: The Case of U.S. Oil Dependence," paper presented to conference on *Energy Security: Indicators and Concepts*, ZEW, Mannheim, Germany, November 29–30.

Greene, D., D. Jones, and P. Leiby P. 1998. "The Outlook for US Oil Dependence," *Energy Policy* 26: 55–69.

Gross, R., P. Heptonstall, D. Anderson, T. Green, M. Leach and J. Skea. 2006. *The Costs and Impacts of Intermittency: An Assessment of the Evidence on the Costs and Impacts of Intermittent Generation on the British Electricity Network* (London: UK Energy Research Centre, March).

Grove-White, R., P. Macnaghten, and B. Wynne. 2000. *Wising Up: The Public and New Technologies* (Lancaster, UK: Centre for the Study of Environmental Change, Lancaster University).

Grubb, M., L. Butler, and P. Twomey. 2006. "Diversity and Security in UK Electricity Generation: The Influence of Low-Carbon Objectives," *Energy Policy* 34: 4050–4062.

Hanley, N. and C. Spash. 1993. *Cost-Benefit Analysis and the Environment* (Cheltenham, UK: Edward Elgar).

Helm, D. 2002. "Energy Policy: Security of Supply, Sustainability and Competition," *Energy Policy* 30(3): 173–184.

Helm, D. 2007. "European Energy Policy: Meeting the Security of Supply and Climate Change Challenges," *EIB Papers* 12(1): 30–49.

Herfindahl, O. 1959. *Copper Costs and Prices: 1870–1957* (Baltimore, MD: John Hopkins University Press).

Hill, M. 1978. "Diversity and Evenness: a Unifying Notation and its Consequences," *Ecology* 54(2): 427–432.

Hirschman, A. 1964. "The Paternity of an Index," *American Economic Review* 54(5): 761.

Hubberke, D. 2007. *Indicators of Energy Security in Industrialised Countries* (Chemnitz: University of Chemnitz, December).

Hughes, T. 1983. *Networks of Power: Electrification in Western Society 1880–1930* (Baltimore, MD: Johns Hopkins University Press).

International Energy Agency (IEA). 1980. *A Group Strategy for Energy Research, Development and Demonstration* (Paris: International Energy Agency).

International Energy Agency (IEA). 1985. *Energy Technology Policy* (Paris: International Energy Agency).

International Energy Agency (IEA). 1991. *Energy Policies of IEA Countries: 1990 Review* (Paris: International Energy Agency).

International Energy Agency (IEA). 2002. *Elecricity Information 2002* (Paris: International Energy Agency).

International Energy Agency (IEA). 2007. *Energy Security and Climate Policy: Assessing Interactions* (Paris: International Energy Agency).

Jacobsson, S. and A. Johnson. 2000. "The Diffusion of Renewable Energy Technology: An Analytical Framework and Key Issues for Research," *Energy Policy* 28(9): 625–640.

Jansen, J., W. Van Arkel, and M. Boots. 2004. *Designing Indicators of Long-Term Energy Supply Security*. Working paper ECN-C-04-007 (Petten, Netherlands: Energy Research Centre).

Jaulin, L., M. Kieffer, O. Didrit, and É. Walter. 2001. *Applied Interval Analysis* (London: Springer Verlag).

Jaynes, E. 1986. "Bayesian Methods: General Background." In L. Justice (ed.), *Maximum Entropy and Bayesian Methods* (Cambridge: Cambridge University Press).

Joint Energy Security of Supply Working Group (JESS). 2004. *Fourth Report* (London: Department of Trade and Industry, May).

Junge, K. 1994. "Diversity of Ideas About Diversity Measurement," *Scandinavian Journal of Psychology* 35: 16–26.

Kauffman, S. 1995. *At Home in the Universe: the Search for the Laws of Complexity* (London: Penguin).

Kelly, J. 1978. *Arrow Impossibility Theorems* (New York: Academic Press).

Keynes, J. 1921. *A Treatise on Probability* (London: Macmillan).

King, D. 2006. "Why we have no Alternative to Nuclear Power," *Independent*, London, July 13.

King, D. 2007. Interview on *The Material World*, BBC Radio 4, December 21.

Knight, F. 1921. *Risk, Uncertainty and Profit* (Boston, MA: Houghton Mifflin).

Kruskal, J. 1964. "Nonmetric Multidimensional Scaling of a Numerical Method," *Psychometrika* 29: 115–129.

Lawson, N. 1992. *The View from Number 11: Memoires of a Tory Radical* (London, Bantam).

Laxton, R. 1978. "The Measure of Diversity," *Journal of Theoretical Biology* 70: 51–67.

Loasby, B. 1976. *Choice, Complexity and Ignorance: An Enquiry into Economic Theory and the Practice of Decision Making* (Cambridge: Cambridge University Press).

Lovins, A. and L. Lovins. 1982. *Brittle Power: Energy Strategy for National Security* (Andover, MA: Brick House).

Lucas, N., T. Price, and R. Tompkins. 1995. "Diversity and Ignorance in Electricity Supply Investment: A Reply to Andrew Stirling," *Energy Policy* 23(1): 5–7.

Luce, R. and H. Raiffa. 1957. *Games and Decisions* (New York: Wiley).

Mackay, A. 1980. *Arrows Theorem: The Paradox of Social Choice: A Case Study in the Philosophy of Economics* (New Haven, CT: Yale University Press).

MacKerron, G. and I. Scrase (eds.). 2009. *Climate of Urgency: Empowering Energy Policy* (London: Palgrave).

Markandya, A., V. Costantini, F. Gracceva, and G. Vicini. 2005. "Security of Energy Supply: Comparing Scenarios From a European Perspective," *Fondatione Eni Enrico Matei, Nota Di Lavoro* 89 (June).

Matthews, M. and F. McGowan. 1990. *Modes of Usage and Diffusion of New Technologies*, FOP 250 (Brussels: European Commission FAST Project).

May, R. 1990. "Taxonomy as Destiny," *Nature* 347: 129–130.

McKeown B. and D. Thomas. 1988. *Q Methodology* (Newbury Park: Sage).

Meyers R. 1997. "Social iInfluence and Group Argumentation." In L. Frey and J. Barge (eds.), *Managing Group Life: Communicating in Decision-Making Groups* (New York: Houghton Mifflin).

Mitchell, C. 2007. *The Political Economy of Sustainable Energy* (London: Palgrave).

Mitchell, C. and B. Woodman. 2006. *New Nuclear Power: Implications for a Sustainable Energy System* (Warwick: Green Alliance and University of Warwick).

Morgan, M., M. Henrion, and M. Small. 1990. *Uncertainty: A Guide to Dealing with Uncertainty in Quantitative Risk and Policy Analysis* (Cambridge: Cambridge University Press).

National Economic Research Associates (NERA). 1995. *Diversity and Security of Supply in the UK Electricity Market*, report to the Department of Trade and Industry, London.

National Economic Research Associates (NERA). 2002. *Security in Gas and Electricity Markets*, report to the Department of Trade and Industry, London, October.

Owen, H. 1997. *Open Space Technology: A User's Guide*, 2nd edn. (New York: Berrett-Koehler).

Oxford Economic Research Associates (OXERA). 2004. *Results of Renewables Market Modelling*, study conducted for UK Department of Trade and Industry, Oxford.

Parkinson, C. 1989. "Statement by Secretary of State for Energy," *Hansard* 275, April 5.

Patterson, W. 1999. *Transforming Electricity* (London: Earthscan).

Pearce, D. and C. Nash. 1981. *The Social Appraisal of Projects: A Text in Cost-Benefit Analysis* (London: Macmillan).

Performance and Innovation Unit (PIU). 2001. *Working Paper on Generating Technologies: Potentials and Cost Reductions to 2020* (London: Cabinet Office).

Pielou, E. 1977. *Mathematical Ecology* (New York: Wiley).

Plummer, J. (ed.). 1983. *Energy Vulnerability* (Cambridge, MA: Ballinger).

Prime Minister's Strategy Unit (PMSU). 2002. *The Energy Review* (London: Cabinet Office, February).

Prindle, B., M. Eldridge, M. Eckhardt, and A. Frederick. 2007. *The Twin Pillars of Sustainable Energy: Synergies between Energy Efficiency and Renewable Energy Technology and Policy*, ACEEE Report Number E074 (Washington DC: American Council for an Energy Efficient Economy).

Rao, C. 1982. "Diversity and Dissimilarity Coefficients: A Unified Approach," *Theoretical Population Biology* 21: 24–43.

Rawls, J. 1997. "The Idea of Public Reason Revisited," *The University of Chicago Law Review* 64: 767.

Renn, O., T. Webler, and P. Wiedemann. 1995. *Fairness and Competence in Citizen Participation: Evaluating Models for Environmental Discourse* (Dordrecht, Netherlands: Kluwer).

Rosenberg, N. 1982. *Inside the Black Box: Technology and Economics* (Cambridge: Cambridge University Press).

Rosenberg, N. 1996. "Uncertainty and Technological Change." In R. Landau, T. Taylor, and G. Wright (eds.), *The Mosaic of Economic Growth* (Stanford, CA: Stanford University Press).

Rowe, W. 1994. "Understanding Uncertainty," *Risk Analysis* 14(5): 743–750.

Rumsfeld, D. 2002. *News Briefing at the Department of Defence*, Washington, DC, February 12.

Runnegar, B. 1987. "Rates and Modes of Evolution in the Mollusca." In M. Campbell, and R. May (eds.), *Rates of Evolution* (London: Allen and Unwin).

Saltelli, A. 2004. *Sensitivity Analysis in Practice: A Guide to Assessing Scientific Models* (Chichester: Wiley).

Scheepers, M., A. Seebregts, J. de Jong, and H. Maters. 2007. *EU Standards for Energy Security of Supply: Updates on the Crisis Capability Index and the Supply/Demand Index, Quantification for EU-27* (Petten: Netherlands Energy Research Centre).

Sen, P. 2005. "Gini Diversity Index, Hamming Distance, and Curse of Dimensionality," *Metron – International Journal of Statistics* 58(3): 329–349.

Simpson, E.H. (1949). "Measurement of Diversity," *Nature* 163, p. 688.

Skea, J. 2007. "Note on Behaviour of Diversity Indices," personal communication to A. Stirling, October.

Smith, A., A. Stirling, and F. Berkhout. 2005. "The Governance of Sustainable Socio-Technical Transitions," *Research Policy* 34: 1491–1510.

Sneath, P. and R. Sokal. 1973. *Numerical Taxonomy: The Principles and Practice of Numerical Classification* (San Francisco: Freeman).

Solow, A. and S. Polasky. 1994. "Measuring Biological Diversity," *Environmental and Ecological Statistics* 1: 95–107.

Spicer, M. 1987. "Energy 1987," address by the Energy Minister to the Conference of the British Institute for Energy Economics, Chatham House, London, December 7.

Stirling, A. 1994. "Diversity and Ignorance in Electricity Supply Investment: Addressing the Solution Rather than the Problem," *Energy Policy* 22(3): 195–216.

Stirling, A. 1995. "Diversity in Electricity Supply: A Response to the Reply of Lucas et al.," *Energy Policy* 23(1): 8–11.

Stirling, A. 1996. "Optimising UK Electricity Portfolio Diversity." In G. MacKerron and P. Pearson (eds.), *The UK Energy Experience: A Model or a Warning?* (London: Imperial College Press, March), pp. 12–25.

Stirling, A. 1997. "Multicriteria Mapping: Mitigating the Problems of Environmental Valuation?" In J. Foster (ed.), *Valuing Nature: Economics, Ethics and Environment* (London: Routledge), pp. 159–184.

Stirling, A. 1998. *On the Economics and Analysis of Diversity.* SPRU Electronic Working Paper Number 28 (Brighton: University of Sussex, October). Available at: http://www.sussex.ac.uk/Units/spru/ publications/ imprint/sewps/sewp28/sewp28.pdf (accessed May 2006).

Stirling, A. 1999c. "Risk at a Turning Point?" *Journal of Environmental Medicine* 1(3): 119–126.

Stirling, A. 2003. "Risk, Uncertainty and Precaution: Some Instrumental Implications from the Social Sciences." In I. Scoones, M. Leach, and F. Berkhout (eds.), *Negotiating Change: Perspectives in Environmental Social Science* (London: Edward Elgar), pp. 33–76.

Stirling, A. 2006a. "Analysis, Participation and Power: Justification and Closure in Participatory Multi-criteria Analysis," *Land Use Policy* 23(1): 95–107.

Stirling, A. 2006b. "Foresight and Sustainability: Reflection and Reflexivity in the Governance of Technology." In J. Voss and R. Kemp (eds.), *Sustainability and Reflexive Governance* (Cheltenham: Edward Elgar), pp. 225–272.

Stirling, A. 2007a. "A General Framework for Analysing Diversity in Science, Technology and Society," *Journal of the Royal Society Interface* 4(15): 707–719.

Stirling, A. 2007b. "Deliberate Futures: Precaution and Progress in Social Choice of Sustainable Technology," *Sustainable Development* 15: 286–295.

Stirling, A. 2008a. "Opening Up and Closing Down: Power, Participation and Pluralism in the Social Appraisal of Technology," *Science Technology and Human Values* 33(2) (March): 262–294.

Stirling, A. 2008b. "Diversity and Sustainable Energy Transitions: Multicriteria Diversity Analysis of Electricity Portfolios." In M. Bazilian and F. Roques (eds.), *Analytical Methods for Energy Diversity and Security* (Oxford: Elsevier), pp. 3–29.

Stirling, A. 2009a. "Risk, Uncertainty and Power," *Seminar* 597 (May): 33–39.

Stirling, A. 2009b. "The Challenge of Choice." In G. MacKerron and I. Scrase (eds.), *Climate of Urgency: Empowering Energy Policy* (London: Palgrave), pp. 251–260.

Stirling, A. 2010. "Multicriteria Diversity Analysis: A Novel Heuristic Framework for Appraising Energy Portfolios," *Energy Policy* 38: 1622–1634.

Stirling, A. and S. Mayer. 2001. "A Novel Approach to the Appraisal of Technological Risk," *Environment and Planning C* 19(4): 529–555.

Suzuki, T. 2001. *Energy Security and the Role of Nuclear Power in Japan* (Tokyo: Central Research Institute of the Electric Power Industry).

Ulph, A. 1988. *Quantification of Benefits of Diversity from Reducing Exposure to Volatility of Fossil Fuel Prices,* evidence to Hinkley Point C Planning Enquiry for Central Electricity Generating Board, October.

Ulph, A. 1989. *Notes on the Use of the CAPM Model to Value Diversity Benefits,* Document S4165, evidence to Hinkley Point C Planning Enquiry for Central Electricity Generating Board.

Umbach, F. 2004. "Global Energy Supply and Geopolitical Challenges." In F. Godement, F. Nicolas, and T. Yakushiji (eds.), *Asia and Europe: Cooperating for Energy Security* (Tokyo: Council for Asia-Europe Cooperation), p. 137–168.

Van den Berg, N., C. Dutilh, and G. Huppes. 1995. *Beginning LCA: A Guide to Environmental Life Cycle Assessment* (Rotterdam: CML).

Verrastro, F. and S. Ladislaw. 2007. "Providing Energy Security in an Interdependent World," *The Washington Quarterly* 30(4): 95–104.

Vincke, M., M. Gassner, and B. Roy. 1992. *Multicriteria Decision-Aid* (Chichester, New York, Brisbane, Toronto, Singapore: John Wiley).

Von Winterfeldt, D. and W. Edwards. 1986. *Decision Analysis and Behavioural Research* (Cambridge: Cambridge University Press).

Wakeford, T. 2002. "Citizen's Juries: A Radical Alternative for Social Research," *Social Research Update*, 37(1), pp. 1–4.

Walker, W. 2000. "Entrapment in Large Technological Systems," *Research Policy* 29(7–8): 833–846.

Weitzman, M. 1992. "On Diversity," *Quarterly Journal of Economics* 107: 363–405.

Werner R. 2004. *Designing Strategy: Scenario Analysis and the Art of Making Business Strategy* (New York: Praeger).

Wicks, M. 2006. "Energy Security & Economic Interaction: Challenges for Government," speech by Minister of State for Energy, Lehman Brothers, London, April 5.

Williamson, O. 1993. "Transaction Cost Economics and Organisation Theory," *Industrial Economics and Corporate Change* 2: 107–156.

Wynne, B. 1992. "Uncertainty and Environmental Learning: Reconceiving Science and Policy in the Preventive Paradigm," *Global Environmental Change* 2: 111–127.

Wynne, B. 2002. "Risk and Environment as Legitimatory Discourses of Technology: Reflexivity Inside Out?" *Current Sociology* 50(30): 459–477.

Yoshizawa, G., A. Stirling, and T. Suzuki. 2008. *Electricity System Diversity in the UK and Japan: A Multicriteria Diversity Analysis*, University of Tokyo, October.

8

THE ENVIRONMENTAL DIMENSION OF ENERGY SECURITY[1]

Marilyn A. Brown and Michael Dworkin

Introduction

Environmental sustainability is rarely discussed as an energy security issue. In some ways this is surprising because in its classic sense, the concept of environmental sustainability encompasses the notion of balancing "the needs of the present without compromising the ability of future generations to meet their own needs."[2] When applied to energy policy, sustainability debates typically focus on ensuring that the harvest rates of renewable resources do not exceed regeneration rates; making sure that waste emissions do not exceed relevant assimilative capacities of ecosystems; and guaranteeing that non-renewable resources are only depleted at a rate equal to the creation of renewable ones. However, these concerns have seldom been seen as constraints in security discussions.

More recently, however, the magnitude of energy impacts on environmental systems suggests an array of additional linkages to energy security. These links are generally based on the assumption that societies can become stressed to the point of collapse when environmental conditions deteriorate to the point that necessary resources are unavailable,[3] Significantly, however, long before we run out of resources, people will start fighting over what is left. As demonstrated by this chapter, the unchecked growth in fossil energy consumption and the ensuing acceleration of global climate change, as well as related air and water pollution, act as "threat multipliers" impinging on energy security worldwide.[4] These three environmental dimensions are just a subset of a larger array of environmental concerns that threaten energy security, including land pollution, forestry, and biodiversity loss.

This broad range of threats to energy security requires a holistic treatment of causes and effects, including energy and climate issues as well as waste, agriculture, water, and forestry.[5] For example, the land required for energy production can compete with food production, leading to tension and instability.

This chapter links three of these environmental dimensions to energy security and suggests a range of metrics. In particular, it focuses on the "threat multipliers" that climate change, air pollution, and water issues add to the energy security challenge, as well as possible mitigation strategies. Derived from this discussion is a set of metrics that measure various environmental dimensions of energy security (Table 8.1).

Table 8.1 Defining and measuring the environmental dimension of energy security

Criteria	Link To Energy Security	Metrics
Climate Change	• Climate change is a "threat multiplier" in terms of energy security • Mass migration of refugees seeking asylum from ecological disasters could destabilize regions of the world, threatening energy as well as national security	• Carbon dioxide emissions and atmospheric GHG concentration levels • Magnitude of global or regional warming, sea level rise, intensification of tropical cyclones, and incidence of drought • Availability of adaptation resources
Air Pollution	• Deterioration of environmental conditions can negatively impact human and ecological health • If resources are not available to prevent or remedy these conditions, political and economic instability can result and energy security could be threatened	• Emissions and concentrations of sulfur dioxide, nitrous oxide (N_2O), and airborne particulates • Mortality and incidence of respiratory diseases from air pollution • Implementation of fuel economy and air pollution standards
Water Issues	• Lack of available safe drinking water can destabilize the security of a region • Because fossil, hydro, and nuclear power plants consume large quantities of fresh water, shrinking supplies of water could threaten the ability to provide electricity and the ability of nations to feed themselves	• Water quality metrics such as dissolved oxygen concentration, phosphorus concentration, nitrogen concentration, chlorophyll-a, and total biomass • Mortality and incidence of diseases from water pollution • Water consumption from power production • Implementation of water conservation and electricity efficiency programs and water quality standards
Other Criteria	• Land pollution, forestry, and biodiversity loss	• Number of brownfields and toxic waste sites • Rates of deforestation and carbon losses from forestry • Rates of extinction of species and number of preserved habitats • Rates of soil erosion

To better understand the metrics used to gauge the environmental dimensions of energy security, it is important to understand the principal beneficiaries of their use. First, institutional investors—that is, large international and non-governmental investors—could rely on this chapter when evaluating a given nation's environmental stability. Climate change directly and indirectly threatens to alter global financial markets, and predictions for future investments will require considerations for energy security. Second, for the same reasons that large investors may develop energy security metrics, smaller investors relying on larger firms for guidance will need to comprehend the energy intersection of security, environment, and economics. Similarly, corporations seeking to expand into international markets should include energy security in any business plan. Identifying the interconnected relationship between energy security and available resources will lead to more informed decision-making and more realistic trade expectations. Finally, increasing geopolitical instability will compel national governments to examine energy and the environment while designing domestic security policy and when making security decisions. This chapter will help policymakers to use climate change, air pollution, and water pollution as broad indicators of energy security, and will identify the risk management strategies related to those environmental concerns.

Climate change

Tackling climate change promises to be one of the most significant socio-technological challenges of the twenty-first century. Access to cheap energy underpins modern societies across the globe. Finding enough energy to fuel industrialized economies and pull developing countries out of poverty without overheating the climate and destabilizing social and political systems is a "wicked problem."[6] The atmosphere has been the world's principal waste repository because the simplest and least costly approach to waste management has been discharging exhaust up through smokestacks, tailpipes, and chimneys.

The earth's atmosphere is currently at a carbon dioxide concentration of about 390 parts per million, and many climatologists have argued that 450 parts per million is the absolute threshold that cannot be passed without risking dangerous anthropogenic interference with the climate system. Projections of future climate change anticipate global temperature increases between 1.1 and 6.4 degrees Celsius by the end of the century, above and beyond the 0.8 degrees Celsius increase that has already occurred over the past century.[7] The atmospheric concentration of carbon dioxide is growing at 2.5 parts per million per year; if untempered, concentrations will surpass 750 parts per million—an extremely dangerous situation—by the end of the century. Highly industrialized countries are responsible for an overwhelming amount of this increased concentration, particularly when one considers that carbon tends to last a century in the atmosphere, so the emissions from the early 1900s still linger today. Industrialized countries such as the US will have to reduce their carbon emissions from about 20 metric tons per capita today to less than 2.5 tons per capita by 2050 to avert this scenario.[8] Reaching that threshold, however, is even more difficult than it immediately appears if one considers the desire to provide electricity to the billions of people with little or no access.

World electricity production approximated 14,800 billion kWh in 2003, which for a contemporaneous world population of 6.3 billion was an average of 2,300 kWh per person. This usage is heavily concentrated in OECD (Organisation for Economic Co-operation and Development) countries.[9] However, the non-OECD population of 5.45 billion used only 5,900 billion kWh,[10] an average of just 1,090 kWh per person per year.

In a world of 6.6 billion people, with 600 million using their current level of more than 10,000 kWh, and the remaining 6 billion provided with 5,000 kWh per person per year, electric usage would be about 31,000 GWh, which is more than twice world electric use for 2003. Bringing all 6.6 billion people to the current levels typical of developed countries would require 66,000 GWh, that is, well over four times the total electricity production of today. Population growth, of course, would exacerbate this problem: providing 8 billion people with 10,000 kWh per year would require 80,000 GWh, a number that is about six times 2003 levels.

Additionally, if the developing world were to achieve consumption levels equivalent to those of North America, the earth would need an atmosphere nine times larger than it is to handle the resulting pollution and carbon emissions.[11] Motorized transport is responsible for *one third* of the US carbon footprint, and emissions are growing. The global proliferation of auto-dominated transportation systems and the monopoly of gasoline and diesel transportation fuels are causing transportation emissions to increase across the developed world; in many countries belonging to the OECD, gains in energy efficiency in the industrial and power sectors have been offset by energy use in the transportation sector.[12]

Personal vehicles have been largely unaffordable for the masses, but this may be changing. Tata Motors, India's leading automobile manufacturer, has recently produced the Nano, a 2-cylinder compact car with a fuel economy of 55 miles per gallon. This is one of the most efficient, environmentally friendly cars in the world and priced at 100,000 rupees ($2,000), it is listed in the *Guinness Book of World Records* as the world's cheapest car. If the Indian government encouraged citizens who currently own vehicles to switch to the Nano, petroleum consumption and carbon emissions would plummet. Instead, the Nano is likely to enable greater car ownership and more widespread car usage in India, resulting in sizable increases in oil consumption and carbon emissions.

To make the same point a different way, if the expected population of the planet in 2030 were to have an energy consumption at the same rate as the US, it would require five times the kWh that now exist. Contemplating the advancements from that enhanced number of kilowatts may be a pleasant thing, but contemplating their production is deeply unsettling for those who consider the levels of greenhouse gasses, heavy metals, and water degradation associated with current electricity generation. Interestingly, reaching worldwide consumption rates equivalent to those of the US has virtually no affect on improving the traditional metrics used to measure energy security.

To a certain extent, increased access to electricity improves the quality of human life. Low level increases in per capita electricity use directly correlate with longer life expectancies, greater education, and higher GDP as defined by the United Nations' Human Development Index (HDI).[13] As Figure 8.1 illustrates, an annual electricity consumption rate of 4,000 kWh per capita represents a real-world benchmark for meeting the basic necessities required for human development. Indeed, below that number, increases in consumption correlate to substantive improvements to human well-being—above that number, increases in per capita electricity use show no signs of significant improvement on the HDI scale. Thus, it is no surprise that the developing

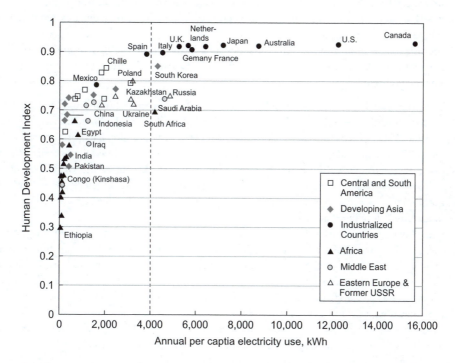

Figure 8.1 The United Nations' human development index and electricity use, 60 countries, 1997.

world will aim to achieve this goal. Considering the threats that global climate change poses to energy security, moving past that threshold may not be worth the slight increase on the HDI scale.

The consequences of climate change are gaining clarity. According to the Intergovernmental Panel on Climate Change (IPCC), there will be at least eight types of negative impacts:[14]

- global warming
- minimum rises in sea levels (0.2 to 0.6m by 2100)[15]
- intensification of tropical cyclones
- meridional overturning of Atlantic Ocean will decrease
- ocean pH will decrease by 0.14 to 0.35 (already down 0.1)
- snow cover will decrease and permafrost and sea ice will melt
- extreme events will become more frequent
- rainfall will increase in the high latitudes, decrease in the subtropics.

The climate change consequences of "business as usual" will be nothing short of catastrophic for the planet. A consensus of studies from the IPCC,[16] United Nations,[17] and numerous top climatologists[18] warn that continued emissions of GHGs will directly contribute to the following:

- major changes in wind patterns, rainfall, and ocean currents, severely altering the distribution, availability, and precipitation of water, possibly leading to drinking water shortages for millions of people;
- destruction of ecosystems, species, and habitats, especially the bleaching of coral reefs and widespread deaths of all types of migratory species;
- a significant loss of agricultural and fishery productivity, along with a shift in the growing seasons for crops and increased drought in areas with marginal soils that have low buffering potential;
- increased damage from floods and severe storms, especially among coastal areas;
- deaths arising from changes in disease vectors, particularly among diseases regulated by temperature and precipitation;
- the risk of abrupt and catastrophic changes such as the sudden release of pockets of deep sea methane or collapse of the North Atlantic Ocean's thermohaline circulation and Greenland's ice sheet.

A research team headed by the NASA/Goddard Institute for Space Studies and the Columbia Center for Climate Systems Research recently confirmed the likelihood of these impacts.[19] These impacts are likely to be of historic proportion, challenging previous global threats such as AIDS, the Great Depression, and global terrorism. The Stern Report projected that the overall costs and risks of climate change will be equivalent to losing at least 5 percent of the world's GDP, or $3.2 trillion, every year, now and forever, and that these damages could exceed 20 percent of GDP ($13 trillion) if more severe scenarios unfold.[20] Stern's figures have since been critiqued for relying on an extremely low discount rate.[21]

The climate change risks faced by developing countries are staggering in magnitude. Containing 80 percent of the world's population, developing countries will be home to 90 percent of the world's population by 2060. Developing economies rely heavily on climate sensitive sectors such as agriculture, tourism, and forestry, meaning that they are directly and significantly affected by changes in temperature, precipitation, and extreme weather events. In addition, developing countries tend to lack resources such as advanced health care and transportation systems, which puts them at greater risk to adverse impacts. They are also, for a variety of geographic and economic reasons, located in regions with the greatest risk of rising sea levels, deteriorating ecosystem services, social tension, and, notably, the creation of environmental refugees. Less affluent countries have fewer ways to recover the economic losses induced by climate change, as their assets are less likely to be fully insured, and the poorest countries rarely have access to systems of recourse other than limited humanitarian aid donations.

Thus, as the climate continues to change, people will be forced to adapt. This adaptation process will take time and impose a number of difficulties—some of which will be easily corrected. Other impacts, however, have no institutional remedy. Global climate change's impending threats will push many families out of their homes.

These climate refugees, or environmental refugees, must relocate due to changes in the climate such as rising sea levels, extreme weather events, drought, and water scarcity. According to The Climate Justice Foundation, "[e]very year climate change is attributable for the deaths of over 300,000 people, seriously affects a further 325 million people, and causes economic losses of US$125 billion."[22] While calamities have been common throughout the ages, the world's population exaggerates the scope of the environmental refugee problem; as the *New York Times* explains: "with the prospect of worsening climate conditions over the next few decades, experts on migration say tens of millions more people in the developing world could be on the move because of disasters."[23] All of this is exacerbated in the context of fresh drinking water, which is not only used for drinking, but also for agriculture. As the groundbreaking report of the Project of the Climate Institute on environmental refugees states,

> [As of 1995] [t]he populations of water-short countries, 550 million, are expected to increase to one billion. Water shortages will be specially adverse for agriculture in general and irrigation agriculture in particular; and for household needs, notably in large urban communities, with all that implies for water-related diseases. In the northern sector of China, with more than half a billion people and producing one quarter of the country's food, virtually all water stocks were already being exploited in 1990.[24]

Another significant challenge for analysts is that there is no agreed upon definition of climate or environmental refugees.[25] Potential climate and environmental refugees could originate anywhere, but concerns are most high in areas with limited resources such as portable water.

Tuvalu, the Marshall Islands, Papua New Guinea, and low-lying parts of the Caribbean and Bangladesh, for example, could be submerged within 60 years if sea levels continue to rise. The Republic of Kiribati, a small island country in the Pacific, has already had to relocate 94,000 people living in shoreline communities and coral atolls to higher ground.[26] India and Bangladesh recently lost an island the two had been fighting over for decades to sea-level rise.[27] The Republic of Maldives could lose 80 percent of its land due to rises in sea level and has already started purchasing land in Sri Lanka for its "climate refugees."[28] Melting glaciers will flood river valleys in Kashmir and Nepal, and reduced rainfall will aggravate water and food insecurity in sub-Saharan Africa, where 182 million people could die of disease epidemics and starvation directly attributable to climate change.[29]

Because climate change is a threat to long-term global stability, it poses both direct and indirect challenges to energy security. Even groups such as the International Energy Agency[30] and former American Defense Secretaries John Deutch and James Schlesinger (2006)[31] have noted that mitigating and adapting to climate change must be considered a part of any attempt to create energy security.

Some metrics of this environmental dimension could be used to measure the causes of global climate change, such as global carbon dioxide emissions and atmospheric GHG concentration levels. Other metrics could reflect climate change impacts, including the magnitude of global or regional warming, sea-level rise, intensification of tropical cyclones, and incidence of drought. Finally, appropriate metrics could reflect the ability of countries and regions to mitigate the impacts of global climate change through the construction of sea walls, hardening of the infrastructure, and other measures. For this, appropriate metrics could be the availability of adaptation funds.

Air pollution

Conventional electricity generation produces a laundry list of environmental damages including radioactive waste and abandoned uranium mines and mills, acid rain and its damage to fisheries and crops, water degradation and freshwater consumption, harmful particulate matter, and cumulative environmental damage to ecosystems and biodiversity through species loss and habitat destruction.

To examine one of the environmental consequences of air pollution more closely reveals the tremendous toll acid rain exacts on the environment. Acid rain can travel for hundreds of miles and thus can cause significant damage across national borders. Specifically, acid rain kills aquatic life, and areas damaged by acid deposition take a long time to recover.[32] Many communities rely on sustenance fishing as the primary source of food and the primary means to a livelihood; thus, acid rain damage can have significant political and socio-economic consequences. Canada and the United States, for example, were involved in a dispute over acid rain—nonetheless, in 2002, the two countries reached an agreement regarding emissions of sulfur dioxide and nitrogen oxide. In Europe, acid rain has been the subject of multilateral negotiations. An important feature of the acid rain problem in Europe was that some countries were net importers and some were net exporters. Eventually, 21 countries signed a Sulfur Protocol, and this was followed by a Nitrogen Oxide Protocol.[33] While the US–Canadian and the European disputes were resolved peacefully, an acid rain problem can lead to more consequential conflicts in less fortunate parts of the world. Less diversified economies, along with less developed political systems, will trigger catastrophic security consequences. For instance, countries that depend on fishing and find water resources threatened by acid rain might take significant aggressive measures against other countries that are the sources of the acid. Likewise, within a country, depletion of fish resources might lead to significant economic dislocation or possible conflicts over the remaining resources. Despite the compelling evidence that there are direct security consequences from burning coal and oil, the future remains dependent on those particulate-emitting fuels.

Indeed, a global new coal build has begun. China currently constructs one coal plant each week, and other developing countries—led by India—are gearing up to reach about one third of that level of coal plant production by 2030.[34] As Figure 8.2 shows, the non-OECD Asian nations as a whole account for the vast majority of this anticipated coal "build-up." "Over their roughly 60-year lives, the new generating facilities in operation by 2030 could collectively emit as much carbon dioxide as was released by all the coal burned since the dawn of the Industrial Revolution."[35]

Similarly, the global proliferation of auto-dominated, petroleum-fueled transportation has already precipitated social and environmental challenges in the developed world that will soon be replicated across the globe unless current trends are altered. Vehicles powered by fossil fuels spew a variety of unhealthy pollutants and particles directly into the air where they become ingested and inhaled by human beings and ecosystems, contributing to acid rain and ozone depletion. Although 85 percent of the world's population does not now have access to a car, they aspire to car ownership, especially residents of the rapidly growing South and East Asia nations. As a result, the use of automobiles across the globe is set to rise dramatically, unleashing significant environmental problems.

Consider emissions of particulate matter (PM), not a specific pollutant itself, but instead a mixture of fine particles of harmful pollutants such as soot, acid droplets, and metals. Conventional

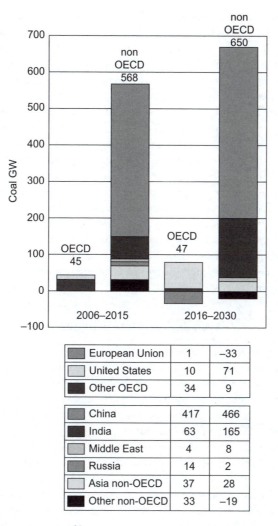

Figure 8.2 Incremental new coal capacity.[36]

automobiles are the largest single human-caused source of PM in many countries, and for those with stringent emissions requirements for vehicles such as California or the European Union (EU) the second largest human source after power plants. (Forest fires and dust storms are the leading non-human sources.) Thousands of medical studies have strongly associated inhalation of PM with heart disease, chronic lung disease, and some forms of cancer. Using some of the most recently available data in the US, deaths from PM pollution are comparable to those from Alzheimer's disease and influenza, and greater than the deaths from breast cancer, automobile accidents, prostate cancer, HIV-AIDs, and drunk driving.[37]

Moreover, global stationary and mobile source combustion and industrial production of acids are the largest sources of nitrous oxide (N_2O) after agriculture. NO_x from combustion is chemically transformed in the atmosphere and deposited in the form of nitrogen compounds, resulting in emissions of N_2O similar to those from fertilizer application. Stationary sources include steam boilers and other systems used for power and heat production, while mobile sources include primarily transportation systems (e.g., trucks, cars, buses, trains, ships).

While indoor air pollution has been substantially addressed in most industrialized nations, the same is not true in much of the developing world where "energy poverty" abounds. Millions of women and children in developing countries spend significant amounts of time searching for firewood, and then burning it or charcoal indoors to heat their homes and prepare their meals. The indoor air pollution that results shortens the life of 2.8 million people every year, almost equal to the number dying annually from HIV/AIDS.[38] It is estimated that even in 2030, about 1.4 billion will still be at risk of having to live without modern energy services.[39] Close to one million of these deaths—910,000—are children under the age of five who must suffer their final months of life dealing with debilitating respiratory infections, chronic obstructive pulmonary disease, and lung cancer. This sustained suffering could destabilize large portions of the world.

Reflecting the cause of air pollution, appropriate metrics could be emissions or concentrations of sulfur dioxide, nitrous oxide (N_2O), and particulates. Reflecting the destabilizing consequences of air pollution, appropriate metrics could include mortality and incidence of respiratory diseases from air pollution. Finally, reflecting the commitment and ability of countries and regions to mitigate these impacts, appropriate metrics could include implementation of fuel economy and air pollution standards.

Availability of safe drinking water

An adequate supply of safe drinking water is a basic prerequisite for human survival. Deficiencies in water supply and water quality already cause about 4,500 deaths throughout the world every day or 1.7 million deaths a year, 90 percent of these children.[40] More than one billion people lack access to clean water and 2.6 billion do not have access to improved sanitation facilities. Some rivers, aquifers, lakes, and other water sources are so polluted that it is more profitable for residents to remove plastic bottles and trash from them for recycling than to fish. The US Central Intelligence Agency believes that more than three billion people will be living in water-stressed regions around the world by 2015 (with a majority concentrated in North Africa and China). According to the Water Resource Management Institute, Pakistan and India will also be water scarce by 2025. Altogether, the World Resources Institute (2000) estimates that by 2025, 40 percent of the world's population will be living in countries experiencing significant water shortages.[41]

Global climate change threatens to worsen these conditions, magnifying the prospect of mass migration of refugees seeking asylum from ecological disasters including drought and coastal flooding from sea-level rise. Water tables for major grain producing areas in northern China are dropping at a rate of five feet per year, and per capita water availability in India is expected to drop 50 to 75 percent over the next decade.[42]

The intimate relationship between electricity generation and water use could cause severe water shortages and crises if population and electricity consumption trends continue. The expansion of power generation can even threaten the ability of nations to feed themselves: for example, the Mekong Dam that China is erecting for electricity would eliminate much of Southeast Asia's agricultural production. Power plants impose a litany of additional environmental impacts on water supplies, including impingement, entrainment, eutrophication, and radioactive contamination.

Research and development activities are ongoing into the development of power plants that use saline, wastewater, or other less pure water sources for cooling. National laboratories and industry scientists are also devoting resources to studying alternative cooling systems that are less water intensive. There are dry cooling plants in operation worldwide, but these power plants are more expensive to build and less energy efficient, which puts them at a considerable economic

Table 8.2 Cooling water withdrawal and consumption rates for common thermal power plant and cooling system types[43]

Plant and Cooling System Type	Water Withdrawal (gal/MWh)	Typical Water Consumption (gal/MWh)
Fossil/biomass/waste-fueled steam, once-through cooling	20,000 to 50,000	~300
Fossil/biomass/waste-fueled steam, pond cooling	300 to 600	300–480
Fossil/biomass/waste-fueled steam, cooling towers	500 to 600	~480
Nuclear steam, once-through cooling	25,000 to 60,000	~400
Nuclear steam, pond-cooling	500 to 1100	400–720
Nuclear steam, cooling towers	800 to 1100	~720
Natural gas/oil combined-cycle, once-through cooling	7500 to 20,000	~100
Natural gas/oil combined-cycle, cooling towers	~230	~180
Natural gas/oil combined-cycle, dry cooling	~0	~0
Coal/petroleum residuum-fueled combined-cycle, cooling towers	~380	~200

Note:
Once-through cooling processes are highlighted in gray

disadvantage.[44] Table 8.2 indicates that once-through cooling has a much higher withdrawal rate than closed-loop cooling (pond cooling and cooling towers), but it consumes less water through evaporation to the atmosphere. Baseline forecasts from the National Energy Technology Laboratory (NETL) project these trends to continue.[45]

The energy–water nexus will play a critical role in the future development of South Asia. Even where cooling water is returned to the environment, it is in a heated and degraded form and can disrupt ecosystems. Water conservation is an added benefit of energy conservation. Although energy efficiency alone will not solve water problems, policymakers should integrate these benefits into resource planning.

Reflecting the energy-related causes of water pollution, appropriate metrics could be dissolved oxygen concentration, phosphorus concentration, nitrogen concentration, chlorophyll-a, and total biomass.[46] Reflecting the destabilizing consequences of water pollution, appropriate metrics could include mortality and incidence of diseases from water pollution. Finally, the commitment and ability of countries and regions to mitigate these impacts could be measured by examining the implementation of water conservation and electric efficiency programs and water quality standards.

Mitigation opportunities: efficiency and renewables

While environmental threats including climate change, water pollution, and air pollution have very real consequences for energy security, those threats can be mitigated. Mitigation, for these purposes, broadly means to reduce or halt detrimental consequences from energy impacts on the environment. Energy efficiency and renewable energy generation can reduce the need for fossil fuels, thereby limiting the environmental repercussions of burning coal and oil. While efficiency measures, such as end-use efficiency and system efficiency, do not provide an energy policy that achieves the goal of minimal environmental impact (in order to promote energy security), such measures do provide a partial solution. Further renewable energy development, such as from wind, solar or geothermal resources, can replace traditional generation. Just as the use of metrics can reveal the risks posed by environmental concerns, metrics may also demonstrate the success of mitigation measures.

Energy efficiency can curb GHG emissions, and as the IPCC noted in its 2007 report, energy efficiency can be the most effective and economic response to the threat of climate change in the immediate future. The idea behind energy efficiency is to use less energy, but also avoid disrupting the way people live or interfering with the quality of products they consume. In fact, according to one leading private consulting group, "Energy efficiency offers a vast, low-cost energy resource for the U.S. economy ... [and] [s]uch a program is estimated to reduce end-use energy consumption in 2020 by 9.1 quadrillion BTUs, roughly 23 percent of projected demand, potentially abating up to 1.1 gigatons of greenhouse gasses annually."[47] End-use energy efficiency achieves these gains by making products more efficient. For example, minimum performance standards can be set for domestic and commercial products, such as washing machines, building materials, and automobiles.[48] Radiant heating systems that are embedded within workshop floors are a more efficient use of energy than warming air and then circulating it.[49] Another popular example is the fact that compact fluorescent lamps use 75 to 80 percent less electricity than incandescent bulbs.[50] In both of these cases—heat and light—the same result is delivered to the consumer, but in a way that uses less energy. Such end-use energy efficiency measures, if and when they are harnessed on a comprehensive scale, directly mitigate the human effects of climate change.

Achieving energy security depends on achieving efficiency at the end-user level as well as broader structural efficiency, such as through government action. A national commitment to energy efficiency "can help reduce ... energy security vulnerability in a timely fashion while improving economic and environmental performance."[51] Structural efficiency is necessary to realize end-user efficiency. The so-called principal-agent problem underscores the need for systematic implementation of measures promoting efficiency. The principal-agent problem arises when the benefits or costs of an action are not borne by the person taking the action.[52] An example is when homebuilders do not install energy-efficient appliances because they would increase the home price, which in turn would turn away potential buyers.[53] If rate structures are amended, however, utility companies could be persuaded to bear some of the costs associated with building highly efficient homes. In return, utility companies can avoid costs associated with building new power plants.[54] Another area where system efficiency could be implemented is fuel efficiency. Currently, a person owning an efficient car may nullify his or her car's efficiency by driving more. To avoid this problem, a fuel tax, or a "pay-as-you-drive" auto insurance scheme could be effective in lowering fuel consumption.

Renewable energy sources also offer attractive means to mitigate the environmental security risks caused by energy. The proliferation of renewable fuel sources will decrease net greenhouse gas emissions and improve overall air and water quality, thus ameliorating some of the potential security risks of global climate change. Furthermore, domestic renewable resources "reduce the dependence from imported entities," assuring sustainability and stability.[55] Additionally, most energy efficiency and renewable generation sources are not mutually exclusive—using solar or wind power in one nation does not prevent other nations from harnessing the same energy. Accordingly, renewable fuels can ease the tensions of energy security by offering a local power source free from the negative political and environmental realities of imported fossil fuels.

Unfortunately, neither energy efficiency nor renewable fuels are a panacea for all the security risks posed by energy-spurred climate change, air pollution, and water scarcity. Physical constraints—such as the lack of available transmission capacity to connect renewables to the grid and the lack of pipeline capacity to bring rural sources of biofuels to urban markets—present barriers to widespread implementation. Varied challenges, such as intermittency and relatively high conventional costs, also inhibit renewable energy development. Political, financial, and regulatory uncertainties also delay both energy efficiency and renewable energy deployment. These obstacles are significant, but not insurmountable. Without a doubt, both renewable energy and energy efficiency are necessary and vital components of the solution to the environmental security problems caused by the expanding energy needs of developed and developing nations.

Conclusion

The use of metrics to assess the risks posed by environmental factors may reveal previously unquantifiable security concerns generated by the need for energy. Traditional security risks inherent to energy consumption and generation are apparent, such as boycotts or oil wars. However, adding the environmental dimension reveals the security risks inherent to climate change, water pollution, and air pollution. Tangible challenges, such as acid rain, environmental refugees, and specific pollutants in drinking water, all present potential metrics.

Once these metrics are established and understood, they may have a significant impact on political and economic leaders. The reasons for their utility seem obvious and compelling—long before rising oceans cover our coasts, disruptive flows of major rivers (such as the Indus, Sutlej, Jumna, and Ganges flowing from the Tibetan plateau) will exacerbate conflicts among major military powers, several of whom possess nuclear weapons. Thus, understanding the full scale of security risks enables policymakers to shape the course of their country's or company's decision-making. Moreover, these metrics could help quantify the potential security impact that energy efficiency and renewable energy measures could have on the decision-making process. As booming demand drives an ever-increasing resource scarcity, the pronounced need for targeted metrics will help determine whether we achieve success or failure in grappling with the challenges of energy security.

Notes

1 Also, special thanks to contributions from the Research Associates at the Institute for Energy and the Environment at Vermont Law School: David Contrada, Clay H.W. Francis, Brian E.J. Martin, and Shahin Milani.
2 Bruntland, G.H. 1987. *Our Common Future* (Oxford: Oxford University Press), p. 43. The Brundtland Commission, named for its chairwoman, Gro Harlem Brundtland, was commissioned by the World Commission on Environment and Development; it established the most widely used definition of "sustainable development" in 1983. The Commission's report outlines the need for all nations to cooperate in the fight against environmental degradation.
3 Jared Diamond, Jared. 2005. *Collapse: How Societies Choose to Fail or Succeed* (New York: Penguin Publisher).
4 CNA Military Advisory Board. 2007. *National Security and the Threat of Climate Change* (Washington, DC: The CNA Corporation), p. 6. Available at: <http:// securityandclimate.cna.org>.
5 Ausubel, J.H. 2007. "Renewable and Nuclear Heresies," *International Journal of Nuclear Governance, Economy and Ecology* 1(2): pp. 232–235.
6 Norton, Bryan. 2005. *Sustainability: A Philosophy of Adaptive Ecosystem Management* (Chicageo: University of Chicago Press).

7 National Academies. 2010. *Advancing the Science of Climate Change* (Washington, DC: National Academies Press), p. 3.

8 International Energy Agency (IEA). 2008. *World Energy Outlook 2008* (Paris: IEA).

9 See Appendix A of U.S. Energy Information Administration, *World Net Electricity Consumption by Region: Reference Case, 1990–2030,* (Washington, DC: U.S. Department of Energy), p. 92. Available at: http://www.eia.doe.gov/oiaf/ieo/pdf/ieoreftab_9.pdf (accessed August 28, 2010).

10 Ibid.

11 United Nations. 2008. *Human Development Report 2007/2008* (New York: United Nations).

12 Sperling, Daniel and Deborah Gordon. 2009. *Two Billion Cars: Driving Toward Sustainability* (New York: Oxford University Press).

13 Pasternak, Alan D. 2000. *Global Energy Futures and Human Development: A Framework For Analysis* (Washington, DC: US Department of Energy, Lawrence Livermore National Laboratory, October), pp. 4–5.

14 Collins, William, Robert Colman, James Haywood, Martin R. Manning, and Philip Mote. 2007. "The Physical Science Behind Climate Change," *Scientific American* (August): 64–73.

15 More recent research suggests that sea levels could potentially rise 0.8 to 2 meters by 2100, several times larger than the IPCC estimate: National Academies. 2010. *Advancing the Science of Climate Change* (Washington, DC: National Academies Press), p. 34.

16 Intergovernmental Panel on Climate Change (IPCC). 2007. "Summary for Policymakers," *Climate Change: 2007* (Washington, DC: U.S Government Printing Office).

17 United Nations, *Human Development Report 2007/2008.*

18 Lackner, Klaus S. and Jeffrey D. Sachs. 2005. "A Robust Strategy for Sustainable Energy," *Brookings Papers on Economic Activity* 2005 (2): 215–248.

19 Rosenzweig, Cynthia *et al.*, 2008. "Attributing Physical and Biological Impacts to Anthropogenic Climate Change," *Nature* 453 (May 15): 353–357.

20 Stern, Nicholas. 2006. *Stern Review: The Economics of Climate Change* (London: HM Treasury), Executive Summary. Available at: <http://siteresources.worldbank.org/INTINDONESIA/Resources/226271-1170911056314/3428109-1174614780539/SternReviewEng.pdf (accessed August 28, 2010).

21 Nordhaus, William. 2007. *The Challenge of Global Warming: Economic Models and Environmental Policy* (New Haven, CT: Yale University).

22 Environmental Justice Foundation 2009. *No Place Like Home—Where Next for Climate Refugees?* (London: The Environmental Justice Foundation, p. 4. Available at: http://www.ejfoundation.org/climaterefugees (accessed August 28, 2010).

23 Kakissis, Joanna. 2010. "Environmental Refugees Unable to Return Home," *New York Times,* January 3. Available at: http://www.nytimes.com/2010/01/04/world/asia/04migrants.html (accessed August 28, 2010).

24 Myers, Norman. 1995. *Environmental Exodus: An Emergent Crisis in the Global Arena,* (Oxford, UK: Project of the Climate Institute, Oxford University), p. 3.

25 Dun, Olivia and François Gemenne. 2008. "Defining 'Environmental Migration'," *Forced Migration Review: Climate Change and Displacement,* Issue 31 (October): 10–11. Available at: http://repository.forcedmigration.org/show_metadata.jsp?pid=fmo:4729 (accessed August 28, 2010).

26 Weir, Kay. 2008. "Don't Cry for Kiribati, Tuvalu, Marshall Islands, parts of Papua New Guinea, the Caribbean, Bangladesh, Africa …," *Pacific Ecologist* (Winter): 2.

27 Available at: http://blogs.discovermagazine.com/80beats/2010/03/25/tiny-island-fought-over-by-india-bangladesh-vanishes-into-the-sea/ (accessed August 28, 2010).

28 Smith, Alex. 2008. "Climate Refugees in Maldives Buy Land," *Tree Hugger* Press Release, November 16.

29 Jagger, Bianca. 2008. "The Threat of a Global Climate Disaster is No Longer Up for Debate," *Testimony Before the House Select Committee for Energy Independence and Global Warming,* testimony in front of US House of Representatives, March 6. Available at: http://globalwarming.house.gov/tools/assets/files/0376.pdf (accessed August 28, 2010).

30 International Energy Agency (IEA). 2007 *Energy Security and Climate Policy—Assessing Interactions* (Paris: IEA).

31 Deutch, J. and James Schlesinger. 2006. *National Security Consequences of US Oil Dependency* (Washington, DC: Council on Foreign Relations Independent Task Force, Report No. 58).

32 Eglene, O. 2002. "Transboundary Air Pollution: Regulatory Schemes & Interstate Cooperation," *Albany Law Environmental Outlook* 7, pp. 128–132.

33 McGee, H.W. 2005. "Litigating Global Warming: Substantive Law in Search of a Forum," *Fordham Environmental Law Review* 16: 371–402.

34 It is, however, important to note that China's net growth of coal-fired plants does not increase at such an alarming rate. Indeed, for every new coal-fired plant that China puts online, an older, less efficient plant must be shut down. These new plants, while not emissions neutral, are an improvement over the older system. Recent technology improvements for coal power ensure that this carbon-based fuel will continue to be the largest component of China's energy mix for the near future. See Bradsher, K. "China Far Outpaces U.S. in Cleaner Coal-Fired Plants," *New York Times*. May 10, 2009, Available at: http://www.nytimes.com/2009/05/11/world/asia/11coal.html?_r=2 (accessed March 31, 2010).

35 Hawkins, D.G., D.A. Lashof, and R.H. Williams. 2006. "What to Do about Coal?" *Scientific American* (September, 2006) . Available at: http://www.scientificamerican.com/article.cfm?id=what-to-do-about-coal-2006&offset=4 (accessed April 19, 2010) (accessed August 28, 2010).

36 Brown, Marilyn A. and B.K. Sovacool. 2011. *Climate Change and Global Energy Security: Technology and Policy Options* (Cambridge, MA: MIT Press).

37 Sovacool, Benjamin K. 2010. "A Transition to Plug-In Hybrid Electric Vehicles (PHEVs): Why Public Health Professionals Must Care," *Journal of Epidemiology and Community Health* 64(3) (March, 2010): 185–187.

38 Holdren John P. and Kirk R. Smith. 2000. "Energy, the Environment, and Health." In Tord Kjellstrom, David Streets, and Xiadong Wang (eds), *World Energy Assessment: Energy and the Challenge of Sustainability* (New York: United Nations Development Programme), pp. 61–110.

39 Modi, Vijay, Susan McDade, Dominique Lallement, and Jamil Saghir. 2005. *Energy Services for the Millennium Development Goals* (Washington and New York: The International Bank for Reconstruction and Development/The World Bank and the United Nations Development Programme). Available at: http://www.unmillenniumproject.org/documents/MP_Energy_Low_Res.pdf (accessed August 28, 2010).

40 Organisation for Economic Co-operation and Development. 2008. *Costs of Inaction on Key Environmental Challenges* (Paris: OECD Publishing), p. 48.

41 Cassara, A., C. Layke, J. Ranganathan, and D. Tunstall. 2000. "Tomorrow's Markets, Global Trends, and Their Implications for Business," *World Resources Institute* (Paris: UNEP), pp. 36–37.

42 Pope, C. 2005. "The State of Nature: Our Roof is Caving In," *Foreign Policy*: 67.

43 Source: Sovacool BK and KE Sovacool. 2009. "Preventing National Electricity-Water Crisis Areas in the United States," with Kelly E. Sovacool, *Columbia Journal of Environmental Law* 34(2): 333–393.

44 Gerdes K. and C. Nichols. 2009. "Water Requirements for Existing and Emerging Thermoelectric Plant Technologies," (National Energy Technology Laboratory). Available at: http://www.netl.doe.gov/energy-analyses/pubs/WaterRequirements.pdf (accessed April 19, 2010).

45 Hoffman, J., S. Forbes, and T. Feeley. 2004. "Estimating Freshwater Needs to Meet 2025 Electricity Generating Capacity Forecasts," (National Energy Technology Laboratory), Available at: http://www.netl.doe.gov/technologies/coalpower/ewr/pubs/Estimating%20Freshwater%20Needs%20to%202025.pdf (accessed April 19, 2010).

46 Hickey, K., M. Greenblatt, D. Gayla, and R. Isaac. 2002. "A Quest for Appropriate Water Quality Metrics to Support a Nutrient TMDL Allocation," *Proceedings of the Water Environment Federation*: *National TMDL Science and Policy,* pp. 357–366.

47 McKinsey & Company Global Energy and Materials. 2009. *Unlocking Energy Efficiency in the U.S. Economy* (Chicago: McKinsey & Company, July), pp. iii.

48 Elkind, J. 2010. "Energy Security: Call for a Broader Agenda." In C. Pascual and J. Elkind (eds), *Energy Security: Economics, Politics, Strategies, and Implications* (Washington, DC, Brookings Institution Press), p. 140.

49 The Institute for Energy and Environment at Vermont Law School. 2007. *The Farmer's Handbook for Energy Self-Reliance* (South Royalton, Vermont: The Institute for Energy and Environment at Vermont Law School), p. 15.

50 Lovins, A. 2005. "More Profit with Less Carbon," *Scientific American* (September): 75.

51 Elkind, "Energy Security: Call for a Broader Agenda," p. 138.

52 Brown, Marilyn A., Jess Chandler, Melissa Lapsa, and Moonis Ally. 2009. *Making Homes Part of the Climate Solution* (Oak Ridge National Laboratory, ORNL/TM-2009/104, June). Available at: http://www.ornl.gov/sci/eere/PDFs/CCTP_PolicyOptions_200906.pdf; Brown, Marilyn A. 2001. "Market Failures

and Barriers as a Basis for Clean Energy Policies," in *Energy Policy*, 29 (14): 1197–1207 (accessed August 28, 2010).

53 Elkind, "Energy Security: Call for a Broader Agenda," p. 138.

54 Elkind, "Energy Security: Call for a Broader Agenda," p. 138.

55 Faulin, J., F. Lera-López, A. Arizkun, and J.M. Pintor. 2009. "Energy Policy in Renewables and its Economic and Environmental Consequences at the Regional Level: The case of Navarre (Spain)." In N. Jacobs (ed.), *Energy Policy: Economic Effects, Security Aspects and Environmental Issues* (New York: Nova Science Publishers), pp. 223–256.

9

THE ENERGY POVERTY DIMENSION OF ENERGY SECURITY

Shonali Pachauri

Energy security is a multidimensional issue. Several definitions of the term have been put forth in the past, but most of them include the dimensions of physical availability, economic affordability, and adequate capacity.[1] As this definition highlights, energy security is often viewed at a regional or national level, and largely defined from a political or economic perspective.[2] However, few analyses exist that assess this from the perspective of individual households and analyze its socio-economic dimensions. In poor households in developing countries, energy security is of particular concern. Such households often lack access to efficient energy sources and appliances; they remain dependent on poor-quality energy types (less efficient and more polluting, like unprocessed biomass and coal) and inadequate amounts to meet their basic energy needs, and often face prices that they cannot afford. To secure reliable and continuous supplies of energy, households adopt a variety of coping mechanisms, one being the use of multiple fuels. Indeed, a dominant feature of energy use patterns in many developing country households is the tendency to use multiple energy–technology combinations.[3,4,5] This may be due to cultural and taste preferences in some instances, but it also often stems from a rational decision to maximize energy security.

From a household perspective, energy security can be defined in terms of access to secure, stable, and reliable supplies of modern energy at affordable prices in amounts adequate to meet demands for energy services in full so as to ensure human health and well-being. In contrast, energy insecurity can be seen as a lack of, or inconsistent access to, sufficient affordable energy of the type and quality necessary for a healthy life. Such a definition of household energy security includes several aspects. Physical availability includes a geographical dimension. In other words, the supplies should be available in proximity to where the household is located. Economic affordability requires that the energy be supplied to households at prices that even the poorest can pay. Sufficiency or adequacy is harder to define as this may vary tremendously from region to region depending on climate, customs, and living standards. However, ensuring adequate energy for a healthy life implies that the types and amounts of energy should meet household needs for cooking, heating, and lighting at a minimum without adverse health impacts. Security from a household perspective also requires that supplies of energy be regular, reliable, and of standard quality, that is, uninterrupted and unadulterated.

For many poor households energy insecurity is a fact of life. The energy needs of the poor are small, but even so supplies are often completely lacking or unreliable, and costs, especially of initial expenditures to assure connections or buy capital equipment needed to use more efficient energy sources, can be significant and constrain adoption. There is a large funding gap in providing energy access for the poor that has not been seriously addressed by existing financial mechanisms and financing institutions. Strong political will and government commitment are also required to prioritize investments in energy critical for development of energy resources for the poorest in the population. In order to address the security concerns of the poor, in particular, the Integrated Energy Policy of India[6] defines energy security whereby "The country is energy secure when we can supply lifeline energy to all our citizens as well as meet their effective demand for safe and convenient energy to satisfy various needs at affordable costs at all times with a prescribed confidence level considering shocks and disruptions that can be reasonably expected." The definition was motivated by a concern to ensure that energy is supplied to all citizens of the nation and that equity in access to and consumption of energy are strived for.

Suppliers, whether public or private, tend to concentrate on meeting energy demands of large and industrial consumers at the cost of the poor whose demands remain unattractively low. The highly dispersed nature of settlements in most rural areas also makes supply and distribution costs relatively high. It is therefore important that the entire range of energy options should be considered for poor communities, such as grid and off-grid solutions for electricity supply, liquid and gaseous fuels for cooking, and renewables wherever appropriate depending on location and opportunities. Even though, at least in the medium term, biomass may possibly continue to be the fuel of choice for poor rural households, new technologies for more efficient and cleaner cooking devices need to be made more widely available to those dependent on these fuels and at affordable costs to increase their energy security.

The energy insecurity of the poor tends to remain a neglected issue. This chapter aims to discuss energy security from the perspective of households and analyze its access and poverty dimensions. Empirical examples and analysis from the case of India will be presented to illustrate many of the issues and indicators highlighted. The chapter is organized as follows. The first section discusses the implications of a continued dependence on traditional fuels for the well-being of households and the multiple benefits that can accrue from access to modern energy. The second section then presents some examples of indicators of household energy security using the example of India. A discussion of policies for enhancing the energy security of the poor follows, and the chapter concludes with some final observations and issues for discussion.

Costs of dependence on traditional fuels and benefits of access to modern energy

Electricity has the potential to completely transform people's lives and can usher in many social and economic benefits.[7] Several changes accompany access to electricity. Immediate applications of electricity in newly supplied households are for lighting and appliances, communications, and entertainment. Among community needs, public/street lighting, refrigeration, health centers and schools, piped water, communication, and the like are the most important. Electrification also benefits productive enterprises and agricultural activities such as irrigation/water pumping and commercial and industrial ventures. Well-lit public and commercial spaces enhance security and can also give people the ability to participate in more community activities. While access to electricity is crucial, access to modern fuels for heating and cooking (thermal) applications is just as important from the household perspective. Most households in developing countries do not use electricity for cooking or heating and therefore require access to modern fuels like Liquefied Petroleum Gas (LPG), biogas, or natural gas to meet these needs.

There is a considerable body of work stressing the importance of cooking practices and gender roles. This underscores the role of power relations in energy access. Among the spectrum of consumers, the poorest have the least influence on what types of energy sources and technologies to choose from. Even within the household, there is no exception to this. Gender relations impact on decision-making in terms of fuel and appliance use, acquisition, and expenditure. In many developing countries, women tend to have limited control over and access to productive assets and income. Therefore they have little say in how much can be spent on energy or new stoves. This is despite the fact that women spend more time in collecting biomass than men and cooking activities are considered an all-female domain in most countries. While not all women would embrace new fuels and stoves if they were given the choice, often a proposed change has to benefit the man in the house to have a chance of being adopted.[8]

A number of health and safety issues relate to cooking with solid and traditional fuels, most notably indoor air pollution, the risk of fires and burns, injuries associated with wood collection and carrying heavy loads, and the risk of attack or violence when collecting fuel-wood. Cooking-related health and safety impacts mainly affect women and children since they have the highest exposure to smoke and the other risks connected to cooking with polluting fuels. The evidence is clear and compelling that pollution from burning traditional biomass fuels in inefficient devices, often in poorly ventilated conditions, causes life-threatening and debilitating illnesses in users, especially poor women and children who are regularly exposed.[9] The World Health Organization's 2009 Global Health Risk Report estimates that acute respiratory infections from indoor air pollution (pollution from burning fuel-wood, animal dung, other biomass fuels, and coal) kills about half a million children annually in developing countries, inflicting a particularly heavy toll on poor families in South Asia and Africa.[10] In India alone, over 500,000 premature deaths are attributed to indoor air pollution-related causes. The time and effort expended in gathering biomass and carrying heavy loads has also been associated with back pain and head-aches.[11] Other risks associated with collecting biomass have also been reported, such as snake bites, various injuries, and violence.[12] The drudgery involved also leaves little time for those involved to engage in other leisure or productive activities that could earn them an income or secure them an education.

In addition to the many health and socio-economic impacts of using traditional biomass and other solid fuels for cooking and heating, the use of these fuels also produces significant quantities of "products of incomplete combustion" (PIC), especially dangerous levels of fine particulate matter (PM2.5, PM10), carbon monoxide (CO), and nitrogen oxides, which have a higher global warming potential (GWP) than carbon dioxide (CO_2).[13] Work by Bhattacharya et al.,[14] also discusses research that provides evidence of the fact that incomplete combustion of biomass in traditional cooking stoves releases particles composed of elemental carbon, or black carbon, and other organic compounds. When the biomass consumed is not sustainably harvested, the use of these fuels has the added disadvantage of no longer being CO_2-neutral. Extensive reliance on fuel-wood can also lead to unsustainable harvesting practices that, in turn, contribute to degradation of soils and forest lands and generate other adverse impacts on local ecosystems. Biomass combustion is responsible for a significant proportion of carbonaceous aerosol emissions and brown clouds over the subcontinent.[15] Recent evidence suggests that the warming effects of black carbon emissions, particularly for Arctic and glacial ice, are larger than previous estimates have suggested.[16]

Indicators of household energy security

Indicators of household energy security clearly need to reflect the many elements mentioned in the introductory section of this chapter. In other words, they should ideally be able to measure and monitor, among other things, physical availability and affordability, the vulnerability of different household groups in securing adequate amounts of quality energy services, inequity in access to and consumption of various energy types across different household groups, and reliability and quality of supply of modern energy services for the poorest. In the following, some examples of metrics and indicators that may be used to measure these elements will be discussed in further detail and illuminated with the actual data for the case of India.

India is used as a case study to illustrate the type of indicators that may be used to monitor energy security at a household level since it is the nation with the largest rural population in the world and still faces a huge challenge in ensuring energy security to a large section of its population, particularly those living in rural areas and urban slums. For the country as a whole, only about 64 percent of the population have access to any electricity and for many more, access remains unreliable or inadequate. In addition, among rural households, about 90 percent still rely on traditional solid fuels like firewood and animal and crop residues for their cooking and heating needs. Even among urban households, over 35 percent continue to use inefficient and polluting biomass fuels. A more pragmatic factor that makes India an attractive case study is the availability of fairly reliable official sources of statistical data. Much of the data used to construct the indicators presented in this chapter are from different ministerial reports and from several rounds of the National Sample Survey Organisation (NSSO) of the Government of India.[17] The NSSO was set up in 1950 by the Department of Statistics, and conducts periodic nationwide surveys on various facets of household consumption using a large representative sample of households covering the entire geographical area of India.

The residential sector energy diversity mix

In 1980–1981 over 90 percent of energy consumed by households in India was from biomass sources (largely fuel wood, crop residues, and dung). While this share declined to just over 80 percent in 2000–2001, the actual quantity of biomass consumed increased continuously over the entire period (Figure 9.1). Currently, about 8 percent of residential energy needs are met from grid sources. The remaining share of residential energy demand is being supplied by liquid fuels (petroleum products). However, overall the continued high dependence on traditional biomass fuels indicates a less than optimal fuel mix for the Indian residential or household sector. While the

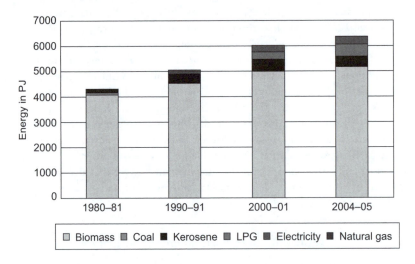

Figure 9.1 Residential final energy consumption mix in India 1980–2005.
Source: Pachauri, S. and L. Jiang. 2008. "The Household Energy Transition in India and China," *Energy Policy* 36(11): 4022–4035.

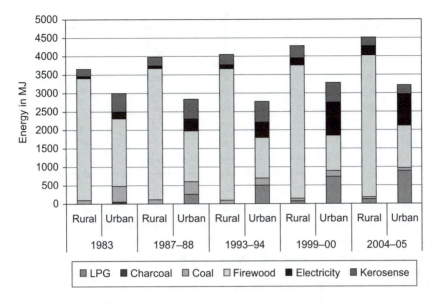

Figure 9.2 Per capita energy consumption patterns in urban and rural households.
Source: Pachauri and Jiang, "The Household Energy Transition in India and China," pp. 4022–4035.

likely increased shift towards petroleum products might have adverse implications for the national dependency on oil imports, it will result in benefits to households from improvements in efficiency, indoor air quality, and well-being.

Trends at the per capita level mirror those at the aggregate level and suggest that in terms of shares of different energy types in total residential energy use, rural households did not witness any striking transition in their patterns of energy use. Biomass use per capita increased in absolute terms, but only slightly, over the entire period. By contrast, a significant increase in the quantity of electricity use per capita occurred. However, the total amounts and the proportions of commercial energy consumed in rural households continue to remain very low. In urban households, a much more rapid substitution of biomass by commercial fuels and electricity is evident. Biomass consumption per capita declined and this decline resulted in a decrease in total per capita household energy consumption in urban households between 1983 and 1993–1994, and between 1999–2000 and 2004–2005 (Figure 9.2). However, during the mid-1990s, a rise in LPG and electricity consumption among urban households drove up per capita energy use. While there is some diversity in the mix of energy types used by urban households, even today within the rural sector there is a preponderance of biomass fuels in the household energy mix. If all the biomass used was being harvested sustainably, and it was being combusted in more efficient and less polluting end-use devices (cook stoves) then the predominant dependence on biomass fuels among rural households would be less worrying. However, the use of biomass in its current form leaves rural households vulnerable and subject to several negative economic, health, and social impacts, as mentioned above.

Household energy access to modern energy

Access has many dimensions. For the purposes of this text, we define access only in terms of actual use, that is, whether a household in fact consumes any of a particular energy type. This is a good indicator of physical availability of energy supplies at the household level, in particular of access to

Table 9.1 Percentage of population using different sources of household energy in India[18]

	1983		1993–94		2004–05	
	Rural	*Urban*	*Rural*	*Urban*	*Rural*	*Urban*
LPG	0	9	2	33	12	61
Coal/coke	3	21	2	8	2	5
Electricity	15	58	36	77	54	91
Kerosene	95	92	95	83	91	55
Fuel-wood	86	61	88	42	88	35
Dung	53	27	53	18	46	10

modern energy forms such as electricity and liquid and gaseous fuels such as LPG. Table 9.1 shows changes in the percentage of people in households using different sources of energy over time. The fact that the columns do not sum to 100 percent provides evidence of the fact that most households use multiple fuels. Major changes are evident in the percentage of persons using different energy types across rural and urban households over this period. The percentage of population using LPG increased from 9 percent to 61 percent in urban areas. However, in rural households the uptake of LPG was much slower, and even in 2004–2005 only 12 percent of the rural population used this fuel. Electricity access also changed dramatically over this period. Whereas 15 percent of the rural population and 58 percent of the urban population were using electricity in 1983, by 2004–2005, 54 percent of the rural and 91 percent of the urban population were doing so. Kerosene is used widely by all households. While the percentage of the rural population using this fuel has not changed much over this period, the percentage of the urban population using kerosene has declined from 92 percent to 55 percent. The share of traditional biomass energy users (both firewood and dung) in rural areas also did not change during this period. However, in urban areas, the percentage of the population using traditional biomass energy halved. These trends reflect that there have been significant improvements in the physical availability of electricity and modern fuels in urban areas. However, in rural areas, electricity access has improved rather slowly and there has been almost no change in the access to modern fuels such as LPG.

Affordability and energy pricing for households

In many countries, the share of the expenditure on energy to the average total income or household expenditure is often used as a measure of affordability. When this ratio falls below a certain threshold, it signifies that energy is affordable and people are not spending excessive amounts on energy or having to reduce their expenditures on other essential commodities. When it exceeds an established threshold, it implies that energy is not affordable and people are having difficulty obtaining enough to meet their needs. While such an indicator may be useful in the case of nations where most energy transactions take place in markets, in the case of many developing countries this is not the case. In particular, in the rural areas of many developing countries, households collect fuel-wood and biomass wastes themselves rather than purchasing it on the market. The non-commercial nature of most of the energy they consume, makes using monetary indicators of the kind described above, less useful in this context.

Several challenges exist with the appropriate pricing of fuels and electricity for the household sector in most developing countries. Most governments provide subsidies on energy to the household sector. The traditional arguments for provision of such subsidies refer to the need to maintain access to essential services for the poorest. However, in many instances the subsidies do not benefit those they are intended to. In India, the average price per unit of energy for petroleum fuels and electricity is similar in rural and urban regions of the country, as prices of both electricity and household cooking fuels (kerosene and LPG) are universally subsidized. However, given the higher share of inefficient traditional fuels being used in rural households, and lower access levels among rural and poorer households, in effect the price per unit of useful energy being paid by the rural populations is in some cases more than that being paid by urban residents (Table 9.2). Table 9.2 also shows that in both rural and urban areas, households that are dependent on fewer

Table 9.2 Energy expenditure shares and energy prices among different segments of Indian households in 1999–2000[19]

Category of Users	Energy Expenditure (Rs. per year)	Energy expenditure as a percentage of total household expenditure (%)	Price per unit end-use-energy (Rs. per Kwh)	Price per unit useful energy (Rs. per Kwh)
RURAL				
Biomass	1227	10.1	0.09	0.46
Biomass & Kerosene	1129	8.8	0.07	0.33
Biomass & Electricity	1477	8.6	0.08	0.31
Biomass, Kerosene & Electricity	1435	8.2	0.08	0.28
Kerosene & Electricity	1388	7.5	0.38	0.70
Kerosene & LPG	1670	6.1	0.19	0.37
Kerosene, LPG & Electricity	2105	7.1	0.18	0.31
Electricity & LPG	1896	6.4	0.20	0.33
URBAN				
Biomass	1328	9.4	0.14	0.68
Biomass & Kerosene	1185	8.8	0.08	0.37
Biomass & Electricity	1261	8.4	0.09	0.34
Biomass, Kerosene & Electricity	1595	8.7	0.09	0.33
Kerosene & Electricity	1461	7.5	0.20	0.42
Kerosene & LPG	2145	6.6	0.22	0.43
Kerosene, LPG & Electricity	2427	7.5	0.18	0.32
Electricity & LPG	2528	7.1	0.21	0.33

energy carriers tend to pay more in terms of the price per unit of useful energy than those that diversify use to many fuels. In addition, households that are dependent on combinations of fuels that include less efficient energy carriers pay more per unit of useful energy than those that use more efficient energy forms.

Accounting for expenditure on all fuels and electricity, rural households in India spent a higher proportion of their total household budget on energy in 2004–2005 (about 10 percent compared with 7 percent in urban households). Studies, such as those by Gangopadhyay *et al.*,[20] conclude that existing subsidies on fuels for the residential sector in India are fiscally unsustainable and also of little help in meeting social policy objectives as they are seriously misdirected and disproportionately benefit richer urban households, who already have greater access to modern energy. Clearly the present system of universal subsidies on kerosene and LPG is not fulfilling its purpose in India. Efforts on designing mechanisms for delivery of targeted subsidies for the benefit of the poor are needed. While in the short run at least, the political pressure to keep prices low is great, in the long run, such artificially low prices hinder the development of new energy supplies, result in fiscal and financial unsustainability of fuel and electricity providers, and can even become an obstacle to an energy transition.

Adequacy or sufficiency of energy consumption

Determining an optimal amount of energy services required to meet the basic needs of a population is fraught with many problems. Goldemberg *et al.*,[21] estimated that the requirement of direct primary energy per time unit to satisfy basic needs is about 500W per person. This kind of calculation rests on a number of assumptions regarding the type of energy-consuming equipment (stove, light bulbs, etc.), their sizes, efficiencies, and intensity of use. In addition, the approach requires, as a first normative step, the definition of a set of basic needs. This is a problematic endeavor since basic needs vary with subjective wants, as well as with climate, region, period of time, age, and gender. Pachauri *et al.*,[22] propose a measure of energy poverty that relates energy quantities and efficiencies of end-use devices to access to different sources of energy by different segments of the population. They estimated that in 1999–2000, 15 percent of the Indian population was "desperately energy poor" (no access to electricity or clean fuels and consuming less than enough to cook two square meals a day and for basic lighting) and over 30 percent were "energy poor" (lacking access to modern energy and consuming amounts that provide minimum services). More recently, the new Integrated Energy Policy of India specifies basic minimum or lifeline energy requirements as 6kg of LPG per household per month and 30KWh of electricity per household per month. According to this benchmark, only 70 percent of LPG users in rural areas consumed sufficient quantities of the fuel, whereas in urban areas about 90 percent of users consumed the fuel in sufficient amounts in 2004–2005. Similarly, only 65 percent of electricity users in rural areas consume sufficient amounts, whereas in urban areas over 85 percent of users are consuming above the lifeline amount, according to 2004–2005 survey data.

Multiple fuel use

Multiple fuels can provide households with a sense of energy security. Complete dependence on commercially traded fuels can leave households vulnerable to variable prices and often unreliable service. An analysis of energy-use patterns in Indian households that compares data on the distribution of households by their reported primary source of cooking energy with the percentage share of those using single, dual, or multiple cooking fuels (Figure 9.3) shows that most households reported using one or more fuels to supplement their primary source of cooking energy. In the full sample for all Indian households, less than 15 percent used a single cooking fuel, about 46 percent

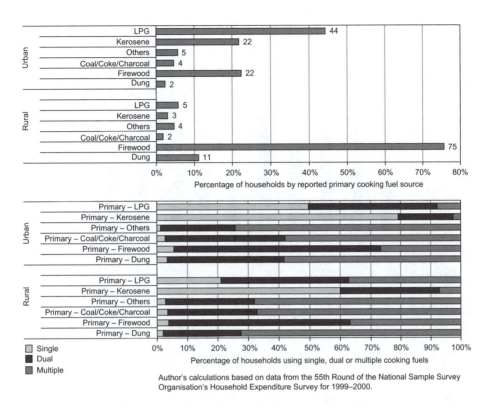

Figure 9.3 Multiple cooking fuel dependency in Indian households in 1999–2000.
Source: Pachauri, S. 2006. "Strategies of the Energy-Poor in India," Options (IIASA's in-house scientific magazine), Summer.

used two fuels, and the rest used three or more cooking fuels. A more detailed breakdown reveals that dual and multiple fuel use is more frequent in poorer households which are more dependent on less efficient non-commercial fuels. Thus, rural and urban households reporting dung, firewood, or coal/charcoal as their primary cooking energy source are more likely to cook using other fuels as well. Households reporting their primary source of cooking energy as commercial fuels like LPG or kerosene are more likely to use only a single cooking fuel, perhaps because supplies of commercial fuels are easier to access, particularly in urban areas. Poorer households face greater uncertainty about their energy supplies. There are bigger seasonal variations in the biomass fuels on which they usually depend, and households are less likely to have access to more secure commercial fuel supplies, particularly in rural and more remote regions.

Equity in energy access and consumption

The indicators on energy access and consumption presented in previous sections have already pointed to the tremendous disparities existing between rural and urban populations in India. Indeed, such disparities are common to most developing countries. In addition to disparities in access levels and consumption across rural and urban areas, variations in patterns of energy use across income classes suggest that the use of modern energy is concentrated among the richest segments of the population (Figure 9.4).

The distribution of final direct energy use per capita for the years 1983 and 1999–2000 can be depicted by a Lorenz curve. If one plots the percentage of direct energy used by various portions of

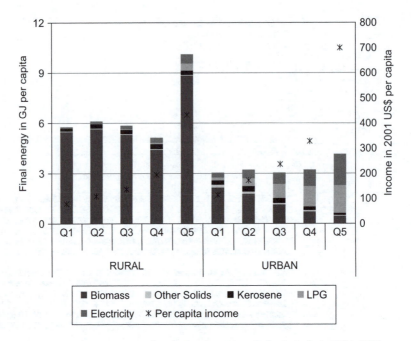

Figure 9.4 Energy use patterns across rural and urban income quintiles in India in 2004–2005.
Source: Pachauri and Jiang, "The Household Energy Transition in India and China," pp. 4022–4035.

the population according to their income, it becomes apparent that significant inequality in the use of direct energy exists, with the bottom 60 percent of the population using only about 33 percent of total direct energy, and the top 10 percent of the population consuming as much as 30 percent of total direct energy in 1983. The inequality in energy use also persists over time, with the Lorenz curve for the year 1999–2000 more or less identical to that for 1983.[23] A comparison of the Gini coefficients of the distributions for the two years (0.57 and 0.54 respectively) also reveals little change in the level of inequality over this time period.

Reliability and quality of energy supply

While physical access to modern sources of energy such as electricity and gas is an important indicator of energy security for households, it says little about the reliability or quality of supply. In India, as in many developing countries, even where physical access is available, reliable electricity supply to rural and poor customers is lacking. As a result of overall shortages, power supply to household and agricultural customers is heavily rationed. Thus the availability, that is, the actual hours of supply received in a given day for a given season, and the reliability, that is, total duration of power cuts during the scheduled hours of power supply are poor and this can have important effects on household livelihoods. In addition, the quality of power supply, measured in terms of its voltage and the variability of this, also impacts customers. According to a World Bank indicator of quality of electricity supply (lack of interruptions and lack of voltage fluctuations), India is ranked 97th out of a set of 125 countries.[24]

The quality of power supply in urban centres is also a matter of concern in India. The prevailing quality of supply is forcing impacted consumers to go in for backup systems which are costly, inefficient in terms of energy throughputs, and also environmentally unfriendly. The proliferation of diesel generating sets, invertors, voltage stabilizers, etc. in Indian cities stands testimony to this.

Poor quality of power supply can also impact energy conservation efforts and the promotion of energy-efficient end-use appliances. Consumers are often reluctant to go in for energy-efficient devices (which are relatively more costly), fearing damage to these in the event of sudden power failures, voltage quality problems, etc.

Unfortunately, well-documented data and indicators on quality of energy supply are hard to come by, but clearly there is a need to monitor these aspects. In addition to some of the indicators of quality of electricity supply mentioned above, similar indicators for reliability and quality of supply in the distribution of fuels also need to be developed.

Policies for enhancing household energy security

Policies to address energy security concerns at a household level clearly need to ensure access to modern energy sources at affordable prices for all citizens. Increasing the physical availability of electricity and modern fuels requires increased supply and distribution of these energy sources. Both the public sector and the private sector have a role to play. Governments, however, need to provide the right incentives and regulations to encourage the private sector to invest in these sectors. In rural areas in many developing countries, the low demand densities and income levels make the supply of energy to these areas rather unattractive to private sector investors. Traditionally, governments have also tended to heavily subsidize energy for poor households and agricultural consumers living in rural areas. While such subsidies may have been justified on social grounds, they have often resulted in market distortions, been appropriated largely by richer segments of consumers, and led to state utilities and energy companies becoming bankrupt due to the heavy subsidy burdens. In the face of the increasingly poor financial performance of the energy utilities and companies, improving distribution to areas and households without access has lagged and is proving to be a huge challenge. Innovative financial mechanisms and the development of appropriate business models are crucial to accelerate access for poor and rural segments of the population and to promote equitable social and economic development.

In many developing countries, including India, policies for improving access to modern energy and household energy security have largely been conceived in a rather centralized fashion. Such centralized energy planning models have typically neglected the energy needs of rural areas and the poor. In addition, the focus has traditionally been on the supply side and less consideration has been paid to understanding patterns of household energy demand or assessing the ability and willingness to pay of poor customers. With a vision to refocus efforts at improving access among the rural population, the Indian government's Rural Electrification Policy 2006 aimed at provision of electricity access to all households by 2009 and a minimum lifeline consumption of one unit per household per day as a merit good by the year 2012. The National Electrification Policy 2005, which preceded this by a year, had as its target the total village electrification by 2010 and total household electrification by 2012. The main program through which universal access objectives of the Electricity Policy are being implemented is the Rajiv Gandhi Grameen Vidyutikaran Yojana (RGGVY), launched in April 2005. A large effort towards grid extension and strengthening of the rural electricity infrastructure has been initiated through the RGGVY.

More recently, however, the Indian government has been mooting options for more decentralized solutions for improving energy access. The Ministry of New and Renewable Energy of the Government of India has recently developed plans to electrify about 25,000 of the remotest villages in India. Because it is inefficient to extend the energy grid to these villages, decentralized, renewable energy systems are being developed instead. The Electricity Act 2003 in India also makes provision for the promotion of private or local community participation in the supply and management of electricity in rural areas through a system of franchisees. Furthermore, the national electricity policy (NEP) for India, announced in February 2005, allows for decentralized electricity generation with local distribution networks, in situations where providing grid connectivity would not be cost-effective. These are welcome steps, but it remains to be seen how effectively these plans will be implemented and what institutional structures will be put in place for these targets to be realized.

In addition to policies to improve the availability of electricity at the household level, the Ministry of New and Renewable Energy (MNRE) of the Government of India launched a new initiative on biomass cook stoves in 2009, with the primary aim of enhancing access to improved end-use devices, especially among rural households who are likely to depend on biomass for cooking for the foreseeable future. The new initiative is based on the recognition that cook stove technology has improved considerably in the past few years. But further advances are still possible and, indeed, essential. The aim is to achieve quality of energy services from cook stoves comparable to that from other clean energy sources such as LPG. Under this initiative, a series of pilot-scale projects are envisaged using several existing commercially available and improved cook stoves and different grades of processed biomass fuels. The goal of the program is to sell 150 million stoves over the next ten years.

The government's role in setting appropriate energy prices requires it to play a delicate balancing act, mixing concerns of ensuring adequate financial returns to energy utilities and companies on the one hand, with issues of affordability and social equity on the other. In India, past policies of setting universal subsidies on electricity for agricultural and household consumers, and on modern cooking fuels like LPG and kerosene, are seen to have largely failed in achieving the social objectives they were put in place for. In addition, these policies have resulted in poor economic returns for energy suppliers, as already mentioned. Putting the electric utilities and energy companies back on a sound financial footing will generally require higher end-user prices and better billing and collection. This could result in an increased financial burden for poor households in particular, if adequate social safety provisions are not put in place. However, concerns about affordability have perhaps been used too readily as an argument against tariff reforms. There are a number of ways through which the social impact of tariff adjustments can be mitigated, chief among them being targeted assistance programs and lifeline tariffs for poor customers. However, setting up and operating these schemes is challenging and will require competent institutions and adequate administrative capacity.

Concluding comments

This chapter has highlighted some of the key elements of energy security from the perspective of households and presented some examples of indicators needed to measure and monitor this, with examples using data for Indian households. India and other developing countries face a tremendous challenge in ensuring energy security for all their citizens. A continued lack of commitment in dealing with this issue can only result in holding back the economic and social development of certain segments of the population. The examples presented in this chapter have highlighted the fact that metrics and indicators constructed to measure energy security are often dictated by the availability of existing data. A necessary step to ensure that the policies announced are implemented is to put in place regular monitoring mechanisms and develop a consistent and complete indicator set that can measure the various dimensions of energy security as highlighted in this chapter. Clearly, much larger efforts need to be made in regard to proper and regular data collection and development of indicators to monitor the various facets of energy security from a household perspective. While improving data and statistics is a significant challenge, it is likely to provide added benefits to the energy sector in terms of better information for other aspects of energy policy and planning.

The indicators presented in this work also emphasize the importance of having information for heterogeneous population groups within a nation. Aggregate indicators at the level of nations cannot adequately capture the various aspects of equity in access, affordability, adequacy, and quality and reliability of energy supply for the poorest segments of the population. Existing sets of indicators are limited and often available only at the national level. For several of the smaller and least developed nations, recent data even on aggregate indicators is often lacking. More detailed data for disaggregate and heterogeneous spatial, demographic, and socio-economic groups within nations are available in the case of some nations. However, these more disaggregate datasets often need to be constructed from detailed analysis of national or regional household surveys that are often conducted with objectives other than energy in mind. An assessment of actual drivers of household energy choices and transitions in different regions and settings, and the development of more decentralized energy plans for improving the energy security of the most vulnerable population groups, requires detailed information on household energy-use patterns, expenditures, and socio-economic drivers at as disaggregate a level as possible. More regular and comprehensive household surveys can go a long way in filling the information gap and providing information on the consumption patterns of heterogeneous groups. Data gathered through such surveys can also be essential for assessing the affordability of different population groups and designing programs that can target the most vulnerable groups more effectively. Further conceptual and empirical work, along with concerted efforts towards the collection of more detailed data, is clearly needed for designing and improving the social safety mechanisms that can enable energy security for all households.

Notes

1 Asia Pacific Energy Research Centre (APERC). 2007. *A Quest for Energy Security in the 21st Century: Resources and Constraints* (Yokyo: APERC).
2 Noronha, Ligia, and Anant Sudarshan (eds.). 2008. *India's Energy Security* (London: Routledge).
3 Reddy, B. Sudhakara and T. Srinivas. 2009. "Energy use in Indian Household Sector: An Actor-Oriented Approach," *Energy* 34 (8): 992–1002.
4 Pachauri, S. 2007. *An Energy Analysis of Household Consumption: Changing Patterns of Direct and Indirect Use in India* (Berlin, Heidelberg, and New York: Springer).
5 Masera, Omar, B. Saatkamp, and D. Kammen. 2000. "From Linear Fuel Switching to Multiple Cooking Strategies: A Critique and Alternative to the Energy Ladder Model," *World Development* 28: 2083–2103.
6 Government of India. 2006. *Integrated Energy Policy of India*, Planning Commission, Government of India.
7 Barnes, D. F. 2007. *The Challenge of Rural Electrification: Strategies for Developing Countries* (Washington, DC: Resources for the Future).
8 Food and Agriculture Organization. 2006. *Energy and Gender in Rural Sustainable Development* (Rome: Food and Agriculture Organization of the United Nations).
9 Smith, K. R., S. Mehta, and M. Feuz. 2004. "Indoor Smoke from Household Use of Solid Fuels." In M. Ezzati, A. D. Lopez, A. Rodgers, and C. J. L. Murray (eds.), *Comparative Quantification of Health Risks: The Global Burden of Disease Due to Selected Risk Factors* (Geneva: World Health Organization), vol. 2, pp. 1435–1493.
10 World Health Organization. 2009. *Global Health Risk Report* (Geneva: World Health Organization).
11 Parikh J, Saudamini Sharma, and Chandrashekhar Singh. 2008. "Energy Access and its Implication for Women: A Case Study of Himachal Pradesh," paper presented at the workshop on *Clean Cooking Fuels and Technologies*, June 16–17, Istanbul, Turkey.
12 Wickramasinghe, Anoja. 2001. "Gendered Sights and Health Issues in the Paradigm of Biofuel in Sri Lanka," *Energia News* 4(4): 14–16.
13 Smith K. R., R. Uma, V. V. N. Kishore, J. Zhang, V. Joshi, and M. A. K. Khalil. 2000. "Greenhouse Implications of Household Stoves: An Analysis for India," *Annual Review of Energy and the Environment* 25: 741–763.

14 Bhattacharya S.C., P.A. Salam, and M. Sharma. 2000. "Emissions from Biomass Energy Use in some Selected Asian Countries," *Energy* 25(2): 169–188.

15 Gustafsson, O., Martin Kruså, Zdenek Zencak, Rebecca J. Sheesley, Lennart Granat, Erik Engström, P. S. Praveen, P. S. P. Rao, Caroline Leck, and Henning Rodhe. (2009). "Brown Clouds over South Asia: Biomass or Fossil Fuel Combustion?" *Science* 323: 495–498.

16 Ramanathan V. and G. Carmichael. 2008. "Global and Regional Climate Changes due to Black Carbon," *Nature Geoscience* 1: 221–227.

17 Available at: http://www.mospi.gov.in/nsso.htm (accessed August 28, 2010).

18 Pachauri and Jiang, "The Household Energy Transition in India and China," pp. 4022–4035.

19 Pachauri, S. and D. Spreng. 2004. "Energy Use and Energy Access in Relation to Poverty," *Economic and Political Weekly* January 17.

20 Gangopadhyay, S., B. Ramaswami, and W. Wadhwa. 2005. "Reducing Subsidies on Household Fuels in India: How will it Affect the Poor?" *Energy Policy* 33: 2326–2336.

21 Goldemberg, J., T. B. Johansson, A. K. N. Reddy, and R. H. Williams. 1987. *Energy for a Sustainable World* (New Delhi: Wiley-Eastern Limited).

22 Pachauri, S., A. Mueller, A. Kemmler, and D. Spreng. 2004. "On Measuring Energy Poverty in Indian Households," *World Development* 32(12): 2083–2104.

23 See Pachauri, 2007.

24 Available at: http://siteresources.worldbank.org/INTEXPCOMNET/Resources/2.05_Quality_ of_Electricity_ Supply.pdf (accessed August 28, 2010).

10

THE SOCIAL DEVELOPMENT DIMENSION OF ENERGY SECURITY

Anthony D'Agostino

Introduction

Existing interpretations of energy security have viewed affordability as the primary means by which energy systems impact societies at the micro level. This is affirmed in energy security metrics that either exclude non-price social dimensions, or disadvantage them vis-à-vis physical, technical, geopolitical, and market dimensions. Among others, metrics developed by Loschel et al.,[1] Blyth and Lefevre,[2] Scheepers et al.,[3] and Jansen et al.,[4] evidence this. Kruyt et al.'s[5] mapping of the energy security indicators and indices in the literature onto an "energy security spectrum" provides implicit corroboration. Only one of the nearly two dozen surveyed indicators/indices incorporates "acceptability" characteristics that the Asia Pacific Energy Research Centre, which created the four As energy security schema,[6] associates with social and environmental considerations.

This preeminence of energy affordability has both macro- and micro-level justifications. At the macro-level, economic growth and energy demand have historically been understood as tightly coupled.[7,8] Affordable energy supplies have therefore been viewed as a prerequisite for industrialization and the social welfare gains brought about by economic development. Developing country governments may hasten the industrialization process by subsidizing energy and intervening in domestic markets. At the macro level, countries may also justify energy subsidies for their role in curbing price volatility. Wildly fluctuating prices discourage capital flows and at their peaks may consume a significant share of household and firm expenditure.

At the micro level, pro-poor arguments are often used to support the case for affordable energy. Since low-income groups devote a large share of their income to energy services, subsidy programs can reduce this burden. Subsidies may also extend access to modern energy sources to households that previously had been priced out. However, subsidy programs designed with such social aims have often led to unintended, negative spillovers at the macro-level. Broad-based policy instruments devised to benefit targeted segments of the population unintentionally can be captured by the rich.[9] Furthermore, subsidies create deadweight loss; the social opportunity cost of tax collections to fund such programs is likely higher than the social benefits they provide.[10]

Conversely, the national and occasionally sub-national nature of energy security assessments obscures the direct effects of the production, delivery, and consumption of energy at lower levels. As a result, policies driven by energy security considerations overlook the acute consequences faced by communities and households, such as the displacement of communities from hydroelectric dams in Laos and Brazil. The numerous coal miner fatalities in China each year provide another example of social costs often neglected by energy security indicators and metrics.

This chapter therefore argues that the social dimensions of energy security are more all-encompassing than heretofore acknowledged. A case study format is used to illustrate examples of broader, social impacts experienced by communities and households that might be incorporated under a more holistic construction of energy security. This entails a recognition of the existing inconsistencies in energy policy formulation. Policies devised to help portions of the population afford energy (i.e., lowest deciles) demonstrate micro-level intervention, with counterproductive effects at the macro level. At the same time, macro-level energy security assessments, and the policies derived from them, often gloss over the micro level, social impacts where state intervention or preemption may in fact be needed.

Fossil fuel subsidies

Fossil fuel subsidies were one item of discussion during the September 2009 Pittsburgh G-20 Summit, underscoring their magnitude and global presence. There, world leaders committed to phasing out "inefficient fossil fuel subsidies" and redirecting funds towards renewable energy development as part of their newly launched Framework for Strong, Sustainable, and Balanced Growth.[11] In November that year, APEC leaders endorsed the Framework goals in their Leaders' Declaration and likewise vowed to "rationalize and phase-out over the medium-term fossil fuel subsidies while providing those in need with essential energy services."[12]

Though it is difficult to get a complete inventory of global fossil fuel subsidy expenditures because of off-budget allocations, a lack of data collection resources, and other transparency constraints, the International Energy Agency (IEA) estimates that 20 non-OECD countries alone spent US$310 billion on energy subsidies in 2007.[13] This more than doubled the total official development assistance awarded the following year (US$128 billion).[14] The estimated fossil fuel subsidy burden for the ten countries comprising the Association of Southeast Asian Nations (ASEAN) is depicted in Figure 10.1.

While most of these programs were instituted to improve access and affordability to energy, their broad-based design fails to differentiate those who can afford to pay the full price from those who cannot.[15] For example, the *Far Eastern Economic Review* in a 2008 analysis calculated that Indonesia's wealthy have absorbed most of the benefits of fuel subsidies. The richest 10 percent consumed 45 percent of the subsidy, whereas the bottom 10 percent saw only 1 percent.[16] Though subsidies are frequently couched as pro-poor policies, they are just as often exploited for political gain. More efficacious policies, like targeted cash transfers, can support pro-poor development and energy access while reducing fiscal outlays.

The effects of fossil fuel subsidies

Collectively, the Organisation for Economic Co-operation and Development (OECD) identifies subsidies as "any measure that keeps prices for consumers below market levels, or for producers above markets levels, or that reduces costs for consumers and producers."[17] As a result, producers and consumers make decisions based on biased price signals that inevitably lead to excessive production and consumption.[18,19] This can have severe social, environmental, and economic spillovers depending on the scale and scope of the subsidy. The following are just some of the negative effects common to countries with significant subsidy regimes:

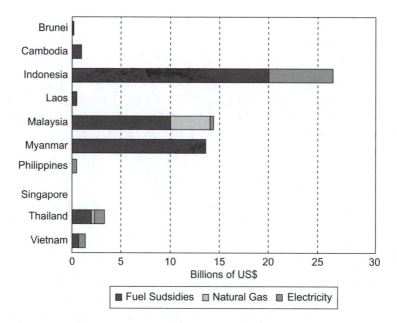

Figure 10.1 Fossil fuel subsidy expenditures across Southeast Asia.
Source: Sovacool, Benjamin K. "A Comparative Analysis of Renewable Electricity Support Mechanisms for Southeast Asia," *Energy* 35(4): 1779–1793.

Social impacts:

- divert spending away from more effective social development sectors like health, education, and infrastructure;
- discourage households from responding to energy price increases by improving efficiency or conserving energy, drawing avoidable expenses on the government, and preventing the creation of jobs in new industries;
- result in inefficient resource use which decreases future resource availability and compromises long-term social welfare.

Environmental impacts:

- favor incumbent energy sources and make it more difficult for new energy sources to attain cost-competitiveness;
- may lead to other forms of environmental degradation, like in Pakistan Punjab and India where free or cheap electricity has greatly accelerated the depletion of groundwater aquifers;[20]
- contribute to climate change and the release of global, regional, and local air pollutants.[21] An OECD/IEA report suggests that a global phase-out of fossil fuel subsidies would reduce greenhouse gas emissions by 10 percent or more by 2050.[22]

Economic impacts:

- decrease country attractiveness to investors who are uncertain about their ability to recover their investment costs quickly;
- for energy-producing countries, inefficient domestic use means reduced availability for exports, impacting a country's ability to raise foreign currency reserves;

- erode country competitiveness and will increase economic vulnerability if a global climate deal imposing carbon costs is passed;
- may contribute to fuel smuggling where borders are porous.[23]

Additionally, subsidized rates undercut an electric utility's revenue base and therefore its ability to perform necessary maintenance on existing facilities or to expand service to non-coverage areas. Chronically neglected utilities are more likely to suffer from unscheduled power outages or rolling blackouts, with consequent social and economic impacts.

Obstacles to subsidy reform

Subsidy reform is considered a "win–win" action that reaps social, environmental, and economic benefits, but the success of such depends on political realities.[26] Recent events in Southeast Asia are compelling evidence that subsidy reform, especially of the "socially sensitive" fuels of diesel, LPG, and kerosene, will incite public outrage, especially if conducted suddenly and without public awareness-raising or involvement efforts.

For instance, gasoline price hikes contributed to Suharto's fall as Indonesian president in 1998 and likewise threatened Megawati Sukarnoputri's presidency when a 2003 measure to link domestic fuel prices with global prices drew mass protests.[25] The policy, along with price hikes for various utilities, was soon retracted. Manila is frequently the site of demonstrations against electricity and fuel prices, such as in June 2008 when hundreds of trucks blocked roads leading to the presidential palace in protest of the fuel products sales tax.[26] Myanmar's eruption of violence in September 2007 was largely ignited by price hikes, not from subsidy reform, but from the 500 percent markup on natural gas which sent food and essential goods prices soaring.[27]

In electoral democracies, a lack of popular support for reform is reason enough for politicians to steer clear when a reelection is at stake. Voters may not understand the long-term economic and social benefits of reform and may remain unconvinced despite policy-makers' best efforts. Opposition candidates are likely to accuse the incumbent of raising the cost of living without having to publicly propose viable, fiscal alternatives. Some special interest groups, such as taxi and lorry unions, stand to lose immensely from reform measures and may exert disproportionate influence depending on their level of political connectedness. Unfortunately, there may be situations where no alternative means of satisfying such groups exists.[28] Reforms may also reduce employment in the domestic energy sector.[29] However, these losses should be compared against the jobs that innovation-stifling subsidies have failed to create.

The barriers to subsidy removal are not restricted to socio-political factors. Benefits from inaction exist, though are likely to be outweighed by its costs:

- For populations who are fueling deforestation from excessive biomass use, a shift to fossil fuels or electricity may be environmentally beneficial.
- Similarly, subsidies may enable such groups to adopt cleaner-burning fuels which pose fewer human health and safety risks.
- Their removal, while improving a country's fiscal position, may contribute to inflationary pressures as energy price markups are passed through to other goods and services in the economy.
- Targeted subsidies, for example in the form of rationalized, increasing block tariffs, may in fact provide a cost-effective safety net for low-volume consumers.

Malaysia's fuel subsidy reform of June 2008

The summer of 2008 prompted numerous countries to revisit their fuel subsidy policies when oil prices climbed to record highs. For Malaysia, the price tag for subsidy inaction was estimated at US$16 billion, from both direct cash transfers and foregone revenue from natural gas sold to power generators at a discount.[30] This bill was exacerbated by cross-border fuel smuggling and owners of foreign-registered vehicles from neighboring Thailand and Singapore taking advantage of cheaper fuel.[31]

In June 2008, the Malaysian government announced subsidy cuts that would raise the price of petrol (then RM1.92 or US$0.60 per liter) and diesel (RM1.58 or US$0.49) by 41 percent and 63 percent respectively, yet would remain low by regional standards.[32] A monthly price review was to be introduced in September 2008 that would link retail prices to market levels with a constant 30 sen per liter subsidy.[33] Cash and road tax rebates of up to US$200 per vehicle were distributed to help offset the fuel premium.[34,35]

This announcement predictably drew reactions from all quarters. Street protests erupted in Kuala Lumpur and Ipoh, with critics calling for Prime Minister Badawi's resignation, many considering the subsidy a rightful transfer from swelling export revenues.[36,37] Analysts were skeptical of reform measures and feared higher-than-anticipated inflation that might command monetary tightening and worsen the country's investment climate.[38] Others welcomed the news and pointed to the fuel subsidy's magnitude (traditionally about 15 percent of the federal budget) which was claimed to exceed development spending on education, health, agriculture and rural development, and transport combined.[39]

Criticism of Malaysia continues, from both private and non-governmental sectors, for its failure to aggressively sustain a subsidy removal program. The 30 sen per liter subsidy for 95 octane is still in place and 97 octane and diesel are subsidized at 16.5 and 32 sen per liter respectively.[40] With lower oil prices in 2009, the year's fuel subsidy totaled RM5.3 billion, but will balloon again in 2010 from bullish prices. As the country works towards improving fiscal discipline and reining in its budget deficit, which reached 7.4 percent in 2009, subsidy restructuring continues to be a policy proposal that has yet to gain traction.

While reform figures prominently in Prime Minister Najib Razak's recently unveiled New Economic Model which aims to confer "developed country" status on Malaysia by 2020, several policy flip-flops on the issue have undermined confidence in its actualization.[41] In January of 2010, a two-tier fuel pricing structure was proposed that would charge foreigners and owners of vehicles with 2,000cc engines and above at the full price.[42] The policy was pulled in March when the Prime Minister explained that "the rakyat (people) does not want it to be done."[43]

Indonesia's kerosene–LPG conversion program

Prior to a reform program introduced in 2007, kerosene had been Indonesia's most heavily subsidized fuel, generating an annual bill of up to US$3 billion and bloated by subsidy abuse. Industry was ineligible for the subsidy and purchased kerosene at Rp. 7500 (US$0.96) a liter, three times the price for households.[44] Incentivized by the spread, an estimated 20 percent of subsidized kerosene sales were smuggled or adulterated.[45]

As deep reforms were estimated to produce annual savings of up to US$2.2 billion, the government in May 2007 launched a kerosene-to-LPG conversion program to encourage households and small businesses to switch to LPG for cooking. Conversion to LPG presented other benefits besides reduced costs for the government (smaller subsidy bill than for kerosene) and households (with projected monthly savings of US$2–11).[46] LPG is cleaner burning, does not require daily refilling, and can be sourced from the country's abundant gas fields. Additionally, kerosene displaced by the program could be refined into more profitable products like aviation fuel.[47]

The program aimed to distribute 42 million packages consisting of a stove set and a 3 kg gas-filled cylinder throughout the country by the end of 2009 and has already achieved this target.[48] Subsidized kerosene in locations where the program was implemented would subsequently be withdrawn from retail sales, though households would still have access at the unsubsidized price. Celebrities, politicians, religious leaders, and other cultural icons were enlisted early on to help raise awareness of LPG's benefits, which soon became self-apparent to the Indonesian public.

However, the program has not been without its implementation problems which contributed to the delay in achieving the distribution target. Various episodes temporarily eroded public confidence in Pertamina, the country's state-owned oil and gas company, and its ability to reliably manage the LPG supply chain.[49,50] As the sole distributor of subsidized fuels, Pertamina was singularly blamed for stove shortages, supply shortages caused by refinery maintenance, extended docking delays experienced by gas-carrying vessels, and a fuel oil depot fire in North Jakarta, which collectively resulted in occasional kerosene price spikes and LPG scarcity.[51] In response, the government partnered with the private sector to lay down an infrastructure network of LPG filling stations, storage, skid tanks, and LPG trucks to decrease delivery times and improve refilling access.[52]

While many kerosene sellers converted to LPG sales with Pertamina's support, small-scale kerosene stove producers were largely neglected and soon went out of business. With LPG stoves primarily being Chinese imports, the conversion program left little room for these producers to maintain a similar line of work. Though a direct cash assistance program was also instituted to help poor households, some were still unable to afford the 3 kg gas refills and claimed they would have to resort to fuel-wood.[53]

Originally launched in East, West, and Central Java provinces, the program will soon have been rolled out across all of Java, the country's most populous island. Expansion to Aceh, Sulawesi, and Kalimantan will take place later this year.[54] The program has been considered highly successful and LPG consumption for 2010 is projected to reach 3 million metric tons, nearly 140 times the volume of just three years previously. As of February 2010, 44 million packages had already been distributed, leaving 10 million to be distributed before the upwards-revised target is met and the program concluded.[55] Through it, the country has transformed into a net kerosene exporter which has created the unforeseen problem of excess inventory. As of February 2010, kerosene stocks were double the government's targeted level, with willing buyers difficult to attract.[56] An additional success has appeared in the possibility of exporting their model overseas. In September 2009, Nigeria expressed interest to the Indonesian government in studying the kerosene-to-LPG conversion program for possible domestic implementation.[57]

Energy systems' impacts on communities

In 2004, the World Bank Group (WBG) published their *Extractive Industries Review*, an assessment of the Bank's involvement in oil, gas, and mining projects. Their findings were clear and consistent with external criticism that its lending portfolio disproportionately favored fossil fuel projects which were environmentally detrimental.[58] According to the *Review*, the Bank would concertedly shift more of its focus to supporting sustainable energy technologies. WBG, at the same time, unequivocally stated that "extractive industries can contribute to sustainable development, when projects are implemented well and preserve the rights of affected people, and if the benefits they generate are well-used."

In general, the broader social impacts of extractive energy industries have traditionally produced a mixed scorecard. Coal mining and oil/gas drilling create jobs, but worker safety protocols are often only loosely implemented, making these job sites more dangerous than they need to be. Fossil fuel resources also produce electricity and transportation fuels whose use creates tangible benefits to the poor, but the poor are usually those most subjected to the airborne pollutants from fossil fuel combustion. In regard to affordability, domestically extracted products may be sold at prices lower than those traded on global markets, either because of reduced production costs, subsidies, or a combination of both (e.g., fuel prices in Venezuela and Iran). Lower prices, in general, facilitate access for the poor so that they too can benefit from energy services.

Additionally, domestic resources that are exported can generate revenues to be earmarked for national development priorities, in education, irrigation, health, and road-construction. Fiscal responsibility of the like is more the exception than the norm for low-income countries entering into resource wealth.

The following two cases highlight the intersection of communities and the energy production value chain. While both are set in Southeast Asia, there are no locale-specific circumstances that preclude similar incidents from occurring elsewhere.

Natural gas drilling in Indonesia: the Sidoarjo mudflow

Nearly four years have passed, but the continuous gushing of 70 °C mud in Sidoarjo, Indonesia remains unremitting. On May 29, 2006, mud erupted from underground near a natural gas drilling well owned by PT Lapindo Brantas, Inc., an oil and gas exploration company, in this East Java town.[59] To date, the mudflow has displaced 40,000 people and inundated more than 1,800 hectares of land—the immediate impacts were even more acute.[60,61]

Within weeks of the May eruption, gas releases of hydrogen sulfide had forced hundreds of villagers to seek treatment for respiratory problems. Water supplies were contaminated and laboratory test results revealed high concentrations of heavy metals. The Sidoarjo Environmental Council declared water from wells and rivers near the mudflow harmful to human health and unsuitable for consumption.[62] The mud forced dozens of factories to shut down, destroyed rice fields and sugarcane estates, and caused the closure of schools and transport links. In November 2006, land subsidence from the mudflow caused a gas pipeline explosion that killed 12 people and injured 15 more.

Numerous attempts have been made to halt the flow, including building dykes, creating a retention pond, redirecting it towards the Madura Straits, dropping concrete balls into the crater, and injecting high-density fluid into neighboring wells in an effort to plug the flow underground.[63,64] All have been unsuccessful and the mudflow has quickened over time. Each day the equivalent of 60 Olympic-sized pools of mud gushes out, several times higher than the rate following the initial eruption, and geologists predict the flow could continue for decades.

Little time passed before employees of the shutdown factories were compensated for lost wages with monthly payments of Rp 700,000, but displaced households experienced numerous and significant delays in receiving compensation. PT Lapindo initially promised families Rp 2.5 million (US$275) a year to cover housing rental expenses until the problem was resolved. President Susilo Bambang Yudhoyono later intervened and signed a presidential instruction in December 2006 ordering PT Lapindo to release a Rp 4 trillion (US$423 million) compensation package in installments, the first 20 percent to be paid by March 2007. Under these terms, the company would effectively buy out displaced households' land and dwellings at predetermined prices per square meter. Dissatisfied with Lapindo's numerous delays in paying out, President Yudhoyono in June 2007 again urged the company to speed up the compensation process for the more than 10,500 families who had been relocated up to then. As of March 2010, victims are still staging periodic protests in Jakarta and demanding the compensation they have been promised.[65]

Responsibility for the incident remains contested despite a May 2009 Supreme Court ruling, consistent with lower court rulings, clearing Lapindo of blame.[66,67] Corporate representatives had maintained throughout that a 6.3-magnitude earthquake two days before in Yogyakarta, 280 kilometers from Sidoarjo, was responsible. In contrast, the majority of international geologists and volcano experts who examined the case were dismissive, calling the earthquake too weak and distant to have instigated the eruption. Others, including some employees of other oil and gas firms, have accused the company of negligence for failing to equip the drill with a safety casing. They say this would have prevented the formation of underground cracks believed to have triggered the mudflow. At the 2008 annual meeting of the American Association of Petroleum Geologists (AAPG), a special session was convened to debate the origins of the mudflow and more than half of the participants considered the drilling either wholly or partially responsible.[68]

In August of 2009, the East Java police ended their investigation citing insufficient evidence to indict Lapindo, a move supported by local prosecutors.[69] Accusations of corruption and misspent public funds have circulated, but the Corruption Eradication Commission has openly refused to conduct an investigation unless a public report alleging bribery charges is filed.[70] Conversely, the National Commission on Human Rights released their preliminary findings in January 2009, stating that clear human rights, including basic rights of living, were violated.[71]

This incident highlights the avoidable hardships faced by local communities when governments and responsible parties fail them. If human error caused the eruption, then additional pre-project and oversight mechanisms should be implemented for similar drilling activities elsewhere. One initial step is to increase the rigor of already mandated environmental impact assessments (environmental impact analyses in Indonesia), and verify they are conducted by impartial and accredited consultants. Another may be to institute a system of random regulatory compliance spot checks. Hotlines where affected stakeholders can anonymously phone in details of alleged violations offer another form of checks and balances. While these measures may raise the cost of doing business, the premium of not doing so is many times higher, as witnessed in the several billion dollars thus far spent on mudflow-related impacts.

The Mae Moh coal plant in northern Thailand

The controversies surrounding the Mae Moh coal-fired power plant, a 13-unit 2,625 MW complex in Thailand's Lampang province, demonstrate the complexities and sometimes intractable challenges arising from the pursuit of energy security. With a worryingly high dependence on natural gas, much of which is sourced from neighboring Myanmar, Thai policymakers have long sought to diversify the country's energy mix and reduce supply-shock vulnerability. Natural gas's 71.4 percent share in electricity production is projected to climb even further unless plants fired by other fuels are built.[72] Lignite, or brown coal, had been considered the solution to these problems and can produce electricity at one-third the cost of natural gas. However, its utilization in northern Thailand has come at the cost of public health and increasing resistance from civil society.

The Mae Moh plant began operating in the 1960s and underwent significant capacity expansion in the 1980s with loan support from the Asian Development Bank and other international lenders, shortening the distance between the plant and Mae Moh district villages.[73] Beginning in 1992, when the eleventh unit was brought online and capacity reached 2,025 MW, thousands of local villagers began experiencing major respiratory problems, dizziness, and rashes as a result of sulfur dioxide and dust emissions from the plant. Over the next six years, several dozen people died from breathing difficulties attributed to poor air quality. Blood tests conducted at the Mae Moh hospital revealed traces of toxic chemicals in patients who complained of dizziness and breath-lessness. Crops and farmland were destroyed by acid rain, while water quality tests in 1999 indicated high levels of arsenic, lead, and nitrogen dioxide in waste water released from the plant into the Mae Moh reservoir and adjacent waterways.[74]

From the onset of these problems, residents of 16 villages demanded relocation and compensa-tion from the Electricity Generating Authority of Thailand (EGAT), the owner and operator of the Mae Moh plant.[75] It was not until 1998 that the first 3,000 people were relocated. The following year, 60 villagers successfully sued EGAT for damages to crops and farmland caused by an incident in August 1998 when the plant's six flue-gas desulfurization systems failed, releasing 150 tons of SO_2 per hour and causing illness for nearly 900 residents.[76]

Further lawsuits were filed, claiming that SO_2 levels permitted by the National Environment Board were exceeded from 1992 to 1998, a charge initially refuted by EGAT but later confirmed by reports from their Pollution Control Department.[77] Last year the Chiang Mai provincial court ruled in favor of villagers demanding compensation for health problems experienced over the same time period and declared the Mae Moh plant's emissions in violation of national standards. Even though the majority of claimants were unsuccessful in proving to the court the plant's responsibility for their illnesses, due to absent medical documents or treatment details, those who did were each awarded ~US$7,000.[78] The verdict also stipulated that EGAT find them new farmland and cover the expenses to relocate them at least 5 kilometers from the plant.

The experience at Mae Moh led to protests against coal plant proposals elsewhere in the country due to concerns over their anticipated health and environmental impacts.[79] Community activists and environmentalists forced the eventual cancellation of two proposed low-sulfur coal plants in Prachuap Kiri Khan that would have added more than 2,100 MW of capacity.[80]

Resistance to new plants, however, may abate, given the recent passage of legislation to compensate people affected by power plants.[81] Through the June 2007 establishment of a Power Development Fund administered by the Energy Regulatory Commission, all power generators are levied an electricity fee collected through a tariff and determined by the energy source. Coal and hydro exact the highest charges at Baht 0.02/unit, whereas wind and solar are assessed none.[82] Accrued funds are distributed to communities living within 5 kilometers of a power plant to cover local development projects in education, public health, and environmental management, relocation expenses, and to compensate for health costs incurred by affected individuals.[83] Since its inception, the funds have accumulated about Bt.4 billion (US$124 million).

Conclusion

The experience of communities in Sidoarjo and Mae Moh vividly demonstrates some of the potential social impacts inherently associated with energy production systems. Such impacts challenge the restrictive conception of affordability as energy security's exclusive social spillover, as based on leading energy security interpretations. While such incidents do not decrease the availability or accessibility of energy supplies and therefore do not undermine "energy security" per se, they do prompt the question of whether such impacts should be excluded from decision-making driven by energy security motivations.

At the same time, the fuel subsidy reform programs in Indonesia and Malaysia suggest avoidable overstretch in the states' attempts to enhance energy affordability. For a host of reasons, energy subsidies may introduce "pernicious effects"[84] at the macro-level, even though micro-level (i.e., specified segments of the population), socially guided reasons may prompt their implementation. These examples call into question the role of governments to safeguard populations against the vagaries of global markets and the unintended consequences such engagement may cause. In addition, they demonstrate a sustained and seemingly irrevocable presence in the one social criterion conventionally embodied in energy security interpretations.

There is therefore scope for expanding energy security considerations to a broader range of social development impacts. The claim can be made that micro-level impacts (those taking place in specific communities and households), or more accurately the *likelihood* of micro-level impacts, cannot be factored into national-level planning. On the contrary, one of the main forces driving subsidy programs is concern for the poor, a micro-level consideration, which demonstrates policymakers' capacity for differentiating policy effects across population groups.

Inclusion of the broader range of potential social impacts into energy security definitions may dovetail with overall human security. Security-driven decisions could then better balance the trade-offs attendant with the selection of any energy technology or source over another, and also provide information about where and how risk-mitigation mechanisms should be instituted. Energy security assessments would indicate when pursuing energy security is contingent on subjecting parts of the population to negative social impacts. At that time, energy policies drawn from security considerations would have more complete information concerning the desirable and undesirable effects to be anticipated from their implementation.

Notes

1 Loschel, Andreas, Ulf Moslener, and Dirk T.G. Rubbelke. 2010. "Indicators of Energy Security in Industrialised Countries," *Energy Policy* 38: 1665–1671.
2 Blyth, William and Nicolas Lefevre. 2004. *Energy Security and Climate Change Policy Interactions: An Assessment Framework*, IEA Information Paper (Paris: IEA).
3 Scheepers, M. J. J., Ad Seebregts, Jacques de Jong, and Hans Maters. 2007. *EU Standards for Energy Security of Supply-Updates on the Crisis Capability Index and the Supply/Demand Index Quantification for EU-27* (Amsterdam: ECN/Clingendael International Energy Programme, ECN-E-07-004/CIEP.
4 Jansen, J. C., W. G. van Arkel, and M. G. Boots. 2004. *Designing Indicators of Long-Term Energy Supply Security*. (Amsterdam: Een onafhankelijk onderzoeksinstituut voor duurzame energie (ECN) ECN-C—04-007.
5 Kruyt, Bert, D. P. van Vuuren, H. J. M. de Vries, and H. Groenenberg. 2009. "Indicators for Energy Security," *Energy Policy* 37(6): 2166–2181.
6 The other As are availability, accessibility, and affordability. Asia Pacific Energy Research Centre (APERC). 2007. *A Quest for Energy Security in the 21st Century* (Tokyo: APERC).
7 Stern, David, I. 1993. "Energy and Economic Growth in the USA: A Multivariate Approach," *Energy Economics* 15: 137–150.
8 Shiu, Alice and Pun-Lee Lam. 2004. "Electricity Consumption and Economic Growth in China," *Energy Policy* 32(1): 47–54.
9 Cust, James and Karsten Neuhoff. "The Economics, Politics and Future of Energy Subsidies," Climate Policy Initiative Workshop, Berlin, March 21, 2010.
10 Alston, Julian M. and Brian H. Hurd. 1990. "Some Neglected Social Costs of Government Spending in Farm Programs," *American Journal of Agricultural Economics* 72(1): 149–156.
11 G-20. 2009. "Leaders' Statement: The Pittsburgh Summit," G-20 Summit on Financial Markets and the World Economy, Pittsburgh, USA, September 24–25. Available at: http://www.pittsburghsummit. gov/documents/organization/129853.pdf (accessed May 5, 2010).
12 APEC. 2009. "Sustaining Growth, Connecting the Region," 2009 Leaders' Declaration, 17th APEC Economic Leaders' Meeting, Singapore, November 14–15. Available at: http://www.apec2009.sg/

index.php?option=com_content&view=article&id=311:2009-leaders-declaration-qsustaining-growth-connecting-the-regionq&catid=39:press-releases&Itemid=127 (accessed May 5, 2010).

13 International Energy Agency (IEA). 2008. *World Energy Outlook 2008* (Paris: OECD/IEA).

14 World Bank. 2010. *World Development Indicators*. (Washington, DC: World Bank Group).

15 United Nations Environment Program [UNEP]. 2008. *Reforming Energy Subsidies: Opportunities to Contribute to the Climate Change Agenda* (Paris: UNEP-DTIE).

16 Bulman, Tim, Wolfgang Fendler, and Mohamad Ikhsan. 2008. "Indonesia's Oil Subsidy Opportunity," *Far Eastern Economic Review*, June.

17 OECD. 1999. *Improving the Environment Through Reducing Subsidies* (Paris: OECD).

18 Saunders, Matthew and Karen Schneider. 2000. "Removing Energy Subsidies in Developing and Transition Economies," paper presented at the 23rd Annual IAEE International Conference, Sydney, June 7–10.

19 Fisher, Anthony C. and Michael H. Rothkopf. 1989. "Market Failure and Energy Policy: A Rationale for Selective Conservation," *Energy Policy* 17(4): 397–406.

20 Shah, T., C. Scott, J. Berkoff, A. Kishore, and A. Sharma. 2007. "The Energy-Irrigation Nexus in South Asia: Groundwater Conservation and Power Sector Viability." In F. Molle and J. Berkoff (eds.), *Irrigation Water Pricing* (Oxfordshire, UK: CABI), pp. 208–232.

21 Morgan, Trevor. "Energy Subsidies: Their Magnitude, How They Affect Energy Investment and Greenhouse Gas Emissions, and Prospects for Reform." Report to UNFCCC Secretariat: Financial and Technical Support Programme. Available at: http://unfccc.int/files/cooperation_and_support/financial_mechanism/application/pdf/morgan_pdf.pdf (accessed April 10, 2010). United Nations Framework Convention on Climate Change.

22 Burniaux, Jean-Marc, Jean Chateau, Rob Dellink, Romain Duval, and Stephanie Jamet. 2009. *The Economics of Climate Change Mitigation: How to Build the Necessary Global Action in a Cost-Effective Manner*. OECD Economics Department Working Paper No. 701, p. 35.

23 UNEP, *Reforming Energy Subsidies*.

24 Victor, David. 2009. *The Politics of Fossil-Fuel Subsidies* (Winnipeg: International Institute for Sustainable Development).

25 Guerin, Bill. 2007. "Kicking the Habit: Indonesia Struggles with its Entrenched System of Fuel Subsidies," *Energy Economist*, May 1.

26 MacKinnon, Ian. 2008. "Philippines Hit by Fuel Price Protests," *Guardian*, June 12.

27 Mydans, Seth. 2007. "Monks in Myanmar Protest for Third Day," *New York Times*, September 21.

28 Victor, *The Politics of Fossil-Fuel Subsidies*.

29 Laan, Tara, Christopher Beaton, and Bertille Presta. 2010. *Strategies for Reforming Fossil-Fuel Subsidies: Practical Lessons from Ghana, France and Senegal* (Winnipeg: International Institute for Sustainable Development).

30 Anon. 2008. "In Flux over Energy Pricing," *New Sunday Times*, May 25.

31 Anon. 2008. "Malaysia to Unveil Fuel Subsidy Reform Plan before Budget 2009," *Asia Pulse*, May 30.

32 Ng, Pauline. 2008. "End of Cheap Fuel as KL Hikes Petrol Price 41%," *The Business Times*, June 5.

33 Ng, "End of Cheap Fuel."

34 Anon. 2008. "Fuel Subsidy Getting to be Untenable," *New Sunday Times*, September 7.

35 Murugiah, Surin. 2008. "Highlights of New Fuel Subsidy Structure," *The Edge Financial Daily*, June 5.

36 Anon. 2008. "Malaysia PM Urges Calm over Fuel," *Al-Jazeera*, June 5.

37 Sam, Ivy. 2008. "Protests Target Malaysian Fuel Price Hike," *Agence France Presse*, June 5.

38 Chew, Elffie. 2008. "Malaysia Central Bank may have to Hike Rates 75bps this Year," *Dow Jones International News*, June 5.

39 Aris, Azam. 2008. "Why We Need a National Subsidy Policy," *The Edge Malaysia*, May 12.

40 Ng, Pauline. 2010. "Malaysia Shelves Two-Tier Pricing Plan for Petrol," *The Business Times*, March 5.

41 Anon. 2010. "Investors Lukewarm on Malaysia's New Economic Model," *The Edge Singapore*, April 5.

42 Grieder, Tom. 2010. "Government of Malaysia Backs Down on Fuel Subsidy Cuts," *IHS Global Insight Daily Analysis*, March 4.

43 Ng, "Malaysia Shelves Two-Tier Pricing Plan for Petrol."

44 Anon. 2010. "Pertamina Mulls Converting Excess Kerosene Output to Jet Fuel," *Platts Commodity News*, February 7.

45 Anon., "Pertamina Mulls Converting Excess Kerosene Output to Jet Fuel."

46 Anon. 2010. "Indonesia's Savings in Kerosene Subsidy Offset Build in Stocks," *Platts Commodity News*, March 15.

47 Anon, "Pertamina Mulls Converting Excess Kerosene."

48 Budya, Hanung. 2008. "Indonesia LPG Kerosene Conversion Program: Challenges and Opportunities," paper presented at 21st World LP Gas Forum, Seoul, September 24–26.

49 Rachmi, Asclepias. 2008. "Kerosene Substitution Programs in Indonesia: Institutions and Public Policies," paper presented at 31st IAEE Pre Conference on Clean Cooking Fuels and Technology, Istanbul, June 16–17.

50 Wisnu, Andra. 2009. "Kerosene Proves Harder to Phase Out," *Jakarta Post*, March 4.

51 Anon. 2009. "Indonesia's Pertamina to Import LPG to Build Up Stock this Year," *ANTARA*, March 16.

52 Budya, "Indonesia LPG Kerosene Conversion Program."

53 International Energy Agency (IEA). 2008. *Energy Policy Review of Indonesia* (Paris: OECD/IEA).

54 Hari, Vandana and Anita Nugraha. 2010. "Pertamina Seeks LPG Storage as Demand Booms; Indonesia Becomes Kerosene Exporter, but Fails to Find Markets," *Platts Oilgram Price Report* 88, February 9.

55 Anon. 2010. "Indonesia's Distribution of LPG Conversion Packs Beat Target," *Asia Pulse*, January 4.

56 Vandana and Nugraha, "Pertamina Seeks LPG Storage as Demand Booms."

57 Indonesian Ministry of Energy and Mineral Resources. 2009. "Nigeria Models Indonesian Subsidy Reduction System." Available at: http://www.esdm.go.id/news-archives/oil-and-gas/47-oilandgas/2863-nigeria-models-indonesian-subsidy-reduction-system.html (accessed April 10, 2010).

58 World Bank. 2004. *Striking a Better Balance—The World Bank Group and Extractive Industries: The Final Report of the Extractive Industries Review.* Available at: http://www.ifc.org/ifcext/eir.nsf/AttachmentsByTitle/FinalManagementResponse/$FILE/finaleirmanagementresponse.pdf (accessed April 5, 2010).

59 Harsaputra, Indra and I. D. Nugroho. 2006. "Hot Mudflow in Sidoarjo Investigated by Police," *Jakarta Post*, June 16.

60 Bayuni, Endy M. 2009. "Documentary Suggests Causes are Clear as Mud," *Jakarta Post*, November 15.

62 Suharmoko, Aditya. 2010. "Government to Revise Rule to Compensate Mudflow Victims," *Jakarta Post*, January 9.

62 ANTARA. 2006. "Ground Water in Sidoarjo Mudflow Area Declared Undrinkable," July 6.

63 Battersby, Amanda. 2009. "No End in Sight to Victims' Woes," *Upstream*, July 24.

64 Harsaputra, Indra and Ridwan Max Sijabat. 2009. "Government Still Seeking Another Way to Stop Mudflow in Porong," *Jakarta Post*, February 9.

65 Anon. 2010. "Mudflow Victims Take Complaint to Komnas HAM," *Jakarta Post*, March 24.

66 Jayakarna, Agnes S. 2009. "Three Years and Counting: No End Yet to Lapindo Mess," *Jakarta Post*, May 30.

67 Bayuni, Endy M. 2009. "'LUSI' Spurs Geologists' Interest," *Jakarta Post*, December 1.

68 Underhill, John. 2008. "Mud Volcano Cause Discussed," *AAPG Explorer* 29: 32–33.

69 Harsaputra, Indra. 2009. "Mud Victims Renew Calls for Payout," *Jakarta Post*, October 26.

70 Harsaputra, Indra. 2009. "Prosecutors Defend Police over Halt to Lapindo Case," *Jakarta Post*, August 26.

71 Maulia, Erwida. 2009. "Rights Body Identifies Violations in Sidoarjo Disaster Areas," *Jakarta Post*, February 26.

72 Energy Policy and Planning Office, Ministry of Energy, Thailand. 2010. *Energy statistics.* Available at: http://www.eppo.go.th/info/5electricity_stat.htm (accessed May 27, 2010).

73 UNESCO. 2009. *Representation and Who Decides in Environmental Planning (with an Emphasis on Energy Technologies).* Report by Ethics and Climate Change in Asia and the Pacific (ECCAP) Working Group 4.

74 Suksai, Somsak. 1999. "Water Near Mae Moh Plant Found to be Contaminated," *Bangkok Post*, March 7.

75 Suksai, Somsak. 1998. "3,000 to be Moved out of Villages," *Bangkok Post*, October 16.

76 Suksai, Somsak. 1999. "Mae Moh Villagers File Lawsuit," *Bangkok Post*, July 16.

77 Anon. 2009. "Court Orders EGAT to Pay Damages to Villagers Affected by Lignite Power Plant," *Thai News Service*, March 5.

78 Anon. 2009. "Villagers Seek More," *The Nation*, March 7.

79 Anon. 2007. "New EGAT Governor Says Local Resistance to Coal-Fired Power Plants Must be Overcome," *Thai News Service*, November 13.

80 Anon. 2008. "Energy and Industrial Projects Face Not-in-my-Backyard Syndrome," *Thai News Service*, January 3.

81 Anon. 2009. "Community Development Fund Seen as a Success," *The Nation*, December 12.
82 Energy Regulatory Commission. 2009. "Thailand Energy Regulatory Developments 2009." Available at: http://www2.erc.or.th/Doc/thailand.pdf (accessed March 12, 2010).
83 Anon. 2010. "Activist Urges Close Monitoring of Fund to Pay Communities for Impact of Electricity Generating Plants," *Thai News Service*, January 12.
84 Victor, *The Politics of Fossil-Fuel Subsidies*.

11

THE ENERGY EFFICIENCY DIMENSION OF ENERGY SECURITY

Nathalie Trudeau and Peter G. Taylor

Introduction

As governments around the world tackle the complex and intertwined challenges of improving energy security and reducing associated greenhouse gas emissions—while also supporting economic development objectives—two things are increasingly clear:

- Ensuring a better use of the world's energy resources will require policies that encompass a wide range of options. There is a growing recognition that improving energy efficiency is often the most economic, proven, and readily available means of achieving this goal.
- Establishing and maintaining sound policy requires the availability of good quality, timely, comparable, and detailed data that go well beyond those currently included in statistics energy balances, and reflect the distinct characteristics of economic activity and resources available in each country.

To support better energy efficiency policymaking and evaluation, the International Energy Agency (IEA) has been working for more than ten years on developing in-depth indicators—tools that provide state-of-the-art data and analysis on energy use and efficiency trends.[1] More recently, using the latest insights from its work on indicators, the IEA published a brochure with the goal of showing policymakers how in-depth indicators can be used to track the progress in efficiency and identify new opportunities for improvements.[2]

A key challenge in developing effective energy policies is that energy consumption is affected by many non-energy factors such as climate, geography, economy, travel distance, home size, and the structure of the manufacturing sector, as well as differences in everyday behavior. No single solution will be equally effective in all contexts and in all countries. Hence, the importance of collecting data to understand energy consumption patterns, and developing state-of-the-art energy efficiency indicators to better inform decision-making and track the progress towards energy efficiency goals.

Recent efforts by several countries to collect more detailed end-use data have helped to develop energy efficiency indicators, which provide important information to understanding past trends, assessing potential for energy savings, and enhancing efficiency policies.

The analysis of long-term past trends using detailed end-use data available for 11 IEA member countries (IEA11)[3] demonstrates that without the energy efficiency policies and measures put in place since 1973, energy consumption for these countries would have been 63 percent higher in 2006—enough to meet the entire energy needs of Russia, India, and Canada in 2006. This represents 5 gigatonnes (GT) of CO_2 emissions avoided—equivalent to global emissions from the industrial sectors in 2006—and US$1.1 trillion of energy cost savings in 2006 alone.

Detailed end-use data and indicators are equally essential for assessing the further contribution of energy efficiency. The IEA estimates show that large potentials remain across all sectors. For example, the global application of best available technologies (BAT) and best practices technologies (BPT)[4] in the five most intensive industrial sectors[5] could lead to energy savings of 15 exajoules (EJ) per year while also reducing CO_2 emissions by 1.3 GT per year.

This capacity to track trends and identify potential savings makes detailed end-use data and energy efficiency indicators key to launching and monitoring any successful energy efficiency policy. An analysis of the impacts to date of energy efficiency policies implemented by IEA member countries reveals that:

- Effective policies do make a difference. In each of the main energy-consuming sectors, there is evidence of improved efficiency, most of which results in reduced CO_2 emissions. In some cases, however, changes in consumption patterns within a given sector or subsector reduce the overall impact of efficiency gains.
- While it is clear that such measures work, the fact is that currently available energy data are a poor foundation for developing an in-depth understanding of how or why – or, indeed, for analyzing which measures are most effective—and warrant broader implementation. This fact underlines the reality that existing data and information are too sparse to analyze precisely the impacts of specific measures.
- Clearly, more data—and different kinds of data—are needed to support the strategic development, implementation, and evaluation of energy efficiency policies.

Overall, energy efficiency indicators enable energy stakeholders to analyze more precisely specific aspects of main energy consuming sectors, while fully accounting for the unique nature of each national context.

Overview of trends in overall energy consumption

Since 1990, global final energy consumption has increased by 28 percent. Energy consumption has grown most quickly in the service and transport sectors, both sectors showing an increase of more than 40 percent. Figure 11.1 shows that, in 2006, transport was the end-use sector that globally consumed the most energy, accounting for 28 percent of final consumption, followed by industry and households.

Energy consumption in industry showed an increase of 21 percent between 1990 and 2006. Most of this increase occurred after 2000, driven by the strong economic growth in major developing countries.

Total final energy consumption is dominated by oil, with a share of 43 percent in 2006, up from 41 percent in 1990. Oil use for transport increased strongly between 1990 and 2006, driving the overall rise in oil demand.

With a share of 17 percent, electricity has overtaken natural gas as the second most important energy commodity in the final energy mix (Figure 11.2). Electricity use increased rapidly in all stationary sectors, with the strongest growth in households and services. Residential electricity

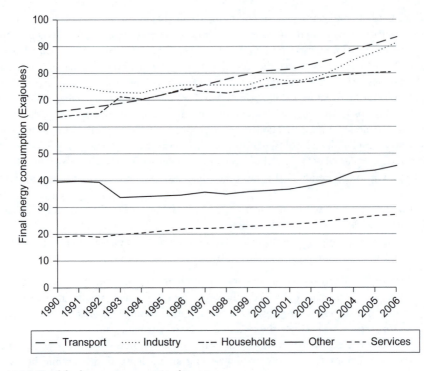

Figure 11.1 Total final energy consumption by sector.
Sources: IEA. 2009. *Energy Balances of OECD Countries, 2009 Edition* (Paris: IEA/OECD); IEA. 2009. *Energy Balances on Non-OECD Countries, 2009 Edition* (Paris: IEA/OECD).
Note:
Other includes agriculture, forestry, fishing, and non-energy use.

demand is largely driven by increased ownership and use of electric appliances. In contrast, coal consumption has declined to 30 percent below the 1990 level in 2000, but its consumption increased again to meet the large energy requirements associated with the strong economic growth in some developing countries. In 2006, coal consumption was 8 percent lower than in 1990.

For decades, countries around the world have used the data contained in standard energy balances as a means of tracking energy consumption according to type of energy commodity and by major sector. While these trends provide a general view of the patterns in energy consumption in the world, they do not provide the reasons behind the development by sector and energy commodity. Coupling energy consumption with other data, such as gross domestic product (GDP) and population, can help to identify factors that drive energy demand.

For the overall economy, two sets of broad, basic indicators are commonly used. Total final energy consumption (TFC) per unit of GDP and TFC per capita.

The ratio of TFC per unit of GDP provides a measure of final energy intensity for a country or a region, and is one of the most frequently used aggregate energy indicators. Trends in aggregate final energy intensity reveal that all countries and regions analyzed have shown a decline since 1990 (Figure 11.3). In general, IEA non-member countries have shown a faster rate of decrease than IEA member countries. In many cases, these reductions can be attributed to strong efficiency improvements due to the introduction of modern, efficient technologies and processes.

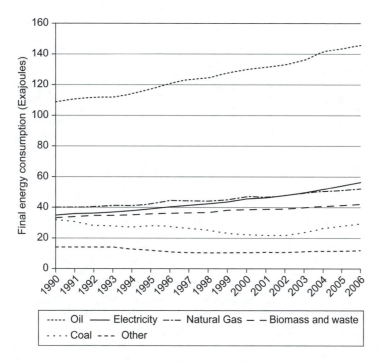

Figure 11.2 Total final energy consumption by energy source.
Sources: IEA. 2009. *Energy Balances of OECD Countries, 2009 Edition* (Paris: IEA/OECD); IEA. 2009. *Energy Balances on Non-OECD Countries, 2009 Edition* (Paris: IEA/OECD).
Note:
Other includes district heat, geothermal, and solar.

An alternative aggregate indicator to TFC per GDP is TFC per capita (Figure 11.4). This indicator measures the amount of final energy used per person in a country or a region. In contrast to aggregate final energy intensity, this indicator shows an increase for most countries and regions. Russia is a significant exception, with energy use per capita having fallen by 34 percent between 1990 and 2006. This is linked with falling wealth, as measured by GDP per capita, following the economic restructuring of the country in the early 1990s.

The two aggregate indicators, TFC per GDP and TFC per capita, are two very different ways of looking at the link between developments in final energy consumption and some of the important underlying drivers. These aggregate indicators have several demonstrated advantages. At the national scale, they can reveal high-level developments in energy use, such as differences in the evolution and absolute levels of final energy consumption amongst countries. More broadly, because they are available for a wide range of countries, they can be constructed to facilitate basic cross-country comparisons.

However, the usefulness of aggregate indicators is limited, and their inappropriate use can lead to misleading results. For example, it would be incorrect to rank energy efficiency performance according to a country's TFC per GDP or per capita as the ratios are affected by many factors such as climate, geography, travel distance, home size, and manufacturing structure, which energy efficiency measures cannot directly influence. Thus, currently available energy data is, in fact, a poor foundation to developing effective energy efficiency policies, or for evaluating their impact.

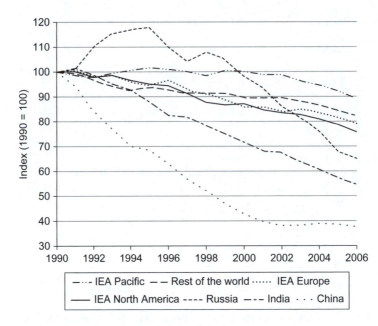

Figure 11.3 Total final energy consumption per unit of GDP.
Sources: IEA. 2009. *Energy Balances of OECD Countries, 2009 Edition* (Paris: IEA/OECD); IEA. 2009. *Energy Balances on Non-OECD Countries, 2009 Edition*, (Paris: IEA/OECD).
Notes:
IEA Pacific includes Australia, Japan, the Republic of Korea, and New Zealand. IEA Europe includes Austria, Belgium, Czech Republic, Denmark, Finland, France, Germany, Greece, Hungary, Ireland, Italy, Luxembourg, the Netherlands, Norway, Poland, Portugal, Slovak Republic, Spain, Sweden, Switzerland, Turkey, and the United Kingdom. IEA North America includes Canada and the United States.

Comparable and disaggregated end-use information about the patterns of energy consumption in all end-use sectors (manufacturing, households, services, and transport) coupled with economic and demographic data are required to construct indicators that identify the factors behind increasing energy use and those that restrain it.

The IEA methodology for analyzing trends in energy

One of the most important issues to understand from an energy policy perspective is to what extent improvements in energy efficiency have been responsible for the declines in final energy intensity seen in the different countries. To understand the role of energy efficiency, it is necessary to separate the impact of changes in subsectoral energy intensities (which are a proxy for energy efficiency) from the effects of changes in economic structure and other factors that influence the demand for energy. This is done using a decomposition approach that separates and quantifies the impacts of changes in activity, structure, and energy intensities on final energy use in each sector and country.

The IEA indicators approach uses the idea of an indicators pyramid, which portrays a hierarchy of energy indicators from most detailed, at the bottom of the pyramid, to least detailed at the top (Figure 11.5). In the IEA approach, the top element (the most aggregate indicator) is defined as the ratio of TFC to GDP. Alternatively, it could have been defined as the ratio of energy use to another macroeconomic variable, such as population. The second row of elements can be defined

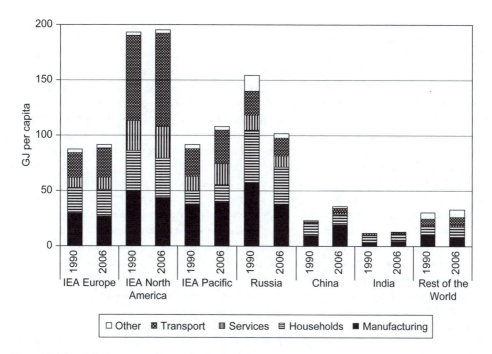

Figure 11.4 Total final energy consumption per capita.
Sources: IEA. 2009. *Energy Balances of OECD Countries, 2009 Edition* (Paris: IEA/OECD); IEA. 2009. *Energy Balances on Non-OECD Countries, 2009 Edition* (Paris: IEA/OECD).
Notes:
IEA Pacific includes Australia, Japan, the Republic of Korea, and New Zealand. IEA Europe includes Austria, Belgium, Czech Republic, Denmark, Finland, France, Germany, Greece, Hungary, Ireland, Italy, Luxembourg, the Netherlands, Norway, Poland, Portugal, Slovak Republic, Spain, Sweden, Switzerland, Turkey, and the United Kingdom. IEA North America includes Canada and the United States.

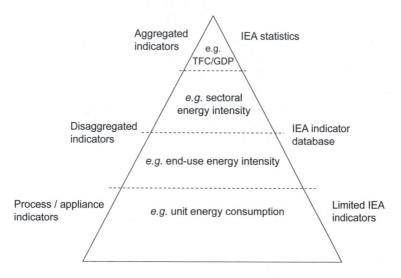

Figure 11.5 The IEA energy indicators pyramid.
Source: Modified from IEA. 1997. *Indicators of Energy Use and Efficiency: Understanding the Link between Energy and Human Activity* (Paris: OECD/IEA).

as the energy intensity of each major sector, as measured by energy use per unit of activity in each sector. Lower rows represent the subsectors or end-uses that make up each sector and progressively provide more details, for example characterizing particular processes or appliances. Joining each level of energy intensities are structural variables that indicate how to weight these intensities to form a more aggregate parameter of intensity or use. Descending lower down the pyramid requires more data and more complex analysis to re-aggregate back up to a higher level. However, each descent also provides a better measure of technical energy efficiency, defined for a specific technology, process, and/or end-use.

This hierarchy is important because it shows how detailed changes (which may be the result of policies, technological progress, structural reform, or behavioral change) can be linked to higher order showing how the former affects the latter. With this hierarchy, one can better explain more aggregate changes in energy use in terms of components and choose more carefully the depth of analysis required. That choice depends on the questions that need to be answered.

In its current work, the IEA draws on detailed end-use information about the patterns of energy consumption in more than 20 end-uses covering the manufacturing, household, service, and transport sectors (Figure 11.6). This information, coupled with economic and demographic data, is used to identify the factors behind increasing energy use as well as those that restrain it. The IEA energy indicators typically reflect ratios or quantities and, at a disaggregated level, can describe the links between energy use and human and economic activities. The indicators include measures of activity (such as manufacturing output or volume of freight haulage), measures of developments in structure (such as changes in manufacturing output mix or modal shares in transport), and measures of energy intensity (defined as energy use per unit of activity).

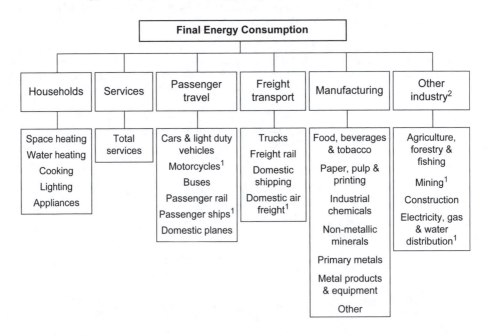

Figure 11.6 Disaggregation of sectors, subsectors and end-uses in the IEA energy indicators approach.
Source: IEA. 1997. *Indicators of Energy Use and Efficiency: Understanding the Link between Energy and Human Activity* (Paris: OECD/IEA).
Notes:
[1] Not included in this study due to lack of consistent and reliable data series.
[2] Other industry is included in the analysis only in the section aggregate trends and is not analyzed separately.

To separate the effect on energy use of various components over time, the IEA uses a Laspeyres decomposition approach that analyzes changes in energy use within a sector using the following equation:

$$E = A \cdot \sum_r (S^r \cdot I^r)$$

In this decomposition, the symbols represent the following parameters:

E: total energy use in a sector;
A: overall sectoral activity;
r: subsectors or end-uses within a given sector;
S^r: share of subsector or end-use "r" in a sector; and
I^r: the energy intensity of each subsector or end-use "r".

The separation of impacts on energy use from changes in activity, structure, and intensity is critical for policy analysis. Most energy-related policies target energy intensities and efficiencies, often by promoting new technologies. Accurately tracking changes in intensities helps measure the effects of these new technologies.

The *energy intensity effect* (E_t^I), which is used as a proxy for changes in energy efficiency, separates out how changes in the energy intensity of each subsector or end-use influence total energy consumption for a particular sector. This is done by calculating the relative impact on energy use that would have occurred between a base year (t = 0) and a future year (t) if the aggregate activity levels and structure for a sector remained fixed at base year values, while the subsector or end-use energy intensities followed their actual development (Eq.(1)). A similar approach is used to calculate the activity and structure effects.

$$E_t^I = A_o \cdot \frac{\sum_r (S_o^r \cdot I_t^r)}{E_o} \cdot$$ (1)

The *hypothetical energy use* (HEU^I) is then defined as the energy use that would have occurred in *year t* if the energy intensities in each sector remained constant at their base year values. It is calculated by dividing actual energy use in *year t* by the intensity effect in that year (Eq. (2))

$$HEU_t^I = \frac{E_t}{E_t^I}$$ (2)

Energy savings from reduced energy intensities can be defined as the difference between the hypothetical energy use and actual energy use (Eq. (3))

$$SAVINGS_t^I = HEU_t^I - E_t$$ (3)

Regional aggregates for hypothetical energy use are calculated as the sum of hypothetical energy uses across all countries in a particular region. Energy savings for a region are then calculated as the difference between the hypothetical energy use and the actual energy use.

The result of the application of this method, combined with the analysis of the different drivers in each end-use sector, provides important insights on the factors impacting energy consumption and the potential to further reduce consumption and to improve energy security. However, the required detailed end-use data to perform such analysis is only available for a few countries. The analysis has been performed on IEA member countries for which the information was available.

Buildings sector

The buildings sector includes the household and service end-users. The household sector includes those activities related to private dwellings. It covers all energy-using activities in apartments and houses, including space and water heating, cooling, lighting, and the use of appliances. It does not include personal transport, which is covered in the transport sector. The service sector includes activities related to trade, finance, real estate, public administration, health, education, and commercial services.

Looking at the reasons for the different trends in the service sector requires energy consumption and activity data disaggregated by subsector and, if possible, end-use. However, such data are scarce, even for IEA member countries. Energy consumption pattern by energy commodity indicates a strong increase in the share of electricity use in the service sector. This increase reflects the growing importance of electricity-using equipments. The limited information available at a more detailed level shows that as there is a wide variation in subsectoral energy intensities, structural effects can be important in determining the overall trends in service sector energy use. Given the limitation of the data to perform detailed analysis for the service sector, this section will focus on the household sector.

Global energy use in the household sector reached 81 EJ in 2006 and accounted for about one-quarter of total final energy use.

Detailed data allowing the analysis of the household sector are available for 19 IEA member countries (IEA19).[6] Given the importance of the climatic conditions in the household sector, which greatly affect the energy requirements for space heating and space cooling, the energy use in the analysis is corrected for yearly variations in climatic conditions. Figure 11.7 shows the energy consumption by countries, before and after the normalization to the same climate conditions. Weather-adjusted energy consumption in IEA19 increased by 15 percent between 1990 and 2006.

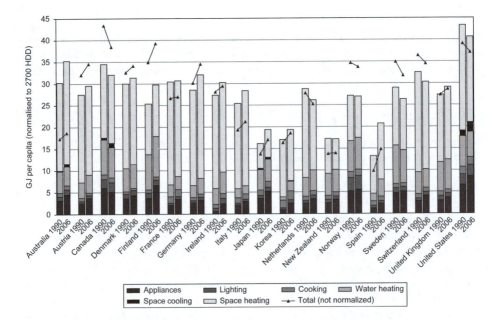

Figure 11.7 Household energy use per capita.

The level of energy use per capita varies significantly across IEA member countries. To a large extent, the high energy use per capita in some countries such as Canada and Finland is due to their cold climates.

In the household sector, space heating is by far the most important energy user in IEA19, accounting for 53 percent of final household energy use in 2006; but it had increased by only 5 percent since 1990. In contrast, appliances' energy consumption (mostly electricity) grew by 52 percent and has overtaken water heating as the second most important energy-consuming end-use. Almost half of the increase in households' energy consumption was due to the important growth in appliances' energy consumption (Figure 11.8).

Several factors affect energy consumption for space heating in households, including dwelling size, the number of occupants, the efficiency of heating equipment, and the demand for useful energy per unit of area heated (useful energy intensity). The impacts of these effects can be investigated through the decomposition analysis (Figure 11.9). From 1990 to 2006, larger dwelling size in the IEA19 countries led to an increase of 0.7 percent per year in energy demand. The reduction in the occupancy of each household puts upward pressure on demand for space heating because a larger number of dwellings are required to house a given population, and the heating needs of a given dwelling are not necessarily reduced because fewer people are living in it.

On average, higher demand for space heating in the IEA19 has been offset by two factors: efficiency gains derived from lower conversion losses in heating technologies and significant reduction in the useful energy intensity for space heating, a proxy for energy efficiency.

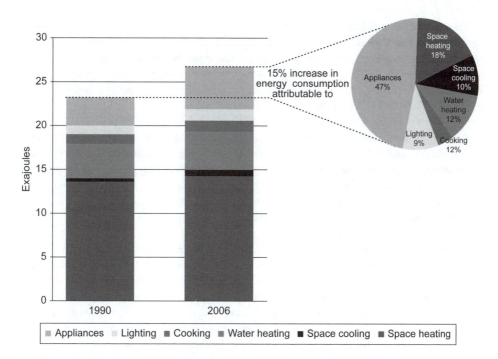

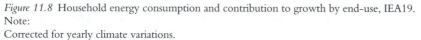

Figure 11.8 Household energy consumption and contribution to growth by end-use, IEA19.
Note:
Corrected for yearly climate variations.

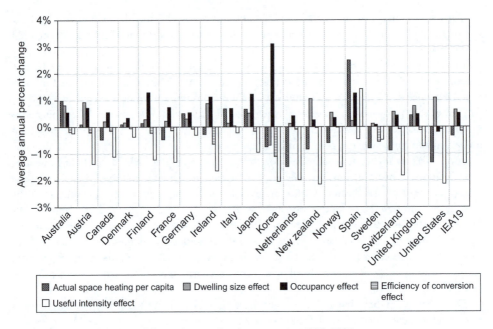

Figure 11.9 Decomposition of change in space heating per capita, 1990–2006.
Note:
Corrected for yearly climate variations.

Energy efficiency policies targeting households in IEA member countries have focused on restraining energy demand from space heating and large appliances through mandatory building codes, energy performance standards and targets, voluntary agreement with industry, and labeling to help guide consumer choices. The analysis on space heating shows that these policies played a key role in achieving energy efficiency improvements, which have averaged 1.3 percent per year since 1990. The low growth in space heating energy consumption reflects this impressive improvement in energy efficiency.

Appliances are another important end-use in the household sector. Electricity use for household appliances in the IEA19 grew by 57 percent from 1990 to 2006, driving the overall increase in household electricity demand. In 2006, electricity consumption by appliances was 59 percent of total household electricity use.

Information on the breakdown of appliances' energy use is not available on a consistent basis, but some data are available for large appliances—refrigerators, freezers, washing machines, and dishwashers. In 2010, these large appliances account for around 50 percent of household electricity consumption by total number of appliances in the IEA, down from 63 percent in 1990.

The declining share of large appliances in total appliance energy consumption (figure 11.10) has been helped significantly by policies implemented in many IEA member countries. For large appliances, information available for 13 IEA member countries shows a 24 percent improvement in the average unit energy consumption since 1990. The impacts of energy efficiency programs can be seen in the marked improvements in unit energy consumption. However, deeper analysis clearly indicates that efficiency gains in large appliances were more than offset by the growing stocks of large appliances and the increased ownership of a wide range of miscellaneous appliances such as personal computers, mobile phones, and other home electronics.

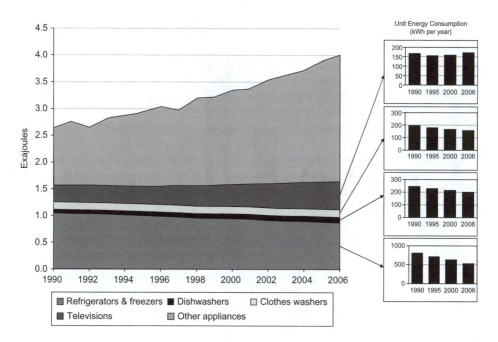

Figure 11.10 Energy consumption by type of appliances, IEA13.

Manufacturing

The manufacturing sector covers the manufacture of finished goods and products, including the energy used as feedstock in the chemical and petrochemical industry and the energy used in coke ovens and blast furnaces in the iron and steel sector.

Within a group of 21 IEA member countries (IEA21)[7] for which comprehensive data are available, recent trends in manufacturing show a marked decoupling of economic activity and energy use. Over the 1990 to 2006 period, output from manufacturing (as measured by value-added) increased by 45 percent. In contrast, total final energy use increased by only 0.4 percent. This decoupling resulted in a 31 percent decrease in final energy intensity.

The energy intensity of manufacturing industry (as measured by dividing total manufacturing energy use by total manufacturing value-added) varies widely between subsectors. The most energy-intensive subsector amongst IEA21 is the production of primary metals. In 2006, energy intensity in this subsector was more than ten times higher than the category of other manufacturing and of metal products and equipment (Figure 11.11). Yet output from the primary metals subsector constituted only 4 percent of total manufacturing value-added, compared with 27 percent from other manufacturing and 36 percent from metal products and equipment. Taken together, the four most energy-intensive subsectors (primary metals, non-metallic minerals, chemicals, and paper and pulp) accounted for almost 70 percent of manufacturing energy use despite representing only 28 percent of total value-added output.

Large differences are also evident in the level of overall manufacturing energy intensity among IEA member countries. Using an indicator approach, it is possible to investigate to what extent these differences among countries can be explained by differences in their industrial structure.

The results of the decomposition analysis (Figure 11.12) are quite striking; even though they do not account for the detailed structural differences within the subsectors of industry (i.e. different

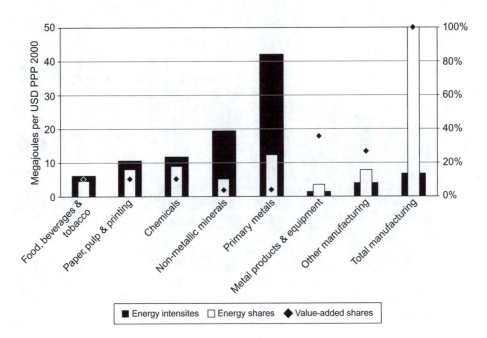

Figure 11.11 Energy use by manufacturing subsector, IEA21.

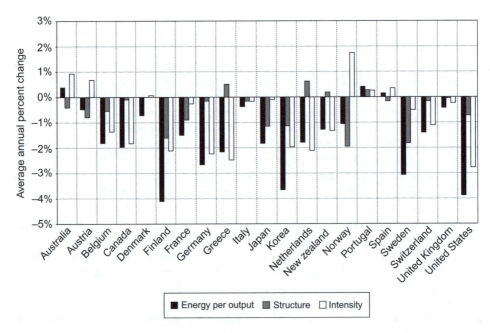

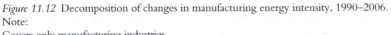

Figure 11.12 Decomposition of changes in manufacturing energy intensity, 1990–2006.
Note:
Covers only manufacturing industries.

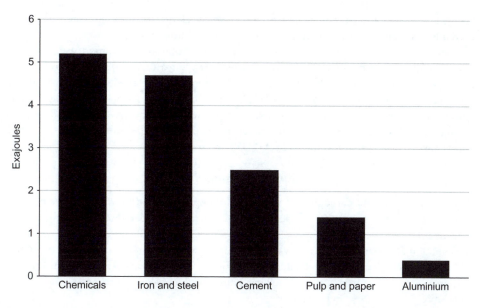

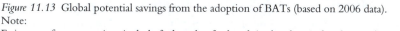

Figure 11.13 Global potential savings from the adoption of BATs (based on 2006 data).
Note:
Estimates of energy savings include fuel used as feedstock in the chemical and petrochemical sector.

product mixes within subsectors), structural effects are responsible for almost half the variation in manufacturing energy intensities that are observed amongst countries.

The decomposition analysis also shows that energy efficiency improvements (as measured by changes in the structure-adjusted intensities) were the main factor restraining energy consumption growth in most countries. Without the energy savings resulting from these improvements, energy consumption in the IEA21 would have been 29 percent higher in 2006.

While the decomposition analysis provides useful insights on the evolution of energy consumption and efficiency in the manufacturing sector, one question remains. Given the important improvements in energy efficiency in the recent past, is there still room for further improvement?

To answer this question, disaggregate indicators have been developed for intensive industries. These indicators are used to track energy efficiency progress over time and also to calculate the technical potential for energy reductions that could be achieved by moving to BAT or BPT in each intensive sector. The conclusion is that the application of these technologies on a global basis could save 15 EJ of energy per year (Figure 11.13), which represents 13 percent of global energy use in industry in 2006.

In practice, the rate of implementation of BATs by industry depends on several factors, including relative energy costs, raw material availability and quality, equipment age, rate of return on investment, and regulations. Governments have at their disposal a wide range of policy instruments—including market mechanisms, fiscal policies, regulatory measures, and information schemes—to stimulate and accelerate the implementation of BATs.

Transport

The transport sector includes the movement of people and goods by road, rail, sea, and air. Between 1990 and 2006, global transport energy consumption increased by 41 percent to

93 EJ. In IEA member countries, the transport sector is taking an increasing share of oil and is currently responsible for over 60 percent of total final oil consumption.

More detailed analysis of the trends in energy consumption in the transport sector required passenger and freight transport to be analyzed separately since they are impacted by different underlying factors. The necessary disaggregated information is only available for a group of 19 IEA member countries (IEA19)[8] in the IEA database. For these countries, indicators that examine consumption per passenger-kilometers (pkm) or per tonne-kilometers (tkm) are developed. Decomposition analyses are also performed to separate and quantify the different factors impacting energy use of passenger light-duty vehicles (LDV) and freight trucks.

Passenger transport

Passenger LDV in IEA19 account for over half of transport demand for oil, and have been the main reason for the growth in oil demand over the last three decades. Light-duty vehicles remained the largest energy consumer, accounting for 87 percent of passenger transport energy consumption. They are also the fastest-growing mode, with an increase of 25 percent between 1990 and 2006 (Figure 11.14). Reducing the fuel intensity of cars (i.e. increasing the fuel efficiency) is therefore a key way of helping both to reduce dependence on oil and to limit CO_2 emissions from the transport sector.

Most policies targeting the passenger transport sector focus on car fuel economy—the energy required to drive 100 kilometers—and programs that encourage consumers to buy smaller and more efficient vehicles. The improvement in energy efficiency reflects, at least in part, that those policies have had a positive impact. According to available data, fuel economy of new cars has improved by 15 percent since 1990.

A number of factors such as vehicle technologies, driving conditions, and fuel efficiency policies have played an important role in both the absolute levels and trends observed. The

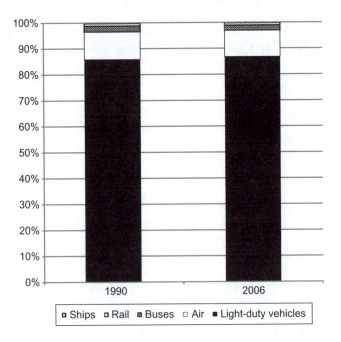

Figure 11.14 Passenger energy consumption by mode.

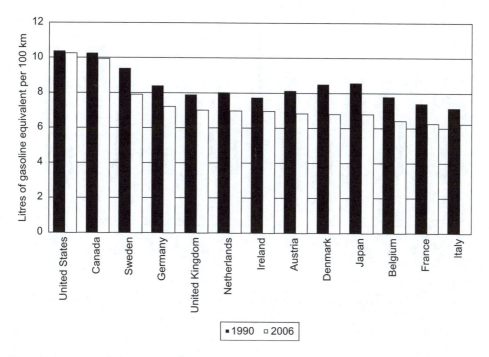

Figure 11.15 Average fuel economy of new cars.

average fuel economy of new cars decreased in all countries between 1990 and 2006 (Figure 11.15). In Europe, this was due to a combination of factors. The 1990s were characterized by the widespread diffusion of vehicles equipped with electronic control systems for fuel management and by stronger consumer demand for more efficient cars—a reaction to high fuel prices. Since the early 2000s, intensities declined further in Europe as a result of increased sales of direct-injection diesel cars.

By combining data on fuel economy with information about car use and ownership, it is possible to examine how different factors influence car energy use across countries (Figure 11.16). All countries belonging to the International Energy Agency, with the exception of Canada, showed increases in car ownership. For most countries, the growth in car ownership tended to increase per capita car energy consumption by about 1 percent per year. The impact of car usage (i.e. the distance traveled by each car) on per capita energy consumption is more varied across countries. In the countries where car usage actually fell, one partial explanation is the trend toward households owning more than one car as the journeys are shared between cars. As a result, travel per car tends to fall.

Freight transport

Detailed information on freight transport energy use and activity is also available for IEA19. Freight transport in IEA19 accounted for 30 percent of total transportation energy consumption in 2006. Between 1990 and 2006, energy consumption in freight transport increased by 31 percent to 13 EJ. The strong growth in freight energy use was almost entirely due to higher energy demand for trucking, which increased by 41 percent. Trucks are by far the largest energy user, accounting for 83 percent of the overall freight transport energy consumption in 2006.

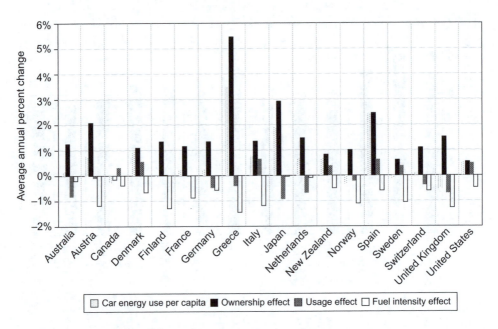

Figure 11.16 Decomposition of changes in car energy use per capita.

The energy intensities of trucks, trains, and ships vary significantly, with trucks being the most intensive (Figure 11.17). The difference in intensity between modes has important implications for energy consumption trends: because of its much higher energy intensity, growth in truck freight haulage drives up energy consumption much more quickly than growth in trains or ships. Consequently, efforts to reduce the intensity of trucking will lead to higher energy savings than reductions in trains and ships.

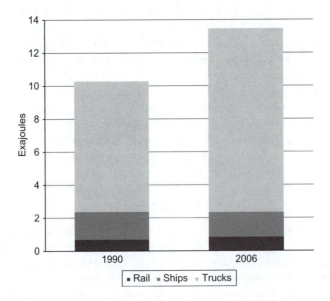

Figure 11.17 Freight transport energy consumption and intensities by mode, IEA19.

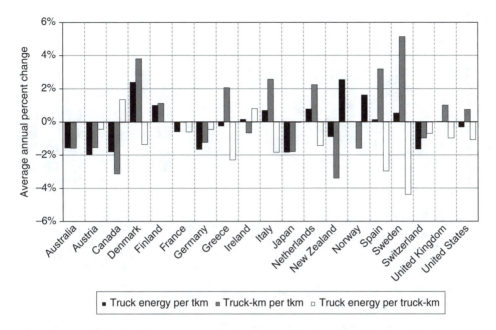

Figure 11.18 Decomposition of changes in truck energy intensity, 1990–2006.

As trucking dominates freight transport use, it is interesting to look in more detail at the factors affecting the overall energy intensity of truck freight haulage. These include: the load factor (average load per vehicle), the share of short-haul freight, vehicle fuel efficiency, driving behavior, traffic congestion, maximum allowable truck weight, and the availability and quality of the infrastructure for freight transport. In order to better assess the impact of such factors, a decomposition analysis of the overall energy intensity has been performed (Figure 11.18). The factors for which consistent information is available across countries are the truck-kilometers per tkm (which is the inverse of the load factor) and the vehicle energy intensity. These reveal that the overall energy intensity of trucking was most strongly influenced by the evolution of load factors.

The overall efficiency of truck freight transport has improved by 0.6 percent per year since 1990. Without the energy savings resulting from these improvements, truck freight transport energy consumption would have been 9 percent higher in 2006.

Overall energy efficiency trends

The previous sections highlighted how different types of indicators can be used to examine trends in energy use and efficiency for individual end-use sectors. This section shows how the decomposition approach can be used to explain how different factors impact total energy use and, in particular, to quantify the role of energy efficiency improvements. Take as an example the large variations among countries in how much energy per unit of GDP has fallen over time. To understand the extent to which this variation reflects differences in energy efficiency developments, it is necessary to separate the impact of changes in subsectoral energy intensities (which are used as a proxy for energy efficiency) from the effects of changes in economic structure and other factors that influence the demand for energy.

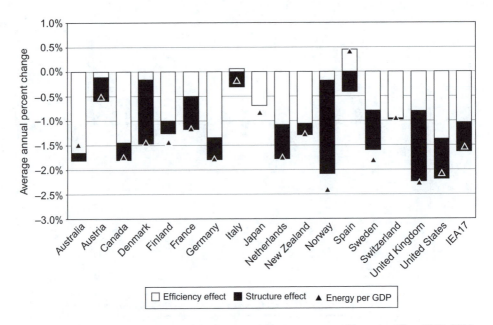

Figure 11.19 Changes in aggregate intensities decomposed into structure and intensity effect, 1990–2006.
Notes:
The figure only shows the relative changes since 1990 and so does not reflect absolute advances in energy efficiency. Some countries had achieved higher levels of energy efficiency than others prior to 1990.

Increased demand for energy services—reflecting increased ownership levels of electric household appliances, bigger houses, more personal travel by car, etc.—drives both energy use and energy use per GDP. Therefore, it is useful to examine how the ratio of energy to GDP is affected by changes in structure (as measured by the ratio of energy services to GDP) and in end-use intensities (such as the energy used to heat a square meter of floor space or car energy use per passenger-kilometer).

The intensity effect for the whole economy is calculated as the aggregate impact of the sectoral intensity effects. The results of aggregate impact calculations show that the energy intensity effect and changes in structure have both contributed to reduced energy consumption per unit of GDP (Figure 11.19). However, declining end-use intensities (the energy intensity effect) have been the most important factor. About 65 percent of the total decline in energy per GDP could be attributed to reductions from the energy intensity effect.

The relative contribution of structural and intensity effects to the overall trend varies among countries. With the exception of Italy and Spain, all IEA countries show that the intensity effect contributed to reducing the ratio of energy use to GDP: for most countries, it was the dominant factor.

It can be informative to compare these results with the information on the absolute levels of final energy intensity. Such a comparison shows that a country's energy intensity is slowly converging. Those countries with a high level of energy use per GDP in 1990 tend to have had the largest reductions in intensity. In contrast, those countries that initially had lower energy use per GDP have generally seen smaller declines in intensity.

Long-term energy savings from improved energy efficiency

The decline in energy intensities (i.e. improvements in energy efficiency) in the various end-use sectors led to energy savings across the whole economy. Without the energy efficiency

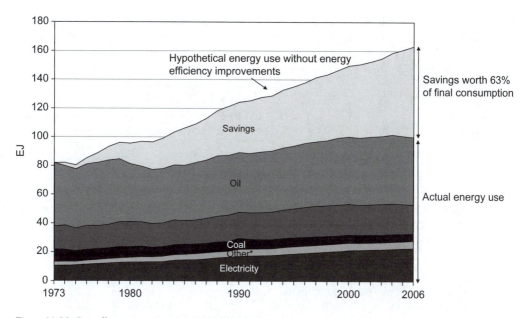

Figure 11.20 Overall energy savings in IEA11 from improvements in energy efficiency from 1973 to 2006 and sectors' contribution in 2006.

improvements that occurred between 1973 and 2006, energy use in IEA11 would have been 63 percent, or 63 EJ, higher in 2006 than it actually was (Figure 11.20). This makes energy savings the most important "fuel" in the IEA11 for this time period—that is, the amount of energy saved in 2006 was slightly higher than the actual consumption of oil, or of electricity and natural gas combined.

However, the rate of improvement since 1990 has been lower than in the period between 1973 and 1990. These findings provide an important policy conclusion: that the changes caused by the oil price shocks in the 1970s and the resulting energy policies did considerably more to control growth in energy demand than the energy efficiency and climate policies implemented since the 1990s. However, analysis shows that the rate of improvement has accelerated in recent years, and is trending toward the rate observed in the 1970s.

Conclusions and policy implications

The benefits of more efficient use of energy are well known and include enhanced energy security, reduced investment in energy infrastructure, lower fossil fuel dependency, increased competitiveness, and improved consumer welfare. Efficiency gains can also deliver environmental benefits by reducing greenhouse gas emissions and local air pollution. One of the first steps in achieving the necessary changes is to better understand how we are currently using energy and the various factors that drive or restrain demand. Influencing the trends in energy consumption requires an understanding of the factors driving it.

Energy efficiency indicators provide policymakers with many important insights about current energy consumption patterns, market developments in the end-use sectors, main drivers of increased energy use, and where the greatest potential for improvements in energy efficiency lies. The analysis presented shows how indicators can be used to help shape priorities for future actions and monitor progress.

Projections published by the IEA in *Energy Technology Perspectives 2010*[9] clearly demonstrate that rates of improvement in energy efficiency will need to be increased substantially to have a realistic chance of a more sustainable and secure energy future. The good news is that this is indeed possible; the results from the indicators analysis confirm that there is still significant scope for energy-efficiency improvements in buildings, industry, and transport. However, a key lesson of the past is that the widespread future deployment of more efficient technologies and practices will require very strong government action. The challenge is to find the right mix of market- and regulation-based policies to achieve cost-effective decisions regarding energy efficiency in all sectors.

Notes

1 International Energy Agency (IEA). 1997. *The Link Between Energy and Human Activity* (Paris: IEA/OECD); International Energy Agency (IEA). 2004. *Oil Crises and Climate Challenges: 30 Years of Energy Use in IEA Countries* (Paris: IEA/OECD); International Energy Agency (IEA). 2007. *Energy Use in the New Millennium: Trends in IEA Countries* Paris: IEA/OECD; International Energy Agency (IEA). 2008. *Worldwide Trends in Energy Use and Efficiency: Key Insights from IEA Indicators Analysis* (Paris: IEA/OECD).

2 International Energy Agency (IEA). 2009. *Towards a More Energy Efficient Future: Applying Indicators to Enhance Energy Policy* (Paris: IEA/OECD).

3 IEA11 countries are: Australia, Denmark, Finland, France, Germany, Italy, Japan, Norway, Switzerland, the United Kingdom, and the United States.

4 BAT is taken to mean that latest stage of development (state-of-the-art) of processes, facilities, or of methods of operation which include considerations regarding the practical suitability of a particular measure for enhancing energy efficiency. In contrast to BAT, BPT is a term that applies to technologies and processes that are currently deployed. BAT could, in many cases, be identical to BPT. In other cases, a new technology may have just emerged, but is not yet deployed. If this is the case, the BAT energy efficiency may be better than BPT.

5 The five most intensive industrial sectors are chemicals and petrochemicals, iron and steel, pulp and paper, cement, and aluminium.

6 For the household sector, IEA19 countries are: Australia, Austria, Canada, Denmark, Finland, France, Germany, Ireland, Italy, Japan, the Republic of Korea, the Netherlands, New Zealand, Norway, Spain, Sweden, Switzerland, the United Kingdom, and the United States.

7 IEA21 countries are: Australia, Austria, Belgium, Canada, Denmark, Finland, France, Germany, Greece, Italy, Japan, the Republic of Korea, the Netherlands, New Zealand, Norway, Portugal, Spain, Sweden, Switzerland, the United Kingdom, and the United States.

8 In the transport sectors, IEA19 countries are: Australia, Austria, Canada, Denmark, Finland, France, Germany, Greece, Ireland, Italy, Japan, the Netherlands, New Zealand, Norway, Spain, Sweden, Switzerland, the United Kingdom, and the United States.

9 International Energy Agency (IEA). 2010. *Energy Technology Perspectives 2010: Scenarios and Strategies to 2050* (Paris: IEA/OECD).

12

THE ENERGY SERVICES DIMENSION OF ENERGY SECURITY

Jaap C. Jansen and Adriaan J. Van der Welle

Introduction

The world energy supply–demand system has all the ingredients in the making for a lasting security of supply problem for humankind. This is poised to bring about a key policy challenge, in the medium and long term if not in the short term.

Worrisome global trends are unfolding with regard to factors determining the long-term cost of energy use. These suggest that the broader issue of supply security deserves urgent and persistent attention by policymakers. Virtually all energy supply chains—for both fossil fuels and non-fossil fuels—are facing huge supply limitations. Supply limitations do not only apply to fossil fuels but also to minerals, resulting in adverse impacts for a range of renewable and energy storage technologies (HCSS, 2009; USGS, 2010). Official projection providers such as the International Energy Agency (IEA) and US Energy Information Administration (EIA), tend to project roughly a 45 percent higher world primary energy use by 2030 than current use (approximately 500 exajoules, i.e. 5×10^{20} joules) and a near doubling by year 2050. Several energy policy analysts (e.g., Turner, 2008; Moriarty and Honnery, 2009; Nel and Cooper, 2009; Rutledge, 2009) question the feasibility of these mainly demand-driven energy supply projections.

The seriousness of limitations to global primary energy use, if true, may provide some comfort to climate change concerns. For instance, the potential for strongly increasing GHG emission from coal combustion seems, typically, to be strongly overrated as seems to be the case with global coal reserves (Rutledge, 2009; Kavalov and Peteves, 2007; EWG, 2007; Tao and Li, 2007). Yet in the absence of strong and enduring effective policy responses, these limitations are poised to be reflected by a steeply upward long-term trend in fossil fuel and electricity prices, along with rising price volatility and more frequent physical supply disruptions.

In low- and medium-income countries, security of supply (SoS) tends to be assigned quite a high priority on the national energy policy agenda. To date, the energy policy issue topping the agenda of policymakers in most OECD countries is "climate change," while in emerging economies the issue is also contemplated closely, although so far allusions to hard commitments are prudently avoided. In OECD countries "energy security" is currently also ranking high on the priority list, whilst certainly in the developing countries, particularly those poorly endowed with fossil fuels, "energy security" is considered important. The latter policy issue tends to go in cycles— typically short-lasting—given prime attention by policymakers in the wake of sudden price spikes in the world oil market or (threats of) market intervention and physical supply disruption of oil or natural gas by major exporting countries. Cases in point are the US$147 per barrel oil price spike in the summer of 2008 and the disruption in Russian gas supplies to the EU through the Drushba gas pipeline in January 2009.

This chapter is structured as follows. Section 2 introduces the concepts of energy security and energy services security. A theoretical framework for analysis of energy services security (ESS) is presented in Section 3. A simple application of this framework, focusing on the delivery of electric energy end-use service, is explained in Section 4, and some major policy-oriented conclusions are drawn in Section 5.

Energy security versus energy services security

An oft-adopted definition of "energy insecurity" is "the loss of welfare that may occur as a result of a change in price or availability of energy" (Bohi and Toman, 1996).[1] This definition considers the economic impacts of energy insecurity. According to this definition, a situation of extreme energy security would be characterized by uninterrupted supply of "energy"—that is, fuel (derivatives) and electricity—at competitive prices.

Another approach considers the policy perspectives of energy security. It aims at a secure energy supply system meeting some key requirements. For example, APERC proposes an energy supply system should achieve (APERC, 2007):

1. *Availability* (depletion, inadequate upstream and midstream investments, etc.).
2. *Accessibility* (restrictions imposed by governments of fuel-exporting countries, exercise of market power, exposure of fuel supply chain components to disruptive events including weather-related ones, technical failures, human errors, or acts of terrorism or war, etc.).
3. *Affordability* (cost per unit of energy to end-users—broken down by the main components of fuel supply chains—might compromise societal security).
4. *Acceptability* (environmental concerns and social/cultural barriers hampering supply because of negative perceptions among the population).

The issue label "energy security" misses a fundamental point: energy is typically not in short supply. Rather, it is *useful energy*, not *energy per se*, that is in short supply.[2] Walt Patterson refers to the First Law of Thermodynamics which implies that no single joule of energy gets lost (Patterson, 2007). By implication, nobody produces or consumes energy. Given these observations, energy security strictly speaking is a non-issue.

This seems trivial but it is not. Patterson observes that ambient energy is, by and large, plentiful across the earth: almost everywhere existing in orders of magnitude above current needs for useful energy. Ambient energy includes sources such as wind power, solar energy, river flow, and marine energy. In principle, ambient energy can be used directly, converted into electricity or into a stored form of energy. The abundance of energy around the world is further enhanced, if rather poorly dispersed globally, by natural resources that embody stored energy such as uranium, coal, natural gas, oil, biomass, and geothermal. At the same time, worldwide expanding conurbations of mega-cities pose local challenges for adequate access to ambient energy sources.

This brings in the direct connection of supply security issues with *energy services*. Energy services can be defined as economic goods produced by the deployment of useful energy.[3] In turn, useful energy is obtained directly from ambient energy flows, for example solar heating, or from energy contained in energy carriers including electricity. A major focal point of this conversion is the part of the energy transferred by energy carriers to deliver useful energy that does not meet this purpose (i.e., "energy losses"). Note furthermore that energy services include outputs from non-energy industrial feedstocks.[4]

The demand for end-use energy services generates final energy demand. This, in turn, impacts activity levels all along the electricity and fuel supply chains up to primary energy supplies. Table 12.1 provides, for the main energy uses, that is, electricity generation, transport, heating, and cooling, some broad avenues for reducing demand for fossil fuels in meeting end-use energy services.

We propose to use the term *energy services security* (ESS) instead of energy security as the notion that covers the central topic of this chapter.[5] Hereafter, ESS refers to *the extent to which the population in a defined area (country or region) can have access to affordably and competitively priced, environmentally acceptable energy services of adequate quality.* This definition implies an end-use orientation to enable a genuinely integrated approach to the multifaceted ESS issue.

Table 12.1 Broad framework of major options for reducing societal dependency on fossil fuels on longer timescales

Main application	Fossil fuel	Major options	
		Demand reduction	Switch away from fossil fuels
Power generation	Oil & Natural gas & Coal	Efficiency standards for generation and power-using equipment	Renewables-based generation
		Reduction T&D losses	Nuclear power (?)
		Demand-side saving behavioral changes	
Road vehicles	Oil & Gas (CNG, GTL) & Coal (CTL)	Fuel/CO_2 efficiency standards	(Hybrid) electric-battery vehicles
			Biofuels
		Demand-side saving behavioral changes	Hydrogen fuel cell vehicles
		Sustainability-oriented spatial planning	Modal shift away from FF, e.g. towards bikes for short-distance trips
Train	Oil & Coal	Fuel/CO_2 efficiency standards	Electrification
			Biomass
		Demand-side saving behavioral changes	Modal shift away from FF
Ships, Aircraft	Oil	Fuel/CO_2 efficiency standards	Biofuels
		Demand-side saving behavioral changes	Modal shift away from FF
Residential & commercial heating	Oil & Natural gas & Coal	Efficiency standards for buildings/heating equipment	Biomass
			Electric heating
			District heating/μCHP on green gas
		Demand-side saving behavioral changes	Solar water heaters
			Heat pumps (ambient/aquifers)
Industrial process heat	Oil & Natural gas & Coal	Efficiency standards	Biomass
		Good housekeeping	CHP
		Process changes	Substitutes and structural demand shifts away from FF-intensive materials/products

Table 12.1 (continued)

Main application	Fossil fuel	Major options	
		Demand reduction	Switch away from fossil fuels
Industrial feedstock	Oil & Natural gas & Coal	(Efficiency standards)	Degradable biomass substitutes (e.g. plastics) Biochemicals substitutes (e.g. biomass-based fertilizer)
		Demand-side savings	DRI based on biogas and electricity Charcoal

Legend:
FF: fossil fuels
CNG: compressed natural gas
GTL: gas-to-liquids
CTL: coal-to-liquids
T&D: transmission and distribution
DRI: direct reduced iron

Theoretical framing

Much recent work on "energy security" focuses on vulnerability to supply disruptions of internationally traded fuels, notably oil and natural gas, affecting fuel prices and even the outright physical availability of fuels (e.g., Bohi and Toman, 1996; Lefèvre, 2007).[6] The main theme in this approach is on (mitigating) supply-side market power and its adverse impact on economic welfare in fuel-importing countries. Other analysts also consider the vulnerability to international trade in fuels for fuel-exporting countries, zooming in on the economic aspects of "demand security" (e.g., Alhajji, 2008) as well as the social and political impacts, investigating the validity of the "resource curse" hypothesis (e.g. Karl, 1997 Bannon and Collier, 2003; Collier, 2008). Analysts considering the politics of (preventing) disruptions in international fuel supply chains examine the destabilizing impacts on international political relationships (e.g., Müller-Kraenner, 2007; Klare, 2008).

Disruptions and vulnerabilities

Recently a useful overarching framework has been proposed by Nicolas Lefèvre (2010) and a consortium of consultants led by Ecofys to map supply disruptions and vulnerabilities, and analyze their effects.Ecofys *et al.* (2009) define three broad categories of root causes of energy insecurity: (1) extreme events, (2) inadequate market structures, and (3) resource concentration. Resource depletion is subsumed by the third category. Table 12.1 illustrates this categorization.

Historic or potential energy security disruptions and vulnerabilities can trigger a chain of knock-on effects in distinct stages, each with (potential) net loss of economic welfare. This is depicted in Figure 12.1. This approach enables a structured identification and analysis of the impacts of vulnerabilities as well as alternative policies and measures on energy insecurity, or rather, as we would phrase it, energy services insecurity.

Table 12.2 Classification of root causes of energy insecurity

Category	Type	Brief description
Extreme events	Extreme weather	Extreme weather events can temporarily disable energy infrastructures and the supply of energy. A recent example is the impact of Hurricane Katrina, which hit the Gulf of Mexico in 2005, disabling a significant portion of the US oil and gas production and processing capacity. There are however many other possible extreme weather events with potential energy security consequences including those which impact on the demand side (e.g. exceptionally cold or hot days) or on the supply side (e.g. reduced cooling water availability).
	Large scale accidents	Much like extreme weather events, accidents can lead to unplanned outages of key energy infrastructures.
	Acts of terrorism	Acts of terrorism against key infrastructures (e.g. refineries or pipelines) or bottlenecks along specific energy trade routes (e.g. the straight of Hormuz) can cause disruptions to energy systems.
	Strikes	Due to the strategic nature of energy, strikes or other forms of social unrest may specifically target the operation of key energy system components.
Inadequate market structure	Insufficient investments in new capacity	Market structures which fail to generate timely investments in key energy system infrastructures can contribute to making the system more vulnerable and ultimately generate energy insecurity.
	Load balancing failure in electricity markets	Because electricity is not storable in any meaningful volumes system operators must effectively balance supply and demand in real time to ensure system reliability. The task is challenging and requires that certain technical characteristics be met. When this is not the case systems sometime fail or do not operate in an efficient manner causing a loss of welfare for users.
Supply shortfall associated with resource concentration		Due to the concentration of resources in certain regions of the world, exploration and production as well as transport of fuels are also concentrated. This generates a certain degree of market power which can adversely affect energy systems.

Source: Adapted from Ecofys *et al.* (2009), p. 12.

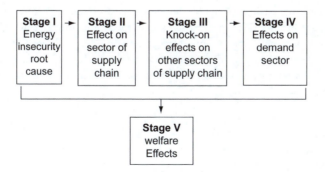

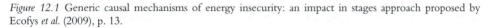

Figure 12.1 Generic causal mechanisms of energy insecurity: an impact in stages approach proposed by Ecofys *et al.* (2009), p. 13.

Resilience as a key concept

Most recent work on energy security fails to consider the resilience of a defined country (or region) to cope with the impacts of adverse ESS ("energy security") trends and events. At best, supply-side security-enhancing measures, such as diversification of the fuel mix, foreign suppliers, and international fuel transport routes and modes, are analyzed. Typically, recent "'energy security" policy research documents may mention some demand-side policies and measures such as energy intensities but with little further elaboration. A notable exception is Scheepers *et al.* (2007) who explicitly consider *inter alia* energy intensity on the demand side.

The magnitude of risks to ESS security is not only determined by exposure to vulnerabilities on the supply side of energy inputs driving the delivery of energy services. The resilience of a recipient society to adverse supply-side vulnerability events/trends works as a cushion that dampens the impacts of supply-side vulnerability.

Energy services security (ESS) is a more inclusive concept than energy security. The timely performance and affordability of desired energy services at quality levels considered adequate by the end-users for the end-use applications concerned is not only affected (in a negative way) by all sorts of supply-side vulnerabilities. The key point is that a broad range of resilience factors that exercise a stabilizing influence on the robustness of the energy services delivery system is identified and thoroughly analyzed as well.

ESS components

Myriad one-event impulses and gradually strengthening or declining forces exercise a negative or positive impact on the level of energy services security. In order to bring structure to the analysis of these ESS aspects, we categorize these ESS-change-initiating phenomena into main ESS-content perspectives, namely *ESS dimensions*.

Each dimension consists of main components and, where appropriate, subcomponents, sub-subcomponents, etc., down to the most elementary dimension attribute level. Components (subcomponents) are also referred to as main (sub-) themes or aspects. Hence, the dimensions have a branch structure, each branch being shaped by the distinct dimension components. Where feasible, we allocate indicators of ESS content attributes to dimension (sub-) components. Many ESS indicators are of a quantitative nature, while others are of an ordinal ranking nature with at least two scoring options. We wish to restate that, for each relevant dimension next to major ESS-reducing vulnerabilities, major ESS-raising system resilience attributes need to be identified to partly/fully/more than offset these vulnerabilities.

On the one hand, each distinct ESS dimension has to bundle a broad range of related ESS content aspects. On the other hand, ESS content aspects encompassed by different dimensions should have no, or at most a fairly remote, logical relationship with each other. Furthermore, a clear differentiation among countries (regions) should be possible in principle with respect to their characteristics regarding each of these ESS dimensions. Based on these criteria we propose the following ESS dimensions:

1. Reliability
2. Energy costs
3. Policy framework
4. Public acceptance.

We have refrained from introducing environmental impact as an additional dimension. In the Trias Energetica (competitiveness, security of supply, environmental impact), this dimension is covered by another principal energy policy domain. Moreover, to the extent that environmental impact is relevant for public acceptance of technologies used in major supply chains enabling the delivery of energy services, it is encompassed under the public acceptance dimension.

ESS contextual attributes

Two principal contextual attributes cross-cut among components of each ESS dimension, that is, *timescale* and *location*. They do not contribute content attributes as such to the ESS concept. Yet they provide essential contextual information needed for interpreting an indicator of an ESS content attribute. The value of certain content attributes of the ESS issue can change substantially, depending on the timescale and the location boundaries that we consider. Key questions in this respect are:

- For which timescale does the metric provide relevant information on the content attribute concerned? Short-term ESS issues as against long-term ESS issues may require rather different policies and measures.
- For which jurisdiction does the metric provide relevant information on the content attribute concerned? This, in turn, is relevant for the level at which possible public interventions should be considered.

The timescale for which energy services security is contemplated is quite relevant. Typically, for very short-term time horizons, disruptions in physical availability of energy services and sudden price spikes attract key attention by private stakeholders and the public sector alike. For long-term time frames the risks of structurally rising fuel and electricity prices and increasing price volatility are key ESS concerns.[7] The reliability or physical availability of energy sources to drive energy services is the prime concern in near-term time frames. This is exemplified by the need for second-to-second balancing of supply and demand by power systems and the need for reliable gas supply in cold winter days in, for example, many European countries where space heating is predominantly gas-based.

Most economics actors are driven by myopic time-bounded behavior. To counteract this serious externality of myopic time-bounded rationality, guidance by policymakers to foster long-term ESS would seem to be of key importance.

Three localization aspects of ESS problems can be discerned relative to the location where the energy services concerned are (to be) provided. First, the "control area," within which jurisdiction the energy services concerned are to be delivered, is of relevance. Second, the location of impacts of an ESS-disruptive phenomenon along the relevant supply chains of energy services is important. We note that the relevant (market) area for certain ESS aspects, for example the price of oil, is the whole world. Alternatively, within power systems proper, the areas in which knock-on impacts of supply disruptions and vulnerabilities can propagate are more regionalized, that is, the synchronized power areas that can cover several countries and the control areas of distinct system operators are of relevance to that effect.

The third aspect regards the localization of the impacts of an ESS-change-initiating factor. A good understanding of the local conditions at each successive impact area contributes importantly to the analysis of ESS. Detailed analysis of each key component/node of the main supply chains that enable the performance of a certain category of end-use service is essential for a good understanding of the risk and resilience factors affecting ESS for the category of energy services considered. Supply chain components/nodes are not necessarily cross-cutting across all ESS dimensions. Hence, consideration should be given to including important supply chain nodes in the composition of those ESS dimensions for which they assume relevance. This might be the case, notably, for some components of reliability (dimension 1) and energy costs (dimension 2).

Applying the framework: a fuel price disturbance

A simple example might help to demonstrate how the theoretical framework can be applied. We analyze in a generic way just one effect of a fuel price disturbance, that is, the knock-on price effect upon the cost of an end-use energy service along the supply chain of a (secondary) final energy carrier.

The fuel supply chain destined for end-use energy services delivered by the electricity supply sector can be structured in a generic fashion as follows (in backward supply chain direction):

- demand for an electricity end-use energy service;
- electricity demand by end-use appliances;
- demand for distribution network and ancillary system services;
- demand for transmission network and ancillary system services;
- demand for electricity generation services;
- electricity generation;
- transport chain of input energy carriers to electricity generation plants;
- (applicable for secondary energy carriers only) PES-SEC conversion plants; transformation of primary energy source (PES; primary fuel) into the secondary energy carrier (SEC) considered used as an input fuel by the power supply sector;
- transport chains of PES (embarkation, haulage, disembarkation), with elaboration of routes and modes (e.g. LNG, piped natural gas);
- production or import of the primary energy source (PES).

The second ESS dimension distinguished in the theoretical framework introduced in the preceding section is energy cost. Several ESS aspects can be categorized as components shaping this dimension. One of these aspects is price escalation. The cost/price change of a primary fuel, for example natural gas, is transmitted to the cost of an electrical energy service, as shown in Table 12.3.

Table 12.3 Generic analysis scheme for determining the impact of (changes in) the unit value (unit cost; price) of a primary energy source on the cost of an end-use energy service, allowing for the various supply chain components

Energy service (ES)	Description	(1)
Unit:	Dimension A	(2)
Unit value:	€2009	(3)
End-use appliance	Description	(4)
Final energy carrier (FEC)	Description	(5)
Unit:	Dimension B	(6)
Unit value:	€2009	(7)
Units required/unit of energy services	Dim B / Dim A	(8)
Cost of FEC input	€2009	(9) = (8) ★ (7)
Cost share of FEC in ES	%	(10) = (9) / (3) ★ 100%
Energy conversion plant	Description	(11)
Input fuel for final energy carrier	Description	(12)
Primary energy source (PES)	Description	(13)
Unit (primary energy source):	Dimension C	(14)
Unit value:	€2009	(15)
Units required / unit of final energy carrier	Dim C / Dim B	(16)
Cost of PES in cost FEC input	€2009	(17) = (16) ★ (15)
Cost share PES in cost FEC input	%	(18) = (17) / (9) ★ 100
Cost share of PES in ES	%	(19) = (18) ★ (10) / 100%

Note that, in principle, the main supply chains can include supply chains for non-energy inputs, for example steel or metallic minerals, and even non-material inputs. Non-energy constraints may also create huge challenges to ESS. Just some examples are: skilled manpower limitations to operate the electricity transmission and distribution networks or to operate nuclear energy cycle facilities; shortages of dry-bulk carriers to transport hard coal; shortages on the steel market to produce various types of power plants, including nuclear power plants and wind turbines; shortages of copper affecting notably T&D networks, wind turbines, and solar photovoltaic equipment; shortage of platinum to produce fuel cells; shortages of lithium to produce lithium-ion batteries, etc.

The above scheme enables the analysis, in a structured way and in a backward chain direction, of how the demand for a unit of end-use energy service ultimately depends on the delivery of a certain volume of primary fuel. Analyzing the upstream dimension of the supply chain, for each of the services needed it can be considered if efficiency, diversification, and/or substitution improvements can be realized. Ultimately, the relationship between the incremental demand for the end-use energy service and the standard requirement for the primary fuel considered can be established. In turn, this paves the way to establish the impact of a change in the price of the fuel on the delivery cost of one unit of the end-use service considered. But it also permits the gauging of the impact of efficiency improvements regarding intermediary supply chain services on, for example, the import dependence for the fuel concerned.

Why should energy services be taken as a point of departure?

This chapter has introduced a theoretical framework for energy-related supply security issues that takes energy services as a point of departure. This diverges from the conventional approach which departs from pre-set demand-driven scenarios. Key parameter values of such scenarios, such as given (high) rates of economic growth, are fed into complex but highly stylized economy-energy-environmental models, which are specified on the basis of observed relationships, including technological progress captured by observed technology learning rates. Next the model provides the required supply of fuels and secondary energy carriers, including, importantly, power and, in turn, the investment needs for the distinct energy subsectors to ensure adequacy of supply, including certain minimum redundancy standards.

To ensure "energy security," most policymakers tend to content themselves by and large with two major activities. These are: (1) standard energy infrastructure planning and plan realization, and (2) diversification of fuel sourcing and fuel transport routing to hedge against resource concentration as their main supply security concerns. In other words, they tend to aim to enable citizens and other private actors within their jurisdictions to enjoy pre-set growth in material prosperity without having to assume any responsibility that the energy requirements will be matched by adequate supply. Where required, the invisible hand of the price mechanism guides private actors towards making their part of the infrastructural investments required.

We posit that the passive, demand-driven, top-down energy systems planning and operational management paradigm is in urgent need of replacement. Energy systems planning and operation is to become a shared responsibility of all actors using energy supply systems, including notably the beneficiaries of end-use energy services. This is to be enabled by regulatory and contractual frameworks making the true time- and location-differentiated cost of all major elements of the energy supply system transparent. This applies to energy end-use services, energy system services all along the supply chain, and, last but not least, energy resources transparent to the maximum extent possible. Flexibility and responsiveness on the demand side are key to raising the resilience of a country to actual and potential vulnerabilities to energy services security. Improved market functioning with transparent price discovery signals and improved and timely public disclosure of relevant market information are key strategy components to raising a demand response. Raising awareness among end-users of the resource intensity and environmental footprint of the choices they make to use their discretional purchasing power is relevant as well. This will help to articulate social preferences in the way of appreciably less resource-intensive portfolios of energy services.

It is evident that raising the level of prosperity and productive employment is receiving top priority by governments throughout the world, including in particular the emerging Asian economies. Doing so proactively over a long-term time horizon, warrants integration of long-term energy services security and environmental sustainability concerns into all other policy domains. This holds true all the more so, as choices regarding investments in buildings, public infrastructure, and spatial planning tend to be characterized by very long capital turnover periods with strong lock-in effects regarding patterns of energy and material use over long periods ahead. High resilience to vulnerabilities regarding energy services security and environmental integrity cannot be achieved without the active engagement of the general public. An energy services security approach, rather than a predominantly supply-side-oriented energy security approach, will help to make this happen.

Notes

1 This section is based on Jansen and Seebregts (2010).
2 A major point in case is that technology for the conversion of many kinds of ambient energy is still lacking commercial, and in certain instances even technical, maturity.
3 Gary Kendall defines an energy service as a useful output of an energy input (Kendall, 2008: 153).
4 The energy resources to meet this category of energy services are also part of the supply security equation. Hence, energy policy legislation neglecting this category—e.g. the newly adopted EU directive on renewable energy sources—weakens the coherence between different domains of energy policy.
5 See also Jansen and Seebregts, 2010.
6 This section is based on Jansen 2009.
7 This also holds for the contract-based segment of the natural gas markets. Such contracts are usually indexed on oil product price benchmarks or on benchmark prices of spot markets for natural gas. In north-west Europe a trend appears to be emerging towards a shift away from oil-based pricing ("gas-to-gas" competition: see e.g. Stern, 2009).

References

Alhajji, A.F. 2008. "What is Energy Security?" *Energy Politics* 4 (Spring).

Bannon, I. and P. Collier (eds.). 2003. *Natural Resources and Violent Conflict: Options and Actions* (Washington, DC: World Bank).

Bohi, D.R. and M.A. Toman. 1996 *The Economics of Energy Supply Security* (Norwell, MA: Kluwer).

Collier, P. 2008. *The Bottom Billion: Why the Poorest Countries are Failing and What can be Done About It* (New York: Oxford University Press).

ECOFYS, ERAS, REDPOINT. 2009. *Analysis of Impacts of Climate Policies on Energy Security: Final Report*. Report prepared for DG Environment of the European Commission (London and Utrecht: European Commission).

The Hague Centre for Strategic Studies (HCSS). 2009. *Scarcity of Minerals: A Strategic Security Issue* (The Hague: HCSS).

Jansen, J.C. 2009. "Energy Services Security: Some Metrics and Policy Issues," paper presented at the fourth ENERDAY conference, Dresden, April 4.

Jansen, J.C. and A.J. Seebregts. 2010. "Long-Term Energy Services Security: What is it and how can it be Measured and Valued?" *Energy Policy* 38: 1654–1664.

Karl, T.K. 1997. *The Paradox of the Plenty: Oil Booms and the Petro-States* (Berkeley, Los Angeles, and London: University of California Press).

Kavalov, B. and S.D. Peteves. 2007. *The Future of Coal*. Report EUR 22744 EN (Petten, the Netherlands: DG JRC and Institute for Energy, February).

Kendall, G. 2008. *Plugged In: The End of the Oil Age* (Brussels: World Wide Fund for Nature).

Klare, M.T. 2008. *Rising Powers Shrinking Planet: The New Geopolitics of Energy* (New York: Metropolitan Books).

Lefèvre, N. 2007. *Security and Climate Policy: Assessing Interactions* (Paris: OECD and International Energy Agency).

Lefèvre, N. 2010. "Measuring the Energy Security Implications of Fossil Fuel Resource Concentration," *Energy Policy* 38: 1635–1644.

Moriarty P. and D. Honnery. 2009. "What Energy Levels can the Earth Sustain?" *Energy Policy* 37: 2469–2474.

Müller-Kraenner, S. 2007. *Energy Security: Re-Measuring the World* (London and Sterling, VA: Earthscan).

Nel, W.P. and C.J. Cooper. 2009. "Implications of Fossil Fuel Constraints on Economic Growth and Global Warming," *Energy Policy* 37: 166–180.

Patterson, W. 2007. *Keeping the Lights On: Towards Sustainable Electricity* (London: Earthscan).

Rutledge, D. 2009. *Hubbert's Peak, The Coal Question, and Climate Change*. PPT presentation. Available at: http://Rutledge.caltech.edu.

Stern, J. 2009. *Continental European Long-Term Gas Contracts: Is a Transition Away from Oil Product-Linked Pricing Inevitable and Imminent?* Report no. NG 34 (Oxford: Institute for Energy Studies, September).

Tao, Z. and M. Li. 2007. "What is the Limit of Chinese Coal Supplies: A STELLA model of Hubbert Peak," *Energy Policy* 35: 3145–3154.

Turner, G.M. 2008. "A Comparison of the Limits to Growth with 30 Years of Reality," *Global Environmental Change* 18: 397–411.

US Geological Survey (USGS). 2010. *Mineral Commodity Summaries 2010* (Washington, DC: United States Government Printing Office).

13

THE INDUSTRIAL DIMENSION OF ENERGY SECURITY

Geoffrey K. Pakiam[1]

Few words so innocently incorporate into their basic meaning as much simplifying illusion as does the word "policy."

Cordell Moore[2]

Introduction

After years of relative neglect, clean energy technologies are once again cultivating widespread public attention. It has become respectable in both the public domain and highest echelons of political office to speak of a "clean energy technology race" involving the world's leading economies. In his latest bestseller, Thomas Friedman asserts that "clean energy is … much more than just electric power … the country that dominates [clean energy technologies] will have … the most national security, the most economic security, and the most energy security."[3] *Clean Edge*, a prominent market research firm, suggests that policies to accelerate the development of clean technologies should focus on the positive gains from "energy and national security, job creation, environmental protection and global economic competitiveness."[4] Within the US government, President Barack Obama has made clean energy development a consistent anchor of his policy agenda, for instance declaring to a joint session of Congress that "[it] is time for America to lead again … to truly transform our economy, protect our security, and save our planet from the ravages of climate change, we need to ultimately make clean, renewable energy the profitable kind of energy."[5] The American Clean Energy and Security Act (ACESA) of 2009 bluntly states that it aims "to create clean energy jobs, achieve energy independence, reduce global warming pollution and transition to a clean energy economy."[6] Companion legislation pending Senate approval also espouses identical goals, virtually word-for-word.[7] According to the logic of these claims then, national economies that lead the growing clean technology industry will eventually accrue a number of interrelated prizes. These include greater economic power, a healthier living environment, better jobs, and a more secure energy future. In addition, it is often assumed that governments have a large role to play in supporting the growth of nascent clean technology industries, using a number of policy levers to aid economic restructuring.[8]

Intuitively and normatively, such claims can be extremely compelling. Few would deny the intrinsic value of a future where material prosperity and comfortable living can coexist with assured access to clean air, water, and other essential natural resources ad infinitum. Evidence of anthropogenic climate change due to rising levels of fossil fuel usage also suggests that current patterns of energy use will eventually have to shift towards less intensive greenhouse gas (GHG)-emitting methods as part of mitigation efforts. On the basis of this shift, new clean energy industries will be established, expanded, and will gradually supplant older, obsolete energy technologies. This chapter, however, will argue that such a trajectory is neither guaranteed nor a natural evolutionary process akin to a "survival of the cleanest." The broad idea of a clean energy race for greater energy security obscures a number of conflicting motives, dynamics, and terms of reference. Disentangling these different strands is crucial if we are to avoid being misled by sweeping narratives that not only fail to account for specific local complexities, but also ignore other compelling normative goals which may be antithetical to clean energy technology development. The vast range of concerns and goals that the clean tech race narrative ultimately encompasses—energy security, environmental policy, technological change, development strategies, poverty alleviation, the roles of governments and markets in resource allocation, natural resources, social welfare, cultural change, inequality, competitiveness, and foreign policy, among others—cannot be discussed extensively within the limits of a single chapter. Instead, we seek to further our general understanding of the narrative by outlining the history of a complex and overlapping relationship between two core terms: *energy security*, and the government policies being used to accelerate the development of clean energy technologies, which we shall call, for the lack of a better term, *industrial policies*.

There are good reasons for narrowing our focus down to these two key terms. Many analysts and policymakers have long discussed how governments and markets might play optimal roles in enhancing the energy security of nation states in an interdependent international system. Few, however, have sought to place this discussion within a broader context which highlights the fact that modern energy services ultimately rely on technologies that are being continuously incubated, commercialized, and produced for deployment. Many of these processes are influenced by state interventions generally known as industrial policies. These include policies for research, commercialization, market development, and maximizing synergies to build productive capabilities. A more systematic approach to clean energy technology development requires us to delve into the nexus between actual policies driven by energy security concerns and those driven by imperatives to build industrial capabilities to produce and deploy energy technologies. This, in turn, requires a deep knowledge of the existing political and economic realities that shape the actual processes of policymaking in specific contexts. In these local contexts, decisions to set agendas and implement policies only surface through struggles over power, different value priorities, and fortuitous circumstances. These micro-level social interactions, in turn, take place against a broader backdrop of shifts in political, economic, and social norms over time.

Seen via this socio-historical perspective, this chapter will seek to demonstrate that the clean energy race narrative downplays a number of major complications and ambiguities in its promises of benefits flowing from clean energy "leadership." For example, it will be shown that it is possible to lead in certain areas of clean energy, such as the deployment of specific technologies and the amount of electricity generated from these sources, while concurrently lag in terms of net balances from the trade of clean energy products. At the same time, it is unclear whether trade deficits in specific clean energy technologies should be seen as a sign of overall economic strength or weakness, unless more detailed economic analysis is carried out. As it stands, the clean tech race narrative is less an accurate reflection of reality and more of an argument designed to support a political consensus for more aggressive and protectionist government measures in clean energy technology. Industrial policies motivated by energy security concerns have indeed made important contributions to the development of clean energy technologies, but great care must be taken to ensure that the right policies are chosen for tasks with multiple goals. For example, industrial policies to support a domestic clean energy technology sector with concurrent aims to ensure greater energy security may be counterproductive if they raise the costs of imported clean energy components as a result. For energy security analysts, efforts must therefore not just focus on security agendas and priorities. They must also seek to confront the complexities of industrial policy formulation and implementation, as they occur both in public policy theory and in the reality of local contexts.

The two key questions that drive this chapter's inquiry are as follows:

1. How do energy security policies influence a government's industrial policies?
2. How do industrial policies influence the production and deployment of clean energy technologies?

The bulk of this chapter is thus devoted to answering these questions, drawing on evidence from a case study of the USA's energy sector between the years 1977 and 2010.

Before we can do so, however, our terms of reference need to be further clarified for better application to the case study. There are three sources of ambiguity. First, defining the scope of the clean energy technology sector is tricky. There is much disagreement over whether certain forms of energy, such as nuclear fission, "clean" coal, and biofuels, should be included in the sector, since many of the supposed solutions to their environmental consequences have neither been found nor definitively proven.[9] Second, industrial policies imply a certain subset of options for government intervention in markets. However, there is little consensus regarding a satisfactory definition of the term, let alone agreement regarding the overall effectiveness of such policies in either theory or practice. Third, energy security, as other chapters in this volume have shown, is a very loose term subject to contestations over its definition and theoretical concept. Our usage of case studies allows us to circumvent this issue to some extent: contextual approaches to energy security analysis focus more on the actual security conceptualizations of policymakers, as opposed to mainly drawing inferences from abstract discussions of energy security. Nevertheless, not only are concepts of energy security often contested by different policymakers, but the actual process of energy security *policymaking* itself can be complex, opaque, and contradictory at times. We see this, however, as less an inherent weakness of the context-specific approach and rather more a reflection of the reality that analysts and policymakers have to face up to if they are to make any significant headway in getting their policy prescriptions successfully adopted in practice.

The issue here is not to attempt the Sisyphean task of resolving these ambiguities for good. Instead, we aim to render them more manageable in ways that can provide useful insights from the case studies, thus helping to answer the two key questions at hand. We can immediately resolve some of these ambiguities by briefly noting two additional limitations of our study. First, we do not attempt to cover the entire clean energy sector, however defined. Our focus is on wind: its technologies and industries, including activities such as research and development, manufacturing, deployment and maintenance, as well as associated ancillary services. It thus follows that most of our discussions regarding industrial policies will focus on policies supporting the US wind sector. We also acknowledge that, in many quarters, industrial policies are understood as instruments geared towards facilitating a process of economic restructuring across an entire economy. Our general discussions will take this view into account. Second, we are less concerned about evaluating the relative effectiveness of different industrial policies in support of the wind power sector's growth, than to simply try and outline the multiple ways in which industrial policies and energy security concerns intersect with regard to clean technologies. However, highlighting these links still requires an investigation of recent sector growth trends and policy outcomes in our case study.

Conceptualizing energy security

"Energy" is viewed with different conceptual lenses by different groups of users. These lenses are often implicitly worn and can be complementary at times, yet incompatible in other contexts. Within the US context, for instance, researchers have argued that there are at least five distinct views of energy usage: scientific, economic, ecological, social welfare, and energy security.[10] Each view frames the "energy" issue in a particular way. Coherently weighing the relative costs and benefits of a possible course of action becomes virtually impossible if these frameworks are not clarified beforehand, because the nature of the "energy problem" tends to change according to the conceptual lens used. Despite these differences, we find that their common focus on the *costs* of energy usage tends to overshadow other aspects of energy's economic utility to society.

Energy as an economic cost

Although modern energy systems are highly capital-intensive industrial sectors in themselves, energy's economic value is more commonly conceived as a commodity feedstock for all other industries. The energy industry's other roles, such as being a source of local employment and domestic revenue generation in itself, have tended to be eclipsed by what is seen as its supportive, albeit critical, role in powering all other economic activities. Likewise, energy security discussions tend to center on policy recommendations to ensure the continued consumption of energy goods for economic and political stability, as opposed to highlighting policies supporting the production systems that make these goods marketable in the first place. For example, geopolitical energy security analysis has focused on the uneven geographical distribution of fossil fuel deposits and whether policies to integrate markets can help to bridge differences of political and economic interest between fossil energy consuming and producing states.[11] The future prospects of fossil energy production levels from regions such as the Middle East, Russia, Central Asia, and West Africa are often highlighted. However, relatively little attention is given to the actual policies which governments of these regions have implemented to help entrench, maintain, and expand fossil fuel industries within their own national economies, or the nature of the domestic economic consequences that have flowed from these developments.[12] To the extent that energy security agendas have been dominated by the concerns of the OECD countries, whose demand for fossil fuels outstrips their own indigenous supplies, this is perfectly understandable. The USA's petroleum imports, for example, made up 30 to 47 percent of net payments for *all* tradables between 2005 and 2009.[13] In 2008, the US economy spent $450 billion on petroleum import purchases alone.[14] When a significant amount of fuel has to be imported from a global market, the "energy" component in "energy security" is usually seen as a cost that somehow needs to be minimized and stabilized, rather than an economic opportunity to be taken advantage of.[15,16]

To be sure, energy security analysis has not been all about threat assessments and supply-oriented geopolitics. In the wake of the oil price shocks of the 1970s, many governments and private enterprises sought ways to quickly lessen their vulnerability to energy supply disruptions. These included attempts to reduce the energy intensity of their economic activities. "Demand-side" energy security analysis looks at how economies can lessen their vulnerability to energy supply disruptions and price hikes through more energy-efficient usage patterns.[17] Again, this line of reasoning tends to emphasize the productivity gains and cost savings arising from more efficient usage of energy in the domestic context, rather than the employment opportunities and revenues that accrue from the production of more efficient energy technologies in the first place.

Energy as an investment opportunity

For every suggestion to change the way energy is used, be it through new supplies, greater energy diversification, or efficiency gains, there are always economic opportunities awaiting investment. Seen this way, energy security discussions take on an added economic dimension. The International Energy Agency's *World Energy Outlook 2009* notes that over US$10 trillion of additional investment in clean energy-related assets will be needed throughout the next couple of decades to avert severe climate change from business-as-usual energy usage, and these will be "at least partly offset by economic, health and energy-security benefits."[18] To fulfill this vision, the report suggests that "[h]ouseholds and businesses are largely responsible for making the required investments, but governments hold the key to changing the mix of energy investment."[19] Yet for all their attention to investment levels, the IEA's predicted economic benefits from these clean energy investments are still framed negatively in terms of fuel cost savings.[20]

The World Economic Forum's (WEF) *Green Investing* report structures the clean investment issue slightly differently. While noting that "enormous investment in the world's energy infrastructure is required in order to address the twin threats of energy insecurity and climate change,"[21] the report devoted an entire chapter to summarizing the scale of returns on clean energy investments for the private sector. It pointed out that "[w]hile the exceptional gains of the past few years may have declined during 2008, the sector as a whole has fared better than any major benchmark over the past five years."[22] It then goes on to detail how these investments could be supported by governments in a number of ways, concluding that "the overarching requirement is for policy stability ... and simplicity, so that the industry is not burdened with unnecessary bureaucratic costs."[23] The WEF report thus links energy security with the profit motive of private capital, while simultaneously reminding governments that they have a key role to play in ensuring that markets are allowed to work as efficiently as possible.

Energy as part of economic leadership

Others, as we saw in the opening paragraph of this chapter, take the relationship between energy security, state policy, and economic returns even further. Governments are assigned with a more mercantilist role based on the view that long-term national economic power will come not just from more secure energy usage, but from their economies' ability to lead in the production and deployment of clean technologies.[24] The Breakthrough Institute, claiming to be "one of America's leading think tanks developing climate and energy policy solutions,"[25] co-authored a report in which it baldly declares that "to regain economic leadership in the global clean energy industry, U.S. energy policy must include large, direct and coordinated investments in clean technology R&D, manufacturing, deployment and infrastructure."[26]

In summary, the concept of energy security is highly malleable. It is not just associated with policies to minimize costs from the improved usage of energy itself, or to catalyze investments in energy infrastructure. Interventionist-inclined policy analysts, writers, and politicians also ascribe national governments with a responsibility to support the domestic development of clean energy technologies for other economic benefits, such as job creation, technological leadership, and new sources of export revenues. The next section discusses one such aspect of government action: industrial policies.

Conceptualizing industrial policies

The rapid rise of so-called "industrial policy states" like Japan, South Korea, and, more recently, China, has led to lively debate about the relative merits of industrial policies in both the developed and developing world.[27] These debates continue to rage, in part because of genuine fears that key sources of prosperity will be irretrievably lost over time (in developed countries), or that they will never be attained in the first place (in developing countries).[28]

The discussion on industrial policies can be complex and convoluted.[29] Here we only wish to highlight some of the main theoretical features of industrial policies that we think are most relevant to the wind energy sector as we see it developing. Below, we briefly outline what we think industrial policies are, why we think industrial policies are important, and key criticisms of industrial policies.

What are industrial policies?

By illustration, consider the following two working definitions of industrial policy:

> a policy aimed at *particular industries* (and firms as their components) to achieve the outcomes that are *perceived by the state to be efficient for the economy as a whole* [italics in original].[30]
>
> restructuring policies in favour of more dynamic activities generally, regardless of whether those are located within industry or manufacturing per se.[31]

Both definitions stress that industrial policies are designed to target selected economic activities for government support, but leave it as open-ended what these policies actually are.[32] To qualify as a deserving industry, in Chang's view, certain "micro" economic activities must be seen as able to contribute and relate to the rest of the economy in ways that help to maximize efficiency at the "macro" national level (which includes processes of technological change and upgrading). For Rodrik, the key criterion for selection is dynamism, which he elaborates on elsewhere as being more productive forms of economic activity brought about through innovation and entrepreneurship.[33] In both these definitions, the need for long-term economic restructuring is either directly alluded to or implied. Industrial policies therefore implicate both the state and market in a symbiotic relationship geared at accelerating positive economic transformations through the construction of more competitive assets. Moreover, while the relationship is meant to be mutually supportive, in Chang's view the state is clearly meant to take a leading, active role in envisioning and enforcing technical change. While these abstractions vastly oversimplify the reality of actual policy practice, they provide a useful reference point from which we can continue to extend our discussion.

Why industrial policies are important

Why might the state be, at times, in a better position than the market to assist in processes of economic restructuring and help build more competitive assets? To answer this question, we need first to acknowledge that there are at least two different problems constantly faced in economic development by different players: one of "catching up" with the rest, and the other of "staying ahead" (we use these terms broadly to allude to both intra-industry competition between sectors, as well as development disparities between different national economies).

It has been pointed out that in technologically advanced industries, certain market failures in the realm of goods and services production are typically both necessary and desirable in order to sustain one's gains from increased productivity and innovation.[34] These include institutional barriers that have been created and upheld by both private firms (such as brand names, differentiated products, firm-specific proprietary knowledge about technology, and management practices) and states (for instance, patent and trademark laws). Productive activities characterized by economies of scale, such as power generation, also tend to favor monopolistic incumbents who can charge much lower prices than new entrants.[35] Seen in this light, the goals of retaining industrial leadership are really more about actions taken to construct and uphold certain desired market imperfections in activities deemed more productive than others. From the perspective of an "outsider" firm that is seeking to enter a lucrative, technologically advanced industry such as power generation, the logical action to take is to find ways to surmount these barriers to entry, either through their own efforts, and/or through enlisting the support of another entity, such as the state. But what constitutes appropriate policy depends on what specific capabilities the firm already has, and the kind of institutional environment it exists in.[36]

If we agree that there is a case for some form of state intervention to build technological capabilities and attain greater economies of scale, such interventions may be better off as being selective in nature, since "in some activities the need for protection may be minimal because the learning period is relatively brief [whereas] in complex activities or those with widespread externalities, newcomers may never enter unless measures are undertaken to promote the activity."[37] Such infant industry policy measures are manifold, and could include targeted domestic content requirements on foreign direct investment (FDI), direct subsidies, or import tariffs.[38] Each of these instruments comes with its own different set of costs and benefits which change according to the particular environment they are being proposed for. In addition, the beneficiaries of such schemes should be subject to some form of disciplining conditionality to ensure that laggards are eventually weeded out, for example performance standards or policy expiry dates.[39]

For industries that are already past the stage of initial experimentation and are fast moving up the learning curve, a wide variety of state-organized support mechanisms may still be necessary to help the most innovative firms attain costs competitive with incumbent rivals.[40] For new technologies that work in the laboratory but have yet to be scaled up commercially due to high fixed investment requirements, states can act as surrogate capital markets in tandem with venture capitalists.[41] In the interests of knowledge diversity, states can also continue to sponsor broad-based basic research initiatives in universities and public laboratories.[42]

Finally, regardless of a country's development status, many new industry projects require simultaneous, large-scale investments in order to be profitable. For example, a large remote wind farm with a high capacity factor may not be seen as worth the considerable sunk costs unless there are credible commitments to lay down complementary investments in transmission lines and other associated infrastructure. These classic coordination problems involving interdependent assets could, in theory, be resolved either within the private sector itself or via state interventions, but much depends on the specific context of the situation.[43] In some cases, complementary infrastructural investments in power lines may be seen as critical to the overall health of the national economy, but will have overly long payback periods that do not justify private sector investment in the current time period and/or amidst expected future market conditions.[44] States could help to bridge such gaps in a number of ways, all of which are essentially signaling devices for the market. First, they could undertake "indicative planning schemes" which provide a focus and shift in expectations for the private sector.[45] Second, states can also redefine and enforce new property rights which, in principle, would reconfigure power relations in favor of cleaner technologies, such as legislative mechanisms to regulate air pollution, or pricing in carbon dioxide emissions. Third, states in both developed and developing countries could also provide direct subsidies to catalyze complementary investments, or re-regulate the electricity infrastructure sector to make it easier for bottlenecks to be alleviated.

Key criticisms of industrial policies

Criticisms of industrial policies tend to run along similar lines as critiques of state intervention in general. There are many of these, chief of which include:

- moral hazards involving excessive risk-taking by private entities, whose risks are borne by the state, and therefore the greater tax-paying society at large;
- insufficient and asymmetric information on the part of the state to make "good" policies;
- state vulnerability to unproductive forms of rent-seeking and special interests;
- a lack of democratic control over policy formed by societal elites;
- not having the "right" set of institutions to undertake industrial policies successfully;
- policies with mixed incentives and unclear goals.[46]

Rather than discuss these in the abstract, we will note some of these criticisms in the context of our case study. Another reason for placing more emphasis on the case study is that the economic arguments both for and against industrial policies in the abstract tend to suffer from some major weaknesses, including the tendency to generalize states and markets as if they were monolithic and separate entities. In reality, this is a false dichotomy; markets and states are imperfect, hetero-geneous, and inseparable. They are social institutions that mediate forms of collective action amongst many other institutions, including civil society, international organizations, and multi-national firms. This is precisely why a long-time proponent of industrial policies has insisted that fixations on particular outcomes and specific policy tools miss the point: what is really needed is "an interactive *process* of strategic cooperation between the private and public sectors which, on the one hand, serves to elicit information on business opportunities and constraints and, on the other hand, generates policy initiatives in response [italics added]."[47] The various forms of states, markets, and nature of the relationships between them are all historically contingent, and therefore are better examined and understood in the context of individual cases.

Energy security and industrial policies in the USA context

Of all countries with the potential to influence global patterns of energy usage, perhaps none inspires as much hope, bewilderment, and frustration as the United States of America. In 2007, the USA remained the world's top energy consumer, accounting for one fifth of total global energy demand.[48] It was also the world's largest producer of carbon dioxide emissions from the burning of fuels, until it was overtaken by China in 2007.[49] Rich in natural resources, the entire country (minus Alaska and Hawaii) is estimated to have the potential to generate at least 36 million GW of electricity from onshore wind power alone; over nine times the total electricity generated in America in 2009.[50] Technical potentials aside, a 2008 study by the US Department of Energy (DOE) has given backing to the view that the USA could realistically source 20 percent of its entire electricity supply from wind by 2030.[51] Despite recent surges in added installed capacity since 2005, actual growth of the wind power sector in the USA has been erratic, in part due to inconsistent, fragmented, and flawed government policy support mechanisms at both the state and federal level.

How exactly have energy security concerns influenced US government policies, including industrial policies, to develop or neglect the wind power sector?[52] Landmark energy legislation, such as the National Energy Act of 1978 and the Energy Policy Acts of 1992 and 2005, as we will see shortly, provide some key reference points that help to link energy security concerns with actual implemented industrial policies. However, these legal documents are, to varying extents, less representative of cohesive energy strategies in practice than the formalized outcomes of extensive deliberations and compromises by individuals representing a vast range of different societal interests.

Policymaking in America is anchored by a diffuse array of tangible institutions (the American Constitution, various elected political offices, the judiciary, bureaucracies, interest groups) as well as more intangible ideological legacies (liberalism, democratic ideals, self-reliance, patriotism, etc.). The process of identifying problems, setting agendas, formulating policies, legitimizing and implementing them—in short, prioritizing and deciding which things matter the most for American society—is historically underwritten by the constitutional separation of powers and bill of rights. The power to set agendas and devise solutions is not only split between the executive, legislative, and judicial wings of federal and state governments, but has also come to rest on the ability of individuals and businesses to organize themselves into effective interest groups, as well as influential bodies like policy think-tanks.[53] Difficulties with power-sharing are, of course, ende-mic to any system of rule. However, the long-term task of governing 50 states, each with its own specific interests and subcultures, suggests that policymaking in America will always be a strenuous process, regardless of what kind of political system is in place.

Early federal support for the wind sector

Identifying core national energy security goals, as well as the means to accomplish them—a fairly thorny task in any country—has become part of a perennial debate in American politics. Many of these disagreements have concerned the role that the federal government should play in energy policy over time.[54] The seesaw-like trajectory of the wind sector has been a partial outcome of this debate. Although wind energy usage has had a long history in the United States, it was only after the first OPEC oil embargo of 1973–1974 that the federal government took a serious longer-term interest in its nascent commercial development, motivated by rising fuel prices, perceived threats to national security, and deteriorating domestic electricity infrastructure performance. By the time President Carter came to power in early 1977, multiple disruptions to energy markets and the mainstreaming of environmental concerns into waves of new government legislation had created compelling pressures for a more coherent and holistic government energy policy that would address all aspects of energy supply, demand, R&D, and accompanying environmental issues.[55,56] The dominant energy security policy concern at the time was America's increasing reliance on oil from an international market vulnerable to politicized disruptions. However, within Congress and other wings of government there was little sustained agreement on which parties should be held responsible for these perceived security risks (OPEC muscle-flexing, greedy oil companies, consumer profligacy, the US government itself, etc.), let alone what should be done about them; a general trend that has continued up to the present time whenever the "oil problem" surfaces in policy discussions.[57]

The Carter administration's first comprehensive energy master plan was overseen by economist James Schlesinger, whose macroeconomic views were, by one account,

> closer to French indicative planning than to the invisible hand of Adam Smith, Alfred Marshall or Milton Friedman. Cultivation of a spirit of cooperation between government planners and industry appealed to Schlesinger: government analysts would provide goals and then perhaps would tailor these goals as a result of feedback from industry. He saw the relationship between government and industry as cooperative rather than adversarial.[58]

However, under pressure from Carter to produce a final plan within three months, Secretary Schlesinger and his small team of staff were compelled to keep other potential contributors and critics at arms' length, despite genuine efforts to seek feedback from other government agencies, industry, and the broad public. The normally powerful "troika" of the Office of Management and Budget (OMB), Treasury, and Council of Economic Advisers (CEA) had no actual inkling as to the full outline of the plan itself before it was made public.[59] The plan, as it was released, was predicated on peak oil assumptions that located the USA in the middle of a broad-based transition away from dwindling global oil and gas resources. Among other things, this would require a long-term capital goods restructuring movement in the 1980s guided by a mixture of targeted taxes, rebates, and price controls intended to incentivize energy conservation and crimp national demand for oil. This would buy more time for America to move on to longer-term technology solutions in the next millennium, based on renewable energy sources and perhaps even nuclear fusion-based energy.[60]

The plan and subsequent bill proposals met with bitter resistance from the Senate and various interest groups. For example, compulsory rate reform proposals and provisions for power companies to burn coal instead of oil and gas were vehemently criticized by both the utility industry establishment and some Congressmen as federal interference on an unprecedented scale.[61] While the eventual passing of the National Energy Act of 1978 and its five component pieces of legislation[62] helped to catalyze the growth of small-scale wind energy technologies, historian Richard Hirsh has persuasively argued that the supportive legislation was by no means guaranteed at the outset and was only passed because of a fortuitous series of events.[63] First, President Carter's genuine desire to see more power being produced from cleaner technologies gained support from several key senators and a clean energy company that was lobbying for greater benefits. Their combined efforts resulted in the passing of critical Section 210 legislation in the Public Utility Regulatory Policies Act (PURPA), which created a guaranteed and well-paying market for small renewable energy-based independent power producers (IPPs) and cogeneration units up to 80 MW in capacity, as well as supportive financial arrangements that utilities themselves were not privy to.[64] That such infant industry policies were successfully pushed through was partly due to the adept negotiating abilities of Congressional renewable energy proponents, coupled with relatively unobstructive committees and interest groups who vastly underestimated the broader significance of such legal provisions for utility restructuring. More importantly in the context of this chapter, the acrimonious and weary atmosphere that characterized the one-and-a-half year-long Congressional deliberations regarding Carter's comprehensive energy security plan had created an unintended political smokescreen through which innocuous-looking radical energy technologies could fly under the radar of entrenched vested interests.[65,66] Through this period, energy security concerns had indeed helped to influence industrial policies in favor of embryonic clean energy technologies such as wind turbines. However, they had done so in a convoluted and, at times, even accidental manner which defies casual generalization.

Four themes of the 1980s

Developments in the 1980s illustrate some of the general themes that would shape the US wind industry until the present day. First, despite (or in the absence of) supportive federal legislature, actual policy implementation was extremely uneven between states. For most of the 1980s, American wind power was practically synonymous with Californian wind power. Even before the 1978 National Energy Act, the Golden State was already facing the looming prospect of an energy crisis due to unrestrained demand growth in the 1960s, increasingly complex bureaucratic hurdles for new conventional fossil power plants, and NIMBY syndrome due to local environmental concerns.[67] Fuel price hikes in the wake of the 1973 OPEC embargo lent additional political urgency to solving California's long-term energy prospects. Energy policy thus quickly moved to the center of governance matters; the energy bureaucracy was restructured and given a broad mandate to address energy security problems comprehensively. By the time the federal government's National Energy Act had come into force, PURPA's Section 210 and federal tax incentives for small-scale renewable technologies represented only several (albeit important) policy tools amongst many that leading interventionist-minded Californian policymakers had at their disposal to increase the supply of energy from IPPs and non-conventional energy sources.

Second, the various federal and state policies of the 1970s and early 1980s were a double-edged sword for wind power developers, since many of these policies were intended to benefit a whole swathe of cleaner and more efficient energy technologies. On the one hand, installed wind capacity in California surged to 1,000 MW by 1985 and 1,799 MW by 1990, in response to tax credits and generous financing from California's interim Standard Offer 4 (SO4) mechanism,[68] a precursor to the more commonly known feed-in-tariff (FIT).[69]

Vertically integrated enterprise US Windpower, for instance, became the largest wind energy firm in the world by the end of the 1980s, in part due to these policies. Power generation costs in some areas fell from about 25 cents/kW in 1981 to about 5 cents/kW by the early 1990s, as key US wind turbine manufacturers moved up learning curves quickly.[70] On the other hand, the non-wind competition also benefitted from government support. Co-generation technologies were able to scale up power production more rapidly and substantially than any other form of non-utility power in the 1980s. Accompanying federal legislation in the National Gas Policy Act of 1978 helped to lower the costs of gas fuels for increasingly efficient combined-cycle gas turbines, while co-generation units, with their already fairly mature technologies, became even more competitive under PURPA provisions because they could mass produce standardized units at lower costs in newly created markets.[71] By the end of the 1980s, wind power was priced more competitively than some large coal and nuclear plants, but was generally still more expensive than gas turbine-generated electricity.[72]

Third, developments in California highlighted some key difficulties that policymakers would face in establishing a politically and economically acceptable rate of return for industries deemed in need of urgent long-term support. Like many others in the late 1970s and early 1980s, state regulators assumed that oil and gas prices were bound to rise in the future. Rather than risk the specter of capacity shortages, they decided to err on the side of caution by drawing up (in conjunction with utilities and IPP representatives) what they considered to be fairly generous incentives for IPPs on the basis of bullish long-term oil and gas price forecasts. The interim SO4 contract, for instance, compelled local utilities to make payments to IPPs over a period of ten years in significant excess of what they would otherwise have handed out. To sweeten the bargain even further, IPPs were not required to make any financial commitments before signing up, and they were allowed a five-year window period for experimentation, during which time no penalties would be enacted if contracts were broken.[73] As implementation began, a miniature gold rush ensued; aside from the already generous terms promised, some entrepreneurs also began to realize that oil and gas prices were likely to head downwards after 1981. Rents offered by the incentives accordingly became higher and even more attractive. By the time California's regulators had realized the margin of their error and closed down the interim SO4 contract for readjustment in 1985, hundreds of rent-seekers had already entered the market, well above initial regulatory expectations.[74] To be sure, some beneficiaries like US Windpower and FloWind Corporation proved to be dynamic cost-competitive players, continuing to expand their businesses and upgrade their technologies even after federal incentives expired in 1985. However, opportunists who often knew more about real estate ventures than wind turbine technologies also entered the market in droves, taking advantage of flawed policies such as investment tax credits that bore no relation to the actual amount of electricity that would be generated from affiliated power projects.[75]

Fourth, federal support for wind technologies and renewable energy could be notoriously inconsistent, depending on the political inclinations and relative power of elected representatives in office. Under the Reagan administration and its strongly held preference for laissez-faire economic policies, the renewable energy industry gradually lost much of the special treatment it had gained during the Carter years. The new administration's categorical rejection of limits on natural resources, coupled with the crash of oil prices in 1986, bolstered the view that America was nowhere near an energy security crisis on the scale purported by Carter and his associates. Federal tax credits for renewable energy were allowed to expire without renewal, and the R&D budget for renewables was reduced and shifted in favor of nuclear energy.[76] Furthermore, the negative public image that "wind turbine tax shelters" had acquired in the wake of unproductive entrepreneurial activity provided additional political justification for Reagan and like-minded members of Congress to remove what they believed to be the root cause of these abuses in the first place. The wind industry underwent its own baptism of fire, which according to Hirsh, left only 6 out of 40 of the most competitive firms standing after the mid-1980s.[77]

Energy Policy Act of 1992 and its aftermath

Like the 1978 National Energy Act before it, the Energy Policy Act (EPAct) of 1992 was both a political compromise as well as a reference point for American energy policy. As in keeping with the previous approach, many of its provisions were based on a national energy plan commissioned by then-president George H. W. Bush (to be known as Bush I henceforth). The need for the plan itself was motivated by a number of contingent factors: America's increasing dependence on imported oil, declining oil production in Alaska, and a general neglect of energy policy during Reagan's time which had, amongst other things, led to rising safety hazards in the nuclear power and weapons sectors.[78] Terminology was indicative. DOE chief James Watkins and deputy secretary Henson Moore decided that the "new" approach should be termed a strategy as opposed to a plan, seeing it not as a statement of broad market-friendly policy principles as had been the general approach during Reagan's time, but an actual blueprint for consolidated action.[79]

One major consequence of the Act was a federal renewable energy production tax credit (PTC) that came into effect in 1994. The PTC reduced the cost of wind-sourced electricity by 1.5 cents/kW (2.1 cents in 2008 US dollar figures adjusted for inflation) on a 20-year levelized basis.[80] It has been viewed by proponents and some analysts as a crucial instrument to accelerate the commercial growth of wind turbine production, deployment, and the building of industrial capabilities.[81] At the same time, the PTC's erratic manner of implementation has frequently been blamed for retarding wind sector growth in years 2000, 2002, and 2004, when the PTC was allowed to lapse for several months in each year before being renewed by Congress.[82] Less noted, however, has been the sluggish growth of the sector from 1995 to 1998, when the PTC was already in full effect and new wind capacity additions were practically only just replacing decommissioned assets (see Figure 13.1).

The difference in growth rates between 1995–1998 and 1999 onwards is potentially significant in terms of the additional insights it may provide for discussions regarding actual energy security and industrial policies. Recall the four themes we drew from developments in the 1980s: policy fragmentation, wind power's cost-competitiveness relative to other energy sources, difficulties with creating productive rent-seeking incentives for firms, and inconsistent federal policy influenced in part by energy price fluctuations. While it is certainly true that, like any industry, wind turbine suppliers will encounter a significant lag in bringing new facilities into the market, it seems

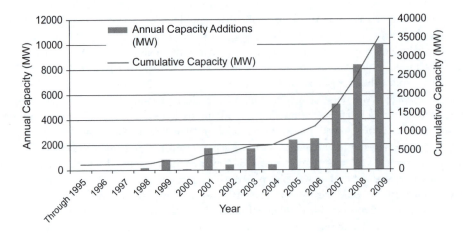

Figure 13.1 Annual and cumulative growth in US wind power capacity, 1995–2009.[83]

too much of a coincidence that wind capacity additions jumped nearly sixfold in 1999 from the previous year after being stagnant for three years running: 1999 was also the same year that previously stable and low oil prices went from less than US$11/barrel in February to US$24.50/barrel in December and then continued on a general upward spiral for the greater part of the decade.[84] Wellhead natural gas prices also began shooting up to uncharacteristically high levels in the summer of 2000, and continued to climb further the following two winters.[85,86] At around roughly the same time, wind turbine capacity once again jumped to new heights in 2001. The DOE itself has also argued that the PTC did little to encourage wind sector growth due to low natural gas prices in the 1990s.[87] Such observations have led to gas being termed wind power's "primary competitor."[88] At the same time, these broad market drivers of fluctuating oil and gas prices had older causes that appear to be at least partly rooted in US federal politics during the 1990s.

The Clinton administration assumed power in 1993, bringing with them widely held expectations that federal energy policies would adopt a more pro-environmentalist and energy efficient orientation (Vice President Gore, had, amongst other matters, co-introduced legislation during his senatorial term in 1989 aimed at mitigating climate change). As is the norm in US politics, little occurred as expected: between 1990 and 2000, US oil consumption and imports rose by several million barrels per day, including imports from OPEC countries.[89] Total energy consumption increased by about 17 percent in the same period, with natural gas increasing its share slightly, and overall electricity intensity rising.[90] For most of the decade, energy supplies were relatively cheap and abundant, while gas and electric power infrastructure was in excess of capacity. The administration was lulled into complacency about its energy supplies, only to receive a rude shock when energy prices began to jump from 1999 onwards, beginning with OPEC's supply cut.[91] Stagliano's account castigates the Clinton administration for what was seen as its highly partisan and negative attitude towards the comprehensive energy legislation approved by a Republican-led administration in 1992, as well as gross neglect of energy policy concerns during a period of relatively cheap and available fossil energy.[92] Joskow's view of the situation is more charitable, noting that the administration's politically naive attempt to distinguish itself by trying to pass a very unpopular top-down "BTU" tax on energy in 1993 roused Congressional Republicans' hackles to the point where they obstructed many subsequent executive and DOE attempts to build on the centrist policies created under the 1992 EPAct and NES.[93]

With hindsight, many recent US energy developments since the 2000s can thus be put into perspective. To be sure, the explosive capacity growth of the US wind sector since 2005 has been unprecedented in its apparent scale and speed. However, are the underlying policy and economic factors that drive this growth still the same ones as in past decades? What is different now? Have US energy security policies indeed helped propel it to become a "clean energy technology leader" in the wind sector, with all the accompanying benefits that such narratives promise? To explore these questions, two interrelated areas are addressed: the nature of recent wind sector growth and recent energy prices and government policies.

The nature of recent wind sector growth

The US wind sector has made significant advances in a number of areas: capacity additions, technological innovation, price competitiveness, and power generated as a proportion of the US share. Nevertheless, the sector still occupies a much smaller share of electricity generation than technical potentials would suggest, faces significant issues with constraints such as increased cost pressures, congested transmission lines, and is also generating a large trade deficit that has tended to increase in tandem with rising capacity deployment levels.

The wind sector in America has attracted much praise for retaking the global leading position in total installed capacity from Germany since 2008. In 2008, cumulative capacity in the USA stood at 25,237 MW, while Germany's stood at 23,903 MW. The gap widened even further by the end of 2009, with the US sector increasing capacity by an unprecedented 9,922 MW to 35,159 MW, while Germany's wind sector made modest gains of just under 2,000 MW in comparison.[94] Wind power's share of electricity generation in the USA has also increased significantly from 0.9 percent in 2006 to an estimated 1.9 percent in 2008. This figure is still relatively small compared with Germany, Ireland, Portugal, Spain, and others, all of whom generated at least 7 percent of their electricity from wind in 2008.[95] In the same year, however, several US states were already generating over 7 percent of electricity from wind within their borders. These included Iowa, Minnesota, South Dakota, and North Dakota, all of which have enacted either mandatory or voluntary renewable portfolio standards of various designs.[96] At the present time, the USA appears to be well ahead of the DOE's scenario path to generating 20 percent of US electricity from wind by 2030.[97,98,99]

In the past decade, wind turbine technology deployed in the USA has also continued to offer improved performance. In 2008, average turbine sizes increased to roughly 1.67 MW, up slightly from 1.65 MW in 2007 and 1.60 MW in 2006.[100] In addition, average capacity factors for wind projects have improved significantly over the past decade, reaching 30 percent in 2000 before hitting the upper 30s by 2005. In some cases, projects managed to achieve capacity factors well in excess of 50 percent in 2008.[101] DOE's wind power database also suggests that the average price of wind power sales has fallen steadily from $63/MW in 1999 (2007 dollars) to $40/MW in 2007, rendering wind power more competitive in wholesale power markets.[102] All in all, these gains strongly suggest that the wind sector is increasing in technological maturity.[103]

The explosive growth of wind power has had mixed results for the US wind industry, revealing a number of hurdles and complications along the way. Just shortly after the US installed wind capacity figures jumped in 2001, a shortage of wind turbine components, rising material costs at various points in the wind supply chain, and weakness of the US dollar led to significant inflationary pressures on wind turbine prices and installed wind project costs which continued into 2008.[104,105] Bottlenecks in transmission line capacity have also resulted in difficulties in getting wind projects realized. By 2008, total wind capacity in interconnection queues amounted to nearly 300 GW.[106] Transmission problems are also being blamed for high-profile project cancellations and project downsizing, such as Mesa Energy's abortion of what would have been then the world's largest wind farm in July 2009.[107]

US wind market growth was estimated to create 35,000 jobs in 2008, bringing total estimated sector employment to 85,000, with potential to grow further into six-digit figures.[108,109] Many of these jobs are related to component manufacturing and assembly, transport, operations, and maintenance of wind turbines. US-domiciled General Electric (GE) Wind remained the top turbine manufacturer in the US market, with a domestic market share of 43 percent of all installations in 2008.[110] However, the sector has become increasingly crowded due to the recent entrance of new vendors such as Acciona, Repower, Fuhrlander, CTC/DeWind, and AWE, as well as existing market share expansions by players such as Clipper and Suzlon.[111] Numerous manufacturing and assembly facilities have been opened all across America by many of these firms, including in states suffering structural changes from deindustrialization such as Michigan and Ohio.[112] Besides new employment opportunities, this increasingly crowded playing field may lead to lower turbine costs, particularly since US project developers downstream have been consolidating their market power for turbine purchases from manufacturers.[113]

Trade-wise, the rapid expansion of the US wind sector has led to increasing deficits. The US is an extremely large importer of wind turbines and components, both in gross and net terms (see Table 13.1).

Large single-sector import figures alone are not necessarily a sign of economic weakness. Major wind manufacturers, including US domiciles, have several global production sites, and can thus import components manufactured overseas "back" into the United States.[115] In any case, no single country is likely to be a net exporter in all clean energy technologies.[116] However, wind sector trade deficits do make it politically harder to sell existing policies that subsidize wind production in the States, since their economic benefits in terms of local job opportunities and payrolls appear to be diluted by a lack of US sales abroad to help offset the larger aggregate US trade deficit. As we saw earlier, export-oriented trade policies in the Energy Policy Act of 1992 were formulated to promote renewable energy exports abroad. But based on current trade figures, these policies either did not succeed for the wind industry, or else they were not implemented properly, if at all. Evidence of such deficits may make it politically easier to advocate export-oriented growth policies or protectionist measures intended to increase the local share of revenue generation from wind manufacturing.

In 2008, just five European countries (Denmark, Spain, Germany, the UK, and Portugal) and two Asian economies (Japan and India) accounted for 98 percent of all US wind set imports.[117] Chinese wind-powered generating set exports to the US began to ramp up in 2006, yet only accounted for less than 2 percent of total imports between 2006 and 2008.[118] Nearly all of these countries' governments have used industrial policy mechanisms in one way or another, either through direct discrimination in favor of local industry players and/or via long-term indirect mechanisms that have helped to provide stable support conditions for emerging markets (see Table 13.2).

Table 13.1 US imports, exports, and net trade balance from wind-powered generating sets

	Import expenditures	Export revenues	Net Trade Balance
2003	$356,000,000	$746,000	–$355,254,000
2008	$2,500,000,000	$22,000,000	–$2,478,000,000

Source: US International Trade Commission.[114]

Table 13.2 Industrial policies supporting the wind sector in selected countries

Direct local support policies		*Indirect support policies*	
Local content requirements	Spain, China.	Feed-in tariffs	Denmark, Germany, Spain, Portugal, China
Financial and tax incentives	Germany, India, Denmark, Spain, USA (some states), China	Mandatory renewable energy targets	USA (various states), UK, Japan
Favourable customs duties	Denmark, Germany, India, China	Government tendering	UK, India, Japan, USA (various states), China
Export credit assistance	Germany, Denmark	Financial and tax incentives	USA, India, China
Quality certification	Denmark, Germany, Japan, India, USA.		

Source: Lewis, Joanna. I. and Ryan Wiser. 2007. "Fostering a Renewable Energy Technology Industry: An International Comparison of Wind Industry Policy Support Mechanisms," *Energy Policy* 38: 1844–1857.

The most prominent industrial policies for wind in the US context have been mainly of the indirect variety, such as the PTC and state-level renewable portfolio standards (RPSs). Unlike the local content requirements used by China and Spain, these do not openly discriminate against foreign firms.[119] The fact that many of the top exporters' governments have used a mixture of both directly discriminatory and indirect policies to support their own local wind manufacturing industries has provided more interventionist-inclined policymakers in America with the political backing to suggest that the USA should adopt a more protectionist stance in order to grow its own firms' local manufacturing capabilities and reduce its trade deficit through increased exports and import substitution.[120] A potential conflict of interests thus arises. US government policies intended to favor local manufacturers more directly, such as raising import tariffs and export credit assistance, might help increase US market share of wind production both domestically and abroad. However, discrimination against imported components could also potentially raise future wind power costs in the USA relative to other power generation industries like gas, since they would presumably raise the prices of inputs like wind-powered generating sets for both local and foreign firms with manufacturing facilities in the USA.[121] A "Buy American" provision would also be likely to provoke a further protectionist backlash by countries such as China, whose markets would be needed for the USA to reduce its wind power technology trade deficit. However, continuing current practices of promoting wind energy production and deployment in the domestic market through indirect policies, such as the PTC, RPSs at either the state or federal level, and the Wind Powering America initiative, will help to increase wind power's share in the electricity mix and even promote local economic development in select regions, but will do little on their own to amend the trade deficit.[122]

Conclusion

This chapter sought to make better sense of the clean tech narrative by discussing the relationship between energy security concerns and industrial policies supporting the wind industry. The US historical narrative provided a rich historical context in which two questions could be discussed:

1. How do energy security policies influence a government's industrial policies?
2. How do industrial policies influence the production and deployment of clean energy technologies?

In the US context at least, energy policymaking has tended to be incremental in effect.[123] It has been easier to make decisions regarding existing policy items already in place. Conflicts are heightened when new policies are introduced, involving large shifts in costs and benefits. These incrementalist tendencies occur not just because of the way US governing institutions have been formally set up based on the separation of powers. Incrementalism also transpires because of the realities of policymaking in energy matters. Making long-term and/or major policy shifts inevitably involves making bets on the future of energy markets based on imperfect knowledge. These bets are more politically acceptable when the country is faced with what appears to be a genuine energy market crisis, such as the oil price shocks of 1973, 1979, and 1990. However, the fact that these shocks dissipated quickly also undercut the view that the market was in long-term jeopardy, putting brakes on the momentum of longer-term policies.

Incrementalism is also reinforced because translating energy security concerns into actual policy decisions has always involved debates over which values should be prioritized, even if these are not always explicitly articulated (national security, freer markets, a cleaner environment, personal liberties, social goods, etc.). The policies that follow from these assumptions each allocate a different spread of costs and benefits based on these values, thus tending to appeal to different groups in society. When this takes place under the shadow of frequent elections, there is always a risk that a political backlash will cause a reversion to the status quo. Related to this is the view that much of what drives US policymaking is underwritten by special interest groups and lobbies. Any major decision to favor a set of new policy approaches is bound to antagonize those who have the most to lose from the proposed shift. All this makes the status quo hard to change for a sustained period of time. This may also explain why the current prolonged climate for higher energy prices has not made it much easier to muster a concerted effort to transform energy markets in ways that will reduce America's vulnerability to oil and work in favor of cleaner technologies. Political conflict is heightened by genuine doubts about attempts to place large bets involving public funding on the future of energy markets, as well as the resistance posed by numerous vested interests in energy-intensive industries and some fossil fuel sectors.

Despite these difficulties, repeated episodes of "security" crises in energy markets (however brief) have provided window periods during which policymakers under the Carter, Bush I, and Bush II administrations have tried (or are currently trying, in Obama's case) to favor longer-term industrial policies that can shift energy economies more in favor of other energy technologies. Under the Carter administration, wind power producers were subsidized by utilities, states, and the federal government, with mixed results due to the experimental nature of the processes involved. Incremental policymaking in the US has meant that once a new item has been passed into law, it becomes easier to get it continued in subsequent years unless there is a substantial political realignment. As we saw during the course of the Bush I, Clinton, and Bush II admin-istrations, this led to some strange episodes where the PTC-supported wind sector could only make substantial gains in capacity additions when Clinton-era energy policies failed to anticipate bottlenecks in gas supplies. Wind became more cost-competitive relative to increasingly expen-sive gas when the lapsing PTC was repeatedly extended into the 2000s. US industrial policies in the energy sector have thus been an amalgamation of broad-ranging aims and watered-down implementation (the EPAct 1992 was arguably rationalist in its formulation but not in subsequent execution). Certain policies such as the PTC might possibly stand a better chance of actually accomplishing multiple goals at the same time (e.g. national security and environmental policy), but much depends on how they are executed and handled over time as circumstances change.

The need for more rational approaches appears particularly pressing in lieu of the manifold expectations being hoisted on clean energy technologies to resolve the issues of climate change, continued economic growth, and energy security. These interests have fused with broader concerns about national economic competitiveness. None of these concerns is particularly novel in the US context. Steps have been taken to try and promote US leadership in clean energy technologies for the past 30 years in the wind sector.

Over this period, it has become clear that supportive policies for wind power motivated by security concerns are de facto industrial policies. This is primarily because the wind sector, from its infancy, has relied on domestic energy sources to generate power, which means that wind power has to be generated by technologies that are entrenched in the local economy in one way or another.[124] But if energy security policies for wind power are industrial policies by definition, the converse is not necessarily true. Many industrial policies in the US context have multiple aims, including social goods provision, economic restructuring, technological upgrading, job creation, environmental protection, and export promotion. These ambiguities in criteria have parallels in Chang's definition of industrial policies, which were policies designed to achieve outcomes "that are perceived by the state to be efficient for the economy as a whole."[125] Systemic notions of efficiency can be inherently problematic because they ultimately involve judgments on which societal values matter and require decisions to consciously widen knowledge boundaries beyond conventional terms of reference. In other words, comprehensive industrial policies suffer from compatibility problems with incrementalist policy approaches. If industrial policies are supposed to help catalyze massive, wide-ranging changes in a nation state's social and economic landscape, evaluating the success of these intentions is made doubly difficult because of the multiple criteria being used to justify these policies. This in turn increases the vulnerability of such policies to politicization. Such issues are of course not limited to the US context; industrial policies face similar difficulties elsewhere because their *raison d'être* is to confront and resolve complex socio-economic problems.

Aside from these general observations, the US case study also suggests that not all industrial policies to promote wind power necessarily increase energy security in the United States. The sweeping narrative of the clean energy race is both its greatest strength and weakness: by seeking to narrow the differences between concepts (energy supply security, environmental protection, economic growth, etc.), it offers an alluring vision of the future. But in doing so, it papers over other trade-offs which may have to occur for these previously disparate concepts to fuse. Industrial policies to promote wind power exports do not directly promote American energy security interests in terms of domestic supply diversification, and may indeed backfire if these policies result in retaliatory measures by other governments with interests in promoting their own wind energy industries. Policy measures to increase the domestic content of US wind turbine manufactures may raise local manufacturing costs and render the sector less capable of delivering increasing electricity loads at cost-competitive prices, unless additional subsidies are provided to reduce consumer prices. These asymmetries in the complex relationship between energy security and industrial policies cannot be ignored, and need to be studied further. However, far from undermining the importance of industrial policies themselves, the US case shows why discussions about government policies to support clean energy technologies still have some way to go in terms of informing current debates. At a time when the clean energy technology race narrative is gaining public influence, the need for more enlightened discussions about the various trade-offs involved is becoming increasingly urgent.

On the basis of these discussions, three recommendations are suggested for readers interested in both energy security and energy policies within and beyond the USA:

1. *Industrial policies should be considered an intrinsic part of energy security policymaking, but wielded with care.* Industrial policies are a critical but little understood policy tool often needed for new and immature energy technologies to compete successfully in a market already

dominated by mature fossil fuel industries. Moreover, tensions between industrial policies and energy security concerns have tended to be glossed over by interventionist-minded politicians, writers, and analysts who have adopted variants of simplistic clean energy race narratives. Wind energy in the USA may be a significant source of employment and manufacturing activity but, like oil, the wind energy trade is still being conducted at a net revenue loss rather than a surplus for the national economy. Aggressive US trade policies to correct this deficit may in turn undermine the efforts of other national governments to grow their own energy industries at home. However, assigning more certainty to these possibilities remains a difficult task unless further investigations are carried out. More research is needed regarding the nature of the wind industry in other countries: its supply chains, supportive government policies, and actual contribution to economic performance relative to other clean energy industries and even the entire economy as a whole. Besides examining whether it would be economically optimal for a particular national economy to have a trade deficit or surplus in the wind energy sector, more attention also needs to be paid to the fact that the beneficiaries of US wind sector revenue outflows appear to be a different set of players as far removed from the Middle Eastern context as one could conceive; most of these former countries are OECD members and/or long-time US allies. Broadly speaking, trade and foreign policy specialists need to pay attention to this complex shift in the international political economy of energy and consider whether current trade policies are beginning to rely excessively on assumptions about energy geopolitics which may be increasingly outdated.

2. *Energy security policy discussions ultimately have to consider the whole range of energy technologies possible at a given point in time.* While serious debates and/or policymaking processes that give consideration to a full range of energy technologies can be extremely costly, time-consuming, and often simply beyond the technical abilities of those involved, this chapter's discussion of the wind sector has shown why such comprehensive approaches are necessary if we are to discuss and anticipate some of the most important policy trade-offs in decision-making. Single-sector approaches may work especially well if they can compare and evaluate performances across multiple-policy environments. But even if this chapter had been formulated along the lines of this approach, it would not have been possible to discuss how a package of different energy technologies could be used to satisfy the energy security priorities of a particular locality/nation state/region in an optimal manner (not to mention the types of industrial policies needed to carry this out). The short-term energy security problem in the USA for the past 30 years has been viewed primarily as an "oil for transport problem," and this is something that the wind sector on its own can do little to solve. Beyond the transport security issue, the growth of gas as a cost-competitive power generation source could be seen by some as a great boost for US energy security, but not necessarily from the viewpoint of the wind sector. Criteria for assessing energy security contributions and policies must therefore involve the full range of energy technologies and acknowledge that each has its own strengths and weaknesses. Trade policy specialists may likewise gain different perspectives when tackling trade balance issues by looking at energy technologies in the aggregate, rather than simply by individual sector breakdowns. In addition, other policymakers beyond the USA may have a different evaluation of their own energy security priorities and a correspondingly different set of solutions. As discussants, we should not fall into the trap of endorsing a single energy technology (or even a particular set) based on criteria that have not taken the particular needs and priorities of local stakeholders into sufficient consideration. Case histories of energy sectors in different countries must give ample attention to the messy realities of policymaking in these countries and not ignore

them in favor of seemingly greater analytical clarity. How one is to decide which stakeholder needs and priorities are more legitimate than others ultimately comes down to questions of contingent political power and value judgments, but a more nuanced understanding of local contexts can help to bridge these typical policy dilemmas to some extent.

3. *Effective energy security policymaking must be grounded in a better understanding of local contexts.* What lessons are there for other countries (or the USA, for that matter) to draw from America's own experiences in policymaking? First, much will, of course, depend on the specific country in question: the peculiarities of its resource endowments, geography, existing energy usage patterns, level of economic development, orientation towards the international trading system, the character of its political system, and policymaking governance structure. Naturally, the well-documented difficulties with anticipating future world market prices for oil and other major fuels suggest that the underlying philosophy of incremental energy policymaking should never be underestimated; but what really matters is the degree to which policymakers can balance the need to make bold choices when opportunities arise with a more cautious world view enriched by the past policy mistakes of previous US administrations. Second, it may also be worth considering the paradox that security policy formulation exhibits in the US context: there is a marked tendency for energy security policies to gain traction only during periods of actual perceived insecurity. Do the policy environments of other countries allow for less reactive and more anticipatory approaches to energy security policymaking to occur? Why is this so? Is the growth of the domestic wind energy sector in other countries better served with backing from national security interests, or is the sector perhaps better left to the vagaries of market mechanisms already in place? Do attempts to reassess energy security prospects and performances of countries through new metrics and indices take these subtle but important differences in local policy environments into account? These are all points that those interested in energy policy may wish to consider further.

Notes

1 The author wishes to thank Hum Wei Mei, Benjamin Tang, and Benjamin Sovacool for useful comments on earlier drafts. The usual caveats apply.

2 Stagliano, Vito. 2001. *A Policy of Discontent: The Making of a National Energy Strategy* (Tulsa, OK: Penwell Corp), p. 282.

3 Friedman, Thomas. 2009. *Hot, Flat, and Crowded: Why the World Needs A Green Revolution – And How We Can Renew Our Global Future. Release 2.0. Updated and Expanded* (London: Penguin), p. 212.

4 Pernick, Ron, Clint Wilder, Dexter Gauntlett, and Trevor Winnie. 2010. *Clean Energy Trends 2010*, p. 7. Available at: http://ww.cleanedge.com/reports/ (accessed February 24, 2010).

5 Obama, Barack H. 2009. "Remarks of President Barack Obama – As Prepared for Delivery: Address to Joint Session of Congress" (Washington, DC: Office of the Press Secretary, The White House). Available at: http://www.whitehouse.gov/the-press-office/remarks-president-barack-obama-address-joint-session-congress (accessed April 3, 2010).

6 Waxman, Henry and Edward Markey. 2009. *H.R. 2454: American Clean Energy and Security Act 2009*, p. 1. Available at: http://www.govtrack.us/congress/bill.xpd?bill=h111-2454 (accessed February 26, 2010).

7 Kerry, John, Barbara Boxer, Benjamin Cardin, and Paul Kirk. 2009. *S. 1733: Clean Energy Jobs and American Power Act 2009*, p. 1. Available at: http://www.govtrack.us/congress/bill.xpd?bill=s111-1733 (accessed February 26, 2010).

8 For example, see Ayee, Gloria, Marcy Lowe, Gary Gereffi, Tyler Hall, and Eun Han Kim. 2009. "Wind Power: Generating Electricity and Employment." In *Manufacturing Climate Solutions: Carbon-Reducing Technologies and U.S. Jobs* (Durham, NC: Center on Globalization, Governance and Competitivenes), p. 35. Available at: http://www.cggc.duke.edu/environment/climatesolutions/

(accessed February 3, 2010); and Tonn, Bruce, K. C. Healy, Amy Gibson, Ashutosh Ashish, Preston Cody, Drew Beres, Sam Lulla, Jim Mazur, and A. J. Ritter. 2010. "Power from Perspective: Potential Future United States Energy Portfolios," *Energy Policy* 37: 1432–1443.

9 Labels aside, whether an energy technology is "clean" or "dirty" is ultimately a matter of degree, since all energy systems, including those powered by wind, solar, geothermal, and hydropower, have negative feedback effects on the environment. For a useful qualitative summary of these effects, see Sovacool, Benjamin. 2008. *The Dirty Energy Dilemma: What's Blocking Clean Power in the United States* (Westport, CT: Praeger), p. 189.

10 Sovacool, *Dirty Energy Dilemma*, p. 195.

11 For instance, see Wesley, Michael (ed). 2007. *Energy Security in Asia* (London / New York: Routledge).

12 For a recent exceptional effort to accommodate a nuanced view of the policies of both fossil energy suppliers and consuming countries within an overarching energy security paradigm, see El-Gamal, Mahmoud and Amy Myers Jaffe. 2010. *Oil, Dollars, Debt, and Crises: The Global Curse of Black Gold* (Cambridge: Cambridge University Press).

13 Energy Information Administration (EIA). *February 2010 Monthly Energy Review*. Available at: http://www.eia.doe.gov/emeu/mer/overview.html (accessed February 28, 2010).

14 Exports of US petroleum products reduced net revenue losses by $61.7 billion that same year. See EIA, *February 2010 Monthly Energy Review*.

15 For instance, see Elkind, Jonathan. 2010. "Energy Security: Call for a Broader Agenda." In Carlos Pascual and Jonathan Elkind (eds), *Energy Security: Economics, Politics, Strategies and Implications* (Washington, DC: Brookings), pp. 121–128; and Yergin, Daniel. 2006. "Ensuring Energy Security," *Foreign Affairs* 85(2): 69–82.

16 This does not exclude the fact that major oil and gas producing states, like Iran, Nigeria, and Russia, also have their own domestic energy security problems. See Elkind, "Energy Security," pp. 131–132.

17 For instance, see Schipper, Lee, Stephen Meyers, Richard B. Howarth, and Ruth Steiner. 1992. *Energy Efficiency and Human Activity: Past Trends, Future Prospects* (Cambridge: Cambridge University Press).

18 International Energy Agency (IEA). 2009. *World Energy Outlook 2009* (Paris: OECD), p. 47.

19 IEA, *World Energy Outlook 2009*, p. 41.

20 IEA, *World Energy Outlook 2009*, pp. 286–289.

21 World Economic Forum (WEF). 2009. *Green Investing: Towards a Clean Energy Infrastructure* (New York / Geneva: World Economic Forum), pp. 9.

22 WEF, *Green Investing*, pp. 19–21.

23 WEF, *Green Investing*, p. 39.

24 For example, see United Nations Environment Program (UNEP). 2004. *Energy Subsidies: Lessons Learned in Assessing Their Impact and Designing Policy Reforms* (Geneva: UNEP), pp. 143–144. Available at: http://www.unep.ch/ETB/publications/energySubsidies/Energysubreport.pdf (accessed February 3, 2010).

25 Atkinson, Rob, Michael Shellenberger, Ted Nordhaus, Devon Swezey, Teryn Norris, Jesse Jenkins, Leigh Ewbank, Johanna Peace, and Yael Borofsky. 2009. *Rising Tigers, Sleeping Giant: Asian Nations Set to Dominate the Clean Energy Race by Out-investing the United States* (Breakthrough Institute and The Information Technology and Innovation Foundation), p. 98. Available at: http://www.thebreakthrough.org/blog/2009/11/rising_tigers_sleeping_giant_o.shtml (accessed February 24, 2010).

26 Atkinson *et al.*, *Rising Tigers, Sleeping Giant*, p. 3.

27 On the concept of industrial policy states, see Chang, Ha-Joon. 2003. *Globalisation, Economic Development and the Role of the State* (London: Zed Books), p. 63.

28 Aiginger, Karl. 2007. "Industrial Policy: A Dying Breed or a Re-emerging Phoenix," *Journal of Industry, Competition and Trade*, 297–323.

29 For useful theoretical overviews, see Lall, Sanjaya. 2004. *Reinventing Industrial Strategy: The Role of Government Policy in Building Industrial Competitiveness*, G-24 Discussion Paper Series no. 28. Available at: http://ideas.repec.org/p/unc/g24pap/28.html (accessed March 2, 2010); and Chang, Ha-Joon. 1994. *The Political Economy of Industrial Policy* (New York: St Martin's Press), pp. 55–90.

30 Chang, *Political Economy of Industrial Policy*, p. 60.

31 Rodrik, Dani. 2004. *Industrial Policy for the Twenty-First Century*. Prepared for UNIDO, p. 2. Available at: http://www.hks.harvard.edu/fs/drodrik/Research%20papers/UNIDOSep.pdf (accessed April 2, 2010) (United Nations Industrial Development Organization).

32 Rodrik, *Industrial Policy* (p. 43) provides a sample list of these industrial policies as he observes them in developing countries: loans for working capital, loans for fixed assets and/or investment projects, equity investment, loans to specific sectors, credit programs for particular regions, horizontal tax incentives, tax incentives to specific sectors, and tax incentives to particular regions. Chang, *Political Economy of Industrial Policy*, takes a more restrictive view, rejecting broader-based measures like horizontal tax incentives and regional tax incentives as industrial policy.

33 Rodrik, *Industrial Policy*, p. 4.

34 Amsden, Alice. 1997. "Editorial: Bringing Production Back In – Understanding Government's Economic Role in Late Industrialization," *World Development* 25(4): 470.

35 We use the term economies of scale broadly, not just referring to cost-efficiency gains from larger-sized products, but also increased manufacturing plant economies of scale, rationalization, spreading overheads, and better financial economies. See Sloman, John. 1994. *Economics,* 2nd edn (New York: Harvester Wheatsheaf), pp. 173–174, 226–227.

36 For example, see UNEP, *Energy Subsidies*, pp. 147–154.

37 Lall, Sanjaya. 2004. *Reinventing Industrial Strategy: The Role of Government Policy in Building Industrial Competitiveness*, G-24 Discussion Paper Series no. 28, p. 11. Available at; http://ideas.repec.org/p/unc/g24pap/28.html (accessed March 2, 2010).

38 Chang, *Political Economy of Industrial Policy*, p. 76.

39 Rodrik, *Industrial Policy*, p. 11.

40 Ibenholt, Karen. 2002. "Explaining Learning Curves for Wind Power," *Energy Policy* 30: 1181–1189.

41 Chang, *Political Economy of Industrial Policy*, p. 78.

42 Chang, *Political Economy of Industrial Policy*, p. 78.

43 Abramowitz, Moses. 1986. "Catching Up, Forging Ahead, and Falling Behind," *The Journal of Economic History* 46 (2): 402; and Ayee *et al.*, "Wind Power," p. 17.

44 Rodrik, *Industrial Policy*, p. 13.

45 Chang, *Political Economy of Industrial Policy*, p. 53.

46 This list was extracted from Chang, *Political Economy of Industrial Policy*, pp. 79–89; Rodrik, *Industrial Policy*; and Bordoff, Jason, Manasi Deshpande, and Pascal Noel. 2010. "Understanding the Interaction between Energy Security and Climate Change Policy." In C. Pascual and J. Elkind (eds), *Energy Security: Economics, Politics, Strategies and Implications* Washington, DC: Brookings), pp. 209–248.

47 Rodrik, *Industrial Policy*, p. 38.

48 IEA, *World Energy Outlook*, p. 76.

49 IEA. 2009. *CO2 Emissions from Fuel Combustion: Highlights. 2009 Edition* (Paris: OECD/IEA) pp. 44–46. Available at: http://www.iea.org/publications/free_new_Desc.asp?PUBS_ID=2143 (accessed December 28, 2009).

50 These estimates are based on all land area with a gross wind capacity factor (without losses) of 30 percent and greater at a height of 80 m above ground, after excluding protected land, incompatible land use, and other spaces. See US DOE Website, "Wind Powering America." Available at: http://www.windpoweringamerica.gov/docs/wind_potential_80m_30percent.xls (accessed April 4, 2010); and US EIA Website, "Net Generation by Energy Source: Total (All Sectors)." Available at: http://www.eia.doe.gov/cneaf/electricity/epm/table1_1.html (accessed April 4, 2010).

51 Office of Energy Efficiency and Renewable Energy (EERE). 2008. "20% Wind Energy by 2030: Increasing Wind Energy's Contribution to U.S. Electricity Supply" (US Department of Energy). Avaialable at: http://www1.eere.energy.gov/windandhydro/pdfs/41869.pdf (accessed March 3, 2010).

52 In the USA, industrial policies are considered politically controversial in many quarters and often viewed as an inaccurate lens with which to frame economic development in the United States. The author realizes that certain present-day parties may wish to avoid associations with industrial policy because of political expediency, and apologizes in advance for any such possible adverse reactions. For some recent general interpretations of industrial policies in the USA, see Fong, Glen. 2000. "Breaking New Ground or Breaking the Rules: Strategic Reorientation in U.S. Industrial Policy," *International Security* 25(2): 152–186; and Ketels, Christian. 2007. "Industrial Policy in the United States," *Journal of Industry, Competition and Trade*: 147–167.

53 For a good introductory overview, see Dye, Thomas. R. 2005. *Understanding Public Policy,* 11th edn (Upper Saddle River, NJ: Pearson).

54 Bamberger, Robert. 2007. *Energy Policy: Conceptual Framework and Continuing Issues*. CRS Report for Congress RL31720 (Washington, DC: Congressional Research Service), p. 7. Available at: http://www.fas.org/sgp/crs/misc/RL31720.pdf (accessed February 24, 2010).

55 Hirsh, Richard. 1999. *Power Loss: The Origins of Deregulation and Restructuring in the American Electric Utility System* (Cambridge, MA: The MIT Press), pp. 55–70.

56 The interventionist thrust of Carter's general energy policies was not novel by any means. It had immediate precedents in the Nixon and Ford administrations as well as Congressional maneuvering during the period and the gradual consolidation of the official energy bureaucracy even before the 1973 embargo. See for example, de Marchi, Neil. 1981. "Energy Policy under Nixon: Mainly Putting out Fires," and "The Ford Administration: Energy as a Political Good." In Crawfurd D. Goodwin (ed.), *Energy Policy in Perspective: Today's Problems, Yesterday's Solutions* (Washington, DC: Brookings), pp. 395–546.

57 Bang, Guri. 2010. "Energy Security and Climate Change Concerns: Triggers for Energy Policy Change in the United States?" *Energy Policy* 38: 1646.

58 Cochrane, James. 1981. "Carter Energy Policy and the Ninety-fifth Congress." In Crawfurd. D. Goodwin (ed.), *Energy Policy in Perspective: Today's Problems, Yesterday's Solutions* (Washington, DC: Brookings), p. 553.

59 Cochrane, "Carter Energy Policy and the Ninety-fifth Congress," pp. 555–556.

60 Cochrane, "Carter Energy Policy and the Ninety-fifth Congress," pp. 560, 577.

61 Hirsh, *Power Loss*, pp. 78–79.

62 The five Acts under the National Energy Act of 1978 are the Public Utility Regulatory Policies Act (PURPA), the Energy Tax Act, the National Energy Conservation Policy Act, the Powerplant and Industrial Fuel Use Act, and the Natural Gas Policy Act (Pub.L. 95–617 to 95–621 respectively).

63 Hirsh, *Power Loss*, p. 88.

64 These policies were partly motivated by the fact that utilities had exercised monopsony power to discourage the growth of IPPs prior to PURPA. Hirsh, *Power Loss*, pp. 87–89.

65 Hirsh, *Power Loss*, p. 88.

66 The technologies themselves were radical, not because they were based on renewable energy sources but because they could be deployed cost-effectively in small modular units that did not have to be hooked up to a utility. Had this potential to overturn previously established electricity industry institutions been realized, Section 210 would likely never have been passed without a much tougher political struggle. Early on, commercial small wind technologies appeared also to exhibit what Harvard Business Professor Clayton Christensen has termed "disruptive" technological character-istics: (1) they tended to underperform relative to established products in mainstream markets, e.g. in terms of reliability and power output, (ii) they had features that fringe customers valued, such as being relatively cheaper, simpler, smaller, and often more convenient to operate and maintain, and (iii) they consisted of mainly components built around proven technologies and put together in a novel manner which offered customers a set of attributes previously unavailable. See Christensen, Clayton. 2006. *The Innovator's Dilemma: The Revolutionary National Bestseller that Will Change the Way You Do Business* (New York: HarperCollins), pp. xviii–xx.

67 Hirsh, *Power Loss*, pp. 93–94.

68 EIA. 2005. *Policies to Promote Non-hydro Renewable Energy in the United States and Selected Countries*, (Washington, DC: U.S. Department of Energy,) p. 10. Available at: http://www.eia.doe.gov/cneaf/solar.renewables/page/non_hydro/nonhydrorenewablespaper_final.pdf (accessed April 2, 2010).

69 In the wake of the 1979 Iranian Revolution and subsequent oil price shocks, the Crude Oil Windfall Profits Tax of 1980 and the Economic Recovery Tax Act of 1981 provided additional tax credit increases and extensions, as well as accelerated depreciation of wind turbine equipment, among other support policies for renewables in general.

70 Hirsh, *Power Loss*, pp. 109–110.

71 Hirsh, *Power Loss*, pp. 101–111.

72 Hirsh, *Power Loss*, pp. 112.

73 Hirsh, *Power Loss*, pp. 97–99.

74 Hirsh, *Power Loss*, pp. 97–99.

75 Hirsh, *Power Loss*, pp. 330–331.

76 Stagliano, *Policy of Discontent*, pp. 43–53.

77 Hirsh, *Power Loss*, p. 337.

78 Hirsh, *Power Loss*, p. 240; Stagliano, *Policy of Discontent,* pp. 70–71; and Laird, Frank. N. and Christoph Stefes. 2009. "The Diverging Paths of German and United States Policies for Renewable Energy: Sources of Difference," *Energy Policy* 37: 2621.

79 Stagliano, *Policy of Discontent*, p. 78.

80 Wiser, Ryan, Mark Bolinger, and Galen Barbose. 2007. "Using the Federal Production Tax Credit to Build a Durable Market for Wind Power in the United States," *The Electricity Journal* 20(9): 79.

81 The touted benefits from such a fulfilled scenario would include greater energy security (through electricity portfolio diversification and less price volatility), environmental protection (through reduced water usage and carbon emissions when generating electricity), and economic development (through income transfers to local wind-hosting communities and domestic wind industry growth). EERE, "20% Wind Energy by 2030," pp. 13, 145.

82 See, for instance, EERE. 2009. *Wind Technologies Market Report* (US Department of Energy), 2009: p. 43. vailable at: http://www.eere.energy.gov/windandhydro/pdfs/46026.pdf (accessed March 3, 2010); and Bird, Lori, Mark Bolinger, M. Tory Gagliano, Ryan Wiser, Matthew Brown, and Brian Parsons. 2005. "Policies and Market Factors Driving Wind Power Development in the United States," *Energy Policy* 33: 1398.

83 Source: American Wind Energy Association, "Wind Industry Statistics," March, 2010, available at www.awea.org/faq/wwt_statistics.html (accessed August 28, 2010).

84 Bamberger, *Energy Policy*, p. 9.

85 Bird *et al.*, "Policies and Market Factors," p. 1399.

86 Joskow, Paul. L. 2001. *U.S. Energy Policy During the 1990s*, NBER Working Paper Series 8454, p. 20. http://www.nber.org.libproxy1.nus.edu.sg/papers/w8454 (accessed February 6, 2010).

87 EERE, *Wind Technologies Market Report*, p. 6.

88 EERE, *Wind Technologies Market Report*, p. 53.

89 Stagliano, *Policy of Discontent*, p. 429.

90 Joskow, *Energy Policy*, p. 19.

91 Joskow, *Energy Policy*, p. 20.

92 Stagliano, *Policy of Discontent*, pp. 426–430.

93 Joskow, *Energy Policy*, pp. 16–21.

94 Global Wind Energy Council (GWEC). 2010. "Global Installed Wind Power Capacity 2008/2009 (MW)." Available at: http://www.gwec.net/fileadmin/documents/PressReleases/PR_2010/Annex%20stats%20PR%202009.pdf (accessed April 14, 2010). There are slight discrepancies in reported annual figures between those compiled by GWEC and those by the American Wind Energy Association, but these are not significant enough to affect the overall conclusions regarding US wind sector growth in this chapter.

95 EERE, *Wind Technologies Market Report*, p. 7.

96 EERE, *Wind Technologies Market Report*, p. 9.

97 EERE, *Wind Technologies Market Report*, pp. 53–54.

98 Consistent underestimation of wind power goals and forecasts (Ayee *et al.*, "Wind Power," p. 24 and EERE, *Wind Technologies Market Report*, p. 52) suggests that forecasts (both DOE and non-DOE) did not fully internalize the large increase in oil and gas prices as they actually occurred in years up to 2008.

99 The DOE's 2030 scenario (EERE, "20% Wind Energy by 2030") is probably as close to a sectoral indicative plan as one can get in the USA. It acts as a key signaling device, setting out a year-by-year trajectory for wind power generation without requiring any mandatory policies. By making more information available as a social good for the broader public, the scenario is being used by advocates and relevant interest groups as a benchmark of progress. It also helps to build support for further evidence of wind power's credibility to generate bulk amounts of clean electricity if performances come close to or exceed the forecast path. This scenario exercise shows that indicative planning and industrial policy do not always have to involve massive subsidies and public funding outlays; what matters more is finding the right set of policy approaches for a particular institutional context. See Chang, *Political Economy of Industrial Policy*, p. 76.

100 EERE, *Wind Technologies Market Report*, p. 17.

101 EERE, *Wind Technologies Market Report*, p. 38.

102 Bolinger, Mark and Ryan Wiser. 2009. "Wind Power Price Trends in the United States: Struggling to Remain Competitive in the Face of Strong Growth," *Energy Policy* 37: 1066.

103 EERE, *Wind Technologies Market Report*, p. 19.

104 EERE, *Wind Technologies Market Report*, pp. 25–36.
105 Bolinger *et al.*, "Wind Power Price Trends," p. 1064.
106 EERE, *Wind Technologies Market Report*, p. 12.
107 Ayee *et al.*, "Wind Power," p. 25.
108 Ayee *et al.*, "Wind Power," pp. 25–27.
109 American Wind Energy Association (AWEA). 2009. "Windpower Outlook 2009." Available at: http://www.awea.org/pubs/documents/Outlook_2009.pdf (accessed February 3, 2010).
110 EERE, *Wind Technologies Market Report*, p. 14.
111 EERE, *Wind Technologies Market Report*, p. 14.
112 EERE, *Wind Technologies Market Report*, pp. 15–16.
113 Bolinger *et al.*, "Wind Power Price Trends," p. 1064.
114 David, A. S. 2009. *Wind Turbines: Industry and Trade Summary (ITS-02)* (Washington, DC: US International Trade Commission), pp. 30, 35. Available at: http://www.usitc.gov/ind_econ_ana/research_ana/ind_trade_summ/documents/ITS-2_Summary.pdf (accessed February 5, 2010).
115 David, *Wind Turbines*, p. 31.
116 Pernick *et al.*, *Clean Energy Trends 2010*, p. 6.
117 David, *Wind Turbines*, pp. 30–31.
118 David, *Wind Turbines*, pp. 30–31.
119 The tendency of the PTC to expire in the USA has led to some rather ironic situations despite its open-ended nature. For example, in the early 2000s, Danish company Vestas postponed plans to set up local manufacturing facilities in America because of market instability created by the haphazard implementation of the PTC. See Lewis and Wiser, "Fostering a Renewable Energy Technology Industry," p. 1850.
120 See for example, Chanda, Nayan. 2010, "Thorns Amid Green Shoots," *The Straits Times*, March 15.
121 The USA at present already enacts a general duty of 2.5 percent on all imported wind-powered generating sets, while China, India, the EU, South Korea, and Taiwan apply their own duties as well, ranging from 2.7 percent to 16 percent. See David, *Wind Turbines*, pp. 36–37.
122 While this chapter does not discuss renewable portfolio standards at the state level or the Wind Powering America initiative in detail, it should be noted that both types of initiatives are variants of industrial policies to promote greater wind energy consumption. They are ostensibly driven by a mixture of objectives geared at great energy security, environmental cleanliness, indirect economic development, and income transfers from the generation and siting of wind power facilities, but do not directly target wind manufacturing industries as a source of economic development.
123 For a classic exposition on the theoretical "branch method" of incremental policymaking, see Lindblom, Charles. 1959. "The Science of Muddling Through," *Public Administration Review* 19: 79–88.
124 To further illustrate this point in the extreme hypothetical case: a completely imported finished turbine product would still require transport, installation, and maintenance services, all of which are likely to involve some local economic opportunities.
125 Chang, *Political Economy of Industrial Policy*, p. 60.

14

THE COMPETING DIMENSIONS OF ENERGY SECURITY

Martin J. Pasqualetti

Navy seals take aim at pirates who have taken control of an oil tanker in the Gulf of Aden. Meanwhile, in England, hundreds of people regularly assemble to protest against the continued operation and relicensing of the nuclear power plants such as Sizewell after it was reported that demand for electricity was rising faster than expected. A few hundred miles to the east, curious grade-school children must march through metal detectors before being allowed to tour a giant coal plant in Germany. Across the Atlantic, oyster fishermen in southern Louisiana fret over their future as a giant oil spill in the Gulf of Mexico washes ashore and threatens their livelihood. Off Cape Cod, Interior Secretary Salazar approves the installation of hundreds of wind turbines in Nantucket Sound, citing the increasing need for electricity in nearby communities. In Southeast Asia, a tense CEO calls an emergency meeting when a power outage at his Intel plant in Penang plunges his entire factory into darkness. To the north in urbanized China, new coal plants are being constructed at breakneck speed despite worries that the carbon dioxide they are emitting endangers climate stability. In the southwest deserts of the US, a pipeline ruptures south of Phoenix, and within minutes cars line up at every gas station in a scene reminiscent of events that followed the infamous 1973 oil embargo. In sub-Saharan Africa, villagers scrounge for fuel to cook meals for their families. All these disparate and far-flung, events connect to one another by a common thread, energy security.

Often running under the radar of public discourse and media attention, energy security has steadily risen to the top of the agenda at all levels of private, corporate, military, and international discussions. It is no longer whether the US should risk environmental damage by drilling for oil in the Arctic National Wildlife Refuge; it is whether such potential oil discoveries there can decrease the need to import oil from unstable or unfriendly countries. It is no longer just a matter of whether nuclear power plants can be operated safely; it is whether alternatives can meet demands for electricity from fossil fuels. It is no longer just a worry that oil spills can occur from offshore drilling; it is whether such drilling can bolster domestic supplies and meet rising demand. It is no longer just a matter of how wind turbines off Cape Cod might interfere with the recreational experience of those at the beach; it is whether Massachusetts can afford to forgo such development and still meet its needs for low-carbon energy. With these and numerous other examples, energy matters are now being skewed by concerns of energy security in all its myriad manifestations.

As a reflection of greater visibility and rising sense of urgency, the John D. and Catherine T. MacArthur Foundation recently funded a meeting of 40 security specialists at the Lee Kuan

Figure 14.1 Gulf of Aden: the Arleigh Burke–class guided missile destroyer USS *Farragut* (DDG 99) passes by the smoke from a suspected pirate skiff it had just disabled. USS *Farragut* is part of Combined Task Force 151, a multinational task force established to conduct anti-piracy operations in the Gulf of Aden. Pirates on the high seas, particularly near the Gulf of Aden, have increased their attacks on oil tankers, jeopardizing supply lines between the Middle East and the rest of the world. In order to provide greater security for these supplies, naval vessels from several countries have been deployed to provide additional security, but with limited success.

Source: Photo by Mass Communication Specialist 1st Class Cassandra Thompson/Released) 100331-N-8959T-308. March 31, 2010. http//www.flickr.com/photos/usnavynvns/4483342235/in/set-7215761800128177/.

Yew School of Public Policy of the National University of Singapore (Table 14.1).[1] The goal of the two-day gathering was to share perspectives and information, to identify metrics and indicators of energy security useful in making national policy decisions, and to sharpen the public debate about how to balance the needs, aspirations, and imperatives of an ever-crowded world.

Table 14.1 List of names and affiliations of attendees

Country	Name	Institution
Austria	Shonali Pachauri	International Institute for Applied Systems Analysis
Austria	Alan McDonald	International Atomic Energy Agency
Canada	Larry Hughes	Energy Research Group, Dalhousie University
China	Li Jinke	Shandong Institute of Business and Technology
China	Shi Dan	Chinese National Academy of Sciences
France	Nathalie Trudeau	International Energy Agency
France	Aad van Bohemen	Head, Emergency Policy Division, International Energy Agency
Hungary	Andreas Goldthau	Associate Professor, Department of Public Policy, Central European University
Hungary/Sweden	Aleh Cherp	Professor, Director of Research, Central European University; Universitetslektor, Lund University
India	Rekha Krishnan	The Energy and Resources Institute (TERI) New Delhi, India
India	Sanjay Verma	Joint Secretary (Energy Security), Ministry of External Affairs

Table 14.1 (continued)

Country	Name	Institution
India	S. Rajagopal	Former Secretary of the Indian Atomic Energy Commission
India	Eshita Gupta	Energy and Resources Institute
India	BG (Ret) Krishnaswamy Srinivasan	Center for Security Analysis (Chennai)
Indonesia	Asclepias R. S. Indriyanto	Executive Director, Indonesian Institute for Energy Economics
Japan	Masanari Koike	Graduate School of Engineering, The University of Tokyo
Malaysia	Gladys Mak	Malaysia Energy Center
Netherlands	Jaap C. Jansen	Energy research Centre of the Netherlands (ECN)
New Zealand	Barry Barton	Professor, Faculty of Law, University of Waikato (correct)
Singapore	Scott Valentine	Lee Kuan Yew School of Public Policy, National University of Singapore
Singapore	Benjamin Sovacool	Assistant Professor, Lee Kuan Yew School of Public Policy, National University of Singapore
Singapore	Hooman Peimani	Energy Studies Institute (Singapore)
Singapore	Geoffrey Kevin Pakiam	Energy Studies Institute (Singapore)
Singapore	Joergen Oerstroem Moeller	Institute of Southeast Asian Studies (ISEAS)
Singapore	Violet Chen	Energy Market Authority
Switzerland	Edgard Gnansounou	Swiss Federal Institute of Technology Lausanne (EPFL)
Thailand	Tira Foran	USER—Unit for Social and Environmental Research
United Kingdom	John Kessels	International Energy Agency, Clean Coal Centre
United Kingdom	Andy Stirling	Professor, University of Sussex
USA	Michael Dworkin	Professor, University of Vermont Law School
United Kingdom	Godfrey Boyle	Professor of Renewable Energy, The Open University
USA	Martin J. Pasqualetti	Professor, School of Geographical Sciences and Urban Planning, Arizona State University
USA	Jack Barkenbus	Senior Research Associate, Vanderbilt University
USA	Marilyn Brown	Professor, School of Public Policy, Georgia Tech University
USA	Christopher Cooper	Oomph Consulting, Alexandria, Virginia
USA	Gal Luft	Co-Director, Institute for the Analysis of Global Security
USA	Anne Korin	Co-Director, Institute for the Analysis of Global Security

While many possible topics are worthy of discussion, the workshop confined itself to just a few, including: What is energy security and how can it be measured? What are the most appropriate metrics to measure various energy security dimensions? Are concepts of energy security appropriate uniformly for all countries? As discussions proceeded, other key questions emerged: Can there be equity in access and usage of energy for countries of the world or is this impossibly optimistic? Given that energy security is closely intertwined with climate security, should the two be addressed together? What is the impact of local and regional energy security on global security? Will energy insecurity lead to political destabilization? How do we tackle the problem of sufficiency while deciding on security? I use these questions to provide the organizational outline for the following summary of the discussion in Singapore, including references to some of the burgeoning literature on the topic of energy security.

Definition

As we consider energy security, we find that there are three basic services most groups work with, namely transportation, space-conditions (i.e., heating and cooling), and applications that need access to a continuous supply of electricity (whether household appliances or computer systems for national defense). All people need at least basic energy services of these types, irrespective of whether a country is long or short on oil or natural gas or electricity. The various stands that governments might take on geopolitical issues as a result of disparate resource endowments do not detract from these shared needs.

Defining energy security is a precursor to considering its many linkages. This task was the earliest and most fundamental topic discussed in Singapore. It was clear from the beginning that the notion of energy security contains substantial complexity and fundamental areas of overlap. For the International Energy Agency (IEA), the definition of energy security is "the availability of an uninterrupted or reliable supply of energy at an affordable price."[2] Ensuing discussion pointed out that this definition has physical, economic, social, and environmental dimensions, as well as long- and short-term dimensions.[3] Barry Barton (one of the attendees) extended on the IEA version by defining energy security "as a condition in which a nation and all, or most, of its citizens and businesses have access to energy resources at reasonable prices for the foreseeable future free from serious risk of major disruption of service."[4]

More elaborate and nuanced definitions are of course available. As these definitions suggest, energy security may be simple in its basic concepts. Nonetheless, improving energy security for specific situations and locations can be a complicated matter. For example, some at the Singapore workshop found the definitions by the IEA and Barton too supply-oriented and too vague. For them, the restrictive wording "for the foreseeable future" would seem at odds with the longer-term view implicit in the Brundlandt definition of sustainable development[5]. Also "sufficient" amount of energy, "reasonable" prices, and "serious" risk of "major" disruption are subjective and bound to vary across countries and communities.

Two suggestions at the Workshop identified the principal ingredients in any notion of energy security. One, by Larry Hughes, alluded to security's "Four 'R's:" Review (understanding the problem), Reduce (using less energy), Replace (shifting to secure sources), and Restrict (limiting new demand to secure sources).[6] Another, this from the Asia-Pacific Energy Research Center, identified the "Four As" of energy security: Availability (of oil, other fossil fuels, and nuclear energy); Accessibility, referring to barriers accessing energy resources; Affordability, which is limited to fuel prices (including price projections) and infrastructure costs; and Acceptability, which refers to environmental issues dealing with coal (carbon sequestration), nuclear, and unconventional fuels (biofuel and oil sands).[7]

Any discussion of energy security must recognize that it varies from one place and one culture to another, especially at the household level. For example, energy security for a simple residential unit in Bangladesh will not be the same as it would be in a plush condominium in Manhattan. It must also recognize that energy security will not mean the same thing for chip-maker Intel as it would for gum-maker Wrigley, or for a resident of tropical Singapore as compared with someone in subarctic Helsinki. Moreover, the energy world is volatile and changing rapidly. This means that what is considered secure today may not be secure tomorrow. Recognizing these disparities is to simply recognize a significant restriction on improving energy security.

It was clear during the workshop that we should differentiate between the concepts of energy security and the implementation of these concepts. Implementation must be relevant to objectives, system limits, context, horizon, and so forth, while accepting that it is generally true to say that energy security means different things to different people, companies, and countries. It should be possible, nonetheless, to develop a common framework which can allow for different perspectives. This framework should begin with vulnerabilities and enhancing resilience in the face of adverse disturbances regarding access of a country's population to energy services.

Finally, the Singapore workshop identified several components that could be included in any discussion of the topic. They included:

1. Reliability and affordability. Every user finds such qualities among the most essential energy services.
2. Diversification. When referring to energy security, diversification primarily means ensuring reliable supply, whether by tanker, transmission line, pipeline, train, or other means. Having such diversification takes into account that that diversity must still be at an affordable cost; when taking geopolitical dynamics into account this can be a very complex process. How do we address this? Primarily diversity provides reliability of supply. One way to achieve this would be to structure the energy supply system in a decentralized fashion leading to reduced length of pipelines, ocean transportation, and so forth. Similar thinking would apply to storage as well. Diversification refers to the basket of energy resources and energy suppliers, both by source and location. While usually included in any measure of energy security, such diversification cannot be applied uniformly for all countries. For example, increased diversity could be less important in Norway, which receives most of its electricity from its own ample and reliable hydropower resources. The case for greater diversity could, however, be stronger for France, which is highly dependent for its electricity on nuclear power despite the absence of significant deposits of uranium reserves within its borders.

    The argument for diversity requires context. Churchill, wishing to make his fleet faster, decided on the eve of World War I to switch from secure coal to insecure oil. As a consequence, of course, the UK immediately became reliant on a diversity of sources for its oil, making availability of this fuel a matter of national energy security.[8] Another way to look at this matter is to consider that solar power is usually considered to be the most secure source of energy we have, yet it is the least diverse, at least as used directly.
3. Resilience. Diversification is a strategy to increase the resilience of energy supplies and decrease the probability of supply disruption (insecurity) for a given demand and set of possible contingencies.
4. Variability. This term refers to resource substitution options. We can discriminate security among importing countries, transit countries, and exporting countries; between industrialized and developing countries; among different socio-economic standards and conditions. We cannot expect energy security to be static over time or space. For the "bottom two billion" of the world's population, energy security is a matter of the minimum levels of energy services necessary for life and health. Everyone needs the same basic services (transport, heating/cooling, and continuous supply of electricity). The question remains: which are the most important services and where will the energy come from to meet these services? The bottom two billion often lack the necessary energy resources needed to provide themselves with many basic services. In these cases, what energy substitutes might be available to satisfy these needs? For heat, for example, there are many options; whereas there are no substitutes for electricity. This means variability can increase energy security for certain purposes but not others.
5. Import independence. This consideration is principal to countries from which imports are sourced; that is, external dependence could be indirect, as in the case of technology dependence, even if fuels or resources are indigenously available. There is an important caution here: the assumption that imports are inherently insecure and domestic supplies are

inherently secure is usually too simplistic; it tends to overlook the counterintuitive fact that some imported energy supplies may be considered secure (e.g., US reliance on Canadian crude oil), while some energy supplies that are available domestically can nevertheless be considered insecure (e.g., UK reliance on North Sea gas).

6. Other topics. Others topics important to the definition of energy security were raised but were not discussed at length. They included: routes and transport and distribution networks, strategic energy storage capacity, peak energy demands, environmental stewardship (the responsibility not to increase environmental damage during development, transport, processing, distribution, or use of energy), adequacy of investment to assure security, contractual terms (e.g., long-term "take-or-pay" versus "spot market," as varying by country and fuel), energy efficiency opportunities, and the distinction between a supplier's energy security and a consumer's energy security.

Figure 14.2 Gulf of Mexico: under pressure to increase domestic oil supplies, President Barack Obama proposed the opening of Gulf waters for expanded oil exploration and development. Just two weeks later, BP's Deepwater Horizon's drilling rig exploded into flames and sank. The accident led to a massive oil spill that in just one week exceeded the size of the state of West Virginia. Drilling in the Gulf is supported as one way to reduce reliance on further oil imports.

Source: Photo by the U.S. Coast Guard. Available at: US Coast Guard — 100421-G-XXXXL-Deepwater Horizon fire.

Developing metrics and indices

One of the principal goals of the Singapore Workshop was to discuss and, possibly, identify metrics and indices of energy security. Some of these metrics were considered fundamental and some were considered variable. Broadly, the metrics came to be organized under these headings:

- import dependence and patterns
- "cleanness" of energy
- access to energy
- economic dependence on energy

Metrics are important because they can provide useful data for analysis and use in technical operations and business decisions across organizations. Whether quantitative or qualitative, metrics are measurements or readings resulting from an operating state or situation. Applying this definition, it must therefore be possible to develop relevant metrics of impacting elements that help make an energy security index. For example, per capita consumption of 700 kW of electricity in a particular country can be utilized to compare with a world average of 2300 kW and thereby help to make a judgment on quality of life, development status, and the need to ensure energy security. A similar approach can be adopted when relevant parameters are identified and agreed.

Any discussion of metrics raises questions, and proceedings in Singapore were no exception. Among the questions raised, two dominated: What ingredients constitute a useful index? How do we identify what should be considered significant? These questions commonly form the basis of deliberative discourse on appropriate ingredients. The inherent shortcoming of this approach is that different groups will gravitate toward different sets of ingredients to make up an index that comports with their cultural views; everyone has their own set of personal criteria to apply. This became apparent at the Singapore Workshop, where many countries and cultures were interacting. The agreed approach was to first identify common services, indicators, and methods, and then to select indicators that can make up a preferably quantitative set of indicators to be used.

Perhaps the most important element in any metric or index of energy security is energy infrastructure. Indeed, substantial discussion at the Singapore Workshop focused on how to improve security by adjusting infrastructure. Participants proposed developing a set of questions about alternative energy futures and then constructing a metric of energy security for each scenario. It was agreed that this approach could be an improvement, and that going through such an exercise could allow a comparison of various options based on security gains. For example, what would be the relative levels of energy security that would attend a nuclear energy future vs. a renewable energy future? This could be construed as an "energy wedge."[9]

Another alternative, one that attracted substantial support in Singapore, was to start with what *the public* in each culture and country might identify as important for their own individual energy security, and to seek to determine which combination of energy supplies would be considered the most secure to them. This method is based on surveys of those who would be affected by each specific policy decision taken to improve security. The validity of such a step will depend on survey design and questions. It will also depend on the level of public understanding necessary to make informed decisions on long-term energy security issues. To some, public education would be a necessary part of such an approach, yet even in its absence, just the *perceptions* of the public can play a strong role in developing policy decisions. This is an argument for using expert opinion rather than public surveys. One way around this problem would be to use a graphical technique for explaining the relationships.[10]

Some argued that energy security can be seen narrowly as the security of the supply of petajoules or BTUs (British Thermal Units) for human needs and wants. It was pointed out, however, that this runs the risk of giving priority to amounts of energy rather than to human security. So a broader view of energy security is obliged to ask questions about energy's contribution to human welfare. For example, have we increased our energy security if we threaten a war to obtain access to some oil field? Is energy security improved when the amount of dirty coal we burn results in the expense of an enormous increase in lung diseases? While these questions cannot be brought into the discussion in their entirety, there must be some qualification to the effect that an increase in the availability of energy is not at the expense of other human (or biospheric) values.

It was argued by some that we should keep climate change and energy security analytically clean and separate. The intent of this recommendation was to only deal with those aspects of

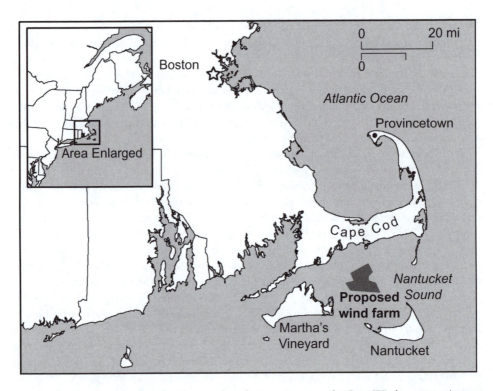

Figure 14.3 Nantucket Sound: proposed as a carbon-free energy source, the Cape Wind energy project was granted approval by Secretary of the Interior Salazar on April 28, 2010. Located in Nantucket Sound, it will be the nation's first offshore wind development. One of the arguments for its approval was greater energy security.

Source: Cartography completed at the School of Geographical Sciences and Urban Planning, Arizona State University.

climate change that may directly affect energy security. This view is logically consistent, but it is based on an important assumption that metrics are being provided to a well-governed polity where climate and security are not only separated but can be reflected upon and managed wisely and rationally, balancing each other. There are such societies. Sweden is one example.

Some at the workshop believed that if a metric is to have worthy practical value it should proceed not from ideal models of governments but from real governments. In most countries climate is indeed separate from energy security in a sense that it is always subordinate and sometimes has no influence on security discourse at all. In such societies one cannot rely on presenting analytically and logically separate metrics and then hoping for sound integration. Those metrics that do not fit the currently powerful discourse will simply be discarded. In other words, if climate change is excluded from energy security, it will most likely be completely ignored rather than taken on board in some mysterious "separate" process.

Time

Although Barton includes the dimension of time in his definition, it is helpful to stress its importance separately. Typical households, especially in expanding economies such as China, Singapore, and India, will use more energy tomorrow than they did yesterday or a decade ago, in part because they are acquiring more appliances, automobiles, and other energy-greedy goods. While this form of "energy creep" occurs in developed countries as well, it is the developing world that is more rapidly accelerating their energy use, something often explained as Jevon's Paradox.[11] Unless there is a compensating improvement in the efficiency of their appliances, it will continue to push upwards per capita consumption, thereby putting further pressure on maintaining supplies. By the same logic, some degree of backcasting would also be beneficial to see how some economies historically have grown faster than others.

Another aspect of the relationship between time and long-term security is the "system inertia" that results from large investments in generation plants, infrastructure, and building stock. These facilities tend to have very long capital turnover periods.

Time also allows a convenient *organizational* tool in defining and categorizing energy security. For example, energy security could address short-term factors (such as unexpected supply disruptions, price fluctuations, emergency storages, and alternative import routes), medium-term factors (such as affordability for industry and households, investments in infrastructure), and longer-term factors (such as, resource depletion, diversity, climate concerns). Despite the fact that time is an important ingredient in energy security, and that short- and long-term issues should be integrated, it is not clear whether such integration is possible. Short-term security is usually caused by an emergency;[12] long-term security can be debated and thought through systematically. One step is to first distinguish between the two and then look at integration.

Environmental quality

Environmental quality as an element in energy security can be viewed from two perspectives. One perspective is that conditions in the natural environment have impacts on the availability of energy. For example, the availability of hydropower is diminished if there is less rain, less storage, or higher siltation. Solar energy is affected by increased cloudiness and the angle of the sun in the sky. Wind power is affected by turbulence and wind speeds. Thermoelectric power plant operation is affected by increased temperatures in cooling waters. In other words, energy production (conversion) is dependent on environmental goods just as other human activities are.

The other perspective is more akin to the fourth "A" of the "four As" mentioned above: acceptability. In other words, in energy security we need to focus largely on energy-related impacts on the local, global, and regional environment. How acceptable is it, for example, to damage the environment in order to meet our energy needs/demands?

A balance must be attained among all three of the following: economic growth, energy generation/availability based on fuel mix, and environmental impact. One benefit cannot be at the cost of another. What is the balance among these three elements, for example, in the case of nuclear energy or renewable energy? Each option has varying applicability within economies depending upon the availability of fuel, the rate of increased energy demand, and the environmental implications of each choice. Can Asian countries afford all types of technologies, can they absorb imported technologies, apply them and build on them successfully? Do they possess technological capability to decide what is appropriate? Technology has a crucial role to play. Technology management is an important factor in energy security.

How will environmental concerns of energy security shift with different policy options? This line of inquiry becomes sharpest when considering whether the specific topic of "climate change" should be included in any definition of energy security. Little agreement exists on this matter from one country to another, but there is essential agreement that there needs to be more consideration of environmental changes, social and behavioral considerations. This is another way of saying that the emphasis of ongoing deliberations on energy security cannot rest solely on issues of infra-structure. One way to assure the place of the environment in discussions of energy security is to put a price on the environmental impacts associated with an energy source. Having taken this step, it will be a measure of the community's acceptance of an energy source. Sweden does this for its carbon emissions.

The discussion of the role of environmental quality in deliberations about energy security comes down to three fundamental questions:

1. Do environmental impacts of energy systems affect energy security and if so how?
2. Do other environmental factors (such as climate change) affect energy security and if so how?
3. What are the analytic and policy benefits of considering environmental impacts of energy systems or environmental factors affecting energy security together with other energy security factors?

Geographic variability

Energy security in all its manifestations will vary from place to place. Factors that are deemed important in one location will not necessarily be considered important in other locations. For example, sea level rise from continued increases in greenhouse gases will be important in the Maldives but not for those who live in Nepal. By some thinking, sea level rise is a climate change issue, not an energy security issue. The heating/cooling question is a good geographic example, as the energy needs for someone living in the tropics are different from someone living in higher latitudes. For someone living in Singapore, heating will not be as important as it is for someone living in northern China. The amount of energy that is needed to maintain health will vary from place to place.

More important, measures taken to provide energy security in one location might well be at odds with measures taken to improve security in another. This perspective covers such events as the usual competition for scarce resources, but it also includes decisions by transit countries (such as Ukraine) that might firm up their own supplies while jeopardizing continued supply to countries further along the pipeline. As Georgia works to facilitate the use of its territory for natural gas transport, Ukraine's leverage to influence gas supplies from Russia could decrease. Another example might involve a country diversifying its oil suppliers with the result of reducing revenues once available from its former supply stalwarts to use for the protection of their oil fields.

The opposite effect might also occur. For example, if individuals in Ukraine pilfer natural gas, parts of the EU might lose their supply when Russia cuts off supply in response. What this can lead to is a shift in how energy security is achieved within a jurisdiction. If natural gas becomes too problematic because of the annual tussle between Ukraine and Russia, a country may turn to other, more secure, sources that might not be acceptable in happier times.

Socio-economic variability

Socio-economic conditions affect individual sense of energy security from place to place. For example, energy security in India might be on the order of the national average of 30 kW/household/month. In the US, in contrast, 30 kW is needed per day, on average. Different people will have different sensitivities and preferences. Some participants in Singapore questioned whether the underlying lifestyle patterns should be taken as given. That is, are lifestyles sustainable in the long run, not only from environmental perspectives but also from sheer supply security perspectives. This might be an issue of availability, accessibility, and affordability (three of the four 'A's). That is, is the energy available? If it is, can the community access it? If accessible, can the community afford it?

The importance of supply reliability will depend upon the critical nature of how the energy is used. A sense of security and reliability will differ from one group to another as locations change. One must address the difference between energy needs vs. energy wants. A person living in a rudimentary manner in the rainforests of New Guinea will have, in most cases, a lower level of energy reliability to provide customary security. If such energy is not critical for survival or comfort for that person, supply on most days can be interrupted without consequence. For someone on a ventilator in a hospital in Singapore, reliability is the key to survival itself.

Topics deserving more attention

Absent in Singapore was any discussion of education. Once we have come to some conclusions about the meaning of energy security, the metrics of energy security, and the measures available to increase energy security, we will need an appropriate educational strategy for disseminating information and educating the public and policymakers. It should be anticipated that this would be an iterative process. That is, as people become more knowledgeable, the sophistication of the discussion can shift.

Indeed, education is important for the discussion of transition towards sustainability- and security-compatible lifestyles for rich population strata in OECD countries and non-OECD Asian countries alike. In many places in Asia, as well as other regions of the world, the desire for large, centralized electricity generation requires extensive grids which are often too expensive to run to rural communities, the result being that the rural poor do not get the same opportunities that those closer to the grid do. There is an interactive relationship between energy security and education that is particularly apparent in this situation, and it might be simpler to be promoting the benefits

Figure 14.4 Phoenix, Arizona, and its surrounding suburbs hold a population of about 4 million people. Only two gasoline pipelines supply this isolated metropolis. When one of those pipelines burst on July 30, 2003, motorists immediately began queuing at petrol stations, some people needing three hours to find the fuel they needed. Photo by the author.

of stand-alone renewable energy such as solar modules in such places. In a broader context, education could be extended to "value formation in society."[13]

In addition to education, another topic that did not figure in the discussions was the crucial role of technology. Appropriate technology is a prerequisite for enabling energy security, especially as it affects such things as improving energy efficiency, reducing emissions, and opening up new resources for potential contribution.

Areas of agreement

Energy security is a big and messy topic. It is big because it involves every level from the individual to the entire globe. It is messy because what it measures and any possible solutions that might be created must consider differences from group to group, from place to place, and from time to time. How do we evaluate it, measure it, increase it? These and other questions were discussed in Singapore. It is not surprising the list of questions that came out of these discussions was longer than the list of answers.

Among the areas of agreement, developing definitions for the key terms and phrases, such as energy security, is critical; without this, meaningful discussion and decision are problematic. The group settled upon that offered by Barton, with only minor dissent about whether to include climate change in the definition.

We also agreed that progress toward increasing security will be slow and undirected unless there is a matching of actions with self-identified themes of importance, even though the specifics will be different in different situations.

A third area of agreement was that nothing breeds suspicion like the lack of transparency. This aphorism applies manyfold to energy security. Despite the truth of this statement, transparency is often avoided for purposes of expediency or disinterest. This suggests that, as in many other instances, the identification of measures to increase energy security should include, and often start with, a thorough understanding of what the public considers to be important. This will be different at the individual level, the personal level, the family level. Thus, it is essential to conduct systematic and statistically significant surveys to find out what the people think before we can embark on any path to remediation. Although such public opinions will often be parochial and self-serving, there are few more important steps in moving toward the most effective course of action.

A fourth area of agreement was that greater energy security requires that energy sources should be secure, sustainable, and preferably environmentally benign. Gaining energy security temporarily or while despoiling the environment is not acceptable. Yet, this very trade-off is common at all socio-economic levels. Poor, developing countries, for example, commonly fell trees for fuel, only to create accelerated erosion and crop failure. Richer countries are willing to risk environmental havoc to secure more energy that would ostensibly improve energy security. In the US, this has been most notable in the decades-long debate over oil drilling in the Arctic National Wildlife Refuge.[14]

A fifth area of agreement was that achieving energy security must recognize the great variability that is inherent in the task. In this vein, geographical diversity will continue to dominate discussion about energy security. We must constantly remind ourselves that a sense of security and the opportunities and strategies to achieve it will vary from one place, one culture, and one location to another; that is, a single person's sense of security will differ from that of another person for a multitude of reasons. The goal of improving energy security will depend upon what is considered sufficient, although affordability creeps into this, as does accessibility.

What is sufficient for one nation may not be sufficient for another. Per capita consumption of electricity in Asian countries is far lower than in Western countries. This means that a single "fix" will never be applicable in every instance. As there are different definitions of energy security for different groups, countries, and cultures, so too must there be different remedies and actions to increase that security from one circumstance to another.

One way to think about this is to consider energy efficiency and the development and availability of renewable energy, particularly distributed versions of such technologies, as plausible paths to greater energy security. These two approaches have inherent appeal for certain societies. Energy efficiency can be a useful strategy to achieve greater security for those people who use energy inefficiently, although this is far less available for people who are impoverished. What is the motivation for the richer people? Probably, saving money, not security, but it could have a similar beneficial effect, assuming their actions do not result in Jevon's Paradox. For impoverished people, whose minimal energy use provides little opportunity for improved security through greater efficiency, renewable energy can have a greater potential for increased energy security. Take, for example, the case of simple farmers in the Petén of Guatemala. Until recently, they had no electric lighting and no reliable source of illumination from liquid fuels. The introduction of solar photovoltaic panels changed that social dynamic by providing electricity for nighttime lighting and the introduction of other low-energy appliances.[15] Renewable energy development is also being touted as a partial solution to national energy security concerns,[16] although its efficacy for that end is often questioned by those who advocate more conventional oil development.[17]

A sixth area of agreement was that we should develop a variety of metrics with consideration of diverse combinations of issues. These issues, for example, might include: cultural differences

Figure 14.5 Africa: The majority use for the world's wood is not for paper or as building material but as fuel, both for warmth and food preparation. Five countries—Brazil, China, India, Indonesia, and Nigeria—account for about half the firewood and charcoal produced and consumed each year. The supply of wood becomes less secure with each year's harvest. This demand is stripping the land of its trees and increasing the potential for soil erosion and floods. The problem stems from the lack of any alternative energy supplies.

Source: http://en.wikipedia.org/wiki/File:Buying_fuelwood.jpeg. Used with permission.

(country by country), time, environmental quality, and how they would each be affected by different energy choices and policy decisions, quality of supply, social-behavioral considerations, and perceptions of risk. In this regard we uncover the most important questions of energy security, namely: At what point do people feel secure? How does energy security differ from actual security? What is energy security?

Recommendations

As we continue to consider matters of energy security, in all its myriad manifestations, ingredients, and importance, there are several steps we can take that seem of paramount importance.

1. Develop an educational program that increases the level of understanding about energy security for decision-makers and the general public. Currently, energy security is but a minor part of the public discourse in any country.
2. Avoid "particularism" that would lead to the consideration that there exist different concepts of energy security for industrialized vs. developing countries, or for energy net exporters vs. energy net importers. As far as adequacy between energy demand and supply is concerned, it is possible to define a unique concept and implement it according to the specificity of each system.
3. In order to avoid confusion, the system must be well defined. For example, the security of energy demand/supply adequacy, when considered as synonymous with energy security, is very different from the "vulnerability of the economy to energy crises." However, the latter case may also be considered when dealing with energy security; in that case, the distinction ("energy net importer" vs. "energy net exporter") should be made.
4. Develop pathways (scenarios) to explain how societies can move from fossil dependence to non-fossil dependence over the next few decades. Already there are indices for human development and environmental sustainability.[18] Can these serve as references and is there a possibility of integrating them in our effort to develop an energy security index? Is not a holistic approach better than developing a stand-alone index? How will this be put to use other than ranking countries on a scale?
5. Develop socio-economic conditions from country to country and place to place in order to have a direct bearing on energy security. Among those conditions are: poverty, availability of supply, affordability, perceptions of security, social status, health, ethnicity, access (particularly to electricity), the *rate* of economic growth in a country and its impact on energy demand, quality of public governance, and the availability of finance for energy infrastructure.

The Singapore Workshop lasted two days. While the discussions were provocative and lively, it was clear at the end of the second day that we had only just started to nibble around the edges of some of the important questions that had brought us together. We had not, in fact, arrived at a single metric or index, nor did it seem likely that one existed to be discovered. We did succeed in producing an outline for further exploration and research, an endeavor represented in this chapter. The workshop also succeeded in validating the notion that improving energy security will be expensive, complicated, and elusive, but also essential. None who use energy can live without a hunger and need for such security; the achievement of sustainability, economic prosperity, and world order is impossible without it. Whether in Asia, Africa, Europe, North or South America, we all need energy security. It is the core principle of our individual and collective freedoms and survival.

Notes

1 For more information see: <http://www.spp.nus.edu.sg/cag/The_MacArthur_Foundation_Project. aspx> (accessed August 28, 2010).

2 International Energy Agency (IEA). 2001. *Toward a Sustainable Energy Future* (Paris: International Energy Agency).

3 As discussed by Constantini, Valeria, Francesco Gracceva, Anil Markandya, and Giorgio Vicini. 2007. "Security of Energy Supply: Comparing Scenarios from a European Perspective," *Energy Policy* 35(1): 210–226: "A *physical* disruption can occur when an energy source is exhausted or production is stopped, temporarily or permanently. *Economic* disruptions are caused by erratic fluctuations in the price of energy products on the world markets, which can be caused by a threat of a physical disruption of supplies … The instability of energy supplies may also cause serious *social* disruption. Today, oil is vital for the functioning of the economy, and any disruption of supply is likely to lead to social demands, and possible social conflict. Lastly, there are many *environmental* concerns about damage to the ecosystems caused by the energy chain, whether accidentally (oil spills, nuclear accidents, methane leaks) or as a result of polluting emissions (urban pollution and greenhouse gas emissions)." (emphasis added).

4 Barton, Barry, Catherine Redgwell, Anita Ronne, and Donald N. Zillman (eds). 2004. *Energy Security: Managing Risk in a Dynamic Legal and Regulatory Environment* (New York: Oxford University Press).

5 World Commission on Environment and Development (WCED). 1987. *Our Common Future* (Oxford: Oxford University Press), p. 43; European Commission (EC), 2000. *Towards a European Strategy for the Security of Energy Supply*, Green Paper, COM, 2000, 769 final (Brussels: European Commission).

6 Hughes, Larry. 2009. "The Four 'R's of Energy Security," *Energy Policy* 37(6): 2459–2461.

7 Asia Pacific Energy Research Centre (APERC). 2007. *A Quest for Energy Security in the 21st Century* (Tokyo: Institute of Energy Economics, Asia Pacific Energy Research Centre). Available at: www. ieej.or.jp/aperc (accessed August 28, 2010).

8 Yergin, Daniel, 2006. "Ensuring Energy Security," *Foreign Affairs* 85 (March/April): 69. However, this assumes that the suppliers have sufficient supplies to meet the requirements of the consumers. For example, see http://dclh.electricalandcomputerengineering.dal.ca/enen/2009/ERG200911.pdf.

9 Hughes, Larry. 2009. "Energy Wedges: A Systematic Way to Address Energy Security and Greenhouse Gas Emissions." A version of this paper was presented at the Fifth Dubrovnik Conference on *Sustainable Development of Energy, Water, and Environment Systems* in Dubrovnik, Croatia, September. It is also available from http://dclh.electricalandcomputerengineering.dal.ca/enen/ (accessed December 16, 2009).

10 Sheth, Niki and Larry Hughes, 2009. "Quantifying Energy Security: An Analytic Hierarchy Process Approach." Available at: http://dclh.electricalandcomputerengineering.dal.ca/enen/2009/ERG200906. pdf (accessed December 21, 2009).

11 Peart, Sandra, 1996. *The Economics of W. S. Jevons* (New York: Routledge); Yale University 2005. "2005 Environmental Sustainability Index Benchmarking National Environmental Stewardship," Yale Center for Environmental Law and Policy, Yale University, and Center for International Earth Science Information Network, Columbia University. In collaboration with: World Economic Forum, Geneva, Switzerland, and Joint Research Centre, European Commission, Ispra, Italy. Available at: http://www.yale.edu/esi/ (accessed December 18, 2009).

12 See Noland, Bob. 2004. *Saving Oil in a Hurry: Oil Demand Restraint in Transport* (London: Centre for Transport Studies, Imperial College); and Hughes, "The Four 'R's of Energy Security," pp. 2459–2461.

13 Hughes, " The Four 'R's of Energy Security," pp. 2459–2461.

14 Debate: "Oil Drilling in the Arctic National Wildlife Refuge." Available at: http://debatepedia. idebate.org/en/index.php/Debate:Drilling_in_the_Arctic_National_Wildlife_Refuge (accessed April 10, 2010).

15 Matthew Taylor, personal communication, November 28, 2009. See also Taylor, M. J. 2005. "Electrifying Rural Guatemala: Central Policy and Rural Reality," *Environment and Planning C*, 23 (2): 173–189.

16 "The Pickens Plan." Available at: http://www.pickensplan.com/act/ (accessed April 10, 2010). "Renewable Energy as a Driver to Ensure Security of Energy Supply for Europe." Available at: <http://www.europeanenergyforum.eu/archives/european-energy-forum/security-of-supply-matters/

renewable-energy-as-a-driver-to-ensure-security-of-energy-supply-for-europe> (accessed April 10, 2010).

17 Shaw, Anup. 2009. "Energy Security." Available at: http://www.globalissues.org/article/595/energy-security (accessed April 10, 2010).

18 Yale University. 2005. "Environmental Sustainability Index Benchmarking National Environmental Stewardship." Available at: http://www.yale.edu/esi/ESI2005_Main_Report.pdf (accessed April 10, 2010).

15

INDICATORS FOR ENERGY SECURITY

Bert Kruyt, Detlef van Vuuren, Bert J. M. de Vries, and Heleen Groenenberg

Introduction

There has been a recent revival of interest in energy security (or its synonym "security of supply") mostly stirred by the high oil prices in the period up to 2008.[1] Governments in different parts of the world have responded to the situation by formulating policy to improve energy security, but in most cases without explicit quantifiable policy goals. One reason for this is that energy security is a rather elusive and context-dependent concept. Issues like the availability of domestic resources, the degree of international cooperation, the degree of risk acceptance, and relationships with other policy targets all determine energy security interpretations. Still, developing a more formalized notion of energy security, including the use of quantifiable indicators, may help to make the concept less vague. Moreover, quantifiable indicators are needed to include energy security considerations in model-based scenario analysis. Such scenarios could be used to study trends in energy security and explore trade-offs with other policy goals. This chapter aims to contribute to the development of more formal notions of energy security, by providing an overview of available indicators for (long-term) security of supply and discussing the strengths and weaknesses of these indicators. First, we define the notion of energy security more exactly (section 2). Next, we discuss indicators for energy security that have been proposed over the years (section 3). In order to evaluate these indicators in a more practical sense, we apply a selection of them to assess the future security of supply, with a focus on Western (OECD) Europe, partly in relation to the consequences of stringent climate policy (section 4). For this, we use scenario results of the TIMER model,[2] a simulation model of the world energy system. A discussion of the methods and results is given in section 5. Finally, section 6 presents the main conclusions.

Energy security—a framework

Background

The interest in energy security (ES) is based on the notion that an uninterrupted supply of energy is critical for the functioning of an economy. However, an exact definition of ES is hard to give as it has different meanings to different people at different moments in time.[3] It has traditionally been associated with the securing of access to oil supplies and with impending fossil fuel depletion. After the 1970s, security concerns also arose for natural gas, widening the concept to cover other fuels.

ES is also not constrained to only physical aspects: it also includes the price of oil and natural gas[4] and the vulnerability of energy conversion and transport.[5] The ability of the system to cope with extreme events, such as hurricanes (Katrina), strikes, and terrorist actions, are also mentioned in the context of ES.[6] Finally, also the political stability of supplying and transit countries is part of ES discussions.[7]

Clearly, the concept and definitions of ES have widened over time. In present-day definitions,[8] four main elements can be identified. The first and most dominant element (included in all definitions) is the availability of energy to an economy. This entails an element of absolute availability or physical existence (fossil resources are essentially finite). Next, there is an element of accessibility due to the large spatial discrepancy between consumption and production of resources. Acquiring access often carries geopolitical implications. Furthermore, there is an element of costs in most interpretations of ES. Finally, some definitions also include an element of environmental sustainability (e.g. related to the availability of tar sands or bioenergy). One may question whether ES should be defined so broadly, as very wide definitions may erode the concept and make it equal to even broader concepts such as sustainable development. However, in this overview we start from the broad definition in order to be able to deal with the full literature on the issue. Therefore, we will adhere to a classification scheme proposed by the Asia Pacific Energy Research Centre,[9] by classifying elements relating to ES into:

- availability—or elements relating to *geological* existence;
- accessibility—or *geopolitical* elements;
- affordability—or *economical* elements;
- acceptability—or *environmental* and societal elements.

It should be noted that these are by no means isolated categories but subject to a complex interplay.

A distinction is often made between short-term and long-term ES.[10] While the former is related to short-term disruptions, the latter deals with more structural aspects of the energy system. In this chapter, we focus on the latter, but it should be noted that the timescales are connected, as underinvestment in long-term ES leads to increased risk of disruptions.[11]

Different perspectives

ES is context and perspective dependent. This can be shown by relating the four aspects of ES to different views on world development. A crucial factor is the question of how the world develops with regard to globalization.[12] One possibility is a trend towards multilateralism and market trust. In such a situation, attention on geopolitical factors is likely to be low, while physical *availability* and *affordability* could be more important. Conversely, increasing competition between regions will raise political barriers between regions and increase focus on energy independence and thus implies a focus on *accessibility* to resources.

There seems also to be a trade-off between *affordability* and *acceptability*. Responding to environmental challenges (climate change, other environmental targets) leads, in general, to higher costs. Different perspectives exists on how to weigh these trade-offs. One perspective emphasizes the need for low energy costs as a condition for economic growth (this often coincides with optimism with respect to environmental threats and resource scarcity). A second perspective, however, emphasizes the need to deal with environmental consequences and physical depletion as they provide a basis for economic growth.

The above dichotomies of (1) regionalization versus globalization and (2) economic efficiency and technology optimism versus a focus on equity and solidarity are also the basis of the

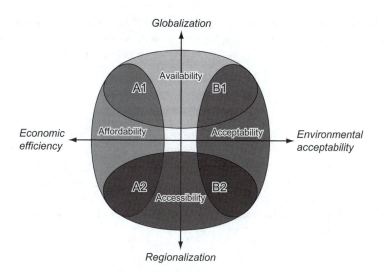

Figure 15.1 The 'energy security spectrum'; the four dimensions of energy security and their relation to global orientations.

Intergovernmental Panel on Climate Change's (IPCC) *Special Report on Emission Scenarios* (SRES).[13] In SRES, they were used to define four different storylines for future scenarios of greenhouse gas emissions. These scenarios are: A1 (high level of globalization and focus on economic efficiency), B1 (high level of globalization and focus on equity), A2 (low level of globalization and focus on economic efficiency) and B2 (low level of globalization and focus on equity) (Figure 15.1). We can use these same axes also to map the four dimensions of ES.

Indicators for energy security

Over recent years there have been a number of attempts to devise indicators for ES. Some of the indicators deal with one aspect of ES, while others attempt to capture several elements in a single aggregated indicator. Here, we provide an overview of the indicators found in the literature. It should be noted that some of the developers of these ES indicators seem to aim at capturing ES in some kind of objective quantitative metric, which could be used in policymaking (allowing the setting of targets in a similar way to setting greenhouse gas reduction targets). Given the discussion above on the different perspectives, we consider most indicators to have a much more heuristic role—capturing a particular aspect of ES and indicating a relative position or direction of change. Most indicators are therefore also only valuable in a certain context. This point is even more important for indices, as these include some form of subjective weighting (see also Section 5: Discussion).

Overview of simple indicators

Resource estimates

The actual availability of energy sources forms a crucial aspect of ES and therefore available (remaining) resources are often used as a direct indicator for ES. Unfortunately, however, large uncertainties surround the amounts of hydrocarbon resources and their extraction potentials.

The best known resource inventory is that of the United States Geological Survey (USGS).[14] Although some regard USGS as "one of the most independent and reliable sources of data,"[15] others (proponents of the peak oil theory) argue that the USGS estimates are overly optimistic.[16] Thus there is no consensus on the available resources.

Reserves to production ratios

Reserves to production ratios (also called R/P ratios or RPRs) are often used as ES indicators.[17] They indicate the size of current reserves expressed in years of current production levels. Obviously, in the future neither reserves nor production rates are fixed so ideally a more dynamic quantity should be used but in practice, constant factors are usually used. While the RPRs are relatively easy to interpret, they ignore issues like a rapidly changing demand and/or uncertainty in reserve estimates. Dynamic RPRs (that account for possible future changes) might be conceptually better but also less transparent.

Diversity indices

Diversity in energy (fuel) type and geographical source can be an important means to hedge against supply risks.[18] A quantitative measure of diversity can therefore serve as an indicator of ES. Stirling argued that diversity indices should consider three key elements:[19] (1) variety (the number of categories); (2) balance (the spread across categories); and (3) disparity (the degree to which the categories are different from each other). In practice, however, it is difficult to define disparity. Hence, so-called "dual concept" diversity indicators are based on two of the three key elements of diversity.

As for most ES indicators, the exact definition of these dual concept indicators (including the resolution) includes some form of subjectivity (or arbitrariness). The relationship between diversity and ES is also not well established. While diversity does provide resilience against physical supply disruptions, physical disruptions more and more are translated into price shocks, which can spill over from one market to another. One may discuss how important these correlations are. Awerbuch and Berger[20] mention significant diversification when correlation coefficients between energy prices are below 0.7.[21]

Import dependence

Measures of import dependence are amongst the most commonly used ES indicators. Various disaggregations with regard to fuels and regions are possible, as well as a focus on physical and/or monetary units. Import dependence is often expressed relative to oil consumption. For ES purposes, it would appear most practical to look at net imports. Also more refined import dependency indicators exist. Besides import shares, the Asian Pacific Energy Research Centre applies a combined measure of diversity and import dependence.[22] To this end, the Shannon index is adapted to measure an economy's import dependence weighted with its fuel diversity:

$$NEID = \frac{\Sigma_i m_i p_i \ln p_i}{\Sigma_i p_i \ln p_i} \qquad (1)$$

with m_i the share in net imports of PES i, and p_i the share of PES i in Total Primary Energy Supply (TPES).[23] Here, a higher value implies a lower ES. With a specification of the fuel's role in the energy mix, this indicator provides a more refined indication of import dependence as the simple import numbers and is useful as such. On a global level, also international trade can be used directly as ES indicator.

The strength of import indicators is that they provide a straightforward and insightful indicator that does not require specific expertise to comprehend. The indicator is used often. In the case of international cooperation, it can be argued that import dependence is less relevant to ES. In a more regionalized world, however, where a paradigm of competition rather than cooperation prevails, import shares form a useful indicator (see Figure 15.1).

Political stability

The political situation in supplier countries is also important for ES. To our knowledge, only three studies have attempted to quantify this element that we have dubbed "political stability." The IEA uses political risk rating.[24] In a follow-up report the IEA bases its political risk measure on the average of two of the six World Bank worldwide governance indicators, that is, "political stability and absence of violence" and "regulatory quality." Jansen *et al.*,[25] in their turn, use the United Nations Development Program's (UNDP) Human Development Indicator (HDI) as a political stability indicator. One may debate whether even more subjective, bilateral issues need to be accounted for as well (such as between the USA and Venezuela). As these examples show, it is not straightforward to identify relevant simple indicators. While indicators like the HDI seem to be too indirect, unfortunately commercial political risk assessments are often proprietary.

The energy price

In a well-functioning market, price functions as an indicator of ES. It is also considered as a measure of economic impacts. Finally, it also reflects scarcity and thus depletion of energy resources. The oil price plays a special role. Being a dominant energy carrier in most parts of the world, the oil price is seen as a crucial ES indicator. A difficulty is that these prices are influenced also by other factors (speculation, strategic communication, short-term shortages). Moreover, for use in scenarios it should be noted that historically it has proven to be extremely difficult to model oil prices accurately. The use of oil prices as an ES indicator is mainly useful relative to other scenarios (what-if types of questions).

Mean variance portfolio theory

Mean variance portfolio (MVP) theory stems from financial economics. It has been applied to electricity generating mixes, not only taking into account the unit generating costs, but also the variance in fuel costs and the correlations amongst different fuel costs.[26] The portfolio analysis provides an "efficient frontier," a limit in the cost-risk domain beyond which (energy) investment portfolios cannot be made less costly without increasing their risk or, vice versa, cannot be made more risk averse without increasing their cost. Moving along this frontier represents different trade-offs between risk and cost. As such, MVP is an optimization method rather than an indicator.

One unique element of the MVP approach is that it assumes past data to form a sufficiently firm ground for future projections. This has been opposed by Stirling,[27] who argues that under conditions of ignorance[28] no basis exists to assume that historic patterns will repeat themselves.[29] Because fuels are substitutes or because prices are coupled (as with gas in parts of Europe, where its price is coupled to that of oil), price shocks in one market can have spillover effects on others. Contrary to "traditional" ways of measuring diversity, the MVP does address this issue.

Share of zero carbon fuels

The Asia Pacific Energy Research Centre (APERC) uses an economy's efforts to switch away from a carbon-intensive fuel portfolio as an indicator for *acceptability* in the conext of ES. This is done by taking into account the share of renewables and nuclear in total primary energy supply.[30] Alternatively, one could also look at the carbon content of fuels (e.g. CO_2/GJ). It should be noted that acceptability concerns also exist regarding other energy options, for example nuclear energy.

Market liquidity

Market liquidity relates to the capacity of markets to cope with fluctuations in supply and demand and is therefore relevant to ES. The IEA includes a market liquidity indicator in its information paper on ES,[31] defined as the exponential function of the ratio of a country's consumption over the total of that fuel available on the market. The concept of market liquidity is linked to price elasticity. For stock markets, it has been suggested to use a coefficient of elasticity of trading (CET) as an indicator of market liquidity,[32] defined as the relative change in trading volume over the relative change in price. Values below unity indicate an inelastic market, while values above unity indicate elastic markets.

Demand-side indicators

A range of demand-side indicators has been proposed in relation to ES, mostly as they are relevant for the impacts of energy shortages. Important indicators include the energy and oil intensity of the economy. It has also been proposed to use energy intensity indicators relative to a benchmark. Another category of demand-side indicators relates ES to energy expenditures.[33] It is assumed that high expenditures are indicative of great difficulties in supplying resources. Moreover, expenditures directly relate to *affordability*. It is useful to monitor expenditures vis-à-vis income measures. For the poor, other demand-side indicators may be envisioned that rely less on monetary values, but rather on physical values such as the availability of traditional biomass in the face of growing food requirements.[34] Such indicators, however, have rarely been used. Finally, some indicators focus on the question of which sector energy is used in, identifying sensitivity to ES problems (e.g. the share of oil used in the transport sector, since the transport sector is specifically inelastic and has little substitution options).

Overview of aggregated indicators

Shannon index based on Jansen et al., 2004

Jansen *et al.* used the Shannon index at the heart of their aggregated indicator.[35] They applied a combined index that captures fuel diversity, but also diversity in suppliers, for the share of imports of each fuel. These suppliers are attributed a political stability factor, based on a modification of the UNDP's Human Development Indicator (HDI): more weight is given to the suppliers that are thought to be politically stable. Resource depletion is also factored in through the inclusion of a depletion index. This index rests on the assumption that markets will respond to information on reserve/production ratios if these drop below a value of 50.

While this aggregated index captures several parts of the ES concept, the balance between different elements lacks a fundamental ground (is arbitrary).[36] A similar critique holds for the assumption of the threshold for reserves-to-production ratios. The import diversity measure emphasizes the *accessibility* element of ES—which might not be as relevant under all scenarios/worldviews.

The IEA's energy security index

The IEA have constructed two aggregated indicators for ES.[37] One deals with the physical *availability*, clearly relevant if prices are regulated. This indicator is defined as the share of a country's total energy demand met by pipe-based gas imports purchased through oil-indexed contracts. The rationale behind this is that pipelines generally do not allow consumers to switch to other suppliers in case of a supply disruption, as opposed to LNG-based trade. The second indicator deals with price risks stemming from supply (or sellers) market concentration. The assessment of supply concentration is done by means of a Herfindhal-Hirschman index. A measure of political stability is also included, giving extra weight to politically unstable countries, based on two of the six "worldwide governance indicators" of the World Bank. The supply concentration measure for each fuel market is weighted according to the fuel's share in primary energy supply to assess a country's vulnerability to these concentration risks.

Also for this indicator, the balance between the parameters for supply concentration and political stability is arbitrary. On a more conceptual level, classifying supply concentration as the sole indicator of ES stems from a particular perspective that has a firm trust in the functioning of (liberalized) energy markets. Dynamics of other aspects of ES, such as depletion, are ignored.

S/D index

The Supply/Demand (S/D) index for long-term ES[38] has been designed on the basis of expert assessments covering all possible relevant aspects of ES (demand, supply, conversion, and transport of energy in the medium to long term). Values of individual elements are determined by scoring rules which are functions of shares, supply origins, efficiencies, reserve factors, network capacity, refinery and storage capacity, to name but a few. The functions are deliberately kept simple in favor of transparency. The factors are weighted on the basis of expert judgments.

The main difference compared with the other indicators is that the S/D index attempts to grasp the whole energy spectrum, including energy demand, as it lowers the overall impact of supply disruptions. Due to its comprehensiveness, however, the S/D index suffers from limited transparency as well as an extensive amount of arbitrary weighting factors, even if these are deliberately made explicit.[39]

Willingness to pay

Bollen has constructed a "willingness-to-pay" function for ES.[40] This indicator represents the percentage of GDP a country is willing to spend in order to lower the ES risks. It is assumed that willingness is higher for higher ES risks, as indicated by: (1) high import quotes, (2) high shares of oil and gas in TPES, and (3) high energy intensities. The function is of the form:

$$IMP_{t,r} = A * i_{t,r}^{\alpha} * c_{t,r}^{\beta} * E_{t,r}^{\gamma} \tag{2}$$

with IMP being the willingness to pay to avoid a lack in ES, i the import ratio of the fuel, c the share of the fuel in TPES, E the energy intensity, A a region-specific calibration constant, relating to the ES at t=0, and finally α, β, γ exponents, with a value of 1.1, 1.2, 1.3, respectively. The indicator is calculated for oil and natural gas only, as these are considered the main sources subject to potential ES risks. The exponents α, β, and γ are greater than 1, based on the assumption that the ES risk increases faster as the dependency increases. The function is calibrated based on the investments nations have made in order to improve their ES in the past.[41] The fact that this indicator is expressed in monetary terms makes it directly comparable to other cost estimates. Obviously, the actual parameter choice is dependent on world views—something that (unfortunately) has not been considered by Bollen. High values for α may, for instance, correspond to an A2 (Figure 15.1) interpretation of ES.

Oil vulnerability index (OVI)

Gupta computes an aggregated index of oil vulnerability based on seven indicators:[42] (1) the ratio of value of oil imports to GDP, (2) oil consumption per unit of GDP, (3) GDP per capita, (4) oil share in total energy supply, (5) ratio of domestic reserves to oil consumption, (6) exposure to geopolitical oil supply concentration risks as measured by net oil import dependence, diversification of supply sources, political risk in oil-supplying countries, and (7) market liquidity. These elements are combined in the overall index, where their weighting is based on a statistical method called principal component analysis (PCA). In this method, the covariance of the indicators above is used to assign weights, rather than (subjective) expert judgments. This greatly increases the robustness of the results. However, as with MVP, extrapolating statistical variance to obtain future projections may lead to concerns over the robustness in relation to changing context and worldview.

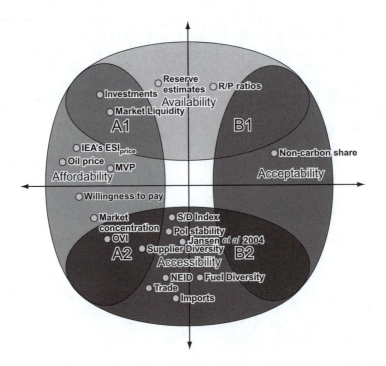

Figure 15.2 The indicators discussed in this study and the elements of the energy security spectrum they focus on.

The indicators in relation to various elements of energy security

Using the previously given four quadrants to outline possible ES interpretations (Figure 15.1), we map the indicators discussed so far onto the raster of perspectives or worldviews behind these four quadrants (Figure 15.2) (see Annex A for arguments for the mapping). The adequacy of ES indicators does depend on the different notions of ES. For instance, energy price and demand-oriented indicators may be considered highly relevant in an affordability oriented perspective (the left part of Figure 15.1), while in this perspective the share of zero-carbon fuels may be considered as irrelevant. Using a set of indicators from different positions in Figure 15.2 may help to broaden ES considerations, and make them more relevant for different worldviews. It should be noted, however, that not only the indicators are context-dependent, but also their elaboration (as briefly addressed for the diversity indicators and the willingness-to-pay index).

Table 15.1 provides an overview of the indicators and their required input data. The table also indicates the applicability of the indicators in large-scale, long-term energy models for prospective analysis. For instance, short-term price variations, such as required for MVP indicators, are not included in global energy models. Finally, we have indicated in the table whether the indicators are currently, to our knowledge, used in energy policymaking.

Table 15.1 Overview of SOS indicators in the literature

Indicator	Input Data Required	Scenario analysis with TIMER?	Current use in policy making?
Simple indicators			
Resource estimates	Quantity and likelihood of occurrence of fossil resources	+	Qualitatively
Reserve to production ratios	Resource estimates and production figures (at country or global level)	+	Qualitatively
Diversity indices	Shares of fuel in TPES or shares of suppliers in import	+	No
Market concentration	Shares of producers in the market	+	No
Import dependence	Import quotes of energy carriers	+	Yes
NEID (Net Energy Import Dependency, APERC)	Import quotes and shares of fuel in TPES	+	No
Political stability	Depending on the paradigm; HDI, various political risk ratings		Qualitatively
Oil price	The oil price		Yes
Mean variance portfolio	share of generating technology/fuel in TPES; (expected) cost per unit of energy; (expected) short term variance in this cost		No
Non-carbon	Share of fuel in TPES; carbon emission (y/n)	+	Yes
Market liquidity	Available fuel on the market/production, consumption/import needs	+	
Energy or oil intensity	PES (total or per fuel), GDP	+	Yes
oil/energy expenditures	TPES, GDP, energy cost (fuel specific)	+	Limited
Energy or oil use per capita	TPES, population	+	Limited
Share of oil in transport sector	Sectoral energy use, total oil use	+	Limited

Table 15.1 (continued)

Indicator	Input Data Required	Scenario analysis with TIMER?	Current use in policy making?
Share of transport sector in total oil use	Sectoral energy use, total oil use	+	Limited
Aggregated indices			
Jansen *et al.* (2004)	Shares of energy carrier in TPES; import quotes, shares of suppliers in imports; HDI and RPR per country/region	+	No
IEA's ESI$_{price}$	share of producer in market (based on net exports), political risk rating per producers, shares of prim. energy carrier in TPES. Additionally supply available on the market; global RPRs for fossil fuels.	+	No
S/D index	Fuel shares in TPES, import shares, supplier shares in imports, long- or short-term contracts, energy intensity, detailed information on conversion and transport not further specified here, see Scheepers et al. (2007)	+	No
Willingness to pay	import quotes; fuel shares in TPES; energy intensity; historic calibration	+	No
OVI (Gupta 2008)	Import quotes, GDP, oil price, TPES, shares of oil suppliers, ICRG	+	No

Application in the model-based scenario context

Application of selected indicators to energy security in Western Europe

To illustrate the actual application of different indicators, we have included some of them in a scenario study on the relationship between climate policy and ES with a special reference to Western Europe. This case study considers two main alternative scenarios: (1) a "business-as-usual" scenario without climate policy (baseline scenario) and (2) a stringent climate policy scenario. Both scenarios are based on the OECD Environmental Outlook. These scenarios have been elaborated using the TIMER model, which is an energy-system model describing long-term developments of the energy system[43] The OECD baseline (OECD-B) scenario describes a world under intermediate assumptions for factors such as economic growth, population, and technology development.[44] It assumes no major shifts in current policy regimes. Under the OECD baseline scenario, global energy demand is projected to increase to 865 exajoules (EJ) in 2050, of which demand for oil constitutes 288 EJ. On the basis of this OECD-B scenario, a second scenario has been developed that aims at stabilization of greenhouse gas concentrations at 450 ppm CO_2-eq by 2100.[45] This stringent climate policy scenario (OECD-CP) is implemented by the forced imposition of a carbon tax which induces emission reduction by means of energy efficiency improvement, fuel switch, and use of technologies with carbon capture and storage. Worldwide, carbon emissions in this scenario are reduced by about 40–50 percent in 2050 compared with 2000. Oil and primary energy demand are lower than in the baseline (132 EJ/yr and 635 EJ/yr by 2050, respectively).

The question we address here is: how adequate are the different indicators as a policy tool for present and future ES developments. Although there is no explicit focus on the differences in environmental indicators between these scenarios (acceptability), it should be noted that the OECD-CP scenario has, by its very definition, a much lower greenhouse gas emission than the OECD-B scenario. As a co-benefit of climate policy, also the emissions of air pollutants are significantly reduced.[46]

Oil

The projected increase in oil demand implies that in the OECD-B scenario, globally the conventional proven oil reserves are depleted around 2035 and production needs to come from less certain and non-conventional occurrences (Figure 15.3). In contrast, the lower oil demand of the climate policy case implies that a considerable part of current reserves is still in place in 2050.

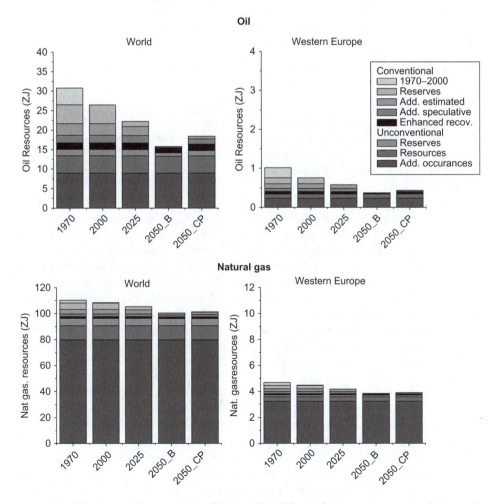

Figure 15.3 Oil and natural gas resources of the world and those of Western Europe. Depletion under baseline (BL) and climate policy (CP) scenario in the period 1970–2050.

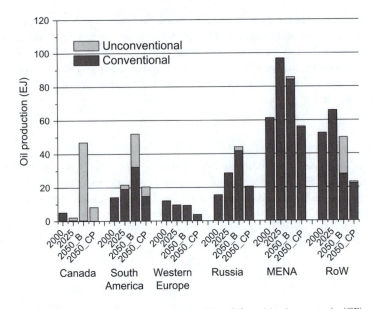

Figure 15.4 Main oil producers for the baseline scenario (B) and the mitigation scenario (CP).

For Western Europe specifically, domestic proven oil reserves are projected to be depleted by 2025 in the baseline and most of the conventional estimated and speculative reserves by 2050. Under the OECD-CP scenario, a small fraction of these uncertain resources would still be in place in 2050. From the perspective of oil security, there are thus clear positive co-benefits of climate policy for ES (B1).

The available indicators show increasing concentration of supply. In the OECD-B scenario, the majority of the increase in oil production from 2000 to 2025 will come from the Middle East (consistent with the IEA's World Energy Outlook[47]). After 2030, however, the TIMER model expects the share of the Middle East in world oil production to decline as unconventional oil production from Canada and South America increases. Furthermore, conventional oil production in Brazil and Russia increases. This implies a declining market concentration after 2030. Interestingly, in the climate policy scenario, lower oil demand leads to a situation where oil production will still predominantly come from the cheaper reserves in the Middle East and Russia. As a result, supply concentration in 2050 is higher than the baseline (Figure 15.4). From a supply concentration perspective (especially A2), the synergy between climate policy and ES will therefore not be as evident.

Natural gas

For natural gas, the global, currently proven, conventional reserves are projected to be depleted under the OECD-B scenario by 2050, with projected world natural gas use of 221 EJ/yr. The projected demand is 184 EJ/yr in the OECD-CP scenario. In both cases, a fair amount of the estimated and speculative conventional resources is expected to be still in place by then. Demand for natural gas is much less impacted by climate policy due to its lower carbon content. Consequently, depletion of natural gas resources is comparable in the two scenarios. For Western Europe, ES issues are also more prominent for natural gas as proven conventional natural gas reserves are projected to be depleted by 2025 in both the OECD-B and OECD-CP scenarios, leaving only speculative resources and/or imports. Again, climate policy has hardly any co-benefits for ES. In terms of concentration, natural gas production in the OECD-B scenario initially becomes geographically more diversified, in contrast to oil, because several potential suppliers have produced relatively little natural gas so far. After 2020, however, Russian and Middle Eastern production is projected to become dominant and both the production and export concentration indicators show a declining ES. Depending on, amongst others, the LNG developments, Middle East natural gas production is projected to increase rapidly, producing by 2050 over one third (37 percent) of world output.

Coal

The global proven reserves of coal are very large and this will still be the case by 2050. Additional recoverable reserves are huge, in the range of 100 Zettajoules. This translates into a high RPR for coal, although it declines from a current 167 years to 81 years in 2050. In the OECD-CP scenario, global coal production is reduced by as much as 139 EJ/yr in 2050 compared with the baseline. Supply is expected to become slightly more concentrated.

Trade

The rising world energy demand implies an increase in internationally traded energy. Figure 15.5 shows the share of total energy demand met through international trade, as well as the shares of dominant fossil energy carriers and modern biofuels. The figure shows that international energy trade increases in both absolute and relative terms, implying an increasing interdependency of regions (with associated ES consequences). The major differences in the OECD-CP scenario

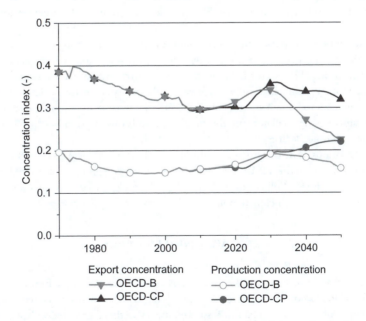

Figure 15.5 Concentration in the production and export market for oil (with 0 a perfect market with equal shares for an infinite number of suppliers and 1 a monopoly) (baseline and mitigation scenario).

compared with the OECD-B scenario are the lower oil and coal trade (-100 EJ/yr and -26 EJ/yr, respectively), partially substituted by an increase in biofuel trade (+40 EJ/yr).

Imports

As a result of mildly declining oil use, under the OECD-B scenario the oil import share in Western Europe remains high (between 60 and 70 percent). The larger part of the oil import is projected to come from the Middle East, with a smaller share coming from Russia. In the OECD-CP scenario, the oil import in Western Europe will decline significantly in absolute terms but only marginally in relative terms with respect to the OECD-B situation. For natural gas, Europe's dependency on imports is projected to increase, reaching over 60 percent in 2050. Most of this demand is met by natural gas from the former Soviet Union and consequently the import diversity for natural gas is rather low. These results of the scenarios suggest, again, that accessibility-oriented indicators show a decreasing ES for oil and natural gas, while climate policy has co-benefits in the case of oil but not, or much less so, for natural gas.

Fuel diversity and demand-side indicators

Fuel diversity indicators such as the Shannon index strongly depend on the number of different energy carriers accounted for (see also Section 3). In the TIMER model (but also in most other global energy models) the number of different energy carriers taken into account is limited. The scenario analysis shows that in Western Europe the growth of electricity from solar/wind and of modern biofuels contributes to an increase in fuel diversity, as measured by a Shannon index of diversity. In the OECD-CP scenario the increase in renewables is much larger, but the resulting benefits for fuel diversity are offset by a substantial decrease in the share of coal in TPES. Contrary to China, for instance, where the share of coal is so large that a decrease actually improves diversity, in Europe a decrease in the coal share does not improve fuel diversity.[48]

Another interesting trend is that in all countries oil use is becoming more and more concentrated in the transport sector (as it is substituted by natural gas and coal in other sectors such as power generation). This sector is rather inelastic with regard to price changes, and as such is vulnerable to disruptions. In Europe, the share of the transport sector in oil use increases from a current 72 percent to 92 percent in 2050 in the OECD-B scenario. According to the OECD-CP scenario, climate policy will not curb this trend (while oil consumption is reduced in transport, it is also reduced in other sectors).

The calculations show that prices for oil and natural gas are projected to rise. It should be noted, however, that prices in the TIMER model are subject to a large number of simplifications and are mainly depletion driven. Still, for oil and natural gas, ES is likely to decline in terms of affordability. This gets even worse with climate policy as it leads to even higher energy costs.

Aggregated indicators

We have calculated the IEA's ESI_{price}-index (describing concentration in fossil fuel supply) but, as shown in Figure 15.6, its value is more or less constant for Western Europe in the OECD-B scenario. Climate policy will lower the ESI a little, with an increased concentration in the oil supply market offset by a decrease in fossil fuel use. Also the aggregated indicators proposed by Jansen *et al.* show a rather stable trend over the projection period in the TIMER results.[49] For these indicators, climate policy tends to lead to a somewhat higher ES (Figure 15.6). For the last

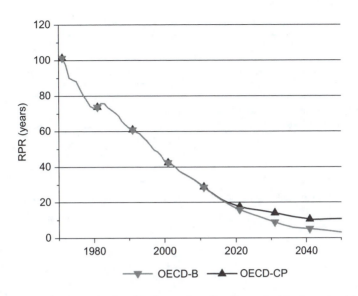

Figure 15.6 Resource-Production ratios for oil and natural gas (baseline and mitigation scenario).

aggregated index, the supply–demand index, a rather stable trend over the projection period is also observed, with little change in the OECD-CP scenario. Groenenberg and Wetzelaer did show earlier that climate policies (energy efficiency and targets for renewables) can lead to as much as a 10 percent increase in the S/D index by 2020 for the EU 25.[50] The much smaller difference observed here may stem from the high level of aggregation.

Alternative scenarios

We have used here two scenarios: OECD-B and OECD-CP. One could use other scenarios such as for instance the IPCC SRES scenarios. An interesting aspect of the SRES set is that they directly relate to the different ES definitions. For instance, under the A1 scenario (see Table 15.2 and Figure 15.1), a major focus of an ES policy would be to ensure a low-cost energy supply and avoid global depletion of resources. At the same time, the high economic growth in this scenario and the reliance on fossil fuels imply that resources would be depleted faster than in the OECD-B scenario. Several trends described for OECD-B may therefore be even more clearly visible in the A1 scenario (earlier depletion, stronger reliance on import). The main ES question in this world would be whether alternatives to conventional fossil fuel supply (renewables, nuclear, unconventional resources) can be developed fast enough to continue provision of low-cost energy.

In the A2 scenario (Table 15.2) a major focus of an ES policy would be to ensure accessibility— given the emphasis on regional economic growth. In the short term, import trends in OECD-B may therefore be very different in an A2 world. A major question here, however, is whether sufficient domestic resources are available. If not, local depletion will, in the future, have to be substituted by increased imports, thus eroding the original policy effort.

In the B1 world the focus on renewables and efficiency leads to a lower fossil fuel use than in OECD-B. Trends with regard to fossil fuel depletion and import dependence are likely to be somewhat delayed. A challenge in the B1 scenario would be whether renewable energy resources

Table 15.2 Position of the OECD baseline and climate policy scenario versus the IPCC SRES scenarios.

	SRES				OECD	
	A1	A2	B1	B2	OECD-B	OECD-CP
Main focus (archetype)	Economic optimism	Regional fragmentation	Global sustainability	Regional sustainability	Business as usual	Reformed market
Environmental policy	Reactive	Reactive	Pro-active; no explicit climate policy	Pro-active; no explicit climate policy	Reactive	Reactive except for stringent climate policy
Openness	Connected world	Competition	Connected world	Regional focus	Connected world	Connected world
Global population (2050)	8.2	10.4	8.2	9.0	9.1	9.1
Global economic growth (2050)	22.7	9.7	18.3	14.5	15.2	15.2
Primary energy use	1250	978	805	863	865	635

are available sufficiently and timely to find synergy between ES and environmental policies. Finally, developments in the B2 world would be similar to the OECD baseline.

Discussion

Capturing a broad notion such as ES in indicators inevitably leads to simplification. While indicators suggest some form of scientific objectiveness, their value cannot be interpreted independently from the context. In this chapter, we have discussed ES in a broad, comparative, and dynamic context in order to include all dimensions of ES in the literature. From the analysis, it is clear that it is hard to make firm, unambiguous statements: a broad approach uncovers the different interpretations and trade-offs in the evaluation of the aspects of availability, affordability, acceptability, and accessibility.

The indicators discussed in this chapter have clear limitations, certainly in combination with the simplifications usually made in large-scale, long-term energy models:

- They do not capture the differences in transport modes that are used (e.g. pipelines or ships; and the associated risks, including flexibility). Moreover, while ES for natural gas critically depends on the available infrastructure, this is typically not captured in ES indicators.
- Geopolitical relations are extremely hard to quantify and one has to rely on expert judgment. Global energy and/or economic scenarios may support such assessments.
- Long-term energy models are unfit to investigate price volatility. Indicators incorporating this (such as mean variance portfolio theory) can only be used in models with short-run dynamics.

- The assumptions with regard to resources and costs of unconventional oil critically determine the (partial) transition from conventional to unconventional oil presented above. The degree to which these resources will be used depends on technology development, associated costs, and public acceptance of the environmental consequences.
- The complicated indices (especially the S/D index) provided rather similar results under different scenarios. In this study we have refrained from a sensitivity analysis, but the use of this indicator could benefit from it, especially since it was originally designed for a cross-member state comparison in the EU 25. The high level of aggregation may contribute to the rather ambiguous results of this indicator.

Given the subjective and context-dependent nature of the ES concept, one may prefer to use a wide range of indicators in assessing ES trends. We argue that such indicators are most useful to point out important trends in a dynamic, comparative framework rather than to focus on the specific outcomes from these factors. It is possible to construct aggregate, multidimensional indices out of these. However, such indices of ES are inherently subjective as there is no fundamental basis on which to assign weights. This is shown here for two indices in Table 15.3.[51] They both measure very similar factors but the effect each has on the final indicator value is significantly different.

Conclusions

In this chapter, we have carried out an overview of indicators of ES in the literature and used them in scenario analysis. We emphasize that there are different perspectives on ES. We have classified these perspectives and the elements of the energy system on which they focus into four categories: availability, accessibility, affordability, and acceptability. We then applied a selection of these indicators in a model-based scenario analysis, with a focus on Western Europe and on the interactions with a low greenhouse gas concentration stabilization scenario. Our main conclusions are presented below.

It is not possible to capture ES in a single indicator

ES as a concept is open to various interpretations. As indicators are designed from specific perspectives on ES, they focus as such on different elements of the ES "spectrum." Therefore, we consider it not possible to assess ES unambiguously based on a single indicator. We have attempted to classify the indicators with regard to the perspective from which they were designed and as a result the elements of the energy system they focus on. Based on the subjective character, one may also argue that ES indicators are useful to depict trend but their exact values have only a limited meaning.

There is a trade-off between comprehensiveness and transparency

Aggregation of various elements into one "aggregated" indicator provides the potential pitfall of hiding the underlying dynamics from sight. The fact that these weights are (to a certain extent) inherently perspective-dependent may also form an objection to their use in policymaking. Thus, there seem to be trade-offs between comprehensiveness, transparency, and subjectivity. The closer one gets to encompassing all relevant elements, the less straightforward the resulting outcome is.

Scenario analyses show diverging trends with respect to ES

We used several indicators in a scenario case study based on a medium-growth scenario and a stringent climate policy case. *Availability* indicators show a decline of ES. Our projections suggest that as a result of increased global demand, the conventional proven oil and natural gas reserves could be depleted in about three to four decades. After this period, oil and natural gas production needs to come from speculative and unconventional resources. In terms of *accessibility*, it is important to note that international trade in energy carriers is projected to increase considerably (by 142 percent in 2050 compared with 2008 under the OECD-B scenario). The percentage of oil that is imported into Western Europe is projected to stay at around 65 percent in the years up to 2050, whereas the import share of natural gas is projected to rise to 62 percent in 2050. As most of this gas will come from Russia, import diversity is also fairly low for Western Europe. These results depend on the development of LNG as an alternative transport mode. *Diversity* in energy carriers, however, is projected to increase due to increased renewable consumption. Under the stringent climate policy scenario, fuel diversity is higher, although partially offset by a decrease in coal consumption. The aggregated indicators that take a number of *accessibility* elements into account (such as the S/D index)[52] show a constant, stable trend under the OECD-B scenario. Their level of aggregation may contribute to this, as different parameters balance out. Finally, for oil and gas, the *affordability* of energy is projected to deteriorate as prices of fossil fuels rise in all scenarios. Next to that, the production of oil is expected to be concentrated in fewer regions in the coming decades, only to diversify again towards 2050 as oil production from Canada and South America increases strongly. The IEA's combined measure, which takes into account the exposure to these supply concentration risks, shows rather steady exposure for Western Europe over the coming decades.

The effects of climate policy on ES are twofold. There are co-benefits as well as undesired consequences

Climate policy may bring ancillary benefits to ES, the most notable being delayed fossil resource depletion due to reduced fossil demand and enhanced fuel diversity. However, supply concentration in the oil and coal markets is projected to be higher under the climate policy scenario compared with the baseline. In the case of oil, this is because with reduced demand for oil, the more expensive and unconventional (both in terms of technology and region) resources are not developed. The different co-benefits and trade-offs imply that the usefulness of climate policy for ES is perspective-dependent. Climate policy reduces the depletion rate for oil (attractive from a B1 perspective). It also reduces energy imports (for instance in Western Europe)—but at the same time increases supply concentration (thus resulting in a mixed evaluation from an A2/B2 perspective). And while climate policy reduces the impact of depletion on oil prices, it also leads to an increased use of more expensive fuel types (leading to a trade-off between climate policy and affordability).

Overall, the analysis presented in this chapter helps in elaborating the concept of ES by providing an overview of available indicators proposed by different researchers. It has been shown that no single ideal indicator for energy security exists—and that the four dimensions of energy security (availability, accessibility, affordability, and acceptability) can be used as a taxonomy to understand the relative position of indicators vis-à-vis each other. Analysts and policymakers may choose to select several indicators from the list (e.g. Appendix A on the basis of the particular interpretation of ES). As the case study shows, several of these indicators can also be used within the context of modeling applications.

Appendix A: Indicator mapping rationale

Table 15.1A provides the rationale for the positioning of the SOS indicators in Figure 15.2. This should not be interpreted in an overly strict way. Roughly eight areas can be distinguished, based on the four dimensions and the combinations of these four into four overlapping areas.

Table 15.1A SOS indicators and their relationships to different SOS dimensions

Indicator	Rationale for position in SOS spectrum	Main dimension of SOS			
Simple indicators		*Av*	*Acs*	*Aff*	*Acp*
Resource estimates	Physical existence of resources forms the basis for potential availability. If a classification based on economic feasibility is made, then a slight shift towards affordability.	X			
Reserve to production ratios	Physical availability and consumption translated into time frame of availability.	X			
Diversity Indices	Depending on the application either accessibility (fuel div, supp. div) or affordability (supply concentration)		X	X	
Supply market concentration	See above		X	X	
Import dependence	A large determinant in accessing resources is the fact whether these are domestic or not.		X		
Net Energy Import Dependency	A combined measure of two elements related to accessibility (import and fuel diversity) will most likely end up in the same realm.		X		
Political stability	The political situation (including the alignment of political orientation between supplier and consumer) is an important determinant in the access to resources.		X		
Oil price	The affordability of energy is in its strictest interpretation almost similar to its (monetary) price.			X	
Mean variance portfolio	Relates the unit generating cost (affordability) to the variance therein.			X	
Non-carbon	The negative consequences of energy consumption may hinder its societal acceptance.				X
Market liquidity (CET)	The (un)willingness to trade translates to price movements and thus the affordability of energy.			X	
Market liquidity (IEA)	When defined as own consumption in relation to amount available on the market, it is an indication of the vulnerability to price movements.			X	
Energy or oil intensity	These demand-side indicators provide an indication of the potential impacts of a disruption, be it physical or economical. As such they can be placed between availability and affordability.	X		X	
Oil/energy expenditures				X	
Energy or oil use per capita			X		
Share of oil in transport sector			X	X	

Table 15.1A (continued)

Indicator	Rationale for position in SOS spectrum	Main dimension of SOS			
Simple indicators		Av	Acs	Aff	Acp
Share of transport sector in total oil use		X		X	
Aggregated indices					
Jansen et al.[53]	With fuel and import diversity at its roots, and a political stability parameter, this indicator mainly focuses on the accessibility element, although the inclusion of a depletion function introduces an element of availability.		X		
IEA's ESI$_{price}$	Focusing on the root causes of market power and resulting uncompetitive pricing, this indicator can be placed in the affordability quadrant. Including political stability introduces an element of accessibility to the indicator, whereas including depletion introduces an element of availability.			X	
S/D Index	Although very elaborate, the emphasis of this indicator is on accessibility, with import shares determining the supply score, and conversion and transport included. Including demand moves introduces an element of availability/affordability, but given the weight of this element it stays predominantly access-oriented.		X		
Willingness to pay[54]	This function translates SOS concerns into monetary terms, and as such can be placed in the affordability quadrant.			X	
OVI	Predominantly monetary indicators and thus Affordability, but also supplier diversity, political risk and reserves i.r.t imports. Based on the weights as described in more towards Acceptability than Availability	X		X	

Notes

1 International Energy Agency (IEA). 2007. *Natural Gas Market Review 2007: Security in a Globalising Market to 2015* (Paris: International Energy Agency); International Energy Agency (IEA). 2007. *Contribution of Renewables to Energy Security* (Paris: International Energy Agency); International Energy Agency (IEA). 2007. *Energy Security and Climate Change: Assessing Interactions* (Paris: International Energy Agency); European Commission (EC). 2006. *A European Strategy for Sustainable, Competitive and Secure Energy*, Green Paper, SEC(2006) p. 317 (European Commission).

2 De Vries, van Vuuren, Den Elzen, and Janssen. 2001. *The Targets Image Energy Model Regional (TIMER) Documentation* (Bilthoven, the Netherlands: National Institute of Public Health and the Environment (RIVM)); Van Vuuren. Detlef 2007. *Energy Systems and Climate Change: Scenarios for an Uncertain Future* (Utrecht: Utrecht University).

3 Alhajji. 2007. "What Is Energy Security? Definitions and Concepts," *Middle East Economic Survey* L (45) (November 5). Available at: http://www.mees.com/postedarticles/oped/v50n45-5OD01. htm (accessed February 20, 2008). While some authors distinguish between the concepts of energy security and security of supply, here we use them interchangeably.

4 IEA, *Energy Security and Climate Change: Assessing Interactions*; Toman, Michael. 2002. *International Oil Security: Problems and Policies.* (Washington, DC: Resources for the future); Jenny. 2007. "Energy

Security: A Market-Oriented Approach," presentation at the OECD Forum on *Innovation, Growth and Equity*, May 14–15, OECD, Paris.

5 Scheepers, Seebregts, de Jong, and Maters. 2007. *EU Standards for Energy Security of Supply: Updates on the Crisis Capability Index and the Supply/Demand Index Quantification for EU-27* (Petten, Netherlands: Energy Research Centre).

6 Chevalier. 2006. "Security of Energy Supply for the European Union," *European Review of Energy Markets* 1 , pp. 4–22.

7 International Energy Agency (IEA). 2004. *Energy Security and Climate Change Policy Interactions: An Assesment Framework* (Paris: International Energy Agency); IEA, *Energy Security and Climate Change: Assessing Interactions*; Jansen, Van Arkel, and Boots. 2004. *Designing Indicators of Long-Term Energy Supply Security*, (Petten, Netherlands: Energy Research Centre

8 Asia Pacific Energy Research Centre (APERC). 2007. *A Quest for Energy Security in the 21st Century* (Japan: . Institute of Energy Economics, APERC; Clingendael International Energy Programme (CIEP). 2004. *EU Energy Supply Security and Geopolitics*, Tren/C1-06-2002 (The Hague: Clingendael Institute); International Energy Agency (IEA). 2007. *World Energy Outlook 2007: China and India Insights* (Paris: International Energy Agency).

9 APERC, *A Quest for Energy Security in the 21st Century*.

10 IEA, *Energy Security and Climate Change*: Assessing Interactions.

11 IEA, *World Energy Outlook 2007: China and India Insights*.

12 Hoogeveen and Perlot (eds). 2005. *Tomorrow's Mores: The International System, Geopolitical Changes and Energy* (The Hague: Clingendael International Energy Programme).

13 Nakicenovic *et al.* 2000. *Special Report on Emissions Scenarios* (SRES) (Cambridge: Cambridge University Press).

14 US Geological Survey (USGS). 2000. *World Petroleum Assessment 2000* (Washington, DC: USGS).

15 Mulders, Hettelar, and Van Bergen. 2006. *Assessment of the Global Fossil Fuel Reserves and Resources for TIMER* (Utrecht: TNO Built Environment and Geosciences).

16 Greene, Hopson, and Li. 2005. "Have We Run Out of Oil Yet? Oil Peaking Analysis from an Optimist's Perspective," *Energy Policy* 34: 515–531.

17 Feygin and Satkin. 2004. "The Oil Reserves-to-Production Ratio and its Proper Interpretation," *Natural Resources Research* 13, pp. 59–65.

18 Jansen, Van Arkel and Boots, *Designing Indicators*; APERC, *A Quest for Energy Security in the 21st Century*; IEA, *Contribution of Renewables to Energy Security*.

19 Stirling. 1998. *On the Economics and Analysis of Diversity* (Brighton: Science Policy Research Unit, University of Sussex).

20 Awerbuch and Berger. 2003. *Applying Portfolio Theory to EU Electricity Planning and Policy Making* (Paris: International Energy Agency).

21 See this chapter, section 4.1.7 on Mean Variance Portfolio Theory.

22 APERC, *A Quest for Energy Security in the 21st Century*.

23 The original definition is formulated somewhat differently, but after rewriting comes down to the above.

24 For more information see: http://www.prsgroup.com/ICRG.aspx (accessed August 28, 2010); IEA, *Energy Security and Climate Change Policy Interactions*.

25 Jansen, Van Arkel, and Boots, *Designing Indicators*.

26 Awerbuch. 2006. "Portfolio Based Electricity Generation Planning: Policy Implementations for Renewables and Energy Security," *Mitigation and Adaptation Strategies for Global Change* 11: 693–671; Awerbuch and Berger, *Applying Portfolio Theory*.

27 Stirling, *On the Economics and Analysis of Diversity*.

28 Stirling starts his elaborate work on diversity with a discourse on incertitude: the whole spectrum of uncertainty and risk, arguing that when it comes to energy systems, we are in a state of ignorance, where outcomes are poorly defined and no basis exists to assign probabilities to them. As such, the idea that past data can provide probabilities on which to base future decisions is rather heroic.

29 An approach has been developed that aims to combine the probabilistic mean variance portfolio approach with a more precautious method advocated by Stirling. This method consists of adding the outcomes of both methods on a weighted basis, where the weight factor represents the level of trust in historic trends as a guide for the future.

30 APERC, *A Quest for Energy Security in the 21st Century*.

31 IEA, *Energy Security and Climate Change Policy Interactions*.

32 Datar. 2000. "Stock Market Liquidity: Measurement and Implications," Fourth Capital Market Conference, New York, December 3–4, 2000.

33 Kendell. 1998. *Measures of Oil Import Dependence* (Washington DC: Energy Information Administration, Department of Energy).

34 van Ruijven, Urban, Benders, Moll, van der Sluijs, de Vries, and van Vuuren. 2008. "Modeling Energy and Development: An Evaluation of Models and Concepts," *World Development* 36: 2801–2821.

35 Jansen, Van Arkel, and Boots, *Designing Indicators*

36 IEA, *Energy Security and Climate Change: Assessing Interactions.*

37 IEA, *Energy Security and Climate Change: Assessing Interactions.*

38 Scheepers, Seebregts, de Jong, and Maters. 2007. *EU Standards for Energy Security of Supply: Updates on the Crisis Capability Index and the Supply/Demand Index Quantification for EU-27* (Petten, the Netherlands: Energy Research Centre).

39 Scheepers, in personal communication with the author, declared that the subjective nature of the concept of ES was a motivation to make the subjective weight factors in the SD index explicit. (Personal communication with Scheepers, August 30, 2007).

40 Bollen. 2008. *Energy Security, Air Pollution, and Climate Change: An Integrated Cost Benefit Approach* (Bilthoven: Netherlands Environmental Assessment Agency).

41 Specifically, France's investment program in nuclear energy starting in the 1970s serves as a reference point. From this it is inferred that France's willingness to pay for avoided ES risks is in the range of a few per mille of GDP per year.

42 Gupta. 2008. "Oil Vulnerability Index of Oil-Importing Countries," *Energy Policy* 36: 1195–1211.

43 De Vries, Van Vuuren, Den Elzen, and Janssen. 2001. *The Timer IMage Energy Regional (TIMER) model: Technical Documentation* (Bilthoven, the Netherlands: National Institute for Public Health and the Environment); Van Vuuren. 2007. "Energy Systems and Climate Policy: Long-Term Scenarios for an Uncertain Future." Ph.D. thesis, Utrecht University.

44 Organisation for Economic Cooperation and Development (OECD). 2008. *OECD Environmental Outlook to 2030* (Paris: OECD); Bakkes, Bosch, Bouwman, den Elzen, Janssen, Isaac, Klein Goldewijk, Kram, de Leeuw, Olivier, van Oorschot, Stehfest, van Vuuren, Bagnoli, Chateau, Corfee-Morlot, and Kim. 2008. *Background Report to the OECD Environmental Outlook to 2030. Overviews, Details, and Methodology of Model-Based Analysis* (Bilthoven, Netherlands: Environmental Assessment Agency).

45 Van Vuuren, Den Elzen, Lucas, Eickhout, Strengers, Van Ruijven, Wonink, and Van Houdt. 2007. "Stabilizing Greenhouse Gas Concentrations at Low Levels: An Assessment of Reduction Strategies and Costs," *Climatic Change* 81: 119–159.

46 Mayerhofer, de Vries, den Elzen, van Vuuren, Onigkeit, Posch, and Guardans. 2002. "Long-Term, Consistent Scenarios of Emissions, Deposition and Climate Change in Europe," *Environmental Science and Policy* 5: 273–305; van Vuuren, Cofala, Eerens, Oostenrijk, Heyes, Klimont, den Elzen, and Amann. 2006. "Exploring the Ancillary Benefits of the Kyoto Protocol for Air Pollution in Europe," *Energy Policy* 34: 444–460.

47 IEA, *World Energy Outlook 2007: China and India Insights.*

48 van Vuuren, Fengqi, de Vries, Kejun, Graveland, and Yun. 2003. "Energy and Emission Scenarios for China in the 21st Century: Exploration of Baseline Development and Mitigation Options," *Energy Policy* 31: 369–387.

49 Jansen, Van Arkel, and Boots, *Designing Indicators*

50 Groenenberg and Wetzelaer. 2006. *Energy Security of Supply under EU Climate Policies* (Petten, the Netherlands: Energy Research Centre).

51 The two indices are Jansen, Van Arkel, and Boots, *Designing Indicators*; and International Energy Agency *Contribution of Renewables.*

52 Jansen, Van Arkel, and Boots, *Designing Indicators.*

53 Jansen, Van Arkel, and Boots, *Designing Indicators*

54 Bollen. 2008. *Energy Security,*

16

MEASURING SECURITY OF ENERGY SUPPLY WITH TWO DIVERSITY INDEXES[*]

John Kessels

Introduction

Coal is the world's most abundant fossil fuel and plays a key role in many countries' energy supply. China, India, USA, Russia, Canada, Indonesia, and South Africa all have large coal reserves. It has been estimated that there are proven coal reserves totaling over 900 gigatonnes which is equivalent to over 160 years of production at current rates.[1] Coal is arguably the most important energy provider in large Southeast Asian countries including Indonesia, Thailand, Vietnam, China, India, and the Philippines. The map at Figure 16.1 shows coal reserves based on the BP Statistical Review of World Energy 2006.

To address energy security in these countries a strategy is needed on the sustainable use of coal. One of the issues confronting these and other countries is providing their citizens with a secure and sustainable energy supply to ensure the stability of their economies and welfare of their citizens. The increasing world population and economic growth results in a demand for all types of energy. According to the 2009 *World Energy Outlook* fossil fuels could remain the dominant source of primary energy up to 2030.[2]

With a balanced approach coal is one of a combination of energy supply options that include gas, nuclear, oil, and renewable energy. The abundance of coal reserves at low cost plus a need to reduce greenhouse gas emissions (GHG) highlight the importance of clean coal technologies (CCT). Without the use of CCT it is unlikely that many Asian countries' energy security and climate change policy objectives for emission reductions will be achieved. The use of supercritical coal combustion (SPCC), integrated gasification combined cycle (IGCC), and circulating fluidized bed combustion (CFBC) is likely to be the most important CCT used in Asia. It is also imperative that Asian countries examine the use of carbon capture and storage technologies.

In both developed and developing countries energy security is an important policy driver.

> Secure, reliable and affordable energy supplies are fundamental to economic stability and development. The threat of disruptive climate change, the erosion of energy security and the growing energy needs of the developing world all pose major challenges for energy decision makers.[3]

[*] The author would like to acknowledge the contribution from B. Wetzelaer and S. Bakker from ECN.

313

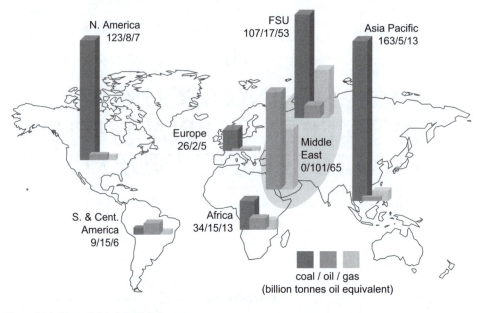

Figure 16.1 Map of global fossil fuel reserves.
Source: *BP Energy Statistical Review of World Energy 2006* (London: BP, 2006).

Historically, oil was the key energy resource of which countries wanted to ensure stability of supply. However, with the growth of coal use in developing countries and with many developed countries renewing their coal-fired power capacity in the coming decades there is much discussion on the role coal can play to increase energy security.

In order for CCTs to play a role it is important that there is a viable international framework to encourage technology transfer and diffusion. Climate change and energy supply security policy are currently not integrated in most countries, despite possible synergies.

As of 2010, little progress has been made since the United Nations Framework Convention on Climate Change (UNFCCC) response to scientific concerns about the increasing atmospheric concentrations of GHG and the possibility of climate change back in 1992. In 1992 an agreement was reached, with the key article number 2 stating the need for the:

> Stabilisation of greenhouse gas concentrations in the atmosphere at a level that would prevent dangerous anthropogenic interference with the climate system.[4]

A considerable first step occurred in 1997, when the Kyoto Protocol required 38 industrialized countries to make legally binding commitments to reduce their GHG by the period of 2008–2012. This was a legal instrument to respond to changes in scientific understanding and political will to achieve the objectives of the UNFCCC.

The ESCAPE approach—Energy Security and Climate Policy Evaluation — suggests that linking climate change policy with security of energy supply may improve climate policy at the national and international levels.[5] The ESCAPE approach explores the options of inclusion of energy security issues into national and international post-2012 climate negotiations. Linking energy security and climate change policy will improve the outcome of other policy areas including transport and mobility, urban planning, air pollution, land use, and poverty.[6]

The chapter emphasizes the importance of energy security with clean coal technologies by showing that measures to reduce import dependency are mostly synergetic with climate policy. On an international level, linkages of energy security into post-2012 climate policy may be possible in sectoral bottom-up approaches or technology frameworks.

Energy security

To address the challenge to provide energy security as well as stabilize carbon dioxide emissions from anthropogenic activities requires a global integrated policy mix that recognizes the different circumstances of each country. In recent years international climate negotiations have clearly shown that to design an effective and acceptable policy mix is a difficult task.

Energy security is normally managed individually by countries although integration of gas and power supplies is being pursued and this is mainly the case in Asia. To improve regional cooperation, individual country interests prevail. This will depend on a countriy's energy resources and whether it is self-reliant, as in the case of Indonesia with large coal and gas reserves, or like Thailand reliant on gas but with depleting gas reserves and with only 12 years of proven gas reserves remaining. In international climate change policy the majority of Asia is a signatory to the UNFCCC. No Asian country has legally binding targeted commitments to reduce their GHG as is the case for the Kyoto Protocol signatories.

To achieve the ultimate objective of the UNFCCC, namely the stabilizing of atmospheric greenhouse gas concentrations, requires cuts in global GHG emissions in the order of 50–60 percent by 2050. It is also accepted that in order to reach the EU goal of less than 2 °C temperature increase compared with pre-industrial levels, global emissions must peak before 2030.[7]

The latest UNFCCC meeting was held in December 2009 in Copenhagen. Little progress was made in new commitments by either developing or developed countries. There is currently an impasse which is unlikely to be broken until after the next meeting in November 2010 in Mexico. The IEA *World Energy Outlook* forecasts that by 2030 coal-fired installed capacity could double with 80 percent of the growth coming from developing countries. Without policies or incentives to build more efficient coal-fired power stations there is likely to be a continual growth in the use of subcritical technology which is considerably less suitable for retrofit with CCS equipment. Supercritical coal-fired power stations, if the location is suitable, are able to be retrofitted. Without an agreement on targets, whether binding or non-binding, there is a danger that the status quo will continue and consequently a further increase in anthropogenic emissions.

Without control technologies in place, conventional coal-based technology will continue to be built in Asia with higher GHG and air pollution emissions. Compared with coal-based electricity air pollutants and GHG emissions, the use of gas-based generation is more attractive to many countries. However, with increasing uncertainty about future natural gas supply against reasonable prices in Asia, this policy objective may induce a shift in thinking towards coal to improve energy security.

Modeling the future for coal

This section presents two approaches to quantify security of supply, the Shannon diversity index[8] and the Supply/Demand Index[9]. Each of the approaches is explained and applied to a High Renewables (HR) and High Coal (HC) scenario. The purpose of the quantifications is to provide an indication of the extent that an increased role of coal or renewables may have on the security of supply in Asia. The Shannon diversity and Supply/Demand indices are applied to the baseline and the HR and the HC scenarios.

Shannon diversity index

The Shannon diversity index is used in order to address the following question: What is our knowledge of types/events of long-term energy insecurity? It seems that our knowledge of possible future energy-related events that can impact our long-term energy security is very limited. According to Jansen,[10] in a state of ignorance well-designed diversity strategies with regard to the portfolio of long-term energy supply options hold out the best promise of energy supply security. In order to develop a tool to help design optimum diversity strategies, Andrew Stirling conceptualized "diversity" with the help of three subordinate properties[11]:

- *Variety*. Refers to the number of categories (e.g. primary energy sources categories) into which the quantity in question (e.g. primary energy in Mtoe) can be divided. The more categories, the greater the diversity.
- *Balance*. Refers to the pattern in the market share across the categories: the more even the spread across the categories, the greater the diversity.
- *Disparity*. Refers to the nature and degree to which the categories differ from each other. For example, it would appear that the categories oil and natural gas are less disparate than oil and renewables, considering the heterogeneity of the latter. Disparity, though, is an intrinsically qualitative, subjective, and context-dependent aspect of diversity.

For the purposes of this chapter, the Shannon diversity index has been used. The Shannon diversity index is applied to the portfolio of sources for primary energy supply and only reflects variety and balance. To include disparity in the Shannon index is too complex and is therefore excluded in this analysis.

The assessment of the fuel mix diversity at the regional level forms the basis of the Shannon diversity index. Five categories of primary energy supply are considered (coal, oil, gas, nuclear, and renewables). The maximum value they can take on indicating maximum diversity in terms of variety and balance is 1.61 (-ln(1/5); 5 is the number of distinguished primary energy sources). The minimum value, if all energy services would be driven by only one primary source, is 0.

Jansen *et al.* proposed to correct this basic fuel mix diversity index (which we call I_1 in this chapter) downwards by integrating three indicators of long-term energy supply security on a step-by-step basis.[12] The second Shannon diversity indicator (I_2) adjusts I_1 for energy import dependency (and therefore has a lower value than I_1). This is done by including correction factors for fossil fuels. These factors are based on projected shares of imports of fossil fuels from a specific region in total import of sources. Correction factors and the corresponding I_2 are low if the world region concerned has import dependencies for fossil fuels that are relatively high and, at the same time, very poorly diversified. It should be noted in this respect that the correction factor for renewable energy is equal to 1, because this primary energy source category is considered to be very diverse in nature of the sources (hydro, biomass, wind, etc.) and the technologies applied.

The third (I_3) indicator entails a correction of I_2 for long-term socio-political stability in export regions. Experts also recommend using the United Nations Development Program's Human Development Indicator (HDI) as an index for long-term socio-economic availability. It is likely there will be a high correlation between countries with long-term future political stability and countries with a high current HDI score.[13]

The fourth indicator (I_4) takes into account the depletion of natural energy sources in the measure of the Shannon diversity index. The assumption made is that the market will react to information on proven reserves and if the reserve to production ratio (R/P ratio) reaches a value below 50 years. However, R/P ratios are hard to project given the partly political character of these ratios. Several OPEC countries tend to cut down upward revisions of official statistics on proven reserves in bullish market conditions, while presenting a more robust reserves situation in lean times to attract foreign investments. Consequently, Jansen *et al.* used projections of ultimately recoverable reserves, and substituted for the R/P ratio the quotient of the ultimately recoverable reserves and production of the selected region.[14]

Supply/Demand index

The Supply/Demand index (S/D index) is based on the probability of an energy supply disruption, and the impact on economy and society depends to a large extent on the structure of the energy system. Elements of the energy system are: fuel mix, origin of primary energy sources, energy transport infrastructure, conversions into secondary energy, and energy demand.[15]

Consequently, the S/D index focuses on the supply and demand of several energy sources, as opposed to the Shannon diversity index, which includes only the supply. The S/D index also covers final energy demand, energy conversion, and transport. The index uses four types of inputs: two objective types and two types of a more subjective nature. Figure 16.2 shows the conceptual model of the elements considered in the overall S/D index. Each individual aspect used in the model (i.e., at the end of the branches) obtains an index value between 0 and 100. So the resulting S/D index ranges also between 0 and 100. An increase in the S/D index indicates a better security of supply (SoS) position.

The italic labels are the objective inputs and concern the *shares* of different supply and demand types (i.e., for demand: industrial, residential, tertiary, and transport use; for supply: oil, gas, coal, nuclear, renewables, and other). The labels in roman font are subjective inputs and concern the *weights* that determine the relative contribution of the different components in the index (such as the relation between supply and demand outputs in the index, or the relation between EU imports and non-EU imports). The *scoring rules* for determining various index values reflect

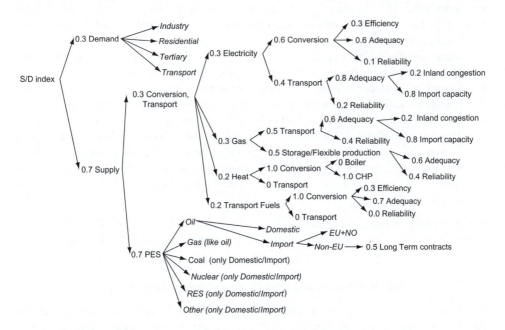

Figure 16.2 Weights (defaults) and shares used in the Supply/Demand index mode.

different degrees of perceived vulnerabilities (lower score with increasing vulnerability). In the next section on assessment of energy supply security, the following *weights* and major *scoring rules* apply that are derived from two reports. [16] The second report provides the details on weighting and scoring rules. [17]

Weights

- 0.3 for Demand (i.e., the score for Demand counts for 30 percent in the overall S/D index);
- 0.7 for Supply; consisting of: 0.3 for Conversion and Transport (consisting of several other branches, see Figure 16.2); 0.7 for Primary Energy Sources.

Major scoring rules

- To calculate the index values for each energy demand sector (i.e., industry, residential, tertiary, and transport) the energy demand in the business as usual scenario could be used. The index should, in particular, value the degree in which the energy used in the industry sector is kept as low as possible. To be exact, the energy demand level should be compared with the "essential energy demand needs" warranted by energy supply. As a parameter to indicate the essential energy demand needs, the energy intensity factor is chosen. The index values for each energy demand sector are calculated from the ratio between the EU27's energy intensity and the benchmark figure. The benchmark is the average figure of energy intensities of the five best performing EU member states. The maximum value will be 100 if the energy intensity is less (i.e., better) than the benchmark value. Weighting the four sectoral indices with the shares of each demand sectors relative to final energy demand results in the sub-index value for demand.
- Index value of 100 for nuclear energy irrespective of the supply of origin (i.e., reliable export partners and unreliable export partners), because supply risks for uranium are relatively low.
- Minimum value of 70 for coal and renewables if the total supply is imported. The score will increase proportionally with increasing domestic supply.
- Minimum value of 0 for oil and gas if the total supply is imported from less reliable regions (in the EU27 case or EU member states cases, the EU and Norway are considered as reliable as domestic production). The score for gas and oil equals the net share of domestic supplies plus the dependency from reliable export regions. Using the net domestic share and import dependency as weigthing factors ensures that the total score will not be higher than 100. The PES sub-index is calculated on the basis of such scoring rules and the relative share in the total primary energy supply of each primary energy source.

It is noteworthy to mention that due to the weights of Supply (i.e., 0.7) and the PES (i.e., 0.7) herein, the total S/D index is for almost 50 percent determined by the PES sub-index.

Quantitative results from the Shannon diversity index

The Shannon diversity index is applied to the High Coal and High Renewable scenarios as described and summarized in Table 16.1. The last variant (I_4) incorporating proven regional reserves with respect to the annual production in the export region concerned, is left out of

Table 16.1 Composition of the Shannon diversity index

Indicator	Description	Input parameters
I_1	Diversification of PES in energy supply	share of PES (coal, oil, gas, nuclear, and renewables) in total primary energy supply
I_2	I_1 + Energy import dependency	import dependencies of coal, oil, and gas due to inter-area movement between net import regions and net export regions
I_3	I_2 + Long-term political stability in import regions	real GDP per capita
I_4	I_3 + Level of resource depletion	reserve to production ratio

the analysis because of a lack of data. The alternative scenarios (HR and HC) are compared with the baseline scenario covering the period 2004–2030. The projected fuel mix in the five world regions needed to calculate the diversity indicator I_1 is sourced from the IEA *World Energy Outlook 2006*.[18]

For the calculation of I_2 and I_3 in 2004, the import dependencies due to inter-area movement between import regions of origin for oil and gas from export regions are provided by the BP statistical energy review of world energy 2004.[19] The import dependencies for coal come from the Energy Information Administration's *International Energy Outlook 2007*.[20] In total the following 13 potential (foreign) regions of origin were identified: North America, Europe, China, India, Japan, Central and South America, Russia, other Eurasia, Middle East, Africa, Australia, Indonesia, and other Asia Pacific).

As stated for the calculation of I_3 in 2004, the UNDP HDI is an ideal proxy for long-term political stability. However, projections of the HDI indicator are not available. Projections of real GDP per capita are used instead as the HDI indicator is highly correlated with a normalized value of the square root of real GDP per capita.[21] Those GDP projections are performed by the World Energy Technology Outlook H_2 — 2050.[22] The actual GDP figures in the base year 2004 data are derived from the World Economic Outlook Database of the International Monetary Fund.[23] Normalization is done dividing the distinct values of the 13 regions of origin by the highest regional value of the same year.

The baseline scenario for the projected year 2030 represents a combination of two reference cases developed by IEA WEO 2006 for oil and gas and EIA IEO 2007 for coal. An important aspect of both cases is that they provide projections on import dependence and fossil fuel production by the five world regions. Due to the difficulty of projecting such data, inter-regional trade by importing and exporting regions figures for the year 2030 can only be found for world coal flows.[24] In the case of oil and gas, the import dependencies due to inter-regional trade are assumed to be equal to the values identified for the base year 2004. Table 16.2 shows the projections of this simple modeling exercise. It should be mentioned that such projections are only based on regions, not on companies as trade participants.

This study also assumes that all projections do not differ between the three different scenarios. Another critical assumption is that we assume a single market risk. Consequently, net exporting regions with a large market share are exposed to the same market risk as regions with no export potential and zero market share.[25] Finally, combining various energy security indicators into a single factor (i.e., I_3) inevitably raises the question of balance between the different indicators. For example, should diversification be given greater importance than import dependency? Hence, the results should be considered as illustrative.

Table 16.2 Projected inter-regional trade in coal, oil, and gas under baseline scenario, HC scenario, and HR scenario in 2030

IMPORT REGIONS

EXPORTING REGIONS / Import shares in %	North America coal	oil	gas	Europe coal	oil	gas	China coal	oil	gas	India coal	oil	gas	Japan coal	oil	gas
North America				9	4		5			4	1		4	2	2
Europe	1	15						2			1			1	
China										7	3		7	1	
Japan								1							
C&S America	68	29		27	2			2							
Russia		3		21	45	65	4	11	50	4	1		4	1	
Other Eurasia				4			2			2			2		
Africa		28	11	25	27	4		37	13		78	100		82	23
Middle East	13	24	70	14	21	31	5	21	25	4	11		4	4	
Australia	11		8				52	1	13	48	1		48	1	15
Indonesia							28			26			26		28
Other Asia Pacific		2	11		1		5	24		5	3		5	10	32

Overall results

The index values in Figure 16.3 are presented as a 100 percent stacked column. To be exact, the figure compares the percentage of each indicator that corrects the final indicator of the Shannon diversity index (I_3). A lower percentage of the Shannon diversity index suggests a worse energy supply situation than a higher percentage. Both the values and the dynamics between the three indicators are interpreted in Figure 16.2 for a couple of regions.

In China, the relatively low scores for I_3 (see Figure 16.3) suggest that long-term energy supply security will be most negatively affected by relatively large dependence on a few primary fuels, leading to a low level of diversification (i.e., relatively large correction for diversity). In contrast to Japan and Europe, dependency on relatively poorly diversified foreign regions of origin (indicated by I_2) and political stability in foreign regions of origin (indicated by I_3) would denote less negative factors in China. This is visualized in Figure 16.3 by the relatively short dark gray and white bars for China compared with Europe and Japan.

North America shows the highest score for I_3 under all scenarios. This is partly caused by a more even spread of the primary energy sources in the PES mix of North America (20 percent for oil, 15 percent for gas, 44 percent for coal, 4 percent for nuclear, and 16 percent for renewables) compared with, for example, the larger spread in the Chinese PES mix (21 percent for oil, 2 percent for gas, 65 percent for coal, 1 percent for nuclear, and 11 percent for renewables). Another explanation can be given by the adequately diversified energy import in North America. In Table 16.3, Africa, the Middle East and Central South America are assumed to be more important sources of oil imports to North America in 2030, while the Middle East and Russia remain by far the most important sources of oil imports to Japan and Europe. A last explanation lies in the fact that North America relies on relative stable foreign regions of origins. This can be seen in Figure 16.2 by the relatively short white bars, although the differences with China and India are not significant.

This study interprets the major projection results for the Shannon diversity index in more detail for each scenario in the next sections. These concentrate on I_3 (covering diversity, import dependency, and stability of import regions) as it gives the most sophisticated results.

The trend of the Shannon diversity index between 2004 and 2030 presents a varied picture across the investigated regions. In all three scenarios the energy security situation, according to I_3 as the most elaborated indicator of the Shannon diversity index, is projected to worsen for North America and Europe (scores presented as normalized values in Table 16.3; i.e., a maximum score of 100 and a minimum score of 0). In contrast, the energy security situation in China and India improves under the HR scenario, whereas Japan experiences an improvement in all three scenarios.

Table 16.3 World region-based scores of the Shannon diversity index I_3 covering diversity, import dependency, and stability of import regions

I_3	Baseline		HC	HR
	2004	*2030*	*2030*	*2030*
Europe	63	59	60	61
North America	80	73	72	78
China	57	54	48	63
India	60	63	55	61
Japan	41	48	49	57

Baseline scenario 2030

Japan yields the lowest score for the most elaborate indicator I_3: 48. Japan scores very low on independency of imports. This can be observed by comparing the adjustments on energy import dependency (I_2-I_1), shown in Figure 16.3 as gray bars, between the investigated countries. On the aspect of resource diversification in energy supply, Japan performs relatively well compared with the other world regions (high I_1). Hence, in the case of Japanese nuclear power plants having operational problems, diversity minimizes the impacts of such failures. The low score on the same aspect (I_1) for China could indicate that fuel switching is restricted in case of environmental restrictions. Alternative dual-firing (coal–gas) plants are scarce. However, China scores relatively high on independency of imports. This is mainly caused by the large indigenous coal production. In the case of Europe, strong dependencies on oil, gas, and coal imports lead to a relatively large difference between I_1 and I_2 compared with North America. In 2030, North America can still rely on relatively large shares of inland gas and coal production compared with India and especially with Europe and Japan.

High coal scenario 2030

Some key features of this scenario are 50 percent of baseline gas and nuclear shares replaced by coal in the power sector and 50 percent of the baseline natural gas consumption replaced by coal or coal-based SNG for all world regions except China, where the fuel mix in the industry sector remains at the 2004 level. However, the energy security situation worsens in North America, China, and India. Europe and Japan only score slightly better than the baseline scenario 2030 for the composite indicator I_3. This is due to two different factors: (1) diversification of the energy mix is projected to evolve quite unfavorably under this scenario, especially for China and India, due to even larger reliance on coal compared with baseline scenario; (2) the adjustments for import dependency with the allowance for political stability (I_1-I_2-I_3) are assumed to be equal under all scenarios in 2030. This can be visualized by the equal shares of I_1-I_2 (dark grey area) and I_2-I_3 (white area) for each column. Hence, under the HC scenario the change in I_3 compared with the baseline 2030 is driven by diversity only.

High renewables scenario 2030

The HR scenario assumes a higher penetration of biofuels in the transport sector. Furthermore, renewables in the power sector take 50 percent of the baseline gas share and 33 percent of the baseline coal share. The industry sectors of all the world regions experience a fuel switch from coal and gas to biomass. Due to these assumptions, the HR scenario yields an improvement of projected energy security for all world regions except for India, as depicted by the projections for Indicator I_3 in year 2030.

Quantitative results Supply/Demand index

Calculation of the S/D index or a sub-index of the S/D index under the baseline scenario is carried out for the USA, EU27, China, India, and Japan for the year 2030. Data from Eurostat was collected for the calculation of the S/D index[26] and IEA statistics[27] and the "EU trends to 2030 — update 2005" baseline scenario.[28] The use of the S/D index in the Directorate-General for Energy and Transport (DG TREN) baseline scenario is illustrated in Table 16.4.

Table 16.4 PES sub-indices, share fuel mix, import dependencies, and share unstable regions for a number of selected regions in 2030 on the basis of WEO baseline scenarios (Base) and alternative scenarios (HC and HR)

PES sub-index and share fuel mix (score | Base | HC | HR per region):

Sub-index	EU27 score	EU27 Base	EU27 HC	EU27 HR	USA score	USA Base	USA HC	USA HR	China score	China Base	China HC	China HR	India score	India Base	India HC	India HR	Japan score	Japan Base	Japan HC	Japan HR
PES Sub-index		58	70	74		83	91	92		86	87	87		78	80	81		50	59	68
Oil	16	0.35	0.23	0.22	56	0.39	0.20	0.17	39	0.22	0.21	0.21	23	0.24	0.22	0.22	15	0.39	0.25	0.24
Gas	63	0.30	0.17	0.17	99	0.20	0.15	0.18	100	0.05	0.02	0.03	70	0.06	0.04	0.03	24	0.17	0.10	0.10
Coal	88	0.14	0.35	0.17	100	0.24	0.45	0.21	100	0.61	0.65	0.43	97	0.41	0.53	0.39	70	0.16	0.39	0.15
Nuclear	100	0.07	0.04	0.06	100	0.08	0.04	0.07	100	0.02	0.01	0.02	100	0.03	0.02	0.03	100	0.22	0.13	0.21
Renewables	100	0.13	0.20	0.39	100	0.08	0.16	0.37	100	0.10	0.11	0.32	100	0.25	0.19	0.33	100	0.06	0.13	0.30

Import dependency and Less secure regions:

	EU27 Import dependency	EU27 Less secure regions	USA Import dependency	USA Less secure regions	China Import dependency	China Less secure regions	India Import dependency	India Less secure regions	Japan Import dependency	Japan Less secure regions
Oil	92	92	74	59	77	79	87	89	100	85
Gas/LNG	63	59	16	5	33	0	30	99	97	78
Coal	40		2			0		11	100	

Note:
Import dependencies for oil, gas/LNG, and coal are given by IEA *World Energy Outlook 2006*. Import dependencies expressed in rounded % (Net Imports/Gross Inland Consumption), (crude & product) oil import/ natural gas & LPG import share of supplies within expected less secure regions expressed in rounded %. As already indicated, the S/D index model uses parameters that are determined by expert judgment. In particular, the region-specific oil import and gas import share coming from expected less secure countries in 2030 can be identified as a subjective parameter and, therefore, should be considered as illustrative.

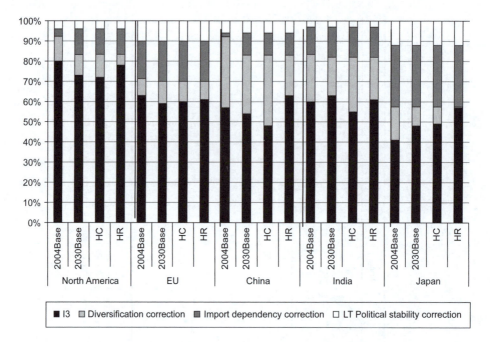

Figure 16.3 Scores of the Shannon diversity index (I_3) and its correction factors (I_1, correcting for diversification, I_2-I_1 correcting for import dependency, I_3-I_2 for political stability of import regions).

The calculation of the primary energy source (PES) sub-index for the baseline scenario is based on objective information contained in tables that show projections of net import and primary energy supply derived from IEA *World Energy Outlook* (WEO) 2006.[29] The WEO 2006 baseline scenario and indicative results across the different regions for the year 2030 are presented in Table 16.4 and displayed in Figure 16.3.

In order to assess future developments in a region-specific energy system, this study constructed two alternative scenarios which can be compared with the baseline scenario:

- high coal scenario (HC)
- high renewables scenario (HR)

All fuel mixes in these scenarios are described in Table 16.5. Both scenarios are applied to the other world regions (PES sub-index). Quantitative results for world regions were applied using the S/D PES sub-index.

Using the sub-index for primary energy sources of the Supply/Demand index illustrates the impact of changing the fuel mix on the energy security of supply situation in world regions. This simplification can be justified as in our scenario approach, and in the two scenarios developed, the demand conditions are not changed. In addition, data requirements for the demand and conversion and transport part of the Supply/Demand indicator are considerable, and in the context of the current study not feasible for all world regions. Therefore we focus on the PES sub-index.

The baseline projections in the *World Energy Outlook 2006* are essential for the calculation of the sub-indices for PES in the different regions. These projections should be considered as a baseline scenario of how regional energy markets would evolve if governments do nothing beyond what they have already committed to doing to influence long-term energy demand.

An important assumption is that the IEA crude oil import price is projected to decline to about $47 per barrel in 2012 (down from $60 per barrel through 2007). It is assumed to rise again slowly thereafter, reaching $55 per barrel in 2030. GDP growth projections are other important assumptions that highly influence the pathway of energy demand in the different regions. Yearly projected GDP growth figures between 2004 and 2030 are highest in China (5.5 percent), followed by India (5.1 percent), the United States (2.3 percent), Europe (2 percent), and Japan (1.4 percent). Finally, the pace of technological innovation can be seen as another important factor that affects the costs of supplying energy and the efficiency of using energy. End-use technologies become steadily more energy-efficient in the baseline scenario, though the pace varies for each fuel and sector depending on the IEA's assessment of the potential for efficiency improvements and the stage of technology development and commercialization. For example, neither CO_2 capture and storage, nor second-generation biofuels are assumed to be economically viable before 2030.

The use of the PES sub-indices in a scenario approach for the year 2030 is shown in Table 16.4 and Figure 16.3, which presents the results for EU27, USA, China, India, and Japan. The results are discussed below.

2030 Scores using the WEO 2006 baseline scenario

On the basis of the scenario data taken from the baseline scenario of the IEA WEO 2006, the PES sub-index for Japan is the lowest. This is mainly a result of 100 percent import dependency for oil and 97 percent import dependency for gas, but a relatively low share of coal in the fuel mix also contributes to a lower PES sub-index value compared with countries like India and China.

The calculated PES sub-index value of the EU27 is 8 points higher than the index value of Japan. This is mainly due to less dependency on gas imports from less stable regions and a relatively better projected coal import dependency of 40 percent.

China benefits from indigenous coal production (with a PES share of 61 percent). In addition, the PES sub-index value is positively influenced by a relatively low share of oil and gas in the fuel mix. Also, based on current insights of BP,[30] our analysis assumes that Australia operates as the only export partner in the LNG trade with China in 2030. Consequently, the Chinese natural gas and LPG import share of supplies within geopolitical unstable regions is determined to be zero.

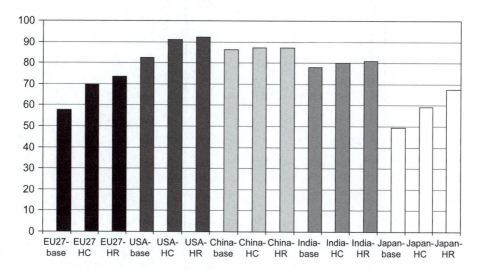

Figure 16.4 PES sub-indices of the Supply/Demand indicator for world regions in 2030.

Table 16.5 Input value for PES sub-indices: region-specific oil import and gas import share coming from expected less secure regions

Countries	Total Import		Imports less secure regions		Less secure regions			
	Oil (Mt)	Gas/LNG (bcm)	Oil (Mt/ % of total imports)	Gas/LNG (bcm / % of total imports)	Oil	Gas	LNG	Gas + LNG
Europe	665	432	608 (92%)	254 (59%)	South & Central America, Former Soviet Union Middle East North Africa West Africa	Russian Fed. Turkmenistan Iran	Nigeria Qatar UAE Brunei Indonesia Malaysia	Oman Egypt Algeria Libya
USA	671	116	397 (59%)	6 (5%)				
China	192	1	152 (79%)	0 (0%)				
Rest of Asia/ India	442	8	193 (89%)	8 (99%)	China			
Japan	257	82	217 (85%)	64 (78%)				

The USA is also one of the best scoring regions because of the relatively high scores on the parts of the origins of the imported oil and gas, 74 percent and 16 percent respectively, despite the high import dependencies for these two PES. Nevertheless, the relatively large shares of oil and/or gas and low share of coal weakens the PES sub-index value compared with China.

2030 Scores using the high coal scenario

On the basis of the high coal scenario, PES sub-index values are calculated for the selected regions. On average, this index value increases by more than 6 points compared with the baseline scenario, caused by an increase in the share of coal in the fuel mix and a relatively high minimum sub-index value for coal of 70. Note that the import dependencies and shares of imported oil and gas coming from unstable regions are assumed equal to the baseline values.

The change in ranking of the regions when compared with the baseline scenario shows that the USA, instead of China, tops the list followed by India, Europe, and Japan. The USA and China are the best scoring regions, because the calculated PES sub-indices improve due to an increasing share of coal and renewables scores presented as normalized values; that is, a maximum score of 100 and a minimum score of 0 in the fuel mix (gas and oil are replaced by indigenous coal production and domestically generated renewable energy). In contrast, Europe and Japan experience the largest increase in the PES sub-indices compared with the baseline scenario of 2030. In other words, these countries profit most from the increased share of coal in the PES mix.

2030 Scores using the high renewables scenario

The high renewables scenario will also lead to an improved energy security situation compared with the baseline scenario, albeit not all to the same degree in the selected regions. The main cause of this improvement is the minimum score of 70 assumed for the diversified sources of renewable energy. The score will increase proportionally with decreasing share of imports. In this study, we assume a 100 percent domestic share for renewable energy and, as a result, the minimum score of 100 is achieved for all regions. EU27 foresees the largest share of renewables in the PES fuel mix. Consequently, the EU profits optimally from the renewable energy index value of 100. The low score for coal (i.e., 70) in Japan results in a relatively large increase of the index value compared with the HC scenario. So, Japan fully takes advantage of the decreased oil and gas PES shares and the increased role of renewables.

Concluding remarks

Coal will dominate the electricity sector in Southeast Asia for the foreseeable future, with Vietnam, China, India, and Indonesia having large coal reserves at low prices. Energy security, air quality, and climate change mitigation can be linked through the use of clean coal technologies and in combination with nuclear, gas, and renewables. In this chapter, two security of supply quantification methodologies have been discussed and applied to the high coal (HC) and high renewables (HR) scenarios. These scenarios cover five world regions, in order to gain insight into the change in long-term energy supply situation under different assumptions. Southeast Asia is at a crossroads regarding which path it takes in terms of energy security. It is likely it will be neither a HC or HR path but rather a combination of the two. However, the IEA WEO scenario indicates that the use of coal will increase, which makes it more important that the most efficient coal-fired power stations are built and planned with the possibility of retrofitting with CCS.

The first methodology, the Shannon diversity index, is elaborated into several variants that cover diversification of energy supply sources (I_1), import dependency (I_2), and political stability in import regions (I_3). These indicators are additional to each other, whereby I_3 is used as the most elaborate indicator, covering all aspects. In the second approach, the S/D index, the assignment of objective shares and subjective weights is instructive for its attempt to balance the different components in the index (such as the relationship between supply and demand types in the index, or the relation between stable regions' imports and unstable regions' imports).

Comparison of the results between the quantitative analysis of the S/D index and the Shannon diversity index is justified because the same overall scenarios are applied. In this study, the WEO 2006 reference scenario (i.e., baseline scenario) and two alternative scenarios developed in the study (high coal scenario and high renewables scenario) are applied to analyze the energy security situation in EU27, China, India, North America, and Japan in 2030. Thereby, in the assessment of the security of primary energy supply, both methodologies incorporate important common factors:

- domestic primary energy production versus imports from foreign regions of origin;
- imports from unstable regions.

There is one main difference between both methodologies. The Shannon diversity index focuses on the notion of diversity and heavily relies on the work of Andrew Stirling (see his chapter in this volume), while the S/D index (i.e., its PES part) is based on index values as a function of the net share of domestic supply and the relative share in the total primary energy supply of each of the primary sources (see chapter from Jansen and his colleagues). Nevertheless, similar conclusions were reached with both approaches:

- In Japan, Europe/EU27, and North America, the HR scenario will lead to an improved energy security situation compared with both the baseline scenario and the high coal scenario in 2030.
- In Japan and Europe/EU27, the HC scenario will lead to an improved energy security situation compared with the baseline scenario in 2030. On the basis of the baseline scenario, Japan ranks lowest among other regions.

The use of the two indicators in other regions yields different results, with an increased share of coal decreasing the diversity in energy mix, but improving the overall import dependency situation. The contrast in results between the Shannon diversity index and the Supply/Demand PES sub-index is most prominent in the case of China for the high coal scenario. This can be explained by the fact that in the baseline scenario the share of coal is already high, and further increased in the HC scenario. This will have an obvious negative impact on the diversity in primary energy supply. However, as China is largely self-sufficient in its primary energy supply, it has a high score in all scenarios for the Supply/Demand index.

The 2004–2030 period, using the analysis of the Shannon diversity index, indicates that the energy security situation in China and India improves under the HR scenario, whereas Japan experiences the same development under all three scenarios. In contrast, the energy security concerns rise in Europe and the USA under all scenarios. For other investigated regions, no calculated overall S/D indices were available. Only PES sub-indices could be calculated. More work is needed to gather data and analyze the situation in other Southeast Asian countries.

Notes

1 BP. 2006. *BP Energy Statistical Review of World Energy 2006* (London: BP).
2 International Energy Agency (IEA). 2009. *World Energy Outlook* (Paris: International Energy Agency Organisation for Economic Co-operation and Development).

3 International Energy Agency (IEA). 2006. *Energy Technology Perspectives: Scenarios and Strategies to 2050* (Paris: International Energy Agency, Organisation for Economic Co-operation and Development).

4 UNFCCC. 2006. "United Nations Framework Convention on Climate Change." Available at: www.unfccc.int (accessed August 29, 2010).

5 Kessels, J. and S. Bakker. 2005. *ESCAPE: Energy Security and ClimAte Policy Evaluation. Linking Climate Change and Energy Security Policy in Post-2012 Climate Strategies*, ECN-C-05-032 (Petten, The Netherlands: ECN).

6 Kessels, J., S. Bakker and B. Wetzelaer. 2008. *Energy Security and the Role of Coal* (London: IEA Clean Coal Centre).

7 Intergovernmental Panel on Climate Change (IPCC). 2001. "Climate Change 2001" In B. Metz, O. Davidson, R. Swart, and J. Pan (eds.) *Mitigation: Contribution of Working Group III to the Third Assessment Report of the Intergovernmental Panel on Climate Change* (Cambridge: Cambridge University Press), pp. 1–45.

8 Jansen, J. C., W. G. van Arkel, and M. G. Boots. 2004. *Designing Indicators of Long-Term Energy Supply Security*, ECN-C-04-007 (Petten, The Netherlands ECN).

9 Scheepers, M. J. J., A. J. Seebregts, J. J. de Jong, and J. M. Maters. 2007. *EU Standards for Energy Security of Supply: Updates on the Crisis Capability Index and the Supply/Demand Index Quantification for EU-27*, ECN-E-07-004/CIEP (Petten/The Hague, The Netherlands: ECN/CIEP). (Een Onafhankelijk Onderzoeksinstituut voor Duurzame Energie [ECN] and Clingendael International Energy Programme [CIEP]).

10 Jansen, *et al.*, *Designing Indicators.*

11 Stirling, A. 1999. *On the Economics and Analysis of Diversity*, SPRU electronic working paper series, Paper No. 28. Brighton, UK: University of Sussex.

12 Jansen, *et al.*, *Designing Indicators.*

13 Jansen, *et al.*, *Designing Indicators.*

14 Jansen, *et al.*, *Designing Indicators.*

15 Scheepers, M. J. J., A. J. Seebregts, J. J. de Jong, and J. M. Maters. 2006. *EU Standards for Energy Security of Supply*, ECN-C-06-039 (Petten/The Hague, The Netherlands: ECN/CIEP).

16 Scheepers, *et al.*, *EU Standards for Energy Security of Supply.*

17 Scheepers, *et al.*, *EU Standards for Energy Security of Supply: Updates.*

18 International Energy Agency (IEA). 2006. *World Energy Outlook 2006* (Paris: International Energy Agency, Organisation for Economic Co-operation and Development).

19 BP. 2004. *BP Statistical Review of World Energy 2004* (London: BP).

20 Energy Information Administration (EIA). 2007. *International Energy Outlook 2007* (Washington, DC: EIA).

21 Jansen, *et al.*, *Designing Indicators.*

22 WETO-H$_2$. 2006. *World Energy Technology Outlook – 2050* (Luxembourg: European Commission, Directorate General for Research, Directorate Energy, Office for Official Publications of the European Communities).

23 International Monetary Fund (IMF). "World Economic Outlook Database" (Washington, DC: International Monetary Fund). Available at: <http://imf.org/external/pubs/ft/weo/2007/01/data/index.aspx> (accessed April 2007).

24 Energy Information Administration (EIA). 2007. *International Energy Outlook 2006* (Washington, DC: Energy Information Administration).

25 International Energy Agency (IEA). 2007. *Energy Security and Climate Policy: Assessing Interaction* (Paris: International Energy Agency, Organisation for Economic Co-operation and Development).

26 Eurostat. 2006. *Energy & Transport in Figures – Statistical Pocketbook 2005* (Luxembourg: European Commission, Directorate-General for Energy and Transport, Office for Official Publications of the European Communities).

27 International Energy Agency (IEA). 2006. *IEA Database on Energy Statistics 2006* (Paris: International Energy Agency, Organisation for Economic Co-operation and Development).

28 European Commission. 2006. *European Energy and Transport Trends to 2030 – Update 2005* (Luxembourg: European Commission, Directorate-General for Energy and Transport).

29 IEA, *World Energy Outlook 2006.*

30 BP. 2007. *BP Statistical Review of World Energy 2007* (London: BP).

17

MEASURING ENERGY SECURITY

From universal indicators to contextualized frameworks

Aleh Cherp and Jessica Jewell

Indicators of energy security and their limitations

The current debate on measuring energy security is largely focused on finding the "right" indicators. In the recent special issue on energy security in *Energy Policy*, six of the eight articles were directly related to indicator development and energy security quantification.[1] Given the complexity of energy security, it is understandable that researchers and policymakers alike seek quantification which can simplify and cut through this complexity. However, in this chapter we will argue that much more attention should be given to the *process* of indicator identification and application as well as to the underlying assumptions and perspectives that shape this process. Thus our discussion starts with the inherent choices and trade-offs surrounding indicator selection which are generally inexplicit and unstated in the literature.

Generally speaking, an indicator is a signal or proxy useful in conveying condensed information about the state of a system. An example is body temperature as a signal of the state of health. An energy security indicator is a signal of the state of an energy system, which conveys information about its potential vulnerabilities. Choosing such energy security indicators faces three challenges:

1. *Complexity.* The complexity of energy systems hides multiple dynamic vulnerabilities, which are difficult to capture with simple understandable indicators.
2. *Uncertain future.* Energy security is about how vulnerabilities will develop in the future, not the present or the past. How can potentially multiple and uncertain futures be presented in indicators?
3. *Conflicting perspectives.* Various actors have different perspectives on energy systems and assign different priorities to their various elements and threats. How can energy security indicators credibly reflect these often conflicting priorities? How can simple, understandable indicators capture these complex dynamics?

This chapter describes how the choices made in the area of simplifying complexity, understanding the future, and balancing conflicting priorities shape the most commonly used energy security indicators. It also describes how dominant storylines relate to indicator selection and framing. It concludes with an energy security framework which builds on indicators to present a contextualized evaluation of energy security.

Making choices, shaping indicators

Complexity of the energy systems

The state of a simple system, for example an internal combustion engine, can be relatively easily described by a limited number of well-chosen parameters: the cooling water temperature, the oil level, the rotation speed. This is because we know the boundaries of the system, its elements, and their interconnections. This is not so with complex energy systems where their external boundaries and internal connections are not always known and are always uncertain and fluid.

As with other complex systems, the external boundaries of energy systems can be drawn in various ways. The choice of boundaries affects the choice of indicators since any quantification is only possible when the system in question is clearly defined. It is often argued, implicitly or explicitly, that national energy systems function relatively autonomously and therefore energy security indicators should reflect national-level parameters. But it can also be argued that local or regional energy systems are autonomous and thus energy security should be discussed at the sub-national level (as Hughes[2] does for Eastern Canada). Energy security of groups of countries such as the EU can also be analyzed.[3] Finally, it is not uncommon to analyze the security of global energy "sectors" (such as the oil sector) spanning national boundaries but operating relatively autonomously of other energy sectors.

Deciding on where to draw the "substantive" rather than "spatial" boundaries of energy systems is more complicated and intricately connected to values and priorities. Energy security indicators should characterize disruptions of energy systems, but what constitutes "a disruption" depends upon our expectations of the "normal functioning" of an energy system. In the most narrow and traditional sense, a disruption affects the ability to provide affordable energy for the normal functioning of key economic sectors. Dealing with energy flows and stocks and immediately related economic factors (prices, investment levels, etc.) may be sufficient for quantifying vulnerabilities under these assumptions.

However, if we expect our energy systems to provide universal access, ensure climate neutrality, safeguard human health, facilitate good governance, guarantee national self-sufficiency, or support rapid economic growth then the meaning of energy disruptions changes. In such cases we might need indicators that reflect connections between the pure energy characteristics and such phenomena as greenhouse gas emissions or local pollution, the distribution of energy consumption among social groups, and corruption, to name just a few.

The internal structure and "mechanics" of energy systems matter as well. What are the most important subsystems and how do they interact? Such subsystems, often called "energy sectors," can be defined in several different ways. They may reflect the structure of primary energy sources (PES) (oil, gas, nuclear, etc.), of end-use sectors (transport, industry, residential, etc.) or energy carriers (electricity, heat, liquid fuels). This division reflects important assumptions about the extent to which fuels, carriers or end-uses are substitutable and to what extent their vulnerabilities can be analyzed separately.

The choice of subsystems or energy "sectors" largely determines the approach to aggregation used in energy security indicators. All energy security indicators are aggregated from individual, more specific parameters. Usually the state of an energy sector is described by indicators aggregated within the boundaries of this sector like the total generating capacity or the average age of the infrastructure. For example, the security of the nuclear electricity sector can be described by the total generating capacity or the average age of the fleet. More ambitious aggregation across different sectors which does not subdivide national energy systems into smaller subsystems is also possible as described later in this chapter. This type of aggregation assumes pretty strong substitutability, flexibility, and links between different components.

The delimitation of energy sectors closely relates to assumptions on how energy systems operate at different timescales. For example, energy demand may be viewed as inflexible with respect to fuels and inelastic with respect to prices (which is most true in the short term). This justifies aggregation at the level of fuel sectors. If, however, a particular end-use sector can switch from one fuel to another then aggregated indicators for all fuels used in this sector may be more appropriate. Naturally, longer timescales may accommodate more profound reconfiguration of energy systems and thus more aggregated indicators.

Thus, the division of energy systems into sectors is very much about the flexibility and dynamics of energy systems. It matters not only for the aggregation of various parameters into energy security indicators but also for measuring the diversity of energy systems. Diversity indices can be calculated based on the "disparity" between fuels (or conceivably other components) which reflects our perspectives and assumptions. Should natural gas procured from two different countries be considered as one or two different sources? Should it be considered as the same source as oil and coal (as all of them are fossil fuels?) Should wind and solar energy be grouped together (as they are renewables) or stand apart in calculating the relevant indicators?

Three mindsets for the future

An indicator of energy security should send a signal about the future. This is more difficult than just measuring the present. First, as we have already mentioned, energy systems are complex and thus we do not know how they will behave in the future. If a motor engine overheats it will likely explode, and the cooling water temperature is a pretty good predictor of such an outcome. But a complex system may or may not "explode" if "overheated." It may instead be able to adjust to the stress by reorganizing.

The capacity to reorganize is particularly relevant when a complex system includes social components and reflexivity, as energy systems do. Social institutions can mitigate threats to energy systems (such as by releasing strategic stocks if a major supplier goes offline) or they can exacerbate them (for example from the increase in price volatility due to price hedging). The response depends upon a number of both "hard" and "soft" factors ranging from technological capacity to socio-economic flexibility and political will.

Complex systems may also change and transform on their own without any external influence. In systems language, they have "emergent properties." For example, new energy technologies can emerge making old threats obsolete and new ones actual. Complex systems may also react to relatively minor disturbances by passing their "tipping point" and collapsing or entirely and rapidly transforming to another state. An example is the cascading failures in the US electricity systems after they have passed a tipping point.[4]

There are several different ways of representing the future of complex systems. For the purposes of our analysis we differentiate three logically consistent mindsets.

The first, "deterministic," mindset focuses on well-known properties of energy systems: resources, flows, stocks, infrastructure, investments, etc. In this mindset, the future is a function of the present: the outcome of the unfolding trends. Future threats and risks primarily resulting from natural or technological factors can be predicted or at least estimated based on the existing properties of the system. Within this mindset, ideal indicators would accurately reflect future risks and vulnerabilities such as resource scarcity, aging infrastructure, demand growth, and rising costs.

The second, "sovereignty," mindset focuses on actor-dependent properties of energy systems which have to do with reflexivity, intentions, and power. In this mindset, the future is uncertain and unfolds as a result of the implementation of competing plans of various actors. Major vulnerabilities arise as a result of clashes of such plans and underlying interests, intentions, and ploys. The key threat in this mindset is that the energy system becomes dominated by malevolent powers such as energy-exporting countries, international energy companies, or even the market. Thus, the sovereignty mindset is more preoccupied with the future behavior of various actors in energy systems rather than with physical factors. However, behavior is impossible to predict, since it depends on highly reflexive intentions. Therefore, as far as metrics are concerned, the sovereignty mindset often seeks to measure what is quantifiable: the power of various actors, their mutual dependency, and their space to maneuver.

The third, "resilience" mindset focuses on self-organizing properties of energy systems. The future is seen as the result of such self-organization rather than merely as a mechanical continuation of the present or as unfolding from actors' intentions and plans. Many of the most important threats are unknown. Thus, the main vulnerability is the inability of energy systems to adapt to challenges: both known and unknown. The metrics most fitting this mindset do not seek to predict future risks but rather aim to characterize the adaptive capacity and resilience of the system.

The challenge of priority-setting

Setting priorities and determining which aspects and vulnerabilities are important is also subject to choice and debate, often in a highly contested political context. Such prioritization has received more extensive coverage in the literature than the other choices made when selecting indicators. Which energy options should be prioritized and which may be allowed to be disrupted? Are short-term intermittent threats or longer-term "creeping" but more enduring vulnerabilities more important? Are "natural" or "political" risks more acceptable? Should energy prices be "fair" and what does it mean? Naturally, such choices affect the indicators: which parameters are selected and how they are weighted, aggregated, interpreted, presented, and used.

Selecting energy security indicators: making politically constrained choices

Table 17.1 summarizes how choices in these three areas affect the assumptions and boundaries about energy systems, representations of the future, and priorities in the process of selecting and defining energy security indicators.

In principle, a large number of such choices and their combinations are possible, but in practice such choices are constrained by political agendas. The choice of indicators is a political process

Table 17.1 Assumptions and priorities essential for selecting energy security indicators

Area of choice		Possible choices
Energy Systems	External boundaries: spatial	Global, supra-national, national, sub-national
	Expectations	Environment, health, equality, competitiveness, security
	Internal boundaries and systems behavior	Division into sectors (by fuel, by end-use, etc.); and the degree of sectors' autonomy and interdependence
	Future	Deterministic, sovereignty, or resilience mindset
Priorities	Critical elements of energy systems	Security of supply, infrastructure or services
	Time-horizons	Short-, medium- or long-term vulnerabilities
	Acceptability of risks	Political, natural or technical risks
		"Catastrophic" low-probability or insignificant high-probability risks

because once agreed such indicators guide decisions affecting significant interests. The nature of such processes varies from one jurisdiction to another depending upon the prevailing political culture and the existing capacities for deliberation on a contested subject.

Energy security agendas are typically formed by elites consisting of more technocratically and market-oriented energy professionals and more politically minded national leaders and politicians. In most cases it is natural for both groups to draw boundaries of energy systems along national borders, transnational energy "sectors" such as "the European gas pipeline network" or "the international oil market," or between international alliances such as the EU, OPEC, or the OECD.

For energy policy elites, it is also most natural to see energy systems as structured along infrastructural divisions including supply versus demand and individual fuel sectors. This reflects the traditional management and conceptual organization of the technocratic elite and it also resonates with the political security elite who tend to be strongly concerned with externally originated disruptions of energy supply.

Thus, the discourse about the future of energy systems is commonly dominated by the deterministic mindset (preferred by technocrats) and the sovereignty mindset (preferred by politicians). As a result, the focus on forecasting and planning often competes with the focus on power and dependence. Elements of the resilience mindset also penetrate the futures discourse through concepts such as markets, innovation, learning, and resilience.

From the energy security standpoint, the highest priority in managing energy systems is achieving a supply–demand balance. However, traditionally, energy policy focuses on the supply side of this equation. This happens for a variety of reasons. Historically, security of energy sources attracts most attention since the very concept of energy security emerged to reflect concerns over supply interruptions.[5] Energy supply is not only the main area of responsibility of energy professionals but also their source of power and *raison d'être*.

Political leaders are often preoccupied with uninterrupted delivery of energy services. In fact, disruption of nationally vital energy services may lead to political instability. At the same time, managing the demand for energy services (e.g. through increasing energy prices or imposing quotas) is often politically more sensitive than securing sufficient supply.

With respect to possible threats to energy supply, it is easier for the elites to mobilize political support for addressing politically motivated, dramatic, and immediate disruptions than longer-term "creeping" threats associated with natural or infrastructural conditions.

Energy security indicators and storylines

The inherent messiness and necessity of assumptions in designing and choosing indicators formulation means that the formulation process is largely influenced by the social context and interests of the actors involved. The importance of social reality in shaping perceptions of the truth dates back to the seminal work of Berger and Luckmann[6] and has become a pillar of many disciplines in social science. The recent work related to energy security indicators within this tradition highlights the importance of the social context in the development of sustainability indicators,[7] the polysemic nature of energy security,[8] and the role of fantasy-creation in shaping energy futures for certain technologies;[9] however, there is little explicit discussion of this in the literature on energy security indicators.

This section maps the existing energy security indicators onto related social constructs which we call storylines or discourses. It describes how different mindsets and perspectives influence the perception of the "truth" about energy security and names some of the dominant agents in each discourse as well as the associated storylines and indicators. Table 17.2 summarizes the most commonly used indicators and related storylines, mindsets, and systemic assumptions.

Table 17.2 Commonly used energy security indicators, associated discourses, mindsets, systemic assumptions, and priorities

		MINDSET			Systemic assumptions and priorities
		Deterministic	Sovereignty	Resilience	
S T O R Y L I N E S	Global scarcity of energy resources	Global R/P ratio	Concentration of resources	Diversity of global PES	Global system; autonomous fuel sectors. Natural threats
	Domestic scarcity of energy resources	Domestic R/P ratio			National systems; autonomous fuel sectors. Natural threats
	Failures of infrastructure	Efficiency for peak power gen. Spare capacity Efficiency			Technical systems; natural or technical threats
	Dependence on unreliable suppliers		Import Dependence*	Strategic Stocks	National systems Political threats
	Volatility of international energy markets	Energy Intensity**			National systems; demand and supply; Low elasticity. Economic threats
	Unaffordable energy prices	Energy Intensity** Vulnerability of economies to high prices		Market Exposure	
	The danger of the least-cost approach	MVP			National systems or sectors (electricity); Economic threats
	Multiple diverse risks to energy supply	Diversity of technical elements (e.g. transport routes, power plants)	Diversity of suppliers and market actors	Diversity of energy technologies	National systems; Diverse threats Strong internal connections or adaptive capacity
	Energy security threats accumulate	Supply/Demand Index			
		Oil Vulnerability Index			

Notes:
* variations include dependence on "unstable," "unreliable" or "unfriendly" countries.
** variations include intensities of individual fuels or individual sectors.

Scarcity of global resources

Humanity has been concerned about global resource scarcity since the time of Malthus, but it was *The Limits to Growth* report[10] that most prominently linked these concerns to certain systemic assumptions and quantitative indicators. This story and related indicators consider global energy systems as relatively autonomous fuel sectors.

Most often these concerns relate to conventional oil consolidated in the so called "Peak Oil" debate. This debate is illustrative because it shows different perspectives—and eventually different indicators—inherent in the three mindsets. The concept of Peak Oil is itself firmly rooted in the *deterministic* mindset. It is based on the assumption that with knowledge of the current reserves and production, we can "predict" with some certainty when the world will run out of conventional oil.[11] Since our understanding of energy systems demonstrates that it cannot operate without massive reliance on relatively cheap oil, this leads to a doomsday scenario in which the world runs out of oil, resulting in widespread economic and social crises. The indicator most firmly associated with this mindset is global reserves or the global R/P ratio for a particular fuel.

The central question of the *sovereignty* mindset is "who will control the last barrels of oil?" Will these countries or organizations be able to dictate their conditions for the rest of the world? Will great and small powers struggle over the last productive wells, possibly sparking a large war?[12] The indicator most relevant to these questions is the geographic concentration of world oil resources. The system boundaries for this indicator are not necessarily global; instead, they may reflect the existing energy clubs, economic or political alliances, spheres of influence of superpower, or even "civilizations."

The *resilience* mindset all but refuses to recognize the "Peak Oil" problem, or at least to express it in such terms. It has much more trust in the adaptability and self-organizing properties of the global energy system. The future of such a complex system surely cannot be predicted based on the past trends. New technologies will emerge to either replace oil or extract more of it. Unconventional resources may become more widely used[13] and/or the markets will force change in behavior and institutions. To be specific, the resilience mindset also considers dependence on oil a problem, but not because we will run out of it one day. The main disadvantage of consuming so much oil is that it suppresses other energy technologies and thus reduces the diversity of the global energy system which is a precondition for its ability to adapt to oil scarcity or other disruptions. The main indicator thus is the diversity of energy options. The system boundaries can be global, national, or even regional or local.

The main agents in this discourse tend to be journalists,[14] a few prominent oil-industry executives (most notably the late Matthew Simmons and T. Boone Pickens), and a handful of scholars spanning both the physical and social sciences.[15] Though most of the "peak" debate relates to oil, similar stories emerge in relation to other energy sectors: "peak gas," "peak coal," "peak uranium," and even "peak water."

Scarcity of domestic resources

Following closely on the heels of the global scarcity story is the fear of domestic scarcity. This story draws the energy system boundary along national borders and at the same time considers fuel sectors as relatively autonomous. Thus the indicators used to illustrate this story generally relate to one energy source within a given national context.

The story of domestic scarcity generally fits in with the deterministic mindset. Adequacy of physical reserves can be reflected by the reserves to production (R/P) ratio. This metric indicates how many years with the current reserves and production a primary energy source will last. The

R/P ratio canbe compared across different energy sources. Due to the simplicity and transparency of the R/P, it can be useful for gaining insight into the long-term production potential for a given resource as well as which international actors will likely play key roles in the development of a given market.[16] In addition, for energy exporting nations (such as the UK or Argentina), the R/P ratio can provide a signal for the imminence of an energy transition.

The deterministic mindset and related indicators are based on assumptions of current technological conditions;[17] however, since the very definition of reserves includes the economic feasibility of a resource (and cannot predict the discovery of new resources), they are inherently fraught with uncertainty and are subject to change. For example, for oil the R/P ratio increased by 41 percent between 1973 and 1997 due to technological advances following the Arab oil embargo.[18] Some researchers, particularly those interested in oil, have tried to address the dynamic factors that affect the R/P by using forecasting techniques to predict how the production level and technological advances will affect long-term global availability of resources.[19] While this approach can potentially provide more realistic predictions (particularly over the long term), the embedded assumptions increase the uncertainty and decrease the transparency.

Another problem with the R/P ratio is that for non-energy-producing nations, it can be quite misleading since countries with low domestic reserves often have negligible production.[20] Some researchers avoid this problem by using the domestic oil reserves to the domestic oil consumption ratio.[21]

Dependence on unreliable suppliers

The energy security agenda is strongly dominated by considerations of import dependency, which is natural since this discourse justifies and strengthens the power of domestic energy elites who usually control the energy discourse in a country. The story of risks associated with import dependency is simple and convenient for politicians, technocrats, and the media. It fits primarily within the sovereignty mindset and draws the boundaries of energy systems along national borders. The main threats within this discourse are political rather than natural or technical.

Thus, one of the oldest and most common measures for energy security is net import dependency, or the proportion of a given fuel that comes from abroad. Given that imported energy supply carries greater uncertainty than domestic supply, the higher the net imports are, the greater the exposure an energy source (or system) has to these uncertainties. This measure can apply to a single fuel type or to the entire fuel mix.[22]

Some modifications to this metric distinguish between different regional sources. For example, Scheepers *et al.*[23] differentiate between EU and non-EU sources of oil and gas, and for non-EU sources between sources that have long-term contracts and those that are purchased on the open market. Similarly, the Asia Pacific Energy Research Centre[24] presents not the total net import dependency of oil but import dependency on Middle Eastern sources; they also scale the net import dependency on oil for the proportion it plays in total primary energy supply of a country. Alhajji and Williams[25] propose the following three measures of oil import vulnerability for OECD countries: percentage of imports from top five oil-producing countries, OPEC share of the world petroleum supply, and the Persian Gulf share of the world petroleum supply. Additionally, some promote differentiating between politically stable and unstable countries. For example, Gupta[26] specifically considers the political stability of supplier countries. Jansen[27] and Lefèvre[28] also use political stability ratings in their diversity indices, which will be discussed in the multiple diverse risks to energy supply section.

In addition to these modifications, some authors, particularly in the oil security debate, have criticized import dependency as misrepresenting the risk associated with dependence.[29,30] While Kendell[31] proposes a more holistic measurement which integrates demand-side indicators into oil vulnerability, Greene[32] suggests measuring oil dependence not by the raw energy flow into a country but rather the affect this flow has on the country's economy and policies. These suggestions either challenge the dominance of the energy supply sector or they expand the substantive boundaries of the energy system to include socio-economic elements.

Another metric related to import dependency is the days of strategic stock of a given fuel. This metric is commonly applied to oil[33] but can also be applied to other fuels such as natural gas or coal. This metric is intrinsically linked to the resilience mindset, implying that imported sources are subject to physical and price disruptions so a strategic stock of a given fuel can shield a country from disruptions from fuel suppliers or the international market.

The discourse of "unreliable" suppliers is very popular in the mass media and often penetrates the vocabulary of policymakers. Many political commentators in the US lament the dependence on "Middle East oil," implying the hostility of Middle Eastern countries towards the USA, and often proposing to replace it by imports from "friendlier" Canadian oil increased domestic drilling,[34] or reducing oil consumption.[35] Similarly, political commentators in Europe coined the phrase "Russia's energy weapon" to point to risks of energy dependency on the Russian Federation.[36] The discourse of unreliability of Russian energy exports is also quite popular among European policymakers. For example it has been used as the key argument in favor of constructing a nuclear power plant in Lithuania and for supporting a variety of gas and oil pipeline projects avoiding Russia.

Volatility of international fuel market

Another story closely linked to energy imports is that of the volatility and unpredictability of international energy markets. Such volatility is especially undesirable from the deterministic mindset perspective as it increases the instability and unpredictability of energy systems. Naturally, those with the prevailing sovereignty mindset are also averse to price volatility which is sometimes blamed on erratic markets or irresponsible speculators.

The import dependency indicator, discussed in the previous section, is in part related to this story. In such a case, it is assumed that domestic energy prices can somehow be "shielded" from international fluctuations (which means a pretty autonomous functioning of the natural energy system). When import dependence is used in relation to the "volatile markets" story it is usually not dependence on particular countries but rather dependence on global markets that causes a threat.

Another relevant indicator within this storyline is energy intensity of the economy or of a given sector (total or in relation to a specific fuel).[37,38,39,40] While historically the end-use part of the energy system has been excluded from measurements of energy security, recently it has been receiving more attention.[41,42] The standard argument is that the more energy intensive a society is, the more vulnerable it will be to energy price fluctuations.

Scheepers *et al.*[43] present a slightly different argument for using energy intensity and propose that it can be used as a measure of "essential energy needs" for each sector. Accordingly, they propose four sector-specific indicators: energy intensity for the residential and transport sectors, and energy intensity of the value-added for the industrial and tertiary sectors (ton-oil equivalents/M€). They also suggest that it would be possible to use energy conservation targets or energy emission targets as a measure of essential energy needs; however, they rule out this approach due to the range of assumptions that would need to be made and practical limitations.

There are also several indicators used to measure market exposure for a given energy source. These indicators use the assumption that the more exposure an economy has to the international market, the higher the risk of negative economic consequences due to price fluctuations. These are mostly used within the oil vulnerability and oil security literature.[44,45,46,47] On the supply side, these market exposure indicators include: the proportion of the total energy supply from oil[48] or gas,[49] the ratio of world oil imports to the net oil imports of a given country,[50] and the ratio of world oil supply to the oil demand of a given country.[51]

The same politicians and policymakers who exploit the fear of dependence on foreign sources use the danger of volatility discourse. The G8 summit commonly condemns volatility of energy and oil prices,[52] and the energy industry states that the lack of energy price stability inhibits sufficient investment in energy resources and infrastructure.

Unaffordable energy prices

Energy prices can rise not only intermittently as a result of short-term fluctuations but also permanently and persistently. It is well documented that high energy prices can hurt vulnerable groups[53] and even undermine national economic competitiveness.[54] Political leaders and techno-crats are well aware of the destabilizing effects of such high prices and therefore maintaining "affordability" has been high on national energy security agendas.

Concerns over high energy prices are strongly linked to the deterministic mindset which considers the inputs and outputs of the energy economic system as a function of prices. From the sovereignty mindset point of view, high prices are often portrayed as a "plot" of energy exporters and are dangerous since they increase the power of exporters and may lead to catastrophic loss of power for elites; most recently this phenomenon was demonstrated by the uprising in Kyrgyzstan which allegedly was triggered by high electricity and heating prices.[55]

These assumptions are naturally not universal. The sovereignty of energy exporters is strengthened as a result of high energy prices. And from the resilience mindset high energy prices may stimulate the innovations necessary for positive transformations of the energy system.

Energy intensity, discussed above, is one natural indicator of vulnerability to high energy prices. There are additional methods proposed to measure this specific kind of vulner-ability. Studies that aim to measure the "vulnerability" to price (or physical availability) variations of a specific fuel often include a crude measure of economic vulnerability such as the value of oil imports,[56] the ratio of the value of fuel imports to GDP,[57,58] or the portion of export earnings that goes to purchasing oil on the international market. The higher the import bill for a given energy source, the more vulnerable a nation's economy to price increases of that fuel.

Another approach that has been proposed is Greene's and Leiby's[59] Oil Security Metrics Model, which models the future US GDP losses due to oil dependence from wealth transfer to oil-exporting nations, GDP losses as a result of higher oil prices, and macroeconomic disruptions due to oil price shocks. Recently, Greene has elaborated on this work to suggest that the US should redefine oil independence as being achieved when "the costs of oil dependence ... [are] so small that they will have no effect on [a country's] economic, military or foreign policies."[60] This definition demonstrates a distinctly different mindset in understanding energy independence, from one based on import ratios to one that tries to approximate the possible damage that high energy prices from imports can have.

This group of metrics also includes more general indicators of economic well-being. The per capita income is one measure of vulnerability to energy price fluctuations and with oil, poorer countries are proven to suffer a higher percentage of their GDP than richer countries from an increase in oil prices[61,62] Another possible metric in terms of oil vulnerability is a country's foreign exchange reserve, since countries with a larger reserve are better equipped to deal with sudden price hikes in imported energy.[63]

The discourse of unaffordable energy prices is commonly promulgated by industrial actors as well as poverty reduction and development organizations. Industrial lobby groups in countries commonly argue that national energy prices must be competitive for the national industry to be able to compete on a national level. Additionally, the high cost of energy in low-income energy-importing countries is a common concern for development organizations, including the World Bank and United Nations Development Programme (UNDP).

The danger of the "least-cost" approach

Related to the previous discussion of risk exposure of an economy is the argument that taking the least-cost approach to energy choices exacerbates energy security risks. This storyline argues that there is a price risk that is associated with fuels and can be determined by measuring historic price-risk volatility. The technique to accomplish this is based on mean–variance portfolio (MVP) theory, whose origin lies in financial literature,[64] which proposes that the relative risk of an individual asset can be determined from its historical price variability and the risk of a portfolio of assets can be minimized through the selection of stocks with low covariance. Since the relative risk of each asset is assumed to be related to its historical price variability, risk of the portfolio is minimized by diversifying into assets whose fluctuations do not follow each other. In the energy sector, by examining the historical covariance of different fuels or suppliers, one can ostensibly calculate the optimal portfolio mix to minimize risk.

This technique has been used most widely for determining the price risk associated with different portfolios of fuel for electricity generation.[65] In addition to applying the MVP to the US electricity sector, Humphreys and McCain[66] apply it to the entire US fuel portfolio to measure the portfolio risk that emerges from the nation's fuel mix. Neff[67] applies the MVP approach not only to price covariance between different fuel types but also to export quantity variation between different fuel suppliers. He makes a case that by examining historical production variation between different supplier countries for oil during times of political unrest (such as the Iraq–Kuwait war) one can gain insight into the most efficient supplier diversification portfolio.

This metric is a result of all three mindsets. It is deterministic in that it assumes future price volatility can be predicted by historical trends. Neff[68] uses it in the sovereignty mindset to evaluate the relative risk of different suppliers. Finally, it falls into the resilience mindset by arguing that energy portfolios can be constructed to have resilience against price risks.

This academic discourse is promulgated by economists who try to influence the energy policy choices in favor of more balanced portfolios. In spite of the aim at policymakers there is little evidence that this approach has been integrated into either the political or industrial spheres.

Failures of infrastructure

If the previous two discourses focus primarily on natural threats (resource scarcity), this storyline focuses on technological risks. In this story, energy systems are primarily technical (i.e., if an electricity or pipeline network spans several countries it is still considered one system). The dominant mindset in this discourse is deterministic: under-maintained or overexposed systems are likely to fail.

There have been a number of indicators associated with this storyline. The spare capacity associated with a given carrier has been proposed to reflect the security of that carrier[69,70] and specifically as an indicator for electricity. Similarly, for gas the marginal spare capacity can be calculated by measuring the proportion difference between the maximum gas supply capacity and the theoretical maximum demand. A related metric is the import capacity of the electricity network relative to the domestic capacity.[71] The main limitation with the spare capacity (and the underlying technically oriented mindset) is that in liberalized markets it is increasingly a "reflexive" economic, rather than an "objective," concept and thus cannot easily be measured. This means that in the case of electricity, the security of supply is not only determined by the absolute installed spare capacity but is also strongly influenced by the regulatory environment.[72]

Another approach to evaluating infrastructural robustness is to compare existing infrastructural attributes with the best available technology. Scheepers *et al.*[73] do this with the efficiency of power plants, boilers, and refineries. In the resilience mindset, the closer a given technology is to the state of the art, the more reliable it is.

This discourse of infrastructural requirements has emerged from certain technocratic research circles[74] as well as the utility and industry groups.[75] This focus on infrastructure is no surprise for these groups given their technocratic nature and the utility groups' interest in garnering investment for electricity infrastructure.

Energy infrastructure and its failures are particularly sensitive to contextual specifics and not always suitable for quantifications allowing international comparison. For example, Le Coq and Paltseva[76] suggest that the ideal data to determine risks for transport of imported energy into the European Union would be to determine the exact path of each import, determine whether or not that import passes through vulnerable areas, and determine what alternatives there would be for that supply if the existing path were disturbed. While these data could be collected, they are context dependent and also require a certain amount of judgment of risk, especially if an international comparison is subsequently attempted.

Multiple diverse risks to energy supply

The previously discussed discourses focused on relatively well-defined risks to energy systems: natural (resource scarcity), technical (infrastructural failures), political (unreliability of exporters), and economic (volatile and high prices). In contrast, this last discourse focuses on multiple unidentified risks which may include all of the above plus extreme natural events, terrorism and sabotage, and a variety of other factors.

The essential approach to such risks is not putting all the eggs in one basket; however, what are our energy "eggs" and "baskets" is subject to different interpretations. It may be various elements of energy infrastructure such as pipelines, refineries, sea lanes, and power generation plants (favored in the deterministic mindset); various suppliers of energy and market actors (favored in the sovereignty mindset); or various energy sources and technologies (favored in the resilience mindset).

While the importance of diversification in the energy sector was recognized by Winston Churchill as early as before World War I,[77] Stirling[78,79] was the first to apply diversity metrics to the energy sector. Stirling[80] argues that the energy field is dominated by uncertainty, both about the range of possible outcomes as well as the probability of these outcomes, and thus reasons that given the ignorance of future outcomes, the best measure of the resilience of a system to disruptions lies in measures of its diversity.

The Shannon-Wiener diversity index (SWDI) has been applied to the diversity of fuel sources for an electricity portfolio[81] as well as the entire primary energy supply.[82] Jansen *et al.*[83] present a series of indicators which include four iterations of the SWDI: the first is a pure rendition measuring the diversity of fuel types, the second rendition modifies the calculation to account for regional diversity in the supply base, the third modification scales the index for political stability of the supplier region, and the fourth adjustment addresses resource depletion of various fuel types.

The Herfindahl–Hirschman index (HHI) has also been applied to the diversity of primary energy sources[84] as well as to the supplier diversity for a given fuel in a given market.[85, 86] The former application mirrors common uses of the SWDI, while the latter use focuses on the market risks associated with supplier concentration for fuel types. Lefèvre[87] also presents a version that is scaled for the political risk of the supplier countries for a given fuel and one that is scaled for the proportion of the market that a given fuel source supplies.

Thus the measure of diversity (as well as the issue of aggregation) entirely rests on how we delimit energy sectors (fuels, etc.). Subjectivity in delimiting the amount of difference between fuel types has been discussed extensively by Stirling.[88] He proposed to calculate "diversity distances" based on surveys, thus explicitly pointing to the subjective nature of any fuel delimitation. However, we face the same difficulty in delimiting the distance between end-uses (and as a result the implicit flexibility between fuel sources).

While this discourse evolved in academic circles, it has been taken up by technocrats and policymakers alike. Additionally, due to the flexibility of how different aspects of energy can be valued, diversity indices have the potential to be used to justify almost any decision from policymakers.

Energy security threats accumulate

The final set of metrics contains aggregated indices that mix elements of different sets of indicators and essentially "add" them together to produce an energy security index. The advantages and disadvantages of aggregated indices have been extensively discussed in research and policy literature.[89] The purpose of this section is not to provide an exhaustive list of aggregated energy security indices but rather to discuss several examples of different approaches to aggregation and the inherent assumptions and mindsets associated with it.

The simplest way to aggregate metrics from different sectors is by normalizing these to a common scale (either numerically or by using a series of thresholds) and then assigning arbitrary weights to each metric. This is the approach that Scheepers *et al.* use in their Supply and Demand index which "aims to review and assess the energy security supply in the medium and longer run."[90] Their system boundary includes all three parts of the energy system: primary energy supply, energy conversion and transport, and final energy demand within national energy systems. They present a series of metrics for each part of the energy sector (all of which are included in the previous sections of this chapter), and for each metric they set thresholds for maximum and minimum values when the value measures the system to be "sufficiently" reliable, adequate, or efficient. Once all their data is normalized to a common scale, they assign weights to various parts of the system: 0.7 to supply and 0.3 to demand.

Another approach that has been proposed for aggregating metrics is to multiply the proportion of each fuel source or fuel type in a diversity index by a constant which characterizes the risk associated with that source. This approach was discussed in section one in relation to characterizing the political instability or the resource depletion of a given fuel source. In addition to these approaches, Le Coq and Paltseva[91] propose an external supply security index for each of the three main fossil fuel types which aggregates data related to supplier and transmission of different supply sources. They do this by modifying the proportion of each supplier's source by a value related to the metrics listed above.

Consider the following modified HHI:

$$\text{Herfindahl-Hirschman Index} = \sum_i (cp_i^2) * d$$

In Le Coq and Paltseva, c is equal to the product of the fungibility of the supply source, the political risk of a supplier country, and the distance between the supplier and consumer countries, while d is equal to the product of the net import dependency of the fuel source and the proportional supply of that fuel source in the total PES. Thus by taking the product of different aspects of a supplier, they assume that both the political stability and lack of fungibility of a source make a low diversity rating worse. Additionally, by scaling this to the demand side, they assume that the risk rating of a given fuel will be greater the bigger the role it plays in a nation's economy.

The final approach to metric aggregation covered by this review is the use of principal component analysis used by Gupta[92] in her oil-vulnerability index for oil-importing countries. She aggregates the following metrics: the ratio of value of oil imports to GDP, oil intensity of the economy, GDP/capita, oil share in the total energy supply, the ratio of domestic reserves to oil consumption, net oil import dependence, diversification of supply sources, political risk of oil-supplying countries, and the ratio of world oil imports to a given country's net oil imports. Thus the index she produces contains metrics related to supply, demand, and societal welfare. In order to aggregate these metrics, Gupta uses the principal component analysis which is a multivariate statistical approach that accounts for covariation between indicators to produce a set of uncorrelated "components." These components are then used to scale the original values for the metrics which ostensibly reduces the dimensionality of the dataset by correcting for covariation between the original metrics.

Aggregating metrics across different system elements and different mindsets implicitly assumes that threats are cumulative. Thus if a metric aggregates import dependency with oil intensity of the economy (as Gupta[93] does), the assumption is that the two elements are cumulative in lowering the energy security (or in this case oil security) of a country. The problem with this approach is that the indicators that are aggregated often represent different *types* of vulnerabilities, thus the aggregation method can actually obscure the vulnerability. In fact, in Le Coq and Paltseva's[94] recent work, they found that even aggregating across different fossil fuel types obscured the risks between different energy sources.

The accumulation of energy security risks typically tends to be in the academic domain where the belief is that policymakers will be unable to understand multiple metrics, thus they need indices which simplify the complexity. This approach is also sometimes used in political circles as a way to increase the space for political maneuver ability. Aggregated metrics may be interpreted more widely, thus allowing more options to "address the problem" than in the case of more specific indicators pointing to exact areas of intervention which may not be politically convenient.

Local universalism vs. global contextualism

As follows from the above discussion, energy security indicators are results of political compromises. These compromises are not only about priorities and perceptions (as noted by Chester[95] and Kruyt et al.[96]), but also about the structure and boundaries of energy systems and their possible future trajectories.

Though political agendas may constrain the choice of energy security indicators, they still cannot explain why so few "storylines" dominate the majority of indicators. Surely, the diversity of contexts in different countries should result in a much larger diversity of compromises, discourses, and eventually indicators. However, there are additional constraints on developing indicators imposed by the capacities of individual countries and by the process of international proliferation of indicators.

Simply speaking, many countries and jurisdictions do not have the resources, time, or platforms for a well-informed deliberation and debate on energy security. In such situations, it may seem easier to adopt indicators already used in another country or internationally rather than go through a protracted and expensive domestic process of indicator development. Naturally for such adoption to take place, energy security indicators should be presented as objective, universally valid measures rather than results of specific compromises only valid in particular contexts. Unfortunately, in international fora and most of the literature they are mostly portrayed in the former rather than the latter way.

The proliferation of generic energy security indicators to very different jurisdictions may thus be explained by "institutional isomorphism" as described by DiMaggio.[97] Isomorphism explains why similar strategies are adopted by very different organizations which find it easier to copy the behavior of successful actors rather than dealing with complexities and uncertainties relevant to their own context. The propagation of energy security indicators is facilitated by the similar processes and actors that are responsible for isomorphism in other areas, namely international organizations, international professional elites, as well as coercive pressures on less powerful actors.

There is certainly nothing wrong with the flows of knowledge and information from one country to another or from international organizations and professionals to individual nations. More worrying, however, is the overall paradigm in which such exchange of knowledge takes place. This paradigm focuses on finding the "right" indicators rather than on stimulating a process through which energy security concerns relevant to specific contexts can be identified, quantified, and dealt with.

The current proliferation of energy security indicators takes place within the paradigm of "local universalism." Most powerful discourses reflecting specific ("local") concerns are translated into indicators which are presented as universal and objective. These indicators are then imposed in contexts which lack the capacity to formulate similarly powerful discussions and discourses that would more accurately reflect their own contexts. Instead of strengthening their capacity to have a useful debate on energy security, less powerful countries and jurisdictions are offered to select from a menu of a few ready-made "objective" indicators. More often than not, it is much easier for them to pick the least controversial and most understandable indicator from the list (e.g. "import dependency") and thus lend further support to the claim of universal validity of this indicator, already the lowest common denominator of previous compromises.

As a result, the local is universalized. Instead of actually transferring and enriching useful knowledge, such a process homogenizes and entrenches existing discourses, forever validating the associated assumptions and simplifications.

This may explain why there are only a few storylines, primarily focused on short-term, supply-oriented concerns, dominating the energy security indicators debate. To be sure, short-term supply-oriented concerns are valid and important for many countries and should be addressed; they should not, however, push all other concerns, which may be more relevant in certain contexts, off the agenda.

An alternative to such "local universalism" might be "global contextualism" where global knowledge is contextualized through an informed local deliberation process. Such a process does not necessarily produce universally applicable indicators (in fact it may produce no indicators at all), but it might contribute to understanding specific energy security challenges as well as to building local capacities. Following this principle, the framework proposed in the next section is not another set of indicators, but rather a series of steps through which a rigorous and systematic energy security assessment may be carried out in diverse contexts which considers contextualized concerns and problems.

From indicators to frameworks

This section presents an energy security assessment framework. The first subsection briefly describes the generic stages and steps of the proposed framework. Subsequently we illustrate the application of the framework with the analysis of energy security from the Global Energy Assessment (GEA).[98]

National energy security assessment framework

The contextualization of global knowledge on energy systems and their vulnerabilities can be enabled through explicit articulation of choices on priorities and assumptions used in an energy security assessment. We structure such choices in three stages, each containing a number of steps. Each step provides an opportunity to relate global generic knowledge to local circumstances, perspectives, and priorities.

The first stage is **framing** the assessment through defining its purpose and the intended uses of its results and agreeing on an operational definition of energy security.

The second stage is making the most important **choices and assumptions** appropriate for the purpose of the assessment, which include:

- agreeing on a model of the energy system including its external and internal boundaries;
- clarifying the nature of potential risks and vulnerabilities;
- agreeing on the appropriate time-horizons and the ways of representing the future: as a forecast, as a plan, as a scenario etc.

The third stage is agreeing on the **methods** (including indicators and analytical tools) most appropriate for the purpose and the assumptions, and **conducting the assessment**.

Although these stages are logically sequential, any of the preceding steps can be revisited as necessary in light of the findings arrived at at any subsequent step.

Assessment of energy security in the world within the Global Energy Assessment

This section illustrates the proposed approach, with the example of assessing energy security in the world within the Global Energy Assessment (GEA). It follows the three generic stages of the proposed assessment process: (1) clarifying the purpose and intended uses of the assessment, (2) articulating assumptions and choices used in the assessment, and (3) presenting the methods and indicators used in the assessment.

Framing: energy security as a national challenge in the global context

The assessment presented here has been carried out for Knowledge Module 5 (KM5), Energy, Security, and Interdependence of the GEA. KM5 is part of Cluster I of the GEA which describes the global energy challenges. Energy security is identified as one such challenge (others being energy access, climate change, health, and investment). KM5 findings are used, together with other findings of Cluster I, to inform the GEA scenarios (Cluster III) and eventually knowledge modules dealing with energy policies (Cluster IV).

The KM5 assessment is framed by the observation that energy security is the most politically prominent energy-related concern. Disruptions of energy systems may affect broader security issues ranging from the viability of national economies and stability of political systems to the danger of armed conflicts. This means that policies developed in the quest for higher energy security have been a key driving force in the transformations of energy systems. Whether they will remain such a global driving force in the future depends upon whether disruptions of nationally vital energy services will be likely or perceived as likely.

Thus, KM5 considers energy security as a national challenge in the global context. Consequently it defines energy security as the uninterrupted provision of nationally vital energy services. It aims to map energy security conditions in the world in order to understand whether they do indeed represent a global challenge, whether they are likely to be a serious driver of energy transformations in the future, how these conditions may change in the medium to long term under different scenarios, and eventually how energy security relates to other energy challenges.

Thus, from the point of view of KM5 it is important to understand which countries are likely to experience energy security problems and what the nature of these problems is. It aims to paint a broad-brushed picture of energy security conditions in the world and that can be used in discussing global developments and scenarios. Thus the results are not intended to be sufficiently specific to affect policy choices in individual countries.

Choices and assumptions: boundaries, structures, and futures of national energy systems

The GEA evaluates energy security as a national-level concern. This is in line with the historic responsibility of nation states for energy security and their currently key role in shaping energy policy. This assumption means both that the analysis is guided by concerns of national policy makers and that the boundaries of energy systems are drawn along national borders.

KM5 focuses on evaluating the vulnerabilities of nationally vital energy services which are essential to the functioning of modern states. Climate change, health, and other externalities, as well as energy access, have been explicitly excluded from this analysis because they are treated elsewhere in GEA.

A starting point of this assessment is that different countries have different energy security priorities. This is because the configuration of their energy systems and the nature of the nationally vital energy services vary from one country to another. Thus, the assessment of national energy security seeks not only a binary evaluation of "energy secure" versus "energy insecure" but also a clarification of the *types* of vulnerabilities faced by individual countries. This aim has implications for how the assessment presents the internal structure and the external connections of national energy systems.

First, given the focus on nationally vital energy services it is important to define what these services are. KM5 considers four types of energy end-use: (1) transport, (2) residential and commercial (R&C), (3) industrial, and (4) export. Whereas transport and the R&C sector are important for virtually all countries, the industrial sector contributes to over 25 percent of GDP in some 60 countries with over 4.5 billion people. The energy export sector, which is defined as the national income and economy from the energy exports, is vitally important for several dozen countries, most of them developed and emerging economies. We assume that the energy security of a nation is compromised if any of these vital energy services is vulnerable.

The analysis further assumes that the vulnerability of the vital services depends upon the vulnerability of primary energy sources (PES) and electricity which are used to provide these services. Thus, energy supply sectors are also delimited. In the vast majority of the countries the latter include fossil fuels (oil, gas, and coal) as well as nuclear, hydro, traditional biomass, and modern renewables. While, theoretically, individual renewable resources and potentials would be ideal, for analytical purposes, it is only possible to analyze the five sectors based on mainstream energy sources (excluding traditional biomass and modern renewables).

Thus our analytical representation of a national energy system consists on the one hand of four "vital services": transport, industry, residential and commercial, and energy for export, and, on the

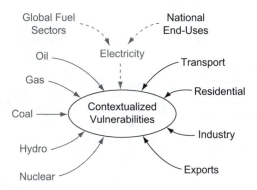

Figure 17.1 Energy sectors used for the GEA energy security analysis.
Note:
Biomass and modern renewables are not shown in this scheme. The GEA contains only a limited analysis of energy security implications of these PES because the data necessary for worldwide quantitative analysis are at present not available.

other hand, of five "supply sectors": oil, gas, coal, nuclear, and hydro. The electricity sector is the tenth of the analyzed subsystems as shown in Figure 17.1.

The delineation of both supply and end-use sectors is important for two reasons. First, it provides an interface between on the global situation regarding the supply sectors and in the local context regarding specific fuel mixes for different end-uses in each particular country. Second, it shows how vulnerabilities propagate between different elements of the national energy system. Most obviously, the vulnerabilities of fuels and electricity propagate to end-uses. In addition, demand-side vulnerabilities such as energy intensity or demand growth may also contribute to the vulnerabilities of particular fuel sectors. Third, as already mentioned, this subdivision helps to clarify the *types* of vulnerabilities of national energy systems by relating these to specific (supply or demand) sectors.

With respect to time-horizons, this framework follows the predominant concerns of national policymakers by focusing on short- (under 5 years) to medium- (5–20 years) term threats. We assume that short- and medium-term vulnerabilities can be reasonably well predicted based on the available information. This places our analysis within the deterministic mindset, where no disruptive changes in energy systems are envisioned.

The GEA analysis of energy security is not limited to the deterministic mindset. Its primary focus is the energy-related interdependence between nations. In this way it responds to the energy sovereignty concerns which top the political agenda in most countries. Where possible, it also refers to resilience of energy systems as reflected, for example, in the diversity of options for electricity generation or the state of the infrastructure and socio-economic exposure. In this vein, the vulnerabilities that are quantitatively addressed by the assessment are aging infrastructure (particularly nuclear power plants which are expensive and slow to replace) and the costs of energy imports.

Assessment method and indicators

The GEA energy security assessment has been conducted in several steps as shown in Figure 17.2. Each step generated results which were not only used at other steps, but were also interpreted in their own right to provide insights into the nature of vulnerabilities of each country's energy systems.

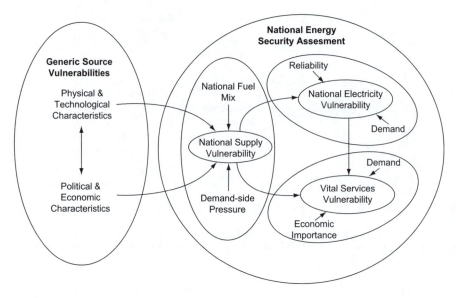

Figure 17.2 The steps of energy security assessment used in the GEA.

1. The first step is the analysis of the generic vulnerabilities of PES: fossil fuels (oil, coal, and gas), nuclear, and hydro energy. These vulnerabilities are identified with reference to both physical/technological and political/economic factors relevant to a particular energy source. This step results in fuel-specific indicators which are used at the subsequent stages of the assessment.
2. The second step is the analysis of the security of the national energy supply in each country based on the national PES mix and the fuel-specific indicators derived in the first step. Vulnerability of supply also takes into account national fuel intensity and demand growth for some fuels.
3. The third step is evaluating the vulnerability of national electricity systems. This takes into account the vulnerabilities of primary energy sources (as evaluated at the previous step) used for electricity production. The other criteria are the adequacy of electricity generation infrastructure as well as growth of demand for electricity and the rates of access to electricity.
4. The fourth step is analyzing the vulnerability of the four nationally vital energy services (industry, transport, residential/commercial, and energy exports). Vulnerability of each energy service depends upon the security of primary energy sources and electricity (evaluated at previous steps) used in delivering this particular service. It also depends upon demand-side factors such as energy intensity of a particular service, and growth in demand for and the adequacy of provision of such a service.
5. The final step is the cross-sectoral evaluation of national energy systems in which data from various sources and end-uses are aggregated to obtain a bird's-eye view of the overall security and resilience of national energy systems.

Table 17.3 lists the indicators that are used for this assessment related to the primary concerns reflected by these indicators which are further explained in the next section. It is important to note that the GEA aims to measure the global conditions and thus relies on indicators available for the majority of the world countries. In particular, this analysis significantly relies on the International Energy Agency (IEA) statistics (2007) which are available for some 130 countries with almost 6 billion people.

Table 17.3 Overview of concerns and indicators of national energy security addressed in KM5 of the Global Energy Assessment

| Energy sector | Energy security concerns (indicators)★ | | |
	Short (<5 years)	Medium (5–20 years)	Long (>20 years)
Oil	**Exposure to the global oil market** (import dependency, cost of imports, *type and diversity of import routes, import origins*)		
	Demand-side vulnerabilities (annual growth in oil consumption, *oil intensity*)		Global conventional oil scarcity ("peak oil")
		Domestic availability of oil (R/C)	
		Environmental acceptability of oil production and use	
Gas	**Exposure to the global and international gas markets** (import dependency, cost of imports, *type and diversity of import routes, import origins*)		
	Demand-side vulnerabilities (*gas intensity*)		
		Domestic availability of gas (R/C)	
		Environmental acceptability of gas production and use	
Coal	**Exposure to the global coal market** (import dependency)		
		Domestic availability of coal (R/C)	
		Environmental and health acceptability of coal production and use	
		Seasonal water availability	
Nuclear		**Aging infrastructure** (average age of nuclear power plant)	
		Capacity to replace existing fleet (start of last plant construction)	
		Access to capital, enrichment, reactor manufacturing, reprocessing	
		Environmental, safety and security acceptability of nuclear power	
Hydro	Reliance on dams which are shared (*trans-boundary dams* or *dams on trans-boundary rivers*)		Effects of climate change on water patterns and availability
		Seasonal water availability	
		Aging and silting of dams and other infrastructure (*average dam age*)	
	Exposure to risk of dam failure or sabotage (diversity of dams)		
Electricity	**Exposure to imported fuels** (dependence on imported fuels)		
	Exposure to a single fuel market (low diversity of energy sources used for electricity production)		

Table 17.3 (continued)

Energy sector	Energy security concerns (indicators)*		
	Short (<5 years)	Medium (5–20 years)	Long (>20 years)
		Adequate capacity (annual demand growth rate, access rate, *deliberate power cuts*)	
		Underinvestment and aging infrastructure (*average age of power plants, annual investment in electricity*)	
Transport	**Exposure to imported fuels** (dependence on imported fuels)		
		Demand-side vulnerabilities (annual consumption growth rate)	
Industry	**Exposure to imported fuels** (dependence on imported fuels)		
	Demand-side vulnerabilities (industrial energy intensity)		
Residential and commercial	**Exposure to imported fuels** (dependence on imported fuels)		
		Demand-side vulnerabilities (annual consumption growth rate)	
		Adequacy of provision (reliance on traditional biofuels in the residential sector)	
Energy for export	**Exposure to price fluctuations** (revenue from energy exports as share of GDP)		
	"Security of demand" (diversity of export routes and destinations)		
	"Dutch disease" and "resource curse"		
		Availability of domestic resources (Resource/export)	
Cross-sectoral	**Exposure to imported fuels** (overall import dependency, cost of energy imports compared with GDP, cost of energy imports compared with export earnings)		
	Overall resilience of primary fuels (diversity of PES)		
	Exposure to energy-price volatility (overall energy intensity)		
		Demand-side pressure (annual growth rate in consumption, consumption per capita)	

Notes:
R/C—resource to consumption ratio; PES—primary energy sources.
*Concerns that are included in the framework are listed in bold. Those indicators that weren't collected in this framework are in italics.

Conclusions

This chapter discusses the three groups of challenges inherent in designing energy security indicators: the complexity of energy systems, the uncertainties over their future evolution, and the competing agendas of actors involved in defining energy security priorities. These challenges are normally addressed through making assumptions about external boundaries of energy systems, their internal structures, the trajectories of their future developments and the most important concerns.

While in principle there is a wide variety of such assumptions and their combinations, in practice only a limited number of these are used in developing energy security indicators. They are generally unstated and inexplicit. We trace most of these assumptions and most of the indicators used in practice to a few dominant discourses on energy security. While these discourses reflect several important concerns they tend to focus on short-term disruptions of a political and economic nature.

Through the overview of existing energy security indicators we show that these tend to represent energy security concerns in a rather narrow and limited way. An explanation for this phenomenon can be found in the process by which energy security indicators are designed. Within this process, the choice of assumptions underlying the indicators is severely constrained by political agendas and capacities for a meaningful debate. The worldwide propagation of energy security indicators is dominated by the paradigm of "local universalism," that is, the quest for metrics valid in most contexts which inevitably becomes the imposition of the "lowest common denominator" on the least powerful actors in the process. Preliminary context-specific concerns and storylines are later promoted as generally valid, and related indicators are portrayed as objective and universal. Instead of the actual transfer of knowledge, such processes homogenize and entrench existing discourses, forever validating the associated assumptions and simplifications.

We propose an alternative paradigm that might be called "global contextualism." The proposed framework for assessing energy security contextualizes global concerns through an informed local deliberation. The proposed framework is not another set of indicators, but a series of steps through which appropriate energy security concerns can be investigated in specific contexts. The three stages of the proposed assessment framework provide opportunities for the deliberate choice of the purpose and intended uses of the assessment, assumptions about the nature of the system and its future articulation of the most pressing concerns regarding potential threats, and finally selection of analytical methods and indicators most appropriate.

The use of context-specific tools of energy security assessment should not be limited to developed countries. In fact, the worldwide energy assessment shows that the least developed and developing countries are among the most vulnerable to energy security threats. Their capacities to monitor their energy security situations and design effective responses should be strengthened by the international community. This will require reorientation of the current regimes for global energy security governance to more inclusive, polycentric, and flexible mechanisms which are able to address complex, systemic, and dynamic energy security challenges at different scales and in different contexts.

Notes

1 "Energy Policy: Concepts and Indicators," *Energy Policy* 38(4) (2010).
2 Hughes, L. 2010. "Eastern Canadian Crude Oil Supply and Its Implications for Regional Energy Security," *Energy Policy*. Available at: doi: 10.1016/j.enpol.2010.01.015 (accessed August 29, 2010).
3 Le Coq, C., and E. Paltseva. 2009. "Measuring the Security of External Energy Supply in the European Union," *Energy Policy*. Available at: doi: 10.1016/j.enpol.2009.05.069 (accessed August 29, 2010).

4 Dobson, Ian, Benjamin A. Carreras, Vickie E. Lynch, and David E. Newman. 2007. "Complex Systems Analysis of Series of Blackouts: Cascading Failure, Critical Points, and Self-Organization," *Chaos* 17(2). Available at: doi: 10.1063/1.2737822 (accessed August 29, 2010).

5 Chester, L. 2010. "Conceptualising Energy Security and Making Explicit Its Polysemic Nature," *Energy Policy* 38(2): 887–895.

6 Berger, P. L. and T. Luckmann. 1966. "The Social Construction of Reality: A Treatise in the Sociology of Knowledge," (Garden City, NY: Anchor Publishing).

7 Mickwitz, P. and M. Melanen. 2009. "The Role of Co-Operation Between Academia and Policymakers for the Development and Use of Sustainability Indicators—A Case from the Finnish Kymenlaakso Region," *Journal of Cleaner Production* 17(12): 1086–1100; Hezri, A. A. and S. R. Dovers. 2006. "Sustainability Indicators, Policy and Governance: Issues for Ecological Economics," *Ecological Economics* 60(1). Available at: doi: 10.1016/j.ecolecon.2005.11.019.

8 Chester, "Conceptualising Energy Security."

9 Sovacool, B. K.and B. Brossmann. 2010. "Symbolic Convergence and the Hydrogen Economy," *Energy Policy* 38. Available at: doi: 10.1016/j.enpol.2009.11.081.

10 Meadows, D. H., D. L. Meadows, J. Randers, W. W. Behrens, and of the Club of Rome, 1972. *The Limits to Growth* (New York: Universe Books); Cavallo, Alfred J. 2002. "Predicting the Peak in World Oil Production," *Natural Resources Research* 11(3). Available at: doi: 10.1023/A:1019856621335. [Accessed August 29 2010]; USGS, *World Petroleum Assessment 2000* (Washington, DC: United States Geological Survey, 2000).

11 Aguilera, R. F., R. G. Eggert, C. C. Gustavo Lagos, and J. E. Tilton. 2009. "Depletion and the Future Availability of Petroleum Resources," *The Energy Journal* 30(1): 141–174.

12 As described in: Klare, Michael T. 2008. *Rising Powers, Shrinking Planet: The New Geopolitics of Energy* (New York: Metropolitan Books).

13 Rogner, H. H. 1997. "An Assessment of World Hydrocarbon Resources," *Annual Review of Energy and the Environment* 22(1): 217–262.

14 Heinberg, Richard. 2005. *The Party's Over: Oil, War and the Fate of Industrial Societies* (Gabriola Island, BC: New Society Publishers); Paul Roberts, Paul. 2005. *The End of Oil: The Decline of the Petroleum Economy and the Rise of a New Energy Order* (London: Bloomsbury).

15 Aleklett, K., M. Höök, K. Jakobsson, M. Lardelli, S. Snowden, and B. Söderbergh. 2009. "The Peak of the Oil Age: Analyzing the World Oil Production Reference Scenario in World Energy Outlook 2008," *Energy Policy* 38(3). Available at: doi: 10.1016/j.enpol.2009.11.021 (accessed August 28, 2010); Greene, David, Janet Hopson, and Jia Li. 2004. "Running Out of and Into Oil: Analyzing Global Oil Depletion and Transition Through 2050," *Transportation Research Record: Journal of the Transportation Research Board* 1880(1). Available at: doi: 10.3141/1880-01 (accessed August 28, 2010); Klare, *Rising Powers, Shrinking Planet*.

16 Cavallo, "Predicting the Peak in World Oil Production."

17 Rogner, "An Assessment of World Hydrocarbon Resources."

18 Salameh, Mamdouh G. 1999. "Technology, Oil Reserve Depletion and the Myth of the Reserves-To-Production Ratio," *OPEC Review* 23(2): 113–125.

19 For an oil-related example see: Greene, *et al.*, "Running Out of and Into Oil ."

20 Gupta, E. 2008. "Oil Vulnerability Index of Oil-Importing Countries," *Energy Policy* 36(3). Available at: doi: 10.1016/j.enpol.2007.11.011. [Accessed August 28 2010].

21 Gupta, "Oil Vulnerability Index"; Turton, Hal, and Leonardo Barreto. 2006. "Long-Term Security of Energy Supply and Climate Change," *Energy Policy* 34(15). Available at: doi: 10.1016/j.enpol.2005.03.016.

22 Alhajii, A. F. and J. L. Williams. 2003. "Measures of Petroleum Dependence and Vulnerability in OECD Countries," *Middle East Economic Survey* 46: 16; Scheepers, M., A. Seebregts, J. de Jong, and H. Maters. 2007. *EU Standards for Energy Security of Supply* (Amsterdam: ECN/Clingendael International Energy Programme).

23 Scheepers *et al.*, *EU Standards for Energy Security of Supply*.

24 Asia Pacific Energy Research Centre. 2007. *A Quest for Energy Security in the 21st Century: Resources and Constraints* (Tokyo: Institute of Energy Economics, Japan).

25 Alhajii and Williams, "Measures of Petroleum Dependence and Vulnerability."

26 Gupta, "Oil Vulnerability Index."

27 Jansen, J. C., W. G. van Arkel, and M. G. Boots. 2004. Designing Indicators of Long-Term Energy Supply Security, ECN-C-04-007 (Amsterdam: ECN).

28 Lefèvre, N. 2007. *Energy Security and Climate Policy: Assessing Interactions* (Paris: IEA/OECD).
29 Kendell, *Measures of Oil Import Dependence.*
30 Greene, D. L. 2010. "Measuring Energy Security: Can the United States Achieve Oil Independence?" *Energy Policy* 38. Available at: doi: 10.1016/j.enpol.2009.01.041.
31 Kendell, *Measures of Oil Import Dependence.*
32 Greene, "Measuring Energy Security."
33 Kendell, *Measures of Oil Import Dependence.*
34 Levy, Janet. 2009. "An End to Dependence on Middle East Oil," *American Thinker* (March 26). Available at: http://www.americanthinker.com/2009/03/an_end_to_dependence_on_middle.html (accessed May 9, 2010).
35 National Resource Defense Council. 2009. "Safe, Strong and Secure: Reducing America's Oil Dependence America's Rising Consumption of Oil Threatens the Economy and National Security," (Washington, DC: National Resource Defense Council). Available at: http://www.nrdc.org/air/transportation/aoilpolicy2.asp (accessed May 9, 2010).
36 2006. "Russia's Energy Weapon," *BusinessWeek* (April 28).Available at: http://www.businessweek.com/mediacenter/podcasts/international/international_04_28_06.htm (accessed May 9, 2010). Simpson, Emma. 2006. "Russia Wields An Energy Weapon," *BBC World News* (February 14). Available at: http://news.bbc.co.uk/2/hi/4708256.stm.
37 Bacon, R. and M. Kojima. 2008. *Coping with Oil Price Volatility*, Energy Sector Management Assistance Programme (Washington, DC: World Bank Group).
38 Gupta, "Oil Vulnerability Index."
39 Scheepers *et al.*, *EU Standards for Energy Security of Supply* .
40 Toman, Michael A. 2002. "International Oil Security Problems and Policies," *The Brookings Review* 20(2): 20–23.
41 Jansen, J. C. and A. J. Seebregts. 2010. "Long-Term Energy Services Security: What Is It and How Can It Be Measured and Valued?" *Energy Policy* 38(4). Available at: doi: 10.1016/j.enpol.2009.02.047.
42 Scheepers *et al.*, *EU Standards for Energy Security of Supply.*
43 Scheepers *et al.*, *EU Standards for Energy Security of Supply.*
44 Greene, D. L. and S. Ahmad. 2005. *Costs of US Oil Dependence: 2005 Update* (Washington, DC: United States Department of Energy).
45 Gupta, "Oil Vulnerability Index."
46 United Nations Development Programme (UNDP)/World Bank *The Vulnerability of African Countries to Oil Price Shocks*. 2005. (Washington, DC: Joint UNDP/World Bank Energy Assistance Management Program,).
47 UNDP/World Bank "Vulnerability of African Countries."
48 Gupta, "Oil Vulnerability Index."
49 Cabalu, Helen and Chassty Manuhutu 2009. "Vulnerability of Natural Gas Supply in the Asian Gas Market," *Economic Analysis and Policy* 39(2): 255–270.
50 Gupta, "Oil Vulnerability Index."
51 Blyth, W. and N. Lefèvre. 2004. *Energy Security and Climate Change Interactions: An Assessment Framework* (Paris: OECD/International Energy Agency).
52 Group of Eight Press Release. "Responsible Leadership for a Sustainable Future" (G8 Summit Meeting) (L'Aquila, Italy: G8 Secretariat, 2009).
53 Bacon, R. 2005. *The Impact of Higher Oil Prices on Low-Income Countries and on the Poor* (Washington DC: World Bank Energy Sector Management Assistance Program).
54 United Nations Development Programme (UNDP). 2007. *Overcoming Vulnerability to Rising Oil Prices: Options for Asia and the Pacific* (Bangkok: UNDP Regional Center in Bangkok).
55 European Forum for Democracy and Solidarity. "Kyrgyzstan, Country Profile" (April 9, 2010), Available at: http://www.europeanforum.net/country/kyrgyzstan (accessed May 9, 2010).
56 Kendell, *Measures of Oil Import Dependence.*
57 Cabalu and Manuhutu, "Vulnerability of Natural Gas Supply."
58 Gupta, "Oil Vulnerability Index."
59 Greene, David L. and Paul N. Leiby *The Oil Security Metrics Model*. 2006. (Oak Ridge, TN: Oak Ridge National Laboratory May).
60 Greene, "Measuring Energy Security," 1614.
61 Gupta, "Oil Vulnerability Index."

62 United Nations Development Programme (UNDP)/World Bank. *The Impact of Higher Oil Prices on Low-Income Countries and on the Poor.* (Washington, DC: UNDP/World Bank).

63 UNDP/World Bank *The Impact of Higher Oil Prices.*

64 Markowitz, H. 1952. "Portfolio Selection," *The Journal of Finance* 7(1): 77–91.

65 Awerbuch, Shimon. 1995. "Market-Based IRP: It's Easy!!!," *The Electricity Journal* 8(3). Available at: doi: 10.1016/1040-6190(95)90201-5. Awerbuch 2006a; Bar-Lev, Dan and Steven Katz. 1976. "A Portfolio Approach to Fossil Fuel Procurement in the Electric Utility Industry," *The Journal of Finance* 31(3): 933–947; Roques, Fabien A., David M. Newbery, and William J. Nuttall. 2008. "Fuel Mix Diversification Incentives in Liberalized Electricity Markets: A Mean-Variance Portfolio Theory Approach," *Energy Economics* 30(4). Available at: doi: 10.1016/j.eneco.2007.11.008; Awerbuch, S.2000. "Investing in Photovoltaics: Risk, Accounting and the Value of New Technology," *Energy Policy* 28 (14): 1023–1035; Awerbuch, S. 2006. "Portfolio-Based Electricity Generation Planning: Policy Implications for Renewables and Energy Security," *Mitigation and Adaptation Strategies for Global Change* 11(3). Available at: doi: 10.1007/s11027-006-4754-4; Bar-Lev and Steven Katz, "A Portfolio Approach to Fossil Fuel Procurement," pp. 933–947; Roques, *et al.*, "Fuel Mix Diversification Incentives."

66 Humphreys, H. B. and K. T. McClain. 1998. "Reducing the Impacts of Energy Price Volatility Through Dynamic Portfolio Selection," *IAEE Energy Journal* 3: 107–132.

67 Neff, T. 1997. *Improving Energy Security in Pacific Asia: Diversification and Risk Reduction for Fossil and Nuclear Fuels.* Project Commissioned by the Pacific Asia Regional Energy Security (PARES) (Massachusetts: Institute of Technology, Center for International Studies).

68 Neff, *Improving Energy Security in Pacific Asia.*

69 Helm, D. 2002. "Energy Policy: Security of Supply, Sustainability and Competition," *Energy Policy* 30(3): 173–184.

70 Yergin, Daniel. 1988. "Energy Security in the 1990s," *Foreign Affairs* 67(1): 110–132.

71 Scheepers *et al.*, *EU Standards for Energy Security of Supply.*

72 Joskow, Paul L. 2006. "Competitive Electricity Markets and Investment in New Generating Capacity," *SSRN eLibrary.* Available at http://ideas.repec.org/p/mee/wpaper/0609.html (accessed August 29, 2010); Kirschen, Daniel and Goran Strbac. 2004. "Why Investments Do Not Prevent Blackouts," *The Electricity Journal* 17(2). Available at: doi: DOI: 10.1016/j.tej.2003.12.005.

73 Scheepers *et al.*, *EU Standards for Energy Security of Supply.*

74 Scheepers *et al.*, *EU Standards for Energy Security of Supply.*

75 Chupka, M. W., R. Earle, P. Fox-Penner, and R. Hledik. 2008. "Transforming America's Power Industry: The Investment Challenge 2010–2030," (Columbus, OH: The Brattle Group.

76 Le Coq and Paltseva, "Measuring the Security of External Energy Supply."

77 Yergin, D. 2006. "Ensuring Energy Security," *Foreign Affairs* 85(2): 69–82.

78 Stirling, Andrew. 1994. "Diversity and Ignorance in Electricity Supply Investment: Addressing the Solution Rather than the Problem," *Energy Policy* 22(3). Available at: doi: 10.1016/0301-4215(94)90159-7.

79 Stirling, "Diversity and Ignorance in Electricity Supply Investment."

80 Stirling, "Diversity and Ignorance in Electricity Supply Investment."

81 Stirling, "Diversity and Ignorance in Electricity Supply Investment."

82 Jansen *et al.*, *Designing Indicators.*

83 Jansen *et al.*, *Designing Indicators.*

84 Neff, *Improving Energy Security in Pacific Asia.*

85 Gupta, "Oil Vulnerability Index."

86 Lefèvre, *Energy Security and Climate Policy: Assessing Interactions.*

87 Lefèvre, *Energy Security and Climate Policy: Assessing Interactions.*

88 Stirling, Andy. 2010. "Multicriteria Diversity Analysis: A Novel Heuristic Framework for Appraising Energy Portfolios," *Energy Policy* 38(4). Available at: doi: 10.1016/j.enpol.2009.02.023.

89 For just one example see: Bossel, H. 1999. *Indicators for Sustainable Development: Theory, Method, Applications* (Winnipeg: International Institute for Sustainable Development), pp. 1–124.

90 Scheepers *et al.*, *EU Standards for Energy Security of Supply*, p. 8.

91 Le Coq and Paltseva, "Measuring the Security of External Energy Supply."

92 Gupta, "Oil Vulnerability Index."

93 Gupta, "Oil Vulnerability Index."

94 Le Coq and Paltseva, "Measuring the Security of External Energy Supply."

95 Chester, "Conceptualising Energy Security."

96 Kruyt, B., D. P. van Vuuren, H. J. M. de Vries, and H. Groenenberg. 2009. "Indicators for Energy Security," *Energy Policy* 37(6). Available at: doi: 10.1016/j.enpol.2009.02.006.

97 DiMaggio, P. J. and W. W. Powell. 1983. "The Iron Cage Revisited: Institutional Isomorphism and Collective Rationality in Organizational Fields," *American Sociological Review* 48(2): 147–160.

98 For more information see www.globalenergyassessment.org.

18

APPLYING THE FOUR 'A'S OF ENERGY SECURITY AS CRITERIA IN AN ENERGY SECURITY RANKING METHOD[1]

Larry Hughes and Darren Shupe

Introduction

The increasing worldwide demand for energy sources such as crude oil, natural gas, and refined petroleum products has resulted in energy supply challenges and volatile energy markets. Unstable prices and potential energy shortages are making energy security an important issue worldwide.[2,3] Methods for ranking a jurisdiction's energy sources in terms of their contribution to its energy security are of interest to many politicians, policymakers, and members of the public as they can assist in both policy development and public education.[4]

A method for determining the ranking of a jurisdiction's energy sources typically requires a list of alternatives (the energy sources), a set of criteria and metrics (one per criterion) to rank the alternatives, and weights (one per criterion) to rank each alternative;[5] some examples of existing approaches include work by Brown and Sovacool,[6] Clingendale,[7] Greene,[8] Hughes and Sheth,[9] Lefèvre,[10] and the World Energy Council.[11] The criteria, metrics, and weights should be justifiable, understandable, and the results reproducible, if the method is to gain acceptance amongst its potential users.

One potential set of criteria are the four 'A's (Availability, Accessibility, Affordability, and Acceptability) developed by the Asia Pacific Energy Research Centre (APERC) in 2007, which focus primarily on fossil energy supplies and nuclear energy.[12] Although this is a very narrow view of energy security, the four 'A's are applicable to the commonly held view of energy security as being a regular (i.e., uninterrupted) supply of affordable energy.[13]

This chapter extends the scope of the four 'A's and associates them with a set of quantifiable metrics so they can be used as the criteria for a general-purpose energy security ranking method. Unlike ranking methods such as that defined by Brown and Sovacool,[14] this method is not restricted to the national level since many nations or supranational federations are made up of distinct regions that do not necessarily have access to the same energy sources. (If the data exists, the method can determine the ranking of the energy sources used in any jurisdiction from a household to a region, to a nation.) Although the method does not produce a single, overall ranking value for the jurisdiction, it does produce a ranking vector that shows the relative security of each of the jurisdiction's energy sources.

Like other ranking methods using weights (for example, see Hughes),[15] this method also produces a ranking vector from a single set of weights applied to the criteria. However, a single ranking vector is one of many and by itself cannot show how sensitive each of the different energy sources are to changes in the weights. To address this, the chapter shows the effect of applying a range of weights to the criteria—the resulting ranking vectors can expose the effects of potentially unexpected changes in the price of energy or supply shortfalls. By producing ranking vectors rather than a single rank, it is possible to examine the effect of the potential changes on the different energy sources.

The chapter demonstrates the method's application and the effect of examining ranges of weights by applying it to the energy sources used in a number of eastern Canadian provinces.

The four 'A's

The Asia Pacific Energy Research Centre (APERC) has developed a set of energy security indicators known as the four 'A's;[16] the following is a brief introduction to the four 'A's, their application, and possible limitations.

Availability

APERC's definition of availability focuses on oil (and other fossil fuels) and nuclear energy:[17]

> Thus, this growing dependence on oil, coupled with current high oil prices, declining oil discoveries, and the low level of spare oil-production capacity worldwide, have generated concern about the future adequacy of oil supply. How much oil do we have in the world? Is that enough to meet the ever increasing global demand and if not, what will be the substitute? These questions have become increasingly important since oil is the dominant source of world energy today and will continue to be so for the foreseeable future.

Availability is meant to indicate the amount of supply of a given primary energy resource in terms of known reserves. Kruyt *et al.* has refined the definition to mean "elements relating to geological existence.[18]

Examples of availability include:

Policy. Offshore exploration for oil or natural gas deposits will increase the availability of energy if successful. In 2006, the United States' Minerals Management Service estimated that there were a total of 86 billion barrels of oil and 420 trillion cubic feet of gas in undiscovered fields on the Outer Continental Shelf (OCS).[19] If accurate, this would be a significant jump in reserves from 19.1 billion barrels of oil and 244.7 trillion cubic feet of gas in proven reserves.[20]

Technology. Further investment in tidal power will increase the availability of electricity. For the Bay of Fundy on Canada's East Coast, the World Energy Council estimated that a potential of 17 TW of electricity could be generated per year. Currently the only generation of tidal electricity in the region comes from a 20 MW facility near Annapolis Royal, Canada.[21]

APERC's definition of availability is too narrow for a general-purpose energy security index as it assumes underground resources only; that is, fossil fuels and radioactive materials. Instead, availability should include all primary energy sources including renewables such as hydroelectricity, biomass, solar, and wind.

Accessibility

APERC's description of accessibility refers to barriers to accessing energy resources:[22]

> Besides the availability of energy resources, the ability to access these resources is one of the major challenges to securing energy supply to meet future demand growth. Barriers to energy supply accessibility [include] economic factors, political factors, and technology.

Accessibility refers to the ease with which a proven energy reserve can be relied upon to supply the market. It refers to the challenges nations face due to required expansion of infrastructure or the need to secure longer-term energy contracts with energy exporters and has been defined as "geopolitical elements."[23]

Examples of accessibility include:

Policy. When completed in 2010, the Nord Stream natural gas pipeline from Russia under the Baltic Sea to Germany will give Western Europe more secure access to Russian natural gas supplies, as it avoids transit countries. The Nord Stream Project is designed to supply up to 55 billion cubic meters of natural gas per year.[24]

Technology. In order for the electric vehicle (EV) market to become established, charging or battery replacement stations need to be accessed and the required infrastructure must be in place to meet the expected demand efficiently. To address this issue, the Province of Ontario in Canada proposes having sufficient recharging infrastructure in place for EVs, representing 5 percent of the province's entire automobile fleet by 2020.[25]

Although it is possible to discuss economic factors in terms of their application to upstream or downstream activities, including these in the accessibility definition can be confusing, as there is also a definition for affordability.

Affordability

APERC's definition is limited to fuel prices (and price projections) and infrastructure costs. Thus, the most affordable policy directions for the energy industry tend to be ones which are able to utilize current technology and resources.

Examples of affordability include:

Policy. When external costs, such as the effects of climate change, are considered, renewable energy is viewed as being cost competitive with non-renewable sources. A number of APEC member nations have developed programs to subsidize the foundation of the renewable energy industry. An example is the Sunshine Project in Japan in which a long-term renewable energy project was carried forward by the Japanese government to create a market for photovoltaics (PVs). Starting in 1974, the project has moved from the early phases of heavy emphasis on research and development to the current implementation phase, with residential PVs generating a total of 931,575 kW in 2005.[26]

Technology. The expansion of liquefied natural gas (LNG) capacity creates challenges to affordability due to the relatively high capital costs of the infrastructure train and security concerns. These factors respond to changes in the energy market and the economic climate.[27]

Depending upon the jurisdiction or service under consideration, the definition of affordability could be expanded to take the cost of energy services into consideration, and could include the cost of energy to the consumer at a time specified by the analysis. Taxation can also influence energy affordability.[28]

Acceptability

APERC considers acceptability to refer to environmental issues dealing with coal (carbon sequestration), nuclear, and unconventional fuels (biofuel and oil sands). The description of acceptability is:[29]

> Energy demand in the APEC region is projected to increase nearly three-fold, as the region experiences robust economic growth. This energy demand trend is expected to increase energy-related environmental impacts. Faced with this impending problem, policy makers around the world are trying to curb pollution from the energy industry by imposing stricter environmental regulations. Strict environmental regulations combined with enhanced environmental awareness for issues related to the energy sector will create fossil fuel use constraints and affect future energy resources mix.

APERC's focus is on changes in the energy market regarding GHG emissions and tax mechanisms for "dirty" fuels that will impact the relative security of a given resource. Kruyt *et al.* define it as pertaining to "environmental or social elements."[30]

Examples of acceptability include:

Policy. The development and utilization of biofuels may be seen as a more acceptable solution in terms of balancing the requirement for liquid fuels for the current transportation fleet and the importance of finding fuels that are seen as carbon neutral or are of domestic origin.[31,32]

Technology. Coal is seen as being a less acceptable energy source given its high carbon intensity. Because of this, emphasis is being placed on developing carbon sequestration techniques to make it a more palatable energy option.[33]

APERC's view on acceptability is important and can be broader than the economic impact of environmental regulations; for example, it could also include social and political issues such as the food–fuel debate, the displacement of indigenous peoples as a result of energy extraction, or the associated risks of dealing with a country or organization. Regardless of the metric used, measuring any of these values can be a challenge.

The ranking method

Decision analysis is a collection of principles and methods aiming to assist individuals, groups of individuals, or organizations in complex decisions and is intended to help make a choice among a set of known alternatives.[34] It was first applied to study problems in the exploration of petroleum in the 1960s and is now used in a wide variety of applications, such as, business, dispute resolution, and energy and environmental issues.[35]

Multicriteria decision analysis is a branch of decision analysis used to solve complex decision problems where several, often contradictory, points of view must be taken into account.[36] Although a number of different multicriteria decision analysis methods have been developed, all use decision matrices to rank a group of alternatives according to metrics and weights associated with a set of criteria.[37,38] Of the different multicriteria decision analysis methods available, perhaps the best known is AHP or Analytic Hierarchy Process.[39]

AHP allows alternatives to be ranked (by the criteria) either qualitatively or quantitatively. Qualitative ranking is obtained from a group of experts well versed in the subject using a technique known as pair-wise comparison. For large numbers of alternatives, the pair-wise comparison technique has proved to be a challenge as the number of comparisons is in the order of n^2; furthermore, to some people the results produced can appear to be arbitrary and are not easily reproducible by other groups of people equally knowledgeable in the subject.[40] However, quantitative ranking using data obtained from publicly accessible sources, such as national statistical agencies, has proved to be more successful as the results are reproducible and their application can be justified.

The decision matrix and ranking vector

A decision matrix is a tool that allows alternatives to be ranked. It is a two-dimensional matrix consisting of alternatives (in this example, the energy "choices" available to a jurisdiction) and criteria (the metrics and weights). The decision matrix consists of c columns (one per criterion) and a rows (one per alternative). Figure 18.1 shows the decision matrix and the metrics vector with c elements (one metric, m, per criterion).

Each element of the matrix contains the ranking, $r_{i,j}$, of alternative i with respect to criterion j and is obtained by applying the criterion's metric to the alternatives in its column; that is, $r_{i,j} = m_j$ is applied to A_i. The rankings are normalized.

Each row contains the rankings of its alternative with respect to the criteria. The final ranking of each alternative is obtained by applying the weighting associated with each criterion to the ranking of each alternative with a row and then summing them to create a ranking vector. The weighting vector, w, contains c elements, one for each criterion; while the ranking vector, v, contains a elements, one for the final rank of each alternative, as shown in Figure 18.2.

The resulting ranking vector contains the overall ranking of each alternative; the larger the value, the higher the overall ranking. If the alternatives are various energy sources or services, the

	m_1	...	m_c
	C_1	...	C_c
A_1	$r_{1,1}$		$r_{1,c}$
...			
A_a	$r_{a,1}$		$r_{a,c}$

Figure 18.1 A decision matrix (including the metrics vector).

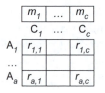

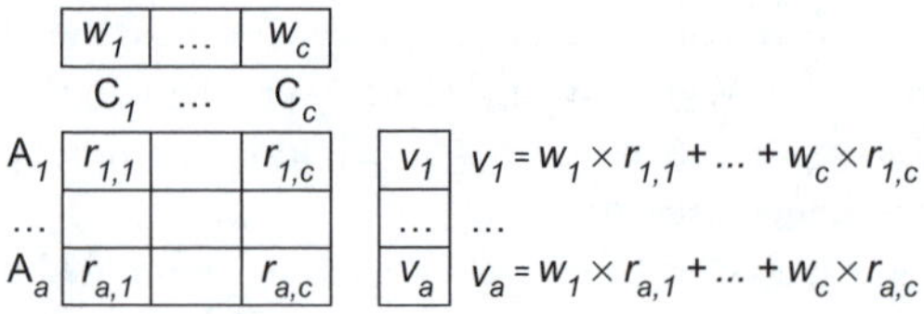

	w_1	...	w_c
	C_1	...	C_c
A_1	$r_{1,1}$		$r_{1,c}$
...			
A_a	$r_{a,1}$		$r_{a,c}$

v_1	$v_1 = w_1 \times r_{1,1} + ... + w_c \times r_{1,c}$
...	...
v_a	$v_a = w_1 \times r_{a,1} + ... + w_c \times r_{a,c}$

Figure 18.2 Determining the ranking vector.

ranking vector can be interpreted as the energy security index, indicating the level of security associated with each alternative—the greater the value, the more secure the alternative is considered to be. The different metrics employed and the weighting chosen for each criterion determines the final ranking.

Creating an energy security ranking vector with the four 'A's

Before a jurisdiction's energy security ranking vector can be obtained it is necessary to identify the alternatives, criteria, metrics, and weights. In addition to discussing the alternatives, this section defines a set of criteria and metrics for energy security based upon the four 'A's, and proposes an alternative approach to determining and applying the weights.

Alternatives

The alternatives can be any group of related energy sources that are necessary for the functioning of one or more energy services in a jurisdiction (for example, a household, community, or region). The choice of alternatives should not be influenced or restricted by the criteria; however, the alternatives may influence the choice and interpretation of the criteria.

Criteria and metrics

There are four criteria: availability, accessibility, affordability, and acceptability. Each criterion defines or explains what part or component of the alternative is of interest, while its metric is a means of comparing the alternatives quantitatively.

This section discusses how the four 'A's can be extended beyond acting as energy security criteria for fossil and nuclear energy supply and be applied to any primary or secondary energy source, including renewables. In all cases, the criteria are associated with quantitative metrics: the higher the value, the more secure the energy source.

Although availability and accessibility are synonymous, they are defined and treated differently.

Availability

At any given time, a variety of energy sources are available to a jurisdiction to meet the needs of some or all of its energy services; each energy source contributes a certain amount of energy to the overall energy consumed by the jurisdiction. The availability criterion (AVA) refers to the relative contribution of each of the jurisdiction's energy sources (i.e., alternatives) for a given time period; for example, data from the most recent year.

The metric for obtaining the ranking of the alternatives is to normalize the values of the energy contribution of each alternative. For example, Table 18.1 shows the different energy sources that were available for Sweden's transportation sector in 2007,[41] their contributions to the sector, and the normalized value of each alternative.

In this example, petrol has the highest ranking with a normalized value of 0.351, followed by diesel and gasoil at 0.321. At the other extreme are natural gas and LPG (0.002) and medium and heavy fuel oils (0.004). The values can be interpreted in a number of ways: the greater reliance on a single source (such as petrol) could suggest a greater level of vulnerability to the jurisdiction should supplies be disrupted or prices change dramatically, while the limited availability of natural gas suggests that its contribution is insignificant to the overall energy security of Sweden's transportation sector. The final importance of the results will depend upon the weight assigned to availability.

Table 18.1 Energy availability for Sweden's transportation sector in 2007 (TWh)[42]

Energy source	2007	Normalized
Petrol	45.8	0.351
Diesel and gasoil	41.8	0.321
Electricity	3.0	0.023
Bunkers oils	25.7	0.197
Medium/heavy fuel oils	0.5	0.004
Aviation fuels etc.	11.1	0.085
Natural gas, incl. LPG	0.3	0.002
Ethanol	2.1	0.016

Accessibility

The availability ranking gives no indication of the changes in an energy source's supply over time as it is simply the current state of the jurisdiction's different energy sources. Understanding the jurisdiction's energy security requires knowledge of the trends or changes that have taken place with an energy source over time.

Energy sources such as oil fields and coal mines are discovered, exploited, and, at some point, their production declines whereupon they are eventually abandoned. Other energy sources, such as hydroelectric facilities, are built and produce at a more or less constant rate over time depending upon factors such as the weather; however, production from seemingly sustainable sources is not immune from decline or closure due to, for example, infrastructure failures or changes in the environment. Public or political pressure can also influence the length of time that an energy source is utilized.

The temporal trends or changes in the production or supply of energy from an energy source or supplier are referred to as accessibility (ACS). A number of metrics can be considered for the accessibility ranking, two of which are discussed here: the reserve-to-production (R/P) ratio and historical supply data.

The reserve-to-production ratio is, as the name suggests, the ratio of an energy source's known reserves for a given year to the production of the energy source for that year. It is used as an indication of future, rather than past, production. However, reserve numbers are notoriously inaccurate as they can be erroneously reported or speculated by the resource owners, whether they are a publicly traded oil company or national oil company.[43,44] Furthermore, the R/P ratio cannot reasonably represent some renewables, as the concept of "reserve" is not applicable to renewables such as wind and tidal.

Historical supply data are often available as time-series from data sources such as the Energy Information Administration (EIA), the International Energy Agency (IEA), and BP Statistical Review of World Energy. The supply data can show long-term trends with respect to the accessibility of the energy source and, as importantly, need not be restricted to energy sources that have reserves. For the purposes of this paper, the historical supply data of an energy source will be used as the criterion for accessibility.

The accessibility metric for the current state of supply can be obtained from a linear regression of the annual energy supply data from some point in the past to the present. A negative value indicates a decline in production, whereas a positive one signifies an increase in production; the regression gives the trend in the supply. The final year is known, the starting year must be determined. One possible starting year is to take the first observed inflection point (that is, the most recent peak or trough in supply); however, this new trend may be a temporary phenomenon that masks a longer-term trend. To illustrate the application of the inflection point as a means of determining the start of the historical trend, consider Sweden's transportation energy supplies, shown in Figure 18.3 (a circle denotes a peak, while a triangle indicates a trough).

The number of inflection points varies between the different energy sources: petrol and electricity have four; diesel/gasoil, bunker oils, and aviation fuels have two; and ethanol, medium/heavy fuel oils, and natural gas have one. Selecting the most recent inflection point for petrol (2006) would suggest an upward trend, while selecting the only inflection point for medium/heavy fuel oils (2005) suggests a downward trend—in both of these cases, the long-term trends taken over ten years (1998 to 2007) are actually the opposite. Similarly, picking different inflection points for each energy source from different years can appear arbitrary and may not be justifiable. The choice of starting year can be validated by selecting a sufficiently long time-series that produces coefficients of determination (R^2) that indicate a reasonably satisfactory correlation for each energy source.

A variation on this is to obtain a time-series, determine the linear regression for each year prior to the final year in the series, and then take the median value of the linear regressions as the trend for each of the energy sources.

If any of the trends are negative, a different approach to calculating the accessibility is needed as negative values cannot be normalized. This can be solved by taking the absolute value of the most negative trend value and adding it to each element in the list, thereby making all elements in the

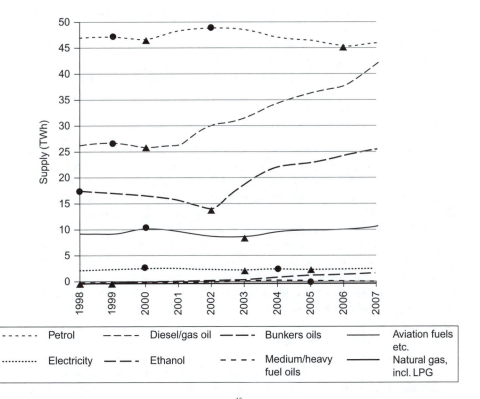

Figure 18.3 Sweden's energy supply for transportation.[45]

Table 18.2 Normalized accessibility values for Sweden's transportation energy sources (1998–2007)

Energy source	Median linear regression values	Shifted	Normalized
Petrol	−0.436	0.000	0.000
Diesel/gas oil	2.256	2.693	0.366
Electricity	0.010	0.447	0.061
Bunker oils	1.435	1.871	0.254
Medium/heavy fuel oils	−0.005	0.431	0.059
Aviation fuels etc.	0.298	0.734	0.100
Natural gas, incl. LPG	0.035	0.472	0.064
Ethanol	0.283	0.719	0.098

list relative to zero. The resulting list can be normalized. An example of this is shown in Table 18.2.

The normalized values show the trend of each energy source: the larger the value, the more accessible the energy source is considered to be relative to the other values in the list. Values closer to zero indicate energy sources that have declined in accessibility over the period in question.

Affordability

Energy affordability can be viewed in a number of ways; for example:

- All energy sources are associated with a cost, either directly in terms of the extraction process or indirectly in terms of the infrastructure required to convert and possibly transport the energy for use by an energy service, or both. In this view of affordability, the criterion refers to the price paid for a unit of energy.
- The impact of the price of an energy source to an individual varies depending upon the individual's income—the lower the income, the larger the percentage of income required to pay for the energy. This view of affordability refers to the ability to pay for a unit of energy.

Although some national statistical services and public interest groups maintain affordability indices for items such as food, clothing, shelter, and heating, it can be difficult to apply such a criterion uniformly across a population.[46] Ranking the different energy sources using the cost of each energy source is perhaps the simplest interpretation of affordability.[47] Although this is not "affordability" in the true sense of the word, the lowest cost-per-unit of energy could be assumed to be the most affordable and hence the most secure.

High energy costs impact low-income households disproportionately,[48,49] suggesting that a high value of affordability (that is, cost) cannot be considered secure. Furthermore, this runs counter to the interpretation of the availability and accessibility metrics, where higher values mean more secure energy sources. Accordingly, it is necessary to reverse the ordering in affordability; that is, higher cost-per-unit energy values are interpreted as being a less secure energy source.

Taking the reciprocal of the value and using it as the affordability metric means that the resulting higher values (i.e., those that are less costly per unit energy) indicate more secure energy sources. Table 18.3 shows the annual space heating costs for a variety of fuel sources and heating plant efficiencies in an average, detached residential home using 70 GJ per year in parts of eastern Canada.

Table 18.3 Residential space heating costs for 70 GJ[50]

Energy source and furnace efficiency	Annual cost	Normalized
Biomass 60%	$1,592	0.220
Natural gas 90%	$1,775	0.198
Fuel Oil 85%	$1,962	0.179
Natural gas 62%	$2,500	0.140
Electricity 100%	$2,570	0.137
Fuel Oil 60%	$2,779	0.126

Affordability (the normalized reciprocal of the annual heating cost) sees biomass ranked highest in terms of affordability (0.220) and fuel oil in a 60 percent efficient furnace ranked the lowest (0.126).

Depending upon the energy service, the affordability criterion can include both operating and capital costs. Affordability need not have anything to do with environmental charges or taxes associated with the energy supply.

Acceptability

The fourth criterion is acceptability (ACC) and refers to how acceptable an energy source is considered to be by the jurisdiction. Unlike the other criteria, the choice of the acceptability metric is more of a challenge in that there are many different ways in which an energy source can be ranked as "acceptable"; these can range from emissions associated with different energy sources to the impact of the energy source on indigenous peoples in the places where the energy is produced. The acceptability metric faces another problem in that what is considered a reasonable metric by one person may be unreasonable to someone else; an example of this is the debate over greenhouse gas emissions and their impact on the climate.

Acceptability can also refer to the associated risk in dealing with the supplier of a particular energy source. Some energy supplying countries are enduring long-running internal conflicts (e.g., Nigeria and Iraq), while others have seemingly arbitrary or inconsistent regulatory environments (e.g., Russia). Using a political or economic risk assessment can act as the acceptability metric of the energy source.

Whatever the choice of metric, it should be normalized so that it can be used in the decision matrix.

It is worth noting that acceptability is often an expendable virtue. What is considered unacceptable one day may be considered acceptable the next; for example, much of the US continental shelf was closed to offshore oil and natural gas development until President Barack Obama decided to lift a large part of the moratorium in the spring of 2010.

Weights

After ranking the alternatives by the different criteria is completed, the ranking vector can be obtained by applying the weights to the rankings associated with each alternative. Like the metrics, the weights should be justifiable and reproducible.

In AHP, the weights are determined by respondents who are expected to have an understanding of the ways in which each criterion relates to, or impacts, the jurisdiction. The pair-wise comparison technique is also used to obtain the weights. Since there are typically fewer criteria than alternatives, the pair-wise comparison is not as onerous, making the results potentially less error-prone and open to debate. The limitation of this approach is not so much that it is qualitative, but that it produces a single ranking vector based upon the current views of the respondents. These views, like those obtained when determining the alternatives' rankings, should reflect the nature of the jurisdiction. However, in some cases they may not be a true reflection of the relationship between the jurisdiction and the criteria. Furthermore, two (or more) groups of respondents may produce different weightings for the same criteria.

An alternative approach to determining the weights is to consider a range of weights for the criteria, thereby generating a range of different ranking vectors. This allows a variety of questions to be asked about the energy sources and their ranking; for example:

- What is the resulting ranking of the alternatives from a given combination of criteria?
- How does one criterion influence the alternative ranking differently from another?
- How sensitive is an alternative's energy security ranking to changes in the weights?
- If certain alternatives are considered more favorable than others, what combination (or combinations) of criteria should be encouraged?

Example

The following example applies the four 'A's to the energy security of Atlantic Canada, the four easternmost Canadian provinces bordering the Atlantic Ocean (New Brunswick, Newfoundland and Labrador, Nova Scotia, and Prince Edward Island). Although the region is endowed with hydroelectricity, biomass, and limited coal, crude oil, and natural gas resources, most of these products are exported to other parts of Canada, the United States, and Europe.[51] As a result, the region relies heavily on imports of coal and crude oil to meet the energy demands of its transportation, heating, and electrical services. Figure 18.4 shows the changes in Atlantic Canada's energy supply for the decade between 1999 and 2008 (electricity refers to primary electricity generated from hydroelectric and nuclear facilities, biomass data is estimated for 1999 to 2001, and "oil" refers to crude oil). Data from the figure can be used to determine the availability and accessibility directly, while affordability and acceptability can be obtained indirectly from other sources.

Ranking methods

The ranking of Atlantic Canada's energy alternatives is determined by applying the four criteria and their associated metrics discussed in the previous section.

Availability is obtained from the most recent annual supply data for each alternative; in this example, it is the data from 2008 shown in Figure 18.4. The data show that the greatest availability levels are from domestic supplies of natural gas, crude oil, and electricity. The sources with the lowest availability are crude oil from Angola and the United Kingdom, and domestic supplies of coal. The availability ranking is determined by normalizing the availability values of each energy source for 2008.

The same data sources are used in determining the accessibility of each energy source. In this case, the linear regression of each alternative is obtained for the decade between 1999 and 2008, giving an indication of the changes in each energy source over this period. These values are then offset to ensure that any negative values are treated as positive values and finally, they are normalized. The ranking shows that the most accessible energy sources are domestic crude oil, the industrial use of local biomass, and hydroelectricity, while the least accessible are supplies of crude oil from Iraq, Norway, and the United Kingdom.

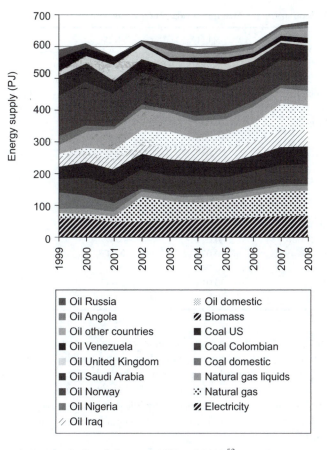

Figure 18.4 Energy supply in Atlantic Canada between 1999 and 2008.[52]

Affordability refers to the price of a unit of energy.[53] Since the units vary between different energy sources (i.e., oil, $/barrel; coal, $/tonne or $/short ton; biomass, $/cord; natural gas and natural gas liquids, $/m^3; and electricity, $/kW), all prices are converted to $/TJ. The reciprocal of the price of each source is used as the ranking since higher prices are considered to be less affordable. Prices are in Canadian dollars.

In this example, environmental and political metrics were not chosen for acceptability as environmental legislation varies widely, both within the region and at the national level. Furthermore, Canada makes no distinction between suppliers based upon politics. Instead, the risk associated with each supplier, as determined by the Economist Intelligence Unit (EIU), was employed as the acceptability metric;[54] since lower values indicate less risk, the reciprocal of each value was obtained and the resulting list normalized. In terms of country risk, Norway is the most acceptable, while Iraq, Venezuela, and Nigeria are the least acceptable.

The decision matrix is completed by listing the different rankings of the alternatives under their respective criteria, as shown in Table 18.4.

Ranking the alternatives

A ranking vector is produced by applying criterion-specific weights to the criterion rankings of each alternative, as described in the section above, "The decision matrix and ranking vector."

Table 18.4 Decision matrix for Atlantic Canada's energy sources

Energy source	AVA	ACS	AFF	ACP
Electricity	0.095	0.078	0.022	0.084
Natural gas	0.119	0.121	0.074	0.084
Natural gas liquids	0.026	0.047	0.107	0.084
Coal domestic	0.002	0.036	0.172	0.084
Coal Colombian	0.094	0.065	0.126	0.032
Coal US	0.084	0.061	0.239	0.070
Biomass	0.078	0.087	0.024	0.084
Oil domestic	0.110	0.132	0.023	0.084
Oil Iraq	0.071	0.028	0.024	0.021
Oil Nigeria	0.027	0.051	0.023	0.025
Oil Norway	0.112	0.000	0.023	0.129
Oil Saudi Arabia	0.071	0.044	0.024	0.036
Oil United Kingdom	0.012	0.009	0.023	0.070
Oil Venezuela	0.025	0.047	0.023	0.022
Oil other countries	0.045	0.081	0.024	0.034
Oil Angola	0.014	0.067	0.023	0.031
Oil Russia	0.017	0.046	0.024	0.028

A simple ranking vector can be obtained by applying a weight of 1.0 to the alternatives under a single criterion, ignoring the others by giving them each a weight of zero. Table 18.5 shows the ranking of the alternatives, from lowest to highest, for each criterion using this approach.

These rankings show the relative security of each alternative with respect to a criterion. In the case of availability, domestic coal is least secure, while domestic natural gas is most secure; in terms of acceptability, crude oil from Iraq is seen as least acceptable, while crude oil from Norway is seen as most acceptable.

Table 18.5 Lowest to highest ranking of alternatives for each criterion (from Table 18.4)

Availability	Accessibility	Affordability	Acceptability
Coal domestic	Oil Norway	Electricity	Oil Iraq
Oil United Kingdom	Oil United Kingdom	Oil Angola	Oil Venezuela
Oil Angola	Oil Iraq	Oil domestic	Oil Nigeria
Oil Russia	Coal domestic	Oil Venezuela	Oil Russia
Oil Venezuela	Oil Saudi Arabia	Oil Nigeria	Oil Angola
Natural gas liquids	Oil Russia	Oil United Kingdom	Coal Colombian
Oil Nigeria	Oil Venezuela	Oil Norway	Oil Other countries
Oil Other countries	Natural gas liquids	Oil Other countries	Oil Saudi Arabia
Oil Iraq	Oil Nigeria	Oil Russia	Coal US
Oil Saudi Arabia	Coal US	Oil Saudi Arabia	Oil United Kingdom
Biomass	Coal Colombian	Biomass	Electricity
Coal US	Oil Angola	Oil Iraq	Natural gas domestic
Coal Colombian	Electricity	Natural gas domestic	Natural gas liquids
Electricity	Oil Other countries	Natural gas liquids	Coal domestic
Oil domestic	Biomass	Coal Colombian	Biomass
Oil Norway	Natural gas domestic	Coal domestic	Oil domestic
Natural gas domestic	Oil domestic	Coal US	Oil Norway

Table 18.6 Energy security vector with equal criterion weights (0.25 each)

Energy source	Ranking
Coal US	0.114
Natural gas domestic	0.099
Oil domestic	0.087
Coal Colombian	0.079
Coal domestic	0.073
Electricity	0.070
Biomass	0.068
Natural gas liquids	0.066
Oil Norway	0.066
Oil Other countries	0.046
Oil Saudi Arabia	0.044
Oil Iraq	0.036
Oil Angola	0.034
Oil Nigeria	0.032
Oil Venezuela	0.029
Oil United Kingdom	0.029
Oil Russia	0.028

By giving each criterion an equal weight of 0.25, a different view of the region's security is obtained. In Table 18.5, crude oil from Norway may be the most acceptable and, after domestic natural gas, the most available; however, because of declining production in the North Sea, and hence supplies to Atlantic Canada, it has the lowest accessibility. Other patterns also become apparent; for example, coal is the least expensive fuel, regardless of the source, yet one of its suppliers, Colombia, has a very low acceptability ranking. The final ranking is obtained using the equations in the section above, "The decision matrix and ranking vector," with a common weight of 0.25 and is shown in Table 18.6.

The values in the table can also be represented graphically. By separating the criteria within each alternative, the relative importance of each can be shown; for example, see Figure 18.5 where each criterion has a weight of 0.25. With this combination of weights, the most secure energy sources are found to be US coal, domestic natural gas, and domestic crude oil, while the least secure are crude oil from Russia, Venezuela, and the United Kingdom. Norway's declining crude oil supply gives it an accessibility ranking of zero; consequently, Norway does not have an accessibility component.

In Figure 18.5, the criteria are associated with weights of equal value (0.25 each); this can be considered the current state of energy security in the jurisdiction. By changing the weights, it is possible to determine the effect that different events can have on the jurisdiction's energy security; for example, a reduction in the affordability of the energy sources as a result of an economic downturn. Reapplying the method with a new set of weights will produce another ranking vector that can be compared with the original.[55]

The challenge with this approach is in determining the new set of weights. Consider the case in which a group of experts decide that the weight associated with affordability is to fall by 40 percent from 0.25 to 0.15 (i.e., energy prices will be less of a concern) and the values of the remaining weights are 0.35 for availability (i.e., short-term energy supply is an increasing concern) and 0.25 for both accessibility and acceptability. Figure 18.6 shows the ranking produced when these weights are applied to the criteria's values associated with the energy sources.

The ranking of each energy source can be obtained from the graph or the data that produced the graph. For example, in Figure 18.6 the security ranking for domestic natural gas is 0.104 (most secure), while the ranking for crude oil from the UK is 0.028 (least secure).

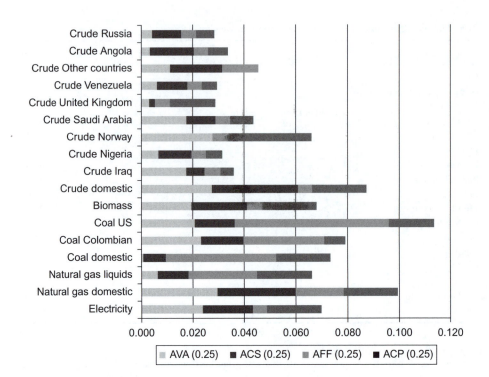

Figure 18.5 Graphical representation of decision matrix with equal weights (from Table 18.4).

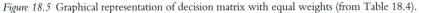

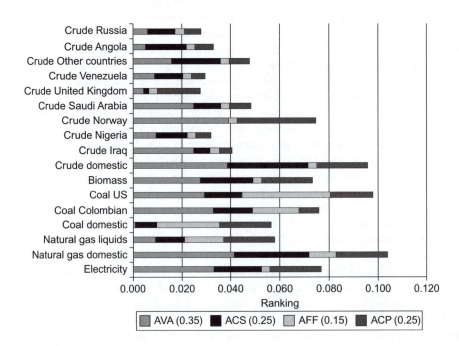

Figure 18.6 Applying unequal weights to the criteria.

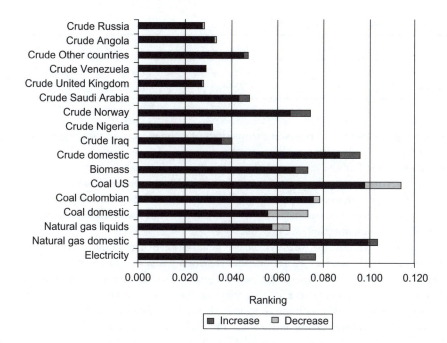
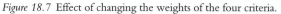

Figure 18.7 Effect of changing the weights of the four criteria.

Although the differences in the rankings shown in Figure 18.5 and Figure 18.6 may appear small, they nevertheless illustrate the fact that when different weights are assigned to the criteria, the overall rankings will change. In this case, increasing availability (0.25 to 0.35), keeping accessibility and acceptability constant (at 0.25), and decreasing affordability (from 0.25 to 0.15), changes the individual rankings by varying amounts, as shown in Figure 18.7; the magnitude depends upon each energy source's sensitivity to the changes. Here, domestic and US coal exhibit the most significant declines in their contribution to the overall security of the jurisdiction, while

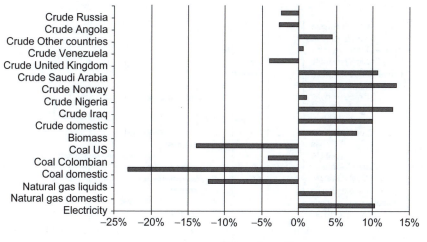

Figure 18.8 Change in ranking expressed as percentage (from Figure 18.7).

Table 18.7 Minimum and maximum weights

Weight	Availability	Accessibility	Affordability	Acceptability
Minimum	0.20	0.20	0.10	0.20
Maximum	0.30	0.25	0.40	0.45

these are largely offset by increases in the rankings of domestic crude, Norwegian crude, and electricity.

An alternate view of the effect of changing the weights is shown in Figure 18.8, where the increase or decrease in the energy source's overall contribution to the jurisdiction's energy security is expressed as a percentage. Domestic coal, US coal, and natural gas liquids experience the most significant decreases in percentage terms, whereas crude from Norway, Iraq, and Saudi Arabia exhibits the most significant increases.

As discussed previously, the weights selected by one group of experts might not be the same as the weights selected by another. As a result, multiple ranking vectors could be produced, reflecting the weights selected by the experts and potentially overlooking combinations of weights that could lead to different rankings. Rather than selecting one set of rankings, an alternative approach is to take the minimum and maximum weights and enumerate all possible rankings associated with the weights. As an example, consider the range of weights shown in Table 18.7.

From Table 18.7, different combinations of weights can be obtained and applied to create new security rankings. The weight values used range from the minimum to the maximum in steps of 0.05 (for example, Availability's weights are 0.20, 0.25, and 0.30); regardless of the combination, the sum of the weights must always be 1.0.

Figure 18.9 shows the least and most secure ranking values obtained from an enumeration of the possible rankings of the different weight combinations. A ranking produced by any weight combination from Table 18.7 will fall somewhere on the ranking range for each energy source; for example, the black lines in Figure 18.9 are the rankings associated with weights of 0.20, 0.20, 0.25, and 0.35 for Availability, Accessibility, Affordability, and Acceptability, respectively.

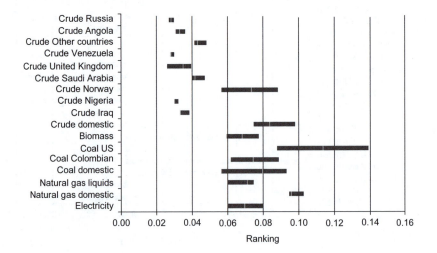

Figure 18.9 Minimum and maximum rankings for weights from Table 18.7.

Figure 18.9 highlights a number of points regarding the choice of weights:

- The weights chosen by an expert need not produce the "best" ranking for a given range of weights. The ranking of an individual energy source will produce a value that falls between the least and most secure values, inclusive.
- The combination of weights that produce the least and most secure energy security values can vary from one energy source to another. For example, the least and most secure ranking for domestic natural gas has Availability, Accessibility, Affordability, and Acceptability values of 0.20, 0.20, 0.40, 0.20 and 0.30, 0.25, 0.10, 0.35, respectively. However, for natural gas liquids, the weights required for the least and most secure rankings are reversed (that is, 0.30, 0.25, 0.10, 0.35 and 0.20, 0.20, 0.40, 0.20).

When an energy source has a security ranking that is less than its most secure ranking, comparing the weights may give an indication of how the security ranking can be improved. As an example, in Figure 18.9, electricity has a rank of 0.0694 (from weights of 0.20, 0.20, 0.25, and 0.35 for Availability, Accessibility, Affordability, and Acceptability), which is less than the most secure rank of 0.0798 (from weights of 0.30, 0.20, 0.10, and 0.40 for Availability, Accessibility, Affordability, and Acceptability). This suggests that increasing electricity's Availability and decreasing its Affordability (i.e., lowering its cost) could increase its security.

To further illustrate the significant impact in the energy security rankings that can result from changing the criterion's weights of the different energy sources, consider the case (albeit extreme) in which the weightings change from affordability, with a weight of 1.0 (all other criteria have a weight of 0.0), to accessibility. In this example, energy sources with high affordability rankings will have a decrease in their security ranking while those with a high accessibility ranking will have an increase in their ranking. The changes caused by ranking decreasing affordability and increasing accessibility are shown in Figure 18.10. Since the criteria rankings are normalized, shifting the

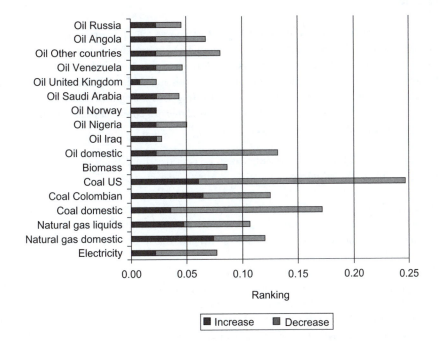

Figure 18.10 Effect of changing ranking from affordability (1.0) to accessibility (1.0).

weight from one criterion to another means that the sum of the increases in ranking is equal to the sum of the decreases. The most significant security decreases occur with US, domestic, and Colombian coal and natural gas liquids, while domestic oil, electricity, biomass, and domestic natural gas all experience marked increases.

This section used Atlantic Canada's energy sources to show how the method can rank a jurisdiction's energy sources in terms of their energy security. By starting with equal weights, the present ranking of the energy sources can be ascertained; in Atlantic Canada, the most secure sources are US coal, domestic natural gas, and domestic crude oil, while the least secure are sources of crude oil from the UK, Venezuela, and Russia. Changing the weights can result in new rankings that can be compared with rankings from other weight combinations, offering potential paths to more secure energy sources.

Discussion

This chapter has introduced a method of producing an energy security ranking for the different energy sources or products used in a jurisdiction. The method has four criteria and metrics based upon APERC's four 'A's and employs a decision matrix for creating the ranking.

APERC's original definitions of the four 'A's have undergone a number of changes with their adoption for the method described in the chapter:

Availability. APERC's description of availability refers to the R/P ratio of a primary energy source, with the focus being on fossil and nuclear energy sources; the greater the R/P ratio, the more secure the source. The description used for the method refers to the present levels of supply of a given energy source from a supplier; the greater the availability, the more secure the source. APERC's view of availability is future supply, whereas the method's view deals with current consumption.

Accessibility. APERC's definition of accessibility refers to how well a proven energy reserve can be relied upon to supply the market; it includes "economic factors, political factors, and technology." The method's definition of accessibility refers to historical supply trends, indicating whether access to the source is increasing, decreasing, or remaining constant. APERC's use of availability and accessibility refers to energy security in terms of future and current consumption, while the method's use of availability and accessibility, if considered together, can give an indication of the relative energy security of each energy source.

Affordability. Both APERC and the described method consider affordability to be the actual cost of the energy source to the consumer.

Acceptability. APERC's view of acceptability refers to the economic impact of environmental regulations with respect to coal, nuclear, and unconventional fuels. In the method, acceptability refers to the political and economic risks of the supplier and its state as a supplier of an energy source.

Ranking energy sources can be done qualitatively or quantitatively. Although both approaches work, ranking metrics based on quantitative data are typically easier to reproduce and can be more justifiable than using qualitative data obtained from a group of respondents. Perhaps the most fundamental difference between the two definitions of the four 'A's is that for availability and accessibility APERC relies on projections and qualitative results, whereas the method uses quantitative values.

The one exception to the objective of employing quantitative data is acceptability, which, because of the way it is produced, is qualitative; however, it is treated as if it were quantitative. This chapter uses data from the Economist Intelligence Unit's Country Risk Model for acceptability primarily because it was readily available, comes from a reputable source, and appears to offer consistent results. The method used in the Country Risk Model to determine country rankings is proprietary and, as with all qualitative data, is open to the biases of its contributors; however, its major shortcoming is that it does not include all countries in the world. Other country ranking services include Coface and Jane's,[56] which, like the Economist's Country Risk Model, are fee-based services; as these were not readily available, they were not considered for this chapter. Other potential ranking services examined were the Central Intelligence Agency's World Factbook (containing quantitative country data but no ranking) and the OECD (a coarse ranking scale that offered little distinction between countries).[57]

Normalization is a commonly used technique in most multicriteria decision analysis methods when ranking alternatives; the method described in this chapter applies it to each criterion's metric (N denotes the maximum number of energy sources, while *Source* refers to an energy source):

Availability. The current supply of each energy source is normalized to obtain the source's availability ranking:

$$Rank_{Source} = \frac{Supply_{Source}}{\Sigma_{i=1}^{N} Supply_i}$$

Accessibility. The accessibility ranking of each energy source is obtained from the source's historical supply data and the application of the following steps:

1   For each energy source, find the linear regression for each year in the historical supply data to the current year and then determine the median of these regressions

$$Value_{Source} = Median \left(Regression_{EarliestYear}, \ldots, Regression_{CurrentYear} \right)$$

2   If one or more alternatives have negative median linear regression values, add the absolute of the most negative value to each alternative:

$$Value_{Source} = Value_{Source} + |Value_{Most\ Negative}|$$

3   Normalize these values to obtain the accessibility rank of each energy source:

$$Rank_{Source} = \frac{Value_{Source}}{\Sigma_{i=1}^{N} Value_i}$$

Affordability. In affordability, low cost energy is considered to be more secure than high cost energy; consequently it is necessary to use the reciprocals of each energy source in order to obtain the normalized ranking for affordability:

$$Rank_{Source} = \frac{1}{\frac{Cost_{Source}}{\Sigma_{i=1}^{N} \frac{1}{Cost_i}}}$$

Acceptability. How an energy source's acceptability is ranked depends on the data and its interpretation: if higher values denote greater acceptability, the values can be normalized directly (as with supply in the availability metric); however, if lower values denote greater acceptability, the reciprocal of the value is to be used (as with cost in the affordability metric).

The four criteria must be assigned weights for use in calculating the ranking vector of each energy source. In most multicriteria decision analysis methods, a single set of weights is obtained from respondents who are aware of the jurisdiction's energy situation. A limitation of this approach is that the respondents must be aware of the state of each energy source with respect to the criteria. An alternative approach, described in this chapter, is to create a range of weights that can show how changes in one or more criteria can affect the ranking associated with an energy source.

Any number of combinations of weight ranges can be applied to the criteria to obtain different ranking vectors for a jurisdiction's energy sources. This allows the user of the method to examine different "what if" scenarios, thereby gaining further insight into the state of the energy sources with respect to each of the criteria. Applying a range of weights to the criteria (rather than a single set of weights) allows more insight into, for example, how sensitive the energy sources are to changes in the importance of the criteria. This approach to obtaining an energy security vector reflects the inevitable changes that take place over time in any jurisdiction as, for example, perceptions regarding different energy sources and economic conditions change. As a result, it is important that anyone studying a jurisdiction's energy security be familiar with the jurisdiction's energy sources, the relevance of each of the four 'A's to the jurisdiction, and be prepared to apply different weights to the criteria. With this level of knowledge, it is possible to develop relevant energy policy for the jurisdiction.

The example demonstrated that the choice of weights for the criteria is dependent upon the person or organization producing the energy security index. If the results are to compare one jurisdiction with another or simply to indicate how the jurisdiction's energy security has changed, the criteria chosen should have both a spatial and temporal continuity. However, the metrics should, as has been discussed, be quantitative rather than qualitative.

Although infrastructure is not explicitly mentioned or measured, changes in infrastructure can be captured in some of the criteria, notably accessibility, which reflects the long-term trends in supply. Disruptions in supply caused by infrastructure failures or geopolitical issues often appear as seemingly unexpected changes in historical supply. The reasons for the changes in accessibility require more than the method, they require analysts with a broader understanding of past energy events.

The results produced by the method are not projections—they are a causal summary of the jurisdiction's current energy supply and what has happened in the past as influenced by applying ranges of weights to the criteria. Analysts and policymakers can employ the resulting ranking vectors and ranges to identify possible future security problems or policy directions.

The four 'A's and the method described in this chapter can also be used in evaluating the energy security associated with scenarios considering different energy futures. Such scenarios must be organized so that the data they produce meet the requirements of the criteria and metrics.

Concluding remarks

A method for developing energy security ranking vectors for the energy sources used in a jurisdiction has been described. It extends APERC's four 'A's: availability, accessibility, affordability, and acceptability by redefining some of the criteria to include historic trends, allow renewables, and employ quantitative data. By relying on quantitative data, the results are reproducible and potentially less open to criticism.

The method can be used to examine the state of energy security in a jurisdiction as a whole or in its energy services (i.e., transportation, heating and cooling, and electricity production), and can include:

- Annual recalculation of the rankings to show the current state of energy security for the jurisdiction or energy service.
- Testing "what-if" scenarios, to examine the projected energy supplies and what this would mean for the jurisdiction or energy service.

By broadening the definition of what constitutes a jurisdiction to include regions within a nation or supranational federations, the method allows energy security issues at the regional level—that could be hidden at the national level—to be considered. This is applicable in jurisdictions where energy supplies vary from region to region.

The chapter's recommended use of a range of weights, rather than single values, offers further insights into the potential impact of changes to criteria, such as availability or affordability, which may prove problematic in the future. Unlike other methods for determining energy security, the method described here produces a ranking vector of the energy sources, rather than a single value, for the jurisdiction.

Our method allows the review of the current state of energy security in a jurisdiction. It is only one of a number of tools needed to measure and improve a jurisdiction's energy security. The rankings can be used in conjunction with other tools to influence energy policy decisions, including energy and infrastructure choices for all energy services. The rankings should be revisited on a regular basis to determine the new state of energy security in the jurisdiction.

We are presently examining other metrics for ranking energy sources within each criterion; for example, diversity and disparity in both availability and accessibility. As part of our community work, we are using the method to educate politicians, policymakers, and the public on the importance of energy security.

Notes

1 The authors would like to thank Hari Lakshminarayanan, Jim Parsons, Dave Ron, Jacinda Rudolph, and Sandy Cook for their contributions to the chapter.
2 Constantini, Valeri. 2007. "Security of Energy Supply: Comparing Scenarios from a European Perspective," *Energy Policy* 35: 210–226.
3 Grubb, Michael, Lucy Butler, and Paul Twomey. 2006. "Diversity and Security in UK Electricity Generation: The Influence of Low-Carbon Objectives," *Energy Policy* 34: 4050–4062
4 Smith, Eric. 2002. *Energy, the Environment, and Public Opinion* (Lanham, MD: Rowman and Littlefield); World Energy Council (WEC). 2007. *Deciding the Future: Energy Policy Scenarios to 2050* (London: World Energy Council).
5 Triantaphyllou, E. 2000. *Multi-Criteria Decision Making Methods: A Comparative Study* (Dordrecht: Kluwer Academic Publishers).
6 Brown, Marilyn A., and Benjamin K. Sovacool. 2007. "Developing an 'Energy Sustainability Index' to Evaluate Energy Policy," *Interdisciplinary Science Reviews* 32(4): 335–349.
7 Clingendale. 2004. *Study on Energy Supply Security and Geopolitics* (The Hague: Clingendale International Energy Programme).
8 Greene, David L. 2010. "Measuring Energy Security: Can the United States Achieve Oil Independence?" *Energy Policy* 38(4)(April): 1614–1621
9 Hughes, Larry, and Nikita Sheth. 2009. "A Graphical Technique for Explaining the Relationship between Energy Security and Greenhouse Gas Emissions." In Zvonimir Guzovic (ed.), *Fifth Dubrovnik Conference on Sustainable Development of Energy, Water, and Environment Systems,* Dubrovnik, October 20–24, pp. 223–241.
10 Lefèvre, Nicolas. 2010. "Measuring the Energy Security Implications of Fossil Fuel Resource Concentration." *Energy Policy* (April): 1635–1644.

11 WEC, *Deciding the Future.*
12 Asia Pacific Energy Research Centre (APERC). 2007. *A Quest for Energy Security in the 21st Century* (Tokyo: Institute of Energy Economics, Asia Pacific Energy Research Centre).
13 International Energy Agency (IEA). 2001. *Toward a Sustainable Energy Future* (Paris: International Energy Agency).
14 Brown, "Developing an 'Energy Sustainability Index'."
15 Hughes, "A Graphical Technique."
16 APERC, *A Quest for Energy Security.*
17 APERC, *A Quest for Energy Security*, p. 7.
18 Kruyt, Bert, D.P. van Vuuren, H.J.M. de Vries, and H. Groenenberg. 2009. "Indicators for Energy Security," *Energy Policy* (June): 2166–2181.
19 Materials Management Service, US Department of the Interior, Offshore Energy and Minerals Management (OEMM). 2009. Available at: http://www.mms.gov/offshore/ (accessed May 3, 2010).
20 Energy Information Administration, US Department of Energy. 2009. "U.S. Crude Oil, Natural Gas, and Natural Gas Liquids Reserves 2008." Available at: http://www.eia.doe.gov/pub/oil_gas/natural_gas/data_publications/crude_oil_natural_gas_reserves/current/pdf/table03.pdf (accessed May 3, 2010).
21 World Energy Council. 2007. "Survey of Energy Resources 2007, Tidal Country Notes – Canada." Available at: http://www.worldenergy.org/publications/survey_of_energy_resources_2007/tidal_energy/country_notes/1918.asp (accessed May 3, 2010).
22 APERC, *A Quest for Energy Security*, p. 17.
23 Kruyt *et al.*, "Indicators for Energy Security."
24 Nord Stream. 2010. "The Pipeline." Available at: http://www.nord-stream.com/en/the-pipeline.html (accessed May 3, 2010).
25 Government of Ontario, Ministry of Transportation. 2009. "A Plan for Ontario: 1 in 20 by 2020." Available at: http://news.ontario.ca/mto/en/2009/07/a-plan-for-ontario-1-in-20-by-2020.html (accessed May 3, 2010).
26 APERC, *A Quest for Energy Security*, pp. 69–72.
27 Parfomak, P. 2003. "Liquefied Natural Gas (LNG) Infrastructure Security: Background and Issues for Congress." Available at: http://www.energy.ca.gov/lng/documents/CRS_RPT_LNG_INFRA_SECURITY.PDF (accessed May 3, 2010).
28 Markandya, Anil, and Malcolm Pemberton. 2010. "Energy Security, Energy Modelling and Uncertainty." *Energy Policy* (April): 1609–1613.
29 APERC, *A Quest for Energy Security*, p. 27.
30 Kruyt *et al.*, "Indicators for Energy Security."
31 Escobar, J., E. Lora, O. Venturini, E. Yanez, E. Castillo, and O. Almazan. 2009. "Biofuels: Environment, Technology and Food Security,"*Renewable and Sustainable Energy Reviews* 13(6–7): 1275–1287.
32 Goldemberg, J. and P. Guardabassi. 2009. "Are Biofuels a Feasible Option?" *Energy Policy* 37: 10–14.
33 de Coninck, H., J. Stephens, and B. Metz. 2009. "Global Learning on Carbon Capture and Storage: A Call for Strong International Cooperation on CCS Demonstration," *Energy Policy* 37: 2161–2165.
34 Brachinger, H.W. and P.A. Monney. 2002. *Decision Analysis* (Johannesburg, South Africa: United Nations Educational, Scientific and Cultural Organization (UNESCO)), pp. 931–978.
35 Huang, J.P., K.L. Poh, and B.W. Ang. 1995. "Decision Analysis in Energy and Environmental Modeling," *Energy* (September): 843–855.
36 Zak, J. 2002. "The MCDA Methodology Applied to Solve Complex Transportation Decision Problems." The 13th Mini-EURO Conference: *Handling Uncertainty in the Analysis of Traffic and Transportation Systems,* Bari.
37 Kiker, G., T. Bridges, A. Varghese, T. Seager, and I. Linkov. 2005. "Application of Multi-criteria Decision Analysis in Environmental Decision Making," *Integrated Environmental Assessment and Management* 1(2): 95–108.
38 Triantaphyllou, *Multi-Criteria Decision Making Methods.*
39 Saaty, T. 1980. *The Analytic Hierarchy Process* (New York: McGraw-Hill).
40 Hughes, "A Graphical Technique."
41 Transportation data from Sweden is used to illustrate both availability and accessibility. Sweden was chosen for a number of reasons, including the quality of its data, its prominence as an industrialized European economy, and (with respect to accessibility of transportation energy sources) its plan to

become an oil-free society (see: http://www.sweden.gov.se/content/1/c6/06/70/96/7f04f437.pdf) (accessed August 29, 2010).

42 Energimyndighet. 2008. *Energiläget i siffror (Energy in Sweden) Facts and Figures 2008* (Eskilstuna, Sweden: Statens energimyndighet).

43 Mortished, Carl. 2004. "How Shell Blew a Hole in a 100-year Reputation," *TimesOnLine,* January 10. Available at: http://business.timesonline.co.uk/tol/business/article991863.ece (accessed January 5, 2010).

44 Simmons, Matthew. 2005. *Twilight in the Desert: The Coming Saudi Oil Shock and the World Economy* (New York: Wiley and Sons).

45 Energimyndighet, *Energiläget i siffror.*

46 Hughes, Larry, and Dave Ron. 2009. "Energy Security in the Residential Sector: Rapid Responses to Heating Emergencies – Part 2: Nova Scotia." Canadian Centre for Policy Alternatives (March). Available at: www.policyalternatives.ca/~ASSETS/DOCUMENT/Nova_Scotia_Pubs/2009/Energy_Security_Part_1_Final.pdf (accessed August 29, 2010).

47 Note that "cost" is being used rather than "price." It is assumed that "price" refers to the price of a unit of energy, whereas the "cost" is what the consumer must pay for the energy units required by the service. Different energy conversion systems may purchase energy at the same price, but because of their differences in efficiencies, the cost to the consumer may differ.

48 Hughes, Larry. 2009. "Energy Security in the Residential Sector: Rapid Responses to Heating Emergencies – Part 1: Fundamentals." Canadian Centre for Policy Alternatives (March). Available at: www.policyalternatives.ca/~ASSETS/DOCUMENT/Nova_Scotia_Pubs/2009/Energy_Security_Part_1_Final.pdf (accessed August 29, 2010).

49 Hughes and Ron, "Energy Security in the Residential Sector."

50 Hughes and Ron, "Energy Security in the Residential Sector."

51 Domestic steam coal is the exception in this list as its high sulfur content means only limited amounts can be used in domestic electrical generation. Export markets have been found for this coal to be used as coking coal. See: http://www.xstrata.com/media/news/2010/02/10/1015CET/ (accessed April 5, 2010).

52 Hughes, Larry. 2010. "Eastern Canadian Crude Oil Supply and its Implications for Regional Energy Security," *Energy Policy* 38(6): 2692–2699; Statistics Canada. 2004. "Table 128-0002 – Supply and Demand of Primary and Secondary Energy in Terajoules, Quarterly (Terajoules) – 'Terminated'." CANSIM (database), Using E-STAT (distributor), January 29. Available at: http://estat.statcan.gc.ca/cgi-win/cnsmcgi.exe?Lang=E&EST-Fi=EStat/English/CII_1-eng.htm (accessed March 27, 2010); Statistics Canada. 2009. "Table 128-0015 – Consumption of Solid Wood Waste and Spent Pulping Liquor for Energy Production, Annually (2002 Onwards)." CANSIM (database), Using E-STAT (distributor), October 30. Available at: http://estat.statcan.gc.ca/cgi-win/cnsmcgi.exe?Lang=E&EST-Fi=EStat/English/CII_1-eng.htm (accessed March 30, 2010); Statistics Canada. 2009. "Table 134–0001 – Refinery Supply of Crude Oil and Equivalent, Monthly (cubic metres)." CANSIM (database), Using E-STAT (distributor), June 15. Available at: http://estat.statcan.gc.ca/cgi-win/cnsmcgi.exe?Lang=E&EST-Fi=EStat/English/CII_1-eng.htm (accessed October 25, 2009); Statistics Canada. 2010. "Table 128-0009 – Supply and Demand of Primary and Secondary Energy in Terajoules, Annually (Terajoules)." CANSIM (database), Using E-STAT (distributor), February 10. Available at: http://estat.statcan.gc.ca/cgi-win/cnsmcgi.exe?Lang=E&EST-Fi=EStat/English/CII_1-eng.htm (accessed April 2, 2010); Crude oil prices from "World Crude Oil Prices (Dollars per Barrel) Period: Weekly," Energy Information Administration – Petroleum Navigator, March 2010. Available at: http://tonto.eia.doe.gov/dnav/pet/pet_pri_wco_k_w.htm (accessed March 18, 2010).

53 Crude oil prices from "World Crude Oil Prices (Dollars per Barrel) Period: Weekly," Energy Information Administration – Petroleum Navigator, March 2010. Available at: http://tonto.eia.doe.gov/dnav/pet/pet_pri_wco_k_w.htm (accessed March 18, 2010); Natural gas from Henry Hub spot price, available at: www.bloomberg.com/markets/commodities/energyprices.html (accessed March 16, 2010); Average open market sales price of US coal in 2008 – report released September 18, 2009. Available at: http://www.eia.doe.gov/cneaf/coal/page/acr/table33.html (accessed March 15, 2010); Average realized price in 2008 for the cost of mining coal, reported by Sherritt – Canada's largest thermal coal producer. Available at: http://www.nrcan-rncan.gc.ca/mms-smm/busi-indu/cmy-amc/2008revu/pdf/coa-cha-eng.pdf (accessed March 18, 2010); Spot price for thermal coal in December 2009. Available at: http://www.e-coal.com (accessed March 15, 2010); US coal prices. Available at: http://www.eia.doe.gov (accessed March 14, 2010); Price for pellets in

Fredericton, Canada and price for birch and maple wood sold in Moncton, Canada, 2009. Available at: http://www.unbf.ca/forestry/centers/documents/WoodEnergy_ChuiGeorge1808.pdf and http://www.tdc.ca/wood.htm (accessed March 15, 2010).

54 Economist Intelligence Unit – Country Monitor (EIUCM). 2008. *Country Risk Ratings* (EIUCM).

55 Since the sum of the weights must always equal 1.0, changing the value of one of the weights will require an adjustment of the values of one or more of the remaining weights.

56 Coface Country Risk. Available at: http://www.coface.com/CofacePortal/COM_en_EN/pages/home/risks_home/country_risks (accessed April 20, 2010); Jane's Sentinel Country Risk Assessments. Available at: http://sentinel.janes.com/public/sentinel/index.shtml (accessed April 20, 2010).

57 CIA World Factbook. Available at: https://www.cia.gov/library/publications/the-world-factbook/docs/profileguide.html/ (accessed April 20, 2010); OECD Country Risk Classification. Available at: http://www.oecd.org/document/49/0,3343,en_2649_34171_1901105_1_1_1_37431,00.html (accessed April 20, 2010).

19

MEASURING ENERGY SECURITY PERFORMANCE IN THE OECD[1]

Benjamin K. Sovacool and Marilyn A. Brown

Introduction

This chapter measures and assesses energy security for 22 countries in the Organisation for Economic Co-operation and Development (OECD). It begins by discussing ten metrics that comprise an energy security index. Using this energy security index, we then measure and track the progress of energy security within the OECD from 1970 to 2007. The third section analyzes the relative performance of four countries: Denmark (one of the top performers), Japan (which performed well), the United States (which performed poorly), and Spain (the worst performer). The chapter concludes by offering implications for energy policy and security.[2]

In attempting to tackle a concept as complicated as energy security, we could have focused on almost any scale and any group of countries. Instead of emphasizing smaller scales (such as the individual and enterprises) or international organizations (such as the World Bank or Organization of Petroleum Exporting Countries), we have focused exclusively on nation states. And instead of looking at countries in a single region, such as the European Union, Asia, the Caspian Sea, or the Black Sea, we have investigated energy security for 22 geographically dispersed countries that belong to the OECD. The first reason for this focus is practical: data on patterns of energy production and use have been collected and compiled for OECD countries since the 1950s, and these countries are involved with a number of multilateral organizations dealing with energy issues such as the United Nations and the International Energy Agency. The next reason is more theoretical: OECD countries offer a sample of different types of energy markets and cultures. The United Kingdom and New Zealand are examples of liberalized and privatized energy markets, while other countries such as Denmark and parts of the United States remain highly regulated. The OECD countries we selected also include cultures as diverse as Australia, Greece, Japan, and Turkey. The final reason is pragmatic: because OECD countries are the most industrialized, they also possess the technical and financial capacity to implement policy changes that can improve their energy security. The OECD countries include many of the world's largest consumers of energy, so their decisions affect the global energy marketplace.

Creating an energy security index

Chapter 1 of this book argued that energy security consists of four interconnected criteria or dimensions: availability, affordability, efficiency, and environmental stewardship. Availability refers to diversifying the fuels used to provide energy services as well as the location of facilities using those fuels, promoting energy systems that can recover quickly from attack or disruption, and minimizing dependence on foreign suppliers. Affordability refers to providing energy services that are affordable for consumers and minimizing price volatility. Efficiency involves improving the performance of energy equipment and altering consumer attitudes. Stewardship consists of protecting the natural environment, communities, and future generations. Recognizing that each criterion does not exist in a vacuum, and that each is of comparable importance, Table 19.1 presents ten indicators that comprise an energy security index. Note that, in each case, the indicator is an inverse measure of security; that is, the higher the value, the lower the energy security.

To reflect *availability*, oil import dependence, natural gas import dependence, and dependence on petroleum transport fuels serve as useful indicators. Oil import dependence and natural gas import dependence reflect how dependent a country is on foreign supplies of petroleum (mostly used in transport) and natural gas (a feedstock for industrial activity, power generation, and some heating), and also document changes in the supply mix for the world's first and third most used fuels (the second being coal). The presence of alternative fuels such as ethanol and biodiesel also reveals how far countries have moved away from dependence on petroleum. To reflect *affordability*, the price of electricity and gasoline at the retail level serve as important metrics. We have decided to track residential prices for electricity and gasoline consumption rather than diesel or jet fuel because homes and passenger vehicles account for a majority of the energy used by ordinary people.[3] To reflect *energy and economic efficiency*, metrics such as energy intensity, per capita electricity use, and on-road fuel intensity of passenger vehicles show different but important dimensions. The most inclusive of these three is energy intensity, a measure that indicates the amount of energy used to produce a unit of GDP. By correlating energy use with economic output, the measure thus encompasses patterns of consumption and use for industries, government facilities, consumers, and multiple sectors all at once. Per capita electricity consumption and on-road fuel economy for passenger vehicles also show how efficient individual technologies have become at the end-user level. To reflect *environmental stewardship*, aggregate sulfur dioxide emissions and carbon dioxide emissions reveal how far countries have gone towards mitigating greenhouse gas

Table 19.1 Defining and measuring energy security

Criteria	Underlying Values	Explanation	Indicators
Availability	Independence, diversification, reliability	Diversifying the fuels used to provide energy services as well as the location of facilities using those fuels, promoting energy systems that can recover quickly from attack or disruption, and minimizing dependence on foreign suppliers	Oil import dependence; Natural gas import dependence; Dependence on petroleum transport fuels
Affordability	Equity	Providing energy services that are affordable for consumers and minimizing price volatility	Retail electricity prices; Retail gasoline/petrol prices
Energy and Economic Efficiency	Innovation, resource custodianship, minimization of waste	Improving the performance of energy equipment and altering consumer attitudes	Energy intensity; Per capita electricity use; On-road fuel intensity of passenger vehicles
Environmental Stewardship	Sustainability	Protecting the natural environment and future generations	Sulfur dioxide emissions; Carbon dioxide emissions

emissions, acid rain, and noxious air pollution. These indicators also help show relative progress in how governments have implemented national climate change programs.

Evaluating performance for the OECD

We collected data on these ten indicators and metrics for 22 OECD countries from 1970 to 2007, with a few exceptions and caveats. First, reliable data for energy intensity were only available for 1980 and 2005; fuel economy data for 2005 instead of 2007; and sulfur dioxide emissions data for 2000 instead of 2007. Second, our index is not meant to imply that quantitative measures of energy security are perfect, or that reducing complex situations to numbers is without problems. Numerical indices often highlight not what is most significant or meaningful, but merely what is measurable. Quantitative measurements, especially those taken out of context, can also conceal important nuances and variability. Does a reduction in the energy intensity of a given country mean that its economy is becoming more energy efficient, or that instead more energy-intense products are being imported from elsewhere and energy-intensive jobs outsourced?[4] Third, collecting the data for this study was tedious and difficult. Most of it was not available online and the data for 1970 involved much searching through libraries. Historical data from International Energy Agency publications and archives are inconsistent, and discrepancies found in data and reports published by different agencies (e.g., the Energy Information Administration, World Resources Institute, United Nations, and the World Bank) are even more troubling.

That said, we do believe that these ten metrics provide a reasonable sense of how well countries have provided energy services and promoted energy security, and the results may be surprising to some. Tables 19.2 and 19.3 present data for each of the ten metrics for the 22 selected countries in 1970 and 2007. Table 19.4 shows the overall energy performance score from 1970 to 2007.

To assess how a country has performed relative to other countries based on an array of indicators that use diverse units of measurement, we rely on z-scoring. Z-scores are "dimensionless" quantities that indicate how many standard deviations a country is above or below the mean of the 22 OECD countries. We created z-scores for each of the ten indicators in 1970 and 2007 by subtracting the mean value for each data point and dividing by the indicator's standard deviation. The z-scores are then summed for 1970 and 2007, giving equal weight to each indicator and providing a total energy security score for each country in both years. This z-scoring exercise indicates that the United States had the lowest energy security of all 22 countries, both in 1970 and still in 2007. In contrast, Figure 19.1 depicts that the United Kingdom, New Zealand, and Denmark had high energy security scores in 2007.

We then assessed the relative progress of each country over time by comparing the sum of their Z-scores on the ten indicators in 1970 and 2007. The results of our analysis indicate that the United Kingdom experienced the largest improvement in energy security over this time frame. Its energy security improved on six of the ten indicators, and was particularly strengthened with respect to oil import dependence, shifting from 100 percent oil imports in 1970 to only 4 percent in 2007. Figure 19.2 illustrates that Belgium, Japan, Switzerland, Canada, and New Zealand also experienced significant improvements in their energy security over this same time frame. In contrast, Ireland, France, Italy, Sweden, and Spain experienced the largest declines in energy security over this same period.

A few general trends are worth noting. First, changes in energy security scores over time have been highly variable within the OECD, implying that the countries examined have taken diverse and divergent paths towards energy policy and security, and also reflecting different natural resource endowments. Second, no country improved along all ten indicators of energy security. The United Kingdom and Denmark both scored better on six indicators over the past four

Table 19.2 Energy security performance index for 22 OECD countries, 1970 (in US$2007)[5]

	Oil import dependence (%)	Dependence on petroleum transport fuels (%)	On-road fuel intensity (gpm)	Energy per GDP intensity (thousand BTU/US$GDP)*	Electricity use (kWh/capita)	Natural gas import dependence (%)	Nominal electricity retail prices (US¢/kWh)	Nominal gasoline prices (US$/liter)	SO_2 emissions (million tons)	CO_2 emissions (million tons)
Australia	67%	96.1%	0.059	10.3	3,919	0%	3.7	0.26	1.6	148
Austria	57%	94.3%	0.048	8.5	3,302	34%	18	1.32	0.4	51
Belgium	100%	98.4%	0.045	12.2	3,399	99%	18.5	1.74	1.2	126
Canada	46%	97.3%	0.071	18.7	9,529	1%	3.7	0.37	4.1	341
Denmark	99%	98.1%	0.042	8.8	3,211	0%	9.5	0.42	0.3	62
Finland	100%	97.7%	0.045	12.6	4,885	100%	5.3	0.53	0.4	40
France	98%	96.3%	0.036	8.7	2,882	35%	7.9	0.74	3.5	439
Germany	92%	96.4%	0.042	9.8	2,962	24%	15.9	1.16	6.9	1,027
Greece	99%	98.3%	0.048	6.0	1,118	0%	2.1	0.58	0.3	24
Ireland	98%	97.2%	0.045	9.0	1,956	0%	6.9	0.58	0.2	19
Italy	97%	98.7%	0.036	7.1	2,262	0%	6.3	0.42	2.6	297
Japan	100%	98.2%	0.050	7.8	3,445	32%	48.6	1.27	5.1	769
Netherlands	97%	98.0%	0.040	12.9	3,110	0%	15.3	1.00	1.4	142
New Zealand	100%	95.6%	0.053	11.0	4,941	0%	3.17	0.48	0.1	14
Norway	100%	97.5%	0.043	16.4	14,785	0%	2.6	0.42	0.2	28
Portugal	99%	98.0%	0.043	4.4	830	0%	20.6	1.59	0.1	15
Spain	99%	97.3%	0.037	7.0	1,623	85%	5.8	0.37	1.1	117
Sweden	100%	97.5%	0.050	13.7	8,048	0%	3.2	0.32	0.9	92
Switzerland	100%	96.9%	0.043	7.6	4,693	100%	4.0	1.59	0.1	40
Turkey	53%	97.7%	0.067	5.0	241	0%	21.1	0.11	0.8	43
UK	100%	97.7%	0.048	9.9	4,489	7%	5.3	0.58	8.6	653
United States	22%	95.1%	0.077	14.7	8,022	4%	7.0	0.42	31.2	4,413
Median	99%	97.5%	0.045	9.4	3,351	1%	6.6	0.56	1.0	105
Mean	87%	97.2%	0.049	10.1	4,257	24%	10.7	0.74	3.2	405

Table 19.3 Energy security performance index for 22 OECD countries, 2007[6]

	Oil import dependence (%)	Dependence on petroleum transport fuels (%)	On-road fuel intensity (gpm)	Energy per GDP intensity (thousand BTU/US$GDP)*	Electricity use (kWh/capita)	Natural gas import dependence (%)	Real electricity retail prices (US¢/kWh)	Real gasoline prices ($/liter)	SO_2 emissions (million tons)*	CO_2 emissions (million tons)
Australia	37%	98.3%	0.038	9.0	11,309	0%	12.5	1.24	2.6	394
Austria	91%	96.3%	0.032	7.0	8,090	95%	22.6	1.81	0.2	66
Belgium	99%	98.1%	0.034	9.2	8,688	100%	16.5	2.20	1.3	103
Canada	0%	98.8%	0.043	13.8	16,766	0%	7.6	1.08	2.9	573
Denmark	0%	97.7%	0.033	5.2	6,864	0%	38.2	2.05	0.1	50
Finland	96%	98.1%	0.034	8.8	17,178	93%	17.1	2.12	0.3	64
France	96%	98.1%	0.031	7.2	7,585	97%	17.3	2.03	1.3	353
Germany	94%	98.1%	0.034	7.0	7,175	79%	23.1	2.10	2.4	790
Greece	99%	98.1%	0.034	6.8	5,372	99%	13.0	1.19	0.8	97
Ireland	100%	98.1%	0.034	4.9	6,500	86%	24.7	1.77	0.1	44
Italy	93%	97.5%	0.030	5.8	5,762	85%	27.2	2.06	1.5	430
Japan	97%	98.2%	0.045	6.5	8,220	93%	17.8	1.46	2.6	1,227
Netherlands	91%	98.1%	0.033	9.8	7,057	59%	24.2	2.28	1.0	179
New Zealand	69%	97.1%	0.034	9.1	9,746	0%	17.8	1.35	0.1	36
Norway	0%	98.1%	0.034	12.8	24,295	0%	17.5	2.32	0.6	36
Portugal	98%	98.1%	0.034	5.9	4,799	100%	23.3	2.07	0.2	55
Spain	98%	98.1%	0.032	7.1	6,213	100%	18.7	1.64	2.1	346
Sweden	99%	98.1%	0.036	9.1	15,230	100%	12.7	1.99	0.3	45
Switzerland	99%	98.1%	0.034	5.8	8,279	100%	15.6	1.65	0.1	38
Turkey	94%	96.3%	0.034	6.1	2,053	97%	15.8	2.60	2.1	266
UK	4%	96.3%	0.032	6.0	6,192	8%	22.7	2.07	1.6	524
United States	59%	97.1%	0.050	9.1	13,515	17%	10.3	0.82	17.8	5,725
Median	94%	98.1%	0.034	7.1	7,838	90%	17.7	2.01	1.2	141
Mean	73%	2.2%	0.036	7.8	9,404	64%	18.9	1.81	1.9	520

Table 19.4 Energy security performance score, 1970 to 2007

	Oil import dependence	Petroleum transport fuels	On-road fuel intensity	Energy per GDP intensity	Electricity use	Natural gas import dependence	Nominal electricity retail prices	Nominal gasoline prices	SO_2 emissions	CO_2 emissions	Final score*
Australia	0.051	−1.731	0.336	−0.455	−0.474	0.835	0.310	0.271	−0.432	−0.169	−1.460
Austria	−1.808	−0.459	0.614	−0.083	−0.031	−0.436	0.140	1.200	0.041	0.000	−0.823
Belgium	−0.117	0.580	−0.050	−0.022	−0.119	1.206	1.108	1.209	−0.139	0.050	3.706
Canada	0.094	−1.388	0.435	−0.232	0.152	0.862	1.050	0.847	−0.140	−0.111	1.568
Denmark	2.436	0.888	−0.155	0.778	0.181	0.835	−3.022	−1.173	0.053	0.026	0.847
Finland	−0.039	−0.036	−0.050	0.261	−1.330	1.395	−0.233	−1.101	0.014	−0.009	−1.128
France	−0.127	−1.269	−0.261	−0.115	−0.059	−0.455	−0.017	−0.473	0.206	0.176	−2.394
Germany	−0.340	−1.181	−0.396	0.273	0.045	−0.337	−0.135	0.237	0.416	0.440	−0.979
Greece	−0.162	0.492	0.147	−0.681	−0.159	−1.447	0.083	1.037	−0.137	−0.054	−0.880
Ireland	−0.232	−0.476	−0.050	0.963	−0.127	−1.147	−1.229	−0.232	0.038	−0.015	−2.508
Italy	−0.093	1.702	−0.063	0.053	0.110	−1.124	−1.664	−1.195	0.017	−0.040	−2.297
Japan	−0.065	0.261	−1.935	−0.058	−0.014	−0.444	3.764	1.863	0.092	−0.200	3.265
Netherlands	−0.040	0.228	−0.307	−0.090	0.113	−0.525	−0.358	−0.486	−0.027	0.004	−1.488
New Zealand	0.670	−0.457	0.605	−0.307	0.140	0.835	−0.541	0.482	0.023	−0.014	1.436
Norway	2.480	−0.212	−0.231	−0.429	0.267	0.835	−0.549	−1.764	−0.098	0.001	0.300
Portugal	−0.135	0.228	−0.231	−0.730	−0.134	−1.470	0.280	1.185	−0.004	−0.028	−1.039
Spain	−0.135	−0.388	−0.352	−0.537	−0.171	0.828	−0.427	−0.379	−0.371	−0.162	−2.095
Sweden	−0.117	−0.212	0.107	0.432	0.005	−1.470	0.233	−1.247	0.089	0.063	−2.119
Switzerland	−0.117	−0.741	−0.231	0.190	0.351	1.233	−0.130	2.104	0.023	0.012	2.696
Turkey	−2.063	2.535	1.886	−0.652	0.225	−1.401	1.460	−3.013	−0.416	−0.175	−1.614
UK	2.375	2.535	0.614	0.733	0.698	0.840	−1.079	−0.889	0.888	0.262	6.977
United States	−2.515	−0.898	−0.431	0.706	0.333	0.551	0.955	1.518	−0.135	−0.056	0.029

* Positive numbers imply overall improvement in energy security.

decades, exhibiting the greatest breadth of improvement. Third, a majority of countries have experienced declines in energy security, with 13 countries scoring worse on a majority of the ten indicators between 1970 and 2007. Fourth, some metrics, such as energy intensity and fuel economy for passenger vehicles, have almost universally improved, while others, such as electricity consumption per capita, electricity prices, and gasoline prices have almost universally deteriorated.

Explaining energy security performance

Using the same statistical data, supplemented by a review of the published literature, we explore four countries in greater detail, focusing on their energy security scores and the strategic actions that have led to them. Figure 19.1 shows that Denmark had one of the highest Z-scores in 1970 and 2007, and the United States had the worst score; Figure 19.2 shows that Spain was one of the countries that improved the least in terms of its energy security from 1970 to 2007 whereas Japan was one of the countries that improved the most. We thus decided to explore these four case studies in greater detail—Denmark, Japan, the United States, and Spain—as they seem to represent two of the best and two of the worst countries in terms of their energy security trends over time. Figure 19.3 breaks down their performance among four particular indicators that saw the biggest changes from 1970 to 2007 within each country.

Denmark

Denmark has exhibited considerable success in improving its energy security compared with the other countries analyzed. Since 1970, Denmark has transitioned from being 99 percent dependent on foreign energy sources such as oil and coal to becoming a net exporter of natural gas, oil, and electricity today. Over the same period, Denmark has improved its reliance on non-petroleum

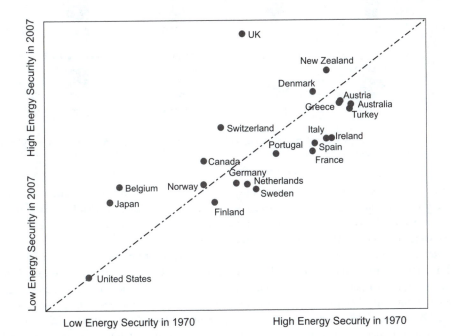

Figure 19.1 Energy security "Z-scores" in 1970 and 2007.

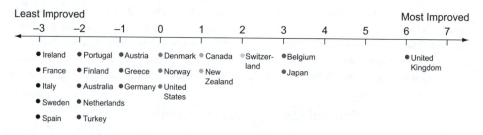

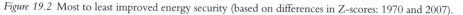

Figure 19.2 Most to least improved energy security (based on differences in Z-scores: 1970 and 2007).

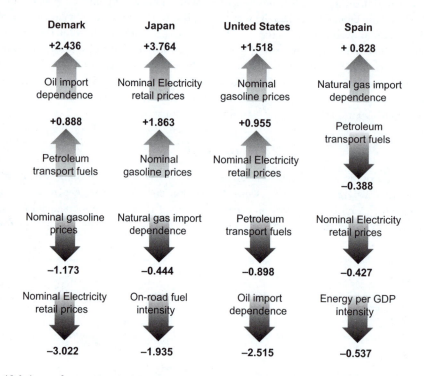

Figure 19.3 Areas of energy security improvement and decline for Denmark, Japan, United States, and Spain, 1970 to 2007.

transportation fuel, decreased its energy intensity by almost a factor of two, and lowered its aggregate carbon dioxide and sulfur dioxide emissions. The only areas where Denmark did not improve were in electricity use per capita, electricity prices, and gasoline prices, and these latter three were areas where almost no country improved.

Denmark is now the unchallenged world leader in terms of wind energy, exporting US$8 billion in wind turbine technology and equipment per year, and Denmark also boasts the lowest energy consumption per capita in the European Union.[7] Primary energy consumption nationally grew just 4 percent from 1980 to 2004, even though the economy grew more than 64 percent in fixed prices. At the same time, more renewable energy replaced fossil fuels, and total CO_2 emissions decreased by 16 percent. Therefore, the carbon dioxide emission intensity—the amount of CO_2 emitted per unit of Gross Domestic Product—was 48 percent lower in 2004 than it was in 1980.

The most obvious factor responsible for such improvement is strong political leadership and well-designed, consistent policy mechanisms aimed at improving energy efficiency and promoting renewable energy. Denmark implemented energy taxes in 1974 as a response to the energy crises, and used the billions in dollars of revenue to invest in wind power, biomass, and small-scale combined heat and power units. The taxes, furthermore, sent price signals that encouraged voluntary energy efficiency measures. Denmark mandated energy efficiency standards for new buildings, and tightened them over a period of 30 years. Danish regulators also designed investment subsidies and feed-in tariffs forcing utilities to buy all power produced from renewable energy technologies at a rate equal to 70 to 85 percent of the consumer retail price of electricity in a given distribution area, and they later regulated that all renewable power providers be given priority access to the grid.[8] The government levied a general carbon tax on all forms of energy, set strict vehicle fuel economy standards, and later adopted European standards pledging to decrease carbon dioxide emissions from automobiles to 140 grams of carbon dioxide emitted per kilometer driven by 2008, which help explain Denmark's lowered emissions of greenhouse gases.

While these efforts have improved many aspects of energy security, they have also made energy more expensive. Denmark's taxes do mean that electricity prices are the highest in the European Union at about 38 cents per kWh, and the price of petrol is more expensive than in 13 other OECD countries. Denmark's experience does suggest that improving availability, efficiency, and stewardship can trade off with affordability, but overall the country appears to be the most energy secure in the OECD.

Japan

A similar pattern of strong government support for energy security exists in Japan, although with less focus on renewable energy and some other notable differences. Since 1970, Japan has lessened its dependence on oil and improved vehicle fuel economy slightly, but increased its dependence on natural gas and significantly increased its sulfur dioxide and carbon dioxide emissions despite its promises under the Kyoto Protocol. Electricity use per capita more than doubled and gasoline prices rose, but Japan was also one of only three countries where electricity prices decreased, and its energy intensity also improved.

Overall, Japan recorded unprecedented levels of economic growth between 1970 and 2007, closing the gap in per capita income, raising standards of living, and improving labor productivity compared with Western Europe and North America, all while drastically improving energy efficiency.[9] Devastated after World War II, Japan's immediate problem was securing adequate supply of energy to fuel reconstruction and industrial growth, and the country's energy needs were met predominately by imported oil and domestic coal. Population density in major cities such as Tokyo, however, made the mounting costs of air and water pollution visible, and environmental awareness was starting to grow at the same time as the Arab oil embargo hit. By 1973, the time of the oil crisis, petroleum accounted for nearly 80 percent of total energy demand, and the crisis precipitated nothing less than panic.[10]

Energy security was given highest priority, and from 1973 to 1975 the government announced a formal energy security strategy that consisted of reducing dependence on petroleum, diversifying domestic energy supply, aggressively promoting energy conservation, and pushing research and development. Japan's Ministry of International Trade and Industry (MITI) began their "Moonlight Project" in 1978 to develop more efficient power technologies and early fuel cells. In addition, the government offered free energy audits for smaller firms and issued standards for combustion and heating devices in industry to improve energy efficiency. These standards applied to more than 3,500 factories in the manufacturing, mining, and energy supply sectors, and the government also required these facilities to hire a certified energy manager and to publicly disclose their energy consumption annually.

The 1980s saw Japan pass an Alternative Energy Law with provisions forcing suppliers to adopt natural gas and renewable power sources, along with the creation of tax incentives and low-interest loans for industrial energy efficiency measures, emphasizing the petrochemicals, refining, cement, and paper industries.[11] The first minimum energy performance standards came in 1983 for refrigerators and air conditioners, and were later expanded to virtually all appliances, including the underrated electric toilet seat warmer. The appliance standards were very successful at reducing electricity consumption. Average electricity use for refrigerators, for example, declined by 15 percent from 1979 to 1997 while average refrigerator size increased by 90 percent. Japanese regulators also applied their performance standards to imported technology ranging from auto-mobiles and televisions to air conditioners and computers, and demanded that the efficiency level of new products had to meet the best performing product in the market, in some cases requiring energy efficiency improvements of more than 50 percent.[12]

Progress in Japan, however, has been more tempered than in Denmark. Energy use per capita in Japan increased from 1973 to 2005 for both households and passenger travel. While the government promoted strict performance standards for appliances, they set only voluntary standards for buildings, and did not ramp up financial incentives until the late 1990s. Japan did require efficiency standards and efficiency labeling for automobiles, and these led to a 12 percent increase in fuel economy from 1979 to 1985 and another 8.5 percent increase from 1990 to 2000. Such improvement, however, was offset by a doubling of transport energy use between 1973 and 2001 due to the growth in vehicle ownership and increases in vehicle size. Private automobile travel rose in Japan from a modest 42.5 percent in 1970 to 55.9 percent in 1987.[13] Moreover, cheap oil prices in the mid-1980s encouraged energy consumption. Energy demand growth as a whole averaged only 0.2 percent between 1973 and 1986, but jumped to 4 percent between 1987 and 1991.[14]

United States

The United States fared poorly compared with almost all other countries—with only Greece, Portugal, and Spain performing worse. The country improved in only three of the indicators from 1970 to 2007—energy intensity, fuel economy, and sulfur dioxide emissions. In contrast, the country has become significantly more dependent on foreign supplies of natural gas and oil, and remains the world's leading emitter of greenhouse gases.

While progress in the adoption of more energy-efficient technologies has saved billions of dollars throughout the economy, most other indicators of energy autonomy demonstrate that the country has become less energy secure over time. Even though energy efficiency has taken root in some sectors of the economy, it has not compensated for the growth in energy consumption that has occurred since 1973, nor will it (if current trends continue) accommodate the growth that forecasters anticipate in coming decades. Moreover, America's dependence on oil from insecure and politically unstable countries has required extensive diplomatic and military efforts that incur huge costs borne by energy users and taxpayers. The country's information economy also remains inextricably tied to reliable power and to just-in-time manufacturing and distribution processes that depend on fleets of petroleum-guzzling trucks and airplanes.[15]

The United States remains more susceptible today to oil supply disruptions and price spikes than at any time in the recent past. It has grown to become the world's largest oil consumer by a considerable margin while, at the same time, its domestic oil production has plummeted. Oil imports have filled the expanding gap, accounting for 59 percent of total US oil consumption in 2007—up from 22 percent in 1970. The United States has so many automobiles that the number of cars exceeds the number of people with drivers' licenses.[16]

The United States also continues to see increasing demand for electricity in a way that threatens its ability to meet customer load requirements. The country consumed about 170 percent more electricity in 2007 than it did in 1970, with power usage growing from 25 percent of the nation's total energy use in 1970 to 40 percent today. Efforts resulting from three decades of clean air legislation have decreased sulfur dioxide emissions from electric generators in the United States. Nevertheless, air pollution remains a serious threat to human and ecosystem health. Americans have experienced a rise in respiratory illnesses, and visibility continues to degrade in formerly pristine areas as a result of pollution from vehicles and coal-burning power plants. Beyond air pollution issues, current energy trends will lead to expanded emissions of greenhouse gases, which most climate scientists believe are contributing to increased global temperatures, recession of glaciers, and more frequent and powerful weather events such as hurricanes.

Because of its huge dependence on imported oil to fuel a transportation sector that has seen little improvement in energy efficiency, the nation could be ravaged by disruptions to oil supplies due to weather, war, or terrorist attacks. At the same time, growing electricity consumption and reliance on power plants employing natural gas, which increasingly come from foreign sources, although this may change with the exploitation of domestic shale gas, thereby reducing import vulnerabilities but creating environmental issues. And while efficiency efforts have successfully slowed the growth rate of fuel consumption in the last few decades, population increases and economic expansion have forced up the nation's overall use of energy, exacerbating the country's environmental problems.

Spain

Tied for last in our energy security index, Spain has shown improvement in only two indicators: a meager reduction in dependence on foreign sources of oil from 99 percent to 98 percent, and a modest improvement in on-road fuel economy from 27 to 31 miles per gallon. Spain has worsened in every other metric, including energy intensity. Total primary energy use per unit of GDP has fallen for 19 other OECD countries (two other exceptions being Greece and Portugal), and overall, major OECD economies used a third less primary energy to generate a unit of GDP in 2006 than in the 1970s.[17]

Spain has defied this trend. The country lacks sufficient supplies of domestic coal, oil, gas, and uranium, has experienced ongoing industrialization, but made little improvement in energy efficiency. Thus, the Spanish energy sector is currently suffering from difficulty in controlling greenhouse gas emissions, high prices, increasing reliance on imported fuels, high levels of growth in energy demand, and stagnating energy efficiency and energy intensity, culminating in a situation even Spanish analysts consider unsustainable.[18] Spain's gradual transition to democracy left intact the prevailing economic structures that had existed during the Franco regime. Unlike in other OECD countries where the comparatively progressive governments were implementing energy reforms during the 1970s, Spanish bankers and industrial managers continued to play a primary role in the country's energy policymaking. Rather than promote energy efficiency or diversification, these stakeholders sought ways to ensure a smooth political transition, maintain economic growth, and retain their political power. From 1975 to 1982, alternative sources of policy such as left-wing parties, environmental groups, trade unions, and consumer advocates were able to exert little influence over Spanish energy policy. The country thus remained committed to developing conventional forms of supply and strengthening agreements to import energy fuels, but neglected energy efficiency and alternative energy.[19] When the Spanish Socialist Workers Party came to power in 1982, energy policy did not break significantly with past patterns.

Whereas energy intensity declined in almost every other OECD country, the late 1980s and most of the 1990s saw sustained growth in energy consumption per unit of GDP in Spain, which increased at an annual rate of 0.75 percent from 1990 to 1997. Per capita electricity consumption and carbon dioxide emissions also increased at rates between 2.3 and 2.8 percent annually over the same period.[20] Spanish regulators heavily focused on building nuclear plants in the early 1980s, but their plans were threatened by high costs and the Chernobyl disaster in 1986. Despite a few early policy documents and royal decrees, the country did not seriously consider energy efficiency and conservation until the early 1990s.[21] At this time, however, a significant number of mergers and acquisitions occurred in the energy sector, creating massive levels of concentration. The newly integrated energy companies, rather than focusing on the domestic Spanish market, initiated plans for international expansion, attempting to privatize and invest in emerging markets in Latin America.[22] Spanish companies established production, refining, and manufacturing centers in Argentina, Brazil, Colombia, and Mexico. The Spanish oil company REPSOL-YPF, the seventh largest in the world, expanded exploration and production to four Latin American countries. Endesa and Iberdrola, two of the world's largest electricity companies, became leading power suppliers for seven countries in South America and Central America. The Spanish company Gas Natural Group also became the largest single investor in Latin American gas markets.

The consolidation and concentration of Spanish energy companies, coupled with comparatively weak political oversight, lack of competition, and a focus on global markets, left little space for consumer advocacy or environmental policy.[23] Throughout the late 1990s, Spanish customers had some of the highest electricity prices in all of Europe, and most consumers generally believed that such high prices reflected a pro-industry bias that allowed large cash flows to be funneled into the international expansion of Spanish firms. The consequence has been a deterioration of energy security in almost every metric. Spanish energy intensity increased by 5 percent from 1990 to 2000, while European intensity decreased by 10.4 percent.[24] The Spanish economy continues to be highly dependent on high-carbon fossil fuels such as oil and coal, which accounted for roughly 60 percent of energy use in 2007, and the situation is further compounded by the mismatch between state, territorial, and national energy policy, which has been very sporadic and irregular, with some regions aggressively pursuing renewables such as wind and solar while other regions have little penetration of renewable power supplies.

Conclusion

This chapter has created an energy security index, utilizing ten metrics that encompass economic, social, political, and environmental aspects of energy security, and analyzed the status of energy conditions in 22 OECD countries from 1970 to 2007. At least four interconnected conclusions can be drawn from our exercise.

First, our energy security index shows that a majority of countries analyzed have regressed in terms of their energy security. This conclusion is discouraging, especially considering that the oil shocks of 1973 and 1974 culminated in the establishment of the International Energy Agency, the creation of strategic petroleum reserves among its members, and the diversification of the fuel base for electricity as most countries moved away from their use of oil to produce electricity. In the United States, the crisis forced sweeping energy legislation through Congress, resulted in the establishment of the Department of Energy, and even provoked President Jimmy Carter to cite the energy challenge as "the moral equivalent of war." Since those times, the international community has seen advances in low-income energy services, efficiency and demand reduction programs, renewable resources initiatives, and market restructuring of the various energy industries. Many individual states in Europe and the United States have implemented aggressive renewable portfolio standards, feed-in tariffs, and systems benefits funds, started emissions trading schemes, and invested heavily in alternative fuels such as hydrogen, ethanol, and biodiesel. Despite all of this effort, our index reveals that most countries have backslid in their efforts to improve energy security.

Second, despite the near universal deterioration of energy security, a great disparity exists between countries. Some clear leaders, such as Denmark and Japan, stand above the rest and offer many lessons. Neither country left the improvement of energy security to the marketplace, and their experience underscores the importance of government intervention through a progression of energy policy mechanisms. First came energy taxes, standards, and R&D, followed by mechanisms such as tariffs and quotas, demonstrating the necessity of using a variety of mechanisms at once to promote sound energy policy. The Danish strategy has promoted "triple diversification": reliance not just on one type of technology, renewables, but also on energy efficiency as well as combined heat and power and district heating to meet energy needs; not just on one type of policy mechanism but a combination of taxes, subsidies, tariffs, and standards; and not just on one type of renewable energy but a combination of biomass, wind, and biogas digestion. Diversification in all three forms—combining supply- and demand-side measures, utilizing a variety of policy mechanisms, and promoting a broad assortment of different types of renewable technologies— is essential. No one approach, no one technology, and no one policy is sufficient alone. Perhaps equally important, the overarching explanation for the success of Danish and Japanese energy policy lies in coordinated and consistent political support and policy. Unlike the United States and Spain, where lack of synchronization between state and federal policy, constant changes in authorization and appropriations, a focus on other priorities, and expiration of programs have impeded energy policy, Japan and Denmark stand as testaments to the importance of consistency.

Third, notwithstanding the progress made by Japan and Denmark (as well as Belgium and the United Kingdom), no nation scored perfectly. This is because efforts to promote energy security, even for the most successful nations, have tended to focus on energy efficiency or increased supply to meet consumer behavior. Strategies have involved increasing the energy efficiency of buildings, appliances, industrial operations, and vehicles, but not on changing consumer patterns, encouraging them to drive less, buy fewer vehicles, or own fewer appliances. Virtually none of the 22 countries tax urban sprawl, heavily promote mass transit and limit personal vehicle ownership; have attempted to change consumer awareness, provided feedback on energy consumption in the form of real time prices, or changed underlying values by encouraging people to value nature, community involvement, and conservation.[25] Thus, no country has successfully promoted true availability and affordability alongside efficiency and stewardship. Trade-offs have often been involved between them, and most countries have seemingly pursued one or two of the criteria at the expense of the others.

Fourth, and finally, the relative success of Denmark and Japan and the relative failure of the United States and Spain serve as an important reminder that creating energy security is as much a matter of policy from within as it is from without. Policymakers need not focus only on geopolitical power structures in energy resource-producing states or draft new contracts with Nigeria and Russia for oil and gas supply. It is not sufficient to build trade alliances and share intellectual property, send more troops to the Middle East, or bolster naval deployments through-out the world's shipping lanes. Equally effective and important can be coordinated and robust domestic energy policy, aimed at changing consumer behavior, promoting energy efficiency, and lowering greenhouse gas emissions. Tools such as subsidies, tariffs, standards, and research expenditures can be just as important, possibly more so, for achieving available, affordable, efficient, and responsible forms of energy supply and use.

Notes

1 The authors would like to thank Yu Wang, a graduate research assistant at the Georgia Institute of Technology's School of Public Policy, for help with the spreadsheet statistical analysis presented in the chapter.

2 This chapter is based on Sovacool, Benjamin K. and Marilyn A. Brown. 2009. "Competing Dimensions of Energy Security: An International Perspective," Georgia Tech Ivan Allen College School of Public Policy Working Paper Series, Working Paper #45 (Atlanta, Georgia, January 13), as well as Sovacool, Benjamin K. and Marilyn A. Brown. In press. "Competing Dimensions of Energy Security: An International Perspective," *Annual Review of Environment and Natural Resources.*

3 For assessments of industrial electricity use, readers are invited to see Adeyemi, Olutomi I. and Lester C. Hunt. 2007. "Modelling OECD Industrial Energy Demand: Asymmetric Price Responses and Energy-Saving Technical Change," *Energy Economics* 29: 693–709. The paper explores the issue of energy-saving technical change and asymmetric price responses for 15 OECD countries over the period 1962–2003. For assessments of fuel economy for freight, rather than passenger vehicles, see Greening, Lorna A., Mike Ting, and William B. Davis. 1999. "Decomposition of Aggregate Carbon Intensity for Freight: Trends from 10 OECD Countries for the Period 1971 to 1993," *Energy Economics* 21: 331–361; and Schipper, Lee, Lynn Scholl, and Lynn Price. 1997. "Energy Use and Carbon Emissions from Freight in 10 Industrialized Countries: An Analysis of Trends from 1973 to 1992," *Transportation Research D* 2(1): 57–76.

4 Brown, Marilyn A. and Benjamin K. Sovacool. 2007. "Developing an 'Energy Sustainability Index' to Evaluate Energy Policy," *Interdisciplinary Science Reviews* 32(4) (December): 335–349.

5 Data for energy intensity starts at 1980 instead of 1970 Specific values for fuel economy for Austria, Canada, Denmark, France, Germany, Italy, Japan, Netherlands, Spain, Sweden, United Kingdom, and United States taken from Schipper, Lee and Lew Fulton. 2009. *Disappointed by Diesel? The Impact of the Shift to Diesels in Europe Through 2006.* Presentation to the Transportation Research Board Annual Meeting, Washington, DC. Values for remaining countries are taken from OECD averages. Values for population figures and Gross Domestic Product (GDP) are taken from US Economic Research Service. 2008. *International Macroeconomic Data Set* (Washington, DC: US Department of Agriculture). Figures for electricity consumption per capita exclude electricity exports, and were calculated by dividing IEA data in total national consumption (in GWh) by the reported national population. Figures for "energy intensity" taken from 1980 data from: US Energy Information Administration. 2007. *World Energy Intensity: Total Primary Energy Consumption per Dollar of Gross Domestic Product* (Washington, DC: US Department of Energy), and presumed market exchange rates adjusted for 2007 US dollars. Values for retail gasoline prices presume premium gasoline, exclude taxes, have been adjusted to 2007 US dollars, and are taken from: Bentzen, Jan. *An Empirical Analysis of Gasoline Price Convergence for 20 OECD Countries*, Working Paper 03-19 (Denmark: Aarhus School of Business 2003), and adjusted according to: Organization of Economic Cooperation and Development. 2008. "Consumer Price Indices: Energy," *Main Economic Indicators* (Paris: OECD). Values for retail electricity prices have been adjusted to 2007 US dollars, are taken from: International Energy Agency. 2008. *Energy Prices & Taxes: Quarterly Statistics* (Paris: IEA), and adjusted according to: Organization of Economic Cooperation and Development. 2008. "Consumer Price Indices: Energy," *Main Economic Indicators* (Paris: OECD). Some data on sulfur dioxide emissions come from: Spiro, Peter A., Daniel J. Jacob, and Jennifer A. Logan. 1992. "Global Inventory of Sulfur Emissions With 1x1 Resolution," *Journal of Geophysical Research* 97: 6023–6036; and Brimblecombe, Peter. 1999. *Historical Sulfur Emissions* (Norwich, UK: School of Environmental Sciences, University of East Anglia). All remaining figures come from: International Energy Agency. 1991. *Energy Statistics of OECD Countries, 1960 to 1979* (Paris: Organisation for Economic Co-operation and Development); International Energy Agency. 1984. *Energy Balances of OECD Countries, 1970 to 1982* (Paris: Organisation for Economic Co-operation and Development).

6 Data for energy intensity and fuel economy is for 2005 instead of 2007. Energy intensity is taken from: US Energy Information Administration. 2007. *World Energy Intensity: Total Primary Energy Consumption per Dollar of Gross Domestic Product* (Washington, DC: US Department of Energy), and adjusted for purchase power parity (PPP). Specific values for fuel economy for Austria, Canada, Denmark, France, Germany, Italy, Japan, Netherlands, Spain, Sweden, United Kingdom, and United States are taken from: Schipper, Lee and Lew Fulton. 2009. *Disappointed by Diesel? The Impact of the Shift to Diesels in Europe Through 2006.* Presentation to the Transportation Research Board Annual Meeting, Washington, DC. Values for

remaining countries were taken from European and OECD averages. Data for sulfur dioxide emissions are from 2000 instead of 2007, and are taken from: World Resources Institute (WRI). 2007. *Climate and Atmosphere Indicators: Sulfur Dioxide Emissions* (Washington, DC: WRI). Values for retail gasoline exclude taxes for the United States and presume unleaded premium or equivalent grade fuel. Data for alternative fuels include only ethanol and biodiesel, report EU targets for most European countries, and come from: Organisation for Economic Co-operation and Development. 2008. *Biofuel Support Policies: An Economic Assessment* (Paris: OECD). All remaining figures are taken from: US Energy Information Administration. 2008. *Country Energy Profiles* (Washington, DC: US Department of Energy); and International Energy Agency. 2008. *Key World Energy Statistics 2008* (Paris: International Energy Agency), with adjustments made according to: Organization of Economic Cooperation and Development. 2008. "Consumer Price Indices: Energy," *Main Economic Indicators* (Paris: OECD) when data were not available for 2007.

7 Sovacool, Benjamin K., Hans Henrik Lindboe, and Ole Odgaard. 2008. "Is the Danish Wind Energy Model Replicable for Other Countries?" *Electricity Journal* 21(2) (March): 27–38.

8 Morthorst, P. E. 2000. "The Development of a Green Certificate Market," *Energy Policy* 28: 1085–1094.

9 Hayami, Yujiro. 1999. "Changes in the Source of Modern Economic Growth: Japan Compared with the United States," *Journal of Japanese International Economics* 13: 1–21.

10 Fukasaku, Yukiko. 1995. "Energy and Environment Policy Integration: The Case of Energy Conservation Policies and Technologies in Japan," *Energy Policy* 23(12): 1063–1076.

11 Yamamoto, Shuji. 1986. "Japan's New Industrial Era: Restructuring Traditional Industries," *Long Range Planning* 19(1): 61–66.

12 Geller, Howard, Philip Harrington, Arthur H. Rosenfeld, Satoshi Tanishima, and Fridtjof Unander. 2006. "Policies for Increasing Energy Efficiency: Thirty Years of Experience in OECD Countries," *Energy Policy* 34: 556–573.

13 Schipper, Lee, Ruth Steiner, Peter Duerr, Feng An, and Steinar Strom. 1992. "Energy Use in Passenger Transport in OECD Countries: Changes Since 1970," *Transportation* 19: 25–42.

14 Fukasaku, "Energy and Environment Policy Integration," pp. 1063–1076.

15 Brown, Marilyn A., Benjamin K. Sovacool, and Richard F. Hirsh. 2006. "Assessing U.S. Energy Policy," *Daedalus: Journal of the American Academy of Arts and Sciences* 135(3) (Summer): 5–11.

16 Schipper, Lee, Ruth Steiner, Peter Duerr, Feng An, and Steinar Strom. 1992. "Energy Use in Passenger Transport in OECD Countries: Changes Since 1970," *Transportation* 19: 25–42.

17 Geller *et al.*, "Policies for Increasing Energy Efficiency," pp. 556–573.

18 Linares, P., F. J. Santos, and I. J. Perez-Arriaga. "Scenarios for the Evolution of the Spanish Electricity Sector: Is it On the Right Path Towards Sustainability?" *Energy Policy* 36(11): 4057–4068

19 Lancaster, Thomas D., 1989. *Policy Stability and Democratic Change: Energy in Spain's Transition* (London: Pennsylvania State University Press); Correlje, Aad. 1991. "Spanish Energy Policy Overview," *Energy Policy* (November): 901–902.

20 Hernandez, Felix, Miguel Gual, Pablo Rio, and Alejandro Caparros. 2004. "Energy Sustainability and Global Warming in Spain," *Energy Policy* 32: 383–493.

21 Perez, Yannick and Francisco Ramos-Real. 2008. "The Public Promotion of Wind Energy in Spain from the Transaction Costs Perspective, 1986 to 2007," *Renewable and Sustainable Energy Reviews*13(5): 1–9; Gonzalez, Pablo. 2008. "Ten Years of Renewable Electricity Policies in Spain: An Analysis of Success Feed-in Tariff Reforms," *Energy Policy* 36: 2917–2929.

22 Arocena, Pablo, Ignacio Contin, and Emilio Huerta. 2002. "Price Regulation in Spanish Energy Sectors: Who Benefits?" *Energy Policy* 30: 885–895.

23 Rio, Pablo and Gregory Unruh. 2007. "Overcoming the Lock-Out of Renewable Energy Technologies in Spain: The Cases of Wind and Solar Electricity," *Renewable and Sustainable Energy Reviews* 11: 1498–1513.

24 Climent, Francisco and Angel Pardo. 2007. "Decoupling Factors on the Energy-Output Linkage: The Spanish Case," *Energy Policy* 35: 522–528.

25 Geller *et al.*, "Policies for Increasing Energy Efficiency," p. 571.

20

MEASURING ENERGY SECURITY VULNERABILITY

Edgard Gnansounou

Introduction

The issue of long-term security of energy supply (SES) is a priority topic on the energy policy agenda worldwide. Several factors contribute to raise concerns about the growing energy insecurity, including the following: the current trends in the evolution of global economy and geopolitical changes, particularly the rapid economic growth in emerging economies (e.g. China, India); the strain on oil and natural gas reserves; the concentration of most of these reserves in unstable regions; the threat of sabotage on energy supply infrastructures; the political tension around the Iranian nuclear program, and, finally, the appropriation of the oil and gas sectors in several oil- and natural gas-producing countries by national governments. The issue of energy supply security has been put under the spotlight, especially in those industrialized countries which are very dependent on external sources for their energy procurement. However, the framework in which SES should be assured is controversial. While some decision-makers trust in market instruments for optimizing the energy supply mix, others demand more government intervention, arguing that the market fails to ensure adequate and sustained levels of energy supply security.

During the last decades, the balance between these two paradigms has changed from one period to another. After the first world oil crisis, public intervention prevailed and energy independence was a top goal of energy policy in most industrialized countries. In the mid-1980s when oil prices were depressed, through to the end of the 1990s, the energy market forces became dominant. Conversely, the financial crisis from 2007 to the present time calls for stronger public regulation. The energy policy in the industrialized countries is often navigating uncertainly between these two paradigms. Notwithstanding the emphasis put on the liberalization and internationalization of energy markets and promotion of free trade, each industrial country or regional group of countries considers energy as a strategic good and develops its own strategy for facing the eventuality of energy supply disruption, as the cases of the European Union (EU), United States (US), and Japan demonstrate.

Several directives have paved the way to the European strategy of energy security. A Green Paper (EC, 2001a) identified physical, economic, social, and environmental risks as the main hurdles to SES and proposed policy options for coping with Europe's dependence on external energy sources. As a follow up to this, the EU introduced several regulations: the Directive 2001/77/EC on electricity generation from renewable sources (EC, 2001b), the regulatory and fiscal incentives to promote biofuels and other substitute fuels (EC, 2001c), and a Directive on energy saving in buildings (EC, 2003). In December 2005, the European Council adopted the Directive on measures for safeguarding security of electricity supply and infrastructure investment that established a framework for ensuring adequacy between electricity demand and supply and an appropriate level of interconnection capacity between European Union member states (EC, 2006a); a similar Directive was adopted for natural gas (EC, 2004). In 2006, the Green Paper *A European Strategy for Sustainable, Competitive and Secure Energy* (EC, 2006b) was issued by the European Commission. It included many measures for developing unified and competitive European energy markets and strengthening Europe's negotiating power with external energy suppliers. In June 2009, the EU enacted a series of climate and energy targets for 2020, known as the 20-20-20 targets, for achieving: 20 percent reduction of greenhouse gas emissions below the levels of 1990, 20 percent reduction of the EU primary energy use compared with the projected levels, and 20 percent share of renewable sources in the EU energy consumption, including a compulsory 10 percent of renewable energy in transport fuels (EC, 2009). The latter target is very challenging and contradictory opinions have been stated by the stakeholders. However, all this policy legislation and proposals prove that a common and interdependent strategy among the EU member states is on the road. But at present, from the point of view of implementation, there is significant diversity among European countries and claims for a monitoring at regional level as well as on a country basis.

In the US the National Energy Policy issued in May 2001 (NEPDG, 2001) was market-oriented. Within this framework, energy security was primarily considered as trade and foreign policy given priority. The US would use its leadership in multilateral organizations (e.g. energy services negotiations within the World Trade Organization) and its bilateral relationships with energy-producing countries for alleviating barriers to trade and investment. The main goal was to contribute to the establishment of internationally open and transparent rules and procedures for investment and trade in energy markets. However, after September 11, the US energy security strategy has moved towards substitution of energy import. The Energy Policy Act of 2005 (EPAct) illustrated that change. The EPAct put forward five main energy strategy goals: diversifying the energy supply by promoting alternative and renewable energy sources, expanding nuclear energy, increasing market share of domestic fuels, and investing in energy R&D; enhancing energy efficiency and conservation in buildings; improving energy efficiency of the national fleet of cars and trucks; investing in the reinforcement and modernization of the electric power infra-structure; and expanding the strategic petroleum reserve (DOE, 2006). Two headlight measures are as follows: the renewable fuel standard (RFS) required that at least 7.5 billion US gallons of renewable fuels (mainly domestic bioethanol) per year be blended with fossil fuels by 2012, and the strategic petroleum reserve (SPR) was allowed to increase from its capacity of 727 million barrels to one billion barrels. Following the Federal energy strategy, the Southern States Energy Board, which includes several southern states governors, issued a comprehensive plan in July 2006 (SSEB, 2006) aiming at strengthening US energy security. That study proposed an ambitious goal of substituting all of the US oil imports by 2030 and envisaged strategic measures including enhanced development of domestic renewable biomass fuels, coal-to-liquid, oil shale, enhanced oil recovery, and voluntary programs for improving transportation efficiency and increasing energy conservation. The Energy Independence and Security Act (EISA) of 2007 reinforced several of these points (CRS, 2007). For instance, the EISA pushed the standard of renewable fuels to 9 billion gallons in 2008 with a further rise to 36 billion gallons by 2022. The Obama administration confirmed the policy orientation of the EISA through the American Recovery and Reinvestment Act (ARRA, 2009) which allocated US$61.3 billion to the energy sector, a significant part of which was for alternative energy. Finally, on 30 March 2010, President Obama announced the energy strategy of his administration with a focus on energy independence: "I want to emphasize that this announcement is part of a broader strategy that will move us from an economy that runs on fossil fuels and foreign oil to one that relies on homegrown fuels and clean energy. And the only way this transition will succeed is if it strengthens our economy in the short and the long term. To fail to recognize this reality would be a mistake" (White House, 2010).

Among the populous industrialized countries, Japan is the most dependent on energy imports. Taking into account its energy resource poverty, Japan, for a long time, has based its strategy of energy security on international interdependence. As a net energy importer, Japan's strength was its high market share in the Asian energy markets and its position as world leader in high-technology provision. The emergence of new energy importers in industrialized countries, as well as in developing countries, has eroded the negotiating power of Japan and favored those forces within the country that demanded strategy revision towards more active government intervention. This tendency to favor energy autonomy was reinforced in May 2006 when the policy council of the Japan Forum on International Relations recommended to the government a "Plan to Establish a Comprehensive Energy Strategy in Keeping with National Interests" (Toichi, 2006). In the same period, the Ministry of Economy, Trade and Industry issued a *New National Energy Strategy* (METI, 2006) that was built on the following quantitative targets for 2030: reduction in the energy intensity of GDP by at least 30 percent; decrease in the oil dependence ratio of primary energy supply from the present 50 percent to lower than 40 percent; decrease in the almost 100 percent petroleum dependence of the transport sector to around 80 percent; maintain or increase the market share of nuclear power generation at the level of 30 to 40 percent or more; increase in the volume of imported overseas crude oil in which Japanese companies have rights and interests from the present 15 percent to around 40 percent. The implementation of this strategy is envisaged through the following specific programs: (1) planning energy conservation, transport energy, new energy innovation, and nuclear power development in order to realize the optimum energy mixes in line with the strategy; (2) comprehensive strengthening of international cooperation in order to assure a stable energy supply; and (3) enhancing emergency measures in order to mitigate or adapt energy supply during critical situations at affordable costs.

While trusting in the market as the most economically effective way to assure an appropriate security of energy supply, all industrialized regions and countries, however, are promoting government intervention to reduce the exposure of their economy to international energy crises. Even though these two paradigms will be reflected through the energy prices in the future, energy supply autonomy is motivated by the threat of a long-term physical collapse of the international energy markets, and so it can be considered as a preventive measure.

Besides the analysis of policies and government intentions, it is worthwhile evaluating the actual energy supply weakness and to benchmark comparable countries against quantified indicators. This chapter aims to propose and evaluate such indicators. In the next section, the concept of energy vulnerability is discussed. The existing work is then reviewed. After presenting selected dimensions of energy vulnerability, a composite vulnerability index is proposed. Using this index, the cases of 37 industrialized countries are benchmarked for the year 2003. Finally, the chapter discusses the complementarities of the market and intervention paradigms for coping with the energy vulnerability issue.

The concept of energy vulnerability

Vulnerability can be defined within the risk theoretical framework that would require the use of probability concepts. When applying this to energy security in the long term, a formal definition is difficult to implement due to the number of possible harsh events and the epistemic nature of their uncertainty. After recalling the formal definition, a resiliency approach is chosen as a proxy to vulnerability in the energy policy framework.

Definition of vulnerability

The vulnerability of a system is the degree to which that system is unable to cope with selected adverse events. As it is not possible to take all harsh events into account, some criteria are needed to govern the selection of relevant contingencies (e.g. likelihood, criticality, and damages). Vulnerability in face of selected events with reasonable likelihood and high damages is of particular interest, especially when these situations are critical. A critical event means that due to its weaknesses, the response of the system to this contingency is inadequate and leads to failure to meet the required mission. Thus the selection of critical events is guided by the analysis of the weaknesses of the system under study to meet the specified goals. However, the selected events should be those reasonably likely to occur. The likelihood could be objectively expressed by probability based on statistics or be subjectively considered with regard to the plausibility of occurrence.

For instance, using the risk approach, the vulnerability of an economy to an energy crisis could be assessed by multiplying the following factors: (1) the likelihood of the occurrence of an energy crisis; (2) the likelihood that the economy will be endangered by the energy crisis, assuming it occurs; and (3) the consequences of the impact, assuming the best policy responses. Actually, the definition and evaluation of these factors are not straightforward. In practice, the context in which the vulnerability is addressed determines, to a certain extent, the relevance of the concept to be applied.

The context of industrialized countries

Globalization and economic integration are increasing worldwide, making public and political attention more sensitive to energy supply security issues such as: the growing dependence on energy imports from insecure regions; the volatility of energy prices due to unstable political climates in the major supplying countries; substantial energy demand growth in emerging economies; the perspective of oil and gas reserves depletion and the global climate change threat that limit the choice of energy supply options. Finally, the uncertainty about the implications of energy market liberalization for the security of energy supply and network reliability leads to government interventions seeking a higher level of energy supply autonomy.

If a peaceful future were expected, relying on energy imports would not be a concern. At present, however, the prospect of an increasing dependency on external sources is perceived as a vulnerability factor in all industrialized regions. In its Green Paper of 2000 on energy security (EC, 2001a), the EU expressed concern about the Europe-30 energy dependence on importation which was expected to increase from 36 percent in 1998 to 60 percent in 2030. That increase in dependency is due to the exhaustion of North Sea deposits of oil and gas, the lack of competitiveness of the European coal industry, and the steady or possibly declining market share of nuclear energy. The US Southern States Energy Board's report (SSEB, 2006) emphasized the hurdle of the cost of oil security to the nation, including elements such as increasing military expenditure, cost of periodic oil price surges, and diversion of financial resources. Finally, Japan's "New National Strategy" also envisaged reducing the oil dependence ratio as one of the strategic options for coping with its energy vulnerability.

Another reason for the reluctance to rely on a high percentage of oil import in the future is the uncertainty that characterizes the evolution of energy prices in the energy transition period. While

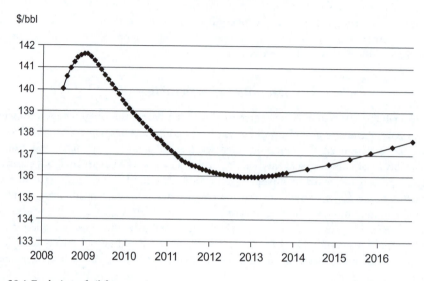

Figure 20.1 Evolution of oil futures prices.
Source: www.nymex.com (accessed on 01/07/08).

oil and gas resources are sufficient for fueling the economic growth to the end of the 21st century, geopolitical vulnerability due to instability in the producing regions is a key factor that could influence the pace and volume of new investments in more expensive oil fields. Thus, the evolution of oil prices in the medium term is uncertain, even if the long-term trend is certain, and the pace and extent of this price increase is unknown.

Assessing likely oil futures prices can be a bit myopic (Figure 20.1). In the long term, the higher production costs of new oil fields and the continuing economic growth in developing countries will maintain a pressure on prices unless oil demand in industrialized countries decreases in a substantial way due to improvements in energy efficiency, oil substitution, or economic recession.

Another factor that produces uncertainty is the liberalization reforms of the energy markets. In Europe liberalization of the electricity and natural gas markets has been facing more skepticism in recent years. According to the European Commission, these reforms aimed to "increase efficiency in the production, transmission and distribution, while reinforcing security of supply and the competitiveness of the European economy and respecting environmental protection." (European Communities 2001a: 14). The goal of efficiency improvement was misinterpreted by some stakeholders as a perspective of a decrease in electricity and gas prices. Higher prices of electricity and natural gas tend to reduce the faith in liberalization as a way to achieving lower energy prices.

Furthermore, the uncertainties during the transition to competitive markets raise additional concerns about several factors, such as the completion of the liberalization objectives in the presence of energy monopolies; mechanisms for ensuring security of supply, in particular investment decisions to adapt capacity of energy infrastructures to new situations within an increasing number of market transactions (i.e., electricity generation and cross-border transmission, gas pipelines); decrease of energy supply diversity, particularly in the case of electricity generation where the market share of natural gas is growing rapidly. Some examples of threats underlying energy vulnerability concerns are: instability in a large oil- or natural gas- producing country which results in an energy shortage over a long period; the creation of a natural gas producers' cartel; reluctance of the private sector to invest in the development of new energy infrastructures; rapid global warming with a forced change in the energy mix; and severe accidents at nuclear power plants that can lead to a poor social acceptance of the nuclear electricity option. In this chapter, long-term energy shortage is emphasized. The strategic reserves are too limited to cope with these kind of events; resiliency of the energy system is the most adequate strategy.

Review of existing work on energy vulnerability

A limited number of research studies have been reported in the literature concerning the design of energy security or the vulnerability concept. Among them, those of the Dutch Energy Research Center (ECN) (Jansen *et al.*, 2004; Scheepers *et al.*, 2007) are the most comprehensive. In the first report, the authors adopted the Shannon-Wiener diversity index as a basic indicator. The following dimensions were then addressed: diversification of energy sources in the energy supply, diversification of imports with regard to imported energy sources, long-term political stability, and depletion of resources in regions of origin. The indicators were applied to four scenarios related to the period 2000–2040. The second study by ECN and the Clingendael International Energy Program (CIEP) proposed EU standards for security of energy supply. Two indicators were proposed for quantifying the concept of security of energy supply. One, based on a weighting system and scoring rules, measured the supply/demand balance (S/D index), taking into account final energy demand, energy conversion and transport, and primary energy supply. The second indicator dealt with the capacity of the country under study to mitigate the effects of sudden energy supply shortfalls. Then the authors defined a SES index as a weighted average of the two indices and applied their method to the cases of the EU member states and to EU-27 as a whole.

Dependence and vulnerability of the European energy systems also have been analyzed by other research groups using, among other indicators, the Shannon-Wiener diversity index (e.g. Costantini *et al.*, 2007). In contrast to the studies where subjective weights were used to derive a composite index, Gupta (2008) applied a principal component analysis (PCA) and used the eigenvalues for estimating the weights of the principal components. According to this approach, the weight of a principal component is as high as its contribution to the total variability of observation. Therefore, it could be questionable whether the weights should be derived either from the subjective perceptions of the decision-makers concerning the contribution of the variables to the vulnerability concept, or from objective measures on the observations' variability.

Selected dimensions of energy vulnerability

Analysis of management options to tackle energy vulnerability

As mentioned above, the envisaged policy measures for reducing energy vulnerability include such options as: reduction of energy intensity in order to make economic growth less sensitive to the volatility of energy prices; mastering dependence on oil and gas by diversifying the fuel mix, as well as the origins of imports, and contributing to the decrease in geopolitical turbulences in the world; decarbonization of energy mixes in order to make the energy system less sensitive to measures concerning global climate change; design of a diversified electricity generation system; diversification of the transport fuel mix; improvement of energy efficiency, particularly in housing; and protection of vulnerable households from a surge in energy prices. In this section, these measures are analyzed using data from the International Energy Agency (IEA, 2007).

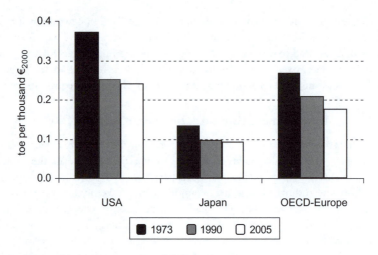

Figure 20.2 Evolution of the energy intensity of GDP.
Source: IEA, 2007.

Reducing energy intensity in industrialized countries

For all the analyses undertaken on energy intensity (EI) in this chapter, the unit of GDP for the different countries used for calculating EI was converted based on market exchange rates (MER). From 1973 to 2005, the energy intensity of industrialized countries decreased by 37 percent due to structural changes in the economies towards less energy-consuming sectors and efforts to promote energy efficiency and rational use. However, as Figure 20.2 shows, this decrease is more significant in the US than in OECD-Europe and Japan where the energy intensity was initially lower Though the effort made by the US and, to a lesser extent, by Europe to decrease energy intensity has been significant, further decreases could result from structural change in the transition economies like Poland, the Czech Republic, the Slovak Republic, Hungary, Romania, and Bulgaria where energy intensity is still high compared with most of the EU member states. Reinforcement of voluntary energy efficiency measures will also contribute to make the European economy less sensitive to the volatility of energy prices.

Decreasing dependency on oil and gas

Oil will continue to play an important role in energy supply during the current century even if its market share has fallen since the energy crisis of 1973 from 45 percent of the world total primary energy supply to 35 percent in 2005. In the OECD countries these figures were 53 percent and 40 percent respectively. Oil is still playing a central role in economic development, and a fair sharing of the declining resources between industrialized countries and the increasing number of developing and emerging countries whose energy demand is growing fast will be a great challenge during the twenty-first century. The concentration of oil production in a few countries and geopolitical turmoil are, more than the depletion of resources, the driving factors for the high volatility of oil prices in the short and medium term. In this respect, the substitution by natural gas is only a transitory solution as the number of exporting countries is also limited and the price of gas is correlated with that of oil. The high volatility of oil prices requires public incentives for investment in new energy options such as synthetic fuels from coal, biomass, and hydrogen, although these options are part of the longer-term solutions.

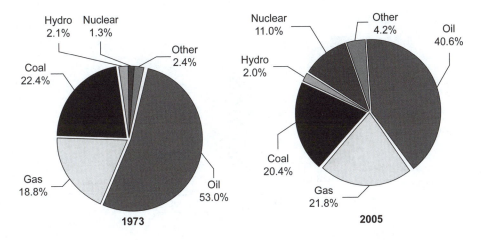

Figure 20.3 Fuels share of the total primary energy supply in OECD countries.
Source: IEA, 2007.

From 1973 to 2005, the share of oil and gas decreased in the industrialized countries from 72 percent to 62 percent, the difference being predominantly captured by nuclear energy (Figure 20.3). In the future, although nuclear power will continue to play an important role, more diversified substitution by renewable energy options must be encouraged for reducing the vulnerability of energy supply. The import ratio of oil and gas and the concentration of import origins are other key factors of vulnerability. This ratio has decreased between 1973 and 2005 in the case of Japan and OECD-Europe, but increased slightly for the US whose ratio stayed lower than those of other OECD regions (Figure 20.4).

Decreasing the CO_2 content of the primary energy supply

The growing concerns about global climate change will make greenhouse gas emissions more and more costly worldwide. The CO_2 content of the total primary energy supply (TPES) obviously

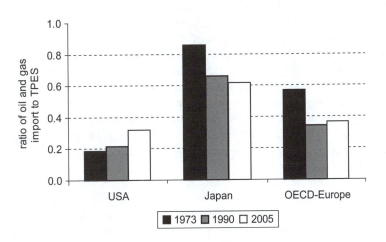

Figure 20.4 Dependence on oil and gas import.
Source: IEA, 2007.

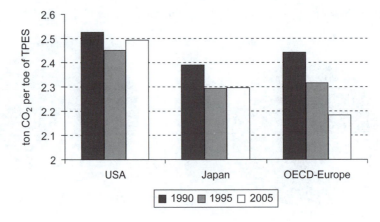

Figure 20.5 Ratio of CO_2 emissions to total primary energy supply.
Source: IEA, 2007.

depends on the reliance of the supply on fossil energy sources. Countries such as Australia, Greece, and Poland, with a significant market share of coal, have a high carbon content of their primary energy supply. From 1990 to 2005, the ratio of CO_2 emissions to TPES decreased by 5.1 percent in the OECD as a whole, while this development varies from one country to another. As Figure 20.5 shows, the ratio was stable in the US, but decreased by 10.6 percent in OECD-Europe. In 1990, the ratio of OECD-Europe to Japan and to the US was 1.02 and 0.97 respectively. In 2005 these figures were 0.95 and 0.88 respectively. The better performance of OECD-Europe was mainly due to the substitution of coal and oil by natural gas and nuclear power. From 1973 to 2005, the share of coal and oil in OECD-Europe decreased from 84.5 percent to 54.5 percent, while natural gas and nuclear energy accounted for 11 percent in 1973 and 37.8 percent of energy supply in 2005.

Enhancing the security of electricity supply

The electrical power supply industry in industrialized countries is facing regulatory uncertainties relative to the responsibility for long-term investment in generation as well as in transmission capacities. According to the Union for the Co-ordination of Transmission of Electricity (UCTE) which groups transmission system operators of 23 European countries, the forecasted reserve margin of the UCTE as a whole is sufficient until 2015 to meet future peak loads, with security being at risk from 2016 (UCTE, 2008). However, the event that occurred in Germany on November 4, 2006, which caused load cuts to 10 million consumers in many countries, proved that the electricity supply in Europe is significantly vulnerable to certain contingencies in the short term. Besides the improvement of cooperation between public authorities and the electricity supply industry in order to assure required investment in new capacities, there is also a need for improvement in operational regulations, particularly for the large interconnected systems such as those in Europe and North America.

From a strategic point of view, the question remains whether electricity can be considered in the same way as a commodity. To what extent is each country responsible for the adequacy between electricity demand and supply within interconnected electricity markets? In the case of industrialized regions where the consumption density is high, should electricity generation be concentrated in a few countries or should investment be encouraged in every state in order to generate electrical power near to consumers? How diversified should the electricity generation mix in each country be and how far should it be clean and safe? In particular, an efficient penetration of renewable energy for electricity generation is one of the diversification options expected in order to make the electricity supply less sensitive to the volatility of oil and gas prices. The future of nuclear energy remains a challenging issue, as along with the development of new technologies for CO_2 capture and sequestration.

Diversifying the fuel mix in the transport sector

Transport is the most vulnerable sector to spikes in oil price. As this sector is essential for the whole economy, it is important to implement voluntary measures in order to introduce alternative fuels. The objective of the European Union to achieve a 10 percent market share for biofuels by 2020 is a great challenge that is presently difficult to take up without importation from producing countries such as Brazil and other developing and emerging countries. Meanwhile, ensuring that this option is sustainable is another important challenge.

Fuel poverty: protecting vulnerable households

The concept of fuel poverty originated in the early 1980s from the UK's and Ireland's grass-roots environmental health movements. With the energy crises of 1973–1974 and 1979, low-income households experienced some difficulty with payment of increased heating bills. They had to spend a large percentage of their income on heating their homes. The concept of fuel poverty is an interaction between poorly insulated housing and inefficient in-house energy systems, low-income households, and high energy services prices. In the beginning of the 2000s, the UK government set up a strategy on fuel poverty aimed at eradicating this phenomenon by 2010 (DTI/DEFRA, 2001) for vulnerable households and by 2016 for all households. According to the standard definition that was adopted in the UK, a household is poor in fuel if it needs to spend more than 10 percent of its income on all fuels used to heat the home at an adequate standard and to meet its needs for other energy services (lighting, cooking, cleaning, etc.). Social measures to cope with fuel poverty exist in many industrialized countries though it is difficult to undertake a comparative assessment concerning their efficiency. The concept of fuel poverty needs to be refined and data should be collected in order to monitor this aspect of energy vulnerability.

Selection of relevant dimensions for modeling energy vulnerability

In line with the analyses made in the previous sections, and taking into account the availability of statistical data, five distinct dimensions were selected: primary energy intensity of the Gross Domestic Product (GDP) (X_1); energy import dependency (X_2); ratio of energy-related CO_2 emissions to the total primary energy supply (TPES) (X_3); electricity supply vulnerability (X_4); and non-diversity in transport fuels (X_5). X_1 is supposed to give an indication of efficient use of energy to produce goods and services. However, this dimension hides several factors. For less industrialized countries, low energy intensity could be an indication of the preeminence of low technology diffusion. Furthermore, the energy embodied in imported goods is not accounted in the statistics; in other words, the substitution of inland production of goods by importation may result in an improvement of X_1. Finally, as far as comparison between countries is concerned, the unit of GDP used to evaluate EI is of the utmost importance. When comparing countries internationally in order to assess their relative welfare, it is common to use GDP at purchasing power parity (PPP), that is a currency exchange rate taking into account the level of prices in each country. Generally, the market exchange rate (MER) is higher than the PPP in economically advanced countries, leading to an underestimate of the primary EI when using MER for these countries. However, PPP focuses more on consumer purchasing power and reflects retail prices rather than prices of intermediate goods. As the manufacturing sectors in more advanced countries generally exhibit a higher productivity, their GDP may be underestimated when using PPP (Suehiro, 2007) and therefore their EI may be overestimated. For this reason, as mentioned in the previous section, the GDP at MER was chosen in this chapter because the case study was on industrialized countries. The consequence of this choice is discussed below.

X_2 is limited in this chapter to oil and natural gas imports because these fuels are the most challenging. As far as energy vulnerability is concerned, the values of positive net exports are not considered, even though a high reliance on energy export may cause economic vulnerability, that is, the Dutch disease. X_3 is supposed to represent the environmental dimension of energy use. However, only a limited aspect of that dimension is represented. Local impacts in particular sites of energy conversion, such as in the case of Canadian oil sands, may induce significant environmental burdens. X_4 mainly denotes a self-sufficiency in electricity supply, coupled with a well-balanced electricity generation mix. Thus, electricity net import countries are penalized and, to a lesser extent, countries with a high share of risky electricity options such as nuclear power plants, do not score high on this dimension. Finally, it is envisaged that X_5 will reward efforts for diversifying the energy mix of the transport sector. The variability within countries is not expected to be high on this dimension for the base year. However, in the future, variability may increase depending on a country's strategy for using alternative fuels in transport.

Design of a composite index of energy vulnerability

The opportunity to design the proposed composite vulnerability index was provided by the World Energy Council's study, *Europe's Vulnerability to Energy Crises* (WEC, 2007). The goal was to design a synthetic index that could help benchmarking and monitoring European countries with regard to their respective efforts to cope with long-term energy vulnerability. Choosing the work by ECN and CIEP (Schaepers *et al.*, 2007) as the current state-of-the-art in the design of indices of energy security risk, the need to propose an alternative method appeared as a response to a few shortcomings in that approach. Indeed, the ECN/CIEP method is oriented towards a comprehensive and analytical representation of the energy supply chain and the review of all possible contingencies included the related probabilities. More than 30 items were studied, resulting in subjective-opinion-dominated weighting systems and scoring rules where the weights and the rules were based on expert judgments. Such a method is mainly qualitative and aims rather at assessing scenarios of the future evolution of energy supply. Compared with that approach, the proposed method is more objective-value-oriented and statistics-based. Even though few subjective parameters are required, their number is very limited as the method emphasizes the most significant determinants of the energy vulnerability. Furthermore, the composite vulnerability index is estimated using a distance concept. The proposed method is summarized below.

For each dimension defined in the previous section, a *relative indicator* was estimated that was finally used to compute a composite index I. The relative indicator of X_1 is estimated by using a scaling technique whereby the minimum value is set to 0 and the maximum to 1. The energy import dependency is estimated in relation to oil and gas net import. Net exports are set to zero. The net import ratio to TPES is then adapted by taking into account the concentration factors in

Table 20.1 Correlation between the relative indicators

Relative indicators	I_1	I_2	I_3	I_4	I_5
I_1	1				
I_2	−0.151	1			
I_3	0.116	0.059	1		
I_4	0.073	−0.028	0.075	1	
I_5	−0.400	0.139	−0.010	−0.046	1

Source: Author's calculation.

oil and gas import origins and geopolitical factors. The ratio of energy-related CO_2 emissions to the total primary energy supply is scaled in the same way as X_1.

The electricity supply vulnerability is defined in terms of three sub-dimensions: the net import of electricity; the concentration and risk of non-acceptance by the public of a dominated technology of electricity generation; and the non-diversification of electricity generation. The indicator of non-diversity in transport fuels is derived from the Shannon-Wiener diversity index. Finally, a composite index of vulnerability was computed as a function of these relative indicators. Many approaches have been tested, including weighted average with subjective parameters and PCA similar to Gupta (2008). These approaches, indeed, gave different ranking orders. In the result, the following method was proposed. (1) The composite index was defined as the Euclidian distance (ED) to the best energy vulnerability case represented by the zero point. (2) When the relative indicators are significantly correlated, the ED is estimated in the orthogonal system defined by the principal components. (3) The ED is standardized in order to obtain a value between 0 and 1.

Case study

Main results

The proposed energy vulnerability index (I) was estimated for the year 2003 for 37 industrialized countries. The estimation revealed no significant correlation between the relative indicators (Table 20.1).

Notwithstanding, the Euclidian distance was estimated in both systems, that is, the $(I_1, I_2, ..., I_5)$ system and the principal components $(P_1, P_2, ..., P_5)$ system. The results were exactly the same. As Figure 20.6 shows, Cyprus (0.749) and Canada (0.439) were found to have the highest and the lowest vulnerability respectively. The mean value and standard deviation of the composite index of vulnerability were 0.576 and 0.080 respectively.

Clustering

Using a univariate clustering function of XLSTAT®, the countries were arranged in three groups according to their composite vulnerability index (I). The top, central, and last elements of each class are presented in Table 20.2.

From a comparison of the inter-class and intra-class variances for each relative indicator, it was apparent that the difference between classes based on average values was significant only for two indicators, import dependency (I_2) and CO_2 emission (I_3) (Figure 20.7).

407

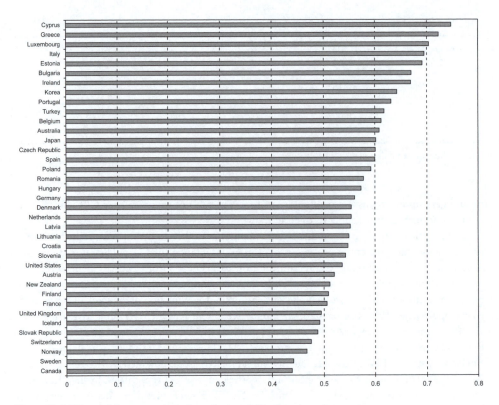

Figure 20.6 Values of the composite index of vulnerability for selected countries.

The importance of each relative indicator in the composite index has been estimated based on the square of the indicators. Due to a low performance of all countries on the dimension X_5, the importance of the transport fuels non-diversity is higher than that of other indicators. This importance decreases from the low vulnerability class to the high vulnerability class, while the I_2 increases its influence. The importance of I_3 increases from the low vulnerability class to the medium class and then slightly decreases. The influences of I_1 and I_4 are less significant (Figure 20.8).

Table 20.2 Results of the clustering analysis

Clusters	Top	Central	Last	Average distance to centroid
Low vulnerability index	Canada (0.439)	Slovak Rep. (0.488)	Austria (0.521)	0.022
Medium vulnerability index	United States (0.536)	Romania (0.578)	Portugal (0.631)	0.026
High vulnerability index	Korea (0.643)	Estonia (0.692)	Cyprus (0.749)	0.025

Source: Author's calculation.

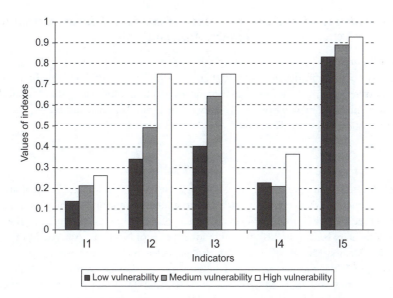

Figure 20.7 Average value of the indicators by cluster.

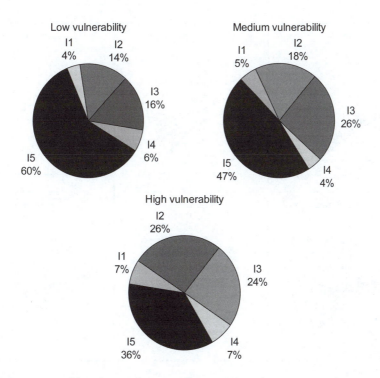

Figure 20.8 Importance of the relative indicators in the composite index.

409

Discussion of selected countries' cases (Canada, US, Japan, Germany, France, Australia)

In order to illustrate the concept of vulnerability proposed in this chapter and to point out its limits, the cases of six countries are discussed (Figure 20.9). These cases also highlight the sensitivity of the composite index to indicators' variations as well as to the influence of geopolitical factors. The data were obtained mainly from the Energy Information Administration (EIA, 2007) and the International Energy Agency (IEA, 2007).

Canada

With regard to the composite index, Canada is the least vulnerable among all 37 countries under study. The strength of this country is on I_2 and to a lesser extent on I_4. Canada is a net energy exporter. Three deposits provide the main source of Canadian oil production: the Western Canada sedimentary basin (WCSB), the oil sands deposits of Northern Alberta, and the offshore fields in the Atlantic Ocean. The WCSB also provided most of the natural gas production (EIA, 2007). In 2003, the net exports of oil and gas for Canada were 49.32 million tons of oil equivelnt (Mtoe) and 75.35 Mtoe respectively (IEA, 2007). Over 99 percent of the total oil and gas exports of Canada were for the US. However, the fact that Canada is considered as independent for its supply of oil should be interpreted with caution. Although a net oil exporter, Canada imports a significant amount of oil and refined petroleum products. In 2003, 44.5 tons of crude oil were imported, representing 56 percent of the intake of the country's refineries (IEA, 2007). This is due to the long distance between the most productive western regions and the most

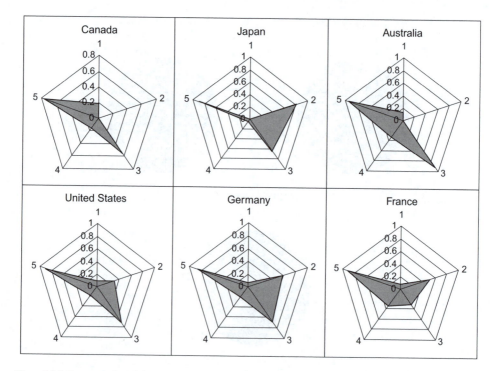

Figure 20.9 Energy vulnerability profile of selected countries.

populous locations in the eastern part of the country which explains the lack of a west–east pipeline. Another consideration is the private nature of the Canadian oil sector, with a growing share of the stake owned by foreign companies, including from China. The proven oil reserve of Canada is second to that of Saudi Arabia. However, over 95 percent of this reserve is in oil sands deposits.

The United States

The US is ranked 12th among all 37 countries and first of the medium range of less energy-vulnerable countries. Compared with Canada, its weaknesses are on I_2 to I_5, the major difference being on I_2. The US is a net oil and gas importing country. In 2003, its net imports were 594.7 Mtoe and 76.1 Mtoe respectively. Oil and gas imports amounted to 29.8 percent of the total primary energy supply. The imported oil came from various geopolitical regions: Commonwealth of Independent States (CIS) 2.6 percent; Middle East (ME) 21.7 percent; Africa (AF) 15.6 percent, and OECD countries 60.2 percent. The importation of natural gas is mostly from OECD countries, at 96 percent. In the baseline, risk factors were attributed to the various geopolitical regions—CIS (30 percent); ME (50 percent); AF (20 percent); OECD countries (0 percent)—resulting in a value of 0.302 for I_2. A change of the risk factors, such as CIS (15 percent); ME (60 percent); AF (15 percent); OECD (10 percent) would result in a slight increase of I_2 (0.315).

Japan

Japan is ranked 25th and its major weakness was on I_2. In 2003 the net imports of Japan were 260.7 Mtoe and 68.4 Mtoe for oil and gas respectively. The origins of oil imports were CIS (0.9 percent), ME (80.5 percent), AF (2.2 percent), OECD and others (16.4 percent); and for gas ME (23.1 percent), OECD, Indonesia and others (76.9 percent). The high dependency of Japan on the ME region for oil import is its major energy vulnerability concern. The strength of this country is mainly on I_1 (energy intensity—rank: 1st) and I_4 (electricity supply—rank: 3rd). The first rank of Japan for I_1, however, is partly the consequence of the choice of MER as the exchange rate for evaluating GDP when assessing EI. If the GDP was estimated at PPP, the rank of Japan would have been 8th. The choice of PPP would have the following consequences: the variability of the EI between countries reduces significantly with a variation coefficient decreasing from 74 percent in the case of MER to 33 percent; Greece becomes 1st in rank on I_1 and Iceland at the bottom of the list. The EI of several less economically advanced countries improves significantly: for example, a 286 percent improvement in Bulgaria, 260 percent in Romania, 183 percent in the Slovak Republic, 171 percent in the Czech Republic, 152 percent in Poland, and 131 Percent in Turkey.

France and Germany

2 and I_3 while it was the contrary for I_1, I_4, and I_5. The main difference relates to I_3, that is, 0.295 for France and 0.614 for Germany. This is due to the high adoption of nuclear power in France and the higher share of coal in Germany. However, this is moderated by a higher risk of public non-acceptance attributed to the French electricity mix in case of an occurrence of an accident at a nuclear plant somewhere in the world.

Australia

Australia ranked just below Japan. Compared with the latter, Australia outranked for energy independency, while Japan outranked on all other indicators. Australia performed particularly low on the intensity of CO_2 emissions due to its high reliance on coal. Fossil fuels represented 94 percent of the TPES in 2003 compared with 84.4 percent for Japan. The difference is mainly due to nuclear energy for electricity generation in the latter country.

Conclusion

Assessing a composite vulnerability index is not straightforward as energy vulnerability is a multidimensional and somewhat qualitative concept. The various dimensions are often correlated, for example low dependence from oil and gas imports could be achieved by increasing the share of coal that could result in increasing the CO_2 content of the total primary energy supply. When the correlations are significant, de-correlated variables were estimated using PCA. Then a composite vulnerability index can be computed as the distance to the best case. In this chapter a Euclidian distance is used allowing a limited compensation between the scores on the various dimensions. The concept was illustrated by a comparison of 37 industrialized countries. The data were not available for all factors of the model and assumptions were sometimes needed for a few countries, especially concerning the sources of oil and gas imports. In these cases, the most favorable values were assumed, for example no penalty for presumed unbalanced import sources. It is worth noting that the proposed concept allows for consideration of geopolitical factors which penalize riskier sources of oil and gas imports. This kind of factor makes the model more or less neutral with regard to the market versus intervention-driven policy options. The market-based security of supply option may lead to securing the sources of oil and gas supply, for example by promoting a peaceful cooperation policy between oil and gas consuming and producing countries. That can be modeled by using lower geopolitical factors. Intervention would therefore focus on the substitution of imported oil and gas by local energy, even if the cost of providing the expected security level is too high. Finally, vulnerability analysis may use either a synchronic or diachronic approach. The latter method aims to monitor the evolution of the energy policy of a given country. The former, which is adopted in this chapter, emphasizes benchmarks of comparable countries for a given year. The two approaches are complementary. The proposed model will be refined and for different countries, and in-depth analyses will be undertaken in order to follow the evolution of the vulnerability indicators with regard to national and international policy objectives.

References

American Recovery and Reinvestment Act. 2009. "American Recovery and Reinvestment Act (ARRA)." Available at: http://www.recovery.gov (accessed August 29, 2010).

Costantini, V., F. Gracceva, A. Markandya, and G. Vicini. 2007. "Security of Energy Supply: Comparing Scenarios from a European Perspective," *Energy Policy* 35: 220–226.

Department of the Environment (DOE). 2006. "On the Road to Energy Security: Implementing a Comprehensive Energy Strategy. A Status Report." Available at: http://www.doe.gov/media/FINAL_8-14_DOE_booklet_copy_sep.pdf (accessed March 17, 2008).

Congressional Research Service (CRS). 2007. *Energy Independence and Security Act of 2007: A Summary of Major Provisions*, (Washington, DC: Congressional Research Service, December 21).

Department of Trade and Industry/Department for Environment, Food and Rural Affairs (DTI/DEFRA). 2001. *The UK Fuel Poverty Strategy* (London: DTI/DEFRA).

European Communities (EC). 2001a. *Towards a European Strategy for the Security of Energy Supply* (Brussels: European Communities).

European Communities (EC). 2001b. "Directive 2001/77/EC of the European Parliament and the Council of 27 September 2001 on the Promotion of Electricity Produced from Renewable Energy Sources in the Internal Electricity Market," *Official Journal of the European Communities* L283/33, October 27.

European Communities (EC). 2001c. "Proposal for a Directive of the European Parliament and the Council on the Promotion of the use of Biofuels for Transport. Proposal for a Council Directive amending

Directive 92/81/EC with Regard to the Possibility of Applying a Reduced Rate of Excise Duty on Certain Mineral Oils Containing Biofuels or on Biofuels." (Brussels: EC).

European Communities (EC). 2003. "Directive 2002/91/EC of the European Parliament and of the Council of 16 December 2002 on the Energy Performance of Buildings," *Official Journal of the European Communities*, L1/65, January 4.

European Communities (EC). 2004. "Council Directive 2004/67/EC of 26 April 2004 Concerning Measures to Safeguard Security of Natural Gas Supply," L127/92, April 29. (Brussels: EC).

European Communities (EC). 2006a. "Directive 2005/89/EC of the European Parliament and of the Council of 18 January 2006 Concerning Measures to Safeguard Security of Electricity Supply and Infrastructures Investment," L33/22, February 4. (Brussels: EC).

European Communities (EC). 2006b. *A European Strategy for Sustainable, Competitive and Secure Energy*, COM (2006) final (Brussels: EC, March 8).

European Communities (EC). 2009. "Directive 2009/28/EC of the European Parliament and the Council of 23 April 2009 on the Promotion of the use of Energy from Renewable Sources and Amending and Subsequently Repealing Directives 2001/77/EC and 2003/30/EC" (Brussels, June 5). (Brussels: EC).

Energy Information Administration (EIA). 2007. "Country Analysis Briefs: Canada. Last Update" (US Energy Information Administration). Available at: http://eia.doe.gov.

Gupta, E. 2008. "Oil Vulnerability Index of Oil-Importing Countries," *Energy Policy* 36: 1195–1211.

International Energy Agency (IEA). 2007. *Energy Balances of OECD Countries 2004–2005* (Paris: International Energy Agency).

Jansen J.C., W.G. van Arkel, and M.G. Boot. 2004. *Designing Indicators of Long Term Energy Supply Security*, (Amsterdam: ECN, ECN-C-04-007).

Ministry of Economy, Trade and Industry (METI). 2006. *New National Energy Strategy (Digest)* (Japan: Ministry of Economy, Trade and Industry, May).

National Energy Policy Development Group (NEPDG). 2001. *Reliable, Affordable and Environmentally Sound Energy for America's Future*. Report of the National Energy Policy Development Group, 20402-0001 (Washington DC: NEPDG, May).

Schaepers M., A. Seebregts, J. de Jong, and H. Maters. 2007. *EU Standards for Energy Security of Supply*, (Amsterdam: ECN, ECN-E-07-004/CIEP).

Suehiro, S. 2007. *Energy Intensity of GDP as Index of Energy Conservation. Problems in International Comparison of Energy Intensity of GDP and Estimate using Sector-based Approach* (Japan: Institute of Energy Economics (IEEJ), August).

Southern States Energy Board (SSEB). 2006. *American Energy Security: Building a bridge to Energy Independence and to Sustainable Energy Future* (Norcross, Georgia: Southern States Energy Board, July).

Toichi, E. 2006. *International Energy Security and Japan's Strategy* (Japan: The Institute of Energy Economics, October).

Union for the Coordination of Transmission of Electricity (UCTE). 2008. *System Adequacy Forecast 2008–2020* (Brussels: UCTE, January 2).

White House. 2010. "Obama Administration Announces Comprehensive Strategy for Energy Security." Available at: http://www.whitehouse.gov/the-press-office (accessed August 29, 2010).

World Energy Council (WEC). 2007. *Europe's Vulnerability to Energy Crises* (London: World Energy Council).

CONCLUSION

Exploring the contested and convergent nature of energy security

Benjamin K. Sovacool and Tai Wei Lim

Introduction

The late biologist Stephen Jay Gould once wrote that the human brain, similar to the eye, cannot focus on all depths simultaneously. One can lose important aspects of the general pattern of a zebra, or the layout of a mountain, by looking too closely upon intricate details or vice versa.[1] His claim appears to hold true for discussion of energy security, a topic that is so complex and dynamic that it is difficult to focus comprehensively on all aspects of it at once. View closely the energy security needs of a home in rural India, and issues such as indoor air pollution and poverty, come to the forefront. Talk about the energy security challenges facing national energy planners in France, and the safety and security of nuclear reactors, will surely come up. Switch to discussing energy security with indigenous people and state-level administrators in the Amazonian part of Brazil, and hydroelectric dams and ethanol production could emerge as key issues. Look too closely on any one of these separate strands, and other threads of energy security tapestry fade into the residual background.

Yet despite the complexity and dynamism inherent in energy security, the 22 chapters presented in this volume do have some common themes. This chapter elaborates on five points of contention and three points of convergence found within the contributions to this book. Points of contention include what energy security is and ought to be, energy fuels and technologies of preference, the role of technology, the role of government, and how an optimal level of energy security ought to be accomplished. Points of convergence include an admission by almost all authors that energy security is a multidimensional concept that involves multiple scales and time frames, that energy security concerns and policies are heterogeneous and differ by types of countries and communities, and that many existing approaches and indicators for energy security suffer from limitations.

Points of contention

The meaning of energy security

Perhaps the most obvious contentious issue within the book has been the definition of energy security. Contributors have advanced different views over how energy security ought to be narrowly or broadly conceived, centering on two key issues: whether *climate change* should be included as an energy security issue, and whether energy security is truly different from *sustainable development*.

In terms of arguing that *climate change* should be separated analytically and practically from energy security concerns, Gal Luft, Anne Korin, and Eshita Gupta present the strongest support. They argue in their chapter that linkage between energy security and climate change may have become an article of faith among government officials, pundits, and academics, creating fertile ground for a new school of thought within the energy security community, but they opined that the link between climate security and energy security may be more tenuous than one might think. They point out that energy security and greenhouse gas reduction have many complementarities, but there may also be many trade-offs between them and, contrary to popular belief, it may not be self-evident that climate change creates energy insecurity, or vice versa. They argue that, important as climate change is, it should not be confused with other, no less pressing concerns. They note that the major energy challenges the world has faced in the past 100 years—the US oil embargo on Japan prior to World War II, the 1973 Arab Oil Embargo, the Iran–Iraq War, the Iraqi invasion of Kuwait and the subsequent Gulf War, Russia's gas cutoff to Ukraine, insurgencies in Iraq and Nigeria, strikes in Venezuela—had nothing to do with to climate change. In their view, it may also be incorrect to contend that one may be able to achieve both reduction in greenhouse gas emissions and improvement in energy security with one strike and, in fact, too much emphasis on one may compromise the other. Their chapter concludes that energy security and climate change may be only two challenges in the menu of issues that dominate policy discourse. In their view, injecting large doses of climate change into every dish on that menu may inevitably cause indigestion, at least to some around the table.

On the other side, chapters by Marilyn A. Brown and Michael Dworkin, David F. von Hippel and colleagues, myself, and others argue that environmental threats including climate change, water pollution, and air pollution may have very real consequences for energy security. Global climate change poses a complex challenge to energy policy because, although there are relatively straightforward (though often not cheap) technical solutions –including flue gas desulfurization devices—to reduce the emissions of acid rain precursors, greenhouse gas emissions may not be so easily abated by "end-of-pipe" methods and therefore a comprehensive approach toward greenhouse gas emissions may be necessary. The climate change issue may also bring in a much longer time perspective than business and governments are used to dealing with. Other environmental issues, such as radioactive waste management, may also require long-term perspectives. In sum, the other side of the debate supposes that environmental issues have to be incorporated into the energy security concept.

A close corollary to the debate over climate change and energy security relates to *sustainable development*. Asclepias R. S. Indriyanto and her colleagues argue that promoting energy security goals is essential if countries such as Indonesia (and other developing economies) are ever to achieve sustainable development. By contrast, Scott Victor Valentine appears to add a caveat to the sustainability argument by pointing out that, while it might be intuitively appealing, there is a valid argument that can be made to justify short-term economic maximization instead of long-term development. In his view, minimizing costs in the short term may provide a nation with the financial leverage necessary to facilitate technological transitions to alternative energy sources in the future. Moreover, Valentine argues that speculating on the prospects of current domestically available energy resources to support the future needs of a nation may also require some speculative analysis of energy system technological development; for example, technological advances in nuclear fusion may theoretically render an analysis of a nation's capacity to support long-term reliance on current energy generation technologies moot. Taking more of a middle ground, Von Hippel and colleagues conclude that no matter how it is defined and measured, sustainable development may require increasing understanding of the interlinked nature of environmental, social, and economic problems—as addressing single problems without consideration of linkages to other areas may be risky. Sustainable development—and addressing energy security—may also require increasing transparency in planning and decision-making of all types, particularly for large projects, and building human capacity (and societal support for such education) to ensure that the capabilities exist in all "stakeholder" groups (those affected by decisions) to address energy security problems and participate in planning processes.

These different dynamics of energy security can create distinct "logics" or "paradigms." To some countries, energy may be an instrument used in conflict, what states fight their wars with. According to this logic a state is secure to the extent that it is not in danger of having to sacrifice core values to maintain supplies of energy fuel. To other countries, sustenance is what matters. Energy is perceived as a precondition to basic sustenance and the functioning of all human beings, societies, industries, militaries, economies, and so on. Since everyone needs it, energy security is a matter of providing equitable access. To a third view, what Felix Ciuta calls "total security," energy affects everything, and everything affects energy. Energy security is therefore about protecting resources and energy systems at all places and locations, from Arctic oil fields and pipelines to energy appliances at homes. Under this broad view, everything is securitized, from resource depletion and global warming to terrorism and even our own personal energy use.[2]

Preferable fuels and focus

Authors have taken remarkably different views on preferred energy technologies, fuels, and systems, with some strongly arguing in favor of renewable energy and energy efficiency, and others looking at oil, gas, coal, and nuclear power. Part of the problem is that energy security risks differ by energy system; each technology has different fuel chains, operating costs, risk structures, externalities, and so on. Electricity security is about infrastructure and reliability, oil and gas security is about reserves and markets. Nuclear energy comes to mind as having the unique risk of weapons proliferation. Energy security indicators can therefore be technology specific: nuclear power would require data related to radioactive releases to the atmosphere and volumes of radioactive waste, hydropower looking at streams and rivers impacted, transmission lines looking at land conflicts. Drawing loosely from a variety of chapters in this book, we can see that each energy system holds different trade-offs and conflicts with the availability, accessibility, acceptability, and affordability dimensions of energy security. Table C.1 elaborates on these further.

Notwithstanding the diversity of these challenges, some chapters do advocate (or at least discuss) preferred energy systems. By far the most recommended technology or practice is energy efficiency. Many contributors recommended energy-efficiency as an easy "least cost," "no regrets" strategy. Gnansounou indicates the importance of building transportation infrastructures that are energy-efficient while Brown and Dworkin focus on associated power plant usage with water conservation. Trudeau and Valentine discuss technological implementation on a global basis for energy conservation. Ami Indriyanto and colleagues prefer examining conservation at the end-user level, while Pachauri recommends household energy conservation. Cherp and Jewell advocate setting energy conservation targets. In terms of economic solutions, Luft, Korin, and Gupta promote proactive investments in conservation. Hughes and Shupe look at the efficiency, availability, and affordability of possible options. Pakiam advocates the use of incentives for energy conservation. Sovacool and Brown highlight the relationship between conservation and research in the OECD.

Table C.1 Security challenges with specific energy systems and technologies[3]

	Availability	*Accessibility*	*Acceptability*	*Affordability*
Oil	Discoveries still possible; but uncertain, nonconventional resources being developed but also uncertain	Rising geopolitical risk, investment barriers, human resource constraints, and poor infrastructure	Rising concerns about dependence on the Middle East and greenhouse gas emissions, as well as pollution related to particulate matter, acid rain, oil spills, rig and tanker accidents	Volatile and often rising prices
Natural Gas	Similar concerns to oil	Slightly less of a geopolitical risk than oil but still constrained by investment, human resources, and infrastructural limitations	Cleaner burning and more efficient than oil and coal, but still carbon intensive; other concerns include methane leakage, accidents and explosions, occupational hazards, and water use	Similar price volatility to oil
Coal	Resources concentrated primarily in ten countries	Some capital and infrastructure constraints due to lack of ports, ships, trains	Rapidly becoming unacceptable due to its environmental impacts and greenhouse gas emissions	Currently cheap but subject to increased costs if a carbon tax is implemented
Hydroelectric Dams	Size is location specific	Some capital and infrastructure constraints	Ecological, social, and historical impacts when implemented without stakeholder consultation and proper social and environmental impact assessments; done improperly displacement of populations, effects on rivers and groundwater, visual intrusion, seismic accidents, downstream effects on ecosystems and agriculture, and methane emissions from reservoirs can result	Higher capital but lower operation costs compared with most other electricity sources

Table C.1 (continued)

	Availability	Accessibility	Acceptability	Affordability
Renewable Electricity	Fuels available in every community but not always feasible at the commercial scale	Limited diffusion of advanced technology in the developing world	Very few greenhouse gas emissions, low direct ecological impact, but some concerns over visual intrusion on sensitive landscapes, noise, avian mortality	Higher capital costs but lower fuel costs than conventional alternatives
Nuclear Power	Uranium processing constrained and uranium reserves uncertain	Limited access to advanced technology	Waste disposal, safety, and proliferation risks	New reactors face extremely high capital and operating costs, existing reactors generally cheap when subsidies excluded
Biofuels	Supply capacity limited to a handful of countries	Natural conditions (land, soil quality, water resource, plant type); and distribution infrastructure constraints	Competition with food, water depletion, deforestation, fertilizer use	Generally more expensive except in select markets (such as Brazil)

Interestingly, oil is perhaps the most-studied energy resource. Gnansounou appears to insist on the conclusion that oil may continue to play an important role in energy supply during the current century even if its market share declines. Gnansounou further points out in his conclusion that the concentration of oil production in a few countries and geopolitical turmoil, more than the depletion of resources, may be the driving factors for the high volatility of oil prices in the short and medium terms. Other chapters that discuss oil include the introduction (articulating energy security challenges around the concentration of oil) and those by Brown and Dworkin (the environmental implications of its use), Liss (marine transport), and Luft *et al.* (serious geopolitical events related to oil over the past few decades).

For John Kessels, the future lies in coal, an idea also iterated by Bert Kruyt and colleagues, who concur that global proven reserves of coal are very large and that coal security will still be important in 2050. Kessels notes that many countries in Asia have large coal reserves and can produce coal at low prices. The need to reduce greenhouse gas emissions highlights the importance of clean coal technologies (CCT); therefore the use of CCT will play a central role in meeting Asian countries' energy security and climate change policy objectives for emission reductions. Coal-fired installed capacity may even double, with 80 percent of the growth coming from developing countries. Kessels cautions that without policies or incentives to build more efficient coal-fired power stations there may be continual growth in the use of sub-critical technology which may be considerably less suitable for retrofit with CCT equipment.

Role of technology

Chapters have differed greatly over the role of technology, whether authors see designing new energy systems and technologies as a solution to energy security problems, or whether they advocate altering consumer behaviors and habits. In classic terms, is the emphasis on energy security to be on the supply side or the demand and services side? Should we be talking about coal, oil, gas, and uranium security, or the security of services such as comfort, mobility, lighting, and cooking? This underscores the multidimensional nature of energy consumption; people, homes, and businesses can be seen as consuming fuels on the one hand, but on the other hand, these are only to provide energy services.

Jaap C. Jansen and Adriaan J. Van der Welle emphasize this point most directly, and argue that energy systems planning and operation should become a shared responsibility of all actors using energy supply systems, including the beneficiaries of end-use energy services enabled by regulatory and contractual frameworks, making the true time- and location-differentiated cost of all major elements of the energy supply system transparent. According to them, flexibility and responsiveness on the demand side may be key to improving the resilience of a country to actual and potential vulnerabilities to energy services.

Closely connected to the discussion about focusing on technologies on the supply side or behavior on the demand side is a discussion about how active people should be in energy planning. Should they be active participants producing their own energy, or passive recipients of energy services? Valentine, in a way, supposes that people should become more involved in decisions about energy use, at least in so far as national energy policies should be participatory and transparent, giving them the option of influencing outcomes. Otherwise, energy decision-making is closed, and the clouds of ideological bias surrounding national energy assessments can cast a gray hue on energy policies.

In the interest of transparency highlighted by Valentine, Jansen and Van der Welle also note that awareness among end-users about the environmental footprint of the choices they make is an essential component of energy security. As choices regarding investments in buildings, public infrastructure, and spatial planning tend to be characterized by very long capital turnover periods with strong lock-in effects, environmental integrity may not be achieved without active engagement of the general public. According to Jansen and Van der Welle, an energy services security approach rather than a predominantly supply-side-oriented energy security approach may help in making this happen.

Martin J. Pasqualetti shares some of the same conclusions about the utilitarian value of public disclosure and dissemination of information. He argues on the need for an appropriate educational strategy for disseminating information and educating the public and policymakers, and that it may be anticipated that this would be an iterative process, that is, as people become more knowledgeable, the sophistication of the discussion can shift. Indeed, Pasqualetti argues that education is important for the discussion of transition towards sustainability- and security-compatible lifestyles for rich population strata in OECD countries and non-OECD Asian countries alike. In many places in Asia, as well as other regions of the world, Pasqualetti argues, the desire for large, centralized electricity generation requires large grids which are often too expensive to run to rural communities, the result being that the rural poor do not get the same opportunities as those living closer to the grid. There is an interactive relationship between energy security and education that is particularly apparent in this situation, and it might be simpler to be promoting the benefits of stand-alone renewable energy such as solar modules in such places. In his view, within a broader context, education could be extended to "value formation in society."

Role of government

Authors disagreed meaningfully over the role of government. Should the primary actors involved in energy security be governments, end-users, investors (in an open energy marketplace), or some mix of them all? The diverging point amongst the authors in this volume appears to be the role of the government and its degree of intervention in the energy market's supply and demand.

Trudeau, for example, concludes that ensuring a better use of the world's energy resources may require policies that encompass explicit intervention by governments. There appears to be a growing recognition that improving energy efficiency may often be the most economic, proven, and readily available means of achieving this goal. Yet achieving efficiency, she argues, requires establishing and maintaining sound policy and the availability of good quality, timely, comparable, and detailed data that go well beyond those currently included in statistics energy balances. A government role is clearly essential.

Looking at the issue from a more global perspective, Goldthau zeros in on how market failures in energy may arise due to imperfect information about energy supply and demand; regulatory uncertainty in key producer and/or consumer markets; or arrangements that render price signals ineffective. Goldthau appears to attribute the oil market's opacity to key producer countries such as Saudi Arabia abstaining from officially reporting output levels, while data from key consumer nations such as China tend to lack accuracy. State companies may have come to control the bulk of global oil and gas reserves but do not to have the same reporting requirements as their stock market listed international, private competitors, which adds to the transparency problem. As a consequence, market participants are left with somewhat educated guesses on key fundamentals. The implication here, as well, is that governments are needed to provide public goods and improve energy security because the market will not do so by itself.

Optimality

A final area of contention concerns what an optimal energy system should look like: is an independent energy security world possible, where each country is energy secure and independent from the others, or should we focus on integration and interdependence? Do energy security challenges lead to conflict, or cooperation? And how do energy security dimensions and issues interact with each other?

Dependence on imported energy, or energy security challenges, does not always create the same results. Energy shortages, for example, can result in coercion (the use of military force and market power), conciliation (dialogue and bilateral partnerships), or cooperation (multinational forms for information exchange and technology transfer).[4] One pertinent aspect of energy security appears to be that various components of it trade off with each other. Here are a few examples, taken from chapters within the book as well as some of the academic literature on energy security:

- Protecting the shipping lanes used by oil tankers with military force secures supply, improving the availability of fuel, but diverts attention and resources from pursuing alternatives to petroleum, failing to promote environmental acceptability.
- Increasing production of corn-based ethanol would reduce petroleum dependence in the transport sector, but would mitigate environmental stewardship through the widespread use of fertilizers and destructive farming practices.
- Stockpiling petroleum and natural gas through strategic reserves can serve as a buffer against price shocks, but also offer just the kind of centralized targets that terrorists and saboteurs find attractive.
- Expenditures on coal-to-liquids as an alternative to gasoline would help countries reduce dependence on foreign sources of oil, but would also make energy supply more carbon intensive.

- Shifting from coal to natural gas in the power sector can reduce greenhouse gas emissions, but it could also exacerbate dependence on foreign sources of natural gas and liquefied natural gas.
- Encouraging demand-side management and energy efficiency can reduce peak congestion on electric power grids, but would directly cut into the profitability of building new power plants.[5]
- Energy taxes can promote efficiency and minimize waste, but also disfavor energy producers, especially Western and Gulf producers of oil and gas and global suppliers of coal.[6]
- Rapid changes in fuel efficiency and fuel economy requirements can lower dependence on oil, but impose costs on automobile manufacturers that can reduce employment and hurt competitiveness.
- Creating a more efficient network of roads could lower congestion and improve automobile fuel economy in Indonesia, but would also only make it easier to extract and distribute coal, accelerating coal depletion and coal-related greenhouse gas emissions.
- More efficient siting for nuclear power plants and associated facilities could increase energy access, again, but could also exacerbate the marginalization of communities living near such facilities and make them dependent on a single industry for income.
- Strategic reserves and stockpiles can serve as an important hedge against price volatility, but can also be used to encourage protectionism and boycotts.
- Low energy prices can facilitate excess consumption, but high prices can hurt the poor and exacerbate energy poverty.
- Shifting from one reliable electricity source (such as hydroelectricity) to wind energy (intermittent and distributed) and coal (prone to volatile prices and greenhouse gas emission) would increase diversification, but could worsen overall system dependability.
- Similarly, shifting from one source of uranium (say Australia or Canada) to a mix of four suppliers (say Namibia, Kazakhstan, Niger, and Russia), or having the United Kingdom switch from relying on domestically available oil from the North Sea (a single source) to sources in Iraq and Venezuela, would also improve diversification but only to a less reliable group of suppliers.[7]
- Diversification from historically cheap sources such as coal and hydro to more expensive ones such as wind and solar can improve availability but conflict with affordability, and can also exacerbate dependence on foreign technologies that local planners may not own.
- Diversification, say from Iranian oil imports to Iraqi oil imports, can also come at the expense of particular countries (in this case Iran loses significant oil revenues).
- Buying reserves or investing in upstream oil and gas projects or bringing in multiple pipelines can ensure security of supply and the availability of fuel, but would be a trade-off with diversification away from oil and gas.
- Improving the energy security of rural homes in India may require the provision of cheap fuels and affordable energy services (which would likely entail considerable emissions of greenhouse gases), whereas improving the national energy security of India might best be served by lowering emissions.
- Hospitals and military installations can receive energy services from multiple feeder lines in order to hedge against interruptions in distribution, but such redundancy can increase costs substantially.[8]

This litany of trade-offs is emblematic of how improving some of the dimensions of energy security inherently conflict with other meaningful dimensions.

Points of convergence

Regardless of energy categories and resource types, there appears to be a converging recognition and centrality of the urgency and importance of energy security. Indeed, the authors writing in this book agree on at least three things: the multidimensional nature of energy security, the heterogeneity of energy security issues, and the limitations with existing energy security research.

Multidimensional nature of energy security

Authors seem to agree that energy security is multidimensional in at least two predominant ways, *scale* and *time frame*.

In terms of scale, a number of chapters noted that energy security is not only a global good, but also a local good, one that differs at scales below the state. What is good for a farmer in France is not necessarily good for a commercial operator in Romania; where one sits, their local geography, plays a strong role, as does the scale of analysis. The energy security concerns presented in this book cut across three primary scales: the household, the nation state, and the global system.

Many contributors to the volume focus on the basic household as a unit of analysis. Despite concerns about the future of energy supply, Shonali Pachauri notes its essentiality used in contemporary household activities. Pachauri argues that electricity has the potential to completely transform people's lives and can usher in many social and economic benefits. Several changes accompany access to electricity. Newly electrified households have access to more reliable lighting and appliances, communications, and entertainment. Among community needs, public/street lighting, refrigeration, health centers and schools, piped water, and communication networks become possible. She notes that electrification also appears to benefit productive enterprises and agricultural activities such as irrigation/water pumping and commercial and industrial ventures. Well-lit public and commercial spaces enhance security and may also give people the ability to participate in more community activities. While access to electricity is crucial, access to modern fuels for heating and cooking (thermal) may be just as important from the household perspective. Most households in developing countries do not use electricity for cooking or heating and therefore require access to modern fuels like liquefied petroleum gas (LPG), biogas or natural gas to meet these needs.

Similar challenges occur at the community level. David von Hippel and colleagues point out that energy production and use also entail common responsibilities and burdens. They note that "not in my backyard" (NIMBY) and environmental justice concerns may be becoming global phenomena, making it increasingly difficult, time-consuming, and costly to site "nuisance facilities" such as large power plants, waste treatment and disposal facilities, oil refineries, or liquefied natural gas terminals. Although people may recognize the need for such facilities, many communities prefer not to have the actual plants in their neighborhood. Von Hippel *et al.* argue that opposition to plant siting may have elevated the importance of local politics in energy policy planning, resulting in questions like: Who has the right to decide where to locate such facilities? Who has the right to refuse? Can any rational policymaking process satisfy all stakeholders? NIMBY appears to epitomize the "social and cultural" risks that may need to be recognized in policymaking agendas.

At the level of nation states, long-term major policy shifts involve making bets on the future of energy markets based on imperfect knowledge, a complicated endeavor. Within both industrialized and developing economies, access to energy services is unequal as the poor may have to expend a larger proportion of their income on energy services even though generally they use less energy than the rich. Pakiam, too, tells us that translating energy security concerns into actual policy may involve intense debates over the role of national security, freer markets, a cleaner environment, personal liberties, and social goods. And D'Agostino points to a clear set of national-level challenges facing countries such as Indonesia and Vietnam, including the resource curse, the environmental cost of fossil fuels, and repealing subsidies.

At the scale of the global system, Gal Luft, Anne Korin, and Eshita Gupta attempt to identify many of the threats to energy security that loom on the horizon—nuclear war in the Middle East, Sunni–Shi'ite violence in the Persian Gulf, successful terror attacks against oil installations in Saudi Arabia, major disruption to energy shipping, the social collapse of Nigeria, energy embargos, to name but a few. Marilyn A. Brown and Michael Dworkin note that traditional security risks inherent to energy consumption and generation may be apparent, such as boycotts or oil wars. However, adding the environmental dimension reveals the security risks inherent to climate change, water pollution, and air pollution. Tangible challenges, such as acid rain, environmental refugees, and specific pollutants in drinking water also represent pressing energy security concerns. Long before rising oceans cover coasts, disruptive flows of major rivers (such as the Indus, Sutlej, Jumna, and Ganges flowing from the Tibetan plateau) may exacerbate conflicts among major military powers, several of whom possess nuclear weapons. Thus, an understanding of the full scale of environmental energy security risks may enable policymakers to shape the course of a country's or company's decision-making. Other macro-effects at the global level include the fact that the poorest quarter of humanity, Africa and Asia, claimed a mere 2.5 percent of the world's energy in 2009, whereas industrialized countries used 70 percent for the same year. Such global inequities will be missed if focus is only given to the energy security risks of individual countries or communities.[9]

Time frame can influence energy security in three ways: whether one is looking forward or backward at energy security challenges; the time it takes energy security issues or incidents to unfold; and the immediacy of external events.

First, some elements or ways of measuring energy security are historic, and include analyzing the past number of blackouts or supply interruptions, price increases for certain fuels, or historical relations with key suppliers. Yet others are future oriented or forward looking, and involve analyzing reserve margins or production ratios, shares of domestic resources, diversification of fuels or suppliers, and the future efficiency of markets.[10]

Second, energy security problems can unfold at different rates. Jansen identified five different time dimensions of energy security challenges:

- near real-time, or less than 1 minute;
- the short term, or less than 2 years;
- the medium run, or 2 to 15 years;
- the long run, or greater than 15 years;
- the very long term, or greater than 50 years.[11]

Termination of electricity service, for example, may last only a few hours, whereas a drought may last years and the impact from pollution can last decades. Short-term energy security concerns involve things like avoiding volatility and shocks, and short-term disruptions are often transitory, caused by equipment failure, human error, storms, crime, and accidents. Long-term energy security concerns, by contrast, will involve structural aspects of energy supply and demand, substituting sources of energy, and diversifying technologies and providers.[12]

These temporary distinctions are proven by history. Short-term physical interruptions of energy supplies have tended to occur due to temporary and non-predictable events such as political events (the Suez Canal crisis), commercial disputes (Russia and Ukraine), meteorological events (Hurricane Katrina), sabotage (Iraqi oil pipelines), technical accidents (the 2003 blackout in the northeast of the United States and Canada), and inadequate domestic generation capacity (the 2002 Californian electricity crisis).[13] Yet medium- and long-term physical interruptions of energy supplies have been related to embargoes (OPEC in the 1970s), protracted political problems (civil war in Iraq), lack of investment (the situation in Africa), and limitations due to overproduction of energy resources (the onshore oil industry in the United States).

Responding to such temporally distinct energy security issues also requires different measures and policies. Short-term solutions might include improving the transparency of the global oil market, strengthening maritime security, and implementing a real-time emergency information sharing system related to energy. Long-term measures would include facilitating investment and trade and technology cooperation in energy infrastructure, researching advanced energy systems, and diversifying the energy sector.

Third, the immediacy of external events can influence the prioritization of energy security concerns. Writing this conclusion in the summer of 2010, the global financial crisis and keeping energy prices low has taken precedence over rapidly transitioning to a more expensive (but also more secure) low-carbon energy system. After the oil shocks of the 1970s, energy security concerns centered on oil. These examples remind us that energy security is also about perceptions, or psychology. Put another way, energy security is not only physical but psychological. The perception of possible interruptions in supply could result in significant policy changes even though in reality their actual risk could be low.[14] Moreover, because energy security risks have a psychological component, people can underestimate them. Security is partially about feeling and emotion, and even in situations where supply and demand of energy remain unchanged, the feeling of security can increase or decrease over time. One study found, for example, that people assume domestic sources of energy are more secure than international ones, even though an analysis of domestic sources of natural gas in Europe showed no difference in energy security terms than for imports from 1980 to 2000.[15]

Heterogeneity of energy security challenges

Commentators all seem to agree that energy security challenges are heterogeneous, and will differ according to the factors of *geographic size, resource endowment, level of economic development,* and *type of energy market.*

First, in terms of *geographic size,* large countries have capacity and technology, whereas small countries do not always have information or access to energy systems. A small country such as the Maldives has energy concerns related primarily to adapting to climate change and weaning off from expensive imported oil, whereas a large country such as Russia is more concerned about adequately distributing its oil, coal, and natural gas; the energy security challenges and needs of countries will therefore differ according to their size.

Second, energy security concerns will differ by *resource endowment* and a country's role as an importer, exporter, or transit country. Nepal's energy strategy will likely be focused on hydro-electricity, Saudi Arabia's on oil, China's on coal. Energy security involves the capacity of each country to cope with changes in supplies using their own resources. Importing countries look to substitute fuels, keep prices low, diversify imports, and diversify energy sources, whereas exporting countries look for security in demand, higher prices, and a stable energy market.[16] Cross-transit countries place a real focus on competition and trade; in fact for them, dependence and lack of diversification are beneficial, as throughput, the amount of energy fuels flowing through their pipelines or transmission networks, is what matters.

Third, and most significantly, energy security differs by *level of economic development.* Developing countries, especially the least developed, islands, or lower middle income countries, typically suffer from a lack of natural resources, economies that spend a significant proportion of their revenue on fossil fuel imports, and lack capacity and planning for energy.[17] Consumers in such countries tend to use smaller amounts of energy, which means these countries do not have the leverage and bargaining power of the United States or European Union. Developed and developing countries also have different access to intellectual property, knowledge, and technology. As one expert told the author, "the needs of Chile and Mexico which have provided reliable and continuous electricity to more than 99 percent of their population are fundamentally different than a Laos or a Congo; layers of development must produce different energy security challenges and therefore metrics."[18]

Fourth, energy security concerns can differ by *type of market*. The International Energy Agency has noted that some markets are well functioning, meaning prices can adjust in response to changes in supply and demand. In these markets, one of the best measures of security is price and the degree of market concentration. The more a country is exposed to a high concentration of markets, the lower its energy security. Yet for markets that are regulated, a monopoly, or pegged to other commodities, prices cannot adjust to imbalances in supply and demand. Therefore another indicator is needed, the physical unavailability of energy, or the higher total share met by imports.[19]

The ultimate point is the heterogeneity of users and energy security dilemmas. Not all customers or countries will be concerned to the same degree with things like continuity, reliability, affordability, and accessibility. Take interruptions in electricity as one example: a factory in China may be on interruptible contracts but merely switch to their own distributed generation or shut down and receive compensation from the utility in the face of a blackout; a home in Ghana used to interruptions in supply may see it as no big deal, whereas a business office in Washington DC will be closed down and in crisis.[20] The key here is recognizing that energy security is intrinsically relative, not absolute. Energy security may be less of a fixed condition; there may be no "energy secure" state. Instead, energy security may always be comparative, acquiring meaning only between countries or classes of consumers.[21] Or, as two authors recently put it, "energy independence is a Sisyphan endeavor, since no country stands apart from international society—importers need countries to buy from, exporters need countries to sell to, and even those that produce just the right amount of energy to meet their domestic demand are also affected by what happens outside their borders."[22]

Limitations with current research

Contributors have much to say about the limitations of existing approaches to energy security as well as the indicators used to measure it. Aleh Cherp and Jessica Jewell distilled a limited number of assumptions used implicitly in developing energy security indicators. Through their exercise, Cherp and Jewell conclude that these discourses tend to focus on short-term disruptions of a political and economic nature in a rather narrow way because the assumptions underlying the indicators are severely constrained by political agendas and capacities for a meaningful debate, dominated by the paradigm of "local universalism," that is, the quest for metrics valid in most contexts which may impose the "lowest common denominator" on the least powerful actors in the process.

Bert Kruyt and his colleagues conclude that there is no single ideal indicator for energy security, as the notion of energy security is context dependent. They point out that issues like the availability of domestic resources, the degree of international cooperation, the degree of risk acceptance, and relationships with other policy targets all strongly determine energy security interpretations. Based on the subjective character of energy security, they argue that indicators are useful to depict trends but their exact values have only a limited meaning.

Other shortcomings may include varying national conditions. Valentine points out that an analyst may employ a benchmarking approach and use the most efficient nation's accomplishments to date (i.e. Japan) in order to estimate potential, but such an approach may ignore disparities in social structure, climatic conditions, geographic characteristics, and political structure, to name but a few influences. Valentine adds that energy efficiency is a fluid measure and somehow methodologies may have to be created to estimate the progress that will actually be made in a given country within the time frame covered by any energy security assessment. He concludes that methodologies for predicting events in the social sciences require the application of critical assumptions which are subject *inter alia* to ideological bias, human error, and predictive inaccuracy.

Pachauri further adds that indicators and metrics might ideally be able to measure and monitor, among other things, physical availability and affordability, the vulnerability of different household groups in securing adequate amounts of quality energy services, inequity in access to and consumption of various energy types across different household groups, and reliability and quality of supply of modern energy services for the poorest. But the main challenge lies in the unavailability of well-documented data and indicators on quality of energy supply in developing economies.

Stirling, too, raises some strong arguments against using simplistic notions of diversification as a way to measure energy security. Where policymaking is based (either contingently or strategically) on a circumscribed perspective of what diversification ought to be, then it risks delivering results that lack robustness. He argues that, at worst, simplistic notions of diversification can be easily manipulated by special interests. To mitigate against this possibility, Stirling urges the need to turn to a general heuristic framework that provides a means to articulate an unlimited variety of different approaches to the assessment of performance and appraisal of disparity, and multicriteria diversity analysis which may help build a framework for more accountable policymaking on energy diversity.

Naturally, we hope that this contribution has been an invaluable first step in uncovering many of these concerns with scholarship on energy security, and also in documenting emerging energy security challenges for developed and developing, importing and exporting, rich and poor communities and countries alike. The next step, of course, will be to devise strategies to overcome these concerns and build on common points of convergence rather than falling prey to contention and inaction.

Notes

1 Gould, Stephen Jay . 2007. "The Power of Narrative." In Paul McGarr and Steven Rose (eds), *The Richness of Life: The Essential Stephen Jay Gould* (London: Vintage Books), pp. 127–142.

2 Ciuta, Felix. 2009. "From Oil Wars to Total Security: Energy in Three Logics of Security." Paper presented at the 2009 International Studies Association Convention in New York, February 16.

3 Apart from relying on arguments presented in the book, the table loosely draws from: US Agency for International Development. 2008. *Energy Security Quarterly: USAID South Asia Regional Initiative for Energy* (Washington, DC: USAID, January).

4 Williams, Paul. 2009. "1970s Redux? Sovereign Resource Activism, Anti-American Reaction, and Consumer Response in the IPE of Energy Seller's Markets." Paper presented for the 50th Annual ISA Convention, February 15–18., New York.

5 Sovacool, Benjamin K. 2008. "The Problem with the 'Portfolio Approach' in American Energy Policy," *Policy Sciences* 41(3) (September): 245–261.

6 Kalicki, Jan H. and David L. Goldwyn. 2005. *Energy and Security: Toward a New Foreign Policy Strategy* (Baltimore: Johns Hopkins University Press).

7 Vivoda, Vlado. 2009. "Diversification of Oil Import Sources and Energy Security: A Key Strategy or Elusive Objective?" *Energy Policy* 37(11) (November): 4615–4623.

8 Vivoda, "Diversification of Oil Import Sources and Energy Security," p. 4616.

9 Smil, Vaclav. 2000. "Energy in the Twentieth Century: Resources, Conversions, Costs, Uses, and Consequences," *Annual Review of Energy and Environment* 25: 21–51.

10 Keppler, Jan Horst. 2007. *Energy Supply Security and Nuclear Energy: Concepts, Indicators, Policies.* Background study in the context of the Ad hoc Expert Group on Nuclear Energy and Security of Supply (Paris: University of Paris–Dauphine, October).

11 Jansen, J.C. 2009. *Energy Services Security Concepts and Metrics* (Vienna: International Atomic Energy Agency Project on Selecting and Defining Integrated Indicators for Nuclear Energy, ECN-E-09–080, October).

12 Glachant, Jean-Michel, Francois Leveque, and Pippo Ranci. 2008. "Some Guideposts on the Road to Formulating a Coherent Policy on EU Energy Security of Supply," *Electricity Journal* 21(10) (December): 13–18.

13 Keppler, Jan Horst. 2007. *Energy Supply Security and Nuclear Energy: Concepts, Indicators, Policies* (Paris: Nuclear Energy Agency, October).

14 Helm, D. 2002. "Energy Policy: Security of Supply, Sustainability and Competition." *Energy Policy* 30 (3), 173–184.

15 Jenny, Frederic. 2007. "Energy Security: A Market Oriented Approach." Paper presented to the OECD Forum on Innovation, Growth, and Equity, Paris, France, May 14–15.

16 Konoplyanik, Andrei. 2004. "Energy Security and the Development of International Energy Markets." In Barton, Barry, Catherine Redgwell, Anita Ronne, and Donald N. Zillman (eds.) *Energy Security: Managing Risk in a Dynamic Legal and Regulatory Environment* (Oxford: Oxford University Press), pp. 47–84.

17 United Nations Economic and Social Commission for Asia and the Pacific (UNESCAP). 2008. *Energy Security and Sustainable Development in Asia and the Pacific* (Geneva: UNESCAP, ST/ESCAP/2494, April).

18 Interview at the International Energy Agency, Paris, France, April 2009.

19 International Energy Agency. 2007. *Energy Security and Climate Policy: Assessing Interactions* (Paris: OECD).

20 Jenny, "Energy Security: A Market Oriented Approach."

21 Kemmler, Andreas and Daniel Spreng. 2007. "Energy Indicators for Tracking Sustainability in Developing Countries," *Energy Policy* 35: 2466–2480.

22 Galgaard, Klaus G. and Asa E.C. Glock. 2009. "The Dialectics of Energy Security Interdependence." Paper presented at the 2009 International Studies Association Convention in New York, February 16, p. 1.

INDEX